ENCYCLOPEDIA
OF THE
STATELESS NATIONS

ENCYCLOPEDIA OF THE STATELESS NATIONS

Ethnic and National Groups Around the World

VOLUME II
D–K

James Minahan

GREENWOOD PRESS
Westport, Connecticut • London

Library of Congress Cataloging-in-Publication Data

Minahan, James.
  Encyclopedia of the stateless nations : ethnic and national groups around the world /
James Minahan.
    p. cm.
  Includes index.
  ISBN 0–313–31617–1 (set : alk. paper)—ISBN 0–313–32109–4 (v. 1 :
alk. paper)—ISBN 0–313–32110–8 (v. 2 : alk. paper)—ISBN 0–313–32111–6 (v. 3 :
alk. paper)—ISBN 0–313–32384–4 (v. 4 : alk. paper)
  1. World politics—1989—Dictionaries. 2. Nationalism—History—20th century—
Dictionaries. 3. Ethnic conflict—History—20th century—Dictionaries. 4. Stateless-
ness—Dictionaries. I. Minahan, James. Nations without states. II. Title.
D860.M56 2002
909.82'9'03—dc21   2001033691

British Library Cataloguing in Publication Data is available.

Library of Congress Catalog Card Number: 2001033691
ISBN: 0–313–31617–1 (set)
        0–313–32109–4 (Vol. I)
        0–313–32110–8 (Vol. II)
        0–313–32111–6 (Vol. III)
        0–313–32384–4 (Vol. IV)

First published in 2002

Greenwood Press, 88 Post Road West, Westport, CT 06881
An imprint of Greenwood Publishing Group, Inc.
www.greenwood.com

Printed in the United States of America

The paper used in this book complies with the
Permanent Paper Standard issued by the National
Information Standards Organization (Z39.48–1984).

10 9 8 7 6 5 4 3 2 1

CONTENTS

Contents

Contents

Contents

PREFACE

This volume is an updated and greatly expanded sequel to the award-winning *Nations without States: A Historical Dictionary of Contemporary National Movements*, which was published in 1996 and contained information on over 200 national groups and their homelands. Since that time, many new national groups have emerged as part of the nationalist revival that began with the end of the Cold War a decade ago. The purpose of this encyclopedia is to provide readers with an easy-to-use, accurate, up-to-date guide to the many national groups in the contemporary world. It is being published at a time when national identity, ethnic relations, regional conflicts, and immigration are increasingly important factors in national, regional, and international affairs.

Encyclopedia of the Stateless Nations: Ethnic and National Groups Around the World follows the development of over 300 national groups from the earliest periods of their histories to the present. That collection of national surveys is an essential guide to the many emerging groups and the national groups that the world ignored or suppressed during the decades of the Cold War, the longest and most stable peace in the history of the modern world. The Cold War did give the world relative peace and stability, but it was a fragile peace and a stability imposed by force. When reading the descriptions of national groups and the analyses of their histories, it is important to keep in mind the broader context—the growing role of national identity worldwide. This encyclopedia, like its 1996 predecessor, addresses the post–Cold War nationalist resurgence, by focusing on the most basic element of any nationalism, the nation itself.

This encyclopedia contains 350 national surveys, short articles highlighting the historical, political, social, religious, and economic evolution of the many national groups that are now emerging to claim roles in the post–Cold War world order. The worth of this encyclopedia in part derives from its up-to-date information on the often virtually unknown national groups that are currently making news and on those that will produce future headlines, controversies, and conflicts.

In this book I have followed the same general approach taken in the previous book for choosing which national groups to cover. Selecting the national surveys to be included in the encyclopedia again presented numerous problems, not the least of which was the difficulty of applying a uniform criteria that could accommodate language, religion, common history, occupational specialization, regional localization, common culture, self-identification, and identification by others. In general, strict adherence to official government lists of ethnic groups has been avoided, as the compilation of such lists is often driven by political considerations. If government criteria were followed, national groups in such states as Turkey or Japan would not be included, because of government claims that there are no national minorities within their borders.

The national groups chosen for inclusion represent a perplexing diversity that share just one characteristic—they identify themselves as separate nations. The arduous task of researching this diversity has been made more complicated by the lack of a consensus on what constitutes a "nation" or "nation-state." There is no universally accepted definition of "nation," "country," or "state." The subject continues to generate endless debate and numerous conflicts.

An attempt to apply the criteria used to distinguish independent states foundered on the numerous anomalies encountered. Size is definitely not a criterion. Over 40 states recognize a building in Rome, covering just 108.7 acres, as an independent state. Nor is United Nations membership the measure of independence; Ukraine and Belarus (Byelorussia) were founding members of the United Nations in 1945 yet became independent only in 1991. Membership in such international organizations as the International Olympic Committee (IOC) or the Organization of African Unity (OAU) does not necessarily signify political independence. Antarctica issues postage stamps but has no citizens; Palestine has citizens and embassies in dozens of countries but is not in practice an independent state; and so on.

Webster's Unabridged Dictionary defines the word *nation* as "a body of people, associated with a particular territory, that is sufficiently conscious of its unity to seek or possess a government particularly its own." On the basis of this definition, the criteria for selecting nations for inclusion was narrowed to just three important factors, modified by the diversity of the nations themselves. The three factors are self-identity as a distinctive group, the display of the outward trappings of national consciousness (particularly the adoption of a flag, a very important and very emotional part of any nationalism), and the formation of a specifically nationalist organization or political grouping that reflects its claim to self-determination. Many stateless nations were eliminated from the encyclopedia when one of these three factors could not be found during the exhaustive research process. National identity is often difficult to define and is very tricky to measure. For that reason this definitive volume of twenty-first-century nationalism contains a number of national groups whose identity is disputed but that met the criteria.

In any compilation, the selection process for choosing which material to include is a complex evolution of subtractions and additions. Estimates of the number of national groups in the world run as high as 9,000, making the selection process truly a process of elimination. The nations included in these volumes therefore represent only a fraction of the world's stateless nations.

Each national survey is divided into several parts or headings: the name and alternative names of the group; population statistics, incorporating the total national population and its geographical distribution; the homeland, including location, size, population, capital cities, and major cultural centers; the people and culture; the language and religion; a brief sketch of the national group's history and present situation; the national flag or other pertinent flags; and a map that places the national homeland in a local geographic setting.

Most of the nations included in this encyclopedia played little or no role in international politics before the end of the Cold War. Some of the national groups will be familiar, historically or more recently as news items, but the majority are virtually unknown and do not have standardized names or spellings in English. Familiar names often were, or are, the colonial or imposed names that in themselves represented a particularly harsh form of cultural suppression. That situation is now being reversed, with scholars, cartographers, and geographers attempting to settle on the definitive forms of the names of national groups, territories, and languages. Until that process is completed, many of the names used in these volumes will not only be unfamiliar but will not appear in even the most comprehensive reference sources.

The population figures are the author's estimates for the year 2002. The figures are designated by the abbreviation "(2002e)" before the appropriate statistics. The figures were gleaned from a vast number of sources, both official and unofficial, representing the latest censuses, official estimates, and—where no other sources were available—nationalist claims. Where important disparities over group size exist, both the official and the claimed population figures are included. Official rates of population growth, urban expansion, and other variables were applied to the figures to arrive at the statistics included in the encyclopedia. Since very few of the world's national groups are confined to one territory, the population statistics also includes information on geographic distribution.

Information on the homeland of each national group includes the geographic location and general features of the territory. Most of the national groups are concentrated in defined national territories—a state, province, region or historical region, department, etc. The corresponding features are included in this section, even though most territorial claims are based on historical association, not modern ethnic demographic patterns, provincial boundaries, or international borders. The geographic information incorporates the size of the territory, in both square miles (sq. mi.) and square kilometers (sq. km). The population figures for the larger cities cover the populations within city limits, and where appropriate, populations of surrounding urban or metropolitan areas. The two figures are included in an effort to reconcile the vastly different methods of enumerating urban populations used by the various governments and international agencies. A list of the principal statistical sources is provided at the end of this section.

Current political events have graphically demonstrated that the overall numbers are much less important than the level of national sentiment and political mobilization. A brief sketch of the people and their culture accompanies each entry, highlighting the cultural and national influences that have shaped the primary national group. A related section covers the linguistic and religious affiliations of each national group.

Each of the stateless nations has its own particular history, the events and conflicts that have shaped its national characteristics and level of mobilization. The largest part of each national survey is therefore devoted to the national history, the historical development of the national group. The national history survey follows the evolution and consolidation of the nation from its earliest history to the present. Although meticulous attention has been paid to the content and objectivity of each national survey, the polemic nature of the subject and, in many cases, the lack of official information have made it impossible to eliminate all unsubstantiated material. The author apologizes for the unintentional inclusion of controversial, dubious, or distorted information gathered from myriad and often unsatisfactory sources.

The national flags and other flags intimately associated with national groups are images of the actual flags; however, due to the informal use of these flags and a lack of information on actual size, all are presented in the same format. In many cases more than one flag is presented, particularly when a national flag has not been adopted or when other flags are equally important. The maps are the author's own, provided to complement the text. They are simple line drawings provided to aid the reader and as supplements to a comprehensive atlas.

The two appendices will allow the reader to develop a better understanding of the historical evolution of national sentiment over the past century and of the rapid proliferation of national organizations that has attended the post–Cold War wave of nationalism. Appendix A sets the numerous declarations of independence in a historical and chronological context, explicitly illustrating the waves of nationalism that have paralleled or accompanied the momentous trends and events of contemporary history. Appendix B provides a geographic listing, by region and nation, of the ever-expanding number of national organizations that herald the mobilization of national sentiment. The number of groups that exist within each national movement graphically illustrates the range of nationalist opinion, although little is known or published about the ideologies, aims, or methods of the majority of these national organizations.

Very few of the stateless nations developed in isolation; they were shaped by their relations with various governments and neighboring peoples. Accordingly, nations mentioned in the various entries that are themselves the subjects of separate entries appear with an asterisk (*). An extensive subject index is provided at the end of the last volume. Each encyclopedia entry also includes a short bibliographic list of sources.

This historical encyclopedia was compiled to provide a guide to the nations in the forefront of the post–Cold War nationalist resurgence, a political process all too often considered synonymous with the more extreme and violent aspects of nationalism. This work is not presented as an assertion that a multitude of new states are about to appear, even though political self-rule is the ultimate goal of many the national groups included in the survey. This encyclopedia is presented as a unique reference source to the nonstate nations that are spearheading one of the most powerful and enduring political movements in modern history, the pursuit of democracy's basic tenet—self-determination.

PRINCIPAL STATISTICAL SOURCES

1. National Censuses 1998–2001
2. *World Population Chart*, 2000 (United Nations)
3. *Populations and Vital Statistics*, 2000 (United Nations)
4. *World Tables*, 2000 (World Bank)
5. *World Demographic Estimates and Projections*, 1950–2025, 1988 (United Nations)
6. *UNESCO Statistical Annual*, 2000
7. *World Bank Atlas*, 1998
8. The Economist Intelligence Unit (Country Report series 2000)
9. *World Population Prospects* (United Nations)
10. *Europa Yearbook*, 2000
11. U.S. Department of State publications
12. *CIA World Factbook*
13. *United Nations Statistical Yearbook*, 2000
14. *United Nations Demographic Yearbook*, 2000
15. *The Statesman's Yearbook*, 2000
16. *Encyclopedia Britannica*
17. *Encyclopedia Americana*
18. Bureau of the Census, U.S. Department of Commerce 2001
19. National Geographic Society

20. Royal Geographical Society
21. *Webster's New Geographical Dictionary*, 1988
22. *Political Handbook of the World*
23. The Urban Foundation
24. *The Blue Plan*
25. Eurostat, the European Union Statistical Office
26. Indigenous Minorities Research Council
27. The Minority Rights Group
28. Cultural Survival
29. World Council of Indigenous Peoples
30. Survival International
31. *China Statistical Yearbook* (State Statistical Bureau of the People's Republic of China)
32. Arab Information Center
33. CIEMEN, Escarré's International Centre for Ethnical Minorities and Nations, Barcelona
34. International Monetary Fund
35. American Geographic Society

INTRODUCTION

The human race has never been a uniform whole, composed of rigorously identical individuals. There are a certain number of characteristics common to all human beings, and other attributes belonging to each individual. Besides the division of the human race by sex, age groups, and class divisions of economic origin, there is another very important separation, which is of a linguistic, ethnic, religious, or territorial type: the division into discernible national groups. Just as social classes are defined by economic criteria, even though they include global human realities and not just economic parameters, national groups are characterized not simply by linguistic or ethnic realities but also by global human realities, such as oppression or other forces of history.

The emphasis on the rights of states rather than the rights of the individuals and nations within them has long dictated international attitudes toward nationalism, attitudes buttressed by ignorance and failure to understand the "nation" versus the "nation-state." The use of condemnatory labels—separatist, secessionist, rebel, splittist, etc.—has been a powerful state weapon against those who seek different state structures on behalf of their nations. The rapid spread of national sentiment, affecting even nations long considered assimilated or quiescent, is attracting considerable attention, but the focus of this attention is invariably on its impact on established governments and its effect on international relations. As the Cold War withered away, it was replaced by a bewildering number and variety of nationalisms that in turn spawned a global movement toward the breakdown of the existing system of nation-states.

Current trends toward decentralization of government and empowerment of local groups inadvertently fragment society into often contending and mutually unintelligible cultures and subcultures. Even within a single society, people are segmenting into many self-contained communities and contending interest groups, entities that often take on the tone and aims of national groups.

The human race was divided into national groups long before the division of labor and, consequently, well before the existence of a class system. A class is defined by its situation in relation to production or consumption, and it is a universal social category. Each individual belongs to a horizontally limited human group (the economic class) and to a vertically limited group (the nation or national group). People have had identities deriving from religion, birthplace, language, or local authority for as long as humans have had cultures. They began to see themselves as members of national groups, opposed to other such groups, however, only during the modern period of colonization and state building.

An offshoot of the eighteenth-century doctrine of popular sovereignty, nationalism became a driving force in the nineteenth century, shaped and invigorated by the principles of the American and French revolutions. It was the Europeans, with their vast colonial possessions, who first declared that each and every person has a national identity that determined his or her place within the state structure. Around the world colonial and postcolonial states created new social groups and identified them by ethnic, religious, economic, or regional categories. Far from reflecting ancient ethnic or tribal loyalties, national cohesion and action are products of the modern state's demand that people make themselves heard as groups or risk severe disadvantages. Around the world, various movements and insurgencies, each with its own history and motivations, have typically—and erroneously—been lumped together as examples of the evils of nationalism.

Over the last century, perhaps no other subject has inspired the passions that surround nationalism and national sentiment. We can distinguish two primary kinds of nationalism, often opposed: unifying or assimilative nationalism; and separatist nationalism, which seeks to separate to some degree from the nationalism of the nation-state. Unifying nationalism shades off gradually into assimilation and imperialism, which reached its apex in the nineteenth century and continues to the present. Nationalism, in its most virulent forms, has provoked wars, massacres, terrorism, and genocide, but the roots of nationalist violence lie not in primordial ethnic and religious differences but in modern attempts to rally populations around nationalist ideas. Nationalism is often a learned and frequently manipulated set of ideas rather than a primordial sentiment. Violent nationalism in political life is a product of modern conflicts over power and resources, not an ancient impediment to political modernity.

The question of what a nation is has gained new significance with the recent increase in the number of claims to self-determination. The legitimacy of these claims rests upon the acceptance of a group in question as a nation, something more than just a random collection of people. The international community primarily regards nations as territorially based, and the consolidation of nations within specific territories has lent legitimacy to self-determination struggles in many areas. Yet this limited definition can give both undue influence to territorially consolidated groups seeking full sovereignty and independence, as well as undermine equally legitimate claims for self-determination among nonterritorial groups that do not aim for statehood but aim, rather, at greater control over their own lives.

National identity becomes nationalism when it includes aspirations to some variety of self-government. The majority of the world's stateless nations have embraced nationalism, but even though nationalists often include militant factions seeking full independence, most nationalists would probably settle for the right to practice their own languages and religions and to control their own territories and resources. Although the nationalist resurgence has spawned numerous conflicts, nationalism is not automatically a divisive force; it provides citizens with an identity and a sense of responsibility and involvement.

The first wave of modern nationalism culminated in the disintegration of Europe's multinational empires after World War I. The second wave began during World War II and continued as the very politicized decolonization process that engulfed the remaining colonial empires, as a theater of the Cold War after 1945. The removal of Cold War factionalism has now released a third wave of nationalism, of a scale and diffusion unprecedented in modern history. In the decade since the end of the Cold War, regionalist movements across the globe have taken on the tone and ideology of nationalist movements. The new national awakening, at the beginning of the twenty-first century, in many respects resembles the phenomenon of the turn of the twentieth century. Ethnicity, language, culture, religion, geography, and even economic condition—but not nationality—are becoming the touchstones of national identity.

Nationalism is often associated with separatism, which can be an offshoot of nationalism, but the majority of the world's national movements normally mobilize in favor of greater autonomy; separatism and separatist factions usually evolve from a frustrated desire for the basic tenet of democracy, self-determination. The conflicts resulting from this latest nationalist upsurge have reinforced the erroneous beliefs that nationalism is synonymous with extremism and that separatism is confined to the historical "hot spots" in Europe and Asia. One of the basic premises of this encyclopedia is that the nationalist resurgence at the end of the twentieth century is spreading to all corners of the world and is likely to mold the world's political agenda for decades to come. Academics too often define nationalism in terms of its excesses, so that its very definition condemns it.

The post–Cold War revival of nationalism is not limited to any one continent, nor is it a product of any particular ideology, geographic area, religion, or combination of political or historical factors. The latest wave of nationalism affects rich and poor, large and small, developed and developing, indigenous and nonindigenous peoples. National diversity is often associated with political instability and the likelihood of violence, but some of the world's most diverse states, though not without internal nationalisms, have suffered relatively little violence between national groups, while countries with relatively little cultural or linguistic diversity, including Yugoslavia, Somalia, and Rwanda, have had the bloodiest of such conflicts.

Nationalism has become an ascendant ideology, one that is increasingly challenging the nineteenth-century definition of the unitary nation-state. The worldwide nationalist revival is an amplified global echo of the nationalism that swept Europe's stateless nations in the late nineteenth and early twentieth centuries, now including the indigenous-rights movements that are major moral, political, and legal issues in many states, and a growing number of groups based on religious distinction that have taken on the characteristics of national groups.

The United Nations estimates that only 3% of the world's 6,000 national groups have achieved statehood. Although the last decade has seen the emergence of an unprecedented number of new states, the existing world order remains conservative in the recognition of new states. There is no perfect justice in dealing with nationalist aspirations; each case should be viewed as separate and distinct. Joining the club of independent states remains a privilege of few of the world's national groups.

The failure to understand national identity and nationalism is often reinforced by the view that nationalism represents a tribal, waning stage of history. The world's insistence that national structures conform to existing international borders for the sake of world peace was one of the first casualties of the revolution brought on by the world's new enthusiasm for democracy and self-determination. Between the end of World War II and the end of the Cold War, nationalism spawned only three new states—Iceland, Singapore, and Bangladesh—while the decolonization process created many more. However, between 1991 and 2001 nationalism accounted for the splintering of the Soviet Union and Yugoslavia, and the partitions of Czechoslovakia and Ethiopia, leading to the emergence of twenty-two new states. The belief that political and economic security could be guaranteed only by the existing political order faded as quickly as the ideological and political divisions set in place after World War II.

The world is in the midst of an extended post–Cold War transition that will last well into the present century. The community of democratic states is expanding, but this era of transition remains complex and dangerous. In much of the world there remains a potentially explosive mix of social, demographic, economic, and political conditions that run counter to the global trends toward democracy and economic reforms. The transition has taken the lid off long-simmering ethnic, religious, territorial, and economic disputes and has stimulated the growth of national identities on a scale unimaginable just a decade ago.

The definition of a "nation" remains controversial and undecided. The nineteenth-century French scholar Ernest Renan stated that a nation is a community of people who have endured common suffering as a people. National identity and nationalism are highly complicated and variable phenomena that resist simple diagnoses of any kind. The most basic premise remains that nations are self-defining. In a broad sense, a nation may be defined as any group of people that perceives itself to be a nation.

The growth of national sentiment can be based on a common origin, language, history, culture, territorial claims, geographical location, religion, economics, ethnicity, racial background, opposition to another group, or opposition to bad or oppressive government. The mobilization of national sentiment is most often a complicated mixture of some or all of these components. No one of these factors is essential; however, some must be present if group cohesion is to be strong enough to evolve a self-identifying nationalism. None of the world's national groups is a hermetically sealed entity. All are influenced by, and in turn influence, other national groups. Nor is any national group changeless, invariant, or static. All national groups are in states of constant flux, driven by both internal and external forces. These forces may be accommodating, harmonious, benign, and based on voluntary actions, or they may be involuntary, resulting from violent conflict, force, or domination.

Democracy, although widely accepted as the only system that is able to provide the basis of humane political and economic activity, can be a subversive force. Multiparty democracy often generates chaos and instability as centrifugal forces, inherent parts of a free political system, are set loose. The post–Cold War restoration of political pluralism and democratic process has given rise to a rebirth of ethnicity and politicized national identity, while the collapse of communism in much of the world has shattered the political equilibrium that had prevailed for over four decades. The Cold War blocs had mostly succeeded in suppressing or controlling the regional nationalisms in their respective spheres, nationalisms that now have begun to reignite old national desires and ethnic rivalries. Around the globe, numerous national groups, their identities and aspirations long buried under decades of Cold War tensions, are emerging to claim for themselves the basic principle of democracy, self-determination. The centrifugal forces held in check by the Cold War have emerged to challenge accepted definitions of a nation and its rights. The doctrine of statism is slowly being superseded by a post–Cold War internationalism that is reshaping the world's view of the unitary nation-state and, what is more important, the world's view of who or what constitutes a nation.

Two main trends are vying to shape the post–Cold War world. One is the movement to form continental or regional economic-political groupings that would allow smaller political units as members. The other is the emergence of smaller and smaller national units as older states are broken up. The two trends are not mutually exclusive. The nation-state, with its absolute sovereignty, is fading and giving way to historical trends—the nation rather than the nation-state in one direction, and supranational bodies, such as the United Nations, the European Union, and even

NAFTA, in the other. The rapidly changing political and economic realities have swept aside the old arguments that population size, geographic location, and economic viability are deterrents to national self-determination. The revival of nationalism is converging with the emergence of continental political and economic units theoretically able to accommodate ever smaller national units within overarching political, economic, and security frameworks.

The third wave of modern nationalism, with its emphasis on human rights and democratic self-determination, is set to top the international agenda for decades to come. The nationalist revival, global in scope, has strengthened submerged national, ethnic, and regional identities and has shattered the conviction that assimilation would eventually homogenize the existing nation-states. The nationalist revival is now feeding on itself, as the freedom won by many historically stateless nations has emboldened other national groups to demand greater control of their own destinies.

A unique feature of this current wave of nationalism is the growing mutual cooperation and support among and between the stateless nations, both nationally and internationally. A number of national groups in countries such as Russia, China, and Myanmar have joined together to work for common goals. Many of the nations selected for inclusion in the encyclopedia are members, or aspiring members, of two organizations that for the first time provide legitimate forums in which to gain strength through numbers and to publicize causes without recourse to violence. The larger of the organizations, the Unrepresented Nations and Peoples Organization (UNPO), was formed in 1991 by six stateless nations, four of which have since been recognized as independent states. The organization, its membership now swollen by the representatives of dozens of stateless nations, is already referred to as an alternative United Nations, representing over 100 million people. The second group, the Free Europe Alliance, is less global in scale but, like the UNPO, is inundated by membership applications.

The political and cultural renaissance spreading through the world's national groups is inexorably moving global politics away from the present system of sovereign states, each jealously defending its authority, to a new world order more closely resembling the world's true national and historical geography. A world community dominated by democracy must inevitably recognize the rights of the world's stateless nations, including the right of each to choose its own future. The twin issues of national identity and self-determination will remain at the forefront of international relations. The diffusion and force of contemporary national movements make it imperative that the nationalist phenomenon be studied and understood. One of the most urgent concerns of our time is to fashion a principled and effective policy toward all national groups.

ENCYCLOPEDIA
OF THE
STATELESS NATIONS

Dagestanis

Daghestanis; Dagestinis

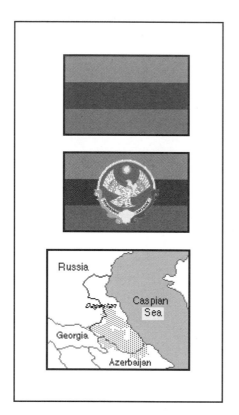

POPULATION: Approximately (2002e) 2,250,000 Dagestanis in Russia, Azerbaijan, and other countries of the former Soviet Union, including 1,527,000 Dagestanis in the Dagestan Republic and over 700,000 in other parts of Russia and in Azerbaijan.

THE DAGESTANI HOMELAND: The Dagestani homeland is a highland region in the Caucasus Mountains and the coastal plains of the Caspian Sea in southern European Russia. Dagestan, meaning "Land of the Mountains," was expanded under Soviet rule to include the northern steppe region, but the Dagestani heartland remains in the highland valleys of the Caucasus. The republic has about 70% of Russia's Caspian Sea coast. The Dagestan Republic is a member state of the Russian Federation, and the most ethnically diverse with 31 official ethnic groups and over 80 nationalities. *Dagestan Republic*: 19,421 sq. mi.—7,496 sq. km, (2002e) 2,211,000—Dagestanis 64%, Kumyks* 12%, Russians 7%, Azeris 4%, Chechens* 4%, Nogais* 2%, Ukrainians, Tatars,* Ossetians* 7%. The Dagestani capital and major cultural center is Makhachkala, (2002e) 336,000, the official capital of the Dagestan Republic. Each of the Dagestani ethnic groups is centered on its own traditional capital and cultural center.

FLAG: The Dagestani national flag is a horizontal tricolor of green, pale blue, and red. The official flag of the Dagestan Republic is the same tricolor with the addition of a central coat of arms, a golden bird on a red background.

PEOPLE AND CULTURE: The term "Dagestani" is a generic name given to all the Caucasian peoples living in the Dagestan Republic, one of the most ethnically diverse regions of the world. The Dagestanis are divided into a number of distinct ethnic groups that often straddle the borders of Russia and Azerbaijan. The largest groups are the Avars* with about 650,000 in the region, Dargins 470,000, Lezgins* 278,000 (in Russia), Tabasarans 122,000, Laks 110,000, Rutuls 27,000, Aguls 26,000, and Tsakhurs 17,000. Each of the Dagestani groups is divided into tribes, clans, subclans, and village communities. Loyalty to the tribe and clan is still generally stronger than that to the national group; Dagestani national sentiment is only beginning to be felt. The mountainous terrain contributes to the ethnic segregation that has developed in the region since ancient times. Daughters are generally not allowed to marry outside their own ethnic group and marriage customs stress ethnic loyalty. Dagestani culture is basically a mountain culture, a mixture of traditional customs and later Islamic influences.

LANGUAGE AND RELIGION: Almost as many languages are spoken as there are Dagestani ethnic groups, some dialects being used by only a few hundred people. The Avar language, comprising thirteen related dialects collectively called Bolmat's, has become the lingua franca and is understood by most of the Dagestani peoples. Russian is also used for communication between the various Dagestani groups and for communication between them and the other national groups in the region. Russian is compulsory in primary and secondary schools. Five of the Dagestani languages have literary traditions—Avar, Dargin, Lezgin, Tabasaran, and Lak. In order to prevent controversy, the republican government has declined to make a decision on an official state language.

The Dagestanis also have strong religious bonds, the majority adhering to the Shafi rite of Sunni Islam. The Sufi orders have remained of central importance to Dagestani social, political, and economic life. The leadership of the orders survived the Soviet persecutions and kept Islam alive during the decades of Soviet suppression. The region has been a center of Islamic learning since the late Middle Ages. Since 1992 classical Arabic and the Koran has been taught in Dagestani schools.

NATIONAL HISTORY: For thousands of years, invaders from Europe and Asia have crossed or conquered the Caucasus Mountains that traditionally divided southeastern Europe and Asia. Each valley in the high mountains became home to a distinctive ethnic group. Influenced by Sarmathians, Romans, Persians, and Khazars, the tribes never united, but remained separate and often warred among themselves. Each tribe retained its own language, culture, and gods.

Conquered by invading Arabs in A.D. 728, the mountain tribes began adopting the Arabs' unifying religious and social system, Islam. A flourishing Muslim civilization developed in the region, centered on Derbent, a major political and cultural center of the Muslim empire known as the Caliphate. The Seljuk Turks overran the region in the eleventh century, forcing many of the Caucasian peoples to retreat to mountain strongholds.

The Mongol hordes devastated the lowlands in the early thirteenth century, but their rule remained nominal in the high mountain valleys of the Dagestani tribes. Persians extended their rule to the coastal lowlands in the fourteenth century, beginning a long rivalry between the Persian and Ottoman Empires that eventually facilitated the Russian conquest of the Caucasus. In 1723 the Russians took control of the plains of northern Dagestan and a weakened Persia ceded the rugged, mountainous south in 1813. Even though nominally subject to foreign rulers, the Dagestani tribes always retained virtual independence under local leaders.

The Dagestanis fiercely resisted Christian rule, which the Russians attempted to extend to the Caucasus following the Napoleonic Wars. Stirred to religious and nationalist fervor, the Dagestanis followed a local *imam*, an Avar political and religious leader known as Shamyl or Shamil, in a long holy war against the Russians. Shamil led the Caucasian resistance to Russian rule for a quarter of a century. During his rule he built a regular army, constructed and developed a state structure, and united for the first time in history a multitude of Dagestani tribal and clan communities. Effective guerrilla tactics during the conflict, called the Caucasian War or the Murid Uprising, in the high mountains halted the Russian advance for over two decades. Thousands died in the final Russian conquest of the region in 1859–60. The last of the fierce Dagestani warriors did not submit to Russian rule until 1877. By the end of the nineteenth century, hundreds of thousands of Dagestanis had been killed or had been forced to emigrate to Ottoman territory.

Openly supportive of the Muslim Turks when war began in 1914, the Dagestanis celebrated the news that revolution had broken out in Russia in February 1917. The Dagestanis were effectively independent as civil administration collapsed, and a Muslim conference elected Mullah Gotinsky as the political and religious leader in May 1917. The Bolshevik takeover of the Russian government in October 1917 created chaos in the Caucasus as local Bolsheviks attempted to take power. The Muslim peoples joined with the Terek Cossacks* to declare an independent Terek-Dagestan republic on 20 October 1917, but the new state, undermined by ethnic, religious, and territorial disputes, collapsed in December 1917.

The Dagestani peoples formed a separate republic in March 1918 and attempted a cooperative defense as the Russian Civil War spread south. On 11 May 1918 Dagestani leaders declared the independence of the North Caucasian Republic. The anti-Bolshevik forces, the Whites, took control of the region in January 1919, but their forced conscription of Muslims incited strong resistance. The routing of the Whites in 1919 brought a bloody suppression of the Terek Cossacks, the major White force in the region, in which bands of Dagestanis often voluntarily assisted the Red Army. Promised autonomy, the majority of the Dagestanis went over to the Reds. The last of the Whites withdrew from the region in January 1920.

The Dagestani leaders, disappointed at their treatment by the Soviet authorities, demanded the autonomy promised during the Russian Civil War. Rebuffed by the Soviet authorities, the Dagestanis rebelled and held out until finally subdued in May 1921, at a cost of over 5,000 Soviet casualties. A hypothetically autonomous Dagestani republic created in early 1921 joined the new Soviet Russian Federation. The new autonomous republic was formed from the former tsarist Dagestan plus several districts of steppe land to the north. In 1922, the republic was extended to the north with the incorporation of former Terek Cossack lands and parts of Stavropol Territory and the Astrakhan *oblast*.

The Soviet authorities suppressed religion among the Dagestanis in the 1920s and 1930s by destroying nearly all mosques and other religious buildings. Under the communists, government posts were judiciously divided according to nationality, often with little regard to ability or education. Power and resources were distributed according to a system of ethnic quotas that conformed to the Soviet idea of divide-and-rule in the region.

The Soviet authorities forced thousands of Dagestanis to abandon their mountain homes and settle among the Turkic peoples of the northern plains. The mountain peoples forced to resettle in the lowlands, mostly Laks and Avars, maintained their culture and tended to embrace nationalism in the face of territorial disputes with the Kumyks and Nogais, who formerly dominated the steppe regions of northern Dagestan.

A religious and cultural revival in the 1970s spread through the thousands of illegal, underground mosques, stimulating renewed Dagestani resistance to official Soviet atheism. Islamic fundamentalism, promoted by revolutionary Iran to the south after 1979, began to make inroads among the younger Dagestanis, who keenly felt the frustration of decades of oppressive Soviet rule. By 1980 an estimated half of Dagestan's male population belonged to illicit Muslim brotherhoods, called *tariqat*.

In the more relaxed atmosphere of the late 1980s, religious and nationalist sentiment emerged as powerful forces in the republic. The rapid religious revival forced the Soviet authorities in April 1990 to authorize charter flights to those Muslims wishing to make the pilgrimage to Mecca. The Soviet authorities had formerly restricted the sacred pilgrimage to just twenty Dagestanis each year.

The attempted Soviet coup and the rapid disintegration of the Soviet Union in August 1991 gave new impetus to the Dagestani national revival. A Dagestani majority in the local parliament unilaterally declared the republic a full member republic of the Russian Federation, while indirectly endorsing the eventual independence of the republic. After 1991 one of the most difficult tasks of the Dagestan government was maintaining the republic's national unity. The Dagestani federation mirrored the Russian Federation, with some national groups, particularly among the Dagestani

Avars and Lezgins,* and the Turkic Kumyks and Nogais seeking separate autonomy.

The Russian military assault on the neighboring Chechnya in December 1994 stirred nationalist and anti-Russian sentiment. Public protests were held in Makachkala and other cities, demanding that the Dagestani authorities condemn the Russian invasion, but the Dagestanis officially remained carefully neutral in the conflict. Interethnic conflicts in Dagestan are generally settled behind closed doors, with the major conflicts arising from the distribution of power and funding. Most interethnic controversies among the Dagestanis are linked to economic issues, such as possession of land and the distribution of jobs and housing.

Islamic militants of the Wahabi sect, which originated in Saudi Arabia, preach Islamic unity and strict adherence to Islamic traditions and Sharia law, but the Dagestanis, mostly traditional Sunnis and having experienced decades of enforced Soviet atheism, have mostly rejected fundamentalism. Violence between the traditionalists and the Wahabis increased in 1998–99. In spite of the renewed vigor of Islam among the Dagestanis, ethnic allegiances are stronger than the idea of Islamic unity, and membership of Islamic organizations follows strict ethnic lines.

In August 1999, several thousand Islamic militants connected to the Wahabi groups crossed into Dagestan from Chechnya in an attempt to gain support for an independent Islamic state. Russian troops defeated the militants, including a second incursion in September, and the Dagestanis showed little interest in following Chechnya into a bloody secessionist war.

The politics of the Dagestanis remain a careful balancing act between the different ethnic groups. Because none of the Dagestani groups is large enough or strong enough to dominate the region, interethnic calm is preserved. Increasingly, however, the Avars and Lezgins are distancing themselves from the other Dagestani groups, while group cohesion is becoming more important as the non-Dagestani groups in the republic, the Kumyks and Nogais, push for separation from the Dagestan Republic. At the turn of the twenty-first century, the Dagestani homeland is Russia's most violent and potentially most dangerous, even as the ongoing war in neighboring Chechnya destabilizes the region.

Discrimination and economic hardships have unified most of the Dagestani peoples, who increasingly see themselves as a separate national group, not just a collection of unrelated Caucasian tribes. The second Chechen War in 1999–2000 increased Russian fear of the Caucasian peoples and a corresponding rise in discrimination and ethnic violence, particularly among immigrant Dagestani groups in Moscow and other areas of Russia outside the Caucasus. Many Dagestanis, formerly employed as laborers or herdsmen in many Russian regions, have returned to their mountain homeland since 1995 because of discrimination.

Dagestan by 1998 was Russia's most violent republic. Gang and ethnic violence continues to mount despite stepped-up military control. In May 1998 a mob took over Makhachkala's major government buildings, and Islamic militants took control of several villages in the south.

The old Russian policy of divide-and-rule remains part of the Russian government's approach to the turbulent Dagestan Republic. The policy has alienated some Dagestani groups, while others have benefited, both in power and land. Several groups in the region, particularly the non-Dagestani groups in the north of the republic, demand separation from the republic and the creation of separate ethnic homelands. The two most nationalistic of the Dagestani groups, the Avars and the Lezgins, have also seen a rise in nationalist sentiment and calls for separate homelands.

The Russian government, following the terrorist attacks on New York and Washington in September 2001, cracked down on radical Islamic organizations accused of having ties to terrorism in the region. In October 2001, the Wahabi movement was outlawed and its religious schools and training camps were closed.

SELECTED BIBLIOGRAPHY:

Bobrovnikov, V. *Dagestan: Land and People on the Land*. 1994.

Chenciner, Robert. *Dagestan: Tradition and Survival*. 1997.

Gammer, Moshe. *Muslim Resistance to the Tsar: Shamil and the Conquest of Chechnia and Dagestan*. 1994.

Krag, Helen, and Lars Funch. *The North Caucasus: Minorities at the Crossroads*. 1994.

Dauphinois
Mountain Occitans

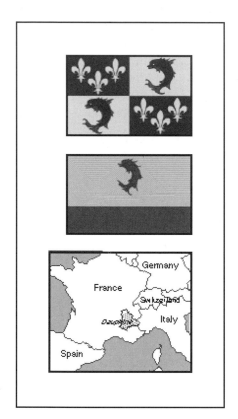

POPULATION: Approximately (2002e) 1,617,000 Dauphinois in France, concentrated in the southeastern regions of Provence-Alpes-Côtes-d'Azur and Rhône-Alpes. Outside the region there are sizable Dauphinois populations in Paris, Lyon, and other large urban areas in France.

THE DAUPHINOIS HOMELAND: The Dauphinois homeland lies in southeastern France, a mountainous region of high valleys dominated by the French Alps. Dauphiné has no official status; historical Dauphiné is divided between the French departments of Isère and Drôme of the region of Rhône-Alpes, and the department of Hautes-Alpes of the region Provence-Alpes-Côtes-d'Azur. *Region of Dauphiné (Province du Dauphiné): 7,685 sq. mi.—19,905 sq. km, (2002e) 1,924,000—Dauphinois 82%, other French, North Africans 18%. The Dauphinois capital and major cultural center is Grenoble, (2002e) 146,000, metropolitan area 504,000.

FLAG: The Dauphinois national flag, the historical flag of the region, is divided into quarters, blue rectangles bearing three yellow fleur-de-lys on the upper hoist and lower fly, and yellow rectangles charged with blue dolphins with red fins on the lower hoist and upper fly. The flag of the Ligue Dauphinois is a yellow field bearing a blue dolphin upper center and a wide blue horizontal stripe across the bottom.

PEOPLE AND CULTURE: The Dauphinois are an alpine people, the descendants of early Celts Latinized by five centuries of Roman rule. The traditions and customs that survived in the high mountain valleys make up the basis of their distinct culture, which has retained many traits that long ago disappeared in lowland French culture. Ethnically and historically the Dauphinois are more closely related to the neighboring Savoyards* than to the French or Occitans* to the west and south. The Dauphinois are known for their tenacity and resistance to authority. Regional alpine costumes, worn at festivals, are part of a cultural revival that has taken hold in the region since the late 1980s.

LANGUAGE AND RELIGION: The language of the Dauphinois, aside from standard French, is a group of dialects of the Occitan language spoken across southern France. The Alpin dialect, often classified as a sub-dialect of Provençal, is spoken from Grenoble south. Gavot is spoken in the northern districts, and Dauphinois (or Dromois) in southern Dauphiné. The dialects are structurally separate and none of the dialects are accepted as standard literary languages, although all are mutually intelligible. The first work published in the Dauphinois dialect was an extract of the Bible in 1830. The Dauphinois dialect shows considerable Provençal influence and borrowings from neighboring dialects spoken in Italy. The use of the dialect is declining, even among the rural population and in the isolated communities in the high alpine valleys. Italian dialects are widely spoken in southern Isère.

The majority of the Dauphinois are Roman Catholic, although there are large Protestant enclaves, including the remnants of a former colony of Waldensians.* The region had a large Protestant population until the massacres of the sixteenth century, when many died and others fled to neighboring countries or to far corners of the French Empire.

NATIONAL HISTORY: Celts began to settle the valley of the Isère River around 650 B.C. The Allobroges, the major tribe of the region, called Gauls by the Romans, developed a reputation as a warrior people due to their resistance to Roman expansion. They were finally conquered by the Romans in 121 B.C.; Roman rule would last for 575 years, leaving a lasting impression on the culture and dialect of the region.

The major Roman center, called Cularo, was renamed Gratianopolis in the fourth century, for the emperor Gratian. The name was eventually corrupted to Grenoble. When Roman power declined, Germanic Burgundians* overran the region, destroying many of the remaining Roman settlements. The Franks later added the region to their growing kingdom, the forerunner of the Holy Roman Empire.

In the ninth century, at the death of Charlemagne, his empire was divided by his sons. Dauphiné was added to the middle kingdom given to Lothair, which was to form the kingdom of Arles from the tenth to the thirteenth centuries. Also in the ninth century, Muslims from North Africa briefly invaded the area, which then reverted to small feudal holdings, most held by vassals of the Holy Roman Emperor.

The nucleus of the region was the countship of Viennois, the county around Vienne, on the east bank of the Rhône. Viennois was part of the original kingdom of Arles and a fief of the Holy Roman Empire. In the early eleventh century the southern part of the countship was separated under the counts of Albon, who extended their domain to other parts of Arles. Guigues IV, the count of Albon from 1133 to 1142, was the first to bear the name "Dauphin." By the thirteenth century, the name, traditional in the ruling house of Viennois, had been transformed into a title, and the fiefs held by the family became known as Dauphiné. The last dauphin, Humbert II, having no heirs, sold all his possessions to the French king in 1349. The agreement, called the "Transport du Dauphiné," stipulated that the heir to the French throne should control the Dauphiné.

King Philip VI of France duly transferred the territory to his grandson, the future Charles V of France. Dauphiné became an appendage of the eldest son of the French king, who assumed the title of dauphin. Dauphiné remained a quasi-independent region with its own government and legislature until it was annexed to France by Charles VII in 1457. The Dauphiné parliament, established in 1453, was an outgrowth of the earlier Delphinal Council. In 1560 the region was made a French province, with a parliament at Grenoble and considerable autonomy in political and cultural matters.

The Dauphiné was made a military quarter due to its geographic position on the Italian frontier, where the French kingdom pressed claims to Alpine territories that divided the French lands from the Italian. The Dauphinois suffered during the Wars of Religion, as well as after the revocation of the Edict of Nantes, as a result of which thousands of Protestants fled to the region between 1562 and 1598 to escape massacres in Paris and other French cities. Later, the relatively large number of Protestants in the Dauphinois were often targeted for expulsion or suppression; many left for Geneva and other Protestant strongholds. The parliament of Dauphiné was suspended by the French government in 1628, and local government was further weakened by the appointment of an intendant, a royal official with power in the region.

The eighteenth century was a period of prosperity and economic development in the region, which gave the new middle class an opportunity to prosper. The government of the French kingdom in the late eighteenth century moved to curb the wide autonomy enjoyed by the historical regions. On 21 August 1787 the province of Dauphiné became the first to demand an assembly of all social classes. In June 1788 the Dauphinois successfully rebelled against a royal decree limiting the powers of the local parliament. The Dauphinois parliament, because of its resistance to the crown, played a major role in the early phase of the overthrow of the French monarchy in 1789. The Revolution, however, was followed by the dissolution of the historical regions and the suppression of the local legislature in Grenoble.

Economic and social change rapidly transformed the way of life of the Dauphinois in the nineteenth century. New roads and railroads were constructed, including the important Paris-Marseilles railroad, which passed through the Dauphinois city of Valence.

Centralization of the French government beginning in the early nineteenth century forced many in the region to migrate to Paris. Writers, artists, and intellectuals were forced in order to work to leave their homeland for the French capital, where all political, economic, and cultural organs were centered. Resentment of the need to leave their homes stimulated a modest regionalist movement in the late nineteenth century.

The population of the region increased dramatically from the middle of the nineteenth century; Grenoble's population increased fivefold from 1860 and 1960 and continued to grow during the 1970s and 1980s. The region, although the first university there was founded in 1339, became a leading university center and research facility only at the beginning of the twentieth century.

The Vercors Plateau was a center of anti-Nazi resistance during World War II. The French resistance—both against the Nazis and against the collaborationist Vichy government that controlled southern France—was particularly active in Grenoble. Groups of partisans operating from hideouts in the French Alps harassed the Nazis and their French allies until the region was liberated by Allied troops. The role of the Vichy government is still a regionalist issue in the region, as the majority of the Dauphinois opposed it.

The stirrings and unrest of the early 1960s fueled student and other protests in Grenoble and other cities in the region. The Winter Olympics held in Grenoble in 1968 coincided with a year of revolutionary turbulence in France. The first stirrings of regional sentiment appeared as visitors from around the globe descended on the city. In 1981 a new socialist government in Paris organized the country into planning regions. Although the regions had very limited autonomy, they were the first taste of self-government since the French Revolution. The division of the historical Dauphiné between two new hybrid regions fueled the growth of regionalist sentiment and demands for the resurrection of an autonomous Dauphiné within its historical borders.

In the 1990s, the Dauphinois supported right-wing political parties, including the far Right. Immigrants, many from North Africa or other areas of France, have been drawn to the Dauphiné, where employment opportunities are better than in Paris or nearby Lyon. Anti-immigrant sentiment and high unemployment were, as in all of France, reasons for increased unrest in the late 1990s.

The return of regional identities after centuries of French centralization paralleled the growth of the European Union (EU). Several regions outside Paris see little value in being represented by Paris when they could, with greater efficiency and influence, represent themselves directly to the EU government in Brussels. Many feel that local economic and infrastructure problems that must now be presented to Paris for solution could be trusted to a regional government with autonomous powers.

A May 1999 poll showed that 67% of the French favored the dismantling of the departmental system and that an astonishing 88% favored autonomy for the historical regions. The Ligue Dauphinois was formed to represent the Dauphinois in their fight to win a constitution for a revived autonomous Dauphiné. A small minority seeks to separate Dauphiné from France and create a separate European state, but there is little support for separatism; however, there is widespread support for a return of the historical autonomy of the region. The rallying call of the nationalist movement is "Not Provençal, not Rhônealpin, but Dauphinois."

SELECTED BIBLIOGRAPHY:

Northcutt, Wayne. *The Regions of France: A Reference Guide to History and Culture.* 1996.

Pinchemel, Philippe. *France: A Geographical, Social, and Economic Survey.* 1987.

Price, Roger. *A Concise History of France.* 1993.

Roux, Stephane, ed. *Alpes-Dauphiné.* 1998.

Dayaks

Land Dayaks; Dyaks

POPULATION: Approximately (2002e) 2,320,000 Dayaks living on the island of Kalimantan (Borneo), which is politically divided between Indonesia and Malaysia. The majority of the Dayaks are concentrated in the Indonesian province of West Kalimantan in the west of the island, with about 40,000 in East Malaysia, mostly in the state of Sarawak.

THE DAYAK HOMELAND: The Dayak homeland lies in central Kalimantan, formerly called Borneo, one of the largest islands of the Malay Archipelago. Mountains and the sea have protected the character and traditions of the interior Dayak tribes. Kalimantan, covering an area of roughly 286,000 square miles (743,325 sq. km), is the world's third-largest island. The Dayak homeland has no official status, with the majority of the Indonesian Dayaks concentrated in the Indonesian province of West Kalimantan. *Province of West Kalimantan (Dayakland/Republik Dayak)*: 60,643 sq. mi.—157,065 sq. km, (2002e) 4,083,000—Dayaks 44%, Malays 37%, Madurese 2%, other Indonesians 17%. The capital and major cultural center of the Dayaks is Pontianak, (2002e) 495,000. The other important cultural center is Singkawang, (2002e) 98,000.

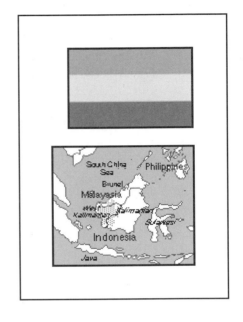

FLAG: The Dayak national flag, the flag of the national movement in Indonesia, is a horizontal tricolor of red, yellow, and blue.

PEOPLE AND CULTURE: The name Dayak until the 1970s was a generic term with no precise ethnic or tribal application; it did not differentiate the non-Muslim indigenous peoples of the interior of Kalimantan from the largely Muslim Malay population of the coastal regions. The related tribes comprise 37 distinct groups collectively called Dayaks. The major tribal groups are the Ngaju Dayaks, Maanyan, Lawangan, Bahau (including Kayan and Kenyah, of central and eastern Kalimantan), and the Bidayuh or Land Dayaks of southwestern Kalimantan and Sarawak. Traditional nomadic cultivation is the basis of the Dayaks' noncommercial societies, which are underpinned by a highly developed set of traditional customs. There are significant variations from one valley to the next, and the Dayaks display a wide range of cultures, although there is a host of similarities, including dwellings, diet, and other cultural traits. Dayak community life is centered around communal longhouses, with several longhouses clustered together to make a village. Historically the Dayaks were head-hunters. The Dayaks have a dynamic and complex legal system, known as *adat*, which dictates their behavior. The Dayaks remain mostly rural; the cities are preserves of Malays and Chinese.

LANGUAGE AND RELIGION: The Dayak languages belong to the Indonesian branch of the Austronesian (Malayo-Polynesian) language family. There are dozens of dialects, most unintelligible to other tribal groups. Dayak activists are working on a standardization of vocabulary and syntax, and the development of a literary language. Other Dayak groups have since begun similar processes. The largest of the Dayak languages spoken in Indonesian Kalimantan are Benyadu, Ahe, Land Dayak (with a large number of dialects), Djongkang, Iban, Kembayan, Kendayan, Maanyak, Malayic Dayak, Ngaju, Ribun, Sanggau, and Selako. English or Dutch are often used as lingua francas, providing common languages for intergroup communications.

The Dayaks' religious beliefs are animistic and polytheistic, with a highly developed and complex set of rituals. The religion, officially called Kaharingan, is listed by the government as an offshoot of Balinese Hinduism. The Indonesian government requires that all citizens adhere to a monotheistic religion; Kaharingan, with its elaborate rituals, is a powerful way to coalesce the Dayaks as a national group. A minority of the Dayaks are Christians, converted to a variety of denominations by missionaries who came to the island in the late nineteenth and early twentieth centuries. Christian beliefs are often mixed with their earlier beliefs and value system. The *adat* system incorporates both the physical and supernatural world. Rituals and beliefs regulate seasonal changes in Dayak life and the Dayaks' relationship with the world around them.

NATIONAL HISTORY: For most of their history, the Dayaks have been isolated from the world. Early in history, immigrant Malays settled the coastal regions, driving the Dayaks into the mountainous interior. Their island, located farther from Indian trade routes than other parts of the Malay Archipelago, was not often the destination of traders and immigrants.

The Muslim coastal peoples united under the powerful sultanate of Brunei, and by the sixteenth century the sultanate controlled most of the huge island of Borneo. The island was visited by Magellan's expedition in 1521, and tales of the opulent sultanate eventually reached Europe. Spanish and Portuguese emissaries reached the coastal regions in the mid-1500s. Soon after, English and Dutch traders and adventurers began to visit the coastal ports regularly. European encroachments greatly weakened the sultanate, leading to a period of lawlessness and piracy.

Before contact with the Europeans, the Dayak tribes often engaged in wars among themselves, frequently in search of ritual trophies—human heads. The tribes, although under the nominal rule of the sultans of Brunei, remained isolated and were relatively untouched by outside influences until the arrival of Christian missionaries during the nineteenth century.

James Brooke, a British subject, arrived in the sultanate in 1839. Brooke offered his military experience to the sultanate and assisted in putting down a serious Dayak revolt and in suppressing piracy in western Borneo. The grateful sultan gave Brooke some 7,000 square miles (18,130 sq. km) of territory and the title "raja of Sarawak." Knighted by the British crown, Sir James created a government and attempted to put down piracy and head-hunting among the Dayak tribes. The Brooke family ruled Sarawak until the outbreak of World War II. The state, a British protectorate from 1888, formed part of the British territories on Borneo. Most of the island of Borneo remained under Dutch colonial rule until World War II.

Modern recognition of the legitimacy of Kaharingan as a religious practice was a milestone in the long history of the Dayak struggles for autonomy. In 1953 the Dayaks, politically and numerically inferior to the Muslims, sought recognition of a territory called Great Dayak in 1953. In 1956, when their efforts failed, a rebellion broke out in Indonesian Borneo among the Christian and Kaharingan Dayaks. In 1957 a new province, West Kalimantan, was created with an ethnic Dayak majority.

The Indonesian government, following an abortive 1965 coup, labeled the Dayaks' indigenous religion as atheistic and, by implication, communist. The Dayaks suffered the madness of the anticommunist fever that swept Indonesia in the late 1960s. In the early 1970s, negotiations began between the Dayaks and the national government over recognition of the Kaharingan religion. The religion, although not related to Hinduism, was finally reclassified as a Hindu offshoot and therefore acceptable to the rigid religious standards set by the Indonesian government.

The Dayak culture was largely able to continue its traditional ways until the 1960s. In 1966, with the coming to power of the "New Order" government of Suharto, the first large logging operations were begun on Dayak lands. The logging companies, with government aid, simply drove the Dayaks from their homes and did little to resettle those displaced. In 1987 Dayak tribesmen in Malaysia began blockading logging roads in an effort to stop the rapid deforestation of their traditional lands. The Dayaks of Sarawak, with growing ties to their kinsmen in Indonesia, mobilized in defense of their common interests, including the rain forests, which provided most of what they needed to live.

Transmigration, a government program to resettle excess population from overcrowded Java and Madura, was implemented in the 1970s, often with the unwitting assistance of international aid organizations. The newcomers, settled on traditional Dayak lands cleared by logging, were from different religious, cultural, and linguistic backgrounds. The destruction of the Dayak habitat and the policy of transmigration aroused the first stirrings of Dayak activism.

Today, logging and mining interests are increasingly displacing the Dayaks and destroying one of the oldest indigenous cultures in the world. The Dayaks are being dispossessed of their traditional lands to allow the unchecked expansion of palm oil plantations, gold mines, and large-scale logging of the virgin forests of interior Kalimantan. The highlands of Kalimantan are believed to be covered by some of the world's oldest rain forests.

Plantation agriculture, controlled by the Indonesian government or private companies associated with the government, has been developed in collaboration with international lenders such as the World Bank. The development of plantations looks good in financial and development reports, but in practice the plantations have proved to be essentially efficient mechanisms for separating the local communities from their natural resource bases. There is a record of Dayak unhappiness with and protest against this mode of production and extraction extending back at least to the early 1980s.

For years the logging companies, many operated by Australian interests, felled vast stands of trees, then burned off the land to leave it ready for replanting. Then came the fires of 1994, which destroyed over 19,000 square miles (50,000 sq. km) of trees. The Indonesian government then banned clearing forests by fire, but illegal logging, with grave consequences for the Dayaks, continued unabated. Pleas to provincial governments to halt logging are mostly ignored, but such protests are increasing. In the late 1990s activists began destroying logging camps and equipment.

The unity of the many Dayak tribes has only begun, spurred by ethnic clashes and their marginalization by logging and mining companies. The frequent clashes between Dayak tribes are almost a thing of the past; their leaders increasingly realize that loss of lands and culture affects all tribes. Activists call the destruction of their way of life and the resettlement of unrelated peoples on Dayak lands cultural genocide, while the Indonesian and Malaysian governments pass laws that make the Dayaks squatters on their own traditional lands. In the late 1980s, a common economic predicament and social status within the state structures of both Indonesia and Malaysia tended to draw the various Dayak groups together for the first time in the long history of the island.

For thousands of years the Dayaks have lived in relative harmony with the world around them, but now their world is threatened by outside interests. Activists talk of the Dayaks' proud culture, a forest culture—but without the forest they are dead. Resistance to the destruction of their lands has so far only slowed logging, mining, and plantation interests for short periods of time. The Dayaks' forests in West Kalimantan are being destroyed at the fastest rate of any in the world.

In West Kalimantan, relative harmony between the Malays and the Dayaks has prevailed for generations. The balance was upset by a massive influx of Madurese, brought to Kalimantan under the *transmigrasi* (transmigration) program. The Madurese first began migrating to Kalimantan in the 1930s, but their numbers now increased sharply. The Madurese, favored by the government, were often employed as managers or workers on the vast government plantations. The Dayak workers on the plantations, economically marginalized and often exploited by the Madurese, resented the newcomers. In December 1996 ethnic violence broke out between the Dayaks and the Muslim Madurese. The violence, which started with small incidents, quickly escalated and spread. In late 1996 and early 1997 the ethnic fighting claimed hundreds of lives and displaced thousands to other areas or to refugee camps run by the Indonesian army.

In March 1997, seven local Dayak leaders were arrested and blamed for the ethnic violence in West Kalimantan. The leaders, accused of belonging to the nationalist organization Republik Dayak Merdeka (RDM), were among 25 people, mostly Dayaks, arrested following confrontations between Dayaks and Madurese in Kalimantan. The seven denied that the Dayaks had established a separatist movement, as charged by the local authorities. The underlying problem was that the Dayaks' confidence in the Indonesian government's policies and abilities to resolve disputes had collapsed.

In the late 1990s, the Malaysian and Indonesian governments stepped up their efforts to stamp out Dayak resistance to logging. The police raided the offices of indigenous organizations, making communication with international organizations and the world press very difficult. Blocking logging roads has been made punishable by an average two years in jail and heavy financial fines. In both Indonesia and Malaysia thousands have been resettled or forced to move to towns, where they crowd into slum dwellings and suffer from poor nutrition, lack of employment, and horrible sanitation conditions.

The issues of language and religion are the major nationalist concerns at the turn of the twenty-first century. Both Malaysia and Indonesia promote their national languages, and also the majority Muslim religion as the state religions. In February 1997 Dayaks from central Kalimantan demanded the creation of safeguards of the rights of the marginalized indigenous Dayaks.

In early 1999 conflicts between Dayaks and Madurese in the Sambas area of West Kalimantan spread across a wide area, producing Indonesia's most vicious ethnic killings in recent years. In October 2000 new violence broke out between indigenous peoples, the Christian and animist Dayaks and the Muslim Malays, and the Madurese migrants in and around the city of Pontianak. The violence, resulting from a traffic accident, spread through the city, leaving several dead and many injured. The conflict between the indigenous peoples and the migrants resettled in the region in government-sponsored migrations is one of the flash points of the growing Dayak national movement. By late 2000, over 1,200 people had been killed, thousands of homes and businesses had been burned, and thousands of Dayaks, Malays, and Madurese had been internally displaced. The government proposed to resettle 30,000 Madurese to an island off Borneo.

Dayak leaders have warned the Indonesian government, already beset by separatist and regionalist movements in several areas of the archipelago, that unless the rights and needs of the indigenous Dayaks are addressed and safeguarded, the continuing ethnic violence will continue, fueling regionalist and nationalist movements in West Kalimantan province. For over three decades the Dayaks have seen their natural resource base steadily eroded by government development policies, to the disadvantage of local communities. Vast amounts of Dayak lands and forests have been destroyed or appropriated for logging concessions, rubber and palm oil plantations, pulp plantations, and transmigration settlement sites.

In March 2001 the ethnic violence moved to Central Kalimantan, where indigenous Dayaks attacked immigrant Madurese groups, sending thousands fleeing by ship from the region. New violence also broke out in Pontianak in Western Kalimantan. The violence has gone on intermittantly since 1997 and has claimed hundreds, probably thousands, of lives and has fueled the growth of Dayak nationalism.

SELECTED BIBLIOGRAPHY:

Davis, Wade Dr., MacKenzie, Ian, and Shane Kennedy. *Nomads of the Dawn: The Penan of the Borneo Rainforest.* 1995.

Lim, Po Chiang. *Among the Dayaks.* 1988.

Perry, Richard J. *From Time Immemorial: Indigenous Peoples and State Systems.* 1996.

Winzeler, Robert L. *Indigenous Peoples and the State: Politics, Land, and Ethnicity in the Malayan Peninsula and Borneo.* 1998.

Dhofaris

Dhufaris; Zhufaris; Zhofaris

POPULATION: Approximately (2002e) 252,000 Dhofaris in the Arabian Peninsula, concentrated in the southern province of Dhofar in Oman. There are Dhofari communities in neighboring areas of Saudi Arabia and Yemen.

THE DHOFARI HOMELAND: The Dhofari homeland occupies part of the southeastern coast of the Arabian Peninsula in southern Oman. Although the province is quite large, only a 160-mile (257 km) crescent between the sea and the high mountains is habitable. By a quirk of nature, a tiny stretch of Dhofar catches the edge of the Indian Ocean monsoon each year. By September, the normally parched ravines are green, and waterfalls tumble through rich foliage. The cool weather, so different from the rest of the Arabian Peninsula, has

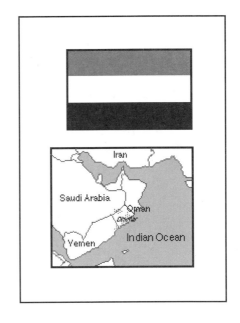

shaped the Dhofaris' national character. The lush district is separated from the rest of Oman by a formidable 400-mile (643 km) stretch of gravel desert. Dhofar forms a province or "governorate" of the Sultanate of Oman. *Governorate of Dhofar (Zhufar/Dhufar)*: 35,126 sq. mi.—90,976 sq. km, (2002e) 276,000—Dhofaris (including Mahra, Qarra, and Sheva) 79%, Yemenis 11%, other Omanis 10%. The Dhofari capital and major cultural center is Salalah, (2002e) 122,000.

FLAG: The Dhofari national flag, the flag of the national movement, is a horizontal tricolor of red, white, and black. The same tricolor, with the addition of the organization's name in black script centered on the white, is the flag of the Popular Front for the Liberation of Oman and Dhofar (PFLOD), the region's largest national group.

PEOPLE AND CULTURE: The Dhofaris take their name from the ruined medieval city of Zufar. Culturally the Dhofaris are divided between the peoples of the plains, mostly Najd and Kathier (or Bait Kathir), and the mountain peoples—the Mahra, Qarra, and Sheva tribes. Despite the teachings of Islam, many traditions persist that uphold different social clas-

527

ses. The highland peoples retain their tribal structures; each tribe is ruled by a sheik, who is responsible for the security and well-being of the tribe. Some of the mountaineers are still seminomadic, moving into settled villages only during the dry summer months. The Dhofaris generally marry only within their tribal and clan groups, although arranged marriages are now less common than in the past. Dhofari society is patrilineal, with inheritance passed from father to son. In the coastal region there has been an infusion of African blood, but in the highlands and the mountains the inhabitants are pure Semites. In the interior Dhofari women still wear traditional velvet dresses decorated with glittering beads and sequins. Some Dhofaris, particularly in the mountains, still practice female genital mutilation, which has been outlawed in Oman.

LANGUAGE AND RELIGION: The Dhofaris of the plains speak Dhofari Spoken Arabic, also called Dhofari. The dialect, related to Hadromi Spoken Arabic, the dialect spoken in the Hadhramawt region of Yemen, is distinct from the Omani dialect spoken in the Omani heartland to the north. The related mountain peoples, the Mahras, Qarras, and other highland tribes, speak pre-Arabic Semitic dialects, although many are now bilingual in the Dhofari dialect of Arabic. The Jibbali and Mehri, or Mahri, languages are also spoken by sizable populations in adjacent regions of Saudi Arabia and Yemen.

The Dhofaris are mostly Sunni Muslims, following the teachings of the Prophet Mohammed. In the mountains, pre-Islamic traditions and customs remain strong, while other religious influences have been introduced in Salalah (ancient Zufar) and the coastal regions. The Dhofaris are not culturally or historically related to the Omanis, and unlike the Omanis, who mostly adhere to the Ibadi sect of Islam, the majority of the Dhofari follow the Sunni rite.

NATIONAL HISTORY: Ancient Semitic peoples drawn to its luxuriant grazing land settled the region over 2,000 years ago. The Semites developed a Persian-influenced civilization in the coastal areas, a cultural island surrounded by desert and accessible only by sea. In biblical times Dhofar was known as the Land of Frankincense. The trade in the aromatic gum resin, burned as incense throughout the ancient world, was controlled by a single tribe, and it brought great wealth to ancient Dhofar. The rare resin, according to the New Testament, was presented to the Christ child by one of the eastern kings who followed the star to Bethlehem.

Ancient South Arabian kingdoms controlled the production of frankincense from the first century A.D. The region remained politically and culturally oriented toward South Arabia and the string of small states that stretched to the Red Sea. The Dhofaris, converted to Islam in the first period of Islamic missionary zeal in the seventh century, remained under the nominal rule of the Muslim caliphate for several centuries. The Islamic religion, as practiced in the isolated region, retained many of elements of the earlier pagan beliefs.

The city of Zufar (Salalah) thrived from the tenth to the fifteenth centuries as a regional trade center. By the close of the twelfth century, the region was ruled as a tributary of Oman by Ahmad ibn-Mohammad al-Manjawa. The first Europeans visited Dhofar in the early sixteenth century. The Portuguese quickly gained control of the coastal towns, which became ports on the European trade routes to the East. The Dhofaris expelled the Portuguese in 1650 and erected an independent, thriving sultanate on the trade routes between Persia, India, and Africa. Though the sultanate was virtually cut off from the rest of the Arabian Peninsula, Dhofari sailors plied the waters of the Indian Ocean.

In 1877 the Dhofari sultanate fell to the Al Bu Sa'id state of the Omanis, invaders from across the northern desert. Neglected by the Omani sultanate, Dhofar rapidly lost its earlier prosperity and became a backward retreat for wealthy Omanis fleeing the desert heat in the north. The Dhofaris, suffering religious and cultural discrimination, rebelled several times in the 1880s and 1890s. Their region, long ignored by the Omani government, became one of the poorest areas of the Arabian Peninsula. It gradually became a political and economic dependency of the British authorities in neighboring Hadhramawt. In 1939 the British, with Omani government agreement, installed in Salalah a garrison that stayed until the end of World War II.

Oppressive Omani rule, particularly after the discovery of oil in the 1950s, sparked a brief rebellion in 1957. Under the rule of Sultan Sa'id bin Taimur, who imprisoned his son, the present sultan of Oman, in Salalah, all newspapers, flashlights, and umbrellas were banned. Royal decrees prohibited dancing, smoking, photography, books, music, sunglasses, and trousers for men or women. The sultan moved permanently to Salalah in 1958. In 1960 Dhofar province boasted only one elementary school and no institutions of secondary education.

In the early 1960s, bands of rebel Dhofari tribesmen formed in the mountains; in 1963, they formed the Dhofar Liberation Front (DLF), which led a Dhofari rebellion against Omani rule. In 1971 the DLF joined with other noncommunist groups to form the Popular Front for the Liberation of Oman and the Arab Gulf (FLOAG), which fought both government troops and the Marxist Popular Front for the Liberation of the Occupied Arab Gulf (PFLOAG). The Dhofari rebellion, sparked by the arbitrary and oppressive rule of the Omani sultan, exacerbated religious tension between the Sunni Dhofari and the Ibadi Omanis.

The rebellion quickly became radicalized, and procommunists took control of the nationalist movement. Many moderate Dhofari nationalists, conservative and fervently anticommunist, fled the region or made peace with the Omani government. The Omani government, to undermine support for separatism, stepped up economic development with the construction of schools, hospitals, roads, and other infrastructure projects. The government also benefited from factional differences among the rebels, with Dhofari tribal leaders generally opposed to the radical socialist doctrine of the groups that had been formed on ideological grounds.

Armed and trained by the communist government of neighboring South Yemen, the Marxist PFLOAG took control of most of Dhofar in 1968 and surrounded Salalah in 1970. The Marxists, with support from the Soviet Union and China, quickly imposed a harsh regime, eliminating the nationalists and the anticommunist Dhofari leaders, outlawing the practice of Islam, and executing people for praying. The Marxist success in Dhofar prompted the British to engineer a coup in Oman that ended the despotic rule of the old sultan and replaced him with his British-educated son, Qabus ibn Sa'id. A combination of coercion and enticement persuaded many Dhofari rebel groups to negotiate, particularly the anticommunist nationalist groups. The Omanis, aided by Britain, Jordan, and Iran, finally crushed the Dhofari Marxists in December 1975.

Oil revenues from wells along the Dhofar-Oman border increased dramatically in the 1970s, bringing prosperity to Dhofar. The new sultan, in an effort to redress the neglect and abuses of his father, increased development and proclaimed a general amnesty. Many Dhofari returned to their homes between 1978 and 1989, although a sporadic rebellion continued. In the 1980s radical regimes in South Yemen and Iran supported Dhofari rebel groups. The growth of Muslim fundamentalism in the 1980s and early 1990s fanned new tension between the Ibadi and Sunni Muslims.

The reforms, particularly the sultan's practice of bringing tribal leaders into government, have muted support for separatism but have not ended the Dhofari demands for political, cultural, and economic autonomy. Fearful of Dhofari unrest, the government severely restricts access to the region. Dhofaris now control tribal and town councils, but the real political power rests with the *wali*, the governor appointed by the Oman government.

The Dhofaris have a relatively short history of association with the rest of Oman, and regionalist and nationalist sentiment is not far below the surface. The Omani government maintains an elite military unit in the region. Called the Cobras, its members are expected to be at their staging area, armed and ready for action, within three hours of receiving notice. Increasing unrest in the region, as in all of Oman, is met by a military response.

The unity of the Omani sultanate, established after the rebellion in Dhofar between 1963 and 1975, is being eroded by the greed of some of the ministers from Dhofar. Every government office now has a duplicate staff in Salalah, diverting resources that might better be used on the Batinah coast, where the bulk of Oman's population lives. Instead funds are being channeled south where staggering profits are realized on chimerical projects. At the same time, the Omani sultan is increasingly distancing himself from the people and the country's problems, allowing the Dhofaris to assume many of the prerogatives of an autonomous state. Anti-Dhofari sentiment in the rest of the sultanate gave rise to a rebirth of nationalist sentiment in the late 1990s. The government has encountered some opposition from small Dhofari guerrilla movements in the mountains.

In 1999 a huge container port opened at Salalah, which is alleviating the high unemployment among the Dhofaris. A free trade zone established in connection with the port, is also contributing to a general well-being in the Dhofar region. The port facilities have opened Dhofar to the rest of the Indian Ocean, helping to end the region's traditional isolation.

SELECTED BIBLIOGRAPHY:

Anthony, John D. *Historical and Cultural Dictionary of the Sultanate of Oman and the Emirates of Eastern Arabia.* 1976.
Arkless, David C. *The Secret War: Dhofar 1971/1972.* 1975.
Janzen, Jorg. *Nomads in the Sultanate of Oman: Tradition and Development in Dhofar.* 1993.
Niven, M. *Special Men, Special War: Portraits of the SAS and Dhofar.* 1992.

Dniestrians

Dniestrian Slavs; Transdniestrians; Transnistrians

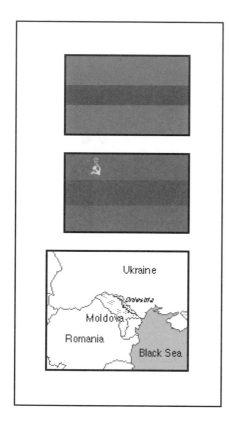

POPULATION: Approximately (2002e) 550,000 Dniestrian Slavs in Moldova, mostly in the breakaway Republic of Dniestria or Transnistria in northeastern Moldova. There are Dniestrian Slav communities in other parts of Moldova, in Ukraine, and in Russia.

THE DNIESTRIAN HOMELAND: The Dniestrian homeland occupies the lowlands on the east bank of the Dniestr River. The region is a rich agricultural area and the most industrialized zone of Moldova. It forms a long ribbon of land between the Dniestr River and the international border between Moldova and Ukraine. The status of the region remains unresolved; officially it is an autonomous republic within Moldova, but it functions as an independent state. *Transnistrian Republic (Pridnestrov'e Respublika/Dniestria):* (2002e) 732,000— Dniestrians 68%, Moldovan 32%. The Dniestrian capital and major cultural center is Tiraspol, (2002e) 216,000. The other major cultural center is Bendery, called Tighina by the Moldovans, (2002e) 149,000.

FLAG: The Dniestrian national flag, the flag of the breakaway republic, has horizontal stripes of red, green, and red. The flag of the Dniestrian national movement has horizontal stripes of green, red, green; it is charged with a yellow hammer and sickle surmounted by a red star, outline in yellow, on the upper hoist.

PEOPLE AND CULTURE: The Dniestrians are mostly Slavs, Russians, Ukrainians, Bulgarians, and Russified Moldovans who inhabit the region of Moldova east of the Dniestr River. They see themselves as a separate people, a Slavic Russian nation even though their homeland lies 375 miles (600 km) from the Russian border. Many are urban, and they tend to be more educated and to hold the managerial and professional positions in the region. Though the Ukrainians have a somewhat different history, they have identified closely with the ethnic Russians in the current conflict. The affinity of the Slav population as a whole has increased since the 1990s, on the basis of dialect and culture. They have formed a united ethnic bloc, which the Moldovan government, appealing to Ukrainian nationalism, has been unable to breach. The Dniestrians have developed a strong sense of regional identity separate from the Russian, Ukrainian, or Moldovan.

LANGUAGE AND RELIGION: The language of the region is Russian, spoken as the first language by most of the Russians, Ukrainians, Bulgarians, and other Slavs in the region. Language has been the primary adhesive for keeping the Ukrainians and Russians, the largest of the Slav groups, together, as the majority of the Ukrainians consider Russian their mother tongue. The majority of the Dniestrians speak a Russian dialect with Ukrainian and Romanian admixtures. The dialect developed its regional character beginning in the eighteenth century, when the majority of the settlers in the region were illiterate.

The Dniestrians, like the Moldovans, are mostly Orthodox Christians, but the two groups are divided between the national churches of Russia and Moldova/Romania. The Russian Orthodox Dniestrians reject control by the Moldovan Orthodox Church and have appealed to the Russian church hierarchy for support, although the ethnic conflict itself has no religious overtones.

NATIONAL HISTORY: The original inhabitants of the region, called Dacians by the Romans, came under Roman sway in the second century A.D. They were overrun by Visigoths and Ostrogoths between 250 and 375; Roman influence ended when imperial authorities abandoned the colonies and withdrew to the territory south of the Danube in 270. Settled by Slav tribes during the great Slav migrations of the seventh century, the region formed part of the first Slav empire, Kievan Rus', from the ninth to the eleventh centuries. Nomadic Cumans, a Turkic people, conquered the region and for almost two centuries carried on intermittent wars with the Byzantines, Kiev, and Hungary.

Devastated by the Mongols in 1242, the depopulated region was settled by Romanian peoples. The region slowly recovered under the rule of Stephen the Great, the creator of the first Moldavian principality in 1359. The Moldavian principality fell to the expanding Ottoman Empire in 1513. Slavic migration to the region resumed in the sixteenth and seventeenth centuries, forming a substantial population east of the Dniestr River in the eighteenth century.

Russia contested Turkish control beginning in 1711 and finally annexed the region called Bessarabia following the Russo-Turkish war of 1806–12. The newly annexed territory, with a Romanian-speaking majority, was subjected to intense Russification and opened to Slav colonization. Tiraspol, founded as a Russian fort in 1792, occupied the site of a Moldavian village and became the metropolis for the expanding Slav population of the region east of the Dniestr River. Ethnic Russians settling in the region usually chose the growing cities, leaving the countryside to the Moldovans and Ukrainians. By the early twentieth century, more than 60% of the Russians had been urbanized. The majority of the settlers east of the river assimilated into the Russian culture, most adopting Russian as their first language.

In the nineteenth century the region, with its mixed population and growing industries, became the object of quarrels and propaganda among and by a number of political groups and the newly organized nationalists seeking to claim the area as Ukrainian, Moldavian, and Russian. During the 1905 Russian revolution, serious disturbances broke out; rival groups fought running street battles and skirmished with Russian troops.

Devastated by nearly three years of World War I, Russia collapsed in revolution in February 1917, leaving the region, and neighboring Ukraine and Bessarabia, effectively independent. As chaos spread across the disintegrating empire, Moldavian and Ukrainian nationalists, and Russian political organizations of every hue, battled for control of the important industrial zone east of the Dniestr River. Following the October 1917 Bolshevik coup, nationalists in both Ukraine and Moldavia laid claim to the area.

Threatened by a Bolshevik advance, the Moldovans voted for union with Romania in April 1918, laying claim to the lands on the right bank of the Dniestr as part of united Romania, but ignoring the east bank with its large Slav population. Romanian army units occupied the area in June 1918 and forcibly annexed the region to Romania. The Romanian military suppressed the vehement opposition of the Slav minority within Bessarabia.

Menaced by the advancing Red Army, the Romanian troops at first withdrew, but stopped the communist advance at the Dniestr River. The Trans-Dniestr area, under Soviet control, became the autonomous Moldavian Autonomous Soviet Socialist Republic created within the Soviet Ukraine in 1924. The autonomous republic became a Soviet showpiece, from which the authorities hoped to export communism to neighboring Romania. In 1930 the Soviet authorities moved the capital of the autonomous republic from Balta, with its mixed population, to mostly Russian Tiraspol on the Dniestr River.

The Soviet army occupied neighboring Bessarabia in 1939 and formally annexed the region in 1940. Enlarged by the addition of Soviet Moldavia on the left bank of the Dniestr, the Moldavian republic became a constituent republic of the Soviet Union. The Slav majority of the Transdniestr region protested the union, citing the historical fact that the left bank of the river had never formed part of historical Bessarabia or Moldavia despite its large Moldavian minority.

Moldavian nationalism, suppressed for decades, grew dramatically in the more liberal atmosphere of the late 1980s, inciting mass demonstrations and demands for linguistic freedom. A nationalist government, elected in February 1990, endorsed in 1989 a strict language law propagated that outraged and alienated the republic's Slavs. Radical nationalists labeled the ethnic Slavs, concentrated on the left bank of the Dniestr River, as enemies, aliens, or invaders, exacerbating ethnic tensions as the instability in the Soviet Union increased. Demands by the republic's Slav population that Russian be made an official state language were ignored. Strikes in the Dniestr area intensified.

A Moldovan flag, adopted in April 1990, was rejected by the Slavs, who continued to fly the Soviet-era flag of red and green stripes. Fighting broke out in the region in September 1990, shortly after the regional *soviet*, or council, proclaimed Dniestria, also called Transnistria, independent. In November 1990, the Moldovan authorities sent troops to clear roadblocks set up by the Dniestrian separatists. In the resulting clashes six people were killed and over 30 wounded, greatly escalating tension in the region. The Dniestrians began forming self-defense units.

The collapse of the Soviet government in August 1991 left local Russian units free to assume political roles independent of political authorities in either Moscow or the newly independent states of the former Soviet Union. The 6,000 troops of the Russian 14th Army in the Trans-Dniestr region took on the role of amateur peacekeepers, a role that was rejected by both the Moldovans and the Dniestrian Slavs. Despite the growing tension, the new Russian government refused to withdraw its troops.

The Dniestrian Slavs categorically rejected Moldovan independence and the imposition of the Moldovan language and the Latin alphabet. Led by Igor Smirnov, the Dniestrian Slavs demanded that Russian be reinstated as an official language and that the Slav majority regions on the east bank of the Dniestr become an autonomous province in Moldova or join Russia.

Moldavia, officially renamed Moldova, became an independent state following the disintegration of the Soviet Union in August 1991. The declaration of independence on 27 August was rejected by the communist Dniestrian leadership. Demands for Dniestrian separation from Moldova escalated as even the noncommunist Slavs supported the communist leaders who promised to protect them from the Romanians. The name of the republic was changed from the Dniestr Moldovan Republic to simply the Dniestr Republic. A referendum held on 1 December 1991, with 98% of the voters participating, showed strong support for Dniestrian separation from Moldova. Armed conflict broke out, pitting the secessionists, backed by the 14th Army, against the new Moldovan army. The Moldovan government lost control of the region; by June 1992 over 700 had died, and 50,000 people had fled the fighting.

On 21 July 1992, following a series of meetings with representatives of Moldova, Romania, Ukraine, and Russia, Dniestria was accorded a special status within Moldova and granted the right to determine its own future should the Moldovans decide to merge with Romania. In late July Russian, Moldovan, and Dniestrian peacekeepers were deployed. In January 1994, the Moldovan government accepted proposals for greater Dniestrian self-government within a Moldovan confederation, but the Dniestrians rejected the offer.

In March 1994 the Moldovan government rescinded the 1989 language law that had begun the alienation of the Dniestrians. Peacekeepers, including Moldovan, Ukrainian, Russian, and Dniestrian troops, deployed in the region under the command of the 14th Army, now known as the Russian Army Operative Group. Agreements between the Moldovan and Russian governments provided for the disbanding of the unit, which was to be withdrawn from the region, but the possibility of renewed ethnic fighting delayed the redeployment of the remaining 2,600 troops indefinitely.

In the late 1990s, as the military stalemate continued, popular Dniestrian demands were modified to call for a more autonomous status, partly due to the majority Moldovan opposition to reunification with Romania. Igor Smirnov, reelected as president, stated at his inauguration in January 1997 that relations between Moldova and Dniestria should be as between separate states. In 1998, an agreement was reached to reduce from 42 to 14 the number of posts in the so-called border security zone that divides Dniestria from Moldova proper; it also allowed for the reopening of a strategic bridge across the Dniestr River.

A new territorial and administrative system was implemented in February 1999, changing Moldova's 40 districts into nine provinces and two autonomous regions, Gagauzia and Dniestria. Financial changes were expected eventually that would cut spending on local officials and make citizens of the autonomous region pay their own expenses. The new territorial arrangement was rejected by the Dniestrian Slav leadership.

There has been little fighting in the region since the civil war in 1992, when at least 1,000 died. Some trade between the region and Moldova has started and the Dniestrians even allowed their footballers (soccer players) to play in Moldova. Many in Moldova and elsewhere see the Dniestrian state as a nest of unreformed communists and gangsters.

The long stand-off has allowed the Dniestrians to build up the trappings of an independent state, including their own currency. No government has extended recognition to the Dniestrian republic, and the question of sovereignty remains unresolved. The Dniestr region is the industrial heart of the region, and the Moldovans can ill afford to lose it. The Moldovan government has agreed to grant the Dniestrians wide political and linguistic autonomy. The continued demands for complete independence is attributed to the political aspirations of much of the Dniestrian leadership.

The Russian government has refused to recognize Dniestrian independence, for fear of encouraging separatists active in many parts of Russia, but the Russians like the idea of a forward base in Dniestria to keep an eye on NATO expansion. The republic, close to Ukraine and Romania, is patrolled by 2,600 Russian soldiers, with a huge arms stockpile.

In early 2001, the Communists regained power following an election in ramshackle Moldova. The new president, Vladimir Voronin, an ethnic Russian, offered two important compromises. One, to give Russians equal status to Moldovan-Romanians throughout the country, and two having Moldova join the Russian-Belarussian union, that would reassure the Dniestrians that Moldova would not seek union with Romania in the future.

Dniestrians feel that they are a group apart, historically part of the great Slav nation, but more recently cut off from their roots and developing a separate Slav culture in the region. In a late 2000 poll, more than 80% of the Dniestrian population were in favor of maintaining independence.

SELECTED BIBLIOGRAPHY:

Dailey, Erika. *Human Rights in Moldova: The Turbulent Dniester.* 1993.
Laitin, David D. *Identity in Formation: The Russian-Speaking Populations in the Near Abroad.* 1998.
Shlapentokh, Vladimir, Munir Sendich, and Emil Payin. *The New Russian Diaspora: Russian Minorities in the Former Soviet Republics.* 1994.
Smith, Graham, ed. *Nation-Building in the Post-Soviet Borderlands: The Politics of National Identities.* 1998.

Don Cossacks
Donskie Kazaki; Kazaki Donu; Kazaky

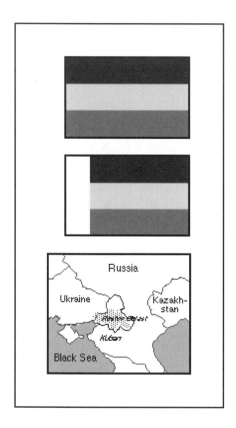

POPULATION: Approximately (2002e) 1,765,000 Don Cossacks in Russia, mostly living in the Rostov-na-Donu region of southern European Russia. Other large Don Cossack communities live in Germany, the United States and Canada, Australia, Siberia, and Central Asia. Population figures for the Don Cossacks are disputed, as they have been classified as ethnic Russians since the 1920s. Don Cossack nationalists claim a population of over two million in the North Caucasus.

THE DON COSSACK HOMELAND: The Don Cossack homeland occupies the basin of the Don River in southern European Russia, a major agricultural region with a narrow outlet, the Gulf of Taganrog, on the Sea of Azov and the Black Sea. The region, once one of three Cossack territories in southern European Russia, formerly the Territory of the Don Cossacks and later the Republic of the Don, is now Rostov Oblast (province) of the Russian Federation. *Rostov Oblast (Territory of the Don Cossacks):* 38,919 sq. mi.—100,826 sq. km, (2002e) 4,318,000—Don Cossacks 44%, Russians 36%, Ukrainians 17%, others 3%. The Don Cossack capital and major cultural center is Novocherkassk, (2002e) 183,000, with a population about 80% Don Cossack. The other important cultural center, the capital of the oblast, Rostov-na-Donu, (2002e) 1,012,000, metropolitan area, 1,328,000.

FLAG: The Don Cossack national flag, the flag of the former Republic of the Don, is a horizontal tricolor of blue, yellow, and red. The official flag of Rostov Oblast is the same horizontal tricolor with the addition of a vertical white stripe at the hoist.

PEOPLE AND CULTURE: The Don Cossacks claim to be the indigenous people of the Don River basin—a living people, not a historical phenomenon, a military caste, or a social class, as many historians argue. The origins of the Cossacks go back to the Tatars of the Golden Horde, who controlled the steppe lands of Ukraine and southern Russia in the thirteenth century. With the breakup of the Mongol-Tatar empire, many Tatars came to terms with the Russians and formed defensive barriers on the expanding Russian borders. From the mid-fifteenth century communities of Russians, Ukrainians, Poles, and other nationalities fleeing serfdom, oppression, debt, or punishment began to form along the Don River. The runaways formed military groups, borrowing traits and structure from the Tatars and developing their skills through brigandage and mercenary service. They began to call themselves Cossacks, from the Turkish *kazak*, meaning "free warriors," and often mixed with neighboring warrior nations, developing linguistic and cultural characteristics that distinguished them from each other. The Don Cossacks, the largest of the Cossack nations, are of Russian and "Eastern," probably Kalmyk, ancestry. They evolved as a separate people in the sixteenth and seventeenth century. The Don Cossacks' claim, not recognized by the Russian government, to separate cultural and ethnic identity is based on their unique history, mode of life, geographic location, and their language.

LANGUAGE AND RELIGION: The Don Cossack language is a distinct Cossack dialect of mixed Russian, Ukrainian, Kalmyk, and Tatar elements. The first Cossack language dictionary was written in the 1960s, but its publication in the Soviet Union was forbidden. Most Don Cossacks are bilingual, speaking their own dialect and standard Russian.

The majority of the Don Cossacks remain devoutly Orthodox, with a higher proportion of believers than among the general Russian public. The Orthodox religion, part of the Don Cossack heritage, is an integral part of their culture. A minority are Old Believers, a breakaway Orthodox sect that was persecuted in the eighteenth and nineteenth centuries, many taking refuge among the Cossack settlements in the Don Basin.

NATIONAL HISTORY: The fertile basin of the Don River has attracted migrants and conquerors since ancient times. Settled by nomadic Slavs around A.D. 880, the region formed a tributary state of Kievan Rus', the first great Slav empire. In the early thirteenth century Mongols and Tatars of the Golden Horde overran the Don River area; ethnic Tatars settled in the depopulated lowlands between 1241 and 1300.

In the early sixteenth century, the Don River valley was sparsely inhabited by nomads and Tatar raiders. Bands of Russians, fleeing oppression and serfdom, began to form in the depopulated region. The number of Slavs fleeing to the Don region increased rapidly during the reigns of Ivan the Terrible and his successors in the late sixteenth and the early seventeenth centuries. In 1570 Ivan the Terrible began to employ Don Cossacks to escort caravans and later to raid Tatar camps and recapture Slavs taken as slaves.

Virtually independent, the Don Cossacks lived by plunder and by selling their military services. A Don Cossack assembly, called the *krug*, was formed to deliberate on important matters; in a structure borrowed from the Tatars, it elected a *hetman* or *ataman*, meaning "leader of horsemen." The Cossack communities of the Don were tolerant of people of other faiths, except for the Jews, and accepted into their hordes Buddhists, Old Believers, Muslims, and pagans. The Cossack communities of the Don freely mixed with the neighboring peoples, particularly the Kalmyks and Tatars. Isolated in the wild country between the Russians and the Muslim lands to the south, they developed a distinctive culture and language that incorporated Russian, Ukrainian, Kalmyk, and Tatar elements.

The Don Cossacks pledged personal loyalty to the tsar in 1614 and received official recognition as a self-governing community in 1623. At the end of the seventeenth century, the Russian frontier had moved closer to the Don Cossack homeland, with newer settlers taking up agriculture. The Cossacks, living in autonomous communities, were allowed to govern themselves in return for military service, but until 1690 their leaders forbade farming. With agriculture came some personal land holdings although most of the territory remained communal lands; the Don Cossacks became a privileged, landowning class employing newly arrived peasants and poorer Cossacks as agricultural workers.

The beginning of the end of the free Cossack bands came with the arrival of Peter the Great at the Sea of Azov to fight the Turks in 1695. His determination to bring the Don Cossacks under his control provoked an uprising in 1707. In 1708 the Don Cossacks lost the right to elect their own atamans. The region, formally ceded to Russia by the Ottoman Empire in 1739, was organized as an autonomous military district, the Territory of the Don Cossacks, in 1790. By 1800 the majority of the Don Cossacks had been reconciled to Russian rule. To centralize the administration of the territory, a new capital was founded at Novocherkassk in 1805.

Fifty thousand Cossack soldiers fought for the Russian Empire during the Napoleonic Wars, of whom 20,000 were killed. A tsarist decree of 1835 established the Don Cossacks as a military caste with special privileges, their loyalty to the tsar ensured by gendarme units garrisoned at Taganrog. Male Don Cossacks were obliged to serve as long as they could sit a horse or shoulder a rifle.

Usually better educated than ordinary Russians, the Don Cossacks prospered on the proceeds of their rich farmlands. Most Cossack communities held the land in common and rented parcels to Russian and Ukrainian peasants. An outflux of freed serfs and urban workers to the expanding industrial cities in the 1860s impelled the Don leaders to establish a modern civil government. The Cossacks, after three centuries of guarding Russia's now-secure frontiers, became a mobile military force to be used within the country. From 1886 the Don Cossacks were dispatched to crush rebellions in other parts of the vast empire, becoming the feared "fist" of the tsar. In the later nineteenth and early twentieth centuries, the tsarist government used Cossack troops to carry out pogroms against the Jews.

In World War I, elite Don Cossack military units were sent to the front in 1914 and many died in heavy fighting. Nonetheless, they greatly resented being pulled back to police an increasingly restive civilian population.

Freed of their oath of loyalty by the overthrow of the tsar in February 1917, the Don Cossacks formed a military government under their own ataman, the first to be elected since 1708. The Don territory, virtually independent as Russia collapsed, remained calm and peaceful, the peace overseen by the Don Cossack military units. Gen. Alexis Kaledin, who became ataman on 30 June 1917, established a Don military government as the only recognized authority in the region.

The Don Cossack government supported the Provisional Russian government, but the Bolshevik regime in Petrograd, taking power in October 1917, quickly proclaimed the expropriation of the extensive Cossack lands. In December 1917 the Don Cossacks declared war on the new Bolsheviks, becoming the first nation to revolt openly against the Bolsheviks. On 10 January 1918, in Novocherkassk, the Don Cossack leaders formally declared the complete independence of the Republic of the Don.

General Kaledin committed suicide following a defeat by the Red Army in February 1918. Another defeat, on 1 March 1918, was followed by the occupation of the Don Cossack republic by Bolshevik troops, but they were quickly replaced by the Germans as a result of the Treaty of Brest-Litovsk between the Central Powers and Soviet Russia. On 21 April 1918 a new provisional government was proclaimed, and the Don Cossack government, reestablished in Novocherkassk, declared the republic neutral in the remainder of World War I.

The Don Cossacks were mostly allied to the anti-Bolshevik White forces as civil war spread across Russia, though a minority joined the Bolsheviks and fought their kin. The Don Cossacks represented one of the Whites' most powerful military units, but strain soon appeared over the Whites' vehement opposition to the secession of any part of Russia. A Don Cossack delegation sent to the 1919 Paris Peace Conference failed to win recognition of the republic or to sway the allies' support of the White position on secession.

Though close to victory over the Red Army in October and November of 1919, the White offensive began to falter and finally to collapse. Refugees flooded into the republic, bringing turmoil, disease, and hunger. Rostov, a city of 200,000 in 1914, had a population of 1.5 million in early 1920. Their frantic appeals to the Allies ignored, the beleaguered Don Cossacks finally suffered defeat by the advancing Red Army in early 1920. Thousands fled, many making their way to Western Europe.

The Soviet authorities, determined to end the Cossack threat to their control, ended all traditional Cossack privileges, prohibited military training, banned the use of the Cossack language, and forbade all references to Cossack culture or history. The Don Cossack population, thinned by war, suffered further losses to the famine that accompanied the forced collectivization of the Don Cossack lands in 1932–33. Still suspect, thousands of Don Cossacks died in purges during Joseph Stalin's dictatorship.

The Nazis, following their sudden invasion of their Soviet ally in 1941, proclaimed the Cossacks descendants of Germanic Ostrogoths, not "subhuman" Slavs, and therefore acceptable allies. Thousands of Don Cossacks joined the Nazis, often facing Cossack soldiers in the Red Army in battle. Some 40,000 Cossacks, including 11,000 women and children, surrendered to the British forces in Austria at the end of the war. The Allies ignored their pleas and forcibly repatriated them to face Stalin's wrath. Most perished in the infamous Gulag. By the early 1950s nearly all traces of Cossack culture in the Don region had been eradicated or suppressed.

A national and cultural revival sprang from an aborted uprising in 1962. Riots broke out in Novocherkassk over the price of basic necessities, but they soon became openly antigovernment demonstrations, accompanied by old Cossack slogans. The region was placed under siege; according to Cossack sources, more than 5,000 died during the insurrection. The violent onslaught triggered a Don Cossack cultural reawakening, accompanied by the publication of the first Cossack-language dictionary and many reference books on Cossack history, culture, language, and nationalist aspirations. The majority of the Don Cossack cultural material was published by exiled Cossack groups in the West.

The liberalization of Soviet society begun in the late 1980s by Mikhail Gorbachev allowed the reculturation of the Don Cossacks to accelerate. When *glasnost* (openness) allowed them to speak out, they first embraced environmental causes, then demanded a voice in local government. A Don Cossack national movement, with roots in the prerevolutionary autonomous state, demanded recognition of the Don Cossacks as a separate people and the indigenous nation of the Don River basin. Claiming that the Don Cossacks formed a majority in the Rostov region, nationalists demanded the replacement of the provincial government with the traditional hetman. As more Don Cossacks declared themselves, nationalist organizations proliferated.

At first the goals of the Cossack associations were cultural and historical in nature—to preserve Cossack traditions and promote historical accuracy of Cossack lifestyles. Don Cossacks then began to demand local self-administration and the return of traditional lands. The Don Cossacks reestablished their traditional Great Circle, the council or *krug*, and selected Mikhail Sholokhov as their hetman. Sholokhov is the son of the Don Cossack writer Mikhail Aleksandrovich Sholokhov, who won international fame for epic novels of his homeland—*The Silent Don, And Quiet Flows the Don*—and other works.

The Russian government, like the former Soviet government, continues to claim that the Cossack nations are ethnically Russian; the claim is disputed by the Don Cossacks. While political scientists, linguists, and ethnologists continued to debate whether the Cossacks constitute a separate national group or are a subgroup of the Russians, the Don Cossacks began, for the first time in nearly 70 years, making their presence felt in their homeland along the Don River.

In mid-1992, a decree signed by Russian president Boris Yeltsin rehabilitated the Cossacks and classified them as "oppressed peoples." The decree granted them the status of an ethnic group and gave them the right to receive land free of charge. The decree also called on Cossack forces to protect Russia's borders; however, some Don Cossacks refused to serve outside their traditional homeland. Don Cossack leaders in March 1993 demanded the creation of an autonomous republic, which would become a member state of the Russian Federation. Decrees in 1993–94 promised special privileges and dispensations, including the restoration of Don Cossack units within the Russian armed forces, but stopped short of endorsing a separate Don Cossack republic. In June 1994 over 150 Don Cossacks, led by their ataman, picketed provincial buildings in Rostov demanding immediate action on the presidential and governmental decrees recognizing their financial and political demands.

In the late 1990s, appointed and elected Don Cossacks became a force in the government of Rostov Oblast. A few Cossack schools were opened, and the Cossacks again became the defining feature in the region. The official flag of the province is based on the Don Cossack flag, and investment and aid from the diaspora has aided local autonomy and increased Don Cossack political power.

Under their elected leader, the Supreme Ataman of the Don Cossacks, small Don Cossack units have fought in ethnic conflicts in Moldova, Bosnia, and Abkhazia. In January 1999, Yeltsin granted the rank of Cossack general, the highest rank available, to the ataman of the Don Cossacks. Although the Don Cossacks are intent on winning recognition as a separate nation, they have identified a modern vocation for themselves—their historical military calling as the protectors of the Slav frontiers. But they also insist on another pillar of Cossack heritage—the independence of the Don Cossack nation, under its elected ataman.

SELECTED BIBLIOGRAPHY:

Feodoroff, Nicholas V. *History of the Cossacks.* 1999.

Groushko, Mike. *Cossack: Warrior Riders of the Steppes.* 1993.

O'Rourke, Shane. *Warriors and Peasants: The Don Cossacks in Late Imperial Russia.* 2000.

Sgorlon, Carlo. *Army of the Lost Rivers.* 1998.

Druze

Druse; Duruz; Muwahhidun; Mowahhidoon

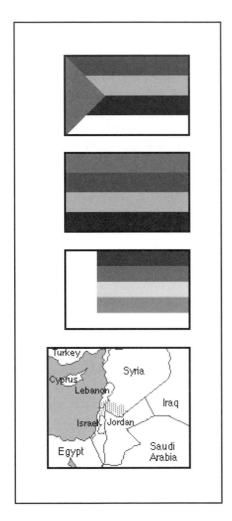

POPULATION: Approximately (2002e) 1,450,000 Druze in the Middle East, including 900,000 in the Jebel ed-Druze region of Syria, 400,000 in adjacent areas of Lebanon, 98,000 in northern Israel, 14,000 in Jordan, and 17,000 in the Israeli-occupied Golan Heights. Outside the region the largest Druze communities live in the United States and Canada. Exact population numbers are difficult to determine, due to the Druze practice of outwardly conforming to the faith of the people among whom they live.

THE DRUZE HOMELAND: The Druze homeland lies in the Middle East, straddling the borders of Syria, Lebanon, Israel, and Jordan. Most of the region is mountainous; Druze communities are traditionally located in the less accessible high mountain valleys. The largest part of the homeland lies in Syria, in a region called Jebel ed-Druze, or Mountain of the Druze. Jebel ed-Druze has no official status; the region comprises the Syrian provinces of Es Suweida, Dar'a, and Al-Qunaytirah. Israel annexed the western districts of the latter two, called the Golan Heights, in 1981. *Jebel ed-Druze (Jabal ad-Duruz)*: 4,328 sq. mi.—11,212 sq. km, (2002e) 1,339,000—Druze 87%, other Syrians 13%. The Druze capital and major cultural center in Syria is as-Suwayda, called Sweida by the Druze, (2002e) 77,000. The other important cultural centers are Dar'a, called Daran, (2002e) 93,000, and Qanawat, the seat of the highest-ranking *jawwad*, or spiritual leader. The major culture center of the Lebanese Druze is Marj 'Uyun, in the Shuf Mountains, (2002e) 17,000. The largest of the Druze villages in northern Israel are Mughar (2002e) 6,000, and Yirka (2002e) 3,000.

FLAG: The Druze national flag, the flag recognized by Druze groups in Syria, Lebanon, and Israel, has four horizontal stripes of red, yellow, blue, and white, with a green triangle at the hoist. Druze groups in the Americas and Australia fly a flag of four horizontal stripes of green, red, yellow, and blue. The flag of the former Druze state in Syria, Jebel ed Druze, has five horizontal stripes of green, red, yellow, blue, and white, with a broad white vertical stripe at the hoist.

PEOPLE AND CULTURE: The Druze are a fiercely independent ethnoreligious group whose exact ethnic origins are unknown but combine both Persian and Arabic influences. Druze national identity and their distinctive religion are closely intertwined. According to Druze legend, the high incidence of tall, fair, and light-eyed Druze results from the mixture of ancient nomads and the Greek soldiers of Alexander the Great. Druze women, although veiled in public, have greater freedom than is usual among Arabic-speaking populations and even participate in the highest circles of Druze religious and political organizations. A large Druze population inhabits the mountains between Beirut and the Syrian border in Lebanon; smaller minorities live in a string of Druze towns in Israel's Galilee region and in the Israeli-occupied Golan Heights.

LANGUAGE AND RELIGION: The Druze speak a North Levantine dialect of Arabic, also called Syrio-Lebanese Arabic. The majority use subdialects called South Lebanese Arabic and South Syrian Arabic (also spoken by the Druze in Israel). The Druze dialect of Arabic retains many pre-Arabic influences and forms associated with their religious writings. In Israel the Druze population also speaks Hebrew, while French is widely spoken by the Druze populations in Syria and Lebanon.

The Druze religion, the defining characteristic of the national group, is characterized by an eclectic system of doctrines and by a cohesion and loyalty among its members that has enabled the Druze culture to survive nearly a thousand years of turbulent history. They call themselves *muwahhidun*, meaning monotheists. The religion developed out of Isma'ilite teachings, with various Jewish, Christian, Gnostic, Neoplatonic, and Persian (Iranian) elements, but with a strict doctrine of monotheism. The Druze permit no conversion to or from their religion and no intermarriage with other groups. Druze society encompasses two distinct groups. The *uqqal* (the knowers, or sages), including women, account for about 10% of the population; the knowers are privy to the secret religious teaching of the *hikma*, the Druze religious doctrine called the Book of Wisdom. The *juhal* or *juhaall* (the ignorant), the majority, are excluded from the secrets and leadership of their religion. The *juhal* attend only the first part of religious meetings, with the remainder reserved for the *uqqal*. Muslims view the Druze as heretical for accepting the divinity of Hakim, the third Fatimid caliph of Egypt, who died in A.D. 1021. The Druze shun mosques, holding their religious meetings on Thursday evenings in inconspicuous buildings. They have also abandoned the Five Pillars of Islam—recitation of the creed, prayers five times a day, donating to charity, fasting during Ramadan, and the pilgrimage to Mecca—and are therefore not regarded by Sunni Muslims as an Islamic people.

NATIONAL HISTORY: Druze traditions trace their origins to an ancient nomadic people, the Auranites, who gave their name to their mountainous homeland in Syria, the Hauran or Hawran. The pagan Auranites, influenced by Jewish and later Greek religious traditions, converted to Christianity under Roman rule in the second century A.D. The Christianity they practiced retained a number of pre-Christian traditions and rituals.

Muslim Arabs invaded the Auranite homeland in the seventh century. The conquerors forcibly converted the inhabitants to their Islamic religion, but many of the Auranite converts secretly continued to adhere to their pre-Islamic traditions. Propagation of the tenets of Druze belief began in Cairo in A.D. 1017, under Hamzah ibn 'Ali, a follower of the caliph Hakim, who had proclaimed his divinity. His sudden disappearance soon after greatly influenced the new sect, whose members still wait for his promised return. Another subordinate, Muhammad ad-Darazi, an Iranian mystic, spread the doctrine in Syria and Lebanon and gave his name to the new religion.

The Druze rejection of Mohammed as the ultimate prophet and of the Koran as the revealed word earned them the enmity of their Muslim neighbors. For centuries they suffered discrimination and persecution by the Sunni Muslim majority. The despised Druze finally withdrew to the mountain strongholds in the Hawran and the Lebanon Mountains, where they evolved a clannish, closed society.

Fierce Druze warriors resisted the sixteenth-century Ottoman conquest of their homeland and the renewed persecution that followed their defeat. Only in the nineteenth century did the Turkish authorities recognize the Druze as an independent congregation. In 1860 the Druze rebelled and attacked both the Turks and the Maronites* of the lowlands. A French expedition sent to protect the Maronite Christians in the Turkish province in 1861 defeated the Druze and drove thousands into the isolated plateaus of the Hawran. The Europeans pressed the Turks to establish a Christian-dominated semi-autonomous province in Mount Lebanon (part of present-day Lebanon) in 1864.

In the isolated Hawran the Druze built a new capital, Sweida, a fortress city ruled by the powerful Al-Atash clan. The Druze warriors, heartened by their religious belief that those who fall in battle are instantly reborn, successfully resisted Turkish attempts to reimpose their rule on Dera, the main town of the Hawran, or Sweida.

Druze attacks on Christians, renewed in the 1890s, provoked a French to send troops to occupy the Druze homeland. The French administration imposed on the Druze region allowed them considerable autonomy under a sultan of the Al-Atash clan. In 1914, when war broke out in Europe, the French attempted to impose direct rule, provoking a Druze uprising that was not fully subdued until after the war had ended and more French troops became available.

In 1920, the French incorporated the Hawran into the League of Nations mandate territory in the former Turkish provinces of Syria, while enlarging Christian-dominated Mount Lebanon to include all of what is now Lebanon, including a large Druze territory. In 1921 the French mandate authorities created an autonomous Druze state, called Jebel ed-Druze, as one of the Levant States. French attempts to replace the Al-Atash ruler with a French governor and to tamper with the Druze tribal hierarchy incited serious revolts in 1925–27, 1937, and 1939 in both Syria and Lebanon. In 1925 the rebels, led by Sultan al-Atash, defeated the French and were later joined by Syrian nationalists. By mid-1927, following the arrival of French reinforcements, the revolt had ended, and Jebel ed-Druze was under tighter military control. The French encouraged the natural tendency of the Druze to isolation, in order to separate them from Arab nationalism and keep them dependent on the French for their security. After the French surrender to the Axis in 1940 the Levant States came under the control of the Vichy government.

Allied troops, mostly British and Free French, liberated the Levant States in 1941 and formally granted Lebanon independence. The Free French also granted independence to Syria but retained the separate French-protected states in Jebel ed-Druze and Latakia, with its large population of Alawites.* In 1942 the Syrian republic incorporated Jebel ed-Druze over strong Druze opposition to domination by their ancient Sunni Muslim enemies. In 1944 the Syrian government, in a conciliatory gesture, guaranteed Druze cultural and religious rights but effectively ended their political autonomy. Since then Druze leaders in Syria have participated in various coups, particularly in 1954.

The Druze in Israel, living in 18 villages in Galilee and on Mount Carmel, long persecuted by the Sunni Muslims, became allies of the Jews and participated in the establishment of the State of Israel in 1948. At the Druze community's request, the Druze have done compulsory military service in Israel since 1957. Druze soldiers have fought alongside the Jewish forces in the many conflicts with the neighboring Arab states. In 1982 Druze soldiers participated in the Israeli invasion of Lebanon, and many were killed in the fighting.

In Syria, Druze opposition to the military government erupted in revolts in 1949 and 1954. Defeated by the Syrian military, the Druze lost all their former autonomous rights. With few economic opportunities, Syria's non–Sunni Muslim minorities joined the military in large numbers in the 1960s. Dominated by the ethnoreligious minorities, the Syrian military purged the officer corps in 1964–65 and replaced most of the Sunni Muslims with

Alawites and Druze. Following the Syrian defeat in the 1967 war with Israel, a power struggle developed; most Druze officers were eliminated by the dominant Alawites in 1969. The expulsion of the Druze and the smaller minorities from the military left Syria under the effective control of an Alawite military clique that continues to rule the Syrian state to the present.

In 1975 civil war broke out in Lebanon between the various ethnic and religious militias. The war, which eventually drew in the Syrians and Israelis, devastated the region and polarized national identities. Druze militias, supported by the Palestinians,* drove all Christians from the Shuf Mountains. In 1987 the leader of the Lebanese Druze established the Civil Administration of the Mountain (CAOM), which provided many services to the Druze of the Shuf Mountains that the Beirut government was unable or unwilling to provide. Since that time, the CAOM has expanded and refined its bureaucracy, increased its services, and generally begun to play an important role in governing the Druze of the Shuf region. Where most states have a dominant majority, Lebanon has only rival minorities guarding their own interests, with the Druze virtually self-governing in their mountain homeland in the south.

The end of Lebanon's civil war in 1990 left the Druze in control of the Shuf region and some suburban areas of southern Beirut. In 1992, the Druze boycotted the Lebanese parliamentary elections. In May 1994, the only Druze radio station in Lebanon was closed, the first casualty of a new government ban on private newscasts. The Druze participated in the 1996 elections; Lebanese Druze leader Walid Jumblatt was the winner in the Druze-dominated regions. Jumblatt strongly criticized the decision to select a Maronite Christian as the president of Lebanon in 1998.

The Druze actively support the return of the Israeli-occupied Golan Heights to Syria, partly to facilitate communication between the various Druze communities. Talks between the Israelis and Syrians, which continued into the new millennium, focused on the disputed region, its Druze population, and the larger number of Israeli settlers.

Israel's good relations with its Druze minority has facilitated contacts between the Druze national leadership and the Israeli government. The very real possibility of fragmented and coup-prone Syria splintering along ethnic and religious lines has become an important element in Druze calculations. Good relations with Israel could be vital to the future of the Druze nation.

The Syrian Druze, having enthusiastically embraced militant Arab nationalism to deflect Sunni Muslim hatred, have seen the value of their support decline rapidly with the end of the Cold War and the splintering of Arab unity. Druze nationalism has gradually superseded the former pan-Arab nationalism the Druze embraced after World War II. The resurgent

Druze nationalism has grown with the renewed contact with the Druze minorities in Lebanon and Israel.

Druze separatism, long suppressed in the heartland in Syria, emerged to some extent with the death of the Syrian dictator Hafiz al-Assad in 1999. His son Bashar, more moderate and less enamored of radical Arab nationalism, has allowed some stirrings of opposition and opinions suppressed for over three decades, although many of the harsh aspects of the dictatorship were reinstated in 2001.

The Israeli withdrawal from southern Lebanon in early 2000 ended strife between the Druze clans, which had been divided between clans allied to the Israeli-backed Southern Lebanese Army (SLA) and others opposed to the Israeli occupation of the region, which includes traditional Druze lands. The conflict had divided the Druze of Lebanon, much as the question of the disposition of Druze-populated Golan Heights pitted clan against clan in Lebanon, Syria, and Israel.

In April 2001 Walid Jumblatt, long a firm ally of Syria, called for the withdrawal of Syrian troops from Lebanon, demanded greater autonomy for the Druze regions of the country, and closer ties between the Druze in Lebanon, Syria, and Israel. In August 2001, he called on members of the Druze community in Israel to refuse to serve in the Israeli army. They are now the only Arab Israeli community required to serve in the Israeli army. He deplored that on the Syrian Golan Heights, occupied by Israel since 1967, many of the Druze still living there have also taken up Israeli nationality.

SELECTED BIBLIOGRAPHY:

Betts, Robert Benton. *The Druze.* 1988.
Hark, Judith. *Change and Continuity among the Lebanese Druze Community: The Civil Administration of the Mountains, 1983–1990.* 1993.
Nissim, Dana. *The Druze: A Religious Community in Transition.* 1980.
Parsons, Laila. *The Druze between Palestine and Israel, 1947–49.* 2000.

East Timorese

Timurese; Tatums; Maubere

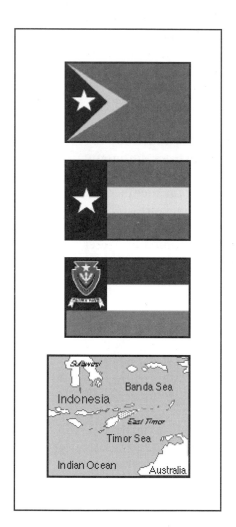

POPULATION: Approximately (2002e) 675,000 East Timorese in Indonesia, mostly concentrated on the island of Timor. There are thousands of East Timorese in refugee camps in neighboring West Timor and in other parts of Indonesia.

THE EAST TIMORESE HOMELAND: The East Timorese homeland occupies the eastern half of the island of Timor in the Timor Sea, in the eastern part of the Malay Archipelago 397 miles (640 km) northwest of Australia. The territory includes the enclave of Okussi (Oé-Cusse), surrounded by Indonesian territory in West Timor, and the small islands of Kambing and Jako. Formerly called the province of Loro Sae by the Indonesia, since late 1999 East Timor has been administered by the United Nations, which is preparing the territory for internationally recognized independence. *East Timor (Timor Timur)*: 5,743 sq. mi.—14,874 sq. km, (2002e) 991,000—96% East Timorese, Indonesian 4%. The East Timorese capital and major cultural center is Dili, 1999 population (prior to the outbreak of violence) 170,000, (2002e) 46,000.

FLAG: The East Timorese national flag, adopted in 1975, is a red field with a black triangle, outlined in yellow, at the hoist bearing a white five-pointed star. The flag of the major nationalist organization, the Revolutionary Front of Independent East Timor (Fretilin) has horizontal stripes of red, yellow, red with a vertical black stripe at the hoist bearing a white five-pointed star. The flag of the National Council of Maubere Resistance (CNRM), which has formed a coalition government under UN auspices, a horizontal tricolor of blue, white, and green, bearing a black canton on the upper hoist charged with a red shield with the national symbols above the motto "Patria Povo."

PEOPLE AND CULTURE: The East Timorese, of mixed Papuan, Malay, Polynesian, and European ancestry, are a distinct nation shaped by their Christian religion and the centuries of Portuguese colonial rule. Non-Timorese and Muslim Timorese from the western half of the island have settled in East Timor since 1975; they accounted for over 20% of the total population of the province until the outbreak of violence following the independence referendum in mid-1999.

LANGUAGE AND RELIGION: The East Timorese speak Tatum (Tetum), a West Indonesian language with a marked Portuguese admixture. About 40 dialects of the language are spoken in the territory. Portuguese is the second language and is proposed as an official language after independence. Bahasa Indonesia, the official language of Indonesia, was imposed during the Indonesian occupation, but few East Timorese speak it.

The majority of the East Timorese are devoutly Roman Catholic, the legacy of centuries of Portuguese rule. Their Catholic religion is an integral part of the East Timorese culture and effectively separates the East Timorese from their mainly Muslim neighbors in Indonesia.

NATIONAL HISTORY: Malays, coming from the islands to the west, colonized the island in the thirteenth century, driving the original inhabitants, small Papuan tribes, into the mountainous interior. The more advanced Malays settled the coastal areas but eventually spread into the interior and gradually absorbed the Papuans into their small tribal groups.

Portuguese navigators came to the island in 1520, followed by the Spanish in 1522. The island of Timor came under permanent Portuguese rule in 1586. The Dutch seized the western half of the island in 1618 and finally defeated the rival Portuguese in a struggle for control of the East Indies in 1641, leaving Portuguese Timor the only Portuguese territory in the vast region of the Malay Archipelago called the East Indies. Portuguese missionaries exerted tremendous influence in the isolated colony, and the Catholic religion became firmly established before Islam spread to the region.

A neglected appendage of Portuguese India until 1844 and later administered from Portuguese Macao, the colony received few European settlers. The Dutch officially ceded sovereignty over East Timor to Portugal in 1859; Portuguese rule over the eastern half of Timor was settled by treaties in 1860 and 1893. East Timor was made a separate Portuguese colony in 1896, the border with Dutch Timor being finally delimited. The actual frontier was decided by the religion of the inhabitants, with the areas populated by Roman Catholics included in Portuguese Timor. The development of the colony, the smallest and poorest of the Portuguese Empire, began only after a serious Timorese rebellion against the colonial administration in 1910–12.

The Japanese took control of Timor during World War II, but the territory was returned to neutral Portugal in 1945. Indonesia, the former Dutch East Indies, including the western half of Timor, gained independence in 1949. The new Indonesian government immediately began to call for the decolonization of Portuguese East Timor, but with little support among the Roman Catholic East Timorese. In 1951 the Portuguese government upgraded the colony's status to that of an overseas territory, and over the next two decades development accelerated, giving the East Timorese a higher standard of living than the inhabitants of neighboring Indonesian regions.

A leftist revolutionary government installed in Lisbon in 1974 moved to free the nation's remaining overseas possessions. Anticipating the end of colonial rule, political parties formed in East Timor—the Revolutionary Front of Independent East Timor (Fretilin), supported by the large rural population, favoring immediate independence; the mostly urban Timor Democratic Union (UDT) advocating self-government and continued ties to Portugal, with a gradual transition to independence; and a small, pro-Indonesian group, Apodeti. In July 1975 elections for local councils, Fretilin took 55% of the vote, UDT received 45%, and Apodeti's calls for union with Indonesia failed completely.

Apodeti activists attempted a coup in August 1975, setting off a civil war in the territory. Fretilin, with the support of the Catholic majority, defeated the Indonesian-backed rebels and on 28 November 1975 declared East Timor independent. The Indonesian government, refusing to accept the declaration or the defeat of its faction, launched an invasion of the new state nine days later. Over 50,000 East Timorese died in the first two months of the Indonesian invasion.

The United Nations refused to accept the legality of the Indonesian occupation. In April 1976, the UN called on Indonesia to withdraw and to allow a referendum on independence. Ignoring the resolution, the Indonesian government annexed the territory in July and embarked upon a brutal campaign to crush widespread resistance. Up to 200,000 East Timorese perished over the next four years, about a third of the 1975 population. A cease-fire was negotiated in 1983, but the fighting resumed less than six months later. Ten years after the Indonesian invasion, the East Timor living standard had not regained the levels of the Portuguese colonial era.

East Timor remained a closed military area until 1988; little official news of the ongoing war reached the outside world. International criticism pushed the Indonesian government to curtail the worst of the military excesses against the civilian population in 1984, although a campaign to defeat the Fretilin insurrection continued. The Indonesian government in

1990 refused a proposal by Xanana Gusmão, the leader of Fretilin, for unconditional peace negotiations aimed at ending the armed struggle.

Stung by international threats of a termination of development aid and calls for an impartial investigation of the harsh conditions in the province, the Indonesian government for the first time, disciplined the military officers responsible for the massacres of civilians. As long as the East Timor situation retained world attention, the repression eased somewhat.

Indonesian troops in November 1992 captured Gusmão, bringing international demands for a fair trial and renewed insistence upon an investigation into Indonesia's administration of East Timor. Gusmão was convicted of possession of illegal arms and other charges and was sentenced to life in prison. In 1995 Indonesian president Suharto reduced the sentence to 20 years.

In July 1994 demonstrators in Dili demanding religious freedom clashed with police seeking to break up the march. In August the Indonesian government banned all protest marches and demonstrations in the province, in an effort to keep the region under tight control—and also out of the news, in order to blunt increasingly strident criticism in the world press.

A November 1994 Pacific nations economic meeting held in Jakarta set off a new round of Timorese demonstrations and pleas to the heads of governments attending the meeting. In spite of the efforts and repression of the Indonesian government, the East Timorese had once again brought the question of East Timor to the world's attention.

The 20th anniversary of Indonesia's annexation of East Timor in 1995 opened a new round of violence and repression. The UN sponsored negotiations between Indonesian governments and East Timorese representatives, but the talks stalled over continuing Indonesian military repression, East Timorese insistence on independence, and government-sponsored settlement of Muslims in the majority-Christian province.

The overthrow of the Suharto dictatorship in early 1999 opened the way for a more democratic government. East Timorese demands for a referendum on their future status were finally granted, and in August 1999 the East Timorese voted 78.5% to separate from Indonesia. The Indonesian military and local Muslim militias refused to accept the vote and rampaged through the province, burning and killing. Over 300,000 fled or were forced into neighboring Indonesian West Timor, while many more fled to the mountains to escape the militias. An unknown number of East Timorese were killed or disappeared, and the region, with its few cities, including the capital Dili, was left in ruins. Catholic priests and nuns were especially targeted by the militias as the province descended into chaos and violence.

An Australian-led UN mission eventually took control of the territory, and by October 1999 many of the estimated 400,000 refugees had begun to return to the devastated area. On 19 October 1999, in an unprecedented vote, the Indonesian assembly agreed that after 24 years of brutal rule, East Timor should be allowed to secede from the Indonesian federation. Recriminations and demands for the arrest of individuals wanted for massive human-rights violations continue to be heard. Indonesian military leaders refuse to investigate the army's role in the systematic, widespread, and flagrant violations of basic humanitarian and human rights. Xanana Gusmão, released from prison by the new Indonesian regime, returned to East Timor as a hero of the fight for independence.

The East Timorese, under UN rule, have begun to rebuild their homeland and to prepare for the independence they have sacrificed so much to achieve. Despite generous humanitarian assistance, the East Timorese lack even basic services and all but the most rudimentary civil administration. The effort of the East Timorese to create an independent nation-state from the ashes will require many years and the full support of the international community. The UN Transitional Administration and the international agencies operating in East Timor currently ensure public order and maintain border security, but the key to a successful transition to full independence will depend on the East Timorese themselves. The slow process of nation building in East Timor has only just begun.

A few East Timorese athletes were invited to participate in the Sydney Summer Olympics in the early fall of 2000. They were allowed to participate, but not under the East Timorese flag, which does not as yet represent an autonomous state. They wore white uniforms and entered the games under the Olympic Games flag.

East Timorese leaders, speaking at a ceremony to mark one year since the fateful referendum on independence in 1999, again thanked the international community for aiding in the reconstruction of the region. They also appealed to the pro-Indonesian militias to end attacks on the territory and to release the thousands of refugees held in camps in Indonesian West Timor.

In early November 2000, the leaders of the small nation pressed the UN to set a date for the independence of East Timor. On 30 August 2001, the East Timorese voted for a government to lead them to full independence and democratic government. Many hope that eventually Xanana Gusmão, the former leader of the independence movement will become their first president. Fretilin took a majority of seats, 55 of 88, in the new assembly and will lead East Timor to independence in May 2002; however, it needed 60 seats to dictate the constitution.

Secret documents released by the United States in December 2001, revealed that prior to the Indonesian invasion of East Timor in 1976, the U.S. president, Gerald Ford, and Secretary of State, Henry Kissinger, met with Indonesian president Suharto. According to the documents, the U.S. administration approved the invasion and annexation of East Timor as an anticommunist measure. On 8 December 2001, East Timorese leaders demanded an explanation and at the very least, an apology.

SELECTED BIBLIOGRAPHY:

Fischer, Tim. *Seven Days in East Timor: Ballot and Bullets.* 2000.
Jardin, Matthew. *East Timor: Genocide in Paradise.* 1999.
McCloskey, Stephen, ed. *The East Timor Question: The Struggle for Independence from Indonesia.* 2000.
Retboll, Torben. *East Timor, Indonesia and the Western Democracies.* 1988.

Eastern Mongols

Khingan Mongols; Mongoll Zizhiqu

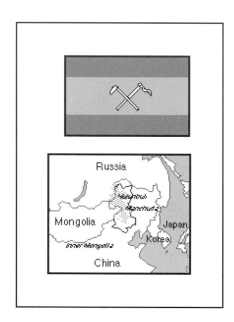

POPULATION: Approximately (2002e) 2,150,000 Eastern Mongols in northern Asia, concentrated in eastern Inner Mongolia and the northwestern part of the province of Jilin in the People's Republic of China.

THE EASTERN MONGOL HOMELAND: The Eastern Mongol homeland, Hulunbuir, the former General Kingan Provinces of Manchuria, lies in northeastern China. The region, formerly part of Manchuria, is a region of fertile farmlands and extensive grazing lands dominated by the forested Greater Khingan Range. Eastern Mongolia is the only part of Mongol territory that receives adequate rainfall. Eastern Mongolia has no official status but forms part of the autonomous region of Inner Mongolia and the provinces of Heilongjiang and Jilin. *Eastern Mongolia/Mongoll Zizhiqu (Hulunbuir)*: 164,235 sq. mi.—425,479 sq. km, (2002e) 6,230,000—Chinese 72%, Eastern Mongols 24%, other Mongols 4%. The Eastern Mongol capital and major cultural center is Hailar, called Khailar by the Eastern Mongols, (2002e) 167,000.

FLAG: The Eastern Mongol flag, the flag of the former republic, has horizontal stripes of red, pale blue, and red, the middle stripe twice the width of the red stripes and charged with a white quirt (riding whip) and pick crossed in the center.

PEOPLE AND CULTURE: The Eastern Mongols are a Mongol people, the eastern branch of the Mongols. Historically the Eastern Mongols are more closely related to the peoples of Siberia, particularly the Evenks,* than to the Mongol tribes farther west. Divided into tribal groups, the Eastern Mongols are the descendants of the Mongols of the eastern leagues or principalities, more influenced by the Manchu and Tungus peoples than were the Mongol peoples to the west. The largest of the Eastern Mongol groups are the Daghur, Solon, Bargut, Oronchon, and Jostu. While a minority still follows the ancient way of life as nomadic herders, the majority of the Eastern Mongols now live in industrial towns and cities. The Eastern Mongols are closely related to the other Mongols of Central Asia, but tribal and historical differences remain important. The eastern tribes are the descendants of the eastern leagues or principalities, tribal hierarchies that remain to the present. The cities are increasingly Han Chinese, while the countryside remains ethnically Mongol.

LANGUAGE AND RELIGION: The Eastern Mongol tribes speak dialects of Eastern or Khingan Mongolian, a peripheral Mongol language with considerable Chinese, Manchu, and Russian admixtures. The language, part of the Mongolian group of Khalka-Buriat family of Eastern Mongolian languages, is spoken in several regional dialects. The most widely spoken of the dialects is Dagur or Daghur, although the name is often applied to all the Eastern Mongolian dialects. Other important dialects are Jostu, Tumut, Khorchin, Uzemchin, and Urat. Most of the Eastern Mongols are bilingual in Mandarin Chinese; many also speak Khalka Mongol, the language of the Republic of Mongolia, and the literary language of most of the Mongols in China. Monolingual Mongol speakers are considered illiterate by the Chinese government.

The religion of the Eastern Mongols, in spite of decades of official state atheism, is the Tibetan form of Buddhism called Lamaism. The Eastern Mongols, like the other Mongol nations and the Tibetans,* revere the Dalai Lama as the spiritual head of the nation.

NATIONAL HISTORY: Nomadic tribes, often warring among themselves, occupied the grasslands as herders. Historically the tribal nomads raided the Manchu and Chinese lands to the east and south. Over many centuries the tribes living in the highlands in the Greater Khingan Range evolved six distinct principalities or leagues—Khingan, Hulunbuir, Nonnimuren, Cherim, Chaota, and Jostu. The leagues remained politically and culturally separate until conquered by Genghis Khan, who united the various Mongol nations in the twelfth century. The Eastern Mongol leagues were absorbed into the huge Mongol Empire, which eventually stretched across most of the known world.

Under Ghenghis Khan's successors the empire weakened, eventually breaking up into many warring states. Politically the Eastern Mongols formed a loose confederation, and in the fifteenth and early sixteenth centuries supremacy passed from tribe to tribe. This period also saw the spread of Tibetan Buddhism into the region, uniting the Eastern Mongol leagues religiously but not politically.

The rise of the Manchus* in the sixteenth century was followed by alliances between the Manchus and the Eastern Mongol leagues. The Eastern Mongol leagues came under direct Manchu rule in 1635. Retaining their own princes and religious leaders, the leagues formed part of Outer China following the Manchu conquest of the Chinese Empire in 1644, in which Eastern Mongol troops participated. To ensure loyalty to the Manchu dynasty, immigration to the region by ethnic Chinese was restricted, and the Eastern Mongol leagues were promised that they could reclaim their independence should there be a change of dynasty in China.

During the nineteenth century, population pressure to the south brought pressure to open up traditional Mongol territories. To relieve severe overcrowding, the Manchu administration opened the Mongol borderlands to Chinese immigration in 1878. Thousands of Chinese moved to the region, most settling in the more fertile southeast. The continuing immigration gradually pushed the native Mongols off the best lands and encroached on their grazing lands, causing serious ethnic clashes and sporadic revolts. In 1904, fears that the Chinese were determined to occupy the remaining league lands sparked violent rioting and attacks on immigration offices and Manchu officials. The Chinese settlers pushed the Mongols north into the dry uplands, while the settlers took control of the fertile lowlands.

Japanese influence in the region increased during the Russo-Japanese War of 1904–1905, with both Russians and Japanese enlisting Mongol mercenaries. By secret treaties after the Russian defeat, the Mongols east of the meridian of Peking were recognized by the Russians as in the Japanese sphere of interest, although many Russians emigrated to the region, eventually forming the second-largest national group, after the Mongols, in many areas.

Eastern Mongolia, ruled directly by the Manchus and not subject to the Chinese administration of Inner China, was the scene of grave disturbances during the Chinese Revolution in 1911. The overthrow of the Manchu dynasty was viewed by the Eastern Mongols as a change of dynasty under the terms of the 1635 Manchu agreement and produced demands for independence. Ignored by China's new republican government, the Eastern Mongol princes announced their intention to secede in 1913. Led by Wangtehfanma, the national leader, the Eastern Mongol leagues attempted to separate from China. The northern principalities of Fengtien and Hulunbuir declared their independence; the Barguts, with Russian assistance, also declared their independence and announced their intention to join neighboring Mongolia. The new Chinese republican government disavowed the Manchu agreement of 1635 and dispatched troops. The Eastern Mongols appealed to the Russians, but with Russia embroiled in World War I, no aid arrived. The republican authorities stripped the Eastern Mongols of their former autonomy except for Barga, in Bargut, which was made an autonomous province. The region came under the authority of the provincial government of Manchuria. Barga's autonomy was revoked in 1920, as Russian power in the region collapsed.

Japanese influence in Manchuria increased in the 1920s during a period of turbulence and chaos in China. On 15 February 1928 the leaders of the Solon League declared the principality independent of China, but Chinese troops again moved in. In 1931 the Japanese took effective control of Eastern Mongolia, making it part of Manchuria; in 1932 they supported a Manchu nationalist declaration of independence from China. In 1933 the Eastern Mongol homeland officially became part of the new state of Manchukuo and was organized as the General Khingan Provinces. First called Eastern Mongols by the Japanese, the authorities organized the Mongol tribes of western Manchuria into separate divisions of Manchukuo's new army—the Mongol Cavalry, the Daghur Autonomous Army, the Solon Self-Defense Army, the Orochon Self Guard, and other units. Thousands of Eastern Mongols, trained by the Japanese to fight with modern weapons, gained practical combat experience during World War II.

The Soviet army occupied Manchuria in August 1945, accompanied by military units of the Mongolian People's Republic. Eastern Mongol nationalists, aided by the Mongol soldiers, formed a national army of 250,000, made up of the units from the former Japanese Manchukuo Army. In November 1945 Stalin ordered the Soviet and Mongol military units to withdraw in deference to the Chinese communists, but on 15 January 1946, before the communists could reach the region, the Eastern Mongol leaders declared the region independent as the People's Republic of Eastern Mongolia. The Eastern Mongol divisions allied to defeated Japan went over to the Soviets, partly because the Nationalist Chinese government of Chiang Kai-shek labeled them traitors and puppets. Payenmandu, the former governor of the General Khingan Provinces of Manchukuo, was elected the new republic's first president.

The nationalists rejected overtures from both the Chinese communists and their civil war enemies, the Chinese Nationalists, and set about erecting an independent Eastern Mongolia. The new state, reorganized into six provinces corresponding to the former leagues, came under increasing pressure from the escalating Chinese Civil War and the Eastern Mongol military units, organized as the Revolutionary Army of Eastern Mongolia, skirmished with both communist and Nationalist Chinese troops.

Factional conflict between groups supporting the Chinese Nationalists and others looking to the Chinese communists or to the Russians destabilized the region, weakening Eastern Mongol defenses as the Chinese civil war spilled into the area. The Eastern Mongol government, its attempt to win allies in Mongolia blocked by Stalin, tried to negotiate a promise of autonomy within China, but both Chinese factions rebuffed the proposal. In mid-1946, right-wing feudal leaders and landlords took power after the leftists failed to win a promise of autonomy. They changed the name of the republic to the Republic of Eastern Mongolia and set about eliminating leftist ideology and symbols, and introducing the Mongol color, blue, to the national flag. Finally defeated by the Chinese communists under Lin Piao in May 1947, the Eastern Mongols came under firm communist rule when the last Chinese Nationalist troops were expelled from the region in

1948. In 1952 the traditional provinces were abolished, and the boundaries were changed to diffuse the Eastern Mongol population.

Severe nationalist disturbances, provoked by government-sponsored immigration to the region, swept the Eastern Mongol districts during the Cultural Revolution in the late 1960s. The authorities, blaming Russian interference in Eastern Mongolia, responded by splitting the region from Inner Mongolia and dividing it among the three northeastern Chinese provinces in 1969. Reduced to minority status by massive immigration, the Eastern Mongols began to assimilate, slowly losing their unique culture and history. In 1979 a less strident Chinese leadership rejoined Eastern Mongolia to Inner Mongolia, therefore restoring some cultural autonomy to the Eastern Mongol population.

The overthrow of communism in the Soviet Union and Mongolia stimulated a cultural resurgence and a parallel growth of nationalism in the region that began to reverse decades of assimilation. The rediscovery of their separate history excited demands for the resurrection of the leagues and the medieval Mongol federation. Modern Eastern Mongol nationalists resolved to return to the traditional values and culture that over five decades of communist rule had nearly destroyed.

In the 1990s, modernization in China alleviated the abject poverty of the region, although it remained far behind the booming provinces of China's Pacific coast. Following renewed unrest and reported violence, the communist government granted a measure of cultural autonomy to the local governments of the Mongol homelands, but in early May 1991 the authorities launched a secret campaign of repression against ethnic Mongolian intellectuals in Inner Mongolia. The campaign began with the suppression of small study groups formed to regenerate the suppressed ethnic and cultural identity. In December 1995 the campaign intensified, with arrests and torture used against activists.

The Eastern Mongol nationalist movement remains small in numbers, poorly equipped, loosely united, and geographically dispersed. Militants based in Europe and the United States remain the most active. Support within Inner Mongolia is ambivalent at best, given the economic situation and memories of the Cultural Revolution and of mass starvation in World War II. The nationalists increasingly encompass environmentalists, antinuclear testing groups, religious organizations, and opponents of the recently imposed limits on the number of children in families. Moderate nationalists work for more autonomy, as promised in the Chinese constitution.

The Chinese government started to develop the economy of Hulunbuir in the late 1990s. The region's abundant basic resources, including coal, timber, and fish, were exploited. Recently discovered oil and natural gas offered new resources for development. As in other minority areas, China's rulers, while exploiting the natural resources, were eager to show their concern for the preservation of local culture. Awards were offered to Han Chinese officials who learned to speak Mongol, though few mastered even basic words. Mongolian script appears alongside Chinese in all public signs. Administrative units, while organized along Chinese lines, are labeled in accordance with traditional Mongol units. Hulunbuir is designated a "league," and the counties are called "banners," a Mongol administrative term.

The Eastern Mongol culture, society, and economy have all been badly damaged under Chinese rule. By distributing grazing lands to herders in the same way that it distributes crop lands to farmers, the Chinese authorities have violated the most basic tenets of pastoral ecology, ruining much of the Eastern Mongol grassland. Culturally, the language has been devalued. Even to pronounce words in Mongolian rather than in the approved sinified pronunciations is to invite dangerous suspicions of "national consciousness." Traditional social mechanisms have been eroded, particularly the unique and ancient customs and traits that long distinguished the Eastern Mongols.

SELECTED BIBLIOGRAPHY:

Curtin, Jeremiah. *The Mongols: A History*. 1996.

Lattimore, Owen. *The Mongols of Manchuria*. 1969.

Pokotilov, D. *History of the Eastern Mongols during the Ming Dynasty from 1368 to 1634*. 2000.

Tang, Peter S. *Russian and Soviet Policy in Manchuria and Outer Mongolia 1911–1931*. 1979.

Eastern Samoans

American Samoans

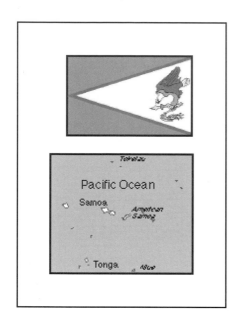

POPULATION: Approximately (2002e) 125,000 Eastern Samoans in U.S. territory, concentrated in the territory of American Samoa, with large populations in Hawaii, California, and other areas of the continental United States.

THE EASTERN SAMOAN HOMELAND: The Eastern Samoan homeland lies in the central Pacific Ocean, comprising the eastern Samoan islands of Tutuila, Aunuu, and Rose; three islands of the Manua group; and Swains Island. Except for the coral atolls of Swains and Rose, the islands are rocky and of volcanic origin. The homeland forms an unincorporated, unorganized territory of the United States. *American Samoa (Eastern Samoa)*: 77 sq. mi.— 199 sq. km, (2002e) 67,000—Eastern Samoans 91%, Tongans 4%, Mainlanders (Caucasians) 2%, others 3%. The Eastern Samoan capital and major cultural center is Pago Pago, on Tutuila, (2002e) 2,000, the center of an urban area with a population of 21,000.

FLAG: The flag of the Eastern Samoans, the official flag of American Samoa, is a blue field with a white triangle edged in red extending from the hoist, bearing a brown and white bald eagle flying toward the hoist carrying two traditional Samoan symbols of traditional authority, a staff and a war club.

PEOPLE AND CULTURE: The Eastern Samoans are part of the larger Samoan national group and form the overwhelming majority of the population of American Samoa. They are a Polynesian nation closely related to the indigenous peoples of New Zealand, Tahiti, Hawaii, and Tonga. The Samoan way of life, called *fa'a Samoa*, is communal; its basic unit of social organization is the extended family. Eastern Samoan society is both communal and authoritarian, with a hierarchy extending up through the village level to the local legislature, the council of chiefs, called the Fono. The Eastern Samoans, with their distinct history and nationality, are nationals of the United States but are not American citizens. Most of the population lives on the largest of the islands, Tutuila, which has the capital and the only large urban population. Due to their status as U.S. nationals, the Eastern Samoans are free to live anywhere in the United States; the number living in Hawaii and the continental United States outnumber those in the home islands.

LANGUAGE AND RELIGION: The Eastern Samoan language is a dialect of the Samoan language, which belongs to the Austronesian or Malayo-Polynesian language group. The language is widely spoken, along with English. Education in the islands is mostly in English. The language is closely related to the languages of the Hawaiians* of the Hawaiian Islands to the north, and of the Maoris* of New Zealand to the south. The majority of the Eastern Samoans are bilingual, and literacy is very high.

The Samoans' traditional religions have essentially disappeared from the islands; the Eastern Samoans today are Christians, more than half belonging to the Congregational Church. The remainder are either Roman Catholic, about 20%, or Methodist.

NATIONAL HISTORY: The islands were probably inhabited by Polynesians more than 2,500 years ago. Around the beginning of the Christian era, migrants left the islands in communal canoes to populate islands as far away as Hawaii and New Zealand. By about A.D. 200, Samoa was at the center of the settled part of eastern Polynesia. As its population grew to the point that the islands were unable to support it, whole families or clans would leave in search of new islands to colonize. Historically Tutuila was subordinate to the ruler of Upolu, now part of Western Samoa (Republic of Samoa), but the Manua Islands were ruled by their own chief.

The Dutch explorer Jacob Roggeveen sighted the Manua Islands in 1722, but he passed them by. French explorers visited the islands in 1768 and again in 1787, when eleven members of the expedition were massacred by frightened islanders. For the next 40 years European navigators avoided the islands, although they became a refuge for runaway sailors and escaped convicts.

The first Christian missionaries, representing the London Missionary Society, arrived in the 1830s. Other missionaries followed; Tutuila and later the Manua Islands came under missionary influence. The Europeans outlawed many island traditions and insisted on "suitable" clothing.

Units of the U.S. Navy visited the islands in 1839, marking the beginning of American interest in the region. In 1872 representatives of the United States signed a treaty with the Samoan kingdom for rights to a naval station at Pago Pago. In the same year a number of chiefs, fearing European colonization, particularly by the Germans, petitioned the United States to annex the eastern islands of Samoa.

A civil war between rival chiefs erupted in 1889. The three powers active in the Pacific—Germany, the United Kingdom, and the United States—

agreed to consider Samoa neutral and created a tripartite protectorate over the islands. A convention between the powers 10 years later recognized the paramount interests of the United States in the islands east of longitude 171° W and of the Germans in the islands west of the meridian. The eastern group of islands was deeded by the high chiefs to the United States in 1904. The cession was not accepted by the U.S. Congress until 1929, although Swains had been granted to the United States by Britain in 1925.

During World War I, German Western Samoa surrendered to the military forces of New Zealand. In spite of some sentiment for the reunification of the islands, Western Samoa continued under New Zealand rule as a League of Nations mandate, while the United States retained control of Eastern Samoa, particularly the strategic naval base at Pago Pago, one of the largest and best protected anchorages in the Pacific.

Other than the harbor area at Pago Pago, the American administration did little to develop the islands, which it administered like the European colonies. The islanders had little governmental power in the first decades of the twentieth century. The islands were under the jurisdiction of the U.S. Navy until 1951, when they were transferred to the Department of the Interior. Agitation for local control mounted in the 1960s and 1970s. In a constitutional convention in 1960, the Eastern Samoans approved the first constitution of the territory of American Samoa. A new constitution was approved in 1967, and in 1978 the first elected governor took office in Pago Pago. Since then, all members of the territory's legislature, the Fono, have been elected by the citizens of the islands. Except for defense, the Fono and the governor control American Samoa.

Since the 1950s thousands of Eastern Samoans have emigrated to Hawaii and the continental United States. Lack of economic and educational opportunity in the islands was the impetus for the migration, along with overpopulation. By the late 1970s the number of Eastern Samoans living outside the islands outnumbered the island population. Tourism and exposure to American culture by the 1970s had broken down the formerly rigid social structure under the *matai*, the chiefs.

Western Samoa was granted independence in 1962, and the new government began a campaign for the reunification of Samoa. The growth of Samoan nationalism began a period of massive development by the American administration. By 1979 the U.S. government had pumped $250 million into the islands, expanding the fishing industry, building schools and health clinics, and creating a viable infrastructure.

In 1981 the first official delegate from American Samoa to Congress was elected. The United States refused to consider independence for the islands, preferring to retain power through a paternalistic welfare state that offers little opportunity to young Eastern Samoans. In 1995 the government of American Samoa was forced to cut public services by 20%. Until the cut, 80% of government income had been tied up in salaries of 4,000 public employees. The government carried a debt of between $20 and $30 million on an annual budget of $140 million. More than half the annual budget is funded by the U.S. government.

The government of American Samoa protested in July 1997 when Western Samoa adopted "Samoa" as its official name. The Eastern Samoans argued that this implied an assumption of predominance over all the Samoan Archipelago.

In spite of a veneer of American culture, *fa'a Samoa*, the Samoan way of thinking and doing things, remains very strong in the islands. Many Eastern Samoans talk of a united Samoan nation, but in view of their ties to family members living in the continental United States, they have shown little interest in taking the last step toward full independence or to unification with the neighboring independent Samoa.

SELECTED BIBLIOGRAPHY:

Faleomavaega, Eni F.H. *Navigating the Future: A Samoan Perspective on U.S.-Pacific Relations.* 1995.
Hughes, H.G.A. *Samoa: American Samoa, Western Samoa, Samoans Abroad.* 1997.
Kristen Katherine, and Kathleen Thompson. *Pacific Islands.* 1996.
Setchell, William A. *American Samoa.* 1976.

Edos

Binis; Benins; Addos; Oviedos; Oviobas

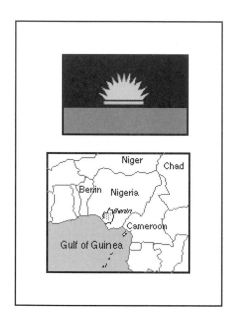

POPULATION: Approximately (2002e) 4,620,000 Edos in Nigeria, concentrated in the historical region of Benin, currently divided between the states of Edo and Delta. Other large Edo communities live in Lagos and other large cities in southwestern Nigeria. Smaller Edo communities live in northern Nigeria, Ghana, and Togo.

THE EDO HOMELAND: The Edo homeland lies in southwestern Nigeria, occupying an upland savanna sloping down to the forest zone and the delta of the Niger River on the Bight of Benin. Mangrove swamps predominate in the oil-rich delta and merge with freshwater swamps farther north before rising to hilly plateaus. The historical Edo homeland, Benin, forms two states of the Federal Republic of Nigeria, Edo and Delta. The Edo dominate in Edo state and form the majority in the northern part of Delta state. *Region of Benin*: 15,361 sq. mi.—39,795 sq. km, (2002e) 7,175,000—Edos 63%, Urhobos 21%, Itsekiris 8%, Ibos (Delta Ibos) 6%. The Edo capital and major cultural center is Benin City, also called Edo, (2002e) 1,046,000. The other important cultural center is Asaba, (2002e) 66,000, the capital of Delta.

FLAG: The Edo national flag, the flag of the national movement, is a black field, with a broad green horizontal stripe at the bottom, bearing a yellow rising sun with eleven rays centered.

PEOPLE AND CULTURE: The Edos are a Bantu people, the descendants of one of Africa's most sophisticated precolonial kingdoms. The Edo nation includes the Edo proper and three subgroups—the Edo-speaking Urhobo (Sobo) south of Benin City; the Bini around the capital city; and the Esan in the east. The Edos mostly live in compact settlements that range in size from small villages to large market towns. The village is the basis of Edo society. Within each village the males are divided into three age groups, which are assigned public works related to community buildings, festivals, and other community concerns. The annual *Igwe* festival, which features all the ceremonies and dances associated with the *oba*, king, is the major cultural festival, but in recent years the festivals have taken on an increasingly nationalistic tone.

LANGUAGE AND RELIGION: All of the Edo subdivisions speak dialects of the same language of the Kwa branch of the Niger-Congo language group. The language is used in local radio and television, and it is the medium of primary and secondary education. The language has an extensive literature, including dictionaries, histories, and fiction.

Many Edos are Christian or Muslim, but traditional religion, worshipping a remote creator and lesser gods, is still a powerful influence in the belief structure of all Edos. The Edos recognize the existence of dual worlds, spirit and physical. They believe that everyone in the physical world has a replica in the spirit world and that the two worlds have great influence over one another. Every 10 years the Edos hold a large masquerade ceremony for the entire community to honor the *edjos*, the spirits.

NATIONAL HISTORY: Very little is known of the early history of the Edos, although early records mention the Edo kingdom of Benin as well established by around A.D. 1000. According to Edo legends the first empire declined, and the Edos, dissatisfied with a dynasty of semimythical kings, the Ogisos, in the thirteenth century invited Prince Oranmiyan of Ife, in Yorubaland, to become their ruler. His son, Eweka, is regarded as the first *oba*, or king, of the Edo kingdom of Benin, although real authority remained with the hereditary local chiefs for many years.

Royal power began to assert itself in the late fourteenth century under Ewedo and was firmly established under the most famous oba, Ewuare the Great. He established hereditary succession to the Edo throne and vastly expanded Benin's national territory. A second empire, thought to have been established between 1390 and 1440, developed as one of the most advanced states in Africa. By the mid-sixteenth century, Benin extended from the Niger River delta in the east to near present-day Lagos in the west.

The Edos gradually incorporated smaller neighboring tribes, although the closely related Urhobo remained separate. Urhobo leaders were officially installed by the oba of Benin. Those who achieved sufficient status within their local community would travel to Benin City to be endowed with ceremonial swords and insignia that confirmed their local authority.

The Portuguese established contact with the kingdom in 1485. Benin was ruled at that time by a revered oba and a council of state, the *Uzama*, and its capital, Benin City, dazzled the Europeans with its wealth, art, and sophistication. The Edos enjoyed good relations with the Portuguese and sent ambassadors to represent the kingdom in Lisbon. One facet of Benin's advanced culture profoundly shocked the European visitors, however—

human sacrifice, an important religious and political ritual performed by state cults.

The kingdom flourished on trade with the Europeans, particularly the growing trade in slaves obtained from the tribes of the interior. Although weakened by violent succession conflicts between members of the royal house in the late eighteenth and early nineteenth centuries, Benin reached its greatest territorial extent between 1816 and 1848, controlling a vast empire that included a number of states inhabited by non-Edo tribes. In the 1850s the empire began to disintegrate; the Itsekiri and other subject peoples broke away to establish relations with the rising power in the region, the British.

The lucrative slave trade, mostly involving the subject coastal peoples, had particularly attracted the Europeans, and gradually the British had taken control of the slave ports. The kingdom's prosperity declined with the suppression of the slave trade, and its rulers increasingly relied on supernatural rituals and large-scale human sacrifice to protect the state from further territorial encroachment. In 1885, the British formally annexed the kingdom's coastal districts, leaving the heartland of the Edo kingdom as the last part of present Nigeria to remain outside British rule. The Edos, in an effort to retain their independence, broke off all contact with the Europeans, but in 1892 the British forced the kingdom to outlaw slavery and human sacrifice and to accept protectorate status.

In 1896, a peaceful British emissary and his escort moving toward Benin City so alarmed the Edos that they attacked and massacred the entire column. The British dispatched an expedition of 1,500 men to subdue them. The Edos deserted their capital; the British found a treasure of magnificent artworks alongside evidence of human sacrifices the Edos had hoped would persuade the gods to help defeat the invaders. The British looted and burned the city, shipping over 2,000 pieces of fabulous Benin art to London. The British captured the king, his family, and his advisers, and had them deported. In 1897 the British installed a new oba under close colonial administrative scrutiny and incorporated Benin into British Nigeria. Oba Obvonramwen, the last of the independent rulers of the Edos, died in 1914 in exile. The defeat of the Edos eliminated the last major obstacle to the consolidation of British rule in southern Nigeria.

Direct British rule gave way in 1914 to more indirect regime through a restored Edo king, Eweka II. In the 1920s, an administrative union of Benin and Yorubaland was opposed by the proud Edo, giving rise to modern Edo nationalism. In 1948 Edo students formed the first openly nationalist Edo organization, the Edo National Union, the forerunner of the later Otu Edo, an organization dedicated to defending Edo interests against domination by the Yorubas. The Ogbomi Society, formed in 1951, was dedicated to protecting the Edo's proud traditional culture in multi-ethnic Nigeria.

A division of Nigeria into three autonomous regions in 1954 spurred rapid growth in Edo nationalism, focused on opposition to inclusion of their homeland in the Yoruba-dominated Western Region—though Benin remained economically independent of the Western Region. Edo nationalist demands were complicated on one hand by the refusal of the non-Edo peoples of the region to support a resurgent Benin, and on the other by Edo refusal to consider a separate region without the non-Edo districts of the old Benin kingdom. The discovery of oil in the Niger Delta gave Edo nationalism a strong economic base in the late 1950s.

British preparations to grant independence to Nigeria strengthened the growing Edo national movement. Serious agitation swept the Edo homeland in 1957–58. In 1960 Nigeria became an independent federation of three regions, Northern, Western, and Eastern. In 1963 the Edos voted to separate their historical homeland from the Yoruba-dominated Western Region. The new Nigerian government, responding to serious Edo threats to secede rather than to submit to Yoruba or Muslim domination, in 1964 created a fourth region, the Midwest, encompassing the traditional Edo lands.

The outbreak of civil war following the secession of the neighboring Ibos* in the Eastern Region, renamed the Republic of Biafra, brought chaos to the region. The ethnic Ibos called on Benin to follow Biafra, but the Edos initially remained loyal to the federal cause. The federal government granted the Edos a major degree of autonomy in 1967, in an effort to undermine nationalists' threats to follow Biafra into secession, taking their petroleum wealth with them. Chaos followed an invasion by Biafran forces on 10 August 1967. The Edos responded by rebelling against both the federal forces and the Biafran invaders. Mutineers from Edo battalions seized Benin City and on 18 August 1967 declared Benin independent of both Nigeria and Biafra. Federal troops ended the secession on 20 September 1967, but the Edo homeland remained a battlefield until the end of the civil war in 1970.

The Edo lands, the only zone not divided and redivided in response to ethnic and religious pressures following the end of the Biafran war, remained intact. However, in 1975 the Edos were forced to accept a new name for their state, Bendel, because the Republic of Dahomey, with no historical connection to Benin, had usurped their ancient name. Nigeria's recognition of Dahomey's new name fueled a resurgence of Edo nationalism, already mobilizing in opposition to the domination of Nigeria by northern Muslim Hausas.* In 1981, citing security concerns, the Bendel state government formed the Bendel State Security System and began recruiting soldiers, but the move was opposed by the federal government as a manifestation of Edo nationalism.

Serious antigovernment rioting swept the region in 1989, fed by demands for greater autonomy and a fairer share of wealth produced by their oil resources. In August 1991, in an attempt to undermine resurgent Edo nationalism and to satisfy the non-Edo populations, Bendel was divided into two new states, Edo in the north and Delta in the south, in the first change in the status of Edo lands since 1964.

In September 1993 most Edo national organizations joined in denouncing Nigeria's new military government. Rising tension resulting from opposition to the Muslim northerners who dominated the military government and from closer political ties to Yorubaland resulted in greater support for Edo autonomy. However, the annulment of 1993 elections believed to have been won by a southern Christian Yoruba, and the imposition of yet another Muslim-dominated military government dashed Edo hopes of greater autonomy and control of their natural resources.

In the mid-1990s violence increased in the region, mostly against the government and international oil companies and their local installations. Edo resentment of the exploitation of their natural resources—oil, land, and water—fueled the violence.

Oral history keeps the ancient traditions of the Edo nation alive. Many young Edos know the history of their monarchs as well as young British students know that of their own rulers. A descendent of Benin's ruling dynasty, Omo 'Oba Erediauwa, still occupies the throne in Benin City, although the present oba has only an advisory role in local government. He is still revered as the spiritual head of the Edo nation and the embodiment of Edo tradition. The present king sponsors bronze castings in the traditional Benin style and leads the campaign to recover the treasures looted by the British in 1897.

The walls of Benin City, considered a heritage site by UNESCO, are in tragically poor repair. As the city grew, the walls were bulldozed and the moat filled in to build roads and houses. Only in the 1990s did organizations, headed by nationalists and historians, begin to agitate to save the legacy of the unique Edo culture.

Ethnic conflicts involving the Urhobos of Delta over the siting of district headquarters and control of potentially rich oil lands erupted in violent conflicts around the city of Warri in 1999. The Edo-speaking Urhobos, seen by the Edo as one of their subdivisions, appealed for support, which led to a mobilization of many Edo volunteers. The spreading ethnic conflict stimulated group nationalism across the region.

In December 2000, the Nigerian government announced the formation of a division of the Nigerian army for the sole purpose of keeping the oil-rich delta states under control; it was to be headquartered in Benin City. The announcement followed a statement by the governor of Edo, Lucky Igbinedion, that his government would take complete control of its oil resources. Igbinedion ruled out confrontation and violence, but the issue of the control of local resources is central to the growing national sentiment. Chief Anthony Enahoro, one of the leaders of the national movement, advised Igbinedion, however, to quit politics and allow the younger generation of Edos to run the affairs of the people. Chief Enahoro accused the governor of spending his time and energies in Abuja, the Nigerian federal capital, while his people lived in poverty and oppression. On 16 December, Chief Enahoro, in the local legislature, presented a motion for the nation's independence.

SELECTED BIBLIOGRAPHY:

Azuonye, Chukwuma. *Edo: The Bini People of the Benin Kingdom.* 1995.
Malaquais, Dominique. *The Kingdom of Benin.* 1998.
Mann, Kenny. *Oyo, Benin, Ashanti: The Guinea Coast.* 1996.
Millar, Heather. *The Kingdom of Benin in West Africa.* 1997.

Emilians

Emellians; Aemilians

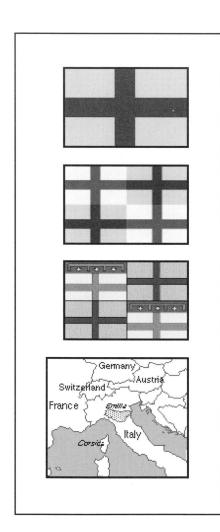

POPULATION: Approximately (2002e) 2,450,000 Emilians in Italy, concentrated in the Emilian provinces of the combined region of Emilia-Romagna. Other Emilians live in Rome and in other areas of Italy. Outside Europe there are Emilian communities in Australia, Argentina, Brazil, the United States, and Peru.

THE EMILIAN HOMELAND: The Emilian homeland lies in north-central Italy, the great Emilian Plain, extending from the Adriatic Sea on the east across the Italian Peninsula to the Po River valley. The region, comprising the provinces of Bologna, Ferrara, Modena, Parma, Piacenza, and Reggio nell'Emilia, forms part of the combined region of Emilia-Romagna. *Region of Emilia*: 6,701 sq. mi.—17,535 sq. km, (2002e) 2,973,000—Emilians 78%, other Italians, non-Italian immigrants 22%. The Emilian capital and major cultural center is Bologna, (2002e) 378,000, metropolitan area 605,000. Other important cultural centers are Parma, (2002e) 168,000, and Modena, (2002e) 176,000.

FLAG: The Emilian national flag, the unofficial flag of the region, is a pale yellow field bearing a blue cross centered. The flag of the national movement has the national flag as quarters on the lower hoist and upper fly, and a white field charged with a centered red cross on the upper hoist and lower fly. The flag of the Emilian League is the same as the national movement, with the addition of narrow blue stripes above the white fields.

PEOPLE AND CULTURE: The Emilians are an Italian people, descendants of the populations of several small but culturally important states that maintained independent existences until the mid-nineteenth century. The Emilians were among the most important contributors to the medieval Renaissance, the rebirth of learning and art following the so-called Dark Ages. Their culture, developed in the centuries since the Renaissance, is among the richest in Italy; their architecture, art, cuisine, and customs are unique. The Emilians have one of the highest gross domestic products in Italy.

LANGUAGE AND RELIGION: The Emilians speak a language called Emiliano-Romagnolo, along with standard Italian. The language, belonging to the Italo-Western group of Romance languages, includes two distinct dialects, Emiliano and Romagnolo. Emiliano is spoken in five regional subdialects—Western Emiliano, Eastern Emiliano or Emiliano-Bologonese, Mantovano, Vogherese-Pavese, and Lunigiano. Structurally, the language is separate from standard Italian, which is based on a Tuscan dialect. Regional activists are pressing for the teaching of the language in primary education.

The Emilians are mostly Roman Catholic, but a growing number adhere to evangelical sects active in the area. The Catholic religion, which lost influence particularly at the height of the communist rule in Bologna and other cities, remains a major cultural influence, but the number of active Catholics has dropped dramatically since the 1960s.

NATIONAL HISTORY: The Etruscans, an advanced people about whom little is known, populated the region in ancient times. Many of the towns on the Emilian Plain are of Etruscan origin. The expanding Romans took control of the region about 200 B.C., Latinizing the population and culture. Most of the now-existing cities were once Roman military colonies.

An ancient Roman road called the Via Aemilia, laid out in 187 B.C. from Rimini to Piacenza, gave its name to the entire region. In popular usage, the name Emilia was applied to the region as early as the first century A.D. After the third century, Ravenna and the Romagna region were not treated as part of Emilia. The decline of Roman rule was followed by invasions of Germanic tribes, particularly the Lombards,* who took control of much of northern Italy in the fifth century A.D. The coastal region, Romagna, and Bologna, fell under Byzantine rule in the sixth century. Ravenna became the seat of a Byzantine exarchate, a local administration, and Byzantine rule extended from the coastal bases to much of Emilia.

A Frankish king, Pepin, took Emilia, Ravenna, and the coastal cities from the Lombards and in 755 gave the coastal region, now called Romagna, to the papacy. The other regions of Emilia eventually formed independent city-states, which prospered. Each of the small states had its own history and cultural traditions. The first European university was founded in Bologna in 1088. Many of the cities became free communes in the twelfth century. The Este family and other noble families established their authority in the thirteenth century.

The feuds between the Guelfs, pro-papal nobles, and the Ghibellines, who supported the Holy Roman emperor, kept the region in turmoil for most of the early Middle Ages. Most of the Emilian cities joined the Lombard League against Emperor Frederick Barbarossa in the twelfth century and helped to break the power of Frederick II. In the fifteenth century, noble families gained control of the cities, ruling them and their surrounding territories as separate and independent states. Papal troops took direct control of the neighboring Romagna in 1503, and by the mid-sixteenth century the papacy had gained control of Bologna, formerly dominated by the Visconti family. Ferrara came under papal rule in 1598. The rest of Emilia was dominated by the Este duchy of Modena and the Farnese duchy of Parma and Piacenza. The two duchies controlled most of present Emilia by the seventeenth century. Rivalries between the city-states prevented the formation of any lasting union in the Emilian region.

The stronger regional states extended their territories at the expense of weaker neighbors. Nearly constant warfare among the many small states resulted in political turmoil but did little to diminish their wealth or to hinder the development of a brilliant culture. The Renaissance, the rebirth of learning and art, reached its peak in northern Italy in the fifteenth century, but much of its progress was undermined by the Italian Wars, in which the major European powers vied for power and territory in Italy in the sixteenth century.

French troops took control of the duchies in the region in 1796. The duchies were disbanded and were added to the French-dominated Cisalpine Republic in 1805 to become part of the Napoleonic Kingdom of Italy. After the period of French rule under Napoleon, the Congress of Vienna in 1815 returned Romagna to the papacy and gave the duchy of Parma to Marie Louise, wife of the deposed Napoleon. Modena was taken by Archduke Francis of Austria, the heir to the last Este ruler. Parma and Piacenza later passed to the Spanish Bourbons. Until the mid-nineteenth century, Emilia remained divided between the duchies of Parma, Piacenza, and Modena, and the Papal States ruled by the pope in Rome.

The Emilians played an important part in the Risorgimento, the unification of the Italian peoples. There were frequent Emilian revolts against foreign or papal rule—in 1821, 1831, 1843, and 1848–49. After decades of continuous unrest and numerous revolts, the Emilians voted for unification with the new Italian kingdom; the entire Emilia region joined almost without resistance in 1860.

In the first decades of the twentieth century, while drought and poverty drove many Italians to emigrate, Emilia was one of the kingdom's leading agricultural regions. The first efforts to organize on a regional basis were made by groups in Bologna and other cities in the years prior to World War I. The Fraternal Association of Emilia, formed in 1911, was the first openly autonomist organization.

The cities of the area were heavily bombed during World War II, particularly in 1944. Its name was changed to Emilia-Romagna in 1948, when it formed the center of the so-called Red Belt, the area controlled by the Italian Communist Party after the war. The cities, particularly Bologna, remained a center of socialism and communism until the collapse of communism across Europe in the late 1980s.

The nationalists, while aiming for eventual independence within a federal Europe, are now demanding political sovereignty within a federal or confederal Italian state, recognition of the Emilian right to self-determination, and Emilian representation at a European level. They also demand that the regional Council of Emilia and Romagna be reformed as a confederal parliament of the two regions. They further call for tax reforms and changes to the pension and health systems, to be controlled by Emilians.

Culturally, the nationalist demands include protection and stimulation of Emilian culture, traditions, and dialects, as well as recognition of the Emilian language as a regional and minority language within the European Union (EU) and the Italian state, and local control of the regional educational system. A wish for tighter control of illegal immigration and the cultural integration of legal immigrants, as well as an end to discrimination, is aimed at sustaining present population levels.

Emilian nationalists formerly part of the Liga Nord, the Northern League, left the organization in May 1994 to protest the league's affiliation with rightist political parties. The new movement, called Nazione Emilia, contested local elections in 1995 and campaigned against the infiltration of the Mafia into Emilia. In 1996 the neofascist MSI-Fiamma Tricolore denounced the Emilian nationalists for attacking Italian national unity and for offending Italian institutions and the Italian nation. The nationalists, supported by the Lega Nord, printed pamphlets claiming Emilian citizenship, rejecting Italian or Padanian identity. The attack by the neofascists was based on laws, still on the books, passed during the Mussolini era prior to World War II.

Other Emilians left the Lega Nord in December 1998 to found Libertà Emiliana, to protest continuing contact between the Northern League and ultrarightist organizations in other parts of Europe. In July 1999 Libertà Emiliana and Nazione Emilia joined together to form one of the largest autonomy groups in northern Italy. The nationalists, with a minority seeking independence within a federal European Union (EU), mostly support the idea of separation from historically and culturally distinct Romagna and of Emilian autonomy within a federal Italian state.

The Emilian nationalists in October 1999 formed a working pact with the autonomists in neighboring Romagna. The two groups are cooperating in efforts to form two new regions, Emilia in the east and Romagna along the Adriatic coast. In early 2000, the Emilians began a campaign for a regional referendum on separation. They also sought primary education in the Emilian language, with new schools open to all, including the growing number of non-European immigrants.

The Emilians have arisen from the inhabitants of a number of independent city-states, each with its culture, dialect, and history. Over the last 150 years the idea of a regional culture has grown as the Emilians discovered that what they shared was more than what divided them. The Emilian nation emerged as one of Europe's newest regional identities in the 1990s, stimulated by confrontation between the northern Italian nations and the culturally, dialectically, and historically distinct peoples of Rome and the south.

SELECTED BIBLIOGRAPHY:

Cervellati, Pier Luigi. *Emilia Romagna*. 1991.
Gioffre, Rosalba. *Emilia Romagna*. 2000.
Leonardi, Robert, and Raffaella Y. Nanetti, eds. *The Regions and European Integration: The Case of Emilia Romagna*. 1990.
Piro, Franco. *Communists at the Door: Economy, Society, and Political System in Emilia Romagna 1945–1965*. 1968.

Epirotes

Epirote Greeks; Northern Epirotes; Vorios Epirotes; Ipirotes; Epeirotes; Epiroteans; Ípirons

POPULATION: Approximately (2002e) 280,000 Epirotes in Albania, concentrated in the southern districts of the republic near the Greek border. The actual Epirote population is a matter of dispute; the Albanian government estimates the population at about 60,000, while nationalists and the Greek government claim a population of over 400,000. Outside Europe there are Epirote communities in Australia and the Americas.

THE EPIROTE HOMELAND: The Epirote homeland, in southern Albania, is characterized by steep limestone ridges that parallel the coast, with high valleys that rise to the Pindus Range in the east. The Epirote homeland, Northern Epirus, has no official status; the region forms the departments of Gjirokastër, Kolonjë, Korcë, Pëmet, Sarandë, Skrapar, Tepelenë, Himarë and the southern districts of Vlorë in Albania. *Northern Epirus (Boreios/Vorio-Epirus)*: 2,108 sq. mi.—5,461 sq. km, (2002e) 547,000—Albanians 47%, Epirotes 36%, Aromanians* 15%, Macedonians 2%. The Epirote capital and major cultural center is Gjirokastër, called Agryrokastron by the Epirotes, (2002e) 26,000. The other major Epirote cultural centers are Sarandë, Saranda or Aghioi Saranda to the Epirotes, (2002e) 18,000, and Korcë, (2002e) 70,000.

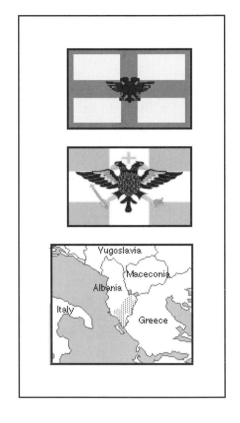

FLAG: The Epirote Greek national flag, the flag of the former republic, is a white field outlined in pale blue and bearing a broad pale blue cross charged with a small, black double-headed Epirote eagle centered. The flag of the national movement is a blue field divided by a broad white cross centered behind a black, double-headed eagle, wings spread and holding in its claws symbols of Epirote sovereignty.

PEOPLE AND CULTURE: The Epirotes, better known as Epirote Greeks, are a Greek-speaking people, descendants of the ancient Epirotes of the southern Balkan Peninsula. Never part of modern Greece, the Greek-speaking Epirotes preserve dialects and cultural traditions that disappeared in Greek Epirus centuries ago. Traditional Epirote music, costumes, and cuisine have formed part of the Epirote revival since the early 1990s. The Epirotes' unique Hellenic culture, which has survived since ancient times, is now threatened by emigration from the region as Epirotes flee economic hardship and government suppression.

LANGUAGE AND RELIGION: The Epirotes speak a Greek dialect, Epirote or Eneipos, that retains many archaic forms and words, no longer used in standard Greek. The dialect, which differs from district to district, is written in the Greek alphabet and can be more readily read than understood by speakers of standard Greek. Education in the language is a contentious issue in the region, as is its use in publishing, radio, and television. Many Epirotes can receive Greek television, which is influencing the use of the dialect.

The Epirotes are overwhelmingly Greek Orthodox, with strong ties to the church hierarchy in Greece, but they also maintain strong ties to the Orthodox Albanians, Aromanians, and Macedonians, who form a compact Christian population of over half a million in predominantly Muslim Albania. Although most of the churches were destroyed or confiscated under the communist government in the 1960s and 1970s, the Epirotes have restored some properties, and many churches have reopened and are in use.

NATIONAL HISTORY: Inhabited by seafaring and herding peoples, the region was an early home of the Greek-speaking peoples of the southern Balkan Peninsula. Epirus was settled by the same nomadic Hellenic tribes that invaded the Greek Peninsula farther south, but they did not share in the cultural development of the Greeks. To the ancient Greeks, the Epirotes were barbarians, and parts of their homeland were colonized by Greek city-states.

Epirus was unified by King Pyrrhus in 272 B.C. and declared a republic in 200 B.C. Overrun by the expanding Macedonian state, Epirus again became an independent kingdom following Macedonia's defeat by the Romans in 197 B.C. The Romans took control of Epirus in 167 B.C., enslaving 150,000 of its inhabitants; they annexed the kingdom to the growing Roman Empire in 146 B.C. The region did not recover its earlier population or prosperity until the Byzantine period, beginning in 476. Under Byzantine rule Epirus was a Hellenized principality, the westernmost province of the Byzantine Empire.

Michael Angelus Commennus erected a resurgent Epirote state at the collapse of the Byzantine Empire in 1204. When the Crusaders set up a Latin state centered on the former Byzantine capital, Constantinople, Epirus remained a Greek state; thereafter the Epirotes played an important part in the preservation of Greek culture in the West. The Turks annexed

Epirus to their expanding Ottoman Empire following a long campaign in 1430–40. The Ottoman conquest of Constantinople marked the end of the Byzantine Empire and ushered in hundreds of years of Turkish rule.

Ali Pasha Tepelenë, a ruler of Yanina (Ioannina) in the late eighteenth century, expelled the Turks and created an independent Epirote state. The Turks soon retook Epirus, but with Greek independence from the Ottoman Empire in 1829 the Turkish hold on Epirus began to loosen. In 1881 the Greeks took the southern Epirus region from the declining Ottomans and pressed their claim to the Greek Orthodox districts of northern Epirus. At the end of the nineteenth century, there were more than 200 schools teaching in Greek in the region.

The First Balkan War of 1912 ended Turkish domination of the Balkans; Albania declared itself independent, and the Greek frontiers again expanded to the north. Greek troops occupied the mainly Christian districts of northern Epirus. The Greek-speaking Epirotes, opposed to Albanian rule, were joined by the leaders of the Orthodox Albanians, who opposed both Greek and Muslim rule. They formed a joint provisional government in 1912. The joint Epirote administration repeatedly rebuffed overtures from both the Greek and Albanian governments.

The Greek occupation troops withdrew under international pressure in February 1914. Rejecting an interim agreement under which the Albanian authorities would take control, the Epirote provisional government, led by Georghios Christaki Zagraphos, declared the independence of the Republic of Northern Epirus on 17 February 1914. The resulting crisis, bringing Greece and Albania close to war, merged into the chaos of the outbreak of World War I. Greek troops moved north to reoccupy Northern Epirus in December 1914 but withdrew under pressure from French and Italian troops in 1916. An autonomous state with its capital at Korcë, supported by the French, collapsed with the French withdrawal. In 1920 Albanian troops occupied the region, and the Epirote districts were integrated into the Albanian state. The 1921 Paris Conference validated the 1913 borders, leaving the Epirote population under Albanian rule.

A League of Nations investigation in 1923 found that the Albanians had failed to implement promises of cultural and linguistic autonomy, and noted growing discontent among the Christian population of the region. The 360 pre–World War I Greek schools were reduced to 78 by 1925, 43 in 1931, and just 10 in 1933. In 1934 the last schools teaching in Greek were closed; thereafter all education was in Albanian. Epirote demands for regional political and religious autonomy in southern Albania were ignored or suppressed over the next decade. In 1935 the Albanian government forcibly closed Greek institutions and removed all Orthodox Christians from official positions. Under the leadership of Ethem Toto, a dismissed government minister, the Epirote Christians rebelled in 1936. Intent on severing Northern Epirus from Albania, the rebels took control of much of the region, but the rebellion collapsed with Toto's mysterious death in 1937.

Fascist Italian troops occupied Albania in October 1939 and attacked Greece from Northern Epirus in 1940. The Greeks counterattacked, driving the Italians from Greece and north from the Epirote region of Albania. The Epirotes again rebelled and with Greek support organized a provisional government, which collapsed with the German invasion of Albania and Greece in 1941. In 1944, near the end of World War II, the Greek government reiterated its claim to the region, but in 1945 the Allied powers reestablished the prewar frontiers.

Albania's postwar communist government, installed in 1946, quickly suppressed all opposition. The radical communist administration instituted decades of harsh rule and exerted intense pressure to assimilate on the Greek Epirote minority. In 1967 the government closed all religious institutions, outlawed public worship, and officially denied the existence of the Orthodox Christian population in Northern Epirus. An estimated 630 Greek Orthodox churches in the southern districts were destroyed or put to other uses.

The communist government's attempts to homogenize the population by restricting religious, cultural, educational, and linguistic rights was particularly harsh on the Greek-speaking Epirotes, whose religion is inseparable from their culture. Internal exile and population resettlements diluted the concentration of Epirotes in southern Albania. Legislation introduced in 1949, updated in the 1950s and 1960s and again in 1979, permitted the forcible relocation of people who "represented a danger to the social system." Between 1949 and 1990 an estimated 110,000 Epirotes were forcibly relocated, mostly to the Muslim northern districts of Albania.

In 1975 the Albanian government ordered that all family names be changed in order to eliminate "alien influences" emanating from the Christian Catholic and Orthodox communities. Muslim names were acceptable, but the Epirotes were forced to select names from an official list. Repression increased as the economy crumbled. In 1977 an Epirote was sentenced to 10 years in prison for showing too much enthusiasm at a performance of a visiting group of Greek folk singers. Another was given 20 years in 1978 for failing to drink a toast to the health of the communist dictator, Enver Hoxha. The communist regime maintained a Soviet-style system of 29 labor camps in remote areas, in which many Epirotes were imprisoned for their religious or cultural affiliations.

Economic and political cooperation between the Albanian and Greek governments increased following Hoxha's death in 1985. In August 1986 the Greek government announced an end to the technical state of war between the two states that had existed since 1940, when Italian forces invaded Greece from occupied southern Albania. Normal relations had not been resumed after the war due to Greek irredentist claims to southern Albania and support of the Epirote community.

The collapse of communism allowed the Epirotes, for the first time in over 40 years, to organize and mobilize. Insisting upon the same rights that the new Albanian government demanded for the Albanian minority in Kosovo, the Kosovars,* in Yugoslavia, in 1991 the Epirotes appealed for assistance to the Greek government. The ensuing crisis polarized the positions even as the Epirotes mobilized also over the linguistic and autonomy questions.

In 1992 attacks on offices of the Epirote national organization, Omonia, and on Epirote shops in the southern cities in Albania raised tension even further. The attacks were reportedly in response to alleged harassment, mistreatment, and deportation of ethnic Albanian refugees from Greece. In 1993–94 hundreds of Epirote military officers, administrators, and teachers lost their positions as the Albanian government moved to suppress the growing national movement following demands for a referendum on independence for Northern Epirus. The government closed Greek-language schools and institutions that, the government claimed, supported Epirote separatism.

The 80th anniversary of the Northern Epirus republic in February 1994 was marked by renewed Greek claims to it, but several Epirote leaders rejected them and demanded an autonomous Epirote state, Greek-speaking but not part of Greece, citing the example of the relation of German-speaking Austria to Germany. The Greek government's advocacy of the Greek-speaking Epirotes often did more harm than good to the Epirote campaign, as it led to accusations of working for the Greek government. Several nationalists condemned the Greek government for "criminal interference" in the fate of the Greek-speaking Epirotes in Albania.

In May 1994, amid a growing crisis between Greece and Albania, the Albanian government arrested and tried for separatism six Epirote leaders. The Epirotes, charged with spying and illegally carrying arms, were arrested and tried but later released following an international outcry. The Albanian authorities continue to regard as disloyal any attachment among the Epirote community to its ethnic heritage.

Greek-speaking populations outside the three southern districts of Sarandë, Gjirokastër, and Përmet are not officially considered as part of the Epirote community. In 1995 the district of Himare, called Chimarra by the Epirotes, whose classification as a Greek-speaking district had been revoked in 1945 for failure to support the establishment of communism in Albania, voted to reclaim its status as an Epirote-majority district. The postcommunist Albanian government has been accused of restricting the Greek-speaking population to just 60,000 by withholding documents identifying Himare as part of the Epirote minority.

Epirote leaders and Greek Orthodox church leaders in late 1991 and early 1992 urged ethnic Epirotes in Greece to return to Albania in order to influence the March 1992 elections. In 1996 local elections candidates of the Unity for Human Rights Party, founded by Epirotes in 1995, took the majority of the elected government positions in the three southern districts of Saranda, Gjirokaster, and Delvina. They also elected six ethnic Epirotes to the Albanian parliament, two representing the Unity for Human Rights Party.

Language and education remain the two most important concerns of the Epirote community. In the summer of 1994, the Albanian government published a directive that mother-tongue education was to be implemented where a certain percentage of the population belonged to a linguistic minority. It also allowed supplementary instruction in the mother tongue where the linguistic minority was less numerous. Talks between the Greek and Albanian governments, which had resumed following Greek accusations that the Albanians had not implemented the prior agreement, collapsed in September 1995 over the issue of the education of the Greek-speaking community in Albania.

The Greek government uses the Epirote question as a counterweight to the estimated 300,000 Albanian nationalists, many ethnic Epirotes, who live and work illegally in Greece. Remittances from these immigrants is one of the Albanian government's major sources of foreign currency; the Greek government threatens to crack down or close the border if the treatment of the Epirote Christians in Albania is not improved.

Political upheaval in Albania in early 1997 led to the flight of thousands of Epirotes to Greek territory. Many arrived at frontier posts without visas or passports. The Greek government mediated between the Albanian government and rebel groups operating in the south, but in March 1997 anarchy engulfed the Albanian capital, Tirana. A new government, including representatives of the Epirotes, ended the crisis and the possibility that the Epirotes would attempt to secede from chaotic Albania. The situation of the Epirotes improved considerably between 1997 and 1999, although cultural discrimination and lack of access to the electoral process continue.

The most immediate goal of the Epirote nationalists is official recognition as a minority within Albania. Secondary goals are unrestricted rights to travel, particularly to Greece, and restoration of cultural traditions of the Epirote community suppressed during the decades of dictatorship. A more militant faction established an Epirote government-in-exile in 1999 and demands a referendum on independence.

SELECTED BIBLIOGRAPHY:

Hammond, N.G.L. *Epirus*. 1981.
Kaplan, Robert. *Balkan Ghosts*. 1993.
Kondis, Basil. *The Greeks of Northern Epirus and Greek-Albanian Relations*. 1954.
Stickney, E.P. *Southern Albania or Northern Epirus in European International Affairs, 1912–1923*. 1926.

Evenks

Evenkis; Evenkys; Ewenkis; Tungus; Evedys; Avankis; Avankils; Chapogirs; Khamnigans

POPULATION: Approximately (2002e) 85,000 Evenks in northeastern Asia, scattered over a vast area of Siberia, northern China, and Mongolia. About 50,000 live in the Russian Federation, 30,000 in northeastern China, and about 5,000 in Mongolia. There is some confusion as to the actual Evenk population, because some Soviet census returns counted only speakers of Evenk, while with respect to culture the numbers were considerably higher.

THE EVENK HOMELAND: The Evenk homeland lies in eastern Siberia, stretching from northern China and Mongolia to the taiga of the Arctic Circle in northern Russia, about a quarter of the whole area of Siberia. Most of the historical Evenk territory lies outside autonomous district—which is popularly called Evenkia, Evedy in the Evenk language—but the scattered Evenk peoples retain close historical and cultural ties. In all of the Russian Federation, only the Russians inhabit a larger territory. The Evenk autonomous district, in central Siberia, occupies part of the Central Siberian Uplands, roughly in the geographic center of the territory of the Russian Federation. *Evenki Autonomous Okrug (Evedy Avtonomdy Okrug)*: 296,370 sq. mi.—767,598 sq. km, (2002e) 27,000—Russians 61%, Evenks 27%, Ukrainians 3%, Sakhas 3%, other Siberians 6%. The Evenk capital and major cultural center is Tura, called Turu in the Evenk language, (2002e) 8,000. The major cultural center of the Even subgroup is Anavgay, in Kamchatka, (2002e) 2,000. The major cultural center of the Chinese Evenki is Aoluguya, (2002e) 5,000, in Inner Mongolia.

FLAG: The Evenk national flag, and the former official flag of Evenkia, recognized by Evenks across Siberia, China, and Mongolia, is a pale blue field bearing the head of a reindeer, in white, on the upper hoist and two white and two darker blue stripes on the lower half. The flag of the Evenk

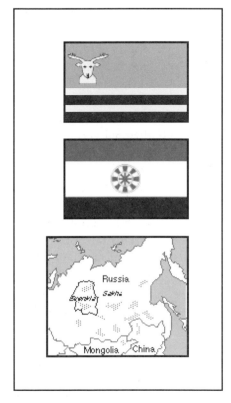

Autonomous Okrug is a horizontal tricolor of pale blue, white, and dark blue, the white twice the width of the blue stripes and charged with a red and white emblem centered.

PEOPLE AND CULTURE: The Evenks are a Tungus nation, one of the indigenous peoples living in north and northeastern Asia. They were formerly known as Tungus, but now Tungus, or Tungusic, is a linguistic name designating a language family. They belong to the Baikal or Paleo-Siberian group of Mongolian peoples, originating from the ancient Paleo-Siberian people, probably a mixture of Tungus and Yukagir cultures. The Evenks are divided into several subgroups, including the Manjagir, Birars (Birachen), Ile, Orochon, and Solon. The major groups in China are the Solon, Tungus, Ainak, Nakagyr, and Orochon. The Evens or Lamuts in northeastern Siberia are a subgroup, divided from the Evenks by the Soviet authorities. The Solons, Tungus, Ainak, Nakagyr, and Orochon or Oro-qen, who are identified with the Eastern Mongols,* live in northeastern China. The Evenki nation and culture are closely identified with the traditional economic activities, especially reindeer herding. Many Evenki activists claim that the cultural survival of their small nation depends on the continued existence of reindeer herding, hunting, and fishing in the traditional ways, though many young Evenks have little interest in the traditional occupations. Reindeer herders and hunters are occupations of the Evenki people; they traditionally practice a system of land tenure based on territorial "obshchinas," communes of small sub-clan groups of one to several families who exercised usufruct rights to particular lands. The obshchina territory was usually defined within watersheds in which the group hunted and pastured its' reindeer. Clan leaders redistributed land to individuals as needed. In many areas of their traditional territory, the Evenki form a small minority of the total population. Alcoholism is a widespread problem among the Evenki, who feel marginalized in many areas.

LANGUAGE AND RELIGION: The Evenki language, called Evedy Turën, is a Tungusic language, the largest of the northern group of the Manchu-Tungus languages. The basic vocabulary has much in common with the Mongolian and Turkic languages. The Evenk language varies considerably from district to district and is divided into three large dialectical groups—Northern, Southern, and Eastern—which are further divided into 26 subdialects in Russia and three in China and Mongolia. In some areas Sakhas and Buryats* have influenced the language, while the influence of Russian is widespread and increasing. In the late 1990s only about 45% of the Evenks in Russia considered Evenki as their mother language. Although knowledge of the language is widespread, particularly among the older generation, many younger Evenks know only Russian. The written language was created in the late 1920s, and in 1933–34 Evenk was introduced into primary schools in Evenkia and some other areas. The Tunguska dialect, spoken around Tura, is the basis of the literary language.

Traditionally the Evenks are shamanists, adhering to rituals involving spirits and reverence of nature. The word "shaman" is itself of Evenk origin. Since 1991 the traditional shamanism of the Evenks has shown signs of revival. Officially many Evenks are Christians, converted to Orthodoxy by missionaries in the nineteenth century, but they have mixed their Christian rituals with the earlier belief system. In the south, many Evenks are Lamaists, having adopted the religion from the Mongols and Buryats.*

NATIONAL HISTORY: The original home of the Evenks is thought to be the area around Lake Baikal, where the ancient Tungusic groups have their roots. The ancestors of the Evenks seem to have had close contacts with the nearby Mongol tribes and peoples speaking Turkic languages. From Lake Baikal the Tungus clans began to migrate to the east, to the Amur River region and the coast of the Okhotsk Sea; to the north, to the Lena River basin; and to the northwest, to the basin of the Yenisey River. Some of the clans moved out onto the vast steppe lands in the south, while others continued north to the tundra and taiga.

One of the reasons for the Evenki dispersal may have been pressure from the Turkic tribes in the Baikal area at the beginning of the first millennium. Any small tribes met on the way were assimilated or forced to retreat. In the southern areas, the Evenks were influenced by the Mongols and came to be known as Horse Tungus. Gradually two large groups of Evenks formed—the northern hunters and reindeer herders, and the southern group, who bred cattle and horses and later took up farming. The domestication of reindeer allowed for the exceptional rate of geographical expansion. A distinctive Evenk ethnic group was identified as early as the fourteenth century in Mongol and Chinese chronicles.

An important turning point in the history of the Evenks was their first encounter with the Russians in 1606. The Russians imposed a fur tax, an annual tribute to be paid in valuable furs. In order to collect the tribute, the tsarist authorities exploited the tribal organization of the Evenks. The Russians brought tools, firearms, and various vices, including alcohol, which has plagued the Evenks even since. They also brought diseases to which the Evenks had never been exposed. Alcohol and diseases led to a rapid decline in the Evenk population.

In the seventeenth and eighteenth centuries, many Evenki clans tried to evade Russian authority by moving to the north and east. Other clans left their home territories when Sakhas or Buryats moved into the region. The traditional Evenki homeland in central Siberia, one of the most remote zones in the Russian Empire, was only under nominal Russian rule and was a place of refuge for indigenous groups and Old Believers, members of a schismatic religious sect persecuted in European Russia. The Orthodox Church attempted to convert the Evenks, but Christianity was accepted only nominally, and shamanism survives to the present.

The Evenks often warred with the Sakhas, formerly called Yakuts, who had settled in the basin of the Lena River in the thirteenth century. In the eighteenth and nineteenth centuries, the Evenks living in the Lena region adopted the Sakha language. In the Baikal region, the Evenks began to speak Buryat and the Mongolian languages, and some even converted to Lamaism.

The Evenks traditionally practice a system of land tenure based on territorial *obshchina*, communes of small subclan groups of one or several families. The clan groups exercised territorial rights to their lands, where the group hunted and pastured their reindeer. Clan leaders redistributed lands to individuals as needed. The Evenks would hunt and herd on other territories only with the permission of local clan leaders.

In the nineteenth century Evenk clans appeared on the lower reaches of the Amur River and on Sakhalin Island, and later they migrated to the Chukchi Peninsula in the far northeast. The Horse Evenks—the Manegirs and Birars—moved into Manchuria, where they were influenced by the Manchus* and Chinese. Most of the nineteenth-century migrations were in search of better hunting grounds or attempts to escape Russian authority and the epidemics brought to the region by Slavic colonists. Evenk protests against Russian aggression and authority were mostly passive, but between 1825 and 1841 there were several rebellions, all ruthlessly crushed. Until the mid-nineteenth century the scattered Evenks did not regard themselves as part of a national group but identified with their dialect, geographic area, or neighboring peoples.

The Russian Revolution and Civil War were remote events for the Evenks of central Siberia. It was not until late 1923 that the first Soviet commissar traveled through the region, organizing local meetings in order to elect the first indigenous governmental councils. The Soviet authorities attempted to create clan councils, but the Evenks were indifferent to these newly imposed institutions. In 1924 a development council for the northern Siberian regions was created to organize the numerically small peoples, who were considered by the Soviet government as classless, primitive societies. Soviet ideology was introduced and explained by propaganda agents who set up centers called "Red Tents." In 1927 the reorganization of the Evenks on a territorial basis began, with the creation of village councils, districts, and territories. In 1930, the Evenk National Territory was formed in the Krasnoyarsk district.

The Soviet aim was to transform the Evenks from a tribe to a society of developed socialism while avoiding the stage of capitalism. In 1931 the official name of the small nation was changed from Tungus to Evenki. At the same time the northeastern Evenks, called the Evens or Lamuts, were officially designated a distinct ethnic group.

Collectivized in the 1930s and 1940s, the Evenks were forced to settle in permanent villages, but fur hunting and reindeer herding remained the major occupations. Many small collectives were consolidated during the 1950s to form large enterprises. Due to their small numbers and the dispersal of the Evenki population, the interests of the Evenks was not taken into account by the local administration and industries.

During the 1950s and 1960s, Evenki youngsters were urged to learn Russian in place of Evenki, and the language was eliminated from most schools in Evenki areas of Siberia. The language was reintroduced in schools in Evenkia in 1980, but only as a subject, not as the language of instruction.

The ethnic composition of central and eastern Siberia changed rapidly after World War II, due to a steady immigration of Slavic workers lured to the region with promises of higher pay and better living conditions. Assimilation, particularly linguistic assimilation, decreased the Evenk population, as counted in the 1959 Soviet census, to less than 25,000. Since 1970 the numbers had been increasing slightly, with a rapid increase as reculturation took hold after the collapse of the Soviet Union.

The Evenks were assimilating in both Russia and China until the late 1980s due to their small numbers, and the Evenki culture was endangered in both countries. Beginning in the early 1990s activists made an effort to strengthen the usage of the Evenki language. Reindeer herding, which makes use of the remote and climatically unfavorable taiga regions in an ecologically sustainable way, is being promoted by Evenki activists. The future of the language and of reindeer herding are the focus of the growing national movement.

Over the last three decades, many oil and gas fields have been discovered in the region. In the near future oil extraction will start in southern Evenkia, but many Evenks are opposed to the exploitation of the resources, fearing that it will mean the end of their traditional way of life. The extraction of oil, coal, and other mineral resources is proceeding steadily and jeopardizing the hunting grounds and pastures of the Evenks. The devastation of the environment by economic development stimulated the Evenk reculturation and the growth of the nationalist movement in the 1980s.

Evenki nationalism, which has developed since the collapse of the Soviet state in 1991, presses for the production of new teaching materials in the Evenki language, creation of a cultural center in Tura, and enhancement of traditional economic activities. Activists support Evenki land claims, rights to traditional land use and resources, and a greater say in local government in areas with Evenki populations. Evenk activists working for self-determination seek to revive the *obshchina* territorial system as the basis for territorial organization.

Presentations by the Evenks to the United Nations Working Group on Indigenous Peoples have emphasized the difficult circumstances in which they find themselves. Since the late 1980s, the Evenks have demanded reforms to reverse the process of alienation from their lands, which in turn would improve their control over their own national destiny.

Recent claims by indigenous Siberians, presented to the United Nations Working Group on Indigenous Peoples, have emphasized the difficult circumstances in which the Evenks find themselves today. Since the late 1980s, the Evenks and other indigenous Siberians have demanded reforms to reverse the ongoing process of alienation from their lands and therefore to improve control over their own destiny. Evenks face enormous problems in preserving their rights to land that they have inhabited since time immemorial. When the question of self-determination as an indigenous people is applied to the Evenks, one issue today is whether the obshchina can be revived as an indigenous institution.

SELECTED BIBLIOGRAPHY:

Fondahl, Gail A. *Gaining Ground? Eveniks, Land, and Reform in Southeastern Siberia.* 1997.

Kennan, George. *Tent Life in Siberia.* 1986.

Mayer, Fred. *The Forgotten Peoples of Siberia.* 1994.

Slezkine, Yu. *Arctic Mirrors: Russia and the Small Peoples of the North.* 1994.

Ewes

Eibes; Ebwes; Eves; Efes; Eues

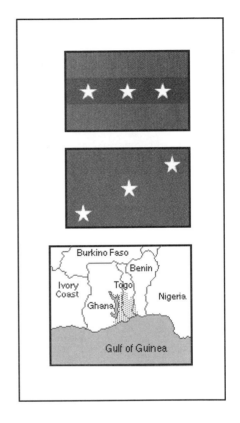

POPULATION: Approximately (2002e) 5,015,000 Ewes in West Africa, occupying a coastal region stretching from the Volta River in southeastern Ghana, with a Ewe population of 2,710,000, through southern Togo, with 2,075,000, into southwestern Benin, with 230,000. There are large Ewe populations in Accra and other parts of Ghana and in other parts of West Africa, particularly in the Ivory Coast and Nigeria.

THE EWE HOMELAND: The Ewe homeland lies in West Africa between the Volta and Koutto Rivers in southeastern Ghana, southern Togo, and southeastern Benin. The region is mainly forested, behind a narrow coastal plain, where the majority of the population is located. The Ewe homeland, called Eweland or Togoland, has no official status but is divided among three distinct African states, forming the Volta Region of Ghana, called Western Togoland; the prefectures of Des Plateaux and Maritime of Togo, called Central Togoland or simply Togoland; and the province of Mono in Benin, Eastern Togoland. *Togoland (Eweland)*: 24,186 sq. mi.—62,643 sq. km, (2002e) 5,593,000—Ewes 66%, Kabyes 10%, Fons 8%, Minas 7%, Avatimes 5%, other Ghanaians, Togolese, and Beninese 4%. The Ewe capital and major cultural center is Lomé, (2002e) 658,000, the capital of the Republic of Togo, metropolitan area 790,000, including suburbs in the Volta Region of Ghana. The major cultural center of the Ghanaian Ewes is Ho, (2002e) 73,000. The major cultural center of the Ewes in Benin is Lokassa, (2002e) 31,000.

FLAG: The Ewe national flag, the flag of the national movement, is a green field with a central red stripe bearing three five-pointed gold stars. The flag used by several nationalist organizations is a green field bearing three gold stars, lower hoist, centered, and upper fly.

PEOPLE AND CULTURE: Ewe unity is based on their language, shared history, and common traditions concerning their origins, which they trace to Oyo in the Yorubaland region of Nigeria. Most Ewes are farmers or fishermen, although a growing number are urban dwellers living in Accra, Lomé, and other cities. The Ewes are a patrilineal people, with inheritance passing from father to son. Sacred stools are symbols of the chiefs' authority and lineage. Clans based on geography and lineage clans remain important parts of Ewe society, although urbanization is breaking down the old traditions. Subdivisions of the Ewes include the Anlo, Bey, and Gen in the coastal districts, the Peki, Ho, Kpando, Tori, and Ave in the interior. The Ewes are further divided into some 120 clans. An energetic commercial people, the famous Ewe market women dominate local commerce across the region.

LANGUAGE AND RELIGION: The Ewe language belongs to the Kwa branch of the Niger-Congo language family. The language is spoken in various dialects. The Ewe language became a literary language during the German colonial period. Although the Ewes claim that their tongue is a single language group, the language is spoken in four major dialects, and there is considerable dialectal variation. Some of the dialects are mutually intelligible only with difficulty. English and French are widely spoken, particularly in the urban areas.

Traditional Ewe religion is organized around a creator god, Mawa, and numerous lesser gods. The worship of the latter pervades Ewe society; believers seek assistance in food production, war, and commerce. Belief in the supernatural powers of ancestral spirits enforces patterns of social behavior and feelings of solidarity among clan members. One traditional practice, particularly in the Volta region, is *trokosi*, a system in which young girls are made slaves to a fetish shrine for offenses allegedly committed by members of their families. About half the Ewes have adopted Christian religions, but traditional doctrines remain important in religious beliefs.

NATIONAL HISTORY: Ewe oral history suggests that they emigrated westward from present-day southwestern Nigeria to settle their current homeland before the mid-fifteenth century. Traditionally small tribal and clan groups, thought to have originated in the Niger River valley in the twelfth century, moved west as part of a gradual migration, displacing earlier inhabitants. Habitually raiding neighboring peoples for slaves and plunder, the Ewes were widely known for their ferocity and aggressiveness. The Ewes never formed a single centralized state, remaining a collection of independent chiefdoms that made temporary alliances in time of war. In the early eighteenth century, several Ewe clans moved west to settle the Volta River region.

Soon after visits by Portuguese explorers in 1482, several European nations established trading posts in the area. The Ewe clans, raiding into Ashantiland in the west and the Fon state of Dahomey in the east, sold thousands of captives to the Europeans through the coastal slave ports. The slave trade earned the region the name "the Slave Coast," and it dominated Ewe activity until the European powers outlawed the trade in the mid-nineteenth century.

European and American missionaries arrived in the Ewe lands in the 1840s. German missionaries, arriving on the coast in 1847, were quite successful among the coastal Ewe clans. Mission education produced the beginning of a national sentiment among the numerous clans. The ties of language and culture began to break down the historical barriers between the clans.

The European competition for colonies divided the Ewe lands in the late nineteenth century. In 1884 Gustav Nachtigal, sent by the German government, induced a number of coastal chiefs to accept German protection. The Germans announced the establishment of a protectorate called Togoland or Togo, meaning "beyond the sea" in the Ewe language. Ten years later the borders of the protectorate were demarcated, with small parts of Eweland included in French Dahomey and British Gold Coast to the east and west of German Togo.

German administration was generally efficient, but it was marred by the harsh treatment of tribal peoples and the use of forced labor. The Ewes prospered under German authority, which fostered education and built towns and roads. The Germans, latecomers in the scramble for European colonies in Africa, made German Togoland a model colony. In 1894 the boundaries of the protectorate were demarcated, with small portions of Eweland left under French control to the east and British administration to the west.

British and French troops moved into the protectorate when war began in Europe in 1914, securing a rapid German surrender. When the war ended in 1919, the French and British occupation troops remained in place, and the partition was formalized by League of Nations mandates in 1922. The partition of their homeland, already divided once by the colonial treaties of 1894, marked the beginning of Ewe national awareness. British and French authorities attempted to enforce the new international border during the 1930s, which led to rioting, but the colonial regimes resisted Ewe unification. Sporadic demonstrations and unrest accompanied demands for reunification up to World War II. After the war, over heated Ewe opposition, the division of Togoland was confirmed; the old British and French mandates became trust territories of the new United Nations.

After World War II Ewe nationalists organized, and in 1946 they formed a coalition of nationalist and cultural groups, the All-Ewe Conference, which established permanent committees to work for the reunification of an independent Togoland within its 1914 borders. In 1947 Ewe nationalists, led by Sylvanus Olympio, later the first president of independent Togo, presented to the United Nations General Assembly the case for a united Ewe state to be called Eweland. The Ewe nationalists kept the issue before the UN and the world for over a decade, but they were continuously blocked by the British and French governments.

In 1956, French Togoland became an autonomous unit of the French Union, the political grouping of France and its colonies, the same year that the United Nations organized a plebiscite in British Togoland on the question of annexation by the British Gold Coast. The overwhelming no vote in the Ewe southern districts of Ho and Kpandu was offset by the yes vote of the more numerous non-Ewe tribes of the northern districts. The Gold Coast, including former British Togoland, called Trans-Volta Togoland, became the first sub-Saharan European colony to win independence, in 1957. The Ewes, never politically united, underwent a dramatic growth of Ewe nationalism as a reaction to the 1956 plebiscite, which had partitioned their homeland between two states without any sense for ethnic unity.

The Greater Togo Movement, a Ewe separatist movement, sought to separate Trans-Volta, now the Volta Region, from Ghana and to unite it with the Ewes of Togo in a single state. The movement was a reaction to the near-total exclusion of Ewes from Ghana's first independence government. Not one Ewe held a position in Kwame Nkrumah's cabinet. In 1958 the Ewes in Ghana rebelled, the uprising spreading to the Ewe population in the west, in the territory incorporated into the Gold Coast in 1894. Forced underground by government police, the national movement received aid and material support from the Ewe-dominated government of neighboring Togo. In March 1960, the Ghanaian government published details of a plot for an invasion of the Ghanaian Togoland from neighboring Togo, and of a draft constitution for a Ewe-dominated Togoland state. In October 1961 over 50 Ewe leaders in Ghana were arrested and imprisoned for secessionist activities. To counter Ewe demands for unification, Nkrumah threatened to conquer and incorporate independent Togo as Ghana's seventh province.

French Togoland gained independence in 1960, under the name Republic of Togo. The first president of the republic, Sylvanus Olympio, won the support of the Ewe population but not of the northern tribes. Support for Ewe reunification grew as Togo's diplomatic relations with neighboring Ghana and Dahomey (later Benin) deteriorated. Separatist groups operating in Ghana since the 1950s became active in Togo after a 1967 coup overthrew the Ewe-dominated government and installed a military regime controlled by the Kabye, a northern Hamitic tribe.

Ghana's president, Nkrumah, was overthrown by Gen. Emmanuel Kotoka, a leader of the Ewes, in 1966. Power was transferred from the coastal Akan peoples to the Ewes and Ashantis.* In 1967 General Kotoka was killed during an abortive coup as anti-Ewe sentiment swelled throughout Ghana. A new government, dominated by the Ashantis, was installed in

1972, again alienating the Ghanaian Ewes. Between 1973 and 1977 Ewe separatism revived with broad support for secession of the Ewe region from Ghana. The major nationalist organization, the National Liberation Movement of Western Togoland, was outlawed in 1976, and advocating secession was made a major crime. In 1979 Flight Lt. Jerry Rawlings, whose mother was Ewe, seized power in a coup, and the Ewes again took many key government positions. Rawlings again took power from a civilian government in 1981, but ethnic tension continued to increase in Ghana.

Gnassingbe (Etienne) Eyadema, in power in Togo since 1967, eliminated most Ewes from government positions and suppressed Ewe nationalism. Existing political parties were banned, and a single-party system was inaugurated. In 1986 Eyadema, the sole candidate, was reelected to another seven-year term. In 1990 mass protests and rioting broke out in Lomé, the worst disturbances among the Ewe population since the early 1960s. Renewed rioting shook Togo in early 1991, forcing the government to legalize opposition political parties, mostly exile political groups in Ghana. A rampage by the northern-dominated army through Lomé in January 1993 set off a mass exodus of about 300,000 Ewes across the borders into Ghana and Benin. During 1993 another 50,000 fled the country out of fear of government security forces. An opposition boycott of the presidential elections later in 1993 allowed Eyadema to be easily reelected. Hundreds died in new ethnic confrontations.

Armed Ewes commandos based in Ghana attacked Lomé's main military base and attempted unsuccessfully to assassinate President Eyadema of Togo. They inflicted serious damage but were driven back into Ghana. The commandos again invaded Togo in an attempt to eliminate Eyadema and the anti-Ewe leadership of the country, but they were again driven back by army troops drawn from Togo's northern tribes.

The international border between Ghana and Togo is often closed, as the two governments alternate support and suppression of Ewe nationalist groups operating on each other's territory. The end of the Cold War and growing demands for multiparty democracy in Africa have fueled a resurgence of Ewe nationalism. The nationalists in all three Togoland territories have coordinated their demands for an end to the divisions imposed on their nation by European colonialism.

During the 1990s, the Ewes of Ghana, enjoying economic and political advantages because President Rawlings is half Scottish and half Ewe, renounced their former secessionist sentiment. Rawlings, was elected president of Ghana in 1993, promoted ethnic harmony, but opposition groups criticized the government for its ethnic bias favoring the Ewes. Rawlings was also accused of harboring plans to unite the Ewes of Ghana, Togo, and Benin under his rule. In Rawlings's home region of Volta, there are good roads and villages with modern bungalows.

Ewe separatist organizations, mostly exiles from Ghana, are tolerated by the Togolese government, which is dominated by the northern tribes and opposed by the Togolese Ewes. Ghanaian Ewes have shown little enthusiasm for unification under the anti-Ewe Togolese government of President Eyadema.

Elections in Togo in June 1998 were blatantly rigged by the Eyadema government. Eyadema's Kabaye tribe, which controls the army, the police, and the bureaucracy, stopped the electoral count and burned the ballots when it became clear that Gilchrist Olympio, the chief opposition candidate and the son of Togo's first president, was going to win. Eyadema was then declared the winner. The continuing rule of terror in Togo has suppressed Ewe nationalism in the Ewe heartland, but sentiment for unification remains a strong impulse in all three regions of historical Eweland.

Presidential elections in Ghana in November 2000 were won by the opposition. Jerry Rawlings, after 20 years in power, stood down and allowed a peaceful transfer of power. The Ewes of Ghana, politically and politically advantaged under the Rawlings regime and fearful of losing the privileges they had enjoyed, gave their support to a democratic system and the creation of a federal state in Ghana.

The peace and relative prosperity of Ghana in the 1990s lessened support by Ewe militants for separation, but nationalism remained strong in neighboring Togo. Demands for the unification of the Ewe nation continues to fuel national movements in all three West African countries. Many Ewe activists, suffering from economic excesses and government corruption in all three countries, claim that their history as the traders and colonial managers of West Africa gives them a basis for the formation of a financially and politically viable state.

SELECTED BIBLIOGRAPHY:

Asamoa, K.A. *Classes and Tribalism in Ghana.* 1990.

Asiwaju, A.I. *Partitioned Africans: Ethnic Relations across Africa's International Borders, 1884–1984.* 1985.

Greene, S.E. *Gender, Ethnicity and Social Change on the Upper Slave Coast: A History of the Anlo-Ewe.* 1996.

Oquaye, M., ed. *Democracy, Politics and Conflict Resolution in Contemporary Ghana.* 1995.

Faeroese

Faroese; Faeroe Islanders; Faroe Islanders

POPULATION: Approximately (2002e) 54,000 Faeroese in northern Europe, most in the Faeroe Islands, but with a sizable population living in mainland Denmark and elsewhere in Scandinavia.

THE FAEROESE HOMELAND: The Faeroese homeland, the Faeroe Islands, is an archipelago of 21 islands, 17 inhabited, lying in the North Atlantic Ocean between Iceland and the Shetland Islands. Strategically located along important sea lanes in the northeastern Atlantic, the islands lie 250 (402 km) miles north of mainland Scotland and 357 miles (575 km) west of Norway. The islands, historically called the Sheep Islands, are high, with rugged cliffs and sparse vegetation. The precipitous terrain limits habitation to narrow coastal lowlands. Fishing, closely tied to the Faeroese culture and

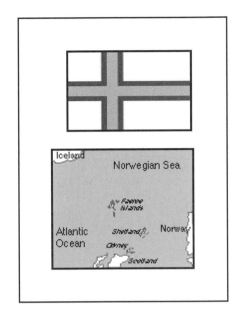

history, accounts for 95% of the islands' economy, as only 6% of the land is suitable for agriculture. The Faeroe Islands form an autonomous state within the Kingdom of Denmark. *Faeroe Islands (Föröyar)*: 540 sq. mi.— 1,398 sq. km, (2002e) 45,000—Faeroese 95%, Danes 5%. The Faeroese capital and major cultural center is Thorshavn, Tórshavn in Faeroese, (2002e) 17,000, situated on the largest of the islands, Stromo.

FLAG: The Faeroese national flag, the official flag of the autonomous state, is a white field bearing a red Scandinavian cross outlined in pale blue.

PEOPLE AND CULTURE: The Faeroese are a Scandinavian nation, the descendants of early Viking colonists and original Celtic inhabitants. Hardy and tenacious, the Faeroese have accommodated to the rugged terrain and damp weather of their homeland and have developed a vigorous culture. The culture of the islands developed in relative isolation, retaining many traits and traditions that have disappeared elsewhere in Scandinavia. The majority of the Faeroese are the descendants of medieval Norwegians who settled the region in the fourteenth and fifteenth centuries. The Faeroese take great pride in their language and culture, particularly in such holdovers as boats made by hand; their archipelago is one of the few places on earth where this skill is still practiced. The Faeroese population nearly doubled in the twentieth century but has now stabilized. Immigration to Denmark and other Scandinavian countries alleviates overpopulation.

LANGUAGE AND RELIGION: The Faeroese speak a separate West Scandinavian language based on the Old Norse brought to the islands by the Norwegian Vikings. The language is related to the language of the Icelanders but is not inherently intelligible with Icelandic. Danish, the language of the controlling state, is widely spoken, along with English.

The Faeroese are overwhelmingly Lutheran and remain one of the more religious of the Scandinavian peoples. The Protestant Reformation, particularly the teachings of Martin Luther, were brought to the islands from the Scandinavian mainland in 1540. Their Protestant religion, like their traditional occupation, fishing, has become an integral part of the Faeroese culture.

NATIONAL HISTORY: The Faeroe Islands, inhabited in ancient times by Celtic tribes from mainland Europe, were the home of Irish hermit monks who came to the island around A.D. 700. The islands were colonized by Norwegian Vikings between the eighth and tenth centuries. Traditionally the Vikings came to the islands around the year 800. In 1035 the islands became part of the Norwegian kingdom. Christianity was brought to the islands from the Norwegian mainland in the eleventh century.

The Black Death, the plague that ravaged Europe in the fourteenth century, devastated the population of the islands. The Norwegian government augmented the surviving population with renewed immigration from the mainland in the fourteenth and fifteenth centuries. The new settlers from the Scandinavian mainland adapted their language and culture to that of the surviving Faeroese, which differed little from the mainland in the Middle Ages.

The islands, as part of the Norwegian kingdom, passed to Danish rule in 1386. Under the Danes the isolated Faeroese retained their language and culture; however, they accepted the Reformation and the Lutheran doctrine brought to the islands by Danish reformers in 1540. The inhabitants of the remote islands, virtually ignored by the Danish government, developed a strong tradition of self-reliance. Sparsely populated and underdeveloped, the islands became almost wholly dependent on fishing. However, in the eighteenth century the islanders discovered a new use for their large fishing fleet—the islands became a notorious center for smuggling goods between the British Isles and Scandinavia.

The Swedish kingdom took control of Norway at the end of the Napoleonic Wars, in 1814, but the Faeroe Islands, long considered an integral part of Norway, remained under Danish rule, ending nearly 1,000 years of close association with the Norwegians. The Danes made the Faeroe

Islands a separate Danish county and introduced a written language, although Danish became the chief language of the islands. Between 1814 and 1856 all island trade came under the control of a Danish royal monopoly, which the islanders circumvented by returning to their traditional smuggling. When the monopoly was ended in 1856, the Faeroese turned to fishing, which remained the main economic activity during most of the nineteenth century.

The decline of the Faeroese language became a major issue of the Faeroese cultural revival of the 1880s. In the 1890s demands for autonomy within the Danish kingdom began among the educated classes. The development of a distinct alphabet, based on that of the Icelanders to the northwest, spurred the development of an extensive Faeroese literature. Faeroese nationalism, growing out of the cultural revival, led to demands for political autonomy. In 1912, as a concession to growing Faeroese nationalism, the Faeroese language was made the second official language of the islands, with equal status to that of Danish.

Faeroese self-awareness and renewed appreciation of their unique culture and history advanced rapidly during World War I, when the islands were briefly granted autonomy. In the first decade after the war the Faeroese experienced a rapid population growth, but for the first time the islanders rejected emigration to the Danish mainland and began to colonize the formerly uninhabited islands of the group. The advanced social legislation of Denmark, extended to the islands, brought increased social services and welfare.

The British military occupied the Faeroes following the fall of Denmark to the Nazis in 1940. Allowed to govern themselves, the Faeroese provided three-quarters of the fish consumed in Britain during the war. The war cost the Faeroese over a third of their fishing fleet and the lives of hundreds of fishermen. Many Faeroese women married British servicemen stationed in the islands and after the war left to live in Britain, strengthening the ties between the Faeroese and the British Isles.

At the end of the war and the return of Danish administrators, there was growing sentiment for full independence. Nationalists pressed for the islands to follow Iceland, which had declared its independence of Denmark in 1944. Following a plebiscite, the Faeroese parliament, the Lagting, declared the islands independent on 18 September 1946; the Lagting ratified the proclamation by a vote of 12 to 11. The inhabitants of Sudhuroy, the third largest of the islands, announced their continued union with Denmark. The Danish authorities then declared the ballot inconclusive and temporarily dissolved the Lagting. A subsequent poll gave the proponents of continued union a slight plurality, and a parliamentary delegation was invited to Copenhagen for further discussions. Faced with continuing separatist sentiment, the Danish government granted extensive autonomy in

1948. The Faeroese government took over all aspects of the island's administration except for defense and foreign relations.

The modernization of the fishing fleet and the expansion of local processing in the 1950s and 1960s gradually raised the standard of living to mainland levels. The prosperous Faeroese, their language firmly established, became increasingly confident and assertive. In 1953 the Faeroese sent two delegates to the Danish parliament, but increasing nationalist demands brought separate Faeroese representation in Scandinavian economic and cultural councils, and recognition as a separate Scandinavian nation. By 1970 the Faeroese were overwhelmingly using the Faeroese language, completing a program begun during the nationalist revival some 90 years before.

Denmark's entry in the European Economic Community in 1973 increased the competition for the diminishing fish stocks by the large fishing fleets of the other member states. Threats to their one important industry, and therefore their culture, reopened the autonomy-versus-independence debate in the late 1970s. The massive over extension of the fishing fleet in the prosperous 1980s led to a collapse of the industry in 1992. Accompanied by a severe recession and high unemployment, the collapse affected the island's autonomous financial institutions. In January 1993, for the second time in many years, the Faeroese government faced the prospect of compromising its independence by accepting a loan from the Danish government.

In 1996 the Faeroese government announced that it had opened bidding for the first drilling rights in newly discovered oil fields in the islands' waters. The first licenses were issued in 1996–97, promising to bring the revenue necessary for the Faeroese to overcome the effects of the financial crisis of the early 1990s.

The Faeroese became skilled at driving hard bargains with the Danish government. In 1998, the Faeroese government opened negotiations with the Danish government with the intention of becoming a sovereign nation under the Danish crown for 25 years. Iceland had in 1917 received that status and a quarter-century later had become an independent state.

The discovery of oil and gas in the waters around the islands promises to end the economic ups and downs of the fishing industry and the accompanying economic problems, like those of the early 1990s. The Faeroese economy has recovered since 1998, with unemployment down to about 5% in 2000. For the immediate future the Faeroese want to continue receiving subsidies from Copenhagen, worth at least $147 million a year in 1998–99, which are needed to keep the islands' schools, hospitals, and social services up to the high Scandinavian standards.

The economic crisis of the early 1990s left many Faeroese angry with fishing quotas and austerity measures imposed by the European Union (EU) and the Danish government. The revitalized national movement has again begun to call for full independence. The Faeroese are already recognized as a separate Scandinavian people, and many nationalists are determined to win official recognition as a separate, independent European people.

In 1998 the Faeroese government began the process of establishing a new constitutional status for the Faeroe Islands as a sovereign state, in continued cooperation with Denmark. A constitutional commission was approved in February 1999. A government support on sovereignty was officially presented to the Faeroese parliament in September 1999. The Faeroese government's intention was to complete negotiations with Denmark on eventual independence and the adoption of a new constitution by the end of 2000. Negotiations between delegations of the Faeroese and Danish governments began on 17 March 2000 with four possibilities discussed: greater autonomy under the existing home rule system; a wider form of home rule within the framework of the present Danish constitution; greater autonomy through an amendment to the Danish constitution; and independence in free association with Denmark. The majority of the Faeroese favor free association, which would allow the Faeroese government to end unilaterally the arrangement and become fully independent.

The Faeroese wish to be recognized as a sovereign state is at odds with an equally fervent desire to maintain ties to the Danish kingdom. The Danish government, which has paid much of the foreign debt accumulated during the economic crisis of the 1990s, is supporting greater self-government and greater fiscal responsibility for the increasingly expensive dependency.

Oil production in Faeroese waters, begun in July 2001, promised financial independence and continued prosperity. Nationalists claimed the proceeds from petroleum will finance the political maturity of the Faeroese—full independence within the European Union.

SELECTED BIBLIOGRAPHY:

Gaffin, Dennis. *In Place: Spatial and Social Order in a Faeroe Islands Community.* 1996.
Levine, Charlotte. *Danish Dependencies.* 1989.
Rutherford, G.K. *The Physical Environment of the Faeroe Islands.* 1982.
Young, G.V.C. *Isle of Man and the Faeroe Islands: Two Similar Countries.* 1981

Far Easterners

Far Eastern Slavs; Dalni Vostochniki; Dalyniaei Vostokiaks

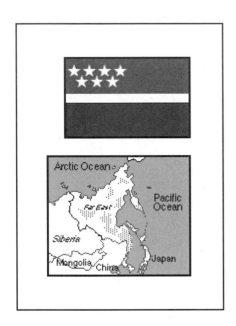

POPULATION: Approximately (2002e) 6,100,000 Far Easterners in Russia, concentrated in the Russian Far East on the Pacific Ocean. Outside the region there are Far Easterner communities in other parts of Siberia, in European Russia, and in the United States and Canada.

THE FAR EASTERN HOMELAND: The Far Eastern homeland occupies the Pacific coast of eastern Russia, a vast region stretching from the Arctic Circle to the border with China. At the closest point, in the Sea of Okhotsk, only three miles separates the Far East from Japan. The Far East forms an economic region of the Russian Federation comprising the Primorski and Khabarovsk territories, and the *oblasti* (provinces) of Amur, Kamchatka, Magadan, and Sakhalin, and the Republic of Sakha (Yakutia). The region includes the autonomous areas of Chukotka, Koryakia, and the Jewish Autonomous Region. *Far East (Dal'nego Vostoka)*: 2,399,958 sq. mi.—6,215,891 sq. km, (2002e) 6,736,000—Far Easterners 78%, European Russians 7%, Ukrainians 5%, Koreans 4%, Sakhas* 4%, Germans 1%, others 1%. The Far Eastern capital and major cultural center is Vladivostok, (2002e) 601,000. The other important cultural center is Khabarovsk, (2002e) 607,000.

FLAG: The Far Eastern flag, the flag of the national movement, is a horizontal bicolor of red over blue divided by a narrow white stripe and bearing seven yellow stars on the upper hoist.

PEOPLE AND CULTURE: The Far Easterners are ethnic Slavs, the descendants of Ukrainian and Russian settlers, Cossacks, and other groups deported from European Russian since the seventeenth century. Thousands of miles and many time zones east of the Slavic heartland in Europe, the Far Easterners developed a unique frontier culture that incorporates Russian and Ukrainian traditions and borrowings from the indigenous peoples. Many cultural traits brought to the region by early settlers remain part of the regional culture but have long since disappeared in European Russia. In customs, foods, and way of life, the Far Easterners are quite distinct from their kin in Europe, having developed in difficult isolation and adapted to a harsh climate. Since the fall of the Soviet Union in 1991, the Far Easterners have seen themselves as a distinct European nation marooned in Asia.

LANGUAGE AND RELIGION: The Far Easterners speak standard Russian along with several regional dialects that combine Ukrainian, Russian, and borrowings from the region's indigenous peoples (including many words for local flora and fauna, foods, and geographical features). Forms and syntax retained by the regional dialects are often archaic, reinforced by the traditional isolation of the Far Easterner communities.

The majority of the Far Easterners are nominally Orthodox Christians, but a history of isolation and decades of official atheism have greatly diminished the importance of religion in the region. A sizable minority are Roman Catholic, mostly the descendants of Ukrainians deported during and after World War II. There are also descendants of religious refugees from European Russia, mostly belonging to the Old Believers who suffered persecution in the eighteenth and nineteenth centuries.

NATIONAL HISTORY: Ruled by the Chinese for centuries, the Far East was a remote region sparsely populated by small tribal peoples. The area was penetrated by Slav explorers and traders in the 1640s, and the expanding Russian Empire soon challenged China's claim to it. The Russians in 1689 abandoned a string of Cossack forts to Manchu China under the terms of the Treaty of Nerchinsk. The treaty, the first between the Chinese Empire and a European power, confirmed Chinese sovereignty and defined the border between the two empires.

Slavic traders and Cossacks, the vanguard of Russian expansion, returned to the region in large numbers in the late eighteenth century. Following the Russian seizure of some western districts, the weakened Manchus* ceded the region north of the Amur River to Russia in 1858. The Russians founded on the Pacific coast a military outpost called Vladivostok, meaning "Rule the East," in 1860, the same year that the Russians forced China to cede the maritime region to the Russian Empire. The main Russian military and naval base on the Pacific was established at Vladivostok in 1872. In 1875 Russian rule was extended to northern Sakhalin Island.

Political prisoners, religious minorities, and criminals, deported to the region's many penal colonies and labor camps, became the first settlers in many districts. Their legacy of antigovernment sentiments and revolutionary ideas became part of the Far Eastern culture. The completion of the Trans-Siberian Railroad in 1892 brought thousands of immigrants from Europe, particularly from the Ukraine. The completion of the Chinese Eastern Railway in 1903 gave the region a more direct rail connection to the rest of the Russian Empire.

Widespread military conscription, introduced with the beginning of World War I in 1914, provoked widespread resentment, as the Far Easterners generally viewed the distant conflict as Europe's war. Soldiers returning from the front and tsarist exiles formed revolutionary organizations that enthusiastically supported the revolution of February 1917. The Social Revolutionary Party, the region's largest, took control of the collapsing civil administration and declared the Far East an autonomous state in May 1917, but it was unable to enforce its authority across the region, as other groups formed rival governments in several of the provinces.

The Bolshevik coup in European Russian in October 1917 inspired local Bolsheviks to attempt to take power. The Bolsheviks fielded a well-armed militia against the more moderate political groups supported by anti-Bolshevik Gen. Vasili Semenov and his 3,000 Cossacks. Pressed by the Bolsheviks, the Far East government appealed for Japanese assistance in February 1918. Aided by 12,000 Japanese troops, the Far Eastern nationalists routed the Bolsheviks and declared the Provisional Government of Priamur at Vladivostok. The Japanese, seeking a buffer between their Korean colony and the Bolsheviks, spread out across the region and sent soldiers to guard the vital railroad. With Japanese support, General Semenov declared the independence of the Far Eastern Republic on 23 May 1918.

Various international military forces intervened as the Russian Civil War spread into the region. The interventionist troops eventually numbering 72,000 Japanese, 7,000 Americans, 6,400 British, 4,400 Canadians, and smaller contingents of French and Italians. The American troops, holding the eastern end of the Trans-Siberian Railroad at Vladivostok, evacuated the famous Czech Legion, thousands of Czech and Slovak prisoners of war who had fought their way across revolutionary Russia in order to return to their homes in Central Europe.

The interventionist forces, except for the Japanese troops, all withdrew following the defeat of the local Bolsheviks in late 1918. Bolstered by troops sent from Europe, the Bolsheviks regrouped and formed a rival Far East Republic, which they declared independent on 6 April 1920. The newly formed Soviet Union recognized the communist-dominated Far Eastern Republic as a sovereign state and the only legitimate government of the region. Gaining strength, the communists took Khabarovsk in February 1922, and they occupied Vladivostok when the Japanese withdrew in October 1922. Most of the defeated White (anticommunist) forces fled south to Chinese territory. On 19 November 1922 the local communists dissolved the Far East Republic and accepted annexation by the Soviet Union.

The war in Europe of 1939 to 1945 was remote from the Far East, but as the Nazis advanced into European Russia many vital industries were transferred eastward, bringing a corresponding increase in population. In August 1945 the government of the Soviet Union, having preserved an armed neutrality with Japan in the region during the war, sent its troops into defeated Japanese-held territory. The occupied territories, southern Sakhalin Island and the Kuril Islands, became part of the Far East region.

The Far East became a dumping ground for political exiles and deportees during Stalin's decades of dictatorship. The exiles, many well educated and often anticommunist, added to the region's distinct character in the 1950s and 1960s. Frustration of a natural orientation to the booming Pacific countries by the control of all economic activity by bureaucrats and ministries in faraway Moscow increased Far Eastern resentment and sense of isolation. Enmity toward the growing number of temporary workers sent to the region from European Russia and attracted by the "long ruble," extra wages they received as hardship pay for working there, initiated the dramatic growth of modern Far Eastern nationalism in the 1980s.

The rapid liberalization of Soviet society under Mikhail Gorbachev in the late 1980s finally allowed the Far Easterners to discuss openly the region's many economic problems. The subsequent disintegration of the Soviet Union exacerbated the problems, as the Far Easterners sought to join their homeland to the fast-growing Asia-Pacific region. Spurred by economic grievances, nationalists in the region began to call for the resurrection of the independent Far Eastern Republic of 1918. In June 1993 the leaders of the Primorski Kray (Maritime Territory), which includes Vladivostok, unilaterally declared the province a member republic in the Russian Federation. The declaration sparked debates in parliaments of the other provinces on reconstituting a separate republic encompassing the entire Far East.

Between 1991 and 2000 an estimated million nonnative Slavs, most of whom had immigrated for the "long ruble," left the region to return to European Russia, to escape economic hardship and the increasing tension between the Far Easterners and the government of the Russian Federation. This continuing emigration, seen by the Far Easterners as the desertion of the European Russians, has reduced the total population of the region from a high of 8.1 million in 1991. The Far Easterners, feeling both ignored and exploited, saw the Europeans as deserting their homeland for an easier life in Europe. However, many Far Easterners welcome the reduction of the European population, who are associated with Soviet policies and are blamed for many of the region's financial, political, and environmental problems.

In 1997 the leaders of the provinces and the republic that constitute the Far East defended Governor Yevgeniy Nazdratenko of Primorsky Kray against pressure from Moscow. Russia's president Boris Yeltsin attempted to remove the governor, who had consistently ignored directives and orders from the central government, but he backed down when faced with opposition from across the Far East. All of the regional leaders were strong supporters of Russian federalism, though many Russian leaders suspected them of separatism. The governor of Sakhalin in September 1998 threatened to withhold tax revenues, starting what he called the "beginning of Russia's dissolution."

Improving ties between Russian and Japan may further weaken the Far Easterners' ties to European Russia. Japanese investment is likely to go to the Far East, with the influx of foreign funds making the already independent-minded leaders there less willing to follow Moscow's lead. Since World War II, relations between Russia and Japan have been complicated by a still-unresolved dispute over the Kuril Islands, a small archipelago (part of Sakhalin Oblast) that was seized from the Japanese in the last days of the war. The Japanese government has always insisted that Russia must return the so-called Northern Territories before the Japanese will become more involved in the economy of the Russian Far East. Despite this impasse, there have been signs that ties are expanding.

At the turn of the twentieth-first century, the Far Easterners consider themselves beyond Moscow's control and are moving rapidly toward market and political reforms. The election of a new Russian president, Vladimir Putin, in 2000 began a new era in relations between the Russian central government and regional leaders. Putin, extremely uneasy about the future of the Far East as its contacts with Moscow became looser with each passing day, reorganized the region, giving it a new regional government with powers over the provinces and republics. The conflict between the local and the federal governments in Moscow, which is to continue for some time, could weaken or strengthen regionalist loyalty and separatist feelings in the region.

Rapid development of the border zones with China and massive immigration from the south led to new anxiety in the late 1990s. The growing penetration of Chinese immigrants and Chinese capital into the Far East is seen by nationalists as symptomatic of Russia's decreasing influence in the region, the danger of Chinese territorial expansion, and the need for a strong Far Eastern government.

From 1991 to 1997, the southern province, Primorsky Krai, was run by an ex-welder, Yevgeniy Nazdratenko, and became awash with graft and crime. The governor simply blamed all the region's problems on the federal government until in June 1997 Boris Yeltsin's representative took over the governor's powers. The takeover, much resented as interference by the central government, was also welcomed, as Nazdratenko's antics were harming the development of the entire Far East.

Trade with neighboring Pacific states has increased dramatically since 1991; exorbitant domestic railroad fares made the Far Easterners further shift their orientation from European Russia to Asian and Pacific countries. The last untapped region in the Northern Hemisphere, the resource-rich

Far East needs to trade its minerals and timber for the manufactured goods readily available in nearby countries, but it must still route every transaction through the appropriate ministry in Moscow. The Far East is an important regional power, both within Russia and within the western Pacific, but nationalists point out that economically little has changed and that the Far East, in order to develop and prosper, must take its place as a sovereign Pacific Rim country.

In September 2001, delegates to a congress in Vladivostok called on the Russian State Duma to declare the Far East a "high-risk" territory. The region's demographic problems are particularly pressing, as more than a million people have left the region and the death rate is double that of the birth rate. Demograghic pressure from China, with 150 million people in the northeastern provinces compared with just 6 million Far Easterners is growing. Currently, there are tens of thousands of Chinese immigrants in the region, but the Far Easterners believe they will become more and more numerous with the threat that the Far East will cease to exist as a Slav region.

SELECTED BIBLIOGRAPHY:

Akaha, Tsuneo, ed. *Politics and Economics in the Russian Far East: Changing Ties with Asia-Pacific.* 1997.

Azulay, Erik, and Allegra Harris Azulay. *The Russian Far East.* 1995.

Kotkin, Stephen, and David Wolff, ed. *Rediscovering Russia in Asia: Siberia and the Russian Far East.* 1995.

Stephan, John J. *The Russian Far East: A History.* 1996.

Flemish

Vlaamsch; Vlaams; Flemings; Flamands

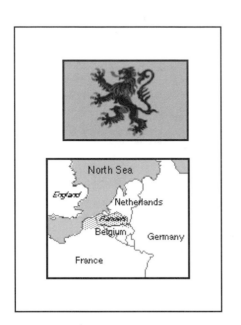

POPULATION: Approximately (2002e) 6,260,000 Flemish in northwestern Europe, 5,770,000 in Belgium, 370,000 in Westhoek (French Flanders), and 120,000 in the southern Zeeland region in the Netherlands. Outside Europe there are Flemish communities in the United States, Canada, South America, and Australia.

THE FLEMISH HOMELAND: The Flemish homeland occupies a broad, flat plain in the southwestern Netherlands, northern Belgium, and northwestern France. Behind the coastline lie the coastal plains, with some of the low-lying areas below sea level. Called "polders," they are protected from the sea by dikes and seawalls. Flanders includes the Flanders Region and Brussels metropolitan area of Belgium, French Flanders, the coastal districts of the French region of Nord-Pas-de-Calais, called Flandre in French and Westhoek in Flemish, and the southern district, Zeeuws Vlaanderen, of the Dutch province of Zeeland. The autonomous Region of Flanders in Belgium includes the provinces of Antwerp, East Flanders, Limburg, Flemish Brabant, and West Flanders. *Region of Flanders (Belgian Flanders) (Vlaanderen/Vlaamse Gewest)*: 5,217 sq. mi.—13,512 sq. km, (2002e) 5,953,000—Flemish 86%, Walloons* 11%, Italians 1%, other Belgians 2%. The Flemish capital and major cultural center is Brussels, called Brussel in Flemish, (2002e) 948,000, metropolitan region 2,399,000 (an autonomous region lying between the provinces of Flemish and Walloon Brabant). The other important Flemish cultural centers in Belgium are Antwerp, called Antwerpen in Flemish, (2002e) 443,000, metropolitan area 1,113,000, Brugge (2002e) 115,000, the historic center of Flanders, and Gent (2002e) 225,000, urban area 525,000 (the official capital of Flanders Region). The major cultural center of French Flanders is Dunquerque, Duinkerke in Flemish, 70,000, urban area 210,000. The major cultural center of the Zeeland Flemish is

Terneuzen, called Neuzen in Flemish, 25 miles (40 km) northwest of Antwerp, (2002e) 34,000.

FLAG: The Flemish national flag, the official flag of the autonomous region, also the unofficial flag of the Flemish populations in France and the Netherlands, is a yellow field bearing the rampant Black Lion of Flanders centered.

PEOPLE AND CULTURE: The Flemish, also called Flemings, are a Germanic people closely related to the Dutch of the Netherlands. However, the Flemish majority remains staunchly Roman Catholic, while Protestant religions prevail in the Netherlands. Formerly a rural people, the Flemish were dominated after Belgian independence in the nineteenth century by the more sophisticated French-speaking Walloons. This domination finally ended in the 1960s, and the Flemish are now the more prosperous of the two major Belgian groups. The Flemish nationalist movement grew from demands for the cultural equality that the Flemings' new economic importance in Belgium warranted. Until the mid-twentieth century the Flemish majority remained rural; only since World War II has a large Flemish urban population developed. The Flemish culture is a legacy of the Flemish Renaissance, and one of the richest in Europe.

LANGUAGE AND RELIGION: The Flemish language, belonging to the West Germanic language group, is a low German dialect closely related to Dutch. In its spoken form, Flemish diverged from Dutch in the sixteenth century but remains nearly identical in its written form. The language, long suppressed in favor of French in Belgium and France, is the focal point of modern Flemish nationalism. In the city and suburbs of Brussels, both French and Dutch are officially recognized. Although the French speakers are the larger group in the city of Brussels, which is surrounded by Flemish-speaking suburbs, they are historically separate from the Walloons and do not identify with Wallonia. In French Flanders, about 90,000 people use the language as the language of daily life, but it has no official recognition and is not taught in area schools.

NATIONAL HISTORY: The Roman province of Belgica, named for the Celtic Belgae tribe conquered by Romans under Julius Caesar in 57 B.C., became thoroughly Latinized in culture and language. The province was invaded by Huns and Salic Franks in the fourth century A.D. as Roman power waned; the Germanic conquerors drove the Latins south to a line approximating the present linguistic division of Belgium, formerly a natural line of dense forests.

The region formed a major part of the new kingdom of the Franks, which began to expand in the late 400s. The Franks eventually established a vast empire, gaining control of most of modern France and southern Germany. The origins of Flanders lay in the Pagus Flandrensis, Brugge and its surroundings, under the Frankish empire. The name "Flanders" appeared as early as the eighth century and is believed to mean "lowland" or "flooded land."

The empire established by the Franks reached its apex under Charles the Great, better known as Charlemagne. The empire began to decline at Charlemagne's death in 814 and was divided by three heirs in 843. Baldwin Bras-de-Fer (Iron Arm) became the first count of Flanders in 862, after marrying the daughter of the Western Frankish king Charles II. At first Flandrensis was an unremarkable district, but in the ninth century an outstanding line of Flemish counts expanded the domain southward to Douai and Arras, and eastward to Ghent and Antwerp. Under Baldwin I and Baldwin II, the basis was laid for later industrial and commercial greatness by the establishment of wool and silk industries at Gent and the inauguration of annual trade fairs at Brugge, Ieper, and other towns.

In the eleventh century, the Flemish lands became a vassal of the Holy Roman Empire as well as of the French crown. The County of Flanders, with its capital at Lille, enjoyed virtual independence from weak French kings; at its greatest extent it controlled Flanders, Westhoek, Artois, and part of Picardy. The county, with power equivalent to that of a kingdom, wielded considerable influence in the political affairs of Western Europe.

In conjunction with the northern Italian cities, the French-speaking Flemish cities led the European Renaissance, a movement little affecting the rural Flemish-speaking peasantry. The Flemish cities, called communes, were granted charters with broad privileges and liberties that reflected their growing prosperity and importance. By the twelfth century the Flemish economy had evolved from a basically agricultural economy to international importance as a center of trade and industry.

In 1191 the direct line of the counts of Flanders died out, and the counts of Hainault, in present-day Wallonia, became the Flemish counts as well, perpetuating the predominance of the French language among the urbanized upper classes. The power of the county was greatly weakened by the departure of Count Baldwin IX on the Fourth Crusade. He was later proclaimed the Latin emperor of Constantinople, as Baldwin I, in 1204.

In the struggle for control of Flanders, the counts gradually lost Artois, Picardy, and other southern territories to the French crown. In the thirteenth and fourteenth centuries, the region was the scene of serious political and economic unrest that often pitted classes, trade guilds, and independent cities in bloody rivalries. The turbulence was worsened by a continuing rivalry between the pro-French and pro-Flemish groups. On 11 July 1302, the Flemish won the Battle of the Golden Spurs against the forces of the French king, who formally recognized Flemish independence. The date, 11 July, is now the official holiday of the Flemish nation. However, civil war in 1322 left Flanders once again little more than a French province. In 1384 the entire region passed to the dukes of Burgundy; Flemish privileges were suppressed but were partially restored in 1477. Under

Burgundian rule, Flemish commerce and Flemish art reached their flower. Protestantism won many adherents in Flanders during the Reformation, but the later military occupation of the Low Countries by the Spaniards mostly reversed Protestant inroads in the southern provinces. Flanders in 1500, then the richest and most populous area of Europe, came under the rule of the Austrian Habsburgs; in 1555 it passed to the Spanish Habsburgs and became part of the Spanish Netherlands. The religious differences between the southern and northern provinces led to a serious division in the Low Countries. In 1566 Protestant activists destroyed statues in Catholic churches, setting off nearly eighty 80 years of sectarian violence.

The Flemish, although separated by religion from the Dutch, united with the Dutch and Walloons to fight first Spanish and later Austrian domination in the seventeenth and eighteenth centuries. The Flemish joined the Dutch in a widespread revolt against Spanish rule in 1576. The Dutch won their independence in 1579, but by 1584 the Spanish had recovered control of Flanders and Wallonia and had imposed an oppressive rule. The expanding French kingdom took control of western Flanders, including the historical capital, Lille, between 1668 and 1678. In 1714 the Flemish homeland again passed to the control of the Austrian Habsburgs.

The military forces of revolutionary France occupied the Flemish provinces in 1792. The Austrian government ceded the provinces to France in 1797, and the provinces were annexed to Napoleonic France in 1801. At the conclusion of the Napoleonic Wars, in 1815, the Low Countries were reunited in the Kingdom of the Netherlands. Rejecting the domination of the kingdom by the Protestant Dutch, the predominantly Roman Catholic southern provinces in Flanders and Wallonia rebelled in 1830 and formed the separate Kingdom of Belgium, under the protection of the major European powers.

The new Belgian kingdom remained a French-speaking state, with Flemish reduced to a peasant dialect. The majority of the nineteenth-century industrialization of Belgium took place in the southern Walloon provinces, leaving the Flemish a rural, agricultural nation dominated by the richer, more sophisticated Walloons. The adoption of French as the official language effectively barred Flemish speakers from most government positions. Much of the history of modern Belgium through the end of World War II consists of the struggle of the country's Flemish community to gain equal status for its language and culture and to acquire a fair share of political influence and economic opportunity.

Flemish resentment of Walloon domination stimulated a cultural and linguistic revival in the nineteenth century. The first works published in modern Flemish appeared in 1837. The revival spread to the Flemish minority in France, and the first cultural organization, in Westhoek, formed in 1852. A sense of Flemish grievance grew throughout the nineteenth century. Flemish became an official language in 1898, but in 1900 dissatisfied Flemish leaders demanded full cultural and linguistic equality with the Walloons.

Belgium was overrun by German troops at the outbreak of World War I, in 1914. Heavy fighting devastated the provinces of West Flanders and French Flanders. The German occupation authorities, to win Flemish support, granted the linguistic and cultural rights long denied by the Belgian government. A faction of the Flemish national movement formed a Council of Flanders in February 1917, and with German encouragement it declared Flanders independent of Belgium on 11 November 1917. The republic collapsed with the German surrender in 1918, and its leaders faced charges of high treason when the Belgian government returned.

In the 1920s, linguistic and economic controversies again caused friction between the Flemish and the dominant Walloons. Flemish extremist groups—many from the first Flemish university, opened at Ghent in 1930—emerged during the turbulent interwar period. Some of the groups, drawn by Nazi propaganda promoting the unity of Europe's Germanic peoples, collaborated with the German occupiers beginning in May 1940, some even joining Nazi fighting units. The German occupation authorities in Belgium again raised the Flemish language to the status of an official language along with French, which lasted until the German defeat and the return of the exiled Belgian government.

The rapid postwar reconstruction of Europe greatly increased the economic importance of the Flemish port cities. By the early 1960s Flanders had surpassed Wallonia as Belgium's economically predominant region. Material prosperity prompted demands for Flemish cultural and linguistic equality. Mass rallies erupted across Flanders in 1961–62. In November 1962, the government adopted Flemish as the sole official language of the Flemish provinces. In 1963 a law was passed establishing three official languages within Belgium: Flemish was recognized as the official language in the north, French in the south, and German along the eastern border. Universities, banks, political parties, and other official institutions split along linguistic lines.

The economic and cultural rivalry between the Flemish and Walloons made weak coalition governments the norm in Belgium. Governments rose and fell on the linguistic issue, with major political parties split into Flemish and Walloon factions. The traditional linguistic and economic grievances of the Flemish population that arose during the nineteenth and early twentieth centuries continue to drive the national movement, which works for an independent Flanders within Europe—a republic that would include Brussels, the so-called Flemish Jerusalem.

In 1970 the first changes were made to the Belgian constitution in a process intended to establish a federal state. The Egmont Pact, adopted in 1977, created autonomous governments in Flanders and Wallonia, and later in bilingual Brussels. Through further reforms to the constitution in

1980, 1988, and 1993, devolution of authority over taxation, culture, and education gradually shifted power from the federal government to the autonomous regions. The status of Brussels, a French-speaking center surrounded by Flemish-speaking suburbs, remains one of the major Flemish nationalist issues.

An even greater devolution of government powers agreed to in February 1993 created a federation and left the Belgian government responsible for little more than finance, foreign policy, and defense. When these limited federal powers are surrendered to a united European federation, as planned for the near future, Belgium will effectively cease to exist except as a geographic area.

Flemish nationalists, on 29 November 1997, proclaimed a provisional government of the Republic of Flanders, with Gert Geens as the first president. The proclamation, made to draw attention to Flemish demands for independence within the European Union (EU), was followed by unofficial parliamentary elections held in February 1998. The unofficial Flemish parliament accepted a constitution for an independent Flemish state in December 1998.

Closer cooperation among the related Dutch and Flemish nations in the Netherlands, Belgium, and France as a regional grouping within the inner core of the EU, an idea often proposed, gained high-level support in 1999. Supporters, including the premier of Belgian Flanders and a Christian Democratic senator in the Netherlands, see the linguistic and cultural region as a natural evolution of closer European integration. The Schengen Accord, implemented in 1998, which opened borders among many of the EU member states, has already caused the Dutch-Flemish border virtually to disappear. On 1 January 2002, the entire Flemish nation, in Belgium, France, and the Netherlands, began using the same currency, the Euro.

Flemish and Walloons are yearly growing farther apart. A new agreement, signed on 29 June 2001, the Lambermont Accord, gives even more autonomy to the two communities, while placating the Walloons with extra funds for a French-language education system. There is growing Flemish resentment of taxes used to support the large number of unemployed in Wallonia hit by the slow collapse of mining and steel.

SELECTED BIBLIOGRAPHY:

Deprez, Kas, ed. *Nationalism in Belgium: Shifting Identities, 1780–1995.* 1998.
Hermans, T.J. *The Flemish Movement: A Documentary History 1780–1980.* 1991.
Pateman, Robert. *Belgium.* 1996.
Strikwerda, Carl. *A House Divided: Catholics, Socialists, and Flemish Nationalists in bibineteenth-Century Belgium.* 1998.

Frisians

Frysk; Friesisch; Fries

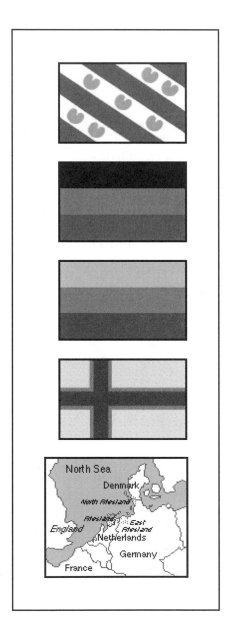

POPULATION: Approximately (2002e) 860,000 Frisians in northwestern Europe, 410,000 in Friesland in the Netherlands, another 300,000 in other parts of the Netherlands, and 150,000 in Germany and Denmark. Outside Europe, an estimated 35,000 Frisians live in the United States and Canada.

THE FRISIAN HOMELAND: The Frisian homeland occupies a region of flat plains and "polders," reclaimed lands, on the North Sea. West Friesland, including the province of Friesland and parts of neighboring Groningen, called Grins in Frisian, also includes a string of offshore islands along the northern coast, the West Frisian Islands. East Friesland, in Germany, including the East Frisian Islands, is separated from Dutch Friesland by the Dollart, an inlet of the North Sea formed by the Ems River estuary. North Friesland, including the North Frisian Islands, lies on the western part of the Jutland Peninsula, on both sides of the Danish-German border. Western Friesland forms a province of the Kingdom of the Netherlands. East Friesland and North Friesland have no official status other than that of distinctive cultural and linguistic regions recognized by the German and Danish governments. *Province of Friesland (Fryslân)*: 1,464 sq. mi.—3,792 sq. km, (2002e) 609,000—Frisians 89%, other Dutch 11%. The Frisian capital and major city is Leeuwarden, Ljouwert in Frisian, (2002e) 86,000. The cultural center of the East Frisians is Strücklingen, called Strukelje in Frisian. The cultural center of the North Frisians is Bredested, Bräist in the Frisian language.

FLAG: The Frisian flag, the official flag of the Dutch province of Friesland and recognized by the Frisian communities in Germany and Denmark, is a blue field divided by three white diagonal stripes charged with seven red devices representing water lilies. The flag of the East Frisians in Germany is a horizontal tricolor of black, red, and pale blue. The flag of the North Frisians in Germany is a horizontal tricolor of yellow, red, and blue. The same flag is used by the North Frisians in Denmark, along with another flag, a yellow field bearing a blue Scandinavian cross outlined in red.

PEOPLE AND CULTURE: The Frisians are a distinct Germanic people with historical and linguistic ties to the Netherlands, Germany, and England. Closely related to the ancient Anglo-Saxons, the Frisians have maintained their unique culture from the time of Roman control in northern Europe, in all over 2,500 years. The Frisians once controlled the whole of the North Sea coast, from modern North Holland to the western Jutland Peninsula. Isolated Frisian minorities still live in the East Friesland region and the East Frisian Islands of Germany, as well as in the North Friesland region and the North Frisian Islands of Germany and Denmark. The Dutch Frisians claim to have erected the first dikes to hold back the North Sea, a method later copied by the Dutch across the Zuider Zee.

LANGUAGE AND RELIGION: The Frisians speak Frysk or Frisian, a language belonging to the Anglo-Frisian branch of the West Germanic languages, the closest of the continental Germanic languages to English, particularly close to the northern English dialects spoken by the Scots* and Northumbrians.* The language is considered a bridge language between English and Dutch. The eastern Frisian dialects, East Frisian and North Frisian, are not mutually intelligible with West Frisian spoken in the Netherlands. At least nine distinct dialects are spoken by the Frisians, although some—such as Fering, spoken on the island of Fohr, Solring on Sylt, and Halunder on Helgoland—are not called Frisian. Since the mid-1980s, as part of the ethnocultural revival, the number of schools teaching in Frisian has significantly increased, and the language is now taught in primary schools throughout the Dutch province of Friesland. Western Frisian is the only dialect of the Frisian language with a developed literary standard.

The Frisians of the Netherlands are about 85% Protestant, belonging to two Calvinist churches, the Dutch Reformed Church and the Reformed Church. The Frisians in East and North Friesland are also Protestant, mostly Lutheran. Minorities in all three areas belong to the Mennonite sect and the Roman Catholic Church. Religion has played a significant role in the development of the modern Frisian culture.

NATIONAL HISTORY: Migrating tribes settled the shores of the North Sea following the breakup of Celtic Europe in the fourth century B.C. The Germanic Frisians eventually controlled the coastal region from present-day Bremen, in Germany, to Brugge in Belgium. The Frisians also conquered and settled the offshore islands lying in the North Sea. In the first century B.C. the Frisians stopped the northward advance of Roman power. The Frisians, called Frisii by the Romans, maintained their independence and even sent raiding parties into the Roman territories to the south. The fierce Frisian warriors became the scourge of the settled peoples on the borders of the Roman Empire in the first centuries of the Christian Era.

Later Germanic tribes, taking advantage of the collapse of Roman power, attempted to invade the region and conquer the Frisians but were unable to subdue the warlike nation. Germanic Angles and Saxons migrated into the coastal region in the fifth century, establishing strong linguistic and cultural ties to the Frisians before eventually crossing the Channel and conquering England.

The Salic Franks invaded the Frisian homeland in the eighth century and gradually brought the Frisians under Frankish control, completing the conquest during Charlemagne's reign. Frankish missionaries introduced the Christian religion to the Frisians, who mostly converted, although retaining many pagan traditions. The Frank's Germanic language replaced Frisian in many areas by the early twelfth century.

Friesland formed the northern portion of the middle kingdom, Lotharingia, that emerged from the division of the Frankish empire by Charlemagne's heirs in 843. The region passed to the eastern kingdom of Louis the German in 870 and ultimately became a fief of Holland. Subjected to Viking raids between the eighth and tenth centuries, the Frisians reverted to their earlier warrior culture, striking fear into their more settled neighbors.

Frisia in the Middle Ages extended from the Scheldt River in the south to the Weser River in the east. In 1248 William of Holland restored the Frisians' ancient rights, but they again revolted six years later. The Frisians were defeated and absorbed into the province of Holland. Although now nominally a part of Holland, the Frisians did not submit but continued to obey only their local headmen; they enjoyed a degree of liberty that was rare in medieval Europe. Feudalism never took root in the region, giving rise to the Frisian saying, "Every Frisian is a nobleman."

In 1433 Holland came under the rule of the house of Burgundy, but the authority of the Burgundian dukes was not recognized by the independent-minded Frisians. In 1498 Emperor Maximilian I bestowed Friesland on Albert, duke of Saxony, whose son, unable to control the wild Frisians, finally sold the Frisian homeland back to the emperor in 1515. Western Friesland, along with the Low Countries, passed to the Spanish Habsburgs and was finally pacified by Spanish troops led by Maximilian's grandson, Charles V, in 1523. East Friesland, created a separate duchy in 1454, was not included in the transfer to the Spanish dynasty, and its history at this point became separate. East Friesland came to be dominated by the city of Groningen in the west, while a separate countship held by the Cirksena family controlled the eastern districts from 1454 to 1744, when they passed to the Prussian kingdom.

The West Frisians joined the rebellion of the United Provinces in 1579, an alliance of the northern Protestant provinces of the Netherlands opposed to Catholic Spanish rule. In 1581 the seven northern provinces of the Low Countries formed an independent Dutch kingdom. Friesland, as part of the Dutch kingdom, retained considerable autonomy, with a separate Frisian *stadholder* appointed by the Frisian people. In 1748 a Frisian prince, William of Orange, became the sole stadholder of all the Dutch provinces. Since that time the Dutch Frisians have remained fiercely loyal to the House of Orange, if not always to the Dutch state.

Geographically separated from the Dutch heartland by the waters of the Zuider Zee and further dispersed across a broad plain and a number of islands, the isolated Frisians retained their language and culture, which the Frisian parliament jealously guarded. In February 1782 the parliament of Friesland became one of the first official organs of a foreign government to extend recognition to the fledgling United States.

The pastoral Frisians remained a mainly rural people but developed a strong culture with an extensive literature. The Frisian metropolis, Leeuwarden, developed as the center of the modern Frisian culture and helped to maintain ties to the Frisian diaspora in northern Europe. Frisians across northwestern Europe still look to Leeuwarden as the center of Frisian culture.

The French forces led by Napoleon overran Friesland in 1794–95, and later formed part of the French-controlled Batavian Republic. Annexed, along with the rest of the Netherlands, by France in 1810, the Frisian territories remained staunchly loyal to the Dutch monarchy. Following French defeat in 1815, the Frisians welcomed back the kingdom of the Netherlands, under their beloved House of Orange.

The Dutch language gradually replaced Frisian as the language of government and education in the nineteenth century and became the first language of the growing urban areas. A Frisian national revival beginning in the 1880s transformed the Frisian language into a modern literary language and slowly reversed the Frisian assimilation into Dutch culture. In the early twentieth century the general cultural revival continued, with Frisian becoming the language of the towns and cities as rural Frisians urbanized. During World War I, Frisian nationals formed the Frisian National Party, called In Fryske Aksyjeploesch in Frisian, to press for the maintenance and wider use of the Frisian language and for increased ties to the East and North Frisians.

Friesland's relative isolation ended with the construction in 1932 of dikes and a highway linking the peninsula to the Dutch heartland. In 1933 the major enclosing dam was completed, calming the Zuider Zee and allowing the opening of a four-lane highway from the other Dutch provinces. The end of Friesland's geographic isolation brought the Frisian heartland into closer dependence on the Dutch economy but gave new impetus to the efforts of Frisian cultural and national groups to protect their language and culture. In the interwar period the Dutch government maintained firm control of the region, especially when the Nazis of neighboring Germany began to make overtures to the Germanic peoples of Europe and to promote closer ties between the Dutch and German Frisians.

German troops overran Dutch Friesland during World War II, but German overtures, including promises of self-rule, failed to sway the Frisians' loyalty to the exiled House of Orange. At the end of the war, Frisian nationalists accelerated the advancement of the cultural movement that had begun at the turn of the century, but receiving major concessions on the culture and use of the Frisian language, most Frisians were content with Dutch rule. During the 1950s and 1960s the Dutch Frisians renewed their links to the German and Danish Frisian minorities. In 1956 the Frisian Council was formed, with the participation of the various Frisian groups in the Netherlands, Germany, and Denmark.

Dutch governments encouraged the Frisian cultural and linguistic movement. Still intensely loyal to the House of Orange, the Frisians have not developed the militant nationalism of many smaller European nations. Following minor disturbances in the 1960s and 1970s, the Dutch government moved to defuse rising nationalism by granting broad linguistic and cultural autonomy, accepting the Frisian language in the local courts, administration, and parliament. Use of the Frisian language in radio and television broadcasting increased dramatically. In 1981, with government approval, the teaching of Frisian became obligatory in the province's 600 primary schools.

The Frisians look back on two and a half millennia of separate history and culture and are intensely proud of them. They enjoy a large measure of local self-government, with their own national flag, anthem, and parliament. Calling themselves the "Scots of the Netherlands," the Frisians maintain a prosperous economy, with 80% of their lands devoted to cattle, sheep, and hogs. In 1989, to further the use of their language, the Frisian parliament passed legislation changing all town, street, and commercial signs from Dutch to Frisian.

The unification of Europe has stimulated interest in independence within a united Europe, but the majority of Frisians are satisfied with the status quo, although there is widespread support for closer cultural ties to the Frisians in Germany and Denmark. The relationship between the Frisian minority and the Dutch government, considered the best of its kind in Europe, has attracted attention from other small nations within Europe and beyond. Free of the tension and quarrelling that preoccupy other small

European national groups, the Frisian culture has flourished, and nationalist organizations turn their attention to other issues, such as the environment and threats to the Frisian coast and the wildlife of the Frisian tidal flats.

In April 2001, a small movement advocating the end of the Dutch monarchy mobilized Frisian public opinion. Traditionally loyal to the House of Orange, but not necessarily to the Dutch government, Frisian activists threatened to separate their homeland from the Netherlands should the monarchy cease to function.

SELECTED BIBLIOGRAPHY:

Mahmood, Cynthia Keppley. *Frisian and Free: Study of an Ethnic Minority in the Netherlands.* 1989.
Markey, Thomas L. *Frisian.* 1994.
Mellink, A.F. *Friesland.* 1995.
Seth, Ronald. *The Netherlands.* 1997.

Friulis

Friuli; Friûl; Friulians; Friulans

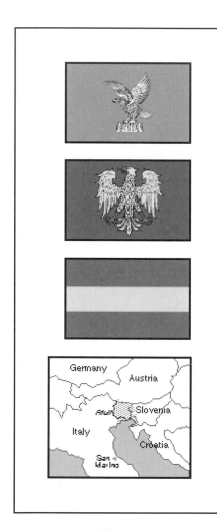

POPULATION: Approximately (2002e) 870,000 Friulis in southern Europe, mostly in northeastern Italy, but with smaller populations in other parts of Italy and in Slovenia and Croatia. Another 700,000 Friulis, considered an integral part of the Friuli nation, live in other parts of the world, mostly in the Americas.

THE FRIULI HOMELAND: The Friuli homeland occupies a mountainous region in the Carnic and Julian Alps and a lowland region bordering the Gulf of Venice and the Gulf of Trieste on the Adriatic Sea, in northeastern Italy and western Slovenia. Friuli has no official status; the Friuli homeland forms part of the autonomous region of Friuli-Venezia Giulia and the Portoguaro district of the region of Veneto in Italy. Officially, Friuli forms the provinces of Udine and Pordenone of the Friuli-Venezia Giulia region of Italy. *Region of Friuli (Friûl)*: 2,777 sq. mi.—7,166 sq. km, (2002e) 797,000—Friulis 91%, Slovenes 8%, Sauris 1%, other Italians. The Friuli capital and major cultural center is Udine, called Udin in Friuli, (2002e) 94,000. The other major cultural center is Pordenone, called Pordenon by the Friulis, (2002e) 48,000. The center of the Veneto Friulis is Portoguaro (2002e) 24,000.

FLAG: The Friuli national flag is a blue field charged with the Friuli national symbol, a golden eagle perched on a gray wall. The flag of the Friuli League is a blue field bearing a yellow eagle with red beak and claws. The flag of the Friuli national movement has three horizontal stripes of blue, yellow, and blue.

PEOPLE AND CULTURE: The Friulis are a Latin people, an ancient nation thought to predate the Etruscans and Romans in northeastern Italy.

Friuli culture, although greatly influenced by centuries of rule by the Venetians,* is a distinct one, combining ancient traditions and customs with the modern trappings of a Rhaeto-Romantic nation. The Friuli consider the large emigrant population, the Fôgalâr, numbering over 700,000, to be an integral part of their small nation. The Friuli are the largest of the Rhaeto-Romantic peoples of northern Italy and Switzerland; others are the Ladins* and the Romansch.* The Sauris, a smaller, closely related people, inhabit the mountainous north of the region and are often counted as ethnic Friulis. The majority of the Friulis are Roman Catholics. The influence of leftist political parties in Italy alarms many moderate Friuli and increases support for the growing autonomy movement.

LANGUAGE AND RELIGION: The Friuli language, Furlan, is a Rhaeto-Romantic language of the Italo-Romance group of languages. The language has been influenced by Venetian and retains a strong Celtic substratum. Furlan is spoken in three major dialects—East Central Furlan, Western Furlan, and Carnico. The majority of the Friulis are bilingual in Italian, the language of government and education, and many of the Italians, Slovenes, and others in the region speak Furlan as a second or third language. Friuli is being cultivated by nationalists as a literary language, although the standardized form of the language is relatively recent and is still debated by scholars and linguists. The language, not recognized as a minority language by the Italian government, is taught in schools on a voluntary basis, depending on the availability of Furlan teachers. Demands for education in the language became a major nationalist issue in the late twentieth century.

The Friulis are mostly Roman Catholics; there are small Protestant groups, mostly in the alpine areas. The history of the region is closely intertwined with that of the patriarch of Aquileia, a political and ecclesiastical center that rivaled Rome in the early years of Christianity in Europe. The spirit of defiance and other historical legacies contribute to religious belief in the region.

NATIONAL HISTORY: The Friuli are believed to have inhabited the area north of the Adriatic Sea before the rise of the Etruscans and Romans, and they are thought originally to have been one of the Celtic peoples that dominated ancient Europe. Roman rule, first established in the coastal plain, was extended to all of Friulia in the first century B.C. The Roman culture and language over centuries replaced the Celtic language and culture of the area, which was known to the Romans as the Julian region.

The Friuli nation took its name from the Roman city of Forum Iulii, the modern town of Cividale, but the center of the ancient Friulia was the city of Aquileia. Aquileia was founded by the Romans as a fortified outpost against the Illyrian peoples in 181 B.C. The town developed as the most flourishing commercial center in northern Italy. The city was ravaged by Attila and the Huns in A.D. 452, forcing its inhabitants to flee to a group of islands in the Venice Lagoon. The city recovered and in the sixth century became the seat of a Roman Catholic patriarch who refused allegiance to the Roman see.

Germanic Lombards* conquered Friulia in 568, following the collapse of Roman power in northern Italy. The area was divided after the barbarian invasion into a coastal zone, dominated by the Byzantines, and an inland zone, ruled by duchy of Friuli and the county of Gorizia. Under Lombard rule Friulia formed a separate duchy; in 801 the region, now called the March of Friuli, entered Charlemagne's Frankish empire. Friuli was later divided into East Friulia and West Friulia, with different rulers and histories.

The political rise of the patriarchate of Aquileia in the eleventh century brought Friuli, the Istrian Peninsula, and the coastal areas under the control of that ecclesiastical sovereign. In the eleventh century West Friulia, the county of Friuli, and its capital, Udine, passed to Aquileia. In the Middle Ages the Friulis' free city-states participated in the great European awakening known as the Renaissance. The cities formed a protective league, a union that greatly aided the preservation of Friuli language and culture.

In 1420 Venice took Friuli, and in 1500, when the line of counts ended, Gorizia passed to the Austrian Habsburgs. The name "Friuli" lost all political meaning but remained a geographic and cultural entity; the Friuli formed a large national minority in the Venetian state. The patriarchate of Aquileia had its seat in Udine from 1238 until it was finally dissolved in 1751. The ancient patriarchate, under its blue and yellow colors, which had survived centuries of turbulent history, was replaced by the archbishoprics of Udine and Gorizia, and its political and secular powers were abolished.

The imposition of foreign rule greatly influenced the development of the Friuli culture and language. In the zone ruled by Venice, the language absorbed many Venetian words and forms, while the east, under Habsburg rule, became essentially Slovene speaking—although Furlan, the Friuli language, remained the second language of a large part of the population. Gorizia retained a large degree of autonomy as the Habsburg crownland of Görz and Gradisca until the eighteenth century.

The Friuilis were reunited when Austria gained control of Venice in 1797; the legality of Habsburg rule in western Friuli was affirmed by treaties in 1814–15, at the end of the Napoleonic Wars. However, at the conclusion of the Austro-Prussian War in 1866, Austria was forced to cede western Friuli, now called Udine Province, to the new Italian kingdom, bringing the Friuli population under Italian rule, with the exception of the

Friuli minority in the Austrian port city of Trieste and its Slovenian hinterland, and the crownland of Görz and Gradisca.

Subjected to intense government pressure during the nineteenth century to adopt standardized Italian language and culture, the Friuli mobilized to resist. Friuli opposition to assimilation inspired a national revival in the late nineteenth century. The growth of nationalism led to demands for autonomy within the Italian kingdom. The unrest spread to the Friuli population of the Austrian Görz and Gradisca, with its mixed population of Friuli, Slovene, and Austrian inhabitants.

Italy remained neutral when war began in Europe in 1914, but allied promises of territory persuaded the Italians to enter the war in 1915. Heavy fighting devastated the Friuli districts, which formed the fluctuating front between the Italian and Austrian troops. Italy lost over 600,000 soldiers before taking Gorizia and eastern Friuli. The Italian government, with allied approval, annexed the captured regions in 1919.

Benito Mussolini took control of the Italian government in 1922, and Fascism became the state creed. The Fascist doctrine stressed Italian nationalism and a uniform Italian culture and language. The Friuli minority, their language outlawed and under intense official pressure, were forced to Italianize all family and place-names and to abandon ancient customs and traditions not approved by the authorities. As repression increased, many Friuli fled to sanctuary among the related Romansch, in southeastern Switzerland.

Friulia was again devastated during World War II, by fighting between Italian and Yugoslav forces. The Friuli faced even greater danger from the postwar territorial claims. Communist Yugoslavia laid claim to eastern Friulia, with its large Slovene minority, while Italy claimed Istria, with its Italian and Friuli minorities. A 1947 agreement partitioned the region, with all of eastern Friulia except Gorizia assigned to Yugoslavia, and an independent Free Territory of Trieste, under United Nations protection, with a mixed population, created in the southeast. While Gorizia remained Italian, the Yugoslav authorities built Nova Gorica in the eastern suburbs of the city, effectively partitioning the Gorizia urban area.

Competing national claims to their homeland inspired the growth of modern Friuli nationalism after World War II. In 1948 Friuli nationalists formed the Moviment Friuli, a nationalist organization dedicated to winning autonomy for the Friuli nation. Demands for autonomy grew after 1954 and the incorporation of the province of Trieste, with its large Italian-speaking population, into the largely Friuli-speaking region to form the new region of Friuli-Venezia Giulia. Protests against Friulia's inclusion in the "hybrid region" fueled nationalist sentiment in the 1960s. In 1963 the Italian government granted the region limited autonomy in recognition of its distinct culture and language.

The Friuli began a second national revival in the 1960s, in which the young, especially, embraced the Friuli culture, language, and history. The Friuli language became a rallying point for the autonomy movement in the 1960s and 1970s. The Friuli nationalists drew on their history as free cities in the Middle Ages as justification for autonomy. In 1975, however, the Italian and Yugoslav governments formally recognized their international border, which runs through the Friuli nation. This, combined with ineffective government response to a devastating earthquake that hit the region in 1976, produced a renewed sense of Friulian national consciousness.

The anti-Roman nationalism sweeping all of northern Italy in the late 1980s fueled the growth of a particularist Friuli nationalism. In concert with other northern Italian peoples, the Friuli increasingly looked to a united Europe as their salvation. The Friuli national movement elected members to the Italian parliament in 1983, initiating a period of voter participation in the political movement for greater Friuli autonomy.

Disgusted with Italy's corruption and its huge, inefficient bureaucracy, Friuli nationalists point to the organized crime that plagues the Italian state and has recently moved into the Friuli heartland. Mafia-related crimes in the region increased 300% in 1990–91 alone. The inequities of the bloated Italian bureaucracy infuriate even the most moderate Friuli, who cite such examples as the 15 men employed to shunt boxcars at the Udine rail center, while 15,000 do the same work in the southern city of Reggio di Calabria.

The independence of Slovenia on Friulia's eastern border, the increasing integration of Italy into the European Union (EU), and the dramatic increase of regional and national movements across northern Italy have encouraged Friuli demands for greater independence and recognition as a separate European people. In 1992 over 100,000 Friulis signed a petition calling for separation from Friuli-Venezia Giulia and the creation of a separate, autonomous Friuli region. In local elections, in June 1992, Friuli nationalists became the largest political entity in the Friuli region.

The Friuli nationalist movement focuses on the creation of a separate region within Italy, but contacts are increasing with other nationalist groups in northern Italy, and there is support for Friuli participation in a federal structure, or as part of a new European region that excludes central and southern Italy. Demands for separation and autonomy rise and fall with the economy; calls for full independence are sometimes voiced, but the Friulis are among Italy's more affluent national groups, and with greater European integration, self-government is a real possibility in the twenty-first century.

Nationalist demands for a referendum on creating a separate Friuli region gained support in the late 1990s. The signatures of 93,500 Friulis demanding a referendum on separation were presented to the government in 1998, but government inaction and opposition to nationalism in northern Italy effectively thwarted Friuli demands.

SELECTED BIBLIOGRAPHY:

Facaros, Dane, and Michael Pauls. *Northeast Italy.* 1990.

Geipel, Robert. *Long Term Consequences of Disasters: The Reconstruction of Friuli, Italy, in Its International Context, 1976–1988.* 1991.

Holmes, Douglas R. *Cultural Disenchantments: Worker Peasantries in Northeast Italy.* 1988.

Muir, Edward. *Mad Blood Stirring: Vendetta and Factions in Friuli during the Renaissance.* 1993.

Fur

Darfuris; Fors; Fours; Fordungas; Furawis; Fortas; Furakangs; Konjaras; Kondjaras; Kungaras

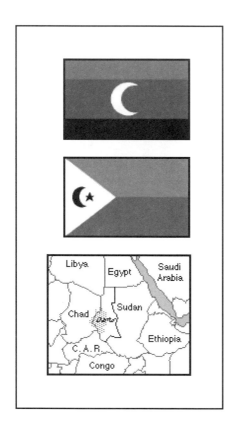

POPULATION: Approximately (2002e) 756,000 Fur in north-central Africa, concentrated in the Darfur province of Sudan, with a small population in adjacent areas of northern Chad. Outside the region there are Fur communities in the Khartoum area of Sudan.

THE FUR HOMELAND: The Fur homeland, Darfur, meaning Land of the Fur in the Arabic language, occupies a high, flat plateau and part of the Libyan Desert in northwestern Sudan. The Fur live in the southern highlands region of Jebel Marra, the highest area of Sudan. The boundaries of Darfur, which have been extended by the Sudanese government, encompass a large non-Fur majority, mainly Arabs in the north. *State of Darfur*: 191,650 sq. mi.—496,371 sq. km, (2002e) 3,805,000—Arabs 61%, Fur 20%, Zaghawas 6%, Bejas 5%, Masalits 4%, Bertis 2%, other Sudanese 2%. The Fur capital and major cultural center is El Fashir, called Tendely in the Fur language, (2002e) 188,000.

FLAG: The Fur national flag, the traditional flag of the region, is a horizontal tricolor of green, red, and black, the red twice the width and is charged with a centered white crescent moon. The Fur national flag, the flag of the national movement, is a horizontal bicolor of red over green bearing a white triangle at the hoist charged with a black crescent moon and five-pointed star.

PEOPLE AND CULTURE: The Fur, of mixed black African, Berber, and Arab background, are generally dark skinned, although physically resembling the Berbers and Arabs. Although they have long been Muslims and dress in Arab clothing, the Fur have not been Arabized. Fur society is divided between landowners and serfs, with smiths, tanners, and other artisans constituting middle classes. Traditional customs still govern marriage, with a bride price paid in cattle and cloth to the daughter's parents.

Polygyny is practiced by the wealthy, and divorce is very common. The Fur are renowned as horsemen, and Fur cavalry was once famed throughout north-central Africa, rivaling that of their close relatives, the Kanuris* of Chad, Nigeria, and Cameroon. Urbanization has been fairly rapid among the Fur since the 1950s.

LANGUAGE AND RELIGION: The Fur language, not related to neighboring dialects, is considered a separate, isolated language group belonging to the Nilo-Saharan family of languages. Many scholars believe that the language is a holdover from the languages spoken in the region before Islam was introduced and Arabic became widespread. The language is largely uniform, with few dialectal differences. Urbanized Fur have increasingly shifted to Arabic as the language of daily life.

The majority religion, Sunni Islam, as observed by the Fur, has incorporated many pre-Islamic and Christian customs. In the more remote areas traditional beliefs are still followed, and traditional local practices coexist with Islamic beliefs. Such practices as the splashing sanctuaries with a flour-and-water paste are carried out to ensure fertility. Rain cults, thought to have been introduced from farther west, make sacrifices at shrines and ancestral tombs when the rains are likely to fall. The office of rainmaker is hereditary.

NATIONAL HISTORY: In prehistoric times the people of northern Darfur were related to the predynastic peoples of the Nile River valley. From about 2500 B.C. the region traded with Egyptian caravans moving southwest from Aswan. Scholars know little of the region's early history, except that ancient Egyptian records mention an organized state trading copper ore and slaves for Egypt's spices, cloth, and luxuries.

Berbers driven from North Africa by invading Arabs in the seventh and eighth centuries settled in the region in large numbers. Early Christian kingdoms rose in the area between the tenth and thirteenth centuries, but they were later destroyed by Muslim Kanuri invaders from Kanem, in present-day Chad and Nigeria. Islam, introduced through the related Kanuris, became the predominant religion.

A small Fur kingdom, established after the demise of the Christian states in the thirteenth century, became the most powerful of the region's Muslim kingdoms. In 1596 Suleiman Solong consolidated the rival tribes and established the Keira dynasty over Darfur. Solong consolidated the rival tribes and expelled the last of the Kanuri invaders. He decreed that Islam would be the state religion, but large-scale conversion did not occur until the reign of Ahmad Bakr in the late 1600s. Ahmad Bakr imported Islamic teachers, built mosques, and compelled his subjects to adopt the new religion.

The Fur sultans controlled the slave trade as a monopoly. They levied taxes on traders and duties on slaves shipped to Egypt, also taking shares of the proceeds of all slaves brought into Darfur. The officials of the sul-

625

tanate used the term "Fur" to refer to the Negroid subjects who accepted both the Islamic religion and the rule of the Keira sultans. As the dynasty became progressively Negroid, its members also came to be known as Fur. The sultanate fought intermittently with the neighboring Wadai sultanate, and periodic attempts were made to subjugate the semi-independent Arabic tribes in the region. The Fur adopted Arab dress and names, although their culture resisted Arabization. Arab incursions gradually forced the Fur into the mountains, where they developed a form of terrace farming, raising cotton, tobacco, apples, and strawberries.

A British explorer, William George Browne, traveling through previously unexplored central Africa, encountered the Darfur sultanate in the late eighteenth century. Browne was forcibly detained in Darfur from 1793 to 1796, but later returned to Britain and published an account of his travels in Africa. His account of the sultanate excited great interest in Europe.

The Keira sultan, often threatened by the Turks through their tributaries, the Egyptians, sent an emissary to congratulate Napoleon on his conquest of Cairo in 1798. Napoleon responded with a demand for 2,000 African slaves, prompting the sultan to break off relations and to abandon hopes of a French military alliance. The desert area just north of the sultanate came under Turko-Egyptian rule in 1821, bringing the threat ever closer. A Muslim brotherhood founded by the Sanussis* of Libya in 1843 gained many converts in Darfur, reinforcing resistance to Turkish or Egyptian domination. For over 50 years the Fur sultanate resisted, finally falling to invading Egyptian troops in 1874.

The Egyptians suppressed various revolts in the region and in 1881 appointed a European, Rudolph Karl Slatin, as governor. He defended the province against the forces of the al-Mahdi, the Arabic religious leader in the Sudan, but was forced to surrender Darfur in 1883. The Fur, discontented under foreign rule, mostly supported the Mahdi and his call for Muslim unity. The Mahdi established a theocratic dictatorship, but weakened by a disastrous famine in 1889–91, his state fell to the Anglo-Egyptian forces of Lord Kitchener in 1898.

A member of Darfur's deposed Keira dynasty, 'Ali Dinar, reclaimed the throne of the sultanate and was recognized by the Anglo-Egyptian government in 1899. He rapidly consolidated his authority and managed to keep Darfur the only region of present-day Sudan not included in Anglo-Egyptian Sudan. The sultan, threatened by the British in the east and the French in the west, built up his army and allied to the Sanussis of Libya. He declared his allegiance to the Ottoman Empire when war began in 1914. 'Ali Dinar led an uprising against the British in 1915, provoking a punitive expedition. In November 1916, 'Ali Dinar died fighting an invading British force. His kingdom, annexed to Anglo-Egyptian Sudan as a province, was the last independent Muslim state in Africa to fall to European rule.

The highland Fur, with long ties to the peoples to the west, had little in common with Sudan's predominant lowland Arab population. The resulting ethnic tension initiated decades of ethnic unrest and attempts to restore Fur sovereignty. After World War I many educated Fur made a point of mastering Arabic, in the hope of making their way in the world in which they found themselves. Their lack of success in the face of Arab intolerance and discrimination led to the formation of a popular regionalist movement and to demands for federal status in the soon-to-be independent Sudan. Fur separatism emerged as a force in 1956, following Sudanese independence and the creation of an Arab-dominated unitary state. In the early 1960s, the Sony Liberation Movement, based in Darfur, began agitation for the separation of the region from Sudan.

The Fur national movement, forced underground in 1966, continued to find substantial support as relations between the Fur and the Arab-dominated government worsened. Coup attempts linked to the Darfur in 1975 and 1979 further alienated the Fur from the Arabic government in Khartoum. Antigovernment rioting in 1980 forced the government to grant limited autonomy and a regional assembly, but the Arab majority in the north of the province continued to dominate the government, politics, and the economy. The introduction of Sharia, strict Muslim laws contrary to many ancient Fur religious practices, exacerbated tension already heightened by bureaucratic attempts to curtail Fur autonomy. Civil strife in neighboring Chad spilled into the region in the 1980s, heightening the historical tension between the Fur and the Zaghawas, the nomadic Arab herders of the lowlands.

Oil, discovered in Darfur in the late 1970s, has yet to be fully developed, partly due to government corruption and inaction, and partly due to resistance by the Fur and other groups living in the area. By the late 1980s, over 25,000 government soldiers were in the Darfur area to protect Sudan's western border and to guard against a resurgence of Fur nationalism.

A new Sudanese government, installed by a coup in 1988 and dominated by radical groups, including Islamic fundamentalists, initiated a campaign to subdue the non-Arab peoples in western and southern Sudan. Arab militias, the Popular Defense Forces, armed by the government and dispatched to Darfur to enforce new language and religious laws, reportedly used indiscriminate violence and participated in massacres of Fur villagers. The Fur retaliated by attacking government facilities and forces in Darfur. The sense of grievance and antagonism against the Sudanese government was reinforced by drought and near-famine conditions that have afflicted the region since 1984.

A Fur rebel movement, with arms from neighboring Libya, has operated in Darfur since 1987, raising government fears of a second front in the country's long civil war in the south. Government bans on trade unions, professional associations, political parties, and on most Fur newspapers remain in effect. Strict censorship has almost completely stifled news of continuing unrest in the region. Visitors, particularly foreigners, need special certificates from the government before they are allowed to enter Darfur. Fur leaders accuse the Sudanese government of attempting genocide, withholding much-needed international famine aid, and using the vicious Arab militias to terrorize the starving Fur into submission.

Much of Darfur was in a state of anarchy by the early 1990s. Severe border clashes along the border with Chad further destabilized the region in 1991. A joint Sudanese and Chadian border commission approved demarcated the disputed border in 1994, but the Fur rejected any adjustments to the borders of their traditional homeland.

Underrepresented in the parliament and other government institutions, the Fur have withdrawn into their ethnic identity, attempting to cope with government hostility by looking back on the greatness of their past. The problems of security and food shortages continue to plague the Fur in the Darfur highlands.

Violence, often at the hands of government-armed Arab militias, created thousands of Fur refugees in the 1990s. Many fled to Khartoum or other areas far beyond their homeland. Accused by the inhabitants of Khartoum of being subversives, the refugees have been treated in a way that has added to the growth of regionalism, with increasing demands for cultural and economic autonomy, withdrawal of government troops and the informal militias from all Fur districts, and creation of a distinctly Fur government with regional responsibilities.

In June 1997, following a tentative agreement between the Sudanese government and several factions of the Southern Sudanese,* parliamentarians from Darful demanded the same for their homeland. The agreement, which provided for a referendum on unity or separation for the southern region, was held up as model for deciding the future of the marginalized, exploited Fur homeland. Fur leaders charged, however, that resources from their region were to be unjustly allocated to the South under the agreement. They also demanded that the government compensate them for the effects of years of civil war.

Violence between Arabs and local groups, involving disputes over grazing and water rights, escalated in 1998. By March 1998, over 100 people had been killed and 50 villages burned in the growing ethnic clashes. The Sudanese government cracked down on political activity in the region from late 1998 to early 1999, seeing the growing conflict as yet another front in the country's long civil war.

Escalating ethnic fighting in Darfur in 2001 led to the flight of over 6,000 Fur into neighboring Chad. The conflict, between Arab groups armed by the government and the non-Arabic Fur, left hundreds dead and dozens of towns and villages destroyed. Land rights and ethnic identity are the basis of the conflict in the last decades.

SELECTED BIBLIOGRAPHY:

O'Fahey, F.S. *State and Society in Dar Fur.* 1980.
Rienner, Lynne. *Sudan, 1898–1989: The Unstable State.* 1990.
Spaulding, Jay, and Lidwien Kapteijns. *An Islamic Alliance: 'Ali Dinar and the Sanusiyya, 1906–1916.* 1994.
Strachan, Peter, and Chris Peters. *Empowering Communities: A Casebook for Western Sudan.* 1997.

Gagauz

Gagauzis; Gagaus

POPULATION: Approximately (2002e) 255,000 Gagauz in Europe, with 178,000 in Moldova and 35,000 in adjacent areas of Ukraine. Another 20,000 live in Bulgaria and Greece, 10,000 in Russia, and smaller numbers in Romania, Turkey, Canada, Brazil, and Central Asia.

THE GAGAUZ HOMELAND: The Gagauz homeland occupies the valleys of the Prut and Jalpug Rivers south of the Roman fortification called Upper Trajan's Wall in southeastern Moldova and southern Ukraine. The region, partly lying in the Bugeac Plain, is mostly agricultural land, particularly suited to the production of white wine, which is the Gagauz national drink. The Gagauz districts of Moldova, Komrat, Cadir-Lunga, Kangaz, Tarkliya, and Vulkanesti, form the Gagauz Republic, an autonomous state within the Republic of Moldova. The Gagauz homeland also includes part of the district of Zaporozh'e of Odessa Oblast in Ukraine. Republic of Gagauzia (Gagauz-Eri): 1,820 sq. mi.—4,713 sq. km, (2002e) 205,000—Gagauz 82%, Moldovans 9%, Russians 2%, Ukrainians 2%, Bulgarians 2%, others 3%. The Gagauz capital and major cultural center is Comrat, called Komrat by the Gagauz, (2002e) 27,000. The city of Cagul, called Kagul by the Gagauz, (2002e) 43,000, is also an important cultural center.

FLAG: The Gagauz national flag, the flag of the autonomous republic, is a blue field bearing narrow white and red horizontal stripes on the bottom and three yellow stars on the upper hoist. The unofficial flag of the national movement is a light blue field bearing a centered yellow disc charged with a black wolf's head.

PEOPLE AND CULTURE: The early history of the Gagauz nation is unclear; there are a number of hypotheses. Some scholars believe that the

Gagauz derive from the Turkic Orguz, Uzy, and Kumans, who roamed the southern Russian steppes until the Mongol invasion of the thirteenth century, when they migrated to the Dobrudja region of eastern Bulgaria. Another hypothesis holds that the Gagauz are the descendants of forcibly Turkified Bulgarians who adopted the Turkish language but retained the Orthodox religion. The most common belief is that the ancestors of the Gagauz fled the continuous Russian-Ottoman wars in the Balkans in the eighteenth century. Culturally and linguistically, the Gagauz are a Turkic people. The small nation, divided in 1945, when the eastern district of their territory was transferred to Ukraine, has developed a strong sense of separate identity. Wine production, the major economic activity, revolves around the yearly growing and production periods. Wine festivals and Orthodox religious observances are closely tied to the Gagauz culture.

LANGUAGE AND RELIGION: The Gagauz speak a Turkic language that belongs to the Orguz-Bulgar subgroup of South Turkic languages of the Uralic-Altaic language group. The language, also called Balkan Gagauz or Balkan Turkic, is spoken in two major dialects, Central and Southern, with the former the basis of the literary language. Other dialects are Maritime Gagauz, spoken in Bulgaria and Romania; Macedonian Gagauz, spoken in southeastern Macedonia; Surguch (Surquch), in the region of Edirne in European Turkey; and Gajal, in the region of Deli Orman in Bulgaria. Gagauz is unique among the Turkic languages for both the large number of Russian, Bulgarian, Ukrainian, Moldovan, and Romanian loanwords and the tenacity and persistence with which the Gagauz people have maintained it. In the late 1990s, 92% considered Gagauz their mother language, but 73% also spoke Russian; only 4% spoke Moldovan (Romanian). The Gagauz assimilated linguistically in order to survive during the Soviet era, but they retained their own tongue as their primary language.

The Gagauz are mostly Orthodox Christians, with a religious tradition that stretches back hundreds of years. Today, of all the Turkic peoples, the Gagauz and the Chavash* are the only predominantly Christian Turkic nations in Europe.

NATIONAL HISTORY: According to Gagauz tradition, their ancestors, a tribe called the Kay-Ka'us, formed in 1256 a small state in the Dobruja region of northeastern Bulgaria with its capital at Karvuna (Kavarna). In the thirteenth century the Kay-Ka'us converted to the Orthodox Christianity brought to their state by Bulgarian monks. Conquered by the Ottoman Turks in 1398, the people, called Gagauz by the Turks, adopted the Turkish language and culture but refused to abandon Christianity for the Turks' Islamic religion. The Gagauz over the next centuries lived as a despised minority, often persecuted by the Turks for their refusal to accept Islam and by the neighboring Bulgars for their Turkish speech.

In the eighteenth century the Gagauz fled to the Russian Empire to escape a concerted Turkish attempt to force their conversion to Islam.

The refugees moved north in small groups, often accompanied by Christian Bulgarians. The first Gagauz arrived in the contested region of Bessarabia in 1750. During the Russo-Turkish war of 1806–12, the majority of the Gagauz took the opportunity to leave Turkish-ruled Bulgaria and settle in Russian-held territory. Bessarabia, ceded to Russia by Turkey in 1812, was later opened to almost unlimited immigration in an effort to dilute the Romanian majority. The remainder of the Gagauz refugees settled in the rural southern districts or Russian Bessarabia between 1812 and 1846. The Gagauz were allowed to settle in Bessarabia on condition that they adopt Russian Orthodoxy.

The Gagauz, reunited in their new homeland in Bessarabia, experienced a dramatic revival of their culture and religion. The production of their famous white wines became an integral part of their culture. A nationalist movement developed from the cultural movement as tsarist rule became progressively onerous, with intense pressure on the Orthodox Gagauz to assimilate. Although the small Christian nation had always looked on the Christian Russians as protectors against the Muslim Turks, in 1848 the Gagauz rebelled against the arbitrary rule of the tsarist bureaucracy. Cossacks sent against the Gagauz rebels ended the uprising with great brutality.

At the end of the Crimean War, in 1856, the region was ceded to the Romanian principality of Moldavia. The Congress of Berlin, convened in 1878, recognized united Romania as an independent state, but the Romanians were forced to cede southern Bessarabia to Russia in return for territory on the Black Sea. The Gagauz, again under tsarist rule, lived peacefully until the upheavals of 1905.

Revolution swept Russia following the empire's defeat by Japan and other setbacks in the early twentieth century. Serious disturbances in the Gagauz homeland in Bessarabia, Gagauzia, broke out during the 1905 Russian revolution but gradually quieted after concessions and promises of increased rights. In December 1905, their authority restored, the local tsarist authorities moved to punish the disturbances, setting off a widespread Gagauz uprising. The rebels drove all tsarist officials from the region and formed a provisional government. On 18 January 1906, the Gagauz leaders declared their homeland the independent republic of Gagauz Khalki. The tiny republic lasted just two weeks before being suppressed by Cossacks and Russian police. The Gagauz, although defeated, again rebelled, along with the Moldovans, in March and April of 1907. The renewed rebellion again brought brutal reprisals.

The Gagauz homeland became a battleground during World War I, particularly after Romania joined the allies in 1916. Many Gagauz, caught up in the fighting, died of disease and hunger. Tsarist Russia collapsed in revolution in 1917, with many Gagauz supporting a movement for autonomy within a revived, democratic Russia. They sent delegates to a Moldovan council, which granted Gagauz autonomy and declared Moldova independent of Russia on 23 December 1917. Before the Gagauz could implement their autonomy within Moldova, their homeland was invaded by Ukrainian nationalists, and later by Bolshevik troops. The Moldovan government, seeking protection from the invading Bolsheviks, voted to unite with neighboring Romania. In November 1918 Moldova, including the reluctant Gagauz, joined the Romanian kingdom.

The Gagauz agricultural region was colonized by Romanian *boyars*, landlords moving north into the new province. The region was treated as an agricultural colony, and the Gagauz were pressured to assimilate into Romanian culture. The 1920s and 1930s were marked by massive corruption and a fall in the Gagauz standard of living. The Romanian authorities refused to build roads in the region during the interwar period, fearing that they could be used by the Red Army should a new war break out—a decision that made marketing Gagauz wines and agricultural products very difficult.

In 1939, after years of tension between the Soviet Union and Romania, the region was indeed invaded by the Red Army. In 1940 Gagauzia, along with Moldova, was ceded to the USSR, but in June 1941 Romanian troops, allied to the invading Germans, reoccupied the region. The Romanian authorities, determined to assimilate the Gagauz, forbade the use and publication of their language, the wearing of their national costumes, or the observance of their national holidays, which mostly celebrated their wines.

In 1944, Soviet reconquest was quickly followed by the collectivization of the Gagauz vineyards and farms. In 1945 the eastern districts of their homeland were transferred to Ukraine, over Gagauz protests. Under Soviet rule, the Gagauz were allowed to use their language, but publication was permitted only in Russian Cyrillic alphabet. The Gagauz, too weak to resist but refusing to assimilate into either Russian or Moldovan culture, withdrew into isolation, preferring to tend their collectivized, yet prosperous vineyards and farms and leave the painful issues of politics to others.

During the Cold War, the Gagauz mostly remained on the land, working as peasant farmers on Soviet collectives. Their refusal to assimilate or urbanize was accompanied by a very high birthrate. Between the 1950s and 1970s, the Gagauz population grew dramatically. Encouraged by the Stalinist Soviet government to retain their Gagauz heritage or to Russify, but not to assimilate into the predominant Moldovan-Romanian culture of the republic, many Gagauz learned Russian; as a result, their culture took on many Russian traits.

In 1982 a few young Gagauz began poetry readings and other cultural events that gradually gathered force in an overall cultural revival. They questioned why their wines, sold in expensive Soviet foreign-currency shops, brought them little in the way of income, and why there were no Gagauz language schools in Soviet Moldova. In 1986, in response to growing pressure from the Gagauz, the Soviet authorities relented and allowed limited Gagauz radio and television broadcasts as well as limited publishing in the language.

Nationalism remained the preoccupation of a few Gagauz intellectuals until late 1988, when Moldovan language demands sparked a rapid spread of national sentiment. In addition to their own language, they had been obliged to learn Russian, but under a new Moldovan language law they would be obliged to learn yet another language, Moldovan (Romanian). The language issue loosened a torrent of grievances—unpaved roads, inadequate drinking water, a total lack of Gagauz schools and kindergartens, and the need for technical and agricultural schools. Of the 41 regions of Moldova, the Gagauz regions ranked 35th through 41st in standard of living.

A national congress convened in May 1989 created a national movement called Gagauz Khalki, demanded autonomy for the Gagauz districts of Moldova, and reunification with Ukrainian Gagauzia. Ignored by the Moldavian authorities, the Gagauz leaders unilaterally declared the region an autonomous republic on 11 August 1990, announcing the republic's secession from Moldovia before petitioning the Soviet government to incorporate Gagauzia as a full union republic. In response, the Moldovan government dissolved and outlawed Gagauzi Khalk. During the October 1990 elections in the breakaway republic, the Moldovan authorities moved to disband the Gagauz government and to retake control of the Gagauz districts, setting off a severe nationalist crisis, as well as violence, in the region.

Soviet Moldavia, renamed the Republic of Moldova, became independent following the collapse of the Soviet Union in August 1991. The Moldovan authorities attempted to end the Gagauz secession and to bring them under the authority of the new republican government, but by early 1992 the Moldovan government's authority in the region had practically ceased to exist. Militant nationalists appealed to the Russian government for incorporation in the new Russian Federation, but the majority of the Gagauz supported peaceful protest and autonomy within Moldova; the hard-liners were quickly isolated.

Fearing the ethnic violence that had broken out in a number of former Soviet republics, the Gagauz accepted an offer to negotiate autonomy within Moldova, with the stipulation that should Moldova decide to reunite with neighboring Romania, the Gagauz would be allowed to secede peacefully. Negotiations began in September 1992 between the Moldovan government and a Gagauz delegation. Negotiations in 1993–94 paved the way for full normalization of relations between the Moldovan government and the Gagauz.

In January 1993 the Moldovan parliament narrowly rejected a proposal to hold a nationwide referendum on reunification with Romania. In elections held in early 1994, the Moldovan nationalists won greater support than did those favoring Romania, which aided relations between the Gagauz and the Moldovan government. In May 1994 Moldova produced a draft constitution providing for a special legal status and broad powers of self-government for the Gagauz nation.

An Act Providing for the Special Status of Gagauzia/Gagauz-Eri was adopted by the Moldovan parliament on 23 December 1994, the first time territorial autonomy had been established for a national minority in post-communist Central and Eastern Europe. In March 1995, 30 of the 36 districts that took part in a referendum on joining the Gagauz Republic voted for inclusion. The Gagauz legislature, the Halc Toplosu, is responsible for the lawmaking within the autonomous republic, with powers in the areas of culture, education, development, taxation, social security, and territorial administration. The Moldovan government declared an end to the five-year separatist conflict.

The Gagauz have established close ties to Turkey and other Turkic states and nations. Gagauz leaders have visited Turkey and the new republics in Central Asia seeking cultural and political ties. The Turks have sent economic assistance and language teachers, and they have even established a satellite link to allow the Gagauz to receive Turkish television. The Turks have encouraged the Gagauz to maintain good relations with the Moldovan government. In mid-1998, President Suleyman Demirel of Turkey visited the Gagauz Republic to reinforce what he called an important relationship between Gagauzia and Turkey. In 1999, the president of Gagauzia visited Turkey, seeking financial help to promote the use of the Gagauz language within the autonomous republic.

Gagauz fear that Moldova would merge with neighboring Romania was one of the reasons for the dramatic growth of nationalism in the early 1990s. In a general referendum on 6 March 1997, 95% of the voters in Moldova favored continued independence from both Russia and Romania. The vote reinforced the wishes of the majority of the Gagauz to maintain their autonomous status within the Republic of Moldova.

The Moldovan government implemented a new territorial and administrative system in May 1999. The country's 40 districts were reorganized into nine provinces and two autonomous regions, Gagauzia and Dniestria. Dumitru Croitoru was sworn in as the newly elected governor of Gagauz-Eri in September 1999. Croitoru took the oath of office in three languages—Gagauz, Romanian, and Russian. The European Union (EU), however, has criticized the agreement between the Gagauz and the Moldovan government as providing too much autonomy.

SELECTED BIBLIOGRAPHY:

Bremmer, Ian, and Ray Taras, eds. *Nations and Politics in the Soviet Successor States.* 1993.

Bruchis, Michael. *Nations-Nationalities-People: A Study of the Nationalities Policy of the Communist Party in Soviet Moldavia*. 1984.

Dima, Nicholas. *Bessarabia and Bukovina: The Soviet-Romanian Territorial Dispute*. 1982.

Van Meurs, Wim P. *The Bessarabian Question in Communist Historiography: Nationalist and Communist Politics and History-Writing*. 1994.

Galicians
Galegos; Gallegos; Galizanos

POPULATION: Approximately (2002e) 3,450,000 in Spain, concentrated in the region of Galicia in northwestern Spain. Outside Spain there are sizable populations in Portugal, France, and Germany. There are large Galician populations, estimated to number 1.5 million, in the Americas, particularly in Uruguay, Argentina, Brazil, and Chile.

THE GALICIAN HOMELAND: The Galician homeland occupies the mountainous northwestern corner of the Iberian Peninsula, just north of Portugal. The region, mostly lying in the Galician Uplands, has a rugged coastline on the Atlantic Ocean on the west and on the Bay of Biscay on the north. The *rías*, fjordlike inlets cutting deep into the coastline, give Galicia a number of good, protected harbors on the Atlantic Ocean and the Bay of Biscay. Most of historical Galicia forms an autonomous region of the Kingdom of Spain made up of the provinces of La Coruña, Lugo, Orense, and Pontevedra. *Autonomous Region of Galicia (Comunidad Autónoma de Galizia)*: 11,365 sq. mi.— 29,435 sq. km, (2002e) 2,735,000—Galician 94%, Portuguese 2%, other Spanish 4%. The Galician capital and major cultural center is the ancient city of Santiago de Compostela, (2002e) 94,000, a center for religious pilgrimages. The largest of the Galician cities—Vigo, (2002e) 287,000, and La Coruña, called A Coruña in Galician, (2002e) 241,000— are also important cultural centers.

FLAG: The Galician national flag, the official flag of the region, is a white field crossed by a diagonal stripe of pale blue, upper hoist to lower fly. The Galician national flag, with the addition of a centered five-pointed red star, is the banner of the Galician national movement. The flag of the

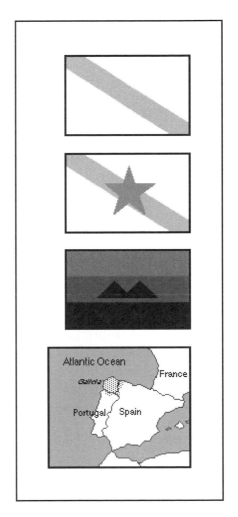

Galicians in the Trás os Montes region of northern Portugal is a horizontal tricolor of pale green, red, and black bearing two black mountains centered.

PEOPLE AND CULTURE: Galicia's name is derived from that of the ancient Celtic Gallaeci. The Galicians, descendants of early Celts and later Germanic Visigoths, are the only Iberian people not of Latin origin. Although the Celtic language is long extinct, Celtic cultural traditions are evident in the Galicians' traditional bagpipes, dances, and music, and in that fact that many Galicians are fair with blond or red hair and light eyes. Traditionally, Galicians lived in small and isolated villages, with the parish as the primary unifier of widely dispersed localities. The system of land inheritance resulted in small, unproductive holdings called *minifundios*. The inability of the land to support a growing population resulted in high emigration from the eighteenth century on. Emigration has been especially high among young men, resulting in serious demographic and economic imbalances.

LANGUAGE AND RELIGION: The Galician language is a Romance language spoken by most of the population of Galicia. The language is spoken in four major dialects, corresponding to the region's four provinces. An intermediate language between Portuguese and Spanish, it is closer to Portuguese, with about 85% mutual intelligibility. The language is spoken in adjacent areas of Portugal and in the Spanish regions of Léon and Asturias. Until the final separation of Galicia and Portugal in 1668, the Galician and Portuguese languages were considered dialects of the same language. The language remains more widely spoken in the rural areas than in the largely Castilian-speaking cities. There are Galician-speaking people in adjacent Spanish regions, including 50,000 in Asturias, 15,000 in Castilla-Léon, and 5,000 in Extremadura. The Galician-speaking population in the Trás Os Montes region of Portugal numbers between 15,000 and 25,000.

The Galicians are devout Roman Catholics, and their capital, Santiago de Compostela, is one of the great Catholic pilgrimage centers of Europe. The pilgrimage route across southern Europe to Santiago remains one of the major religious pilgrimages left in Europe. The Galicians are among the most religiously conservative peoples of Spain, and the liturgical calendar continues to modulate the rhythm of their daily life.

NATIONAL HISTORY: The northeastern corner of the Iberian Peninsula was early inhabited by the Celtic Gallaeci tribe, which left large stone monuments in the rocky highlands. The Romans conquered the Gallaeci in 137 B.C. and included the region in the province of Hispania Tarraconensis. The Celts, except those in the more mountainous regions, mostly adopted the Romans' Latin language and culture. Christianity, introduced by missionaries from Italy, began to make converts in the region around A.D. 100.

The decline of Roman power left the region nearly defenseless in the fourth and fifth centuries. A Germanic tribe, the Suevi, invaded the region and established an independent kingdom in 411 A.D. In 585 the Suevi kingdom was overrun by invading Visigoths, who settled the region and mixed with the earlier Suevi and Celts. Traditionally, the Visigoths adopted Christianity in 587. A substantial Germanic population settled in the region during the Visigothic period, but the basic Celtic character of the population remained. In Roman and Visigothic times Galicia extended beyond the present-day city of León and south to the Duero River.

Moors invading the Iberian Peninsula from North Africa overran most of Visigothic Spain in 711–12. Christian knights held the Muslim Moors to the lowlands in the northwest while forming the Christian kingdom of Asturias in the mountains. The Christians eventually began to expand, reconquering lands from the Moors, including all of Galicia. The reconquered areas united with the kingdom of Léon in 866. Léon, including Galicia, in turn united with the kingdom of Castile, newly liberated from Moorish rule in 1037. In 1157 Léon, including Galicia, again became an independent kingdom, but it reunited with Castile in 1230.

Isolated as they were in a rugged region, the Galicians developed a unique medieval culture, uniting Celtic, Germanic, Latin, and Iberian elements. The Galician language, originally a dialect very close to Portuguese, diverged in the fourteenth century to become the foremost literary language of the Iberian Peninsula. The Galicians developed a lyrical, poetic literature, the first in a Romance language.

The devoutly Roman Catholic Galicians, caretakers of the important medieval shrine of St. James at Santiago de Compostela, maintained contact with all of Europe through a constant stream of religious pilgrims. Santiago developed as the center of the vibrant Galician culture and the object of religious pilgrimages from all over Europe.

The Galicians lost much of their former political autonomy with the merger of the kingdoms of Castile and Aragon in 1479. Galicia came under the administration of the royal Junta del Reino de Galicia in 1495, with little real autonomy. Opposition to the centralizing tendencies of the Castilian kingdom prodded the Galicians to follow the Portuguese in an attempt to leave the Spanish kingdom in 1640. Crushed by Castilian troops, the Galicians embarked on a long cultural and economic decline.

By the eighteenth century the Galician language had degenerated to a peasant dialect, and the upper classes had adopted Castilian speech and culture. The Galician tradition of splitting lands among heirs resulted in a backward, fragmented agriculture that forced many to emigrate, mostly to South America. The French attack on Spain in 1808 allowed the Galicians to regain nominal independence, but the region again came under Castilian rule, under the restored Bourbon monarchy, at the end of the Napoleonic Wars.

In the mid-nineteenth century the Galicians entered a period of cultural vibrancy, accompanied by a literary revival. The Galician language again became the first language of the majority and gradually replaced Castilian as the language of the upper classes. The cultural revival paralleled a growing regional consciousness. Early Galician nationalism, which appeared in the 1840s, was based on a mythical "golden age" of the kingdom of Galicia.

The region's severe economic problems, mostly blamed on the highly centralized government in Madrid, provoked widespread resentment and in the 1880s and 1890s fueled a movement to revive the Galician culture and nation. Among the demands was cultural and economic autonomy and the reopening of the Galician *cortes*, or parliament, which had functioned, if with little real power, until the early nineteenth century. The region's poverty, the history of dividing lands among all sons, and lack of economic opportunity fed a continuing stream of emigrants to the New World, largely to Brazil, where they rapidly assimilated into Portuguese-speaking Brazilian society.

In the early years of the twentieth century, Galicia was one of the most conservative and traditional areas of Spain. Economically backward, Galicia was mostly ignored by the government in Madrid, which concentrated on the industrialization of other areas of the country. In 1931 the Galicians demanded autonomy from Spain's new republican government; in 1932 they established a Galician parliament and pressed for greater linguistic autonomy. Serious nationalist demonstrations rocked the region between 1932 and 1936, until the nationalist resurgence was overtaken by the outbreak of the Spanish Civil War.

A plebiscite in 1936 overwhelmingly supported Galician autonomy, but it was later nullified by the strongly centralized government established by Gen. Francisco Franco. Franco, born in El Ferrol, looked to his native Galicia for support for his fascist rebels, but the majority of his countrymen joined the antifascist forces. Following Franco's 1939 victory, the Galicians suffered severe punishment—their culture was suppressed, and edicts were issued forbidding the speaking, teaching, or publishing of books or newspapers in the Galician language. Only one book was published in the Galician language between 1936 and 1945.

The Galician culture and language began to revive in the 1950s, however, despite the official restrictions. Publishing in the Galician language began tentatively with poetry; later publications included fiction, the sciences, philosophy, and economics. Renowned poets and writers, such as Rosalia de Castro and Antonio Castelao, fostered the rebirth of the Galician language. The postwar revival increased friction with the Franco authorities and spurred the growth of Galician nationalism. Openly nationalist organizations, beginning in the 1960s, gained widespread support in Galicia, which benefited little from the rapid modernization of

Spain in the 1960s and 1970s. By 1975 the average income in Galicia was only half the Spanish average.

In early 1975 Galician nationalism exploded with an outbreak of violence and demonstrations. Several nationalist organizations, supported by demonstrators in the major cities, called for immediate independence. In August 1975 the elderly Franco unleashed a reign of terror accompanied by mass arrests, unexplained deaths and disappearances, and widespread torture. Franco's death in November 1975 brought an end to the terror as liberated Spain rapidly embraced democracy under a restored Bourbon monarchy.

The new democratic government in Madrid granted autonomy to the region of Galicia in 1980, but old habits remained. In July 1981, Francisco Cabrallo, a Galician priest and historian, was sentenced to six months in prison and fined 20,000 pesetas for slandering the Spanish police. The charge stemmed from a single passage in his *History of Galicia* in which he referred to the 1975 reign of terror.

By the late 1980s, 90% of the Galician population spoke the Galician language. Growing ties to other Celtic nations in France and the United Kingdom resulted in cultural exchanges and strong support for the Galicians' campaign to win greater freedom. Small, militant nationalist groups turned to violence in 1988, though the majority of the conservative Galicians continued to support more moderate nationalist policies, which they hoped would eventually establish their small nation within a united, democratic Europe.

In early 1989, a bomb claimed the first victim of the nationalist upsurge. The group responsible threatened more attacks, but the majority of the Galicians rejected the violent methods and pressed for autonomy by peaceful means. Since then the nationalist movement has avoided violence.

Autonomy has been popular with the Galicians, though the Galician regional government is expensive. The region's cities remain upper and middle class, while the rural population continues to farm small, unprofitable holdings. Urbanization of the population, begun in the 1960s, accelerated in the 1990s, even as the population of the region continued to fall due to emigration and economic problems. Emigration from the region between 1900 and 1990 was estimated at more than 850,000 people. Being a relatively underdeveloped region, Galicia has not attracted large numbers of Spanish-speaking migrants, as have the wealthier Catalonia and the Basque Country.

In October 1997, Spain's ruling conservatives won the largest number of votes in regional elections, but the Galician nationalists also made impressive gains, supplanting the socialists as the second force in the region. The leader of the Galician National Bloc, Xose Manuel Beiras, led the nationalist upsurge, taking 26% of the vote, as opposed to just 18% in 1993. The region's conservative-dominated government, in spite of its centralizing tendencies, has promoted the Galician language and culture, supported greater autonomy, and has pushed for development funds from Madrid. The only point on which the conservatives and the socialists agree is that the regionalists forces are gaining ground, which makes both the Spanish Right and Left very nervous.

In 1998, an estimated 94% of the population used Galician in their daily life; only 5% of the population of the region had no understanding of the Galician language. Although the larger cities remain mainly Spanish-speaking, Galician is recognized as an official language, and younger Galicians, looking to greater self-determination within the European Union (EU), now take pride in the Galician language and culture. The national movement emphasizes the Celtic spirit of the Galicians.

The economic progress in the rest of Spain has been felt in Galicia, but the unemployment rate, 17% in late 2000, is still very high; 16% are employed in agriculture and 3% in fishing. The precarious state of the local economy continues to fuel regionalist sentiment and demands for greater Galician control over natural resources.

In October 2001, the Galicians again voted for the conservative People's Party, the party that also controlls the central government in Madrid. Although the nationalists gained additional support, the Galicians are currently more interested in continuing the economic growth than in greater self-government.

SELECTED BIBLIOGRAPHY:

Facaros, Pauls. *Northern Spain*. 1999.
Kern, Robert. *The Regions of Spain: A Reference Guide to History and Culture*. 1995.
Slater, Bert. *Across the Rivers of Portugal: A Journey on Foot from Northern Spain to Southern Portugal*. 1991.
Truscott, Sandra, and Maria Garcia. *A Dictionary of Contemporary Spain*. 1998.

Gandas

Gandans; Baganda; Waganda; Bugandans; Bagandans

POPULATION: Approximately (2002e) 3,835,000 Gandas in East Africa, concentrated in the central districts of Uganda, north and northwest of Lake Victoria. There is a sizable community in the adjacent areas of Tanzania, numbering an estimated 30,000.

THE GANDA HOMELAND: The Ganda homeland lies in East Africa, occupying the southern and southeastern Ugandan districts near Lake Victoria. The Nile River forms the eastern border of the kingdom. The land is lush and fertile, growing a variety of crops. The kingdom of Buganda, partially restored in 1993, is traditionally made up of the present-day districts of Kampala, Mpigi, Mukono, Masaka, Kalangala, Kiboga, Rakai, and Mubende. *Kingdom of Buganda*: 17,295 sq. mi.—44,793 sq. km, (2002e) 5,661,000—Gandas 82%, Sogas 13%, Nyoros* 3%, Asians 1%, other Ugandans 1%. The Ganda capital and major cultural center is Kampala, (2002e) 942,000, metropolitan area 1,347,000. Kampala is also the capital of Uganda.

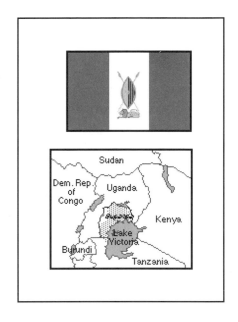

FLAG: The Ganda national flag, the flag of the former kingdom, is a blue field with a narrow, vertical white stripe centered, bearing a gold reclining lion surmounted by a gold shield and crossed gold spears.

PEOPLE AND CULTURE: The Gandas, popularly called Bagandas or Bagandans, are the largest single national group in Uganda. They are a Bantu people who have existed as a distinct nation for nearly a thousand years; they are descended from a mixed population of Bantu and Nilotic peoples. In the Ganda's Bantu language, *Ganda* (or *Baganda*) refers to the people or nation, *Luganda* the language, and *Buganda* the state. The Gandas have a higher standard of living and are more literate and modern than any other national group in Uganda, but they have retained much of their traditional culture. Descent, inheritance, and succession are patrilineal. About 50 exogamous clans are recognized, each having principal and secondary totem animals that may not be killed or eaten. The identity of the

643

Ganda nation remains focused on the king, the *kabaka*, to the extent that Ganda society cannot be imagined without the institution of the monarchy. The average life span, in the mid-1990s, was just 42 years, 10 years less than in 1980.

LANGUAGE AND RELIGION: The Ganda language, Luganda, is an Eastern Lacustrine Bantu language. The language is a Bantu dialect of the Nyoro-Ganda group of the Southern Bantu group. English is widely spoken as a second language. Luganda is spoken in four major dialects, corresponding to historical regions of the kingdom—Kooki or Olukooki, Sese or Olusese, Luvuma, and Ludiopa. The language is the most widely spoken second language in Uganda, next to English. Luganda is used in primary schools in the kingdom and in radio programs, television, and newspapers.

A majority of the Ganda, about 80%, are Christians, about evenly divided between Protestant denominations and Roman Catholicism, with small animist groups and a Sunni Muslim minority making up about 15% of the Ganda population. Traditional Ganda religion, still practiced, recognizes ancestors, past kings, nature spirits, and a pantheon of gods who can be approached through professional mediums. Reverence for clan totems remains an important part of daily observance.

NATIONAL HISTORY: The Ganda are thought to be the descendants of migrants from the east between the tenth and thirteenth centuries. According to their oral history, the Ganda were united under their first king, Kintu, in the fourteenth century. Kintu is believed to have descended from heaven and landed at Podi, in present-day Bunyoro. The kingdom, one of the most advanced in the lakes region of East Africa, fell to migrating Nilotic peoples in the sixteenth and seventeenth centuries. The tall, nomadic warrior peoples were eventually absorbed by the more sophisticated, settled Bantu.

The kingdom came under the domination of the powerful neighboring kingdom of Bunyoro in the seventeenth century, beginning a long rivalry for power between the Gandas and the Nyoros in the lakes region. Reestablished under hereditary kings in the late eighteenth century, by 1800 Buganda had regained its former glory as one of the most sophisticated and politically advanced states in precolonial Africa. The Gandas established contact with the coastal Arabs to the east in 1844. A lucrative trade developed in slaves and ivory, exchanged for imported luxuries and manufactured goods. In the 1850s the Gandas barred Arab slave traders from the kingdom.

The first Europeans visited the kingdom in 1862. They were amazed to find a cultured, developed state, then evolving from a feudal monarchy to a modern, bureaucratic administration. English Protestant missionaries arrived in Buganda in 1877, followed by French Catholics two years later. Ganda Christian converts rapidly became a political force in the kingdom, their power rivaled only by the important Muslim minority. A Muslim uprising in 1888 provided the British with a pretext to intervene in Buganda. In 1893 the British proclaimed the kingdom a protectorate under the Swahili name for Buganda, Uganda, and in 1897 they put down a serious rebellion led by the Ganda king.

Under British colonial rule, the Ganda enjoyed considerable autonomy and were favored by the British administration of Uganda. The British and their Christian Ganda allies subdued Buganda's ancient rival, Bunyoro, and imposed nominal British rule on the neighboring kingdoms. The Ganda kabaka, for his assistance to the British authorities, received a tract of land taken from defeated Bunyoro, setting off a "Lost Counties" dispute that plagued relations between the Gandas and Nyoros for decades.

Cotton, introduced by the British authorities from Egypt, began to be cultivated in 1904, establishing the basis of a prosperous modern economy. A land law passed in 1908 provided a firm legal basis for land ownership in Buganda. The Crown Lands Declaration Ordinance, adopted in 1922, transferred title to most land to the British.

British policy in the 1920s and 1930s greatly reduced the power of the king and spawned the first stirrings of Ganda nationalism. Threats to the rights of their beloved kabaka and resentment of British moves to integrate proud Buganda into a random collection of cultures in the Uganda protectorate incited periodic demonstrations and rioting, particularly serious in 1945 and 1949. Ganda leaders demanded price controls on exports of Ganda cotton, the removal of the Asian monopoly on cotton ginning, and the right to have their own representatives in the Buganda government rather than those appointed by the British authorities. The Ganda demands were rejected.

A tentative British plan for a federation of Uganda and white-ruled Kenya in 1953 prompted the Ganda king to demand a timetable for separate Buganda independence. The British authorities, alarmed by the strength of Ganda national sentiment, deposed the British educated kabaka, Sir Edward Mutesa II, affectionately called "King Freddie," in November 1953. Two years later the king returned from exile, but British permission for his return stipulated that he not oppose Buganda's remaining part of Uganda.

Preparations for Ugandan independence provoked a resurgence of Ganda nationalism in 1960, incited by fear of domination by Uganda's non-Bantu northern tribes. Nationalists of the Kabaka Yekka (King Only) political party proclaimed the kingdom independent on 31 December 1960. The British authorities immediately dispatched the colonial army, drawn mostly from the northern tribes, to occupy Kampala and to force the Ganda to accept federal status within a united Uganda. Prior to Uganda independence, on 9 October 1962, the Ganda had the highest standard of living and the highest literacy rate in Uganda.

The first independent Ugandan government—that of the first prime minister, Milton Obote, who formed an alliance between Ganda nationalists and Obote's United People's Congress—named the Gandas' kabaka the first head of state. Obote created a strong central government and was eventually able to free himself from the coalition with the Gandas. Obote's rule became increasingly dictatorial and brutal; political opponents and Ganda nationalists were murdered or disappeared. In 1964 the Obote government agreed to restore territory claimed by Buganda to neighboring Bunyoro, throwing the Ganda kingdom into disarray.

Obote abolished the autonomy of Buganda and the other Bantu kingdoms in 1966, setting off serious rioting in Kampala. The government, accusing the kabaka of promoting secession, sent troops led by a young northerner named Idi Amin Dada to storm Twokobe Palace. Over 2,000 Gandas were killed, and King Freddie and many other prominent Gandas fled to exile in Europe. In 1967 the Obote government completely abolished the historical kingdoms. Buganda was divided into four districts and placed under martial law. In 1969 the kabaka, the 35th of his line, died in lonely exile.

Idi Amin, with initially widespread support in Buganda, overthrew the hated Obote regime in 1971. A northern Muslim, Amin soon proved to be more brutal than the deposed Obote. Whimsical dictatorial rule gave way to the systematic persecution of the Bantu peoples, Christians, regional leaders, the wealthy, and all suspected or imagined opposition. Massacres, torture, and atrocities became the norm as Uganda, the former "Pearl of East Africa," collapsed into terror and devastation. In 1972 Amin expelled most of the 50,000 Asians in the country and seized their property. Approximately 300,000 Ugandans, including over 100,000 Gandas, were killed under Amin.

Invading Tanzanians and exiled Ugandans finally overthrew Amin in 1979. After several attempts to form a new government, Milton Obote again gained power in spite of the vehement opposition of the Gandas and the other southern Bantu national groups. A Bantu guerrilla army gained support in the southern provinces and in 1986, after a long bush war, drove Obote into exile and installed Uganda's first Bantu-dominated government. Its head was Yoweri Musaveni, belonging to the western Bantu Ankoles,* with strong support in central and western Buganda.

Musaveni tried to rule under a system without political parties, but his efforts at reconciliation have not ended the bitter north-south rivalries that have plagued Uganda since independence. The return of relative peace and freedom allowed Ganda nationalism to reemerge demanding restoration of the kingdom. The Ganda demands, initially rejected by the government on the grounds that restoration would threaten the stability and integrity of Uganda, gained popular support in the 1990s.

In January 1990, 43 people, all but one of them ethnic Gandas, were charged with plotting a coup against the Musaveni government. Some of those arrested were former supporters of Musaveni. Six of the 43 were sentenced to death for their part in the plot in August 1990. The plot exposed the growing opposition to Musaveni among the Gandas. Musaveni despised the idea of monarchy, but to channel Ganda discontent into something other than multiparty politics, he allowed the restoration of the Ganda king, on the condition that he play only a cultural and symbolic role.

In August 1993 the government restored a degree of autonomy to Buganda and allowed Prince Ronald Muwenda Mutebi II to take the throne of the restored monarchy as the 36th kabaka of Buganda. Affectionately known as "King Ronnie," he has become hugely popular among the Gandas. Far from dampening feeling of separatism in Buganda, the restoration of the kingdom has encouraged the growth of nationalism, with many groups pushing to win real power for the kabaka under a federal constitution.

The government in December 1994 responded to the rapid growth of Ganda nationalism by ordering authorities to shut down any meeting or rallies called by the nationalists and federalists that they considered threatened Uganda's unity and national integrity. Although President Musaveni refused to consider their plea for autonomy, most Gandas leaders supported him during the 1996 presidential election. Voting generally split along regional lines between the Bantu south and the Nilotic north of the country. The Gandas fear a return of the terror imposed when Uganda was dominated by northern non-Bantu tribes.

Several Ganda rebel groups emerged in 1995, following rejection by the Ugandan Assembly of legalization of political parties and restoration of political power to the Ganda kingdom. It also rejected proposals for granting Uganda's four hereditary kingdoms federal status. The National Democratic Alliance, led by Herbert Itongwa, skirmished with government troops in early 1995 but was defeated. In 1996 several antigovernment groups, led by a Ganda, Godfrey Binaisa, a former Ugandan president, formed a united front.

In June 1998 the national parliament passed a law that gave about 9,000 square miles (23,000 sq. km) of crown land to the peasants who currently farm it. The Gandas saw the move as an assault on their traditions and their king. Another new land-reform bill that Gandas feared would give parts of their traditional homeland to other groups fueled the growth of Ganda nationalism in the late 1990s. Ganda nationalists claimed that the new land bills favored other tribes, including the Ankole of Uganda's President Yoweri Musaveni. In August 1998 the Gandas, instead of celebrating the coronation day of their monarch, chose to mourn the loss of the kingdom's land due to the controversial land act.

Musaveni's government has returned stability to southern Uganda, but his refusal to grant Ganda autonomy has led to demonstrations and agitation for his removal and for the restoration of the autonomous kingdom that was abolished in 1967. The movement at the turn of the new century remains peaceful, but the potential for violence exists.

The government talked of allowing multiparty politics in 2001, which gave the Ganda some hope that their most pressing political issue, regional autonomy, would again be addressed, but the liberalization of government was not implemented. The Gandas are disillusioned with the political process in Uganda, which has ignored their demands. Currently the Gandas are not in a position to press the government farther, but the issue remains and could lead to political confrontation in the future, as Uganda increasingly divides between the northern non-Bantu districts and the southern Bantu peoples.

The Gandas often blame other tribal groups for their problems, pointing out that had Buganda managed to secede from united Uganda, they would have been spared decades of terror and devastation. After the marriage of Kabaka Ronald Mutebi II in late 1999, passions again ran high in the kingdom for federal status.

The Ugandan government sent 15,000 troops into neighboring Congolese territory to support rebels fighting the government in 1999. The military intervention in the Democratic Republic of Congo raised tension in the country, where 40% live in poverty despite the economic growth of the 1980s and 1990s.

Uganda's continued intervention in the Congolese civil war, with increasing expenditures on the military, became the focus of Ganda discontent. Demands for political devolution, an end to the military adventure in Congo, and decreased spending on arms led to demonstrations and confrontations with the police in late 2001.

SELECTED BIBLIOGRAPHY:

Kasozi, A.B.K. *The Social Origins of Violence in Uganda 1964–1985.* 1994.
Kiwanuka, M.S.M. *The Kings of Buganda.* 1971.
Kiwanuka, S. *History of Buganda: From the Foundation of the Kingdom to 1900.* 1972.
Wrigley, Christopher. *Kingship and State: The Buganda Dynasty.* 1996.

Garifunas

Garinagu; Gari'funa; Karaphunas; Garifune; Black Caribs; Caribes; Black Karibs

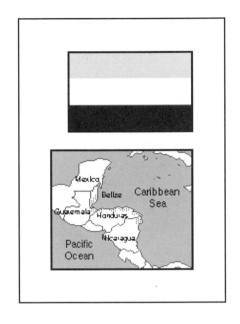

POPULATION: Approximately (2002e) 180,000 Garifunas in Central America, including 120,000 in Honduras, 30,000 in Belize, 25,000 in Guatemala, and 2,000 in Nicaragua. Other large communities live in the United States (New York, Los Angeles, and New Orleans) and the United Kingdom (London), with a small population estimated at 6,000 on the island of St. Vincent in the eastern Caribbean. Some sources claim a total population of up to 450,000 in the Caribbean region.

THE GARIFUNA HOMELAND: The Garifuna homeland lies on the Caribbean Sea in northern Central American, occupying a narrow coastal strip from central Belize to northern Nicaragua. The narrow coastal plains occupied by the Garifunas are called the Patria Chica, the "little homeland." The Garifuna homeland has no official status, forming parts of administrative districts in Belize, Guatemala, Honduras, and Nicaragua. The region has some of the most beautiful beaches in the Caribbean, which are now being developed for tourism. The capital and major cultural center is Dangriga, formerly called Stann Creek, in Belize, (2002e) 15,000. The other important center in Belize is Punta Gorda, (2002e) 5,000. The major cultural center of the Honduran Garifunas in Trujillo, (2002e) 11,000. The major center of the Garifunas in Guatemala is Livingston, (2002e) 10,000, and in Nicaragua the major center is Pearl Lagoon, (2002e) 500.

FLAG: The Garifuna national flag, recognized by Garifuna communities throughout the western Caribbean, is a horizontal tricolor of yellow, white, and black.

PEOPLE AND CULTURE: The Garifunas, formerly called Black Caribs, are a unique Caribbean cultural and ethnic group. They call themselves Garinagu, a corruption of the name of the Arawak Kalinagu tribe. The descendants of a mixture of black slaves, indigenous peoples, and Europeans; they more closely resemble their black ancestors in skin color and features, but culturally they have incorporated traditions and customs from Africa, Europe, and the South American rain forest to produce a unique culture and language. Music and dance, the main Garifuna artistic expressions, are well developed and involve group participation at seasonal festivals. The Garifuna have been able to retain their ethnic identity due to an ability to absorb foreign influences and to change their cultural patterns as needed. Family ties are extremely important, and one of the Garifuna values they most want to save in the modern world. Intermarriage is common, but outsiders are generally incorporated into the Garifuna culture.

LANGUAGE AND RELIGION: The Garifuna language is a patois based on the Arawak language formerly spoken throughout many of the Caribbean islands. The language is mostly of Arawak origin, with admixtures of African languages, French, English, and Spanish. The Garifuna also speak English, the second language of much of the Caribbean coast of Central America, and Spanish where it is the predominant language. Most Garifunas also speak the local Spanish Criole as a second or third language. An English-oriented orthography is used in Belize, with a Spanish-oriented orthography in use in Honduras, Guatemala, and Nicaragua.

Roman Catholicism is the religion of the majority of the Garifunas, because it is the predominant religion in the Spanish-speaking Central America. The church, established in Belize in 1851, remains an integral part of the Garifuna culture. Portions of the Bible were published in the Garifuna language in 1847, the first important publication in the language. There are smaller Protestant groups, mostly converts to evangelical and fundamentalist churches, many based in the United States. Many pre-Christian rites, particularly those associated with death and veneration of ancestors, have been retained as part of the Garifuna popular culture, emphasizing the concept of life after death, continuity of family lines, and mutual assistance between the living and dead.

NATIONAL HISTORY: According to Garifuna traditions, their origins stem from the Kalinagus or Kalifunas, an Arawak agricultural culture based on yucca or cassava farming, hunting, and fishing in the dense South American forests. By about A.D. 1000 some of the Kalinagus had moved up the Orinoco River to the Caribbean coast. Eventually they spread from the coast to the chain of islands in the Caribbean Sea. Later the warlike tribes called the Caribs also migrated from the South American mainland, raiding the Arawak islands and eventually absorbing the peaceful Arawaks.

Europeans increasingly visited the island in the sixteenth and seventeenth centuries, eventually conquering the indigenous peoples of all but two of the islands, Dominica and St. Vincent. In 1635 two Spanish ships carrying slaves from Africa were shipwrecked in the small Grenadine Islands. The surviving slaves, rescued by the indigenous Kalinagu people, were brought to the larger island, later called St. Vincent. The rescued slaves adopted the language, culture, and traditions of the Carib-Arawak people. The mixture of the black slaves and the Indians was to form the basis of the Garifuna nation.

This people of mixed black and Indian background flourished on the island, raising cassava and fishing in the warm Caribbean Sea. They grew in numbers and began to compete with the island's Caribs for land and power. They eventually drove the Caribs into a small zone on the east shore of the island, where they remain to the present. The Europeans called the Garifuna Black Caribs, to distinguish them from the Red or Yellow Caribs, the original indigenous peoples.

The Black Caribs of St. Vincent were numerous and quite prosperous by 1750. They traded tobacco and farm produce for arms, munitions, and other European manufactured goods. Some began to grow cotton for export, using captured African slaves to supplement the labor of the women of the community. The French colonists of the island, few in number, were content to leave the Black Caribs to their traditional pursuits. The Black Caribs later signed a treaty with the French, but the British, victorious over the French in 1763, took control of the island.

The British authorities sought the fertile lands for sugarcane plantations, trying persuasion, trickery, and purchase before provoking the Garifuna into war in 1772. Aided by the French, the Garifuna held off the British at first, but the well-armed Europeans gradually began to gain. A treaty signed with the new British colonial administration in 1773 surrendered the island except for a reserve about 14 miles (22.5 km) long by three or four miles (4.8 to 6.4 km) wide, but the conflict continued for over 30 years. The British, ignoring the treaties, increasingly marginalized the Black Caribs, encroaching on their best lands and attempting to press captured rebels into slavery.

Finally in 1785, the British authorities determined to end the conflict and take over the entire island. Troops were brought in, and a major military campaign was begun. By the summer of 1796 the French gave up, but the Black Caribs continued to fight. The British soldiers burned their villages and crops, forcing the starving people to surrender. Nearly 5,000 men, women, and children were taken prisoner and sent to camps on the island of Baliceau until their fate could be decided. In the dreadfully crowded camps more than half the captives died of disease.

In February 1797 an order came to ship all remaining Black Caribs to the British-held island of Roatán, in the Bay Islands just off the coast of Honduras, where other rebellious blacks had previously been sent. The island had no water and little arable land. Weak and miserable, the Black Caribs got word to the Spaniards on the mainland, and on 19 May 1797 the Spanish attacked and took control of the Bay Islands. The Black Caribs were settled on the Spanish-held mainland of Central America in small village communities.

British loggers to the north and the Miskitos* to the east aided the Black

Carib settlements. Increasingly calling themselves Garifunas, after their ancestors, they spread along the coast. Disgusted with the corrupt and inefficient Spanish authorities in Honduras, many Garifunas began to migrate to other areas in 1807. In the years that followed, the Garifuna slowly established villages on islands and along the coasts of southern Belize, Guatemala, and northern Honduras. Slavery was abolished in Central America in 1824 and many freed slaves joined the Garifuna communities.

The Spanish frequently used the Garifunas as soldiers, even after the independence of Central America in 1821. The Garifuna backed the losing side in an effort to overthrow the president of the failed Central American Federation, Francisco Morazan. Pressed by loyal soldiers, many Garifunas fled the settled areas to less-populated areas. Most went to British territory to settle around Stann Creek in 1832, but others settled the inaccessible lagoons of eastern Honduras and northeastern Nicaragua.

In 1862, British Honduras became a crown colony, but an unfulfilled provision of a treaty between the United Kingdom and Guatemala in 1859 led Guatemala to claim the region. Whatever the border politics, the Garifunas went where they could find work. With the beginning of the commercial fruit industry in the late nineteenth century, they began to settle new areas where banana and fruit cultivation provided employment. They settled villages, in which the women and children stayed farming while the men traveled as necessary to gain livelihoods.

The British authorities in British Honduras in the 1930s established agricultural reserves in the Garifuna area for subsistence-oriented farmers and fishing people. The Honduran government, fearing the Garifuna ties to the British authorities, attempted to suppress the culture along the northern Honduran coast in the 1920s and 1930s. President Tiburcio Carías in March 1937 offered to meet with Garifuna leaders from all the Honduran communities at the town of San Juan near Tela. When the Garifunas arrived they were massacred on government orders. The murder of a dozen Garifuna leaders left the Honduran Garifunas without effective leadership for many years.

Emigration of Garifunas from Honduras and Belize, mostly to the United States and the United Kingdom, began in the 1950s, followed by the Garifunas of Guatemala and Nicaragua in the 1960s and 1970s. In the large American cities and in London, the various Garifuna groups lived in separate areas and mixed little until the reculturation of the late 1970s and 1980s. The rise of ethnic consciousness in the 1960s led to calls for closer cultural and economic ties among the scattered Garifuna communities. The cultural rebirth was led by publishing in the language, including a dictionary, a working orthography, and a growing literature. The Belize town of Stann Creek, historically called Carib Town (for the Black Caribs), was renamed Dangriga in 1975 to honor the Garifuna founders. The Honduran government finally recognized the Garifunas as a distinct ethnic group in 1975.

Contemporary Garifuna nationalism stems from the political and cultural repression of the 1960s and 1970s, when the Garifunas were accused of supporting Central American revolutionary groups. Although the majority of Garifunas are not political, leaving the painful political processes to the Spanish-speaking majorities, they began to press for closer ties between all the Garifuna communities and for cultural and economic autonomy.

The British granted independence to Belize in 1981. The new nation's security remained threatened by neighboring Guatemala, which saw Belize as a "lost province" to be retaken by force. British troops were sent to protect the small country, but were withdrawn in 1994 following the establishment of better relations between Belize and Guatemala. In 1996, after years of neglect, the Guatemalan government officially recognized the Garifuna minority in the country.

The Garifunas suffer the modern ills—drug problems, poor transportation and unpaved roads, and very high unemployment. Emigration, mainly to New York and London, has been a traditional outlet for frustration and a lack of opportunities. Young Garifunas have been immigrating since the 1970s, when the Central American economies began a serious downturn. Funds sent by family members working overseas are one of the major sources of income in the Garifuna homeland.

Migration has provided a temporary solution, but new restrictions in North America and Europe are beginning to close that traditional outlet. In the 1990s, Garifuna leaders pressed for an end to migration, either overseas or to regional cities, as detrimental to the small nation. The smaller towns and villages in the Garifuna coastal areas are trying to find ways to improve opportunities and services. New technologies and methods are improving fishing and agricultural output, and they are producing surpluses for sale. Pensioners returning to live in the homeland have brought a new prosperity to add to the important funds sent by overseas Garifunas. Electricity arrived in the more remote Garifuna villages in the early 1990s.

In the 1990s, experts believed that the Garifunas were one of the least known and most unusual black cultures in the Americas, and one of the most threatened by immigration and tourism. The Settlement Day festival in Dangriga, the Garifuna capital in Belize, is the most important event in Belize. Delegations from all Garifuna communities in Central and North America attend the annual event to reaffirm their cultural identity. The Garifunas are united by history and memory. Activists have established language programs and cultural organizations in all Garifuna areas, and an effort to reculturate the 6,000 Garifunas still living on St. Vincent accelerated in the late 1990s.

The Garifuna community outside Belize have suffered the neglect, indifference, injustice, and ignorance of the culturally and linguistically distinct Latino governments. In spite of decades of government pressure to assimilate into the Latino culture of the Central American countries, the Garifunas have resisted acculturation. Historically distrustful of government authority, modern Garifunas are aggressively maintaining their culture and ethnic identity.

The Garifunas, having lost faith in the existing political system in Central America, see their salvation in emigration or in the growing tourism industry, but nationalists contend that either solution will lead to a transculturation, and adaptation of their historical culture, or a deculturation, its total loss. Nationalists recognize that the preservation of the Garifuna nation depends both on the preservation of their traditional language and culture and on social and economic development. As an indigenous people, the Garifunas claim the basic right of autonomy and self-determination as a distinct nation that straddles established national borders. In 1997, the Garifunas celebrated the anniversary of 200 years of settlement on the Central American coast.

Hurricane Mitch stalled over the region in October 1998, wiping out entire Garifuna communities. Community leaders feared that the destruction of their homes would weaken their already tenuous claims to the land, already threatened by changes to the Honduran constitution that would allow foreigners to purchase coastal lands.

Garifuna leaders from all settlement areas presented a plan for the creation of an autonomous Garifuna homeland, a plan modeled on that of the Miskitos in eastern Nicaragua. In addition, they requested official recognition of their right to bilingual education, greater representation in elective posts, and an end to job discrimination and protection of land rights.

In 2001, the Garifunas were named a World Heritage culture, a new United Nations designation that recognizes and urges protection for endangered heritages. Garifuna leaders welcomed the designation in the hopes that their small nation, with international help, would survive.

SELECTED BIBLIOGRAPHY:

Cayetano, Sebastian R. *Garifuna History, Language, and Culture of Belize and Central America*. 1989.

Garcia, Victor. *Sunset Bay and the Garifuna Massacre of San Juan*. 1994.

Gonzalez, Nancy L. *Sojourners of the Caribbean: Ethnogenesis and Ethnohistory of the Garifuna*. 1988.

Rivas, Ramon D. *Indigenous Peoples and the Garifuna of Honduras*. 1993.

Gauchos

Gaúchos; South Brazilians; Geralians

POPULATION: Approximately (2002e) 20,105,000 Gauchos in Brazil, concentrated in the three southern states of Paraná, Santa Catarina, and Rio Grande do Sul. Other sizable communities live in São Paulo, Rio de Janiero, and around the Brazilian capital, Brazilia. Outside the region there are Gaucho communities in the United States and Europe.

THE GAUCHO HOMELAND: The Gaucho homeland lies in the temperate zone of Brazil, occupying the flat plains called the Pampas. The region, bounded by coastal mountains, the Serra do Mar and the Serra Geral, borders the Atlantic Ocean on the east, Uruguay on the south, and Argentina on the west. The population is concentrated along the coast, although movement to the interior has accelerated since the 1980s. The region, popularly called Geralia, forms the Southern Region of Brazil, comprising the states of Paraná, Santa Catarina, and Rio Grande do Sul. *Geralia (South Brazil)*: 222,836 sq. mi.—577,214 sq. km, (2002e) 25,820,000—Gauchos 81%, Uruguayans 6%, Argentinians 2%, other Brazilians 11%. The Gaucho capital and major cultural center is Pôrto Alegre, (2002e) 1,351,000, metropolitan area 3,622,000, the capital of Rio Grande do Sul. Other important cultural centers are Curitiba, the capital of Paraná, (2002e) 1,637,000, metropolitan area 2,740,000, and Florianópolis, (2002e) 349,000, metropolitan area, 704,000, the capital of Santa Catarina.

FLAG: The Gaucho national flag, the flag of the national movement, is a red field bearing a black cross, outlined in yellow, surmounted by

a centered blue disc, outlined in yellow, charged with thirteen small white five-pointed stars. The flag of Paraná has green, white, and green diagonal stripes bearing the state seal centered. The flag of Rio Grande do Sul is a diagonal tricolor of green, red, and yellow with the state seal centered. The flag of Santa Catarina has red, white, and red horizontal stripes bearing the state seal on a green diamond centered.

PEOPLE AND CULTURE: The Gauchos, named after the legendary cowboys of the Pampas in the south of the region, are mostly the descendants of nineteenth and early twentieth-century European immigrants. Blue eyes, light skin, and lank hair are common features. The Gauchos, unique in Brazil, have retained a basically European culture and their original languages, now widely used as second languages. The European-influenced Gaucho culture has not been assimilated into the Portuguese-Brazilian culture, with its roots in the north of the country, but has retained its distinct European roots and traditions. The Gaucho population has expanded in this century without losing population at the center, an unusual phenomenon in Latin America. Largely middle class and urbanized, the average Gaucho enjoys a standard of living and way of life remarkably similar to those of Western Europe and North America. Ties to Europe remain stronger than elsewhere in Brazil, particularly among the many Italians and Germans. Folkloric tradition centers upon the gaucho and his life on the southern plains, which stretch south from the Itararé River into Uruguay and Argentina. The Gauchos have the longest life expectancy and the highest literacy rate in Brazil.

LANGUAGE AND RELIGION: The Brazilian dialect of Portuguese is spoken throughout the region, with important admixtures of German, Italian, and Spanish borrowings. Many claim that the mixed variety of Portuguese constitutes a separate dialect. The closeness of the Spanish-speaking territories in neighboring Argentina and Uruguay has had a strong influence on the local dialect. The languages of the immigrants, particularly Italian and German, are widely spoken as second languages and in homes. In cities with large German populations, the German language is taught in primary schools.

The majority of the Gauchos are Roman Catholics, often adhering to the religious traditions of northern and Eastern Europe rather than the predominant customs of Latin Europe. There is an important Protestant minority, mostly among the descendants of the German immigrant population, as well as smaller Jewish and Buddhist minorities. Since the 1970s evangelical Protestant sects and groups related to the African-influenced religions of northeastern Brazil have been making inroads in the region.

NATIONAL HISTORY: The original inhabitants, small Tupí-Guaraní tribes, had virtually disappeared under the impact of colonization by the seventeenth century, decimated by conflict and disease. Spanish colonists founded settlements on the coast, including Santa Catarina in 1542. Other

European settlers, moving south from the Portuguese colonies and north from the Spanish colonies, began to settle the interior grasslands, the Pampas.

Much of the territory was explored and occupied by the forces of a Portuguese emissary, Gabriel de Lara, in the 1640s. In 1675 the region passed to Portuguese control. The Portuguese authorities organized the captaincies of São Paulo, Santa Catarina, and Rio Grande do Sul. The captaincies, equivalents of feudal principalities, enjoyed much local autonomy under the rule of powerful Portuguese governors. Portugal's rival in the New World, Spain, finally recognized the southern Brazilian colonies as Portuguese territory in 1790.

Neighboring Uruguay, included in Brazil as a province in 1821, shared the Gaucho tradition, and the regions had much in common. When the Uruguayans revolted in 1825, they were aided by nationalist turmoil in the neighboring Gaucho provinces. Uruguay was recognized as an independent state in 1828, but a group in Rio Grande do Sul sought to secede from Brazil and to incorporate Uruguay in a new Gaucho state.

The Portuguese and Spanish introduced cattle and horses but made little attempt to develop the interior Pampas. The animals were rounded up by gauchos, the cowboys of the Pampas, who were celebrated for their horsemanship, lawlessness, and independence. In the early nineteenth century, landowners began to cultivate the region. During the colonial period, after Indian slavery failed, the colonists imported slaves from Africa for labor on the large plantations, but slavery in the south never reached the scale of the sugar regions of northern Brazil. As slavery became politically less feasible after 1850, Italian immigrants began replacing slaves on the coffee and fruit plantations.

Economic and settlement inequities in huge São Paulo captaincy in the late eighteenth and early nineteenth centuries were exacerbated by the differences in the immigrant populations in the districts. The economic and cultural affiliations of the southern districts were increasingly to the south, to the Gaucho country in Santa Catarina and Rio Grande do Sul. In 1853, the leaders of the southern districts demanded separation from São Paulo, which was finally arranged after some violence. In 1853 Paraná, named for the Paraná River, became a separate province of the Brazilian Empire.

Small numbers of European immigrants, mostly Italians, Germans, Portuguese, Poles, and Spanish, had been settling the coastal districts since the early nineteenth century. Rejecting Brazil's pervasive slavery and plantation agriculture, the European immigrants mostly settled on small family farms, in the European manner. Gradually expanding into the virgin lands of the Pampas, the immigrants created farms, towns, and cities remarkably similar to those of their European homelands.

Feeling little affinity with the culturally and economically separate north, the southerners attempted to take the Pampas provinces out of Brazil in 1835, setting off an ultimately unsuccessful ten-year war. The war, called the War of the Farrapos (ragamuffins), or the Farroupilha Rebellion, was concentrated in Santa Catarina and Rio Grande do Sul. The southerners, beginning to call themselves Gauchos after the legendary cowboys of the pampas, united in opposition to domination from the ethnically and economically distinct north. The growth of separatist sentiment and the development of a distinct *pátria*, or homeland sentiment, marked the beginning of the Gaucho national movement.

European immigration to the region accelerated after the revolutionary upheavals that swept Europe in 1848, becoming a flood after 1870. Immigrants poured into the southern region of Brazil from every country in Europe, as well as from Japan and Lebanon. By 1900 over five million immigrants had settled in the three southern states, including over a million Italians and over 400,000 Germans.

Centralization of Brazilian government in the 1880s ended the traditional autonomy of the states and provoked widespread resistance in the southern states. In 1892 the Gauchos of Rio Grande do Sul rebelled; the rebel leaders declared the state independent of Brazil on 8 September 1892. As the other southern states moved toward secession, federal troops invaded. The rebels finally surrendered in 1894.

The "lieutenants' rebellions" of the 1920s involved both dissatisfied southerners and a minority of officers who were in revolt as much against their senior officers as against the central government. The officers continued to conspire, causing an uprising in São Paulo and Rio Grande do Sul in 1924. Rebellion again spread across the southern states in 1930, the lieutenants joining disgruntled former officers. In what was called the Great Southern Revolt, the rebels followed the governor of Rio Grande do Sul, Getulio Vargas, who finally overthrew the Brazilian government and installed himself as the new president. His authoritarian rule incited renewed revolt in the three southern states, which continued sporadically until 1937. The autonomy of the states was ended and a strong central government created. All political parties were banned until 1944, limiting opportunity to organize. Vargas became the region's most famous son and was Brazil's nation-building dictator for 50 years.

World War II was a difficult time for the Gauchos, with Italy and Germany fighting the democracies. Brazilian troops, including many Gauchos, participated on the Allied side in the Italian campaign in 1944–45, but conflicts between pro-fascist and anti-fascist groups at home continued until the end of the war.

The Gauchos began to expand outward from the original settlements after World War II, but without losing population in their homeland. New interior settlements arose, such as Maringa, founded in 1947; by 1960 Maringa had grown into a city of over 50,000 inhabitants, and by 1990 it had become a metropolis of over 200,000, with wide boulevards and soaring skyscrapers.

Immigration continued during the twentieth century, as did an immense internal movement from the rural areas and the impoverished northeastern states of Brazil. Many of the immigrants settled in the burgeoning cities. Urbanization of the Gaucho population accelerated in the 1970s; a massive building program was carried out in response. The major cities, particularly Curitiba, underwent extensive rejuvenation, including new parks, recreational facilities, recycling programs, zoning regulations, and specialized busing services; Curitiba became a model of urban planning. The lifestyle of the urbanized Gaucho population emulated that of the cities of North America and Western Europe in the 1980s and 1990s. The region remained a mixture of big cattle ranches and modern industrial cities.

Decades of dictatorship and central-government mismanagement pushed the three Gaucho states to establish close economic and political cooperation in the 1960s. An influx of landless peasants from Brazil's poor and backward northeast kindled a strong regionalist reaction. A cultural revival, emphasizing the region's unique history, spawned the growth of nationalist and anti-immigrant groups. The more radical of the groups advocated restrictions on internal immigration and even the forced repatriation of poor, culturally distinct northeastern immigrants.

Brazil's return to democracy in 1985, greeted with tremendous enthusiasm, has disappointed the Gauchos. Hope soon gave way to despair as Brazil's severe economic and social problems continued to multiply. The dream of an advanced, prosperous twenty-first-century Brazil, the one dream shared by all Brazilians, rapidly disappeared. The dramatic decline in the region's living standards that accompanied Brazil's grave economic problems and hyperinflation in the early 1990s gravely damaged the long-held view that Brazil, in the twenty-first century, would take its place among the advanced states of the world. Resentment of the need to emigrate to find work added to the growing national sentiment in the region. The nationalists, dismissed as a fringe group just a decade before, gained support with each new Brazilian crisis.

Citing the example of Uruguay—which, historically and ethnically similar to Geralia but without its impressive resources, achieved the continent's highest gross national income—the nationalists in 1990 advanced a plan for an independent Republic of the Pampas. A poll of the inhabitants of the Gaucho states in December 1991 showed overwhelming support for some form of economic and political autonomy. Two-fifths of those polled favored complete independence.

The Pampas states, their proud residents claim, constitute a country apart. Blue eyes, light skin, and lank hair are the reigning features, and the telephone books are flush with German, Italian, and Slavic names. This region is the "Brazil that works," according to regional leaders, so unlike the nation of mongrels to the north, where carnival and chaos reign. During the long Vargas dictatorship, the southern states were keen to prove their Brazilian-ness, but by the late 1990s they were again emphasizing regional identity and their Gaucho past.

The three southern Brazilian states began the new century with Brazil's highest average incomes, but they still lagged far behind equivalent regions in North America or Europe. Most of the important farming sector, characterized by small farms, has high levels of productivity, and there are important industries in the region. The frustration of being held back by Brazil's inefficient bureaucracy and the need to finance development in other regions of the country, particularly the extremely poor northeast, has swelled the numbers of Gauchos seeking greater control of local government and their economy, and the preservation of their unique cultural institutions.

SELECTED BIBLIOGRAPHY:

Bell, Stephen. *Campanha Gaucha: A Brazilian Ranching System, 1850–1920.* 1994.
Bender, Evelyn. *Brazil.* 1998.
Eakin, C. *Brazil: The Once and Future Country.* 1997.
Oliven, Ruben. *Tradition Matters: Modern Gaucho Identity in Brazil.* 1996.

Gibraltarians

Yanitos

POPULATION: Approximately (2002e) 36,000 Gibraltarians in Europe, mostly in Gibraltar and Great Britain.

THE GIBRALTARIAN HOMELAND: The Gibraltarian homeland lies in southwestern Europe, a narrow peninsula 2.5 miles long surrounding the Rock of Gibraltar, an enclave on Spain's southern Mediterranean coast, just northeast of the Strait of Gibraltar. The Rock of Gibraltar, once considered one of the Pillars of Hercules, lies at the western entrance to the Mediterranean Sea. Gibraltar, popularly called "the Rock," is a self-governing British colony. Only Gibraltarians have the right to live in the colony; all others must obtain residence permits. *Dependency of Gibraltar (Calpe)*: 2.3 sq. mi.—6 sq. km, (2002e) 29,500—Gibraltarians 68.5%, other British, Spanish, Moroccans 31.5%. The Gibraltarian capital and major cultural center is the city of Gibraltar, (2002e) 29,500, which is coextensive with the colony and including British air and naval bases.

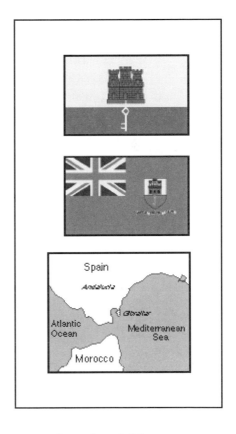

FLAG: The Gibraltarian national flag is a horizontal bicolor of white over red, in the proportions two by one, charged with the red three-towered castle of Gibraltar from which is suspended a golden key. The official flag of the colony is a red field bearing the Union Jack as a canton and the Gibraltarian coat of arms on the fly.

PEOPLE AND CULTURE: The Gibraltarians are a European people collectively of Italian, Maltese, British, Spanish, and Portuguese background. Most Gibraltarians are of Italian or Maltese heritage, although ethnic divisions have been blurred by extensive intermarriage and the formation of a distinct Gibraltarian nationality. National self-awareness, a recent phenomenon, is based on Gibraltar's unique history and culture, a blend of British and Mediterranean traditions.

LANGUAGE AND RELIGION: The majority of the Gibraltarians speak English, along with a variant of Andalusian Spanish called Yanito. Increasingly Yanito and standard Spanish are the languages of daily life, although most Gibraltarians are proud of their bilingual abilities.

The majority of the Gibraltarians are Roman Catholic (75%), with important Protestant (8%—mostly Anglican), Muslim (6%), and Jewish (2%) minorities. Due to extensive intermarriage between the Gibraltarians, many families observe the rites of more than one religion.

NATIONAL HISTORY: The two large promontories at the eastern end of the Strait of Gibraltar—the Rock of Gibraltar on the north and Jebel Musa, called Mount Hacho by the Spaniards, at Ceuta in Africa, known in ancient times as the "Pillars of Hercules"—were believed by the ancient Mediterranean peoples to mark the edge of the world. The Gibraltar Peninsula, guarding the entrance to the Mediterranean and the shortest route from North Africa to Europe, has attracted conquerors since boats first ventured into the Mediterranean Sea. The peninsula, with its easily defensible rock, was conquered or controlled by Phoenicians, Carthaginians, Romans, Vandals, Visigoths, and Moors.

Gibraltar received its name from the Arabic name for the Rock of Gibraltar, Jebel-al-Tarik, the Mountain of Tarik, named for the Moorish leader Tariq ibn Ziyad, who crossed from North Africa to capture southern Spain in A.D. 711. Fortified by the Muslim Moors, Gibraltar served as the southern defense of the opulent Muslim state of Al-Andalus, later called Andalusia by the Spaniards.

The Christian Spaniards, during the reconquest of Muslim Spain, captured the citadel in 1462. The Christians took control of the Moorish fortifications, and the peninsula became a Spanish stronghold, controlling the entrance to the Mediterranean Sea. Isabella I officially annexed Gibraltar to the Spanish kingdom in 1501.

During the War of the Spanish Succession, which eventually involved most of the European powers, the peninsula was captured by English and Dutch troops in 1704. The Peace of Utrecht confirmed British possession of Gibraltar in 1713, over strong Spanish objections. Heavily fortified by the British authorities as a naval base, it was several times unsuccessfully besieged by Spanish forces. During the American Revolution, Spanish troops, assisted by the French, imposed a three-year blockade, which ended in 1783 with the end of hostilities in America. Spain made several attempts to recover the peninsula during the nineteenth century, clouding British-Spanish relations during most of the century.

Gibraltar was officially designated a British Crown Colony in 1830, in spite of Spanish objections. The impregnable fortress, Britain's major Mediterranean base, developed as a flourishing trading center and attracted immigrants from Italy, Malta, and other parts of Mediterranean Europe. The Spanish population of the colony dwindled, while the immigrant population, schooled in English, gradually developed as a distinct Mediterranean people.

The opening of the Suez Canal in 1869 increased Gibraltar's strategic importance and greatly enhanced its position as a port. The base at Gibraltar became one of Britain's most important military and naval facilities. Numerous caverns and galleries extending two to three miles in length, of sufficient width for vehicles, were cut through solid rock, providing sheltered communications from one part of the garrison to another.

The citadel and naval base protected Allied shipping during both world wars. During the Second World War, Spain's dictator, Francisco Franco, resisted Hitler's demand to attack the Rock, fearing that the British would retaliate by taking control of the Canary Islands in the Atlantic. Nonetheless, the Spanish government sought to regain control of the peninsula, which it considered an integral part of the Spanish state, after World War II. Despite Spain's protests that the move contravened the 1713 Treaty of Utrecht, Britain granted autonomy to the Gibraltarians in 1964, giving them their own elected government and control of the colony's booming economy. The Spanish government proposed an Anglo-Spanish condominium as a transition leading to eventual Spanish sovereignty. The British government refused to cede the colony to Spain against the wishes of the inhabitants. In 1967 the British authorities agreed to a referendum, but only 44 out of the 12,762 voters chose Spain and the Franco dictatorship.

A new constitution granted in 1969 created a Gibraltarian legislature, the House of Assembly, with substantial powers. In retaliation the Spanish government closed the border and forbade Spanish citizens to hold jobs in the colony. Because the colony was almost wholly dependent on the Spanish mainland for food, the British authorities were forced to mount an extensive effort to provision the colony by sea and air; further, they allowed a substantial number of laborers, mainly from Italy and Malta, to settle in the colony. The blockade hardened the Gibraltarians' resistance to Spanish claims.

By the 1970s, in the nuclear age, the colony lost its strategic significance, but as a naval base guarding the entrance to the Mediterranean, Gibraltar retained its importance. The colony's economy, formerly dependent on military spending, diversified into banking and international trade. In 1981 Gibraltarians were granted full British citizenship.

The Spanish state's return to democracy in 1975 greatly decreased tension between Spain and Great Britain. Spain reopened the border between Gibraltar and Spain to foot traffic in 1983 and to vehicles in 1985, following a British threat to veto Spain's entry to the European Community (EEC). Following Spain's entry into the EEC in 1986, the Spanish government again raised the question of sovereignty. In 1988 the Gibraltarians again voted to retain their ties to the United Kingdom.

Rising prosperity in the 1980s and 1990s, based on banking and trade, gave the colony's inhabitants new confidence. The results of an August 1991 poll showed a majority desired to be known as Gibraltarians, a separate European people. For the first time the poll showed a majority of Gibraltarians wishing for independence, with support for retaining ties to Britain down to 47% from 62% in 1988. In late 1991 the British government confirmed Gibraltar's right to independence, the only hindrance being Spain's continuing territorial claims.

The government of Joe Bassano, facing tight border controls by the Spanish government and intense pressure from the United Kingdom, approved legislation designed to end drug and cigarette smuggling. The legislation triggered demonstrations both by groups who supported the crackdown and others who opposed it, but the Spanish government, agreeing that the smuggling problem had been addressed, eased border restrictions.

In 1996 elections the Gibraltarians chose a new chief minister, removing Joe Bassano from office after eight years. Peter Caruana, a business advocate and less abrasive than his predecessor, campaigned for better ties to Spain, although he vowed to establish Gibraltar as a major "offshore" banking center. One of the first things he tackled was smuggling, which affected both Gibraltar and Spain. The Spanish government reiterated its offer of autonomy under its decentralized system, but that was an option few Gibraltarians would contemplate. Despite Caruana's more conciliatory style, he insisted that Gibraltar's sovereignty was not negotiable.

Gibraltar's tax laws brought a new industry to the Rock in 1999–2000. Bookmakers from Britain began to transfer their operations, operated by telephone and Internet, to Gibraltar, fleeing a 9% tax on bets levied by the British government. By early 2000 the bookmaking operations accounted for over 10% of the economy.

The Spanish and British government continued talks, often under the auspices of the EEC, later the European Union (EU), during the 1990s. In March and April of 2000, Spanish and British diplomats put final touches to an accord to settle some of the outstanding differences, though not the biggest ones. The agreement precluded independence for the Gibraltarians or even full autonomy but granted them the right to deal directly with the European Commission and the other countries of the EU.

Under the terms of the accord, Peter Caruana agreed that any EU-related matter would be handled through Britain. That would make it easier to implement a number of EU directives, particularly those having to do with company takeovers, which have been stymied by the colony's unsettled status within the Union. (Over the objections of the EU, many Gibraltarians still want the Rock to become an "offshore" banking haven.) The agreement was intended also to resolve lingering complications over passports and driving licenses issued by Gibraltar but until then not recognized by Spanish authorities. The deal also made provision for greater police cooperation in the straits between Gibraltar, Spain, and North Africa. The Spanish government was increasingly worried by an influx of illegal immigrants and by smuggling of drugs and tobacco.

The 2000 agreement continued to skirt the true Gibraltar issue—sovereignty. The Spanish grudgingly acknowledge the status of the Rock as a British colony but refuse to contemplate Gibraltarian independence. The British authorities adamantly maintain that the Gibraltarians themselves must decide on their future. Under the 1969 constitution, the Gibraltarians have the last word on their future.

At a meeting of British and Spanish ministers in November 2001 to discuss the Gibraltar issue, Peter Caruana refused to participate as part of the British delegation. He demanded a Gibraltarian presence and the right to veto any agreement but was ignored. The ministers discussed joint sovereignty, with Spanish control sometime in the future, perhaps in 50 years, but the British government reiterated its pledge to allow the Gibraltarians to vote on any accord. Most Gibraltarians, including chief minister Peter Caruana, claim that they feel Gibraltarian rather than British or Spanish and that they want a non-colonial status that retains their traditional ties to Great Britain.

SELECTED BIBLIOGRAPHY:

Harvey, Maurice, and Richard Van Emden. *Gibraltar.* 1996.
Jackson, William G. *The Rock of the Gibraltarians: A History of Gibraltar.* 1991.
Morris, Dennis S., and Robert Henry Haigh. *Britain, Spain, and Gibraltar, 1945–90: The Eternal Triangle.* 1992.
Shields, Graham J. *Gibraltar.* 1996.

Gilakis
Gelakis; Gilanis; Ghilans; Guilans; Gilanians

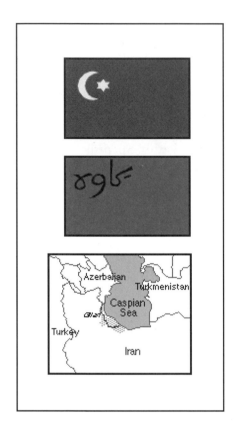

POPULATION: Approximately (2002e) 3,550,000 Gilakis in Iran, concentrated in the northwestern province of Gilan. Smaller communities live in neighboring provinces and in the Iranian capital, Tehran.

THE GILAKI HOMELAND: The Gilaki homeland lies on the southern shore of the Caspian Sea in northwestern Iran. The region is a well-watered and heavily forested plateau lying between the Elburz and Talish mountain ranges and the Caspian Sea. The population is concentrated in the coastal regions and the foothills of the mountain ranges. Traditionally, Gilan is divided into the Caspian and Golha regions. The Golha region corresponds to the mountainous interior that is used for tea production. The coastal areas are devoted to olive groves and terraced rice paddies. Natural barriers, dense forests, and many rivers surround the region. Gilan forms a province of the Islamic Republic of Iran, including the Zanjan Governorate in the southwest. *Province of Gilan*: 14,115 sq. mi.—36,567 sq. km, (2002e) 3,244,000—Gilakis 72%, Talysh* 16%, Mazandaranis 6%, Southern Azeris* 2%, other Iranians 4%. The Gilaki capital and major cultural center is Rasht, called Resht by the Gilakis, (2002e) 427,000, metropolitan area, 825,000. Zanjan, in the interior, is the capital of Zanjan Governorate, (2002e) 302,000.

FLAG: The Gilaki nationalist flag is a green field bearing a white crescent moon and six-pointed star on the upper hoist. The flag of the largest national organization, the Hizb-i Jangali (Jangali Party) is a red field bearing the name "Kaveh" in black on the upper hoist, referring to a legendary Gilaki, a medieval blacksmith, who led the Gilakis against a local Persian ruler.

PEOPLE AND CULTURE: The Gilaki are an Iranian people of mixed

Caucasian, Turkic, and Persian background, speaking a West Iranian language that is of the Indo-Iranian language group but shows a marked Turkic admixture. Historically protected by the Elburz Mountains, the Gilaki culture developed separately, incorporating elements from the Persians, the Turkic peoples, and the Caucasians to the north. Gilaki culture includes a distinctive cuisine, literature, and architecture. The architecture of the Gilakis is unique, primarily because of the abundance of wood as a building material. Most Gilaki houses are wooden with red tile roofs and are surrounded by wooden verandahs. Though the Gilakis are bilingual in the Farsi language and have adopted many Farsi cultural traits, they clearly see themselves as a distinct nation.

LANGUAGE AND RELIGION: The Gilaki language, often called Gilani, is a Caspian language of the West Iranian group of the Indo-Iranian languages. The language, with considerable Turkic and Kurdish admixtures, is not written. Educated Gilakis use Farsi, the national language of Iran, as their literary language, and the majority also speak Western Farsi as a second language. The language has three major dialects — the coastal dialect, Rashti, and Gelashi, which is spoken in the more remote mountain areas. The Rashti dialect, spoken in the capital region, is significantly different and has been heavily influenced by Farsi. Rashti is not intelligible to speakers of "real" Gilaki. Many scholars link the Gilaki language to the neighboring Mazandarani language, but others disagree. Radio broadcasts in the language were begun in the early 1980s.

The majority of the Gilakis are Shi'a Muslims, of the official sect of Iran, with a sizable Sunni minority. Although the Gilakis are devout in basic Islamic practices, they have been subtly influenced by the secularism from the former Soviet Union. Most Gilakis belong to a branch of the Shi'ites known as the Ithna-Asharis. There is reportedly a small Christian population that has operated underground since 1979. Both politically and religiously the Gilakis are unique in Iran for their independent character.

NATIONAL HISTORY: Nomadic Caucasian tribes as early as 1500 B.C. migrated south from the Caucasus Mountains to settle the fertile plains and marshlands along the Caspian Sea. By the sixth century B.C. the region formed a satrapy (province) of the ancient Persian Empire. Conquered by the Greeks of Alexander the Great in 334–31 B.C., it later formed part of the Greek province of Media Atrophene. In the second century B.C. the Persians reconquered the Caspian region, and the Persianization of the population began.

The Apostle Bartholomew, who evangelized the early Gilakis around A.D. 50, brought Christianity to the region. Christianity became a strong presence, but its influence ended with the Arab conquest of Gilan in 641 A.D. Included in the Muslim empire, the Caliphate, the majority of the Gilakis converted to the new religion. From the tenth century Gilan formed part of the newly established linguistic frontier between the Turkic and Iranian peoples.

After conquest by Turkic peoples in the ninth century, the Gilaki culture and language absorbed many Turkic borrowings. During the rule of Malik Shah in the eleventh century, a secret sect of Ismaili Muslims formed the core of Shi'a resistance to Seljuk Turkic rule. The sect, established in Gilan, eventually became known as the Assassins.

The Mongols devastated Gilan in the thirteenth century, and again by Tamerlane a century later. The invasions resulted in a huge influx of refugees, particularly Turkic peoples, into the sparsely populated area. By the fifteenth century, Gilan had declined and lost its earlier civilization; it was poor and backward when the Persians regained control of it in 1592. Gilan was often a battleground in the wars between the Turks and Persians, with religion one of the major causes. The Persian peoples are mostly Shi'a Muslims, but the Turkic peoples farther west are mostly Sunni.

English traders, moving south from Russia, reached Gilan in the late sixteenth century and opened trade to the West, particularly in silk, the region's major export. Russian explorers and Cossacks spearheading the Russian expansion into the Turkish and Persian lands soon followed. Cossacks overran Gilan in 1636 and caused considerable damage before withdrawing. In 1722 the Russians took Gilan from Persia and held the region for ten years, finally returning it to Persia in exchange for territorial concessions in the Caucasus. Under treaties of 1813 and 1828 that ceded their Caucasian territories to Russia, the Persians were obliged to grant the Russians economic and naval establishments in Gilan.

Silk production, introduced in the Middle Ages, flourished in the nineteenth century and accounted for most of Persia's silk exports. Influenced by British and Russian silk traders, Gilan began to modernize in the 1880s and 1890s. Over the next decades the region advanced more rapidly than the rest of decadent, feudal Persia. A small number of Gilakis, schooled by foreigners, formed an intellectual elite that embraced nationalist ideals coming from Europe in the late nineteenth century.

Opposition to the excesses and neglect of the Persian monarchy erupted in open rebellion in 1905. Led by discontented farmers, the Gilakis formed guerrilla groups called Jangli; the rebels were known as Jangali (men of the jungle), for the dense forests that gave them refuge. A British-Russian agreement signed in 1907 divided the weak Persian state into spheres of influence. In 1909 Russian troops crushed the Gilaki rebellion, which in 1912 re-formed as an anti-Russian movement. The Jangali movement emerged as the leading nationalist organization in 1914. In 1917, with their country collapsing in revolution, the Russian troops withdrew from Gilan, and Gilaki rebels took control of much of the countryside.

Gilaki rebels led by Mirza Kuchek Khan, called the "Robin Hoods of the Caspian Marshes" for their generosity to the poor, demanded Gilaki autonomy and also assistance for the region's hard-pressed farmers from the Persian administration, which returned in 1918. Their appeals rebuffed, the Gilaki resumed their rebellion and returned to strongholds in the mountains and forests. German, Austrian, and Turkish officers were recruited to train the Jangali volunteers. The rebellion, joined by Azeris, Kurds, and Armenians, spread across Gilan and a great part of neighboring Mazanderan to the east.

The rebels signed a treaty with the British on 12 August 1918. The treaty granted to Mirza Kuchek Khan the domain of Gilan; the foreign military instructors were expelled. The British withdrew at the end of World War I. In 1919, Cossacks in the pay of the Persian government seized the region. The Gilaki rebels later clashed with British troops that had landed to counter a growing Bolshevik threat to the region. A Red force in May 1920 invaded the region in support of the rebels and with Bolshevik military assistance the Gilaki rebels dislodged the British from their base at Enzeli on the 19th of that month. The next day the Gilaki leader, Kuchek Khan, declared the independence of the Persian Soviet Socialist Republic of Gilan. A separatist government of Gilaki nationalists and communists began to redistribute lands traditionally held by absentee Persian landlords, religious bodies, the Persian state, and the crown.

A 1921 revolution in Tehran installed a new Persian dynasty, the Pahlevi. Faced with a large rebel force preparing to march on Tehran from Gilan, the Iranian government hastily granted generous oil concessions to the new Soviet Union in exchange for the withdrawal of the Red Army from Gilan and the northwest. Imperial troops then invaded the breakaway state in December 1921. The Gilaki leader, Kuchek Khan, was captured, and his head was displayed in Tehran to prove to all that the long Jangali rebellion had finally ended. Many communists and Gilaki nationalist leaders fled to the Soviet Union.

Iran remained neutral during World War II, but the Soviets, citing security reasons, occupied the northern provinces. Encouraged by the occupation force, Azeris and Kurds set up breakaway states, but the Gilakis, having been betrayed by the Soviets in 1921, refused Soviet suggestions for a separate Gilaki state under Soviet protection. In 1946, when the Soviet troops finally withdrew, the Azeri and Kurdish states collapsed.

Rapid post–World War II modernization transformed Gilan; its economic advance was financed by the growth of tourism to the plush Caspian Sea resorts. Agricultural reforms in the middle 1970s aided the establishment of large-scale, mechanized farming, particularly of rice. The oil boom encouraged industrial investment and urbanization.

Greater prosperity incited new appeals for regional autonomy. Gilaki agitation against the repressive rule of the shah resulted in a brutal crackdown by the feared secret police in 1975.

Most Gilakis supported the revolution that overthrew the hated monarchy in 1979. Soon disappointed by the installation of an even more repressive Islamic government in Tehran, the Gilaki again rebelled against the central government. With widespread support—particularly among Gilan's modern, liberated women, and the Sunni Muslim minority—the Jangli movement was revived to fight the new government. In 1981, Gilaki guerrillas, posing as Iranian Revolutionary Guards, killed the government religious leader of Gilan. The Gilaki rebellion was driven underground by mass executions and the imposition of a dictatorship of strict Islamic law.

The Gilakis were terrorized by government gangs for over a decade, but national sentiment revived after the government's poor response to a severe earthquake that devastated the region in June 1990. The isolated villages of flimsy, mud-brick houses were unable to withstand the shock. The quake killed more than 30,000 people in the region, which has still not fully recovered.

Gilaki nationalism, still underground, drew new support following the breakup of the Soviet Union in 1991 and the establishment of new national states where oppressed provinces had formerly existed. Gilan, potentially rich from Caspian Sea oil, caviar, and rice production, remained impoverished and underdeveloped. The province was closed to most foreigners, so little information is available on events in the late 1990s; there are reports of skirmishes between government forces and Gilaki rebels hiding in the forests and mountains. At the turn of the twenty-first century, political executions became rare, but Gilaki exiles claim that the high number of executions of criminal offenders in the region was a cover-up for the repression of nationalist and dissident political views.

A Gilaki mobilization emerged from three days of demonstrations in Rasht on 14 April 2000. The clashes between young Gilakis and the Basijis, the security forces, erupted after the Basijis stopped a young woman, who was with a man, for inappropriate attire. A scuffle ensued between the Basijis and angry Gilakis. Mobs attacked banks and other buildings, and blocked streets with burning tires. The clashes ended following a number of arrests. The violence resumed the following day, when Gilakis tried to observe the Sham-i-Qariban religious ceremony; they were attacked by hard-liners under the pretext of "promoting virtue and prohibiting vice." The demonstrations underlined the Gilakis' impatience at waiting for the civil society and the rule of law they have heard so much about since 1997. The revival of the Jangali movement, which came about as a result of the violent confrontations, marked the first serious threat to the hold of the Islamic government on Gilan since 1979–80.

The Gilaki nationalist movement mostly dispersed or destroyed in Iran, is maintained by the growing exile community. Groups living as far apart as Azerbaijan and California sustain both the Gilaki culture and their national aspirations.

SELECTED BIBLIOGRAPHY:

Chaqueri, Cosroe. *The Soviet Socialist Republic of Iran, 1920–1921: Birth of the Trauma*. 1995.

Foran, John, ed. *A Century of Revolution: Social Movements in Iran*. 1994.

Kashani-Sabet, Firoozeh. *Frontier Fictions: Shaping the Iranian Nation, 1804–1946*. 2000.

Vaziri, Mostafa. *Iran as Imagined Nation: The Construction of National Identity*. 1993.

Giulians

Giulianos; Triestini; Giulians and Gorizians

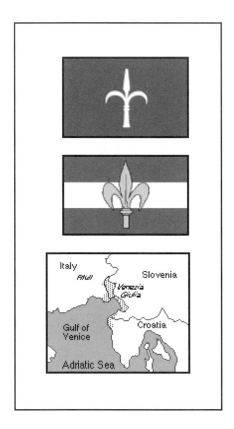

POPULATION: Approximately (2002e) 370,000 Giulians in Italy, concentrated in the northwestern province of Trieste. Outside the region there are Giulian communities in other parts of Friuli-Venezia Giulia, in the Veneto region, and the Milan area of Lombardy.

THE GIULIAN HOMELAND: The Giulian homeland, Venezia Giulia, lies at the head of the Adriatic Sea, occupying a narrow coastal plain on the Gulf of Trieste extending northwest of the Karst limestone plateau to the foothills of the Julian Alps in northwestern Italy. Trieste Province—the city of Trieste and its suburbs—is situated on the northwestern side of the Istrian Peninsula and is surrounded by Slovenian territory, except for a short land corridor to Gorizia Province. Venezia Giulia forms the Trieste and Gorizia Provinces of the region of Fruili-Venezia Giulia of Italy. *Region of Venezia Giulia*: 261 sq. mi.—676 sq. km, (2002e) 396,000—Giulians 72%, Slovenes 18%, Friulis* 8%, other Italians 2%. The Giulian capital and major cultural center is Trieste, (2002e) 215,000. The other major cultural center is Gorizia, the center of Venezia Guilia, (2002e) 37,000.

FLAG: The Giulian national flag, the flag of the former Trieste state, is a red field charged with a white spearlike halberd centered. The flag of Venezia Giulia has three horizontal stripes of red, white, and red, bearing a centered gold halberd.

PEOPLE AND CULTURE: The Giulians are an Italian people of mixed ethnic background, their language and culture the product of centuries of close contact with Germanic and Slav peoples. The region, among Italy's most un-Italian, is a crossroads of the languages and cultures of Central Europe. The population of the province includes the majority Giulians; the Slavic Slovenes, related to the people of neighboring Slovenia; the

Friulis, a Rhaeto-Romanic people more numerous in the adjoining Italian region of Friulia; and Austrians, the remnant of a formerly large Austrian population.

LANGUAGE AND RELIGION: The Giulian dialects form a cluster of northeastern Venetian dialects heavily influenced by German, Slovene, Croat, and Friuli. The dialects remain the language of daily life, with standard Italian spoken by the majority of the population. Slovene, spoken by about 100,000 people in the region, is spoken by many Giulians as a second language. Standard Italian, although the official language of the Italian republic, was not widely spoken in the Giulian region until the 1950s, when radio and television brought it.

The Giulians are overwhelmingly Roman Catholic, with a religious tradition that has flourished since the third century A.D. The influence of the Roman Catholic Church, although still powerful, began to decline with the modernization of the 1950s. In recent years evangelical sects have been active.

NATIONAL HISTORY: The Romans, who knew the head of the Adriatic Sea as the Julian region, extended their authority to it in 177 B.C. Trieste, fortified and expanded, served as the port of, and protection for, the more important Roman commercial city of Aquileia, 22 miles to the northwest. Overrun by barbarian tribes as Roman power collapsed, the Julian region was divided into a coastal zone under Byzantine rule and an inland zone ruled by the dukes of Friuli and counts of Gorizia.

Aquileia, whose inhabitants fled to the islands of the Venetian Lagoon in A.D. 452, was superseded by Trieste as the major city in the region. Slavic migrants occupied the Karst Plateau in the sixth century. Trieste and Gorizia, retaining their Latin cultures, formed a linguistic and cultural frontier between the Latins and the Slavs.

Incorporated in the Carolingian Empire in 788, Trieste and the Julian region passed to the Holy Roman Empire, while the hinterland to the west and south came under Venetian rule. The Roman Catholic patriarchate of Aquileia came to prominence in the eleventh century, bringing the Julian region and Trieste under ecclesiastical sovereignty. A line of count-bishops of Trieste ruled the city as an episcopal see from 948 to 1202, when it became a free imperial city under Venetian authority. Following two centuries of struggle against rival Venice, Trieste finally accepted autonomy under Austrian rule in 1342. In 1420 Trieste was annexed to the Austrian Empire, and in 1500 Gorizia was added to the Hapsburg territories.

The region developed as a meeting point of Latin, Slav, and Germanic cultures. The mixing of cultural and linguistic influences led to the emergence of a regional culture, unique in Europe that combined traits and customs from all three cultures. The inhabitants came to see themselves as Giulians—not Italian, not Austrian, and not Slav, but a mixture of the three.

As Austria's most important outlet to the sea, Trieste became the primary port and naval base of the vast multi-ethnic Hapsburg Empire. The city's rapid expansion replaced the essentially Italian town with long, straight Austrian-designed boulevards lined with stately and ornate Hapsburg architecture. Declared a free port in 1719, Trieste's importance increased with the extension of Austrian administration to surrounding Venetian territory in 1797. Gorizia was the capital of the Austrian crownland of Görz-Gradisca from 1815. In 1867 Trieste became the capital of the newly created crownland of Kustenland, a province of mixed Italian, Slovene, Croat, Friuli, and Austrian populations.

The Italia Irredenta movement, formed after Italian unification in 1870 and dedicated to the recovery of Italian-populated regions outside the kingdom, gained Italian support in Trieste in the late nineteenth century. In 1910 serious anti-Austrian demonstrations erupted in the region, in which Italian-speaking Triestines and Giulians demanded union with Italy.

During World War I, the allies, in a secret treaty signed on 26 April 1915, offered the Julian region, including Austria's primary naval base at Trieste and territories in the Alps, to Italy as an incentive to declare war on Austria-Hungary. The Italians, pressed by the powerful Italia Irredenta movement, joined the allies. The Julian area, especially around Monte San Michele, was the scene of heavy fighting between the Austrians and Italians in 1915–16; the city of Gorizia and other regional towns were heavily damaged.

As Austrian defeat loomed, rival nationalists clashed, and chaos erupted in Trieste and Gorizia. Italian irredentist groups attempted to take control of the cities, setting off serious violence in the region. South Slav troops, supported by Russia, also threatened.

Giulian nationalists took control. Rejecting plans to separate the Italian-majority cities of Trieste and Gorizia from their non-Italian hinterland, the local legislature in Trieste in October 1918 voted to form a separate autonomous republic to be called Venezia Giulia, under the protection of the new League of Nations. The republic—proposed as an Italo-Slovene state that would incorporate Trieste, the Julian region to the north, including Gorizia, and the Istrian Peninsula—collapsed when Italian troops landed on 3 November 1918. The fate of the region remained undecided until 1920, when the reduced Austrian state ceded Trieste and Gorizia to Italy. Trieste was made the capital of the new province of Venezia Giulia and Zara, which included territory now in Slovenia and Croatia.

The region's economic importance declined rapidly with the departure of thousands of Austrian civilians. The Fascist Italian government after 1922 pressed the Italianization of the polyglot region. To counter Slav territorial claims and to reduce the Giulian majority, the government sponsored immigration from culturally and dialectically distinct regions of southern Italy. Ethnic tension flared into violence in the 1920s and 1930, both between Italian-speakers and Slavs, and between the Giulians and the newcomers from southern Italy.

The region's decline reversed with the outbreak of World War II, but the long-smoldering tension flared in violence between Fascist, anti-Fascist, and Yugoslav-supported communist groups in Trieste and Gorizia. The Yugoslav communists used the large urban Slovene minority as an underground, fighting both the Fascist Italian government and the anti-communist Giulians.

In the spring of 1945, Josip Broz Tito's Yugoslav communist partisans took control of Trieste and Gorizia. Thousands of inhabitants, real or imagined Fascist collaborators and anticommunists, were rounded up. Many of the detainees, men, women, and children, were thrown alive into an abyss in the Corso Mountains during the 40 days of Tito's terror. The Italian government's failure to protect the Giulians against the communist terror before the British liberated the area stimulated the growth of modern regionalism and nationalism. Many of the region's Slovenes crossed into Yugoslavia to escape rising ethnic tension and reprisals for wartime activities.

Conflicting postwar Italian and Yugoslav claims to the territory were presented to the new United Nations in 1946. A compromise, grudgingly accepted by the claimants and welcomed by the Giulians, created a Free Territory of Trieste under UN protection. The state was proclaimed independent on 10 February 1947. The free territory comprised two zones, called A and B, under U.S.-British and Yugoslavian administration, respectively. The region flourished as a neutral trading state in the early years of the Cold War.

By the 1947 treaty, Yugoslavia received districts of Venezia Giulia, including the northern suburbs of the city of Gorizia, where it developed the Yugoslav town of Nova Gorica. The city lost its commercial importance after a border settlement by which the Italian government detached Udine Province from Veneto and united it with Gorizia to form Friuli-Venezia Giulia. A London agreement of 1954 restored the city of Trieste and part of Zone A to Italy. Trieste became the capital of the expanded region of Friuli-Venezia Giulia. A statute of autonomy was passed on 31 January 1963.

Outstanding territorial claims delayed the treaty formalizing the division of Trieste until 1975. The signing of the treaty incited a Giulian revival, led by a populist coalition that denounced the accord and demanded autonomy. Steadily gaining support as the province's population and economic importance declined, the nationalists blamed the Giulian region's growing problems squarely on Italy's notoriously inefficient and corrupt government.

The overthrow of communism in 1989 ended the area's long isolation, and ties to old *Mitteleuropa* resumed. Trieste was the only Italian city to have lost population since 1965; Triestine activists seized on the rapid changes sweeping Europe as a last chance to avert stagnation as an Italian backwater. The Giulians began to engage in offshore banking, relying on an old privilege granted under Hapsburg rule. The Italian government rejected the privilege following protests from European Union (EU) countries.

Since 1990 nationalist factions have put forward several proposals—the revival of the independence of 1947–54; autonomy within a federal Italy; or a European region grouping the provinces of Gorizia and Trieste, with their traditional hinterland in a neutral free zone open to the EU and the fledgling democracies in Central and Eastern Europe. The one point all of the factions share is a desire to be free of Italy's huge and hugely inefficient government, which they claim stifles the region's potential. In local elections in November 1993 the nontraditional parties, including nationalists, autonomists, and federalists, took more than 50% of the vote. Trieste's trade is smaller than it was in 1914, when it was a port serving most of Central Europe.

The growing Giulian national movement, part of the Padania movement, which has strong support across northern Italy, wants to reassert the Giulian region's role as a meeting point of diverse cultures, prevent ethnic conflicts, and demonstrate its ability to hold its own in the modern world. To become the gateway to the new Europe is the Giulian goal.

Ricardo Illy, a coffee magnate, has led the Giulian revival while sprucing up the rather faded splendors of Trieste during his term as mayor in 2001–2. In November 2001, Trieste hosted a meeting of representatives of the countries of Central Europe in an effort to resurrect the trade and cultural ties that prevailed before the world wars and the Cold War put up barriers across the continent.

SELECTED BIBLIOGRAPHY:

Levy, Carl, ed. *Italian Regionalism: History, Identity and Politics*. 1996.
Morata, Francesc. *Regional Autonomy and European Integration*. 1993.
Novak, Bogan C. *Trieste Nineteen Forty-one to Nineteen Fifty-four: The Ethnic Politics and Ideological Struggle*. 1970.
Sluga, Glenda. *The Problem of Trieste and the Italo-Yugoslav Border: Difference, Identity, and Sovereignty in Twentieth-Century Europe*. 2001.

Gorkhas

Gurkhas; Ghurkhas; Gorkhalis; Gurkhalis; Khaskuras; Nepalis

POPULATION: Approximately (2002e) 6,360,000 Gorkhas in northeastern India, concentrated in the northern districts of West Bengal State. Other sizable communities include over 300,000 in adjacent areas of Bhutan, and in the Indian states of Sikkim and Assam.

THE GORKHA HOMELAND: The Gorkha homeland, popularly called Gorkhaland, lies in northeastern India, partly in the Sikkim Himalayas in northern West Bengal state of India. Mountainous Gorkhaland is connected to the Indian heartland by a narrow 12-mile-wide corridor of land between Nepal and Bangladesh. The region, with plentiful rainfall, has a wide range of climates, from tropical to subalpine, owing to its varying elevations. The local economy is based primarily on tea, which is grown on plantations up to 6,000 feet (1,800 meters). Gorkhaland, a semi-autonomous region with its own government, the Darjeeling Gorkha Hill Council, comprises the districts of Darjeeling, Jalpaiguri, and Cooch Behar. *Darjeeling Gorkha Hill Council (Gorkhaland)*: 4,888 sq. mi.—12,663 sq. km, (2002e) 6,210,000—Gorkhas 81%, Bengalis 10%, other Indians. The Gorkha capital and major cultural center is Darjeeling, called Dorje-ling by the Gorkhas, (2002e) 95,000. The other major cultural centers are Shiliguri, called Sili-guri by the Gorkhas, (2002e) 298,000, and Kalimpong, called Kalim-pang, (2002e) 48,000.

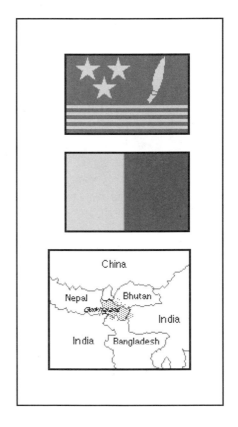

FLAG: The Gorkha national flag, the flag of the national movement, is a green field with four narrow horizontal yellow stripes at the bottom and bearing a yellow *kukri*, a Gorkha sword, on the fly and three yellow five-pointed stars on the hoist. The flag of the Gorkha rebel militias is a vertical bicolor of yellow and pale green; the guerrillas are called the "yellow-greens" after their military flag.

PEOPLE AND CULTURE: The Gorkhas, popularly called "Gurkhas," after their historical military units, are the descendants in India of Magar and Gurung immigrants from eastern Nepal. The ethnic term "Gorkha" comes from the town of Gorkha, or Gurkha, in central Nepal. First used by the British, the name is now applied to all of the Gorkhali-speaking peoples in northeastern India. The Gorkhas in India have consolidated their distinct culture, which developed over many years and incorporates the major activities of tea plantations. The violent struggle against Bengali domination in 1986–88 consolidated the Gorkha national identity. The military aspect of Gorkha life, after years of recruitment into the British and Indian armies, has also become part of the Gorkha culture. All Gorkha men normally wear the military short sword called a *kukri*. Returning and retired soldiers often become teachers or leaders, bringing their experiences in far-off places to bear on local problems. There is a continuing controversy over whether the name Gorkha (or Gurkha) is an ethnic or political designation.

LANGUAGE AND RELIGION: The Gorkha language, called Gorkhali or Khas, is a Nepali language belonging to the Eastern Pahari group of Indo-Aryan languages. The language is Rajastani dialect of the West Indic group, incorporating many borrowings from the Tibeto-Burman languages of the region's original Buddhist inhabitants. The language is spoken in three dialects, with the Gorkhali dialect predominant in India. The Gorkhas, due to decades of British and Indian military schooling, have a high literacy rate compared to neighboring peoples.

The majority of the Gorkhas are now Hindus, although a sizable minority are Buddhists. Buddhist teachings, particularly in the northern districts, in Sikkim and Bhutan, have influenced the traditional Hindu beliefs, with many Buddhist festivals and traditions having been incorporated into the Gorkha belief system. Many of the traditionally Buddhist Gorkhas, after military service in India, adopted Hinduism but retained many of their pre-Hindu beliefs and traditions. Most shrines in the region are sacred to both the Hindus and Buddhists.

NATIONAL HISTORY: The town of Gorkha, the ancestral home of the ruling house of Nepal, was seized by Drabya Shah, leading a group of Rajputs driven from their homeland. Drabya Shah established his own kingdom at Gorkha in 1559. His descendant, Prithvi Narayan Shah, created a powerful military force from the ethnically diverse peoples of the region. The force, known as Gurkhas, conquered neighboring kingdoms and petty principalities, which were consolidated as the kingdom of Nepal. Over the next two centuries they extended their rule over much of present-day Nepal, and in 1791 they invaded Tibet. Raiding south into British territory, the fierce Gurkha warriors threatened Britain's hold on the Himalayan foothills.

The British authorities sent an expedition against the raiders, provoking the Gurkha War of 1814–16. The British forces were mauled in two separate campaigns. In 1815 the British overran many of the Gurkha hill forts, and the next year the Gurkha defenders sued for peace. The war established a strong British influence in Nepal and the Himalayas. Impressed by the ferocity and fighting ability of the Gurkhas, in 1816 the British military formed the first Gurkha units within the colonial Indian Army.

The British forced independent Sikkim to cede the Darjeeling region in 1835 and to cede further territories in the foothills in 1849. The town of Darjeeling, in the cool highlands, soon became a favorite resort of the British colonials of Calcutta and the humid lowlands. Encouraged by the colonial administration between 1859 and 1918, migrants from western Nepal settled in the uplands to work in the important British tea industry. The British called the Nepalese migrants "Gurkhas" whatever their ethnic or cultural origins. The migrants later took the name as their own, calling themselves Gorkhas and their language Gorkhali.

Darjeeling tea, first grown in the nineteenth century, gains its flavor from a combination of soil, altitude, and winds that stunt the growth of the tea bushes. The tea produced in the region is the most exclusive variety, costing over twice as much as other good teas.

Gurkha military units served with distinction in many parts of India, although their use by the British provoked ethnic animosity in India that continues to the present. When the First World War began in 1914, the British shipped thousands of Gurkha troops to the European and Middle Eastern theaters. Over 20,000 Gurkhas died in campaigns in France, Gallipoli, Suez, and Mesopotamia. British military pay and pensions became the prime source of income for the Gurkha peoples of Nepal and northeastern India.

Beginning in 1947, independent India from 1947 also recruited Gurkha units, mainly from the large immigrant population that moved into northern West Bengal State in the early decades of the twentieth century. Despite their loyal service to the British and Indian armies, ethnic tension grew in the northeast between the Gorkhas and the ethnic Bengalis, called *Kala Log* (black folk) in the Gorkhali language. Responding to Bengali demands, the Indian government moved to restrict further immigration from Nepal in the 1970s. The confrontations between the Gorkhas and Bengalis marked the first show of Gorkha strength and the beginnings of the Gorkha national movement.

The expulsion of some 10,000 ethnic Gorkhas from the neighboring state of Meghalaya during an anti-immigrant campaign in 1986 sparked a Gorkha rebellion that rapidly spread across northern West Bengal. The rebels formed the Gorkha National Liberation Front (GNLF), under an ex-soldier, Subhas Ghising, and demanded the separation of the northern districts of West Bengal and the creation of a separate Gorkhaland state. Activists called for the adoption of Gorkhali as one of India's official languages, on a par with its other sixteen official languages.

Their demands were punctuated by strikes and mass demonstrations in the summer of 1986, and the attitudes of many Gorkhas were polarized following a number of deaths in violent clashes with West Bengali police. Over 80,000 Gorkha tea plantation workers refused to harvest the valuable crop as the separatist violence spread across the region with attacks and counterattacks. Tea plantations were burned, as were the housing estates of their workers. By late 1988 over 350 people had been killed, and millions of dollars in damages had been sustained. The damage to the regional economy was still evident 10 years later. Thousands fled the region—the Gorkhas into high-protected valleys, the Bengali refugees to the lower plains.

Their appeals and petitions for separation from West Bengal ignored or rejected, Gorkha nationalists began to advocate the creation of a "Greater Gorkhaland," a sovereign state independent of both India and Nepal and encompassing the Gorkha-populated areas of West Bengal, Sikkim, Bhutan, and Assam. The West Bengal government, controlled by local communists, responded with force. Claiming the support of over 40,000 ex-soldiers, the Gorkhas threatened to escalate the conflict if attacks by Bengalis and the West Bengal police continued. Troops dispatched by the federal government finally occupied the tea plantations in 1987 and moved on to the main separatist centers in Darjeeling and Kalimpong, over the objections of the West Bengal government. Two years of virtual civil war between the Gorkha rebels and the forces of the government of West Bengal devastated the region.

Before 1986, Gurkha soldiers in the Indian army had been patrolling the Punjab, where a violent separatist campaign had been carried out by militant Sikhs.* After that year, the Gurkhas found their own homeland in Gorkhaland being patrolled by Sikh soldiers of the Indian army. In 1987 there were disturbances in Hong Kong, the main Gurkha base of the British army, between Gurkha soldiers and their British officers over Gurkha support of their compatriots in India. In 1988, the Gurkhas celebrated 172 years of service in the British army, but the celebrations were dimmed by the controversy. When Hong Kong reverted to China, two of the three Gurkha battalions were transferred from Hong Kong to the United Kingdom, and the third was disbanded.

The Gorkha rebels accepted an offer of negotiations, and an autonomy agreement reached in July 1988 provided for a semi-autonomous "hill council" to take over the local administration from the West Bengali authorities. The agreement required members of the Gorkha National Liberation Front (GNLF) to drop their demands for a separate state, end agitation, surrender their arms, and cooperate with agents of the federal government. In return the pact provided for limited autonomy in the hill districts of West Bengal, excluding the Gorkha-populated districts of western Assam.

On both sides of the international border between India and Nepal, the Gorkhas, including the thousands of ex-servicemen of the British and Indian armies, demanded a better deal. In 1997 the British government raised the Gorkha soldiers' pay to the level of other soldiers in the British army, but their pensions remained lower. The pay and pensions were based on a 1947 treaty signed by the British government with the Indian and Nepali governments.

Elections to the new legislative body, won by the GNLF, split the nationalist movement. Activists rejected the autonomy agreement, vowing to settle for nothing less than full statehood within India. The more militant groups threatened a terrorist campaign in support of full independence for the Gorkha homeland. In spite of the declarations and statements, separatist violence abated under the rule of the autonomous council.

The increasingly authoritarian West Bengal government, stifling dissent with violence and confiscation of property, inadvertently rekindled the separatist movement in 1990. The Gorkha majority renewed its demands for separation from West Bengal, while a vocal minority again called for independence. In return for dropping territorial claims to western Assam, the militants reportedly received arms and training from Assamese* separatists of the United Liberation Front of Assam (ULFA) during the 1990s.

The Gorkha nationalists, increasingly militant, called a boycott of the autonomous-district elections in August 1993. Only 20% of those eligible voted. The Bengali communists won; the nationalists denounced the new communist-dominated district council as illegal. The nationalists have refused to consider new elections until their demands for separation and autonomy are met. The Gorkha nationalists have become yet another ethnic threat to India's control of its turbulent northeastern states.

In 1994, in an effort to appease the Gorkha nationalists, the Indian government granted more territory and powers to the autonomous hill council. Although the council's powers were limited, it gave the Gorkhas some degree of local autonomy and a say in the affairs of the region. The Gorkha national movement lost support; the government considered the problem solved and the Gorkhas pacified. In the late 1990s, as the Indian government began to plan for the creation of new states in other parts of India, the Gorkha national movement revived and put forward new demands for a separate Gorkhaland state, taking territory from West Bengal.

In 1997 the major tea-producing companies were accused of financing insurgent groups in exchange for peace on the plantations. The government had proved incapable of protecting the tea estates or the people who work on them. The estate owners would rather pay protection money than risk guerrilla attacks or organized strikes. Officials of the tea companies complained in 1999 that their employees were being kidnapped and used to extort ransoms, but that if they paid they were accused by the West Bengal state government of financing terrorism. The region was brought to a standstill in July 1999 by striking tea workers, demanding better living conditions, hospitals, schools, and other amenities.

The demand for a separate Gorkha state within the Indian union has widespread support, with militants continuing to press for separation from India and the creation of a Gorkha republic, to include parts of the Indian states of West Bengal, Sikkim, and Assam, districts of Bhutan, and parts of western Nepal.

In 2000, following the formation of three new states, Jharkhand, Uttaranchal, and Chattisgarh, Gorkha demands for separation increased. In February 2001, the GNLF called an indefinite strike in the region following an attack by opposition Gorkha politicians on the Gorkha national leader, Subhas Ghising. The strike was called off in mid-April to facilitate Gorkha participation in local elections to the West Bengal assembly.

In July 2001, Subhas Ghising said he was withdrawing all political demands, including that for a separate state of Gorkhaland, in "disgust" and pronounced the Darjeeling Gorkha Hill Council (DGHC), of which he is chairman, "dead." He also stated that this was the last term of the Council and that there would be no elections in the future, the next election due in November 2002. He accused the Indian and West Bengal governments of treating Darjeeling as a colony, just as the British had done. He urged the Gorkhas to protect their cultural heritage and "get ready for the future."

SELECTED BIBLIOGRAPHY:

Baskota, Purushottram. *The Gurkha Connection*. 1998.
Khanduri, Chandra B. *A Re-Discovered History of Gorkhas*. 1997.
Parker, John. *The Gurkhas*. 1999.
Smith, E.D. *Valour: A History of the Gurkhas*. 1997.

Greenlanders
Greenland Inuits; Grønlanders; Greenlander Eskimos; Kalaallisuts

POPULATION: Approximately (2002e) 55,000 Greenlanders in Danish territory, mostly living in the coastal regions of Greenland. About 15,000 Greenlanders live in Denmark, in other parts of Scandinavia, and in Canada.

THE GREENLANDER HOMELAND: The Greenlander homeland, considered part of the North American continent, is the world's largest true island. Most of the island's territory lies above the Arctic Circle, and all but a narrow, mountainous, barren, and rocky coast is covered by an enormous ice cap. The ice cap covers 84% of the island, sometimes up to 14,000 feet (36,260 m) deep. The island dominates the North Atlantic between North America and Europe. The sparse population is confined to small settlements along the coast. Greenland has been a self-governing dependency of the Danish kingdom since 1979. *Greenland (Kalaallit-Nunaat)*: 839,999 sq. mi.—1,176,163 sq. km, (2002e) 57,000—Greenlanders 75%, Danes 13%, Inuits* 12%. The Greenlander capital and major cultural center is Godthåb, called Nuuk by the Greenlanders, (2002e) 15,000.

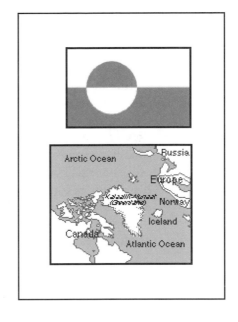

FLAG: The Greenlander flag, the official flag of the autonomous state, is a horizontal bicolor of white over red charged with a large bicolor disc, red over white, offset toward the hoist.

PEOPLE AND CULTURE: The Greenlanders are a people of mixed Inuit and European background, although in the northern districts there is a sizable population of seminomadic Inuits. Over centuries the indigenous Inuits have mixed with Norwegian and Danish colonists from Europe, with the result that the Greenlanders have a variety of features, from Inuit to European. The Greenlander culture incorporates both Inuit and European influences and traditions; an important part of the culture concerns the traditional pursuits of whaling and fishing. Some 90% of the population inhabits the ice-free coastal regions in the south of the island.

The large Danish minority is concentrated in the capital and the other important settlements.

LANGUAGE AND RELIGION: The Greenlanders speak an East Inuit dialect called Greenlandic or Greenlandic Inuktitut, which mixes Inuit and Scandinavian words and forms. The language, intelligible with difficulty to speakers of Inuit, is a unique blend of influences, with many words for different conditions of weather, snow, ice, and other natural phenomenon. Greenlandic became the official language of the state in 1979, but Danish must still be taught so that Greenlandic youngsters can attend universities in Denmark. News in the language is broadcast daily in Denmark and Greenland. English is increasingly popular, particularly among younger Greenlanders.

The majority of the Greenlanders are Protestants, mostly Evangelical Lutheran. Many pre-Christian traditions and beliefs have been retained and have become part of the Greenlander belief system. Traditional beliefs connected with hunting and fishing are particularly revered.

NATIONAL HISTORY: In about 3000 B.C. a Greek sailor, Pytheas of Massila, brought back stories of a great northern land six days' sail north of Britain. The story of Pytheas was the first mention of the island in European chronicles and the first reported contact by Europeans. Stories about the island, often fanciful, became part of folklore and fable. Called Thule or Ultima Thule—the "Farthest Land"—by the Romans, the island gradually faded into myth and legend.

Norse Vikings from the Norwegian coast, led by Eric the Red, rediscovered the island in A.D. 982. Two colonies were established beginning in 985, one near Godthåb and one near Julianehåb, where a few thousand Norsemen engaged in cattle breeding, sealing, and fishing. The most important export became walrus tusks, valued across Scandinavia. In an effort to make the island more attractive to potential colonists, Eric named the frozen land "Greenland." The Vikings established other settlements on the narrow coastal plains in the south, where agriculture was possible. The number of Viking settlers grew to some 10,000 by the twelfth century. A bishopric and two cloisters became the centers of the island's religious life. The Vikings in the thirteenth century reported the first contacts with the Inuit, the vanguard of the Inuit migration across the polar lands to northern Greenland.

The colonists, lacking wood and iron for shipbuilding, could not support communications with Europe and were forced to rely on traders and shipping that arrived from time to time. In 1261 the colonists submitted to the Norwegian king, who promised a yearly voyage to provision the colonies in exchange for taxes and local products. The Norwegians ruled the island through a separate Greenland assembly called the Althing. In 1380 the Danes took over the island's administration but did not attempt further colonization.

Sometime in the fourteenth century the weather grew colder, and agriculture and livestock breeding declined. Plagues brought from Europe decimated the colonial population. The Black Death alone is estimated to have killed half the inhabitants of the colonies. The only ships that sailed to Greenland in those years belonged to outlaws and pirates. Around 1350 the colony at Godthåb was apparently deserted and subsequently occupied by the Greenlander Inuits. In 1379 the colonies in the Julianehåb region came under Inuit attack. The last official notice of Norsemen on Greenland came in 1410; afterward there was only silence from the Norse colonies. Sometime during the next 150 years the Norse colonists disappeared without trace from Greenland; their fate is still not fully known. Theories variously claim that they returned to Europe, joined the Inuits, succumbed to plague or Inuit attacks, or simply died out as agriculture collapsed.

In 1721 the Norwegians, then ruled by Denmark, began to resettle the island; however, the European influence remained slight. In 1815 Denmark lost Norway to Sweden, but it retained Greenland through an oversight by the Congress of Vienna. Underpopulated and economically unimportant, the island remained a forgotten outpost, mostly ignored by the Danish government. Danish rule was neither progressive nor consistent, and the indigenous peoples of the island suffered from tuberculosis and other European diseases.

An American naval officer, Matthew Perry, who would be famous for opening Japan to foreign trade in 1853–54, explored the northern coast of the island in the early nineteenth century, claiming the northern part of the island for the United States. The U.S. government in 1917 relinquished all claim to the territory when it purchased the Virgin Islands from Denmark. The United States, however, established military bases on the island during World War II, when Denmark was occupied by the Nazis. At the end of the war the Americans offered to purchase Greenland; the Danes refused but allowed the maintenance of American military bases, as part of a mutual defense treaty.

The Norwegian kingdom put forward claims to part of the island in 1931, on the basis of the Norwegian-descended population on parts of the coast. The Norwegians took the issue to the World Court in 1932. The World Court decided the case in favor of Denmark, which then reaffirmed ownership of the entire island.

The island's status changed to that of a Danish county on 5 June 1953. The benefits of the Danish welfare system that flowed from this change helped to eradicate the tuberculosis and other European diseases that had ravaged the population. Immigration from Denmark increased during the 1950s and 1960s, the influx generating an extensive ethnic mixing and intermarriage.

The generous Danish welfare system by the late 1960s was supporting many of the island's inhabitants, who felt that it did not pay to work.

Greenlander activists increasingly opposed welfare because of the culture of dependence that it created. The controversy sparked the first moves toward creating a regionalist movement. The Greenlanders, dependent on the products of the land and sea, actively opposed foreign investment and the development of the Arctic oil deposits. In 1972 the Greenlanders voted against Denmark's joining the European Community (EEC).

The opposition formed the first nationalist group, Siumut (Forward Party), in 1977, at the same time that the Danish government appointed a commission to work out home-rule statutes. Fearing that unchecked development threatened their culture and way of life, the nationalists mobilized. In a 1979 referendum 70% of the Greenlanders voted for home rule. On 1 May 1979, under the Greenlander name Kalaatdlit-Nunaat, Greenland became an autonomous state in association with the Danish crown.

Modern technology has brought much frustration to the formerly seminomadic Greenlanders, including urban living in the high-rise housing estates around the major towns, high rates of alcoholism, and venereal disease. The European lifestyle, imported from Denmark, has raised the standard of living and literacy, but the loss of the traditional culture has become a major nationalist issue.

Nationalists vehemently opposed the Danish government's retention of mineral rights in Greenland, as the island is the world's only source of cryolite, a mineral important in the manufacture of aluminum. By the early 1980s dissatisfaction was widespread and had won the support of many of the European inhabitants. In 1982 the islanders voted 52% to 48% to withdraw their autonomous state from the European Economic Community—the first, and so far only, territory to do so.

The island's three major political parties have different visions of the future. Siumut, a moderate socialist party, advocates a more distinct Greenlandic identity and greater autonomy from Denmark, possibly eventual independence. Atassut (Solidarity), with the support of the Danish minority, is pro-European and favors continued close ties to Denmark. Ataqatiqiit (Inuit Brotherhood) favors independence from Denmark and restriction of citizenship to the Greenlandic and Inuit population as the first step to the establishment of a transpolar Inuit state uniting all Inuit peoples. In March 1991 the Greenlanders rejected a move to renew their membership in the European Community. The defeat of the pro-European faction moved the island a step closer to eventual independence.

The Greenlanders suffered an economic downturn in the early 1990s, but since 1993 their economy has improved. The Greenland Home Rule Government (GHRG) has pursued policies that have produced low inflation and helped create surpluses in the public budget. However, since 1990, with the closing of the last remaining lead and zinc mine, the island has had a foreign-trade deficit.

In 1996, the Greenland government signed an oil-exploration agreement that gave four companies the concession to explore and extract oil from the Fylles Bank, 90 miles (150 km) west of Nuuk. The companies, including the government-backed Nunaoil, Inc., were optimistic about the quantity and quality of the region's reserves.

The Greenlanders are critically dependent on fishing and fish exports; about half the government revenues presently come in the form of grants from the Danish government. Although pro-independence forces have widespread support, the Danish subsidies will be difficult for the Greenlanders to renounce unless the oil reserves prove as rich as many hope.

SELECTED BIBLIOGRAPHY:

Caulfield, Richard A. *Greenlanders, Whales, and Whaling: Sustainability and Self-Determination in the Arctic.* 1988.
Nuttall, Mark. *Arctic Homeland.* 1992.
Smiley, Jane. *The Greenlanders.* 1994.
Steltzer, Lilli. *Inuit: The North in Transition.* 1985.

Guadeloupeans

Guadeloupéens; Guadeloupians

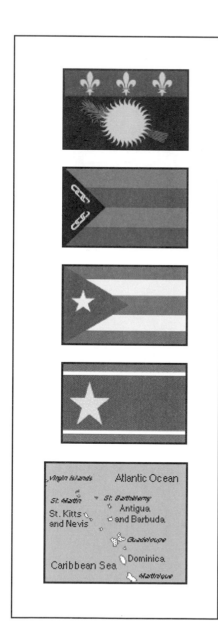

POPULATION: Approximately (2002e) 455,000 Guadeloupeans in the French Caribbean and metropolitan France. Most of the Guadeloupean population lives on the major island, Guadeloupe, with smaller populations on the dependent islands. The only sizable population outside the Caribbean is in France, mainly in the cities of Paris and Marseilles.

THE GUADELOUPEAN HOMELAND: The Guadeloupean homeland includes nine inhabited islands—Guadeloupe, made up of Grande-Terre and Basse-Terre, Marie-Galante, Desirade, the three Îles de Saintes, Saint Barthelemy, and the northern two-thirds of the island of Saint Martin. The islands of the Guadeloupe region are of volcanic origin—except for Grande-Terre, which is a low, limestone formation. The major island, Guadeloupe, is actually two islands, Grande-Terre and Basse-Terre, divided by a narrow channel. Guadeloupe, with its dependencies, forms an overseas department of the French republic. *Department of Guadeloupe:* 687 sq. mi.—1,779 sq. km, (2002e) 432,000—Guadeloupeans (including Creoles) 90%, French 5%, Chinese, East Indian, and Lebanese 3%, others 2%. The major cultural center is Pointe-à-Pitre, (2002e) 22,000, urban area 152,000. The other major cultural center is the capital of the region, Basse-Terre, (2002e) 13,000.

FLAG: The unofficial flag of the Guadeloupeans is a black field bearing a yellow sun over palm fronds with a broad blue stripe at the top charged with three yellow fleur-de-lys. The three major nationalist organizations have distinct flags. The People's Movement for an Independent Guadeloupe (MPGI) flag has four horizontal stripes of green and red with a black triangle at the hoist bearing a broken yellow chain. The Groupement des Organisations Nationalistes Guadeloupénnes (GONG) has a flag with five green and white stripes bearing a red triangle charged with a five-pointed white star at the hoist. The flag of the Popular Union for the Liberation of Guadeloupe (UPLG) is a red field with narrow green and white stripes at the top and bottom bearing a large five-pointed yellow star on the hoist.

PEOPLE AND CULTURE: The Guadeloupeans are mostly descended from African slaves imported to work the French plantations in the seventeenth and eighteenth centuries. A minority, called Creoles, is of mixed African and European ancestry and forms an economic elite. The population of the dependencies is more mixed, with a sizable European population descended from Bretons* and Normans* settled on Marie Galante and Les Saintes. The population of Saint Martin is also mixed, but with a Creole majority. There is a substantial French population, both native-born and from metropolitan France, called Metros. The population is growing at a slower rate than those of most island groups in the Caribbean. The birthrate is well below the average for the region, and the death rate is also comparatively low. Nearly a third of the population is younger than 15 years of age, and over half live in urban areas. The social-welfare system in effect in metropolitan France is also available in the islands, so health conditions are good, life expectancy is high, and education is widespread.

LANGUAGE AND RELIGION: The Guadeloupeans mostly speak a French patois called Creole or Lesser Antillean Creole. The patois, also called Patwa, is the language of daily life. French is the medium of government and education; it is spoken by an estimated 99% of the Guadeloupeans, with varying degrees of competence. The dialect spoken on Saint Barthelemy, popularly called St. Barts Creole, is distinct in grammar and usage and is not intelligible to the Creole speakers from other islands.

Most Guadeloupeans, an estimated 95%, are Roman Catholics, but traditionally they have mixed traditions brought from Africa into their religious belief system. Adherence to customs brought to the islands by the early African slaves is widespread; even members of the European-descended population participate in rituals and festivals. Protestant sects represent about 1% of the population, but evangelical groups incorporating African rituals and beliefs are gaining converts. There are small groups of Hindus, Muslims, and sects that were originally brought from Africa.

NATIONAL HISTORY: Christopher Columbus discovered the island in 1493 and named it for the monastery of Santa Maria de Guadelupe in Spain. Several Spanish attempts to colonize the islands in the sixteenth century were repulsed by the indigenous population. Due to the resistance of the inhabitants, fierce Caribs, the Spanish authorities ignored the island for over a century, formally abandoning attempts to colonize Guadelupe in 1604. In 1626, the Spaniards finally established a settlement on the coast, but they were driven away by French forces, who had established a trading post.

A French colony founded in 1635 survived and laid claim to the entire island, its claim contested by the English from the neighboring islands. After several years of conflict with the Caribs, the colony began to prosper. In 1674 Guadeloupe became part of the French Empire. Sweden, participating in the European scramble for colonies, sent settlers to St. Barthelemy, and Dutch, Danes, and other Europeans fought for island territories in the region.

The prosperity of the French islands, particularly Guadeloupe, required imported labor, because the native peoples disappeared under the impact of colonization. Norman and Breton farmers settled the smaller islands and worked small plots in the European manner, but Guadeloupe developed a plantation economy and an aristocratic planter society, dependent on slaves imported from Africa to work the vast sugar plantations.

The revolution in France in 1789 divided the island; the French royalists were aided by the British, who occupied the islands. Victor Hugues, an official of the French revolutionary government, arrived in Guadeloupe in 1794 and forced the British to withdraw. He proclaimed the abolition of slavery and set up a guillotine in the center of Pointe-à-Pitre. A reign of terror virtually eliminated the island's plantation aristocracy, leaving a population of a few poor whites and thousands of freed black slaves.

Slavery was reintroduced to Guadeloupe by Napoleon's government in 1802, setting off a serious slave revolt. Again occupied by the British in 1810, during the Napoleonic Wars, the islands returned to French rule in 1816. Economically devastated by the revolution and its aftermath, the colony became a neglected outpost of the French Empire.

Slavery was finally abolished in 1848, and the 93,000 slaves on the island were freed. The freed slaves adopted many aspects of French culture, but their native languages so changed the spoken French that a new dialect, called Creole, developed as the language of daily life. African influences also changed religious practices, as traditional beliefs became part of Christian services. The majority of the islanders remained poor subsistence farmers, generally ignored by the French colonial administration that controlled all aspects of the island's life and economy.

The Guadeloupeans supported the resistance movement of Gen. Charles de Gaulle during World War II. The government of metropolitan France at the end of the war moved to end the colonial status of its Caribbean islands. In 1946, Guadeloupe became a department of the French republic, theoretically equal to the departments of metropolitan France; however, the reality of island life remained the same—poverty, unemployment, and subsistence farming.

In the late 1950s, educated Guadeloupeans began to mobilize as the neighboring British islands moved toward independence. Appeals by the popular de Gaulle, who visited Guadeloupe in 1956, 1960, and 1964, managed to curtail the independence movement and convince many Guadeloupeans to remain within the French union. However, several nationalist organizations emerged to denounce French rule as disguised colonialism and to demand independence. The nationalists, critical of the region's high unemployment, underdevelopment, and overpopulation, won widespread support. In 1968 serious rioting and pro-independence violence rocked the island and led to mass arrests and the suppression of all nationalist activity. In order to alleviate the population problem, the French government encouraged the Guadeloupeans to migrate to metropolitan France.

Talks on greater autonomy, begun in the 1960s, slowed to a standstill during the 1970s. Disappointed nationalists abandoned the autonomy movement to join separatist organizations, which became increasingly violent. To curb the growth of national sentiment, the government stressed common French citizenship and dramatically increased economic subsidies. In 1974 Guadeloupe was given the status of a region of France. Economic aid eventually gave the islanders one of the highest standard of living in the Caribbean, but nationalist violence escalated notwithstanding, with attacks on French authority extending to Paris and the French heartland. Guadeloupean nationalists admitted that French citizenship and departmental status greatly benefited the islands. However, unrelieved poverty and unemployment continued to fuel nationalism.

The socialist victory in French elections in 1981 gave the island's government additional autonomy under a new socialist program of government decentralization. Numerous nationalist organizations, supported by the black majority, the Creoles, and the poorer whites, increasingly turned to violence during the 1980s. The nationalists, allied to the leftists and labor unions, instigated numerous strikes and demonstrations. In 1984 the French government rushed gendarmes to the islands to quell serious separatist violence. In 1987 separatist leaders established a National Council of the Guadeloupean Resistance (CNRG), which organized a provisional government of a future Republic of Guadeloupe.

The nationalists enjoyed widespread support in Guadeloupe, but nationalism was tempered by the knowledge that an end to the generous French government subsidies would bring tremendous economic hardship. The right-wing Guadeloupe Objective Party succeeded in obtaining an absolute majority, with 22 of the 41 seats in the regional assembly, in January 1993. The benefits of French departmental status may be too great a sacrifice for the majority of the Guadeloupeans, but that did not stop the nationalists from disrupting the region, calling a general strike in coordination with Martinicans* and Guianese* in January 1994 to protest French Government policies in the Antilles-Guiana region.

The region's economy remains heavily dependent on subsidies from the

French government, which account for as much as half of the island group's budget. Although Guadeloupean incomes are among the highest in the Caribbean, to a considerable extent they are provided by the French welfare system. Agriculture employs the majority of the population, with bananas as the major export, but local agricultural production cannot provide for the population, and food imports from metropolitan France remain a major governmental expense. In spite of the French government's often-reiterated determination to maintain Guadeloupe's present status, the lack of economic progress provided new stimulus to the separatists during the late 1990s.

Nationalist sentiment, although widespread, is tempered by economic reality. Few Guadeloupeans see much of a future for their islands should the generous French government subsidies end. Unemployment, underdevelopment, and subsistence farming remain the realities of daily life; separation from France promises self-determination but also a worsening economic situation.

SELECTED BIBLIOGRAPHY:

Goslinga, Marian. *Guadeloupe*. 1999.
Knight, Franklin W. *The Caribbean: The Genesis of a Fragmented Nationalism*. 1990.
Langley, Winston E. *The Troubled and Troubling Caribbean*. 1989.
Reno, Fred, ed. *French and West Indian: Martinique, Guadeloupe, and French Guiana*. 1995.

Guernseians

Guernesíais; Guernseians; Dgernesíais; Channel Islanders

POPULATION: Approximately (2002e) 67,220 Guernseians in the United Kingdom, most living in Guernsey and its dependencies and in England. There are sizable Guernseian populations, estimated to number over 30,000, living in other parts of the United Kingdom.

THE GUERNSEIAN HOMELAND: The Guernseian homeland forms part of the Channel Islands, Îles Normandes in the local dialects, which lie off the coast of Normandy in the English Channel. Guernsey is the westernmost of the islands, lying just 46 miles southwest of Cherbourg. The major islands are Guernsey, which covers 24 sq. mi. (62 sq. km) and has a population of (2002e) 60,500; the smaller islands of Alderney; and Sark. The Bailiwick of Guernsey includes all of the Channel Islands except Jersey and forms a crown dependency legally independent of the British government. The bailiwick is made up of the major island of Guernsey and the dependencies of Alderney, Herm, Sark, Brechou, Jetou, and Lihou. *Bailiwick of Guernsey:* 30 sq. mi.—78 sq. km, (2002e) 65,500—Guernseians 87%, English 10%, Normans* 2%, others 1%. The Guernseian capital and major cultural center is St. Peter Port, (2002e) 16,500, urban area 30,000.

FLAG: The Guernseian national flag, the official flag of the bailiwick, is a white field with a centered red cross bearing a gold Norman cross, the cross of William the Conqueror, superimposed on the red. The flag of Alderney, called Aurigny in the local dialect, is a white field bearing a centered red cross bearing a round green crest charged with a rampant gold lion. The flag of Sark, called Sercq, is a white field with a centered red cross bearing two Norman lions on the red quarter on the upper hoist.

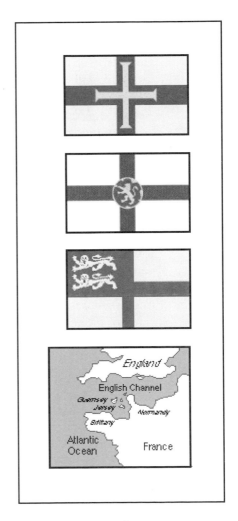

PEOPLE AND CULTURE: The Guernseians, Guernesíais in the local dialect, are the descendants of refugees from ancient Gaul, medieval Norman settlers, and a later admixture of English immigrants as well as Breton and Norman refugees from the medieval religious wars in nearby France. The majority of the population claim Norman ancestry, but on Alderney the English form a majority. The customs and traditions of Norman ancestors are still maintained. The modest national revival of the 1970s and 1980s began a concerted effort to revive the traditional culture and language. The Guernseians fear that without these efforts their culture and language will disappear within 50 years. Although the Guernseians appreciate the protection their ties to the United Kingdom provide, they remain very protective of their island and its culture, even to the point of claiming to dislike all "foreigners," particularly the English and the Jerseians.*

LANGUAGE AND RELIGION: The traditional language of the Guernseians is a local variant of Channel Island Norman French. The language is an archaic dialect of Norman French, the language spoken on the nearby French mainland. Isolated from the mainland, the dialect is quite different, with forms and words not found in standard Norman French. Although English has replaced French as the official language of the state, a group of closely related Norman dialects is still used in daily life, especially in rural districts. Each of the languages is a form of the Norman patois, and they vary from island to island. The dialects, which are older than modern French, are not part of the formal educational system, but increasingly language classes and schools are reviving them. A distinct dialect of English is the most widely used language on Guernsey and its dependencies, with the Guernsesías dialect still spoken in the rural districts. Standard French is also spoken in the islands. Aurignais, the dialect formerly spoken on Alderney, has already died out, the victim of the German evacuation of the island during World War II.

The majority of the Guernseians belong to the Anglican Church, with smaller numbers of Roman Catholics, Presbyterians, Baptists, Congregationals, and Methodists. The islands, often refuges for persecuted groups, have absorbed the religious beliefs of the refugees and now encourages tolerance of all religions.

NATIONAL HISTORY: The islands were inhabited in prehistoric times by Celts from the mainland. Such structures as cromlechs and menhirs indicate that an organized tribal society dominated the islands, but no central authority was ever developed. Under Roman rule, the islands formed part of the province of Gaul and were known as Sarnia. With the decline of Roman power the islands fell to invading Franks, Germanic tribesmen moving into the former Roman provinces in the fifth century A.D.

Christianity came to the islands in the sixth century, introduced by the island's patron saints, St. Helier and St. Sampson. The conversion of the population began the development of a culture and dialect distinct from those of the mainland, a process fostered by the isolation of the islands.

Norsemen, later known as Normans, who came to the islands from the region they had conquered on the mainland, seized the Channel Islands in the ninth century. In 1066 the Normans crossed the English Channel, today still called the Norman Channel by the Guernseians, and conquered England. Guernsey and the other Channel Islands were attached to the Norman kings of England. In 1204 Philip II of France annexed Normandy, but the islands, known as the Norman Islands, remained under English authority, the only part of historical Normandy to remain part of the English kingdom. The Channel Islands were put in charge of a warden and sometimes were granted to favored lords.

The French, claiming the islands as historical parts of Normandy, attempted to take control of the islands in the fourteenth century, but the English defeated the invasion; Guernsey, along with the other islands, remained English fiefs, except for 1338 to 1340, when they were held by the French. The English crown's claims to the islands were recognized by the French in the Treaty of Bretigny in 1360.

The Guernseians retained their Norman law, dialects, and culture in spite of increasing cultural and linguistic assimilation. The islanders, historically self-governing, remained subjects of the English monarchy but were not under the authority of the English parliament. Their personal union with the English crown reinforced their long tradition of independence and local self-government. From the end of the fifteenth century onward, Guernsey, with Alderney, Sark, and the smaller islands, were put under the rule of a captain, later a governor. From the restoration of the British monarchy after the Commonwealth period until 1825, the government of Alderney was separated from that of Guernsey, being granted in 1660 to Edward de Carteret.

Feudal customs were retained on Guernsey and the smaller islands as part of the traditional agricultural society. The famous Guernsey breed of cattle was developed in the eighteenth century, and dairy farming became a mainstay of the economy. To the present day, the breed is kept pure by law, which forbids the importation of other breeds.

The office of governor was abolished in 1835, and its duties were devolved to a lieutenant governor and eventually a bailiff. The bailiff presided over the Royal Court of Guernsey. Local law was declared by 12 *jurats*, permanent jurors. The Royal Court has survived substantially unchanged, administering laws founded on Norman traditions and local usage.

In the late nineteenth century Guernsey became a popular Victorian resort and retirement center. The island's subtropical climate, unique foreign culture, and beautiful scenery drew many English visitors and immigrants. The writer Victor Hugo, exiled from France, lived in St. Peter

Port from 1855 to 1870. By the turn of the century, Guernsey had developed as one of the premier resorts of the British Isles.

The Guernseians during World War I remained loyal to the British monarch, and many volunteered to fight in the British military, often in the trenches of nearby France. The islands were used as staging areas for British troops being sent to fight on the continent.

The Germans overran France in early 1940, forcing the British government to evacuate many of Guernsey's inhabitants before the Germans in July occupied the islands, the only British territory to fall to the Nazi tyranny. During five years of occupation, the Germans were unable to sway the Guernseians' loyalty to Britain. Severe German reprisals, including sinking barges filled with prisoners, became common as sabotage and anti-German activity increased. The population nearly starved, as food was confiscated by the occupation authorities. In May 1945 the islands were finally liberated by British troops, after the liberation of the French mainland.

In the postwar period, the islands quickly recovered. The inhabitants evacuated to the British mainland were repatriated. It was necessary to re-create the island economies, mainly on the basis of dairy farming and tourism. French claims caused long-standing dispute until the International Court of Justice confirmed British sovereignty in 1953.

The mild, sunny climate attracted new residents from Britain, bringing a substantial English minority into the population. During the 1950s and 1960s the islands flourished, on tourism and the export of early crops, mainly vegetables and fruits, for the British market. In 1958 Guernsey began to issue its own currency and stamps.

In the 1960s low taxes made Guernsey a major offshore tax haven and banking center. The traditional enmity between the Guernseians and Jerseians accelerated as rivalry in financial activity grew. Guernseians claim to dislike the inhabitants of Jersey even more than they dislike the mainland British.

In 1968 the British government appointed a commission to consider the relations of the Channel Islands with the Crown. The islanders lobbied for the status quo, preferring to remain a self-governing state, but with the British government retaining responsibility for defense and foreign affairs.

Until the 1970s, vegetable cultivation, particularly early tomatoes for the British market, was the major industry, but by the 1980s the Guernseians had diversified into other industries, such as precision instruments, kiwi fruit, flowers, and butterflies for collectors. Guersey's income tax has remained a flat 20% for over four decades, a much lower percentage than on the British mainland. In the 1980s the Guernseians became alarmed at the growth of population and severely restricted immigration, even for millionaires, with only a few self-supporting immigrants being allowed to settle in the islands each year.

The status of the bailiwick again came into question following the United Kingdom's entry into the European Economic Community (EEC) in 1973, but the islanders preferred to maintain their present status. The Guernseians remain attached to the British crown, in personal union, but not subject to acts of Parliament unless specifically mentioned. The British government is responsible for defense and foreign affairs; otherwise, Guernsey is an independent state. In the 1990s several groups formed specifically to encourage and protect Guernsey's independence and its distinct culture and dialects. The largest of the groups, L'Assembllaïe d'Guernesíais, gained widespread support. A minority favored full independence and membership in the European Union (EU).

The islands are not only a financial paradise but to the Guernseians an earthly one as well. There is almost no crime, pollution, or unemployment. The citizens of the bailiwick can still invoke "clameur de hars," invoking the help and protection of the feudal lord by reciting an old Norman plea.

A French flotilla of fishing boats sailed into the harbor at St. Peter Port in March 1993 to protest restrictions on fishing near the Channel Islands. Fishing boats from Guernsey and Jersey sailed into Cherbourg harbor on the French coast in protest a few days later, after officials repudiated the informal agreement reached in St. Peter Port by the local fishermen.

In the 1990s, French claims were revived, as sovereignty of the islands affects the allocation of economic rights, including to petroleum, on the continental shelf. The Guernseians, to counter French claims, have begun strengthening their autonomy and their ties to the British crown. Extended claims to territorial waters, opposed by the French government, were proposed in mid-2000, to include possible oil reserves.

SELECTED BIBLIOGRAPHY:

Briggs, Asa. *The Channel Islands: Occupation and Liberation 1940–1945.* 1995.
Carel, Toms. *Guernsey.* 1991.
Marr, L. James. *Guernsey People.* 1984.
Ogier, D.M. *Reformation and Society in Guernsey.* 1997.

Guianese

Guianans; Guyanais; Guyanes; Guyane Creoles

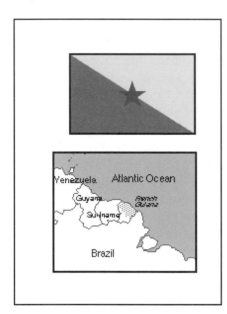

POPULATION: Approximately (2002e) 153,000 Guianese in French territory, mostly concentrated in French Guiana, but with a sizable population living in metropolitan France, particularly in Paris and Marseilles.

THE GUIANESE HOMELAND: The Guianese homeland, called French Guiana, lies on the northwestern Caribbean coast of South America. About four-fifths of the low-lying region is covered by dense jungle of hardwood trees. A fertile coastal plain lies along the Caribbean Sea, where the majority of the population is concentrated; the interior is largely uninhabited. French Guiana, popularly called Guyane, is a dependency of the French state, forming an overseas department of France. *Department of Guiana (Département de la Guyane)*: 33,399 sq. mi.—86,504 sq. km, (2002e) 177,000—Creole (mulattos and blacks) 66%, white Guianese 7%, French 5%, Amerindians 12%, East Indians, Chinese 10%. The Guianese capital and major cultural center is Cayenne, (2002e) 52,000, urban area 108,000. The other major center is Kourou, (2002e) 23,000, the center of the European Space Agency.

FLAG: The Guianese national flag, the flag of the national movement, is a diagonal bicolor of yellow over green, divided from the upper hoist to lower fly and bearing a large red five-pointed star centered.

PEOPLE AND CULTURE: The Guianese population is principally Creole, mulattos of mixed origins, with smaller populations of blacks, Europeans (many the descendants of prisoners released from the former prison colonies), Amerindians, the indigenous population of the territory, Haitians, and representatives of various Asian groups, including Chinese. Other groups, less tied to the territory, are the French administrators, police, and military, collectively known as "Metros." The culture of Guyane reflects the diverse background of the Guianese, a mixed Creole culture highlighted by brilliant, distinctive costumes; dances reflecting

African, Amerindian, East Indian, and eighteenth century French influences; and festivals, particularly the annual pre-Lenten carnival.

LANGUAGE AND RELIGION: The language of daily life, spoken by 90% of the population, is Creole (also called Guyane Creole), Guyanais, or simply Patois or Patwa. Even in Cayenne, the major urban area, over a third use the dialect as their first language. The language is a French patois incorporating borrowings from African and Amerindian languages. Most Guianese are bilingual to some degree, speaking Creole and standard French. Educated Guianese can speak the patois but try to avoid doing so, as it is perceived as a low-status dialect. A countermovement to standardize the dialect and win acceptance as the second official language gained support since the 1990s. Literacy in the region is about 83%. The black population also speaks a dialect called Taki-Taki or Sranan, which preserves many elements of the languages brought from African homelands.

Many religions are represented in Guiana, but the majority of Guianese are Christian, 90% Roman Catholic, with important Buddhist and Protestant minorities; some smaller groups, particularly the Amerindians, continue to adhere to traditional religious beliefs.

NATIONAL HISTORY: Sparsely inhabited by Amerindian peoples, mostly living in the jungle interior, the region became one of the last in South America to be colonized by Europeans. Amerigo Vespucci sailed along the coast in 1499, but Europeans thereafter avoided the region until 1604, when the French landed at the site of present-day Cayenne and claimed the territory for France. The native Amerindian people wiped out the first group of colonists, who had settled at Cayenne in 1643, but the French reestablished the colony in 1664. Captured by the Dutch in 1676, the region later returned to French control but remained largely unexplored and underpopulated.

During the eighteenth century, French authorities made several unsuccessful attempts to establish settlements in the territory. In the years after the French Revolution of 1789, the remote colony became a place of exile; the first penal colony there was created in 1834. Slavery was outlawed in 1848, increasing the demand for penal labor in the territory. Gold was discovered in 1853, but further settlement from Europe was deterred by the establishment of more penal colonies in 1854. The region became France's largest penal colony, with seven separate prison areas; the most notorious was known as Devil's Island, where deported convicts were imprisoned in dreadful conditions. Thousands of criminals peopled the vast penal colonies following enlargement of the system in the 1880s. More than 70,000 French convicts were deported to the penal colonies of French Guiana between 1852 and 1937. The nonprisoner inhabitants of the territory were granted French citizenship in 1877.

The colony, controlled by continental French administrators and police, grew slowly, its population augmented by freed slaves and released prisoners. French criminal law dictated that prisoners sentenced to eight years or more had to remain in Guiana after their release. The last prisoners arrived from France in 1937, as the government began to phase out the penal colony system.

In 1946 Guiana became an overseas department, and in 1951 the last of the penal colonies, Devil's Island, closed forever. General postwar stagnation in the region was offset by increased French government spending. In the 1960s the French government constructed a space research center at Kourou; the center and related facilities became the mainstay of the departmental economy, along with the generous government subsidies.

Autonomist sentiment spread in the mid-1970s. Nationalists demanded a loosening of the tight control of the department exercised by administrators and police sent from metropolitan France. Ordinary Guianese began to criticize the "Metros" (as they were called, to distinguish them from white Guianese born in Guiana), who received hardship pay during their terms of duty in Guiana. The continental French dominated all local government and virtually all economic activity.

In the late 1970s, *le Plan Vert*, the Green Plan, was adopted to encourage increased agricultural and forestry production. The vast hardwood forests, just beginning to be exploited, exemplified the wealth of natural resources. Increasing demands for greater local control of these resources marked the beginnings of the Guianese national movement, which began with organizations dedicated to winning control of the department's natural resources.

Newly organized political parties reflected the dispute over the control of local government. Diverse organizations represented pro-French unionists, autonomists, pro-independence nationalists, and later organizations employed violence and terrorism in campaigns to win independence for the territory. During the late 1970s and the 1980s, South American countries pressed France to decolonize the territory, the last European possession on the continent.

The French space center, considerably enlarged in the 1980s, became an issue of pride for the French government, a part of its attempts to compete with the other major powers. The center, increasingly thought of and used as a European space center, also became a major source of income—countries, industries, and government departments paid for to have their experiments and equipment launched into space; still, the facilities remained under the firm control of the French government, with little local participation other than as lower-level workers. Nationalist groups, led by the more radical activists, threatened to attack the French Space Center in 1983 and 1987.

The French government adopted a proposal to settle 30,000 French colonists in the territory by 1990, but only about 5,000 willing colonists were found. The colonists, mostly French civil servants, were given hardship pay and other incentives that caused great resentment among the local population. Nationalist demonstrations and violence increased in the 1990s. The French government dispatched military reinforcements to the region to quell separatist violence. Growing racism in France, including attacks on non-European Guianese, increased support for nationalism.

Nonetheless, the French budget subsidies and the income from the space center may be too much to give up. The local economy is tied closely to that of France, through subsidies and imports. Besides the French space center, now used by the European Union, at Kourou, fishing and forestry are the most important economic activities. The Guianese are heavily dependent on imports of food and petroleum, and inflation is high. Unemployment remains a serious problem, particularly among the young, where nationalist groups increasingly find willing recruits. A claim by neighboring Suriname to the area between Rivière Litani and Rivière Marouini threatens the territorial integrity of the department, with pro-French groups citing security as one of the major reasons to retain ties to metropolitan France.

The principal political party in the department is the Guianese Socialist Party (PSG), a pro-autonomy party allied to the French Socialists. Nationalist parties, such as the openly Marxist and pro-independence group Unité Guyanaise, are allowed to operate and have won considerable support; however, the violent nationalists of the National Liberation Front of Guyane have been banned, and their organization has been outlawed.

SELECTED BIBLIOGRAPHY:

Crane, Janet. *French Guiana*. 1998.
Miles, Alexander. *Devil's Island: Colony of the Damned*. 1988.
Redfield, Peter. *Space in the Tropics: From Convicts to Rockets in French Guiana*. 1994.
Reno, Fred, ed. *French and West Indian: Martinique, Guadeloupe, and French Guiana*. 1995.

Hadhramis

Hodromis; Hadramawtis; Hadramautis; Hadhramoutis; South Yemenis

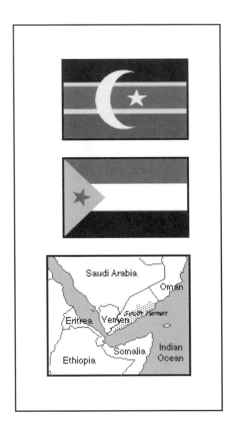

POPULATION: Approximately (2002e) 1,923,000 Hadhramis in Yemen, concentrated in the southern and eastern districts of the country. Outside the region there are large Hadhrami communities in Saudi Arabia, North Africa, and the Persian Gulf region.

THE HADHRAMI HOMELAND: The Hadhrami homeland lies in the southeastern Arabian Peninsula. The region is arid and hilly, with a long, sandy coast, from five to 10 miles (eight to 16 km) wide, on the Arabian Sea, climbing to the Hadhramawt Highlands and the Arabian Desert beyond. The highlands are divided by several wadi basins, the basins of seasonal rivers, including the perennial Wadi Hadhramawt. The Hadhrami homeland, popularly called South Yemen, has had no official status since the union of North and South Yemen in 1990. *South Yemen (Hadhramawt/Hadhramaut/Hadhramout)*: 128,559 sq. mi.—333,054 sq. km, (2002e) 2,586,000—Hadhramis 69%, Indians 10%, Somalis 7%, Adeni Arabs 7%, other Yemenis. The Hadhrami capital and major cultural center is al-Mukhalla, called Mukalla by the Hadhramis, (2002e) 156,000. The other important cultural center is Aden, called Adan locally, (2002e) 509,000, the former capital of South Yemen.

FLAG: The Hadhrami flag, the flag of the former Federation of South Arabia, is a horizontal tricolor of black, green, and blue, the stripes divided by narrow yellow stripes, and overall is imposed a large white crescent moon and five-pointed star. The Hadhrami flag, the flag of the former South Yemen republic, is a horizontal tricolor of red, white, and black, with a pale blue triangle at the hoist bearing a red five-pointed star. Both flags are used by various cultural and national groups.

PEOPLE AND CULTURE: The Hadhramis comprise a number of tribal groups representing various cultural and linguistic backgrounds. They are the descendants of the inhabitants of a number of distinct sultanates and emirates and are the most conservative of the Yemeni national groups. The Adeni minority is made up of the descendants of non-Yemeni Arabs who settled in Aden under the British. One of the legacies of British rule and the liberal policies of the former communist government is that Hadhrami women are among the most liberated and best educated in the Arab world and deplore the religious rules and tribal conventions that now restrict their freedom.

LANGUAGE AND RELIGION: The majority of the Hadhramis speak Arabic, with the Hadhramawt (Hodromi Spoken Arabic) and Adeni dialects of Yemeni Arabic the most frequently used. The Hadhramawt dialect is spoken in a number of regional varieties and has retained many archaic words and expressions. English is widely spoken by the Adenis and the non-Arab peoples.

The predominant religion is Sunni Islam, with the Shafa'i rite the most widespread. Religion is one of the major differences between the peoples of North and South Yemen; the northern tribes are mostly Zeidi Muslim, belonging to a Shi'a Muslim sect that the Sunnis consider heretical. There are small Ibadhi Muslims in the northern Hadhramawt. Many of the Hadhramis' pre-Islamic customs have survived. The traditions and customs of all Hadhrami Muslims are similar, and they freely worship in each other's mosques. The secular society that developed under the Marxist government remains influential; the number of atheists and nonpracticing Muslims in the region is unusual for the Arab world.

NATIONAL HISTORY: In ancient times an advanced civilization evolved, leaving behind extensive ruins in Hadhramawt; otherwise, however, the region's early history remains a mystery. In the first millennium B.C., Yemen was generally divided between the Qataban and Hadhramawt kingdoms. The ancient kingdom of Saba, or Sheba, had its capital at Marib in the Hadhramawt, a region that flourished before 800 B.C. The queen of Sheba is believed to have visited Solomon's Jerusalem around 950 B.C. The importance of the region in ancient times stemmed from its part in the incense trade. Ancient Adana, later called Aden, prospered as a port under Roman rule, but the interior tribes resisted entry by foreigners. The Hadhramis became part of the Himyarite kingdom that flourished from about 100 B.C. to A.D. 525. Around A.D. 400 the incense trade was diverted to the newly opened sea route via Aden and the Red Sea, isolating the overland trade routes and starting the decline of the Himyarite state, which eventually disintegrated into a number of small tribal entities.

In 525, Christian Abyssinians invaded from Africa, encouraged by the Byzantines to protect local Christians in the Himyarite kingdom. The Abyssinians destroyed the kingdom and converted many of the survivors to Christianity. Local rulers, opposed to rule from Africa, called on the

Persians, then active around Aden, for assistance. Around 570 the Persians took control, but the region continued to decline. The once-extensive irrigation system dried up, and the population dispersed throughout Arabia and beyond.

Muslim Arabs, in the first rapid expansion of Islam, overran the region and introduced the new religion to the pagan tribes between 628 and 632 A.D. The Persian governor of Sana'a, in northern Yemen, was the first important official to accept the new religion, which slowly spread throughout the tribal areas of the south. Many Hadhramis joined the great Arab armies that overran North Africa and invaded Europe through the Iberian Peninsula.

In the middle of the eighth century, a religious leader from Basra, in present-day Iraq, introduced the Ibadhi rite of Islam to the region. The rite was predominant for the next 200 years in the Hadhramawt states. Around 951 Sunni Muslims of the Shafa'i rite invaded the region, eliminating Ibadhism.

The expanding Ottoman Turks established a nominal rule over the region in 1538. Aden's port became a center of the Arab dhow trade between Africa and India, and a prized way station on the newly opened European trade routes to the East. In 1630, the local rulers asserted their authority, while remaining under nominal Turkish rule. The Hadhrami tribal peoples were ruled by a number of sultans and sheiks hostile to the outside world. Aden, under the autocratic rule of the sultans of Lahej, declined in the seventeenth and eighteenth centuries.

In 1809, puritanical Wahabi tribesmen invaded from the interior desert in present-day Saudi Arabia. They destroyed all mosques, seen as heretical, devastated many communities, and burned or dumped into wells valuable books and documents. The Wahabis soon withdrew under the threat of an Egyptian invasion. Many Hadhramis emigrated, becoming mercenaries in Muslim India or in other parts of the Arabian Peninsula.

Aden was an insignificant village when the British occupied the place in 1839, forcing the sultan of Lahej to cede it. The town slowly revived under British rule to emerge as a major entrepôt on the Indian and Asian trade routes, particularly after the opening of the Suez Canal in 1869. Aden rapidly became Britain's most important port east of Suez, and a major military base. The city, populated by non-Yemeni Arabs and non-Arabs, was administered as part of British India. To safeguard the port the British authorities between 1882 and 1914 signed protectorate agreements with the 19 tribal states of Hadhramawt. The tribal states were grouped into a Protectorate of Aden under a separate colonial authority. An Anglo-Turkish agreement in 1914 attempted to settle the boundary between Yemen (North Yemen) and the Aden Protectorate, but the border was not resolved until 1934.

After Turkey's defeat in World War I, Yemen gained independence under the feudal Zaydi family, which claimed all of historical Yemen, including British Aden and the protectorate (the Hadhrami states). The British rejected Yemeni demands and made Aden a separate crown colony in 1935, separating its government from British India in 1937.

During World War II the city, now a heavily fortified naval base, was granted a legislative council with limited autonomy, and in 1947 it became fully autonomous. In February 1959 the western Hadhramawt states united in a British-organized Federation of South Arabia, joined by the remaining states between 1959 and 1965. British moves to create a federation of tribal states and a separate Aden colony provoked impassioned opposition in Aden. By 1960 Aden was a city of 100,000, of which 75% were non-Yemeni Arab, 20% Hadhramawt Yemeni, with the remainder British, Indian, Pakistani, and Somali.

The sophisticated Adenis of the city-state, fearing domination by the reactionary leaders of the tribal Hadhrami states, demanded separate independence. Nationalists organized rival groups—the Front for the Liberation of South Yemen (FLOSY) and the National Liberation Front (NLF). In 1963 British preparations to merge Aden into the surrounding federation sparked a revolt by Adeni nationalists. On 7 September 1963 the nationalists declared Aden independent. British troops quickly ended the secession, and Aden became part of the federation, but with provision for renewed separation after seven years if the Adenis felt that their interests were being harmed. Friction between the Adenis and the Hadhrami majority immediately provoked violence. The NLF and FLOSY nationalists mounted terrorist campaigns against the British and the federation government, while also fighting each other for control of Aden and its port. Many Hadhramis in the city and from the tribal states joined, hoping to fight for the modernization of the region.

British troops withdrew from the entire federation, except turbulent Aden, in September 1967. In November fierce battles erupted in the city between the rival nationalist groups, and between the nationalists and the British military. Unable to control the situation, the British withdrew from Aden as well. The National Liberation Front, having eliminated all rivals, seized control of the city and on 30 November 1967 declared the independence of South Yemen. Leftists in control of the city, many from Hadhramawt, moved to overthrow the rulers of the various Hadhrami states and to impose their version of socialism on all of Hadhramawt.

In 1969 a radical faction of the NLF seized control, rapidly nationalizing the economy and strictly regimenting daily life. After 1970, North and South Yemen developed in radically different directions. North Yemen became an Arab republic based on the Egyptian model, while South Yemen, controlled by a radical Marxist faction, became the People's Democratic Republic of Yemen—the first Marxist state in the Arab world. Many Hadhramis who lost possessions through the nationalization policies of the Marxist government sought sanctuary in North Yemen. In 1979, following a second border war with the North Yemenis, the South Yemeni government granted the Soviet Union the right to use the abandoned British naval base at Aden.

The Marxist regime liberalized Muslim life but ruined the economy of the region. The sophisticated, urbanized Adenis abhorred the excesses of the Hadhrami-dominated government, labeling its policies "Bedouin socialism." In January 1986 a coup attempt provoked fierce fighting between rival factions in the city, leaving over 10,000 dead. In early 1989 the government admitted that the 21-year experiment in Marxism had failed.

The collapse of communist ideology in the Soviet Union forced the bankrupt Marxist government of South Yemen to accept unification on terms proposed by the rulers of North Yemen. The economic ruins left by Marxist experimentation made the union amount nearly to absorption. On 22 May 1990 the two Yemeni states merged. The Hadhramis, however, particularly the liberated women, were modern in comparison to the nearly feudal northerners, and though impoverished vehemently resisted the strict controls imposed by North Yemen.

In 1990 the Saudi government ordered the repatriation of all Yemeni nationals in retaliation for the anti-Saudi stance of the newly united Republic of Yemen, causing a major crisis. At the same time, a new oil field was found at Masila, between the coast and Wadi Hadhramawt. Large sums were invested to develop the infrastructure to support oil production, but the political situation prevented development.

The rifts between North and South widened immediately after unification. In the South the legacy of 137 years of British rule had shaped a separate national identity. In elections in May 1993, the more populous North prevailed, largely because the Socialist Party, the largest Hadhrami political party, boycotted the elections. In August 1993 the southern leaders, buoyed by increasing oil revenues, pushed for the decentralization of the Yemeni government. Rebuffed by the central government, the Hadhramis, led by Ali Salim al-Baidh, the former president of South Yemen, attempted to secede. On 4 May 1994 fighting broke out between rival military units. On 21 May 1994 southern leaders, supported by the Saudi government, declared the independence of South Yemen. After two months of civil war, victorious North Yemeni troops besieged Aden, bombarding the city from hills around the port. The civil war left over 10,000 dead in just 10 weeks of fighting.

Violent clashes broke out in May 1998 in Mukalla between police and supporters of a president of pre-unification South Yemen, Ali Salim al-Baidh, a native of Mukalla. The demonstrators protested death sentences passed in absentia on al-Baidh and 14 other Hadhramis who had led the secession attempt in 1994. Another eight defendants received long prison sentences. Police fired on the crowds in Mukalla, killing two people. The defendants were living in exile in neighboring states, but the trial allowed the government to grant a general amnesty to the thousands of Hadhramis who participated in the 1994 rebellion, in an effort to reconcile the two Yemeni peoples.

The demonstrators also protested falling living standards caused by cuts in state subsidies on essentials. Yemen is the most populous and poorest of the states of the Arabian Peninsula, with the limited development funds mostly going to projects in North Yemen. A system of patronage that favors the progovernment tribes of the North boosted the number of civil servants in the country from less than 600,000 in 1994 to over 900,000 in 1998.

Renewed unrest in Mukalla in 1998–99 stemmed from a government plan to divide the province of Hadhramawt. Soldiers fired on crowds, killing at least two people, and arresting a number of demonstrators, particularly following a series of bomb explosions in Aden and the Hadhrami cities of Lahej and Abyan. In October 1998, three Hadhramis were sentenced to death for involvement in an armed group in Hadhramawt and for having links to governments abroad.

The Socialist Party, which represents the southern Hadhramis, who resent northern Yemeni domination, again boycotted presidential elections in 1999. The Hadhramis remain politically fractured and do not present a united front to northern domination, but the resentment and anger that erupted in open rebellion in 1994 could repeat itself at any time, as conditions remain basically the same.

In May 2000, Yemen marked the 10th anniversary of the unification of the two Yemeni states, but resentment continues to simmer among the Hadhramis, a dangerous sentiment where the number of guns outweighs the population by three to one. Democracy has been declining since the attempted secession of South Yemen in 1994 and the civil war that followed. Extremist groups are gaining support. In October 2000, extremists bombed the USS Cole in Aden harbor, a crime tied to Osama bin-Laden, the terrorist leader suspected of planning and executing the terrorist attacks on the United States in September 2001.

SELECTED BIBLIOGRAPHY:

Bidwell, Robin. *The Two Yemens.* 1983.
Ismael, Tareq Y. *The People's Democratic Republic of Yemen: Politics, Economics and Society.* 1992.
Kostiner, Joseph. *Yemen: The Tortuous Quest for Unity, 1990–1994.* 1996.
McKinston-Smith, Tim. *Yemen: The Unknown Arabia.* 2000.

Haidas and Tlingits

Haadas; Kolosh; Haida and Tlingit Nation

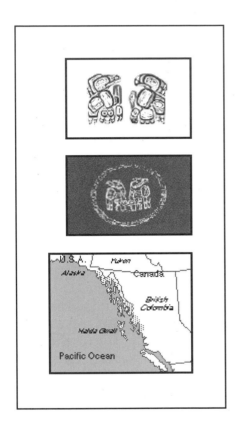

POPULATION: Approximately (2002e) 35,000—Haidas (11,000), Tlingits (18,000), and Tsimshians (5,000)—in northwestern North America, concentrated in the coastal regions of southern Alaska in the United States and northern British Columbia in Canada.

THE HAIDA AND TLINGIT HOMELAND: The Haida and Tlingit homeland lies in north-western North America, occupying the mainland and the 1,100 islands of the Alexander Archipelago in southeastern Alaska in the United States; and the mainland and the Queen Charlotte Islands of British Columbia in Canada. The coast is quite mountainous, and the climate is humid and tempered by warm ocean currents. The tribal lands, call Haa Ani (Our Land), have no official status pending the resolution of land and sovereignty claims in Canada and the United States. The Haidas call their homeland Haida Gwaii. The major cultural centers include the region's important cities, Juneau and Sitka in Alaska and Prince Rupert in Canada. Other important cultural centers are the chief villages of the Haidas, Skidgate and Masset; the settlements of Yakutat and Pelican in the Tlingit territory; and Metlakatla in Tsimskian territory.

FLAG: The flag of the Central Council of Tlingit and Haida is a white field bearing the tribal totems centered. The Haida flag is a red field bearing the national symbol centered, elaborate totem birds surrounded by a white oval of traditional Haida design.

PEOPLE AND CULTURE: The Haidas and Tlingits, including the Tsimshians, are a closely related group of tribes that inhabit the mainland and islands of southern Alaska and northern British Columbia. Although physically and culturally very closely related to the Tlingit and Tsimshian peoples of the mainland, the Haidas, due in part to the isolation of their island homeland have been able to preserve their culture, including customs and traditions that have disappeared on the mainland. The ancient tradition of the *potlatch* continues as an important example. The Haidas in Alaska are called Kaiganis. Among the Haida and Tlingits there are two major clans, or moieties, assigned at birth and based on maternal lineage. Each moiety consists of many local segments interconnected with the three closely related peoples. The Tlingits comprise 14 subdivisions, which may reflect a former era when they were independent tribes. The tribal groups traditionally produced elaborate totem poles carved with crests representing important events in family or clan histories. The totem poles were often used as memorials or housepoles in the large wooden structures that housed extended families. Potlaches, ceremonial distributions of gifts, still mark important events today.

LANGUAGE AND RELIGION: The Haida language, called Xaadas, is an isolated language, the only representative of the Skittagetan language family of the Na-dene language group. Haida is spoken in two major dialects, Skidegate and Masset, or Northern Haida. Tsimshian is divided into Southern Tsimshian, Coastal Tsimshian, Niska, and Gitksian. The Tlingits and Tsimshians speak closely related languages of the Na-dene group. In 1990 only about 500 people could still speak the Haida language. In 1991 language courses in the indigenous languages were begun in local schools. English is more widely used than the indigenous languages, particularly among the younger population. There has been a growing interest in reviving the languages in recent years.

The Haidas, Tlingits, and Tsimshians are now mostly Christians, as the result of the presence of missionaries in the nineteenth century. Many of the Tlingits and Haidas in Alaska are Russian Orthodox. Pre-Christian beliefs, including the veneration of spirits, continue to be important. Spirits are thought to have inhabited the world before the coming of man. Traditionally, ceremonies passed the time during long, rainy winters, as well as provided for the social needs of the people. At one time laws stopped the traditional ceremonies, but since their repeal there has been a renaissance of local culture and religion.

NATIONAL HISTORY: The islands off the coast of North America, settled tens of thousands of years ago by migrants crossing the ancient land bridge from Asia, formed the center of a sophisticated culture. Thickly wooded and with temperate climates and heavy rainfall, the islands supported a large population, with abundant salmon as the staple food. Skilled artisans, the indigenous peoples erected elaborately carved totems and built cedar-plank canoes, some measuring up to 70 feet in length. The Haidas, Tlingits, and Tsimshian, living in a resource-rich region, had time to develop elaborate ceremonies and craft ritual objects. They occupied the region for tens of thousands of years before the arrival of the Europeans. Fiercely territorial peoples, the Haidas, Tlingits, and Tsimshian, in carved war canoes, defended their territories and engaged in the cannibalistic rituals associated with warfare in that place and time.

The northwestern peoples evolved a highly stratified society of chiefs, nobles, commoners, and slaves. The potlach, a public dispensation of personal wealth, was a winter ceremony characterized by the giving of gifts, usually copper plates and elaborate goat-hair blankets. The ceremony brought the giver of the gifts great community respect. Custom demanded that a gift be acknowledged by an even larger or more valuable gift. The potlatch formed a basic feature of the highly evolved culture of the tribes of the islands and coastal region.

Skilled boatbuilders, the Haidas, Tlingits, and Tsimshian traveled great distances up and down the coast. In the early seventeenth century a group of Haida warriors drove the Tlingits from the islands to the north of Haida Gwaii, later called the Queen Charlotte Islands. A group of Haida colonists settled the southern part of the large island, later Prince of Wales Islands, calling themselves Kaigani. The streams of the new land were too small for the traditional salmon harvest, forcing the northern Haida, like the Tlingits, to take to the sea in search of halibut and cod.

The tribes constructed some of the largest gabled houses in ancient America, many measuring up to 60 feet by 100 feet. Haida society was organized in households, in which dozens of extended families lived together in large cedar houses. The Tlingits and Tsimshians relied on whales for fuel and food. The Haida never pursued whales but relied on candlefish for cooking and lamp oil.

Exploration of the northern area by Vitus Bering and Aleksei Chirikov in 1741 prompted the Spanish to send an expedition of their own, under Juan Pérez Hernández, from Mexico up the coast in 1775. Over the next decade other Europeans visited the region, marveling at the sophisticated society and trading for the valuable furs. An Englishman, George Vancouver, surveyed the coast in detail from 1792 to 1794.

Russian traders and trappers established posts in the northern islands about 1775. In 1799 a fort was constructed in Tlingit territory, but the Tlingits drove the Russians out. Russian troops led by Alexandr Baranov later recaptured the fort, killing many of the Tlingit defenders and beginning a long history of conflict between the Russians and the Tlingits of the northern districts. The Russians extended their authority south to Haida and Tsimshian territory in 1802, setting off intense European rivalry for control of the region.

Sitka, founded as Novoarkhangel'sk in 1804 in Tlingit territory, became the center of Russian America. In 1821 the Russians laid claim to the entire region south to the 51st parallel. A compromise in 1824 set the boundary at 54°40' north latitude, the present boundary between Alaska and British Columbia. The compromise partitioned the homelands of the Haidas, Tlingits, and Tsimshians. The largest area, under British administration, experienced a more lenient rule than the harsh authority exercised by the Russians over the Haidas and Tlingits of the northern districts.

In 1780 the indigenous population numbered about 30,000. Although not greatly affected by European influences until the arrival of fur traders and hunters in the early nineteenth century, the tribes were decimated by the diseases, the loss of traditional community relationships, and alcohol introduced by the Europeans. In the north, the brutal Russian colonial rule was particularly hard on the indigenous peoples. A century after European colonization only 6,000 Tlingits, 4,000 Tsimshians, and 2,000 to 2,500 Haidas survived.

Missionaries set up stations and schools in the region between the 1850s and the 1870s, gaining considerable influence over the survivors and aiding in a cultural and national revival. Mission schools introduced many of the survivors to the English language and European customs.

A long decline began to reverse after World War II. Employment in the factories established for the processing and canning of the region's rich fishing harvest stabilized the economic base. In the 1950s the tribes began to press land claims in both Canada and the United States. The campaign to win control of their ancient homelands stimulated demands for tribal sovereignty and promoted closer ties to other native American peoples and indigenous groups in Alaska and British Columbia.

The 1985 Pacific Salmon Treaty between the United States and Canada regulated the salmon fishing in the entire North Pacific coast. The U.S. states of Alaska, Washington, and Oregon, and the Canadian province of British Columbia, as well as the indigenous tribes that ply the northwestern fisheries, were required to agree on measures taken under the accord. The need for such wide consensus has effectively precluded specific agreements, so the Haidas, Tlingits, and Tsimshians have ignored treaty strictures. The chronic failure of dozens of negotiators representing commercial, sport, and tribal fishermen to reconcile their differences on exploiting salmon resources has frustrated the tribal peoples, who consider salmon fishing an integral part of their culture.

In 1991 a judge in British Columbia ruled that aboriginal title to lands in the province had been extinguished by the simple fact of colonial rule. The ruling stimulated new demands for a compromise with the provincial government over the pending land claims and tribal sovereignty. Tribal activists in the late 1990s organized demonstrations, boycotts, and strikes.

The border between the United States and Canada, which divides the three small nations, is still in dispute. Canada recognizes the 1903 boundary at 54°40', known as the "AB Line"—the Alaska–British Columbia Line. The United States contends that the boundary lies some 25 miles south, equidistant from Canada's Graham Island and Prince of Wales Island. The prize is the rich fishing zone of a strait called Dixon Entrance, traditional fishing grounds of the indigenous peoples of the area. The tribal claims to sovereignty include the control and management of the natural resources of the area under dispute. Destruction wrought by mining, whaling, and timber companies has outraged activists, who seek control over the development of these rich natural resources. The activists refuse to recognize the boundary between Alaska and British Columbia and continue to press their ancient right to the land and sea, rights that if recognized would make academic the disagreement over the exact placement of the international border.

The Central Council of the Tlingit and Haida is a sovereign entity, with a government-to-government relationship with the U.S. government. Headquartered in Juneau, Alaska, the council is increasingly becoming a voice for all three of the tribes that straddle the Canadian-U.S. border. The council evolved over the last 50 years from the knowledge that alone the tribes were weak but that united they gained strength. The government of British Columbia, which has so far refused to recognize indigenous land claims, is a particular target of activists associated with the council.

One of the most emotive nationalist issues is the desire of the indigenous peoples of the region to change officially the names of the islands, territories, and other landmarks of their homeland from what they consider to be absurd monarchical names, such as the Queen Charlotte Islands and Prince of Wales Island. The campaign to restore indigenous names, arguing that two centuries of colonialism is embodied in the foreign names, has won widespread support among all groups in the region.

SELECTED BIBLIOGRAPHY:

Ames, Kenneth M., and Herbert D.G. Maschner. *Peoples of the Northwest Coast: Their Archeology and Prehistory.* 1999.
Durlach, T.M. *The Relationship Systems of the Tlingits, Haida, and Tsimshian.* 1974.
Goldschmidt, Walter Rochs, ed. *Haa Aani, Our Land: Tlingit and Haida Land Rights and Use.* 1999.
Kosh, A.M. *Alaska Native Cultures: Tlingit, Haida, Tsimshian.* 1994.

Hausas

Habes; Haussas; Haoussas; Hausawa

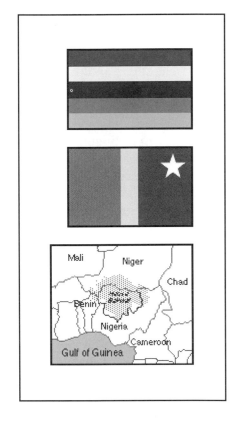

POPULATION: Approximately (2002e) 39,315,000 Hausas in West Africa, 30,435,000 in Nigeria, 5,883,000 in Niger, and smaller populations in Benin, Togo, Cameroon, Ghana, Sudan, and Burkina Faso. There are sizable Hausa communities in the United Kingdom and the United States.

THE HAUSA HOMELAND: The Hausa homeland, called Hausaland, occupies an upland area of plains in Nigeria in West Africa, drained by the Niger River and its tributaries. The region, lying north of the Jos Plateau in Nigeria, extends into Niger and west into Benin. Lying just south of the Sahara, the area is mostly dry savanna, with more fertile land along the rivers. The Hausa heartland comprises the Nigerian states of Bauchi, Jigawa, Kaduna, Katsina, Kano, Sokoto, Kebbi, Niger, Zamfara, and the Federal Capital Territory. *Hausaland (Hausa Bakwai)*: 134,204 sq. mi.—347,587 sq. km, (2002e) 45,160,000—Hausa 70%, Fulani 21%, Nupe 4%, other Nigerians 5%. The Hausa capital and major cultural center is Kano, (2002e) 1,594,000, metropolitan area 2,615,000. The major cultural center of the Hausas in Niger is Zinder, (2002e) 191,000. Other important cultural centers are Zaria, (2002e) 888,000, Kaduna (2002e) 1,452,000, Katsina (2002e) 389,000 and Sokoto (2002e) 503,000 in Nigeria; and Maradi, (2002e) 176,000, in Niger.

FLAG: The Hausa national flag, the flag adopted by nationalists in 1966, has five horizontal stripes of red, yellow, indigo blue, green, and khaki (beige). Some nationalists use the Kano flag, a vertical bicolor of red and blue divided by a narrow yellow stripe and bearing a white, five-pointed star on the upper fly.

PEOPLE AND CULTURE: The Hausas are the largest national group in Nigeria and one of the largest in West Africa. Their culture, displaying obvious Arabic influences, is a Saharan culture incorporating Islam as an integral part of its traditions and customs. The Hausas are mostly rural or live in small towns, though they have a long urban tradition and large, ancient cities, such as Kano and Sokoto. Hausa social organization is characterized by a complex system of stratification, based on occupation, wealth, birth, and important patron-client relationships. The Hausas are divided into three distinct subgroups: the Hausawa, forming the majority; the Tazarawa; and the non-Muslim Maguzawa. By Hausa tradition, all Hausas are descended from the legendary Bayajida (Abuyazidu), although the modern Hausas are racially diverse due to their long history of mixing with other ethnic groups. Many Hausas, often called Hausa-Fulanis due to their close historical and ethnic ties to the Fulanis, are of mixed sedentary and pastoral backgrounds. A Hausization of the Muslim populations of neighboring regions is progressing. Hausa is spoken as the second or trade language, and dress patterns, residential arrangements, and other cultural features are being adopted by non-Hausa groups. It is now difficult to distinguish between the Hausa and the originally lighter-skinned Fulani, as extensive mixing has blurred the ethnic, cultural, and linguistic differences between the two Muslim peoples.

LANGUAGE AND RELIGION: The Hausa language is a West Chadic language of the Afro-Asiatic language group. The Hausa language is the lingua franca of much of West Africa, spoken or understood by over 55 million people. The language is spoken in three major dialects—Eastern, Western, and Northern Hausa—and in numerous subdialects. The dialects are infused with many Arabic words as a result of Islamic influences. Standard literary Hausa is based on the dialect of Kano. Formerly written in an Arabic-based Ajami alphabet, since the early decades of the twentieth century much of the written material has been written in an orthography based on the Roman alphabet.

The majority of the Hausas are Sunni Muslims, but they incorporate many pre-Islamic traditions and customs into their Islamic rituals. The traditions of Islam are very strong, and Hausa men and boys, no matter what they are doing, stop and pray five times a day as required. Islam governs the Hausa outlook as well as daily activities. A minority who do not follow Islam are called Maguzawas. They worship native spirits known as *bori* or *iskoki*. Belief in witchcraft and sorcery remain part of daily life, particularly in the rural areas.

NATIONAL HISTORY: The Hausa, according to oral tradition, migrated from the northwest in ancient times. Settling along the northern tributaries of the Niger River, they developed an advanced civilization with a strong urban tradition, which was unusual in sub-Saharan Africa. Their settlements, at the crossroads of the trade routes of western and northern Africa, developed as independent city-states with centralized governments. The Hausa city-states united between the eleventh and thirteenth centuries to form a confederation of seven states—Kano, Zaria or Zazzau, Katsina, Daura, Rano, Gobir, Biram—and later Kebbi. Wars between the various city-states over trade and territory were common.

The Hausa cities, at the southern terminus of the Saharan caravan routes, carried on extensive trade with North Africa. Arab traders coming south with the caravans introduced Islam in the mid-fourteenth century. A Muslim prohibition against enslaving fellow Muslims facilitated the rapid spread of the religion. Muslim slavers, often employed by the Hausa emirs, raided the pagan tribes to the south, sending thousands of captives north. Islam strengthened Hausaland's monarchical systems and distant commercial contacts.

Fulani nomads from the northwest began to move into the region in the seventeenth century. Refusing to pay tribute to the local emirs, the nomads in 1801 took control of the leading Hausa state, Sokoto, in a *jihad*, or holy war, under the leadership of Uthman dan Fodio. The Fulani conquerors firmly established the predominance of Islam in the Hausa territories even beyond the traditional Islamic strongholds in the urban centers. The Fulanis established the Sokoto Caliphate, an empire that ultimately incorporated some 15 emirates, each headed by a ruling dynasty of Fulani origin. The major commercial center developed at Kano, which was the greatest commercial power in West Africa by the 1820s.

The deposed Hausa dynasties of Zaria and Katsina set up new states at Abuja and Maradi, and a third Hausa state was established at Argunga. In these three Hausa states, north and south of the traditional ones, Hausa culture survived largely untouched by Fulani influence. Many Hausas moved to the west or north to escape domination by the less sophisticated, pastoral Fulanis. The Fulani conquerors progressively adopted the sedentary ways, language, and other customs of the Hausas, and intermarriage between the two Muslim peoples became common. Gradually the term "Hausa" came to be used for both the original Hausa population and the acculturated Fulani aristocracy.

The supremacy of the Hausa region began to decline by the 1880s due to a reduction in trade caused by changing political conditions, the end of the slave trade, and the arrival of Europeans. The British, after decades of controlling the southern coastal regions, began to establish relations with the Hausa emirs in the mid-nineteenth century. In 1885 the sarduana of Sokoto, the spiritual and temporal leader of the region, signed a treaty with the British. The treaty marked the beginning of the British penetration of Hausaland.

French forces moved into the northern Hausa states, capturing Zinder and other cities in 1899. In 1903 the British authorities took direct control of the southern Hausa states, which were joined in a newly created Kano province. In 1906 British forces defeated a Hausa attempt to expel them.

The British admired the Muslims and preferred to control the region indirectly, retaining the traditional administrative structures. Christian missionaries, forbidden to enter the North, concentrated their efforts among the southern pagans; missionary education gave the southern tribes a definite advantage over the northern Hausas. On 1 January 1914, Northern Nigeria was amalgamated with the Protectorate of Southern Nigeria to form the colony and protectorate of Nigeria.

The northern Hausa-dominated region remained traditional and feudal, while the southern Yorubas,* Ibos,* and other mainly Christian peoples rapidly modernized. Educated Christians from southern Nigeria, more familiar with European ways, moved north in large numbers to fill northern administrative and clerical positions spurned by the proud Hausas. Feudal and traditional, the Hausas paid education little attention; only 251 students were attending secondary schools in Northern Nigeria in 1947.

Between 1945 and 1950, rioting occurred resulting from protests of the northern amalgamation with the southern regions. The Hausa leaders belatedly realized that the Northern Region had fallen behind the Western and Eastern Regions of the Christian south. In 1949 the Muslims launched their own political party, the Northern People's Congress (NPC). The postwar political mobilization is considered the beginning of modern Hausa nationalism. When oil was discovered in the Ibo-dominated Eastern Region, the Emirs of Zaria and Katsina demanded a share for northern development projects and 50% of the seats in the newly formed Central Legislature. The emirs threatened to secede if their demands were not met. The acceptance of these demands by the colonial authorities signaled the beginning of Hausa domination of Nigerian national politics.

In the 1950s the Muslims made an effort to catch up with the South, but they were already decades behind. The economic and political disparity between the Muslim northerners and the Christian southerners incited a growing resentment and provoked increasingly violent incidents. The Hausa leaders, claiming that the British favored the southern regions, threatened secession in 1953 as African nationalism and anticolonial sentiment took hold in Nigeria.

British Nigeria's three regions, each dominated by rival tribes, joined a political confederation in 1954 and won full independence from the United Kingdom in 1960. The new Nigerian government, dominated by the numerically predominant Hausa, incited strong opposition in the Christian south. In 1966 a coup by southern officers overthrew the government, and a new regime, dominated by the southeastern Ibos, took control. Rioting swept the North; violent attacks on southerners, especially Ibos, left hundreds dead.

The Hausas, vehemently opposed to domination by a tribe they had once taken as slaves, prepared a plan, code-named *Araba*, meaning Secession Day. The northern leaders planned to reassert Muslim control of Nigeria or, alternatively, to proclaim the secession of a Republic of Hausa.

Before the chosen day, 29 July 1966, a new Nigerian government, headed by a northern Christian, considered a neutral in the regional conflicts, proposed a compromise acceptable to the Hausa leaders—a loose confederation of the Nigerian regions. In September 1966, before the compromise took effect, rioting again spread across the North, with the rioters joined by Muslim soldiers. Over 30,000 Ibos died in the riots, and a million fled back to their homeland in the Eastern Region. The Hausa leadership evacuated all northern civil servants and military personnel from the federal capital at Lagos and prepared to declare Northern Nigeria independent of Nigeria. The proclamation, overtaken by the Ibo declaration of the secession of the East as the Republic of Biafra, was put aside. The Muslims regained their predominance in the government and military, which finally defeated the Ibo secession after a three-year civil war that ended in 1970, leaving over a million dead and hundreds of thousands injured or displaced.

Muslim fundamentalism rekindled Hausa nationalism in the 1980s. The new Hausa militancy, spurred by rising Islamic fundamentalism, set off periodic ethnic and religious clashes across the Hausa homeland. International pressure to restore democracy after decades of Muslim-dominated military governments inserted new strains into the relationship between Nigeria's Christian south and the Hausa-dominated Muslim north. The volatile mix of religion and ethnic tension, exacerbated by political segmentation, renewed the nationalisms that nearly tore Nigeria apart three decades ago.

The precolonial emirates that dominated Hausaland remained major features of local government in the 1990s. Hausa society, to a large extent, remained feudal, politically and socially. Local loyalty and regionalism fractured the Hausa national movement.

Fundamentalist Islam and the increasing resentment of the Hausas by other Nigerian ethnic groups threatened to divide Nigeria along ethnic and religious lines. Thousands died in ethnic rioting in the Hausa states of Northern Nigeria in 1991. The Hausa domination of the military, which has ruled Nigeria for much of the period since independence in 1960, has allowed the Hausas to dominate the country. Their influence began to wane when a new president, Olusegun Obasanjo, began to purge the military in June 1999. The threat to the Hausa domination of Nigeria was one of the reasons behind bloody ethnic rioting that spread throughout Hausaland in July 1999, mainly directed at the mostly Christian Yorubas.

The adoption of strict Sharia law in October 1999 by one of the Hausa-dominated northern states set off a new round of ethnic and religious violence. In February 2000, violence between Hausa Muslims and immigrant Christian groups in the region left hundreds dead or injured. Thousands of Christians fled south or sought refuge in military or police bases. Sharia law became part of the revival of Hausa nationalism at the turn of the twenty-first century. The growing religious element in the opposing nationalisms in Nigeria is making reconciliation and compromise ever more difficult, as the major national groups, divided by historical and religious factors, increasingly go their own ways. On 21 June 2000, the largest and most important state in Northern Nigeria, Kano, held a ceremony and a public holiday to celebrate the introduction of Sharia law. The proclamation prompted many of the state's Christians to leave for the Christian southern states. In late 2000, the Nigerian government asked several northern states to suspend the imposition of Muslim Sharia law, but despite that and Christian protests, Sharia was imposed in a number of Hausa-dominated states.

The Hausas increasingly complain of being marginalized by the Obasanjo government. After decades of Hausa-dominated military governments in Nigeria, many Hausas now see their power draining away toward the Christian southern provinces. The volatile mix of religion, ethnic nationalism, and perceived marginalization has stimulated the growth of nationalism across the region. Disgruntled military officers, serving and retired, are reportedly providing the growing number of private Hausa armies with sophisticated weapons. These paramilitary forces seriously threaten the country's new democratic government.

Severe rioting followed the American attack on the Taliban administration in Afghanistan in October 2001. The attack, in response to the terrorist attacks of September, were seen by many Hausa religious leaders as an attack on Muslims. Fighting and attacks on Christians left many dead and injured before the Nigerian miliary was able to restore order. Disgruntled Hausa military officers, serving and retired, are said to be providing the growing "private armies" with sophisticated weapons, which seriously threaten Nigeria's budding democracy and territorial integrity.

SELECTED BIBLIOGRAPHY:

Badru, Pade. *Imperialism and Ethnic Politics in Nigeria, 1960–96.* 1998.
Kirk-Greene, A.H. *The Hausa Emirates.* 1972.
Miles, F.S. *Hausaland Divided: Colonialism and Independence in Nigeria and Niger.* 1994.
Okehie-Offoha, Marcellina Ulunma, ed. *Ethnic and Cultural Diversity in Nigeria.* 1996.

Hawaiians

Hawai'ians; Kanaka Maoli

POPULATION: Approximately (2002e) 350,000 Hawaiians and part-Hawaiians in the United States, concentrated in the Hawaiian Islands, but with a sizable community, estimated at over 100,000, living on the U.S. mainland. Nationalists claim a much higher population identifying with Hawaiian culture and the Hawaiian Nation; the legal definition of Hawaiians is limited to those with at least 50% Hawaiian blood.

THE HAWAIIAN HOMELAND: The Hawaiian homeland is an archipelago lying in the central Pacific Ocean, 2,397 miles (3,857 km) west of San Francisco just south of the Tropic of Cancer. The islands (eight major islands and 124 islets) are the tops of a chain of submerged volcanic mountains. Hawaii is one of the fifty states of the United States of America. The islands are dominated by Oahu, with the majority of the population, the seat of government, and the state's only large city. *State of Hawaii (Ka Pae 'Aina O Hawai'i/Hawaiian Archipelago)*: 6,471 sq. mi.—16,764 sq. km, (2002e) 1,213,000—Japanese 24%, Caucasians 23%, Hawaiians (and part-Hawaiians) 20%, Filipinos 11%, Chinese 5%, Eastern Samoans* and other Pacific Islanders 3%, others 14%. The Hawaiian capital and major cultural center is Honolulu (2002e) 371,000, metropolitan area 889,000. The other important cultural center is Hilo (2002e) 41,000, the major city on the largest of the islands, Hawaii (Hawai'i).

FLAG: The Hawaiian national flag is a horizontal tricolor of white, yellow, and black, the yellow twice the width of the white and black, and bearing a Kahili symbol centered. The flag of the largest national move-

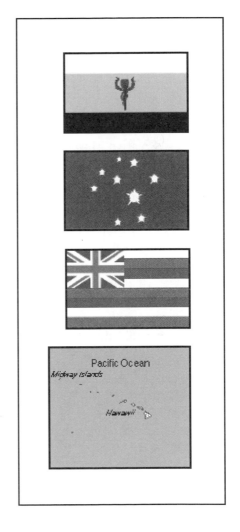

ment, Ka'lahui Hawai'i, is a dark blue field bearing a constellation of nine white 15-pointed stars. The official flag of the state has eight horizontal stripes of white, red, blue, white, red, blue, white, and red; it is charged with a canton on the upper hoist bearing the British Union Jack. It is the only U.S. flag to have flown over a kingdom, a republic, a territory, and a state.

PEOPLE AND CULTURE: The Hawaiians, including the part-Hawaiians who identify with Hawaiian culture and history, are now the third-largest ethnic group in the islands, and the state's least advantaged. Only about 10,000 are full-blooded Hawaiian; the remainder are part-Hawaiians. Nationalists claim that people of pure Hawaiian blood account for 10% of the total population of the islands. The Hawaiians are Polynesians, known for fine physiques and attractive features. Historically the ruling classes tended to inbreed; polygyny and polyandry were practiced, especially among the chiefs. Rank traditionally descended through the maternal line. Over 40 ethnic groups are now represented in the islands. Native Hawaiians are generally poorer and less well educated than other residents of the state. They also suffer disproportionately from health problems and are overrepresented in the state's prison population. The Hawaiian culture emphasizes living off the land, but they are denied the right to live on almost any of their ancestral lands.

LANGUAGE AND RELIGION: The Hawaiian language, 'Olelo Hawai'i or 'Olelo Hawai'i Makuahine, is a Polynesian language of the Marquesic branch of the Malayo-Polynesian language group. The language resembles that of the Maoris* of New Zealand, which was also colonized from the Polynesian heartland in Tahiti and Samoa. In 1900 there were 37,000 Hawaiians who considered it their mother tongue, but by 1990 only about 8,000 fluent speakers remained. The majority of the Hawaiians are trilingual, speaking their own Polynesian language and English plus a mixed dialect called pidgin or Hawai'i Creole English, which is understood by 60% of the state's population, including between 100,000 and 200,000 who do not speak standard English well. Teaching in the Hawaiian and pidgin languages has become widespread since the 1980s.

The majority of the Hawaiians are Christians; Protestant denominations brought to the islands in the nineteenth century claim the largest congregations. Traditionally the Hawaiians had a vague belief in a future existence, four principal gods, and innumerable lesser gods. Hardly anything was undertaken without elaborate religious ceremonies.

NATIONAL HISTORY: Hawaiian tradition places the arrival of Polynesian colonists from the Marquesas sometime between the fifth and ninth centuries A.D., although they may have discovered the islands about A.D. 400. The settlers slowly spread through the uninhabited islands of the chain. A later wave of colonists, from Tahiti, reached the islands between the twelfth and fifteenth centuries. Once established in their new land, the new colonists had no need to obtain supplies from their old homeland; centuries of isolation began, and a degree of racial separation arose. Separate kingdoms, established on each of the major islands, carried on sporadic wars.

Without metals, pottery, or beasts of burden, the Hawaiians made implements and weapons from stone, wood, teeth, and bone. Great skill was displayed in the arts and in local industries, such as fish farming. Their year was based on 12 lunar months, beginning on 20 November, with an occasional intercalary month. The early Hawaiians excelled at sports, including surfboarding, swimming, and wrestling. Music, both vocal and instrumental, was well developed, as was dancing, especially the many varieties of the hula.

Without a written language, knowledge of all sorts was preserved and taught by persons specially trained as the keepers of wisdom and tradition. They were often part of a religious hierarchy that included powerful priests and sorcerers. On important occasions there were human sacrifices. There were places of refuge to which people accused of crimes might flee and be safe. The Hawaiian religious and political systems were closely interwoven. During the years before the arrival of the Europeans, the nobility and priesthood tended to become more and more tyrannical, causing increasing unrest among the commoners, who were the majority of the population.

Capt. James Cook of the Royal Navy, leading a British expedition, encountered the islands in 1778 and christened them the Sandwich Islands. British attempts to explore their find met with fierce resistance from the islands' kings; Cook himself died in a skirmish in 1779. Capt. George Vancouver obtained the islands for the United Kingdom in 1793–94, but the British government took little notice of them—though the British flag was adopted as the first flag of the kingdom. The introduction of European firearms dramatically increased the destructiveness of the internecine wars, further decimating a population already ravaged by European diseases.

King Kamehameha I, called the Great, the ruler of the largest of the islands, Hawai'i, finally conquered the neighboring islands and established a unified kingdom in 1810. The king welcomed American and European traders and whalers, learning from them and encouraging the introduction of technology. During most of the nineteenth century the islands were known both as the Sandwich Islands and as the Hawaiian Islands.

The first American missionaries arrived in the 1820s, and Western influences began to change the Hawaiian culture. There was a liberalization in the arbitrary religious practices, including the abolition of human sacrifice and the more repressive laws and taboos. The overthrow of the priests and a loss of faith in the old gods brought about a swift adoption of Christianity by the Hawaiians. Other missionaries came to the islands in the 1830s and 1840s. By the mid-nineteenth century the Hawaiian kingdom was a largely Christian state. Soon engaging in trade, the missionaries laid the foundations of the islands' most important family fortunes. Plantation agriculture drew in Japanese, Portuguese, Filipino, and Chinese labor. The foreign population soon overwhelmed the native Hawaiians.

Influenced by native advisors, King Kamehameha II established a constitutional monarchy in 1840. The Hawaiian constitution was modeled on various American and British documents. Two years later, the kingdom received recognition as a sovereign state from the United States and the major European powers, although the British occupied the islands for several months in 1843. A Hawaiian "revolt" preceded the British withdrawal in July 1843. The revolt consisted of the Hawaiians' totally ignoring the presence of the British in the islands and claiming victory when the British left—though the occupation had never been sanctioned by the British government. In 1848 the king abolished the feudal landholding system, allowing investment and economic exploitation. Intrigues by the British and French prompted King Kamehameha III to place his kingdom under U.S. protection in 1851.

The Hawaiian population, estimated to number between 300,000 and 500,000 in 1778, had dropped to just 70,036 in 1853. The Hawaiians, once virtually disease free, had no natural immunity to the diseases introduced from both East and West. They soon fell ill with venereal diseases, cholera, measles, bubonic plague, and leprosy.

In 1887 the United States obtained the right to establish a naval installation at Pearl Harbor, near Honolulu. The American's growing commercial and political influence in the kingdom, opposed by King Kalakaua, prompted demands for his abdication in 1889. His more amenable sister, Lydia Liliuokalani, became queen amid rising American demands for constitutional reform. Many Hawaiian and U.S. interests favored annexation of the kingdom, but many in the American government, including President Grover Cleveland, opposed it.

The American residents, mostly sugar planters, on 17 January 1893 staged a coup and deposed the queen. The coup leaders, supported by the American ambassador to the kingdom, requested annexation by the United States following the landing of U.S. troops. A commission sent from Washington reported that the majority of the islanders opposed annexation, and the commissioners, acting for the U.S. Congress, refused the appeal. The provisional Hawaiian government, dominated by American planters, then declared on 4 July 1894 the islands independent, as the Republic of Hawaii. The declaration set off a Hawaiian revolt; the deposed queen traveled to Washington seeking aid from an increasingly unsympathetic American government convinced by economic interests of the need for American control of the islands. In 1897 the new Hawaiian republic signed with the United States a treaty that laid the groundwork for a formal transfer of sovereignty on 12 August 1898. In 1900 Hawaii became a territory of the United States.

By 1910 only some 40,000 ethnic Hawaiians remained, including the growing number of part-Hawaiians. The poorest segment of the population, the former rulers of the islands retained only small subsistence plots. Just 40 individuals, the majority of them descendants of early missionaries, held 97% of the land. A 1921 law granting 200,000 acres to native Hawaiians for homesteading has still to be implemented in a meaningful way.

The territorial government applied for statehood in 1937, but the federal government denied the application, on the grounds that the ethnically mixed population made statehood impossible. The islands remained an exotic outpost until the surprise attack on Pearl Harbor in December 1941. Hawaii became crucial to the war in the Pacific, and the influx of mainlanders during and after the war greatly changed the ethnic composition. On 21 August 1959 Hawaii finally won statehood. Commercial jet service, inaugurated the same year, quickly made mass tourism the mainstay of the island economy.

Tourism remains the state's largest industry, with more than six million visitors a year in the 1990s. The federal government is the second-largest source of income, much of its spending being on defense-related projects. The multi-ethnic population is prosperous and well educated, but the native Hawaiians remain its least advantaged sector.

The Hawaiians, with incomes some 15% lower than the state average, experienced a cultural revival in the 1960s and 1970s, a reculturation highlighting their unique history, language, and traditions. Younger, more militant Hawaiians began to demand cultural rights and economic equality, including compensation for 1.4 million acres of land stolen from the Hawaiians over the last century. In response, at the federal level, a Bureau of Hawaiian Affairs came into being in 1976, but in 1983 the U.S. Congress rejected responsibility for the seized lands. The decision provoked a dramatic growth of Hawaiian nationalism.

The first openly nationalist organizations and advocacy groups formed in the early to mid-1970s, but they were not accepted by mainstream Hawaiians until the late 1980s. The renewed interest in Hawaiian sovereignty was associated with successful independence movements in the former Soviet Union and Eastern Europe as well as the achievements of indigenous nationalists around the globe. The various groups represent views ranging from sovereignty on the lines of the native peoples of the mainland United States, to full independence. There is considerable friction between the various organizations, which detracts from their ability to unify and organize effectively.

The land issue remains central to the national movement. In Hawaiian tradition the land is sacred, and the state's unbridled growth, environmental destruction, and growing pollution are considered blasphemous. In

1988 the nationalists rejected an offer of aid from Libya's dictator, but in 1991 several groups asserted that the Hawaiians are citizens of a sovereign nation, subverted and annexed illegally by the United States.

The Hawai'i Advisory Committee to the U.S. Commission on Civil Rights issued in 1991 a report documenting 73 years of civil rights violations against Hawaiians. U.S. Public Law 103–150, adopted by Congress on 23 November 1993, formally apologized to the Hawaiian nation for the illegal overthrow of the Kingdom of Hawaii 100 years before. On 16 January 1994, activists proclaimed the independence of the Sovereign Nation State of Hawai'i at 'Iolani Palace, the former royal palace in Honolulu. The proclamation, not officially recognized, asserted the rights of the Hawaiians as the indigenous population of the islands and called for the end of the foreign military occupation of their homeland.

Support is growing for the creation of a "Hawaiian Nation," similar to the other Native American nations. The move would give the Hawaiians certain legal protections and rights in their fight for self-determination. In 1996 the Hawaiians organized a vote among the indigenous population on the question of sovereignty; 73% of the 80,000 eligible voters favored Hawaiian sovereignty. Governor Ben Cayetano, in his state of the state address in 1998, actively supported Hawaiian self-determination. The Hawaiians are the only native people in the United States who are not recognized as at least a partially autonomous community.

A 1997 survey showed that the numbers of people identifying themselves as having Hawaiian blood and learning or speaking the Hawaiian language were increasing, in part due to the greater awareness of programs that benefit only people of Hawaiian descent. In January 1999 indigenous Hawaiians across the United States chose 85 delegates to a Hawaiian-sovereignty conference to determine what actions should be taken.

In 1999, activists, particularly on the largest of the islands, Hawai'i, put forward a plan for the restoration of the Hawaiian kingdom. Most native Hawaiians in the 1990s supported some form of sovereignty, but the majority favored autonomy as a "nation within a nation" and did not wish to lose their rights as American citizens. The government sponsored reconciliation hearings on the major islands in 1999, looking for ways to offset the growing support for radical solutions to the sovereignty question. An August 1999 poll showed increased public support for Hawaiian independence, with around a third of all residents supporting the complete restoration of Hawaii as an independent country, up from just 12% in 1996. Several militant groups call for a unilateral declaration of independence before beginning state-to-state negotiations with the United States as an occupying power.

The Hawaiian sovereignty movement is gaining momentum and is now recognized as an important political issue. Hawaiian politicians at all levels of government support the movement. Prolonged deliberations into the potential form of sovereignty have removed the issue from public debate, but the discussions became a public debate in 2001. The questions of entitlements and the preservation of sacred objects (whose destruction has increased tension between settlers and indigenous Hawaiians) have come to play important roles.

SELECTED BIBLIOGRAPHY:

Becket, Jan, ed. *Pana O'Ahu: Sacred Stones, Sacred Land.* 1999.
Coffman, Tom. *Nation Within: The Story of America's Annexation of the Nation of Hawaii.* 1998.
Dudley, Michael Kioni, and Keoni Kealohe Agard. *A Hawaiian Nation II: A Call for Hawaiian Sovereignty.* 1991.
Maenette, K.P., and Ah Nee Benham, eds. *Cultural and Educational Policy in Hawai'i: The Silencing of Native Voices.* 1998.

Hazaras

Hazarahs; Hezarehs; Hezare'i; Hezarehs; Berberis; Taimuris; Timuris

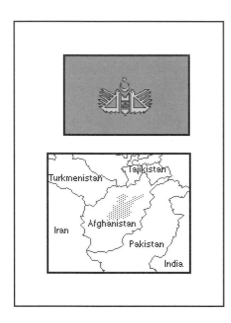

POPULATION: Approximately (2002e) 4,720,000 Hazaras in Central Asia, most in the Hazarajat and Firozkoh regions of Afghanistan. Other large communities include 610,000 in Iran, mostly in the province of Khorasan south of Mashhad, and 105,000 in Pakistan, concentrated around the city of Quetta in Pakistani Baluchistan. Other groups live in Tajikistan, Europe, and North America. Nationalists claim a national population of over six million in central and southern Asia.

THE HAZARA HOMELAND: The Hazara homeland, called Hazarajat, occupies the dry, mountainous central region of Afghanistan. Because of the scarcity of agricultural land, many Hazaras have migrated to other parts of the country, particularly the capital, Kabul, just east of Hazarajat. The Hazarajat consists of valleys, towering rugged mountains, cold winters, beautiful scenery, and raging rivers. The majority of the Hazaras live in the Hazarajat region but due to war and segregation by the discriminatory Afghan governments, some of the Hazara people live in cities throughout Afghanistan. The Hazaras live in nine distinct enclaves in the highlands. *Hazarajat (Hazaristan)*: 56,697 sq. mi.—144,254 sq. km, (2002e) 4,550,000—Hazaras 56%, Pushtuns* 28%, Chahar Aimaks 10%, Tajiks 4%, other Afghans 2%. The Hazara capital and major cultural center is Bamian, called Bamiyan by the Hazaras, had a population of about 40,000 prior to its destruction by retreating Taliban fighters in November 2001. The other major cultural center is Mazar-e Sharif, (2002e) 220,000, in northern Afghanistan. The major cultural center of the Iranian Hazaras is Torbat-e Jam, (2002e) 72,000.

FLAG: The Hazara national flag, the flag of the national movement, is a pale blue field bearing the Hazara national symbol in yellow outlined in black, including two stylized birds surmounted by a crescent moon and five-pointed star.

PEOPLE AND CULTURE: The Hazaras are a people of mixed Turkic and Mongol background, with the Mongol strain most evident in their physical appearance. The name "Hazara" originally referred to a Mongol fighting unit of 1,000 men, but now it means simply "mountain tribe." Traditionally the Hazaras preferred to marry first cousins of their paternal families and seldom mixed with outsiders. Most Hazaras live in villages of from 30 to 100 families, generally in houses of baked mud bricks. About a third of the Hazaras are herders, living seminomadic lives following their herds into the highlands, where they live in *yurts*, circular tentlike dwellings made of horsehair felt. The Hazaras are known for their toughness; their culture is steeped in religion and colored by tribal history and relics. They are traditionally divided into two major subgroups—the Eastern Hazaras of the Hazarajat, and the Western Hazaras in the northern foothills of the Parapamisus Mountains and in Iran. The subgroups are further divided into at least 11 geographically based groups. In recent decades, due to increased poverty, many of the Hazaras have migrated to the cities seeking work as day laborers. The Hazara willingness to perform menial work has earned them a reputation as a hardworking people but has also resulted in their being looked down upon and discriminated against.

LANGUAGE AND RELIGION: The Hazara language, called Hazaragi, is a Farsi dialect, although the Hazaras are physically Mongol. The intermixture of the Indo-European and Mongol linguistic groups resulted in a dialect of Dari Persian that contains extensive words and forms from Farsi, Turkic, and Mongol. Use of the language has been curtailed under Taliban rule, and educational opportunities, particularly for females, have declined dramatically. Most Hazaras also speak Dari Persian, one of two official languages in Afghanistan, as a second language. In Iran most are bilingual, speaking both Hazaragi and Farsi, the language of the Iranian majority. Illiteracy is very high, due to a lack of educational opportunities and traditional attitudes to teaching other than that related to religion. In Iran and Pakistan there are radio broadcasts in the Hazaragi language. Until the 1980s educated Hazaras used Farsi or Arabic as the literary language, but a movement to create a Hazaragi literary language has gained momentum.

The Hazaras are mostly Imani Shi'ites, also known as Ithna Ashari or "Twelvers." They hold a particular reverence for the son-in-law of the prophet Mohammed. Minorities include Ismaili Shi'ites, also known as "Seveners," making up about 5% of the population, and a Sunni population, mostly among the Western Hazaras. The two groups have often fought in the past, but persecution under the Taliban has drawn the two groups closer since 1996. Historically the Shi'a population has been branded as heretical by the orthodox Sunni majority. Following the victory of the radical Taliban in the mid-1990s, teaching in the Hazara language has been curtailed, and education was centered on Sunni Islamic teachings.

Following the overthrow of the Taliban in November 2001, the Hazaras again instituted education in their own language.

NATIONAL HISTORY: Hazara history tells of their ancestors entering the region with the forces of Genghis Khan in the thirteenth century. The descendants of soldiers left to garrison the area became the Hazara nation. Mongol soldiers, often accompanied by their families, spread across the mountainous region following the collapse of the Mongol empire in the thirteenth century. Their physical characteristics long distinguished them from the other national groups in the region.

Tamerlane's forces overran the region in the fourteenth century, forcing the majority of the Hazaras to seek shelter in highland strongholds. The Hazaras retained their military traditions, as invaders from both east and west overran their homeland. They are thought to have adopted Shi'a Islam from the Persians during the rule of Shah Abbas Safavid, who controlled the Hazara homeland in the early seventeenth century, although some scholars believe that they had adopted Shi'a Islam before the spread of the Shi'ite sect from Iran, as early as the middle eighth century.

The Persian king Nader Shah took control of the region in 1737, supporting the Shi'a Hazaras against their Sunni neighbors. The Hazarajat was later included in the territories consolidated by the Pushtun ruler Ahmad Shah Durrani, at whose death in 1773 the Afghan empire included eastern Persia, Afghanistan, Baluchistan, Kashmir, and the Punjab. As a result of the Pushtun expansion and Sunni discrimination, in the late eighteenth and early nineteenth centuries the Hazaras were driven into the barren, dry mountains of the Hazarajat.

The Afghans lost territory to the Europeans and Iranians in the nineteenth century. In 1809 the Afghan government signed an agreement with the British to oppose the Iranians and Russians. The British invaded the region in the First Afghan War in 1839–42, and again in the Second Afghan War in 1878–79. The Hazaras, seeking to avoid conflict, remained in their mountain homeland, resisting efforts by either the British or the Sunni Afghans to control their territory.

In the nineteenth century many Hazaras moved west to the Parapamisus Mountains and into Persian or British territory in present-day Pakistan, to escape the consequences of a failed revolt against the Afghanistan government and to search for better pasture for their herds. From the 1880s, the Hazaras suffered severe political, social, and economic repression. During the reign of Abdur Rahman, from 1880 to 1901, the Hazaras were declared "infidels," and therefore could be killed with impunity. A *jihad*, or holy war, was waged against them by government troops. Thousands died in massacres instigated and carried out by government officials. Although slavery was outlawed in 1919, some Hazaras were kept as slaves by the Pushtuns; the practice continued until after World War II.

Economic deprivation and religious persecution stimulated the political mobilization of the Hazaras in the 1960s and 1970s, in a movement that concentrated on gaining political autonomy within the Afghan kingdom. The symbols of the Hazara nation, the huge Buddhist statues at Bamian that pre-dated the Hazara settlement became the symbols of the Hazara fight for equality within Afghanistan.

The Afghan monarchy was overthrown and a republic proclaimed on 17 July 1973. A bloody coup overthrew the government in April 1978, and a communist government was installed in Kabul.

To support the shaky hold of the communists, Soviet troops invaded Afghanistan in 1979, beginning a decade of brutal occupation and increasing polarization of various Afghan national groups that fought the Soviet occupation and often each other. The Soviets abandoned any pretense of controlling the Hazarajat. The Hazaras succeeded in liberating much of their homeland early in the war; during the 1980s, they reached an agreement with the Afghan government by which, in exchange for not attacking the government, the Hazaras were allowed to live a relatively independent existence in their mountain homeland. From 1982, with increased support from the new Islamic Republic of Iran for some groups, internal fighting between Hazara groups left thousands dead and wounded. The conflict, called the Hazar-Afghan War by the Hazaras, devastated the Hazara homeland and created tens of thousands of refugees.

Soviet forces finally withdrew from the country in early 1989, leaving millions of land mines and a country seriously divided among its ethnic groups. In 1992 the Soviet-backed government was overthrown, and the Afghan capital became a battlefield for the various groups of Islamic guerrillas, including the Hazara Hizb-i-Wahdat, a coalition of eight mainly Hazara Shi'a organizations formed in 1987. The organization received considerable diplomatic, material, and moral support from the Iranian government. The fighting spread in 1992–93, and by 1994 the Hazaras had become more active in fighting against the Sunni government and against non-Hazara Shi'a militias.

Traditionally the Hazaras carried on a comparatively peaceful pastoral existence, following the grazing herds from their winter quarters to summer camps on the upper slopes of Hazarajat. The Hazaras only cultivated enough crops for their own use, forcing many to seek seasonal employment in southern Afghanistan or in northern India during the winter. After a decade of Soviet occupation, followed by a seemingly endless civil war, much of the land of the Hazarajat lies barren and unusable. Thousands of Hazaras had taken refuge in Iran or Pakistan and were unable to return to Afghanistan due to the continuing hostility of the Taliban government.

The Taliban, mostly ethnic Pushtuns, first appeared on the political scene of Afghanistan in 1994 in the southern province of Kandahar. It quickly overran about 90% of Afghanistan, including most of Hazarajat. In September 1996 the Taliban soldiers marched into Kabul. The Taliban zealots enforced a radical form of Sunni Islam, including beards for all men, seclusion for women, and the banning of music, sport, and television. The mostly Shi'a Hazaras were particularly targeted as heretics; the Taliban hierarchy used the historical enmity between the Sunnis and Shi'as to eliminate the fierce resistance of the Hazaras to the Taliban military advance in the central and northern provinces. Thousands of Hazaras fled to refugee camps in Pakistan or Iran.

A Taliban commander, Maulawi Mohammed Hanif, announced during the fighting in northern Afghanistan in 1995 that the policy of the Taliban was to exterminate the Hazaras. He told a crowd, "Hazaras are not Muslim. You can kill them. It is not a sin." In March 1995 10 leading Hazaras were slain by members of the Taliban, creating a pantheon of martyrs to the Hazara cause. The Taliban, on 10 August 1998, declared a fitwa, a religious edict, that the Hazaras were infidels. Following the conquest of Mazar-e-Sharif by the Taliban in mid-August, an estimated 8,000 Hazaras were murdered in round-ups, in homes, and shot down in the streets. On 13 September 1998, Bamiyan, the unofficial Hazara capital, fell to the Taliban, and the horrors of Mazar-e-Sharif were reportedly repeated.

Hazara women, traditionally enjoying a greater degree of social freedom than women of neighboring Muslim groups, were particularly affected by the Taliban prohibition of education, health care, or work for women. The traditional discrimination practiced by most Afghans against the Hazaras was augmented by the Taliban hostility to their Shi'a religion and to their Iranian support. Taliban activists, through the Department of Virtue and Suppression of Vice, were free to search private houses and to destroy all radios, televisions, video recorders, and computers. Ironically, although computers in private homes are forbidden, the Taliban itself maintained two Web sites until November 2001.

The world's failure to condemn the massacres or to bring the Taliban perpetrators to justice fueled the rapid growth of Hazara nationalism. In 1999, in response to increasing international isolation, the Taliban began to modify its harsh Islamic rule, but relations with the Hazaras remained hostile.

The Hazara struggle for independence has been very costly for them. They began the new century as allies of the anti-Taliban Northern Alliance, but with their nation in turmoil and still fighting a seemingly never-ending civil war. Their economy is completely shattered; the only crop that will grow in their valleys with little water and cultivation is opium. The Hazarajat has become one of the major opium-producing areas of the world. In early 2000, a small group of activists called for the independence of Hazarajat as a new state, to be called the Islamic Republic of Hazaristan.

The Taliban government, citing Islamic strictures against human likenesses, destroyed the Buddhist statues at Bamian in March 2001. Internationally condemned for their wanton destruction of the historic statues, the Taliban claimed they were being used as superstitious talismans by anti-government Hazaras. The Buddhas of Bamian were claimed as the work of early Hazaras and were considered the heart of the Hazara nation. The Taliban dynamited the monumental treasures, carved into the Hindu Kush Mountains, claiming that all statues were false idols and contrary to their Islamic beliefs.

The terrorist attacks on the United States in September 2001 began a new era in Afghanistan. Aided by many world governments, the U.S. miliatry attacked Taliban positions across Afghanistan. Following weeks of bombings, the Taliban collapsed. In November, the Taliban evacuated the Hazara regions, but looted and burned every building in Bamian and other important towns. In the wake of the Taliban defeat, the residents, many having spent years in the hills or living in caves away from Taliban control, began to return to their shattered homes.

The Hazaras fear that once the Afghan civil war ends they will no longer be valued as allies and will again be shut out of government and suffer religious and ethnic discrimination. They are determined not to lose the independence they gained in their war with the former communist and Taliban governments.

Hazara delegates participated in the Afghan congress called by the United Nations in Germany in mid-November 2001 in an effort to organize a multi-ethnic government to replace the Taliban. Many Hazaras support the creation of an autonomous Hazaristan as part of a federal Afghanistan, but others feel that after so much suffering that the Hazaras would have a better future should they now separate from war-torn Afghanistan and create a sovereign Hazara homeland.

SELECTED BIBLIOGRAPHY:

Goldstone, Jack, Ted R. Gurr, and Frank Moshiri, eds. *Revolutions of the Late Twentieth Century*. 1991.
Harpviken, Kristian Berg. *Political Mobilization among the Hazara of Afghanistan*. 1998.
Musawi, Askar. *The Hazaras of Afghanistan*. 1989.
Nassim, Jawad. *Afghanistan: A Nation of Minorities*. 1992.

Hejazis
Hijazis; Hejazehs; Hedjazis; Hejazi Arabs

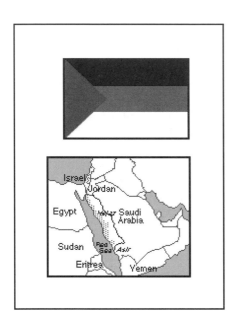

POPULATION: Approximately (2002e) 6,820,000 Hejazis in Saudi Arabia, most concentrated in the Hejaz region by the Red Sea. Outside the region there is a sizable Hejazi community in the Saudi capital, Riyadh, and in other parts of the Middle East, including Jordan, Egypt, and Yemen.

THE HEJAZI HOMELAND: The Hejazi homeland lies on the Red Sea coast of the Arabian Peninsula in southwestern Saudi Arabia. The region is mostly an arid mountainous plateau with several fertile interior oases and a fertile but narrow coastal plain on the Red Sea, called the Tihamah. The relatively well-watered, fertile upper slopes of the mountains are extensively terraced to allow the most intensive possible use. Hejaz has no official status; it forms the Western Province of Saudi Arabia, comprising the districts of Madinah, Makkah, and Tebuk. *Western Province (Hejaz/Al-Hijaz)*: 174,205 sq. mi.—451,190 sq. km, (2002e) 7,868,000—Hejazis 81%, blacks 8%, non-Saudi Muslims 7%, other Saudi Arabians 4%. The Hejazi capital and major cultural center is Mecca, Makkah in Arabic, (2002e) 1,258,000, the holiest city of Islam. The other important cultural centers are Medina, al-Madinah in Arabic, (2002e) 792,000, the second-most-important city of Islam, Jeddah, (2002e) 2,670,000, the major commercial center, and Tabuk, the center of northwestern Hejaz, (2002e) 380,000.

FLAG: The Hejazi flag, the flag of the former kingdom, is a horizontal tricolor of black, white, and green bearing a red triangle at the hoist. The colors of the flag of Hejaz, the first independent Arab state in modern times, became the colors of Arab liberation and appear on the flags of many Arab countries.

PEOPLE AND CULTURE: The Hejazis are a distinct Arab nation, the only nontribal people in Saudi Arabia. The population of the region, particularly in the pilgrimage cities of Mecca, Medina, and Jeddah, has for centuries included descendants of foreign Muslims who stayed in the region. Substantial Indonesian and Indian Muslim populations, as well as Persians and Yemenis, form the largest of the immigrant populations. The Hejazis, as a nontribal people, have suffered discrimination by the *qabila*, or noble tribal families that dominate the Nejd, the Saudi heartland. The tribal peoples consider themselves distinctly superior to the *khadira*, nontribals. Marriage between *qabila* and *khadira* was formerly not considered, although this has begun to change. In Hejaz, status based on education and economic advantage began to undermine the importance of tribal affiliation in the 1960s. Hejazi culture remains the sophisticated product of long contact with foreign cultures, very much unlike the Arab culture developed by nomads and villagers in the Arabian Desert. One of the most urbanized societies in the Arab world, the Hejazis have assimilated many cultural and linguistic influences brought by religious pilgrims.

LANGUAGE AND RELIGION: The Hejazis speak a dialect of Arabic called Arabiya or Hejazi Spoken Arabic. The dialect, although based on standard Arabian Peninsual Arabic, has absorbed many words and expressions brought to the region from other Arabic-speaking regions and from non-Arabic countries. The Hejazi dialect, formerly used as a trade language throughout much of the Red Sea region, has evolved as a distinct language, closely related to the recent regionalist sentiment in the region.

The majority of the Hejazi nation adheres to the Sunni branch of Islam, but a more tolerant sect than the puritanical Wahabi rite, the official branch of Islam in the Saudi kingdom. Other sects are also well represented. Religious clashes, increasingly frequent in the late 1990s, were based on the differences between the orthodox Sunnis and the intolerant creed of the Wahabis, a creed that is enforced across Saudi Arabia, but is often flaunted by the wealthy Nejdis and the corrupt bureaucracy of Riyadh in the interior of the country.

NATIONAL HISTORY: Nomadic Semitic tribes began to settle the region in ancient times. An urbanized culture developed along the coast and among the inland oases with the growth of trade. The northern part of the region was occupied as early as the sixth century B.C., when the Chaldean kings of Babylon had their summer capital at Tayma'. Later Hejaz became part of the Nabataean kingdom, from about 100 B.C. to A.D. 200.

The city of Mecca early acquired importance as a center of commerce and a place of worship for the region's multitude of pagan sects. At the time of Mohammed's birth in A.D. 570, the region had a mixed population of urbanized pagan tribes, Judaized Arabs, Christians, and Zoroastrian merchants.

Mohammed, at age 40, experienced a revelation of his destiny as the Arab prophet. Mohammed's teachings at first attracted a small group of followers but met fierce resistance from the pagan majority. In 622 Mohammed and his followers fled to Medina to escape a pagan plot to murder him. Mohammed's flight, the Hegira, marked the beginning of the Muslim era. By the time of his death in 632, all of Hejaz had come under Muslim rule. The Hejazi people, united by Mohammed, formed the core of the vast Muslim empire, which eventually controlled much of the known world.

Hejaz declined following the transfer of the center of Muslim power, the caliphate, to Damascus in 661, though Mecca and Medina remained pilgrimage centers for the Muslim faithful. In 762 the caliphate was moved from Damascus to Baghdad, even farther from its roots in Hejaz. The Muslim empire, after the Persian conquest of Baghdad in 1258, disintegrated rapidly, splitting into a number of antagonistic territories. Hejaz came under the rule of the Egyptian Mamelukes but remained the spiritual focus of the divided Muslim world. After Hejaz was absorbed by the expanding Ottoman Empire of the Turks in 1517, imperial authority there rested with the sharif of Mecca, the protector of the holy cities and the chief of the powerful Hashemite clan.

Wahabi Muslims, a puritanical sect from the harsh interior Nejd Desert, began to raid the holy cities and oases of Hejaz in the early nineteenth century. On the pretext that the Muslim holy cities had to be protected, the Turks brought Hejaz under direct Ottoman administration in 1845. The sharif of Mecca retained only his religious office as the caretaker of the holy cities. To consolidate their hold on Hejaz, the Turks built a Damascus-Medina railroad in the early twentieth century.

Arab nationalism emerged in the late nineteenth century, on the basis of demands for a separate Arab state within the multi-ethnic Ottoman Empire. In 1908, amid rising Arab opposition to Turkish rule, Husein ibn Ali succeeded to the position of Sherif of Mecca. With the outbreak of war in 1914, British agents, especially T.E. Lawrence, urged Husein to lead the Hejazis in revolt against the Ottoman Turks. The British promised to support the creation of an Arab state at the end of the war.

Sharif Husein ibn Ali, who claimed lineal descent from the Prophet Mohammed, was widely respected as the guardian of the Muslim holy cities. The Arab revolt, led by Husein and supported by British gold, began on 5 June 1916. He later destroyed the Turkish railroad to Damascus, with British aid. On 27 June 1916 Husein declared himself "king of the Arab countries," although the allies formally recognized him only as king of Hejaz. In September 1918 the Hejazis defeated the Turks in the region, but contrary to earlier promises of Arab unity and independence, the victorious allies, the United Kingdom and France, took control of Palestine, Syria, and other Arab territories of the defeated Ottoman Empire.

Hejaz participated in the 1919 Paris Peace Conference as the representative of an allied nation; however, Husein's representative, his son Emir Faisal, accused the British of duplicity and refused to sign the Versailles Treaty. In retaliation, the British withdrew their military support of the kingdom, just as tension began to mount between Hejaz and Nejd—the realm of Ibn Sa'ud, the leader of the Wahabi sect.

The conquest of Hejaz by Ibn Sa'ud had been foreshadowed by the victory at the battle of Turabah in 1919. Ibn Sa'ud led his tribal warriors to victory over the neighboring state of Jebel Shammar in 1921, thus bringing the Wahabis within striking distance of the Hejazi heartland, the holy cities. In 1924, after three years of skirmishing, the Wahabis invaded. The last Hashemite strongholds, the holy cities of Mecca and Medina, fell to Ibn Sa'ud in 1926. Ibn Sa'ud, the sultan of Nejd, assumed the title of king of Hejaz in 1926.

The United Kingdom recognized Saudi control of Hejaz in 1927. To compensate their former Hashemite allies for their defeat by the Nejdis, the British installed Husein's sons as rulers of the British-administered Iraq and Trans-Jordan. Formally incorporated into the kingdom of Saudi Arabia in 1932, Hejaz retained a degree of autonomy until the centralization of the Saudi kingdom in 1952.

The puritanical Wahabis, long opposed to the *haj*, the annual Muslim pilgrimage to Mecca and Medina, as a blasphemous rite, quickly revised their religious views in light of the revenue brought to their expanded state by the hundreds of thousands of religious pilgrims. The major port of entry for the pilgrims, Jeddah, emerged as the major commercial center of the new Saudi state, and the Hejazi merchant class gained power and influence. Cosmopolitan Jeddah, the traditional site of Eve's tomb, grew from a sleepy Red Sea port to a glittering metropolis and the center of sophisticated Hejazi culture. In 1947 the city's population was about 30,000; the population explosion began in the 1950s, as Jeddah's position as the gateway to the holy cities solidified.

When Adb al Aziz, better known as Ibn Sa'ud, died in 1953, he left more than 40 sons and a tribal confederation held together by handouts and the force of his remarkable personality. His heirs continued the handouts and assumed that with time and oil wealth, the country would knit itself together into a normal state. That has not happened. The ruling Saud family has created the trappings of a modern state, but most Saudi citizens remain loyal to units either bigger and smaller than the Saudi nation-state. Sharp differences remain between the Hejazis, who see themselves as the guardians of the holy cities, and the Nejdis, the tribal peoples of the Saudi heartland.

Jeddah remained the commercial center of the Saudi kingdom until the 1960s, and in all the Hejazi cities, mercantile families formed a powerful, educated elite. The traditional merchant class lost influence as Saudi rulers ceased borrowing from them and instead began to compete with them, using oil resources to create a new merchant class in Nejd in the 1970s. The Saudi rulers also favored Nejdis for administrative posts; the appointees in turn used their positions to favor other Nejdis and Nejdi commercial interests. The Hejazi mercantile elite, known as the *awaali*, or first families, became increasingly resentful and anti-Nejdi in the late 1970s and early 1980s.

Hejazi nationalism began to reemerge in the 1970s, spurred by growing radical fundamentalism and tension between the Sunni and Wahabi sects. The Hejazi belief that the oil-rich Saudis cared more for their overseas investments than for the well-being of Hejaz spurred regional and nationalist sentiment. A peace and orderliness of the annual *haj*, viewed by the Hejazis as a continuing test of Saudi legitimacy, began to unravel with attacks on Mecca's Great Mosque by fundamentalists in 1979 and with violence that has often marred the annual pilgrimage since 1987.

The Wahabi interpretation of Islam is rooted in that of the tribal Nejd. To the more sophisticated Hejazis, it is a harsh and alien creed. They regard the current contest between the Saudi ruling family and its increasingly strident Islamic critics as an essentially Nejdi affair, having little to do with their homeland on the Red Sea.

In the past, oil wealth served to reduce the regional differences. In the late 1990s the government's role as the great provider waned. The traditional Saudi practice of stifling dissidence with generous bounties was a custom the Saudi government could no longer afford. The era of Saudi opulence was over. Water shortages and power outages, increasingly common, increased Hejazi resentment of the 10,000 members of the Saudi royal family, who control the kingdom's commerce and administration amid massive abuses and royal privilege. The economy of Hejaz, once dependent on gold mining, is now based on the pilgrimage; it relies less on the wealth generated by oil deposits in eastern Arabia, a fact that has decreased the influence of ministries based in the Saudi capital, Riyadh, in Nejd.

The fall in 1991 of the Soviet Union, another state put together by force, gave new impetus to the Hejazi national movement in the 1990s. The movement, anti-Saudi and anti-Nejdi, has gained support as the cracks in the Saudi state widened. More than six decades after the proclamation of the present-day Saudi state, there is still not yet a Saudi nation, but there is a Hejazi nation, and it increasingly resents its second-class place in the stratified Saudi society. The Saudi state's weakness is its tribal and regional division. Should the Saudi's lose control, the country would most likely splinter along regional lines. The increasing weakness of the Saudi dynasty is its lack of preparedness for peaceful reform. Centrifugal and religious forces have begun to gnaw at the edges of the Saudi fabric.

The Saudi government continued to suppress opposition movements that have surfaced since the 1990 Gulf crisis and war. The Iraqi invasion of neighboring Kuwait focused attention on Saudi Arabia's sharp polarization between two competing forces, the powerful Wahabi religious establishment and liberal reformist elements, many based in Hejaz. By 1997 most domestic dissidents, including the Hejazi nationalist movement, had been silenced or forced into exile. The Hejazi political opposition is fragmented between those seeking a liberalization of cultural and economic strictures, those seeking greater autonomy for the Hejaz region, and the small number of activists who are openly against the Saudi kingdom and the Wahabi religious hierarchy.

The terrorist attacks in the United States in September 2001 threatened the Saudi family's increasingly tenuous hold on the country. A leading Wahabi cleric issued a fatwa, a religious edict, in effect excommunicating the 30,000 al-Saud family. Saud legitimacy is based on support from the puritanical Wahabi movement of the desert Nejd region. The Saud-Wahabi partnership has kept the Saud family in power, but looks increasingly strained as the Sauds lean on American power and the Wahabis increasingly support radical Islamic movements throughout the Muslim world. The Saudi government refused to support the American attack on the Taliban movement and Osama bin-Laden in Afghanistan. The Wahabis, unpopular in Hejaz, have tried to spread their brand of Islam to the Hejazis, the protectors of the holy places, but with only limited success.

SELECTED BIBLIOGRAPHY:

Alangari, Haifa. *The Struggle for Power in Arabia: Ibn Saud, Hussein and Great Britain, 1914–1924.* 1998.
Hogarth, David G. *Hejaz before World War I.* 1978.
Ochsenwald, William. *Religion, Society, and State in Arabia: The Hijaz under Ottoman Control, 1840–1908.* 1975.
Zwemer, Samuel M. *Arabia: The Cradle of Islam, Studies in the Geography, People and History of the Peninsula.* 1980.

Hmongs

Hmungs; H'moongs; Hmu; Miao; Meo; Man; Mong

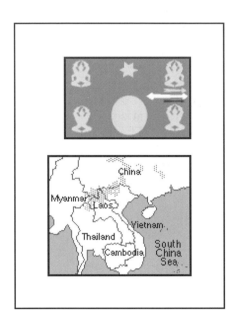

POPULATION: Approximately (2002e) 5,200,000 Hmongs in Southeast Asia and China, including 250,000 in Laos, 740,000 in Vietnam, 125,000 in Thailand, and 3.8 million scattered across southwestern China. Outside Asia the largest communities are the 150,000 in the United States (concentrated in Minnesota), 40,000 in France, and a smaller communities in Australia and French Guinea. The Hmong population in China is variously estimated at between three and eight million, the disparity due to whether one counts only Hmongs or all related groups as well.

THE HMONG HOMELAND: The Hmong homeland lies in southeastern Asia, in northern Laos, Vietnam, and south-central China. Much of the region is characterized by rugged mountains. The Hmong villages in Laos, Vietnam, and Thailand are traditionally found on mountaintops or ridges. The Hmong homeland, lying in the so-called Golden Triangle, is one of the world's major producers of raw opium. In China the Hmongs live in Guizhou, Hunan, Sichuan, and Yunnan Provinces. The capital and major cultural center of the Hmongs in Laos is Non Het, the traditional Hmong capital. The major cultural center of the Chinese Hmongs is the city of Guiyang. In Thailand the major Hmong center is Chiang Rai.

FLAG: The Hmong national flag, the flag of the Chao Fah movement, is a red field with yellow figures in each corner and a centered yellow six-pointed star over a large yellow circle in the center and three arrows—of yellow, white, and pale blue—on the fly.

PEOPLE AND CULTURE: The word "Hmong" means "free," although in China they are commonly called Miao or Meo, meaning "savage." Because of the many years of warfare and forced assimilation, the Hmongs have been divided into five major branches, Hong (Red), Hei (Black), Bai (White), Hua (Flowery), and Qing (Green). The legends, folk tales, and music of all Hmong groups are similar, and all venerate the legendary

Chiyou. Although their culture and traditions are very similar, a few major cultural practices are peculiar to Hmongs in Southeast Asia or in China. Economically and educationally, the Hmongs in China remain undeveloped and backward, especially in remoter parts of Yunnan. The Hmongs now comprise between 70 and 80 separate groups, each with its own style of dress and its own dialect and customs. The Hmongs normally do not mix with other ethnic groups but prefer to live in exclusively Hmong regions or villages. Hmong society is divided into a number of patrilineal clans. Almost all activities of the Hmongs are regulated by customs and taboos. Hmong nationalists in Laos claim that "Miao" is derogatory and should not be used, but a majority of the group in China use it, only a minority calling themselves Hmong. The Hmongs in Laos are grouped with other non-Laos and are called Lao Sung, "the Lao of the mountain tops," with six distinct ethnic groups. The Hmongs in all areas have evolved cultures and economies dependent upon opium cultivation.

LANGUAGE AND RELIGION: The Hmong language belongs to the Hmongic branch of the Hmong-Mien group of the Austro-Thai family of Sino-Tibetan languages. The language is spoken in three major dialects— Eastern, Central, and Western—further subdivided into 30 to 40 mutually unintelligible subdialects. The Hmong are one of the most widespread minority groups in southeastern Asia, a fact that has led to the development of many regional dialects. The Hmong dialects, like the Chinese dialects, are tonal, the numbers of tones varying from dialect to dialect. The Hmu dialect was chosen by the Chinese government as the standard.

The majority of the Hmongs practice their own animist religion, which involves the worship of demons, nature spirits, and ancestral spirits. The spirits are appeased through animal sacrifices and the burning of "paper money." Every Hmong village has at least one shaman, who exorcises evil spirits. Each Hmong home contains at least one altar to ancestral spirits. The "showing the way," *qhuab ke*, is a funeral song meant to guide the soul of the deceased to the original homeland of its ancestors. There have been few converts to Buddhism; a small number have converted to Christianity as a result of contact with Protestant and Roman Catholic missionaries.

NATIONAL HISTORY: According to Hmong oral history, they originated in northeastern China, where they were called Jiuli, 5,000 to 6,000 thousand years ago. The Jiuli, led by the legendary Chiyou, often fought with the ancestors of the Han Chinese, who lived to the northwest of the Jiuli kingdom. As the Chinese population grew, they expanded southward into the Hmong lands. A major war was fought near present-day Beijing. The Hmong legends tell of Hmong victories in the first nine battles but a devastating defeat in the 10th. After their defeat, the Hmong migrated south into the lower reaches of the Yellow River, where they established a new kingdom some 4,000 years ago.

The kingdom, called San-Miao, was led by two Hmong heroes, Tao Tie and Huan Tuo. History repeated itself; the Han Chinese expanded into the region, encroaching on the Hmong lands. In the ensuing war in about 2200 B.C., the Hmongs were defeated and largely exterminated by the Han Chinese leader Yu the Great. The Hmong survivors dispersed across the south and southwestern parts of present-day China. The Hmongs never again united as a nation, according to the majority of scholars.

Most scholars believe that the Hmong predated the Chinese in south-central China although the rest of the Hmongs' oral history cannot be proved or disproved. They were slowly driven south into their present homelands by the continued expansion of the Han Chinese. By about A.D. 220, the term Miao, perhaps after the ancient kingdom of San-Miao, was applied to the tribal peoples by the Chinese in early chronicles of the Han dynasty. They are next mentioned in writings of the Song dynasty period, between the late tenth and the late thirteenth centuries A.D. For several thousand years, until the thirteenth century, the central Chinese governments basically left the Hmongs to govern themselves, demanding only tribute. However, the last dynasty in China, the Qing dynasty, established by the Manchus,* sought direct control. During the Qing dynasty several major wars with the Han Chinese pushed hundreds of thousands of Hmongs into present-day Laos and Vietnam, but also into Burma and Thailand. Qing armies and officials oppressed the Hmongs and attempted to force them to assimilate into Chinese society.

The first important war during this period broke out in 1735, the result of the Chinese southward expansion and the forced assimilation of the Hmong population of the region of Guizhou. The Hmong were defeated in 1738; reportedly over 17,000 were killed, 11,000 captured and executed, and another 13,500 forced into slavery. Half of the total Hmong population was affected by the war. The second war was fought between 1795 and 1806 in the provinces of Sichuan, Guizhou, and Hunan. As in the earlier war, the Hmong fought to resist Chinese expansion and the loss of their lands. The first Hmong migrants left Chinese territory for Southeast Asia in the early nineteenth century.

As a result of the Taiping Rebellion, the Manchu Qing government demanded more taxes and labor from the Hmongs. Led by Xiu-mei Zhang and other leaders, the Hmongs revolted in southeastern Guizhou in 1854. The war involved an estimated million people and spread to many areas of south-central China. Only an estimated 30% of the Hmongs survived when the war finally ended in 1873. Zhang was captured and tortured to death. Hundreds of thousands of the Hmong left the region for Southeast Asia.

At the end of the nineteenth century the French moved into Southeast Asia, taking control of Laos and Vietnam and extending their influence into southern China. French colonial authorities introduced coffee and cotton as cash crops, but opium became the major export crop of the highland Hmongs. In 1904 and 1907, Siam, later called Thailand, ceded further territories in Laos to French control. The French authorities, with little interest in the mountainous regions of northern Southeast Asia, did little to develop the region, other than to require taxes or labor from the inhabitants and to establish a government monopoly on opium in 1899. Profits from the opium monopoly contributed between 15 and 40% of the French colonial budget in Indochina at any given time.

In 1919, led by a national hero, Chao Bat Chay, the Hmong rebelled against French taxes and forced labor. The revolt began around Dien Bien Phu in northern Vietnam. When Chao Bat Chay and his followers were driven across the mountains into Laos, they gained many adherents among the Hmongs of Laos by calling for the establishment of an independent Hmong kingdom. The insurrection ended in 1921, when Chao Bat Chay was betrayed to the French military. In an effort to prevent further revolts, the French established an autonomous district near the Laotian-Vietnamese border. By the early 1920s, mutual trust had developed, and the Hmongs became mostly pro-French.

During World War II, Japanese troops overran Indochina, offering an alliance to Hmongs who would fight alongside them. Most Hmongs refused, seeing the Japanese as yet another alien force in their homeland. Toward the end of the war, the Free French parachuted commandos into the Plain of Jars to prepare for the French recolonization of Laos. They were aided by the Hmongs, who preferred French to Japanese or Laotian domination.

The French, during the First Indochina War, which began in 1946, against Vietnamese and Lao forces, organized the pro-French Hmong majority into guerrilla units called the Meo Maquis. The French withdrew from Indochina following their defeat by the Vietnamese at Dien Bien Phu in 1954.

The Americans, having supported the French with aid and military equipment, decided to support the anticommunist forces in the region. The Hmongs, renowned as warriors, were recruited by the Americans from 1960 onward and formed a secret army. According to some reports, the Central Intelligence Agency encouraged the Hmongs to continue opium production as a source of income.

The pro-Western Hmongs declared the independence of Meoland, an independent Hmong homeland in 1966, but the declaration was generally overtaken by the spreading war. The Americans used the Hmongs against communist forces in Laos and Vietnam until the collapse of the South Vietnamese* in 1975. At its peak in 1969, the anticommunist Hmong secret army numbered about 40,000. The Hmongs suffered so many casualties that new recruits were brought in from the Hmong population in Thailand. An estimated 17,000 Hmong soldiers and over 50,000 Hmong civilians died during the war. Other Hmongs joined the communist forces and later served in official positions in the Lao and Vietnamese governments.

Many Hmongs adopted the Chao Fa religion, a nationalistic creed created in the 1960s by the Hmong prophet Yang Chong Leu. Chao Fa preached a return to the traditional Hmong ways and self-government. Yang Chong Leu also promoted a traditional system of writing known as Pahawh Hmong, which is now widely used. The religion, closely tied to the Hmong struggle for sovereignty, has become an integral part of Hmong culture.

Until the Americans withdrew in 1973, the Hmong heartland in Southeast Asia, on the northern border between Laos and Vietnam, was one of the most fiercely contested zones of the long Indochina war. The victorious communists after 1975 took their revenge on the pro-Western Hmongs, driving many deeper into the mountains and forcing thousands to flee abroad. Between 1975 and 1980, 70,000 Hmongs, a third of the Hmong population of Laos, fled the communist Patet Lao forces; many eventually settled in the United States, Europe, Australia, or in French Guiana in South America. Several Hmong leaders derided the United States over what they claimed had been promises by the Americans not to abandon the Hmongs and to support the creation of an independent Hmong state in Southeast Asia.

The Hmongs in Laos, from strongholds in the mountains, have continued to fight the Patet Lao, from 1975 to the present. Hit-and-run attacks and skirmishes have left much of northern Laos outside of government control. The rebel groups in southern Laos were defeated in 1978–79, but groups in the north and west, supported by China, continued to fight the communist governments of Laos and Vietnam. The Laotian government stopped hunting down and killing Hmong in 1980.

The Hmongs of China, with a long history of resistance to Han Chinese expansion, endeavor to live separately from the Chinese population, who refer to them as barbarians or dogs. In the 1980s, there were reports that the Chinese government had allowed Hmong leaders in China to aid the Hmong rebels in Southeast Asia, particularly in Vietnam, which fought a border war with China in 1979.

Many Hmong refugees chose to return to Laos following its liberalization toward the ethnic minorities in the early 1980s. Others were forced to return by Thai authorities intent on closing camps that by 1995 still held the last 50,000 Hmong refugees. The returnees, generally better educated than those who had stayed behind, quickly moved into leadership roles among the Hmong population, with many later joining the rebels fighting the still-repressive policies of the Laos government. The prejudiced attitudes of the Lao majority have stifled development and caused widespread resentment in the northern Hmong districts. Opium production has been indirectly supported by the Lao government in an attempt to pacify the Hmongs.

The Hmong rebels of northern Laos, led by the Chao Fah movement, continue to fight the communist government of Laos. By 1992, over 30,000 Hmongs were living in refugee camps in Thailand. Interethnic relations in Laos continue to deteriorate, and competition for land has become more critical since the early 1990s. Logging of the valuable timber resources, mostly by Thai companies, has put even more pressure on the arable lands in the Hmong regions. In the late 1990s, the Hmong rebels increasingly moved out onto the plains of southern Laos to set off bombs in Vientiane and other Lao cities and to strike at military targets. In June 2000, the Vietnamese government sent troops into Laos to bolster the Laotians' response to the Hmong rebels. The Vietnamese fear that the growing insurgency will spill across the border into the Hmong-populated districts in northern Vietnam.

To finance their fight for freedom, the Hmongs follow the French and later American policy of financing their activities with opium production. The Hmongs, often with the financial aid of the Hmong diaspora, continue their struggle for regional autonomy and the overthrow of the communist government in Laos. The large Hmong diaspora, particularly in Europe and the United States, increasingly supports the idea of a sovereign Hmong state as the only way to ensure the survival of the their nation.

SELECTED BIBLIOGRAPHY:

Bonner, Brian, and Yee Chang. *Holding Out for a Homeland.* 1995.
Cooper, Robert, ed. *The Hmong.* 1998.
Dao, Yang, and Jeane Blake. *Hmong at the Turning Point.* 1993.
Hamilton-Merritt, Jane. *Tragic Mountains: The Hmong, the Americans, and the Secret Wars for Laos, 1942–1992.* 1993.

Hui

Huais; Hweis; Hui-Hui; T'ung-kan; Tonggans; Dungans; Chinese Muslims

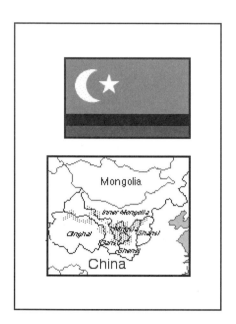

POPULATION: Approximately (2002e) 10,200,000 Hui in China and Central Asia, concentrated in northwestern China, in the Ningsia-Hui Autonomous Region, Inner Mongolia, Xinjiang, Gansu, Qinghai, Shanxi, and in Yunnan in southern China. Smaller numbers live in Anhwei, Liaoning, and in the Chinese capital, Beijing. Outside China there are Hui communities in Myanmar, Kazakhstan, Uzbekistan, and Kyrgyzstan.

THE HUI HOMELAND: The Hui homeland lies in northwestern China, a vast region collectively known as Muslim Territory, included in a number of Chinese provinces and regions. The Hui heartland occupies a highland region, the Ningsia Plateau, just south of the Alashan Desert of Inner Mongolia. Ningsia forms the Ningsia Hui Autonomous Region of the People's Republic of China. *Ningsia-Hui Autonomous Region (Ningxia Huizu)*: 30,039 sq. mi.—77,921 sq. km, (2002e) 6,263,000—Han Chinese 48%, Hui 37%, Tibetans* 8%, Manchus* 2%, Southern Mongols* 2%, other Chinese 3%. The Hui capital and major cultural center is Yinchuan, called Ningsia by the Hui, (2002e) 247,000, metropolitan area 641,000. Other important Hui cultural centers are the large Chinese cities of Xian, Lanzhou, and Xining.

FLAG: The Hui national flag is a pale blue field bearing a white crescent moon and five-pointed star on the upper hoist and two narrow stripes of black and red at the bottom.

PEOPLE AND CULTURE: The Hui are an ethnoreligious (Muslim) nation descendants of early Arab, Persian, and Turkic settlers who took Chinese wives and adopted Chinese speech and culture. Now physically similar to the majority Han Chinese, the Hui are distinguished by their dress, including turbans, and their Muslim religion. Traditional Hui cultural life was intimately related to their Muslim religion. Veiled Hui women traditionally stayed at home, but under the communist regime women were forced to renounce the veil and to do farm work in the communes or production work in the factories. Most Hui engage in agriculture and live in rural areas. The Hui's Muslim religion and related practices and customs, such as refusing to eat pork, continue to separate them from the Han Chinese. The Hui were dispersed in the eighteenth century; Hui minorities live in many parts of China, with the largest concentration in their heartland in Ningsia. Many younger Hui only nominally practice their religion, but they continue to resist assimilation into Han Chinese culture.

LANGUAGE AND RELIGION: The Hui, unlike the other Muslim minorities in China, do not have their own language but speak the Chinese dialect of their locality. The spoken dialects contain various borrowings from Arabic and Persian, particularly the Arabic associated with their Muslim religion. Arabic is spoken as a second language by many educated Hui, especially the Muslim religious leadership. The majority of the Hui speak Mandarin Chinese, the official language of the People's Republic of China.

The Hui are officially Sunni Muslims, although many Islamic sects are represented among them. The older factions evolved from the need to adapt Islam to Chinese culture. To retain their religious purity and group identity, the Hui have always remained socially segregated. Such Hui Muslim traditions as early and arranged marriages and polygamy have been outlawed, and women now officially have the same divorce and inheritance rights as men. According to Muslim custom, Hui women are forbidden to marry non-Hui, but Hui men may marry women of other groups who follow or are willing to follow Islamic practices. An estimated 90% of the Hui claim to be practicing Muslims, and the Chinese government continues to allow the Hui to bury their dead in Muslim cemeteries, while all Han Chinese must now be cremated. The Hui are also exempted from some aspects of China's draconian birth-control program.

NATIONAL HISTORY: Islam arrived in China both by sea and overland, establishing small Muslim communities in the seventh and eighth centuries. In the eleventh century, the kingdom of the Tanguts, called Hsi Hsia, in western China welcomed Muslims as scholars and traders. During the rule of the Mongol Yuan dynasty, installed in China in 1260, a flood of Arabs, Persians, and Turks fleeing the Mongol conquest of their homelands settled in the remote region south of the Alashan Desert. The refugees married Chinese, Uighur, and Mongol women and gradually assimilated, generally adopting Chinese culture and language. Eventually the Muslims, called Hui, took on the appearance and many of the cultural characteristics of the dominant Han Chinese.

The Muslims of the Alashan region expanded, in the fourteenth and fifteenth centuries, and converted surrounding peoples. Only nominally under the rule of the Chinese Empire, the Muslims maintained a separate state ruled by Hui sultans, a source of irritation to successive Chinese dynasties. Following the Manchu conquest of China in 1644, the Hui attempted to throw off infidel rule. Invaded by Manchu troops in 1648, the Hui fought a long and violent campaign but finally fell to overwhelming Manchu military power.

Sporadic Hui disturbances again erupted in open rebellion against Manchu domination in 1785. The Manchu rulers, determined to eliminate the Hui threat to their authority, loosed imperial troops on the region to carry out savage massacres, unprecedented in the East. The Hui homeland, an area larger than modern France, was left virtually depopulated. Hundreds of thousands fled into the desert or to other parts of China. After the Manchu campaign ended, a remnant slowly consolidated in a corner of their devastated former homeland. The Manchu government settled excess population from the eastern provinces in the region.

The Hui in the southern province of Yunnan, many refugees from Ningsia, came into conflict with the majority Han Chinese in 1821, and violence resulted. A rivalry between Chinese and Hui miners in central Yunnan triggered a severe clash in 1855, which developed into a massacre of Muslims in and around the provincial capital, Kunming. This led to a general Hui uprising in Yunnan, which lasted until they were finally defeated in 1873.

Another Hui uprising broke out in Shanxi province in 1862, promptly spreading to Gansu and to the Muslim Uighurs* of Xinjiang. The uprising lasted for 15 years and left thousands dead and displaced. The revolt, begun as resistance to discrimination and official persecution, left a legacy among the Hui of lasting hatred of the imperial government. The pacification of the Hui was delayed because the imperial army was preoccupied with the Taiping rebels in the eastern provinces; it lacked the funds and troops to mount an expedition to the remote outer provinces until the early 1870s.

Excluded from government and certain professions, the Hui lived as a despised minority, suspect due to their religion and their ties to the peoples to the west. Indiscriminate attacks by Han Chinese, paralleled by growing intolerance of their Muslim religion, provoked renewed Hui rebellions in several provinces. The evolution of Islamic movements at the end of the nineteenth century is closely linked to a great surge of social movements as the Manchu Qing dynasty began to crumble. Western and Japanese influences further fanned the flames of Hui discontent. Crushing defeats by imperial troops in the 1870s and again in 1895 dealt severe blows to the burgeoning Islamic movement.

Hui nationalists seized the opportunity presented by the Chinese Revolution of 1911. The nationalists, led by Muslim warlords, drove all Chinese officials from Ningsia, the Hui heartland, and created an autonomous government, but before they could consolidate their independence troops loyal to the new republican government overran the region. The lack of a unified policy weakened the Hui nationalist movement; the Hui rebellion was ended partly through the government's policy of playing off rival rebel leaders against one another.

Tension between the Hui and the Han Chinese continued to mar relations between the two peoples in many areas. Ningsia became the political base of the Ma clan of Ho-chou, a Hui clan that was wooed by the Nationalist Party, the Kuomintang, when civil war spread throughout China. The weak Chinese government only occasionally exerted authority in Ningsia during the turbulent 1920s and 1930s, although a separate Ningsia province was established in 1928 to give the Hui a degree of self-government.

The Hui mobilized to protect themselves from rampaging warlords and the militias of various political factions, many joining a private army recruited by the Ma clan. The Nationalist government of Chiang Kai-shek extended its authority to Ningsia in 1936 but relaxed its former harsh restraints on the Muslim religion to win Hui support as civil war with the Chinese communists escalated. Hui leaders were also courted by communist agents but ultimately refused their overtures, emphatically rejecting the communists' antireligious stance.

During the Sino-Japanese War, fought from 1937 to 1945 as a theater of World War II, communist authorities appealed for minority support by, for among other things, proclaiming Hui cultural and political rights. A government-sponsored Hui brigade was active in the resistance to the Japanese. Although some Hui leaders joined the communists and rose to positions of influence, most Hui supported the pro-Nationalist Ma clan. China's long civil war resumed after World War II.

A communist victory over the Hui armies of the Ma clan in 1949 initiated a strong movement for secession or even mass emigration to another country. Hui guerrillas fighting the advancing communists formed the Chungkuo Islam Djemiyeti (Chinese Islamic Association) in 1953. Pressed by the attempted collectivization of the Ningsia Plateau and the suppression of Muslim religious rights in northwestern China, Hui nationalists declared the Hui-populated districts south of the Alashan Desert independent of China on 9 August 1953, naming it the Chinese Islamic Republic. The republic lasted for less than a month before government troops retook the region. Dubbing the Hui "revisionists," "splittists," and "bandits," communist troops carried out a wholesale slaughter of captured Hui rebels and civilian supporters. The authorities dissolved the Hui autonomous region, which had been created in 1949, and incorporated Ningsia into the neighboring Chinese province of Gansu. After closing most mosques, communist officials first tried a combination of persuasion and pressure to separate the Hui from their Muslim religion, but later they instituted a campaign of harsh repression to force the stubborn Muslims to conform.

In 1957 the Hui demanded the benefit of socialist self-determination preached by communist leaders. Official reprisals sparked a renewed Hui uprising between April and June 1958. Defeated, the rebels, and all Muslims in China, lost their religious rights as a result, when the government enforced the state's official atheism. Communist officials closed all but a few of the remaining mosques and religious schools, but in a bid to undermine Hui nationalism they established autonomous Hui regions in eastern and western sections of the irrigated Ningsia plain and in the foothills of the Liu-p'an Mountains. In 1958 these areas were combined to form the Hui Autonomous Region of Ningsia, but with boundaries carefully drawn to ensure Han Chinese majorities.

The Cultural Revolution of the late 1960s led to violent confrontations between Hui and Han Chinese. Mobs led by fanatical Red Guards destroyed most of the Hui mosques, shrines, and monuments. Hui self-defense groups formed in an attempt to resist the chaotic attacks on turbaned men and forced marriages of Hui women to government functionaries. The official government policy aimed at the eradication of Islam eased only in the early 1980s, when China increased its efforts to establish ties to the wealthy Muslim states of the Persian Gulf.

Religious tolerance, again curtailed after the crushing of the prodemocracy movement in 1989, stimulated a renewal of Hui nationalism. The preoccupation with economic matters that has spread across China since 1990 has become a nationalist issue in Ningsia. In 1992 Hui incomes were less than the Chinese average and considerably less than in China's favored southeastern provinces. In August 1993, the publication of a book with an illustration depicting Muslims praying near a pig, anathema to Muslims, set off riots that spread to Ningsia in October. Only the rapid deployment of troops and police averted a serious crisis.

The relaxation of laws governing religious practices after 1991 allowed the Hui again to practice their religion openly. In April 1993 a ceremony marking the graduation of Hui Muslim students from the School of Islamic Theories was held at the largest mosque in the city of Xian. It was the first such ceremony in China since they had been banned in the early 1960s.

A newly published dictionary has put forward a new theory as to the origins of the Hui—that they originated from dozens of ancient ethnic groups, not from Arabs or Persians as is commonly believed. The theory asserts that the Hui evolved from groups from central, south, and southeastern Asia, as well as from Africa. In this view, the ancient maritime and land routes known as the silk roads facilitated the entrance into China of peoples from many different parts of the world.

There is a strong tradition, continuing to the present, of social ostracism of the Hui and ample historical precedent of periodic violent rebellions against discriminatory treatment. Since 1979 there has been a liberalization of government attitudes toward minority cultures and, at least officially, a more tolerant view of the Hui's Muslim religion. Current government policies have assuaged historical Hui resentment, but full social integration remains a theory only. The Hui continue to be economically disadvantaged, and their heartland in Ningsia is severely polluted; many are obliged to leave in order to earn livelihoods. The gap between the Hui and the more prosperous Han Chinese is widening, and poverty is widespread among the Hui population. Increased contact and trade between the Hui and the Muslim Middle Eastern countries, officially sponsored by the central government, has begun to slow migration from the Hui heartland in Ningsia, but it has also brought increased awareness and contracts with Islamic fundamentalism and Muslim nationalism.

The relationship between Islam and communism in China remains uneasy. Contradictory government policies seek to stimulate ethnic identity on one hand—the government's new policy to allow open religious activity aims at promoting solidarity among the Muslim minority groups—while applying pressure for cultural assimilation and national unity on the other. Official support for religious activity is balanced against efforts to adhere to official atheism. Both the central and regional governments emphasize the Chinese character of the Hui's Muslim religious practices.

In 1994, in a rare confirmation of minority unrest, government sources confirmed that 49 people had been killed in confrontations with paramilitary police units sent into Ningsia to suppress fighting between rival religious groups. Twenty-two Hui leaders were later sentenced to prison on charges of murder and of illegally stockpiling weapons and ammunition. There are reports that the training of future religious leaders has been severely restricted and that the regional government in Ningsia has obstructed the construction of new mosques as centers of discontent and secessionism. The Chinese authorities in January 1996 required all places of worship, including mosques, to register with the government.

Hui protesters demonstrated in early 1996 in several cities in Ningsia against the publication of a book on sexual practices that the Muslims deemed offensive. The book was subsequently banned. In July of 1996, China's first-ever official magazine dealing exclusively with religion was published, including an article outlining the government's intention to enforce restrictions on foreigners setting up religious groups or offices in China or recruiting Chinese followers. These prohibitions also severely limited the *haj*, the Muslim pilgrimage to Mecca.

The economic problems of the Ningsia region make emigration one of the few choices open to younger Hui. Greater economic contacts with Muslim countries could provide a much-needed economic boost and end the need for migration in search of work. The Chinese government committed itself to providing all minorities with the basic necessities by the year 2000, but the Hui are still waiting.

In September 2000 a Han Chinese meat seller displayed pork in Muslim northern Shandong province. Protests by Hui demonstrators continued for weeks, leading to a confrontation between Hui and local police in early December. The police fired on the Hui protesters, killing at least six and injuring over 40. The protests and demonstrations spread beyond Shandong to other Hui regions in several provinces. The disturbances, the most serious involving the Hui since the Cultural Revolution, showed that Islamic radical ideas had infiltrated the region in spite of tight government controls.

SELECTED BIBLIOGRAPHY:

Gladney, Dru C. *Muslim Chinese: Ethnic Nationalism in the People's Republic of China.* 1991.

Heberer, Thomas. *China and Its National Minorities: Autonomy or Assimilation?* 1989.

Lipman, Jonathan N. *Familiar Strangers: A History of Muslims in Northwest China.* 1998.

Schwartz, Henry G. *The Minorities of Northern China: A Survey.* 1984.

Ibans

Sea Dayaks; Sarawakians; Serewakians

POPULATION: Approximately (2002e) 855,000 Ibans in northeastern Borneo (Kalimantan), concentrated in the Malaysian state of Sarawak, with about 75,000 in adjacent areas of Indonesian Borneo and about 20,000 in neighboring Brunei. The related indigenous peoples of Sarawak, numbering over 1.2 million represent 37 closely related groups.

THE IBAN HOMELAND: The Iban homeland occupies a tropical lowland backed by mountains in the northeastern part of the large island of Borneo, also called Kalimantan, in the central Malay Archipelago. Much of the region is forested. Sarawak produces about a third of Malaysia's crude oil and gas, but the state receives just 5% of the royalties from the sale of the two commodities. All revenues from logging go to the state government, which has encouraged indiscriminate logging and timber exports—which, along with deforestation and plantation agriculture, is destroying the rain forests. Sarawak forms a state of the Federation of Malaysia and together with Sabah forms the region of East Malaysia. *State of Sarawak (Negeri Serewak)*: 48,342 sq. mi.—125,325 sq. km, (2002e) 2,219,000—Ibans 33%, Chinese 29%, Malays 17%, Dayaks* 8%, Bidayuh 5%, Melanaus 5%, other Malaysians 3%. The Iban capital and major cultural center is Kuching, (2002e) 371,000.

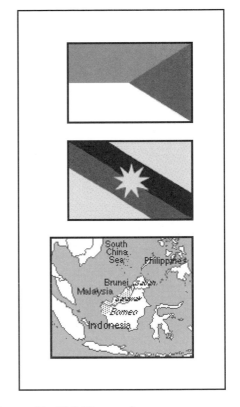

FLAG: The flag of the Iban national movement is a horizontal bicolor of red over white with a green triangle on the fly. The official flag of Sarawak state is a yellow field divided by diagonal black and red stripes upper hoist to lower fly, bearing a centered nine-pointed yellow star.

PEOPLE AND CULTURE: The Ibans, also (mistakenly) called Sea Dayaks, are the largest of the 37 indigenous groups of Sarawak. They were first called "Sea Dayaks" by the British, who came into contact with them in the 1840s. Traditionally the Ibans have referred to themselves by the names of the longhouse villages or rivers where they live; until the 1960s, they had no collective name. Their culture has evolved over thousands of years a distinctive belief system, customs, language. The Ibans often live in communal longhouses, often large enough to house an entire village. Traditionally the Iban culture has been intimately tied to the land and forest, the source of their food and other material needs. There is a closeness, respect, and interdependence between indigenous people, the land, and the forest. Before the advent of large-scale logging, plantation agriculture, and dams, the lifestyle of the Ibans and other Dayak peoples was simple but rich in tradition, food, and all basic necessities. Today, young Ibans are increasingly migrating to urban centers to find work. Oral traditions, such as myths and legends, and traditional recreations are slowly dying out. The effects of growing urbanization, radio and television, and consumer advertising have reached even the most remote groups in the interior. Although Iban society is classless, it is very status conscious, and personal achievement is important for status and prestige in the community.

LANGUAGE AND RELIGION: The Ibans speak a language of the Bornean subgroup of the Malayan group of Austronesian language family. The language includes smaller Ibanic dialects such as Balau, Milikin, Sibuyau; although related to the other Bornean languages, it is not intelligible to those of other Dayak groups. Iban proper is spoken in seven major dialects based on geographic region. Iban contains many loanwords from other Bornean languages and from Sanskrit. The Iban language is the lingua franca of the region and is understood by most of the diverse groups. The state's indigenous peoples speak a number of related Bornean languages of the Malay-Polynesian language group. In 1995, a meeting of more than 110 Iban leaders in Sarawak arrived at standardized guidelines on usages and spelling in the Iban language.

The traditional Iban religious beliefs are largely based on the integration of spirituality and the land, the source of all life. The traditional Iban religion is a fusion of animist and Hindu-Buddhist teachings. All objects have an indwelling spirit, and spirits inhabit the natural environment; therefore all living things must be respected. This spirituality once guided everyday life. Such beliefs have been diluted or even lost as Christianity spreads among the indigenous peoples, although most converts have adopted Christianity in addition to, rather than in place of, traditional religious beliefs. Many Christian leaders and missionaries condemn indigenous practices as evil or backward, often influencing the Ibans to abandon their traditional practices and beliefs. Some Christian groups, however, now attempt to integrate certain elements of their indigenous beliefs, such as traditional plant remedies and respect for the forest.

NATIONAL HISTORY: Early migrants inhabited the region from the interior of Borneo and by sea from the Asian mainland. Divided into tribes, the early settlers lived independently and self-sufficiently. The inhabitants, divided into tribal groups, engaged in chronic warfare, particularly among the coastal and highland tribes, of whose culture ritual head-hunting was an integral part.

In the fourteenth century Muslim sailors and traders introduced Islam to the coastal areas. Many of the coastal tribes embraced the new religion—partly to escape slavery, as it was forbidden for Muslims to buy and sell fellow Muslims. The Muslim coastal peoples eventually united under the powerful sultan of Brunei. By the sixteenth century the sultanate controlled most of the huge island of Borneo.

The Ibans originated deep within the interior of Kalimantan. They first crossed into Sarawak in the mid-sixteenth century, a mass migration that lasted until the early twentieth century. The first Iban settlements in Sarawak were north of modern Kuching, in the river valleys, where rice cultivation was possible. A second wave of migration in the 1800s settled the region south of Kuching. By the early 1900s, the Ibans had absorbed many smaller Dayak groups and had migrated as far across Sarawak as the coastal lowlands along the South China Sea.

The sultanate of Brunei was visited by Magellan in 1521. Tales of the opulent sultanate drew European adventurers to the island in the sixteenth and seventeenth centuries. European encroachments greatly weakened the sultanate, leading to a period of lawlessness, chaos, and piracy. A British subject, James Brooke, who arrived in 1839, offered his military experience to the sultan and assisted the Bruneis to defeat rebel Iban tribes and to suppress piracy. In 1841 a grateful sultan gave Brooke the title of raja and some 7,000 square miles of territory, the western portion of present-day Sarawak. Knighted by the British crown, Sir James proceeded to create a government and to put down head-hunting and piracy. In 1850 the United States recognized Sarawak's independence, and in 1864 the United Kingdom extended diplomatic ties.

In the late nineteenth century, the Ibans were often in rebellion against efforts to extend administrative control to their longhouses along the major rivers. The Brooke government's use of Muslims as mercenary soldiers in the conflicts set the stage for later disagreements between the indigenous Dayaks and the coastal Muslims. Additional lands, traditionally the homelands of the Ibans and other Dayak peoples, were added to the Sarawak state in 1881, 1885, 1900, and 1905.

Sir James's nephew, Charles Johnson, rechristened Brooke, succeeded as the second raja. Charles abolished slavery, encouraged commerce, and greatly extended the authority of his government. In 1888 Raja Charles Brooke accepted the protection of the United Kingdom. Charles Vyner Brooke succeeded his father in 1917, inheriting one of the most prosperous states in the Far East. To celebrate the centenary of the Brooke family's rule, a new constitution was adopted in 1941. The constitution provided for a legislature and a degree of representative government, including representatives of the Ibans and other Dayak groups. Before the administrative changes could take affect, however, Japanese forces invaded the state, forcing the Brooke family to flee.

During the Japanese occupation many Ibans were conscripted as forced labor. Sarawak, after liberation came under British military rule in September 1945. The economy in ruins, the Sarawak legislature voted 18 to 16 to become a British colony, in order to avail itself of British economic assistance for the task of reconstruction. On 1 July 1946 Raja Brooke ceded Sarawak to the United Kingdom, ending over a century of rule by the legendary "white rajas."

Customary land rights were recognized legally in Sarawak, but provisions that effectively resulted in the removal or questioning of these rights were adopted increasingly after 1958. Formal education and the introduction of mass media greatly changed the traditional Iban way of life. Learning a curriculum that had little to do with indigenous knowledge and ways led to a separation between real life and schooling, and a growing gap between the older and younger generations.

Newly independent Indonesia, which occupied most of the island of Borneo, laid claim to Sarawak in 1949. The discovery of oil increased tension between Indonesia and the British administration during the 1950s. British plans to include Sarawak in a proposed Malaysian federation incited strong resistance by the state's non-Malay Dayak majority, led by the Ibans. Ibans and dissident Chinese formed nationalist organizations across the border in Indonesian territory. In 1962, to forestall Sarawak's inclusion in predominantly Muslim Malaysia, the Ibans of the North Kalimantan Liberation Front (TNKU) revolted and occupied several towns. The rebel aim was an independent Iban state, eventually to include Brunei and Sabah as the Unitary State of North Kalimantan. The revolt was quickly suppressed by British troops, and the rebels fled across the border to Indonesian territory.

Sarawak joined the Malaysian federation on 16 September 1963. The accession agreement included safeguards for the non-Malay indigenous populations and offered considerable autonomy to states. The Indonesian government, however, refused to recognize the federation and actively supported attacks on the state by TNKU and communist groups from bases near the border in Indonesian territory. Violent antigovernment rioting brought intervention in the mid-1960s. The Ibans demanded that their language be adopted as an official language, leading to Sarawak's exclusion from the national language law.

Vast oil reserves and bauxite production converted Sarawak into Malaysia's most prosperous state, though a majority of the state's revenues were siphoned off for development projects in poorer mainland Malaya. Iban support for secession, a growing force in the state, rose and fell with the economic and political situation in the 1970s and the early 1980s.

Development projects, often benefiting the Malaysian government or large commercial companies—such as mining, logging, single-crop plantations, dams, airports, and tourist facilities—led to an increasing loss of land and resources among the Iban communities in the 1980s. At the same time, the traditional Iban social, religious, and political systems came under great stress as systematic religious proselytization, centralized educational systems and governmental decision making, and the mass media imposed themselves in ways both obvious and subtle.

The efforts of successive Malaysian federal governments to create a common political community meant in effect the promotion of cultural traditions of the politically dominant group, the Malay Muslims. Government politics favoring the Malay majority led to a rapid spread of nationalist sentiment in the 1980s. An ethnonationalistic consciousness, in the form of "Dayakism," emerged, an alliance of the Ibans and the smaller Dayak groups. The nationalist Parti Bansa Dayak Sarawak (PBDS) was formed in 1983. The Iban national organizations demanded greater linguistic, economic, religious, and political autonomy. Environmental concerns, particularly the increasing deforestation sanctioned by the government, became nationalist issues.

Demands by fundamentalist Muslim Malays for the creation of an Islamic state in Malaysia raised tension in 1989. Amid increasing demands for independence in the state, the Malaysian government cracked down on Iban nationalism in 1989–91 and detained many tribal and community leaders. Iban nationalism became a potent force in the 1990s, demanding more political control and changes to the government policies that siphon off too much of the Ibans' wealth for development projects in mainland Malaya.

The Sarawak state government, controlled by organizations allied to the political parties, continues to give out logging concessions and approve the setting up of new plantations by corporate bodies. To the Ibans, land cannot be separated from their history, identity, and future security. They view the loss of their lands to logging and plantations as loss of their identity and their way of life. Violence spread to the interior of the state, where tribal peoples opposed to the massive logging operations clashed with Malay police. The destruction of Sarawak's forests, one of the most controversial ecological attacks on a virgin forest region of the 1990s, galvanized Iban nationalism. The nationalists charged the Malaysian government with the wanton destruction of the habitat that the Iban and other Dayak tribes had guarded for thousands of years. Until the 1990s, the Ibans' independent spirit and their inability to work closely together kept them from gaining political power commensurate with their numbers.

In spite of a 1990 agreement on sustainable logging in Sarawak, timber exports increased every year during the 1990s. In 1999, exports increased 23% over 1998, and indiscriminate logging continued to decimate the region's forests. The Ibans, in March and April 2000, protested against the logging activities and the establishment of palm oil plantations on their customary lands. The growing economic gap between the more industrialized peninsula Malaya and the less prosperous East Malaysia has exacerbated Iban nationalism. Although protests and demonstrations are peaceful, according to Iban traditional *adat*, or custom, the growing frustration and resentment could lead to violence.

The Ibans, never effectively integrated into mainstream Malaysian society, feel marginalized and frustrated by the desecration of their traditional lands. The conflict between national integration and assertion of indigenous Iban cultural rights is increasingly complicated by the rise of Islamic fundamentalism among the large Muslim minority in mainland Malaya and by the rapid urbanization and shifting political loyalties of the Iban leadership. The Ibans, politically dominated by the Malays and economically dominated by Sarawak's Chinese minority, have nonetheless made great strides in education and are demanding more control over their own affairs and over their traditional territories.

SELECTED BIBLIOGRAPHY:

Bruton, Roy. *Farewell to Democracy in Sarawak*. 1996.
Jawan, Jayum A. *The Iban Factor in Sarawak Politics*. 1991.
Searle, Peter. *Politics in Sarawak 1970–1976: The Iban Perspective*. 1984.
Sutlive, Vinson Hutchins, Jr. *The Iban of Sarawak: Chronicle of a Vanishing World*. 1988.

Ibibios

Ibibio-Efiks; Calibaris; Kalibaris

POPULATION: Approximately (2002e) 5,750,000 Ibibios in West Africa, concentrated in the Nigerian states of Cross River and Akwa Ibom in southeastern Nigeria, with large communities in other parts of Nigeria and a small group in adjacent areas of Cameroon. Outside Africa there are sizable communities in the United Kingdom, Germany, Canada, and the United States.

THE IBIBIO HOMELAND: The Ibibio homeland, called Ibibioland or Calabar, lies in southeastern Nigeria just west of the Cameroon border, a densely populated region that rises from the delta of the Cross River on the Bight of Biafra to the Oban Hills and the spur of the Adamawa Mountains in the north. The main population concentrations are in the forest belt west of the Cross River and in the western half of the far north. Parts of Ibibioland are among the most densely settled areas in Africa south of the Sahara. The Ibibio homeland has no official status; the region, called Ibibioland, forms the Nigerian states of Akwa Ibom and Cross River. *Ibibioland (Calabar):* 10,534 sq. mi.—27,282 sq. km, (2002e) 7,636,000—Ibibios 71%, Ibos* 10%, Ekoi 6%, Cross Rivers tribes 5%, other Nigerians 8%. The Ibibio capital and major cultural center is Calabar, (2002e) 418,000. The other major cultural centers are Ugep, (2002e) 186,000 in Cross Rivers, Ikot Ekpene (2002e) 213,000, and Uyo (2002e) 105,000 in Akwa Ibom.

FLAG: The Ibibio flag, the flag of the national movement, is a horizontal bicolor of red over green divided by a centered yellow cross and bearing a white or yellow five-pointed star on the upper hoist. Another version of the flag is a horizontal bicolor of red over green divided by a centered yellow cross and bearing a multipointed white star on the upper hoist.

PEOPLE AND CULTURE: The Ibibio is not a single group but several

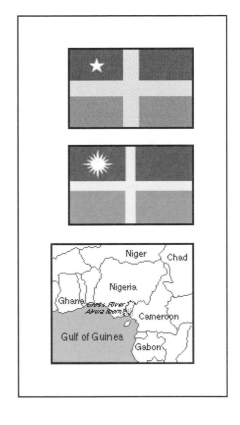

networks of independent communities, with local unity achieved by secret associations. The Ibibio nation includes six major divisions: Efik, Enyong (Northern), Eket (Southern), Anang (Western), Andoni-Ibeno (Delta), and the Ibibio proper (Eastern). Polygyny (multiple wives) was once widespread among the Ibibios but is now relatively rare. Groups of households related through male descent form a "house," led by the eldest male member. A group of related houses form a ward, of which several form a settlement. A chief, the *obung*, is elected from among the heads of various houses; he exercises his authority as the head of a secret society that cuts across clan or tribal lines. Secret societies, both male and female, are prominent in Ibibio life. The origins of the Ibibios remain disputed, but as the Ibibios are generally shorter than neighboring peoples, theories suggest that they represent a pre-Bantu or a mixed Pygmy and Bantu people.

LANGUAGE AND RELIGION: The Ibibio language, often called Efik-Ibibio, is a Kwa language of the Benue-Congo group of Niger-Congo languages. There are several major dialects, including Anaang or Anang, with 1.2 million speakers, taught in schools in the western districts. Efik, spoken around Calabar by about 375,000, is the major dialect and the literary language of all Ibibio speakers. Efik is used in radio, television, and in education. Around four million speak Ibibio proper, which is divided into two major dialects, Enyong and Nkari. Efik is decreasing as the major literary language, while Ibibio has become the main trade language over a wide area of southeastern Nigeria.

The majority of the Ibibios are Christians, mostly Protestants, with an important Roman Catholic minority. The largest of the Protestant sects is the nationalistic Brotherhood of the Cross and the Star. Traditional Ibibio religious beliefs involve a supreme creator god, ancestral and other supernatural beings, magic, sorcery, and witchcraft.

NATIONAL HISTORY: The Ibibios, believed to have inhabited a much larger area prior to the Bantu migrations, settled in the coastal areas on the Gulf of Guinea in the fifteenth century (oral tradition has them in the region much earlier). The Ibibio tribes, divided into clans and societies, founded a number of city-states along the coast, the most important of them Calabar, Bonny, Okrika, and Owome.

The Ibibio were among the first people in the region to come into contact with the Europeans. Visited by Portuguese expeditions in 1472–73, the city-states eventually established trading relations with several European countries. The original trade in local products soon gave way to a lucrative slave trade. The coastal peoples raided the interior tribes—the Ibos, Ekoi, and smaller tribes—for slaves to sell to the Europeans.

Calabar, the most important port on the West African coast in the seventeenth century, formed the center of a great commercial empire based on powerful trading houses. The various Ibibio city-states formed a loose political and mercantile union similar to the Hanseatic League of northern

Europe. The Ibibio secret societies, which controlled commerce and group relations, held the union together through a system of patronage.

A dispute over a royal ax, a symbol of local power, led to the division of the Ibibio tribe in the eighteenth century. The Efik clan, living around the city of Calabar, separated from the Ibibio and established the Ekpe Society, which assumed control of Calabar. Thereafter the Efik secret society, the Ekpe Society, controlled neighboring tribes, but the more numerous Ibibio continued to provide the manpower for the powerful Efik Calabar state before the European takeover of the region. The king of the Efiks still resides in Calabar and is greatly respected throughout Ibibioland.

The Ibibio mercantile houses, dependent on slavery for trade with the Europeans, passionately opposed the United Kingdom's abolition of slavery in 1807, but lax enforcement until 1875 assured continued prosperity. Calabar, superseded by Lagos as the region's major slave market in the nineteenth century, turned to palm oil products as an export.

The Ibibios, the first to establish relations with the Europeans, were also the first to be educated. The first church school was established by the Rev. Hope Waddell of the Free Church of Scotland in 1846. Christian missionaries, spreading the doctrines of their sects, also influenced the Ibibios in other ways, such as persuading the secret societies to prohibit human sacrifice in 1850.

Educated Ibibios entered the colonial government and engaged in commerce in many areas of Nigeria. Able to thrive in the European-dominated civil service and in trade, the Christian Ibibios developed a feeling of superiority toward neighboring peoples, particularly those in the less-developed interior. The Ibibio homeland, included in the British Oil Rivers Protectorate in 1884, remained the most advanced region of British Nigeria. The Efik language became the medium of instruction in the colony's early schools, and the first African language in Nigeria into which the Europeans translated the Bible. The first secondary school in Nigeria opened at Calabar, under the guidance of Scottish missionaries, in 1895.

The Ibibio actively resisted colonial encroachments, and it was not until after the end of World War I that the British were able to gain a strong foothold in Ibibioland. The British found it necessary to impose indirect rule, through the Ibibio Ekpe Society traditions. Under British rule the secret societies and the mercantile houses retained their paramount importance among the Ibibios.

The Ibos began to migrate to Calabar in the early 1900s to work in the lucrative palm oil trade. During World War I, trade was cut off with neighboring German Cameroon, leading to the collapse of the industry. During the course of the war a Christian breakaway prophet known as Elijah II secured a huge following by taking advantage of rumors that the British were going to leave the region because of the war. He claimed to be helping the Germans and promised independence for Calabar, but the

British occupation of the neighboring German colony revived the palm oil trade, and Elijah's nationalist movement faded.

After the war, population density forced many Ibibios to migrate to cities in western and northern Nigeria, where they proved successful as clerks, railway workers, and shopkeepers. The Ibibios tended to gather in separate areas of the foreign cities; in the early 1920s they formed self-help groups, which flourished as substitutes for the secret societies of their homeland.

Tension between the Ibibios and Ibos erupted in violence in October 1929; the rioting quickly took on serious anti-British overtones. Anticolonial incidents spread throughout the Cross River country, threatening the British hold on southeastern Nigeria. A fierce riot by the Ibibios in the port of Opobo was ended when colonial troops fired on a crowd, killing 32 and wounding many more. The incident is considered the origin of the modern Ibibio national movement. Ibibio nationalists formed the Ibibio State Union in 1944 to press for restrictions on Ibo immigration to their traditional lands, and to demand the creation of a separate Calabar region within Nigeria. In 1949 the growing domination of southeast Nigeria by the more numerous Ibos again set off nationalist rioting and fueled Ibibio demands for separation.

Nigeria became an independent state in 1960, a federation of three regions, each dominated by one of Nigeria's three largest tribes. The Ibibio homeland, forming part of the Eastern Region, came under the control of the Ibos, who inherited the commercial and bureaucratic structure in the former British zone. Ibibio agitation for separation increased as Nigeria's tribal tension worsened in the first years after independence. In 1965 the largest of the Ibibio nationalist organizations began a campaign for separation, not just from the Eastern Region but from increasingly chaotic and tribally divided Nigeria.

The Nigerian government, amid rising tribal tension, adopted a new constitution in 1967 that divided the three regions into twelve ethnic states. A new South-Eastern State, created for the Ibibios, provided a focus for loyalty to the federal government when three days later the Ibo proclaimed the Republic of Biafra and withdrew the entire Eastern Region from the Nigerian federation. The Ibibios rejected Ibo rule and generally refused to support the secession. When the Calabar region fell to federal troops in March 1968, however, the Ibibios were dismayed at the attitude of the soldiers. The occupation army treated Ibo and non-Ibo alike, not caring that the Ibibios had supported the federal cause from the beginning. Resentment flared into violence, but the disorders lasted only a short time before federal troops intervened.

The early 1970s were a period of reconstruction and reintegration into the federal Nigerian state. Spurred by the booming petroleum industry, Ibibioland quickly recovered, although the profits from its natural resources were siphoned off for development projects in other parts of the country, adding to the growing list of Ibibio grievances. In 1976 the Ibibios demanded the breakup of the South-Eastern state into two separate ethnic states, giving the Ibibio peoples their own state without the burden of the less-developed northern tribes. The federal government refused, agreeing only to rename the state Cross River.

The Ibibio national movement, dormant for nearly two decades, resurfaced in the late 1980s, fanned into life by renewed tribal tension and the frequent conflicts between Nigeria's southern Christian nations and the Muslim peoples of northern Nigeria, who dominated the military governments that had ruled Nigeria for most of the time since independence. The Ibibioland region, comprising Cross River state, was finally divided in 1987 to produce the new state of Akwa Ibom in the southwest; the new state boundaries also divided the Ibibio nation.

The once proud Ibibios now live in shacks without electricity, surrounded by the filthy and polluting oil industry. Increasingly bitter, the Ibibios, the former "Hanseatics" of Africa, still dream of their past glory. Nationalists assert that the Ibibios' national wealth (in the form of abundant oil), their separate language and culture, and their long history provide both the economic and spiritual resources for the creation of a viable independent Ibibio state. The growing ethnic animosity between the Ibibios and the Ibos to the west and north is rooted in the days of the slave trade, when the Ibos were the source of slaves.

In the late 1990s, the economic climate of Nigeria continued to cripple the Ibibio nation as a cooperative entity. Developments, both individual and communal, were and remain at a virtual standstill throughout Ibibioland. The necessity for Ibibios to migrate to Nigeria's western states to work as laborers in the cacao and rubber industries or as tenant farmers is a source of great resentment. Increasingly the Ibibios are emigrating, mostly to Europe and North America, but they retain strong links to their homeland.

The Ibibios only recently came to consider themselves a distinct nation. When the British gained control, the region was divided into a large number of autonomous towns and villages. In the twentieth century solidarity was promoted by the secret societies, which promoted Ibibio interests in multi-ethnic Nigeria. The Ibibios have been very successful in promoting cultural and political solidarity, which is fostered by the elites of the secret societies, which include cultural, nationalist, and economically based groups.

SELECTED BIBLIOGRAPHY:

Noah, Monday Efiong. *Ibibio Pioneers in Modern Nigerian History.* 1988.

Offiong, Daniel A. *Witchcraft, Sorcery, Magic and Social Order among the Ibibio of Nigeria.* 1991.

Udo, Edet A. *Who Are the Ibibio?* 1989.

Udoma, Udo. *Story of the Ibibio Union.* 1981.

Ibos

Igbos; Biafrans

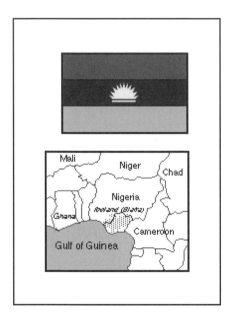

POPULATION: Approximately (2002e) 23,200,000 Ibos in Nigeria, concentrated in the southeastern states of Abia, Anambra, Enugu, Imo, with sizable Ibo populations in neighboring states, and in western and northern Nigeria. Outside Nigeria there are Ibo communities in Europe and North Africa.

THE IBO HOMELAND: The Ibo homeland lies in southeastern Nigeria east of the Niger River. Most of the region is upland savanna, with an extensive forest zone in the south, and lowlands of the Niger River delta, on the Bight of Biafra. Iboland, formerly called Biafra, has no official status. Except in the northeast, the region is mostly rain forest. The region claimed as Iboland comprises the Nigerian states of Abia, Akwa Ibom, Anambra, Cross River, Ebonyi, Enugu, Imo, and Rivers. *Iboland (Biafra)*: 29,848 sq. mi.—77,306 sq. km, (2002e) 29,876,000—Ibos 65%, Ibibios* 19%, Ijaws* 9%, other Nigerians 7%. The Ibo capital and major cultural center is Enugu, (2002e) 595,000, metropolitan area 665,000. The other important cultural centers are Onitsha, (2002e) 511,000, metropolitan area, 1,003,000; Port Harcourt (2002e) 1,047,00, metropolitan area, 1,205,000; and Aba (2002e) 792,000, metropolitan area, 940,000.

FLAG: The Ibo national flag, the flag of the former Biafran republic, is a horizontal tricolor of red, black, and green bearing a gold bar surmounted by a rising gold sun with eleven rays centered.

PEOPLE AND CULTURE: The Ibos, also called Igbos, are Nigeria's third-largest ethnic group, a Bantu people speaking a Niger-Congo language. Known for their energy and industry, the Ibos are often called the "Scots" of Nigeria, a tribute to their business sense and willingness to live outside their homeland for commercial purposes. The Ibos are loosely grouped into five main cultural divisions—the Onitsha in the north, the Owerri in the south, the Ika in the west, the Cross River in the east, and the Abakaliki in the northeast. Traditionally living in autonomous communities, by the mid-twentieth century a strong sense of ethnic identity had developed. There are numerous subgroups based on clan, lineage, and village affiliations. The majority of the Ibos are farmers, and their staple crop is yams—which are cultivated by men, while all other crops are tended by women.

LANGUAGE AND RELIGION: The Ibo language forms the Ibo branch of the Iboid group of the Kwa languages of Benue-Congo group of Niger-Congo languages. Due to the historical divisions of the Ibos, the language is spoken in at least 11 major dialects and dozens of subdialects. A standard literary language is developing from the dialect spoken around Owerri and Umuahia. The language is spoken as a trade language across a large part of southern Nigeria and is an official language in the southeastern states. The Ibos are among the most literate nations in Africa, largely because of a strong tradition of attending Christian missionary schools that emerged after the British conquest of Iboland in the early 1900s.

Many converted at that time to Christianity, especially Catholicism. Traditional Ibo religious beliefs included a creator god, an earth goddess, numerous deities and spirits, and a belief in ancestors that protect their descendants. Christian religious beliefs are now dominant, but traditional customs and beliefs remain strong, particularly ancestor worship and a belief in herbal cures.

NATIONAL HISTORY: Scholars believe that the Ibos originated in an area about 100 miles (160 km) north of their present-day heartland at the confluence of the Niger and Benue Rivers. The first Ibos may have moved into the region between four and five thousand years ago. Divided into over 200 autonomous tribes, the Ibos never developed a central authority like those of neighboring peoples. Cultural influences, particularly from the sophisticated kingdom of Benin to the west, shaped Ibo customs and art. Unified only by language and traditions, the over tribes remained subject to raids by slavers from the Muslim north and from the coastal tribes trading with the Europeans.

Europeans, pushing inland from the slave ports, made direct contact with the Ibo tribes in the seventeenth century. One tribe, the Aro, developed a vast commercial trade network with the Europeans and eventually engaged themselves in the lucrative slave trade, preying on the related tribes in the densely populated region. By the eighteenth century the needs of the slave trade began to encourage the emergence of a more united monarchical structure in Iboland. To protect themselves, many Ibo tribes organized to get new slaves taken from tribes farther north rather than from among themselves.

Christian missionaries, arriving in the early nineteenth century, found the Ibo particularly receptive to both Christianity and the educational opportunities offered by mission schools. By the 1830s Christianity had gained a foothold and spread over the next decades throughout the region

known as Iboland. Missionary education led to the evolution of an educated elite, one of the first in present-day Nigeria.

The Ibo homeland came under British rule in 1884, and a year later the
authorities consolidated the territory as the Oil Rivers Protectorate, administered by the British Royal Niger Company. Enthusiastically adopting
European culture and education, the Ibos quickly overtook the formerly
more advanced coastal peoples. Population pressure and a lack of opportunity pushed many educated Ibos to seek administrative and commercial
positions in other parts of British Nigeria. Favored by the British to fill
low-level civil service and military posts, many Ibos were placed in positions of authority in the north and southwest. Substantial Ibo communities
grew up in the coastal regions and in the Muslim north.

The dynamic Ibos, in the 1920s and 1930s, began to abandon clan and
tribal divisions and to think of themselves as one people. The name "Ibo"
came to symbolize the unity of the many related tribes. In the 1940s the
Ibos became politically active, though Ibo nationalism had no historical
tradition. In 1944 the first Ibo nationalist organization, the Ibo Federal
Union, formed to promote Ibo interests in multi-ethnic Nigeria.

Three regional governments, created by the British authorities in 1953,
were dominated respectively by Nigeria's three largest ethnic groups—the
Ibo in the Eastern Region, the Yoruba in the Western Region, and the
Muslim Hausas* and Fulanis in the Northern Region. Anti-Ibo riots broke
out in the Muslim north in protest of preceived Ibo domination of social,
political, and commercial institutions in the colonial government. Ibos
were hunted down and attacked in Kano; 245 were injured and some 53
murdered.

As independence neared in the late 1950s, the Ibos supported the National Council of Nigeria and the Cameroons (NCNC), which became the
voice of Ibo nationalism. The NCNC formed a coalition with the Hausa-
supported Northern People's Congress (NPC). which led Nigeria to independence in 1960. Ethnic and regional rivalries among the three regions
increased dramatically following independence, particularly as the Ibos lost
their privileged status, while the more numerous Hausas gained affluence
and increasingly controlled the federal government.

Oil production, begun in the Ibo's Eastern Region in 1958, stimulated
rapid economic growth and bolstered Ibo nationalism and confidence. By
the mid-1960s, economic and political rivalry and ethnic friction characterized Nigerian public life. Resentment of the dominant position of the
Northern Region, dominated by the Hausas, and the extravagant use of
the East's oil revenues for northern development projects, finally erupted
in an Ibo rebellion in January 1966. Ibo military officers staged a bloody
coup and replaced the Muslim-dominated Nigerian government with a
new administration under an Ibo president. Anti-Ibo rioting in the Muslim
north of Nigeria, pitting Ibos against Hausas, left many dead.

The northern Muslims in July 1966 launched a countercoup, killing many of the new Ibo leaders. The coup plotters installed a northern Christian, Maj. Gen. Yakubu Gowon, considered a neutral in the regional rivalries, as the new president. Before he could act, serious anti-Ibo rioting spread across the Northern Region; tens of thousands of Ibos were killed or injured. Fleeing the massacres, over a million Ibos fled south to the safety of the Ibo homeland in the southeast. Thousands of Ibos, unable to flee, were massacred by northern militias and civilians.

The anti-Ibo violence led many to believe that they could survive only if they seceded and formed their own country. Mistrust frustrated efforts at a political compromise. Following a futile attempt to win autonomy, Odumegwu Ojukwu, the Ibo leader, declared the Eastern Region independent on 30 May 1967. The new republic took its name from the body of water known as the Bight of Biafra, the part of the Atlantic Ocean that bordered the new state.

General Gowon, the leader of the federal government, refused to recognize Biafra's secession. Federal troops invaded the breakaway state in June 1967, and heavy fighting broke out. Most countries continued to recognize Gowon's government as the legitimate authority in Nigeria; the United Kingdom and the Soviet Union supplied it with arms. On the other side, the plight of starving children in Biafra brought airlifts of food and medicine from many countries. Côte d'Ivoire, Tanzania, Zambia, Gabon, and several non-African states recognized Biafra as an independent state. The French became the principal suppliers of arms to the breakaway Ibo state.

The Ibo troops were at first successful, but soon the numerically superior federal forces began to overrun the south, west, and north. In spite of the overwhelming odds, the Biafrans fought on through 1968 and 1969. Starvation struck the helpless civilian population, and hundreds of thousands died of hunger. The Biafran government, pressed into a tiny fraction of its former territory, finally surrendered in January 1970, ending the most savage war in African history, and the first major televised conflict. An estimated 100,000 casualties resulted from the war itself, and an additional 500,000 to two million civilians died, mainly from starvation as a result of a blockade by federal forces. Following the Biafra war, the Ibos were further marginalized from government positions, though Gowon's government attempted to reintegrate them back into Nigerian society.

The Nigerian regions, officially divided into twelve states in 1967, were further divided in 1976 in an effort to dilute continuing ethnic nationalism. The civil war, which completed the consolidation of the Ibo nation, has become a component of Ibo nationalism, nourished by the legends and memories of the war of independence. The military governments of Nigeria, mostly dominated by ethnic Hausas, banned all political activity but favored northern Muslims for government positions and development projects. The Ibos continued to be excluded from many government ministries and positions.

Regional nationalism, exacerbated by the rapid growth of Muslim fundamentalism in northern Nigeria, took on strong religious overtones in the 1980s. Following the 1979 elections, which once again resulted in northern Muslim dominance of Nigerian politics, there were increased claims of the "forced Islamization" of Nigeria. In 1986 the Nigerian military government allowed the country to join the Organization of Islamic Conferences (OIC), leading to widespread rioting throughout Iboland in the southeast. Tension increased in 1987 as northern Muslims called for the imposition of Shari'a law and Islamic courts. The Hausa-dominated Nigerian government announced that Nigeria would remain a secular state, but allowed Shari'a law to be adopted in Muslim-majority states in northern Nigeria.

Serious ethnic and religious conflict again threatens to tear Nigeria apart. An attempted coup by Christian military officers in 1990 led to many arrests and the execution of 69 plotters. The continuing Muslim-dominated military government, renewed in 1993 following the annulment of presidential elections, has provided resurgent Ibo nationalism with a cause—to free the mostly Christian Ibo from decades of Muslim rule.

Anti-Christian riots in several northern Muslim-dominated states in 1990–91 were the first of a series of violent clashes that continued into the twenty-first century. The riots, which accompanied Christian objections to the introduction of Islamic law in the states, were compared to the anti-Ibo riots of the late 1960s. Hundreds of Christians, mostly Ibos, were killed and injured in the ongoing violence, which again raised the level of ethnic tension and fueled the growing nationalist sentiments among Nigeria's major ethnic groups. An Ibo man in Kano was beheaded for supposedly defaming the Koran, by Muslims who took him out of the local police station in June 1995. The incident, widely reported in Iboland, where it is widely thought that the man was unjustly accused, led to a new round of ethnic and religious violence. The Nigerian government has refused to intervene in the growing ethnic and religious violence.

Discontent and nationalist sentiment in Iboland is growing in direct relation to the economic problems plaguing Nigeria. After decades of extracting oil worth hundreds of billions of dollars, the Nigerians have the same per capita income of $300 that they earned in 1960. Nigeria pumps about $40 million worth of oil per day, but the funds are wasted, stolen, or used for development in the Muslim north. Soon after the Biafran War, oil revenues were officially divided, 50% for the federal government and 50% for local development. The figure in late 1995 is officially 3% for local development, and even that small amount mostly disappears through corruption.

The former Biafra leader, Emeka Odumegwu Ojukwu, declared himself the king of the Ibos in May 1995. The title, conferred by a leading chief, was later rejected by the Oha-na-Eze, the highest body in Iboland. It claimed that there is no king in Iboland and that Ojukwu wished to use the title for political gain. In 1997 Ojukwu announced that it was the turn of the Ibos to present the next civilian president, but his leadership of the Ibos was increasingly challenged by younger nationalists. The Ibos remain politically fragmented, with numerous factions resulting from their geographic differences.

In August 1999 the Igbo National Council of Chiefs threatened that the Ibos would pull out of Nigeria should the Nigerian administration fail to correct what they called an imbalance in ministerial and other political appointments. Few Ibos hold positions in the Nigerian government beyond local or state levels.

Increasingly, ethnic tension in the region are taking on a religious element. The Ibos living in northern Muslim towns continue to be harassed and sometimes killed by the Muslim Hausas. The Ibos have retaliated with violence against the Muslims, but many are returning to the Ibo homeland in the southeast, mirroring the events of 1965–67. Ibo leaders claim that the situation has been exacerbated by the government's refusal to intervene. The Ibos continue to feel marginalized from the central government and are in danger because of their antigovernment sentiments.

Renewed religious and ethnic violence broke out in the northern city of Kaduna in March 2000, with several hundred Ibos murdered by mobs. In retaliation, up to 450 predominantly-Muslim ethnic Hausas were killed in a massacre by mainly Christian ethnic Ibos in the city of Aba. There were also deaths in a number of other towns in Iboland. In May 2000, young militants of Massob (Movement for the Actualization of a Sovereign State of Biafra) marched through several Ibo cities to mark the 30th anniversary of the defeat of Biafra and to call for the resurrection of a separate Ibo republic.

In January 2001, the leaders of the Ibos met in Enugu to discuss their future in Nigeria. The meeting of traditional leaders, politicians, businessmen and youth leaders is expected to discuss relations with President Olusegun Obasanjo's government and the degree of political and fiscal autonomy that might be granted to regions under a constitutional review. The Ibos feel they have been under-represented in central government since the defeat of their breakaway state of Biafra in the civil war thirty years ago. The governors of the Ibo-majority states are pressing for more autonomy while trying to placate younger nationalists calling for separation from Nigeria.

Many Ibos were among the victims of attacks on Christians in northern Nigeria following the American attack on Afghanistan following the September 2001 terrorist attacks in the United States. The Muslims, believing that the attack was an attack on Islam, turned on the Christian minorities.

The religious violence added to the already tense ethnic and regional situation in Nigeria.

SELECTED BIBLIOGRAPHY:

Achuzia, Joe O.G. *Requiem Biafra*. 1986.
Bleeker, Sonia. *The Ibo of Biafra*. 1988.
Ekwe-Ekwe, Herbert. *The Biafra War: Nigeria and the Aftermath*. 1990.
Emecheta, Buchi. *Destination Biafra*. 1994.

Ijaws

Ijos; Izons; Izos; Uzos

POPULATION: Approximately (2002e) 13,120,000 Ijaws in Nigeria, concentrated in the Niger Delta of southern Nigeria, scattered across the states of Rivers, Bayelsa, Delta, Ondo, Edo, and Akwa Ibom. Outside the region there are sizable Ijaw communities in Lagos, the country's major city, and in Europe, principally the United Kingdom and Ireland, and in the United States.

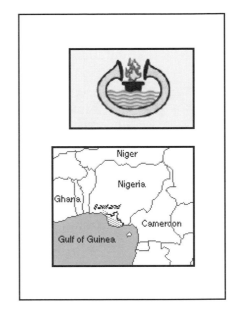

THE IJAW HOMELAND: The Ijaw homeland, locally called Ijawland, occupies the vast delta of the Niger River in West Africa. The region, traversed by the many branches of the Niger, is mostly flat—coastal plains and mangrove swamps stretching for nearly 200 miles along the Bight of Biafra. The defined Ijawland is contiguous, except for mixed Ijaw and Itsekiri communities on the Benin and Escravos Rivers, and culturally homogenous, but it is administratively divided among several states. The Ijaw heartland comprises the Nigerian states of Rivers, Bayelsa, and Delta. *Ijawland*: 27,821 sq. mi.—72,056 sq. km, (2002e) 10,931,000—Ijaws 48%, Ibos* 22%, Urhobos 11%, Isekiris 10%, other Nigerians 8%. The Ijaw capital and major cultural center is Port Harcourt, (2002e) 1,047,000, metropolitan area, 1,205,000. The other important cultural center is Warri, (2002e) 498,000.

FLAG: The Ijaw national flag, the flag of the Ijaw Youth Congress and the flag used by nationalists, is a white field bearing a centered gold bracelet enclosing blue and white wavy lines and red and gold flames.

PEOPLE AND CULTURE: The Ijaws are a Bantu people comprising a number of formerly autonomous groups. Outside the major cities, each group occupies a cluster of villages linked by loose ties of cooperation, particularly against common enemies. At group and village levels, authority is exercised by assemblies of elders, often presided over by priests. The Ijaws have only recently begun to see themselves as a nation, and many still identify with clans or regions. They remain divided into a number of

769

subgroups, including the Kalabari, Nembe, Ogina, Yenegoa, Ikwere, and Warri. Regional cultural differences remain strong, but recent history has fostered mobilization and unification as a nation.

LANGUAGE AND RELIGION: The Ijaw language is a language of the Ijoid group of the Kwa branch of the Niger-Congo language group. The language is spoken in five major dialects—Central-Western, Southeast Ijo, Kalabari, Ibani, Okrika. The Central-Western group is spoken in western Rivers state, in the Burutu, Warri, and Ughelli regions of Delta state, and in Ikale and Ilaje Ese-Odo regions of Ondo state. The Central-Western group is made up of seven separate languages and about 30 mutually intelligible dialects. The Kolokuma dialect is used in radio, television, and in education. Kalabari, Ibani, and Okrika, all spoken in Rivers, form a dialect cluster within the Ijo language region. English is widely spoken in the region.

The majority of the Ijaws claim to be Christian, the result of nineteenth-century missionary activity, mostly in various Protestant denominations. Adherence to traditional religious beliefs, however, remains strong. Cults of water spirits and aquatic animals, especially the hippopotamus and crocodile, are still widespread.

NATIONAL HISTORY: The Ijaws are thought to have migrated to their present homeland in the Niger Delta in the thirteenth century. Following the river south, they spread across the delta in self-governing villages. The decentralized pattern of life, focused on self-contained villages or federations of village communities, was perpetuated by the sharing of various governmental functions among societies of elders and age-grade associations, with groups of youngsters educated together, which creates strong bonds. Secret societies also played an important role in local administrations. The traditional economy was based primarily on fishing; each Ijaw group claimed a distinct culture, as well as political autonomy.

Following contact with European merchants about 1500, communities such as Bonny, Okrika, and Nemke (Brass) began trading with the newcomers, mostly in slaves imported from the interior. Initial Portuguese contacts were focused on Warri in the delta, but other Europeans made contact with other coastal towns, which developed into active trading centers. Various coastal communities organized as middlemen in the trade, partly so they would not become its victims.

Wealthy traders became very powerful in the city-states. The new class of Ijaw merchants, who freed themselves from some of the restrictions of traditional society, were able to accumulate personal wealth and power to rival that of the local kings and often governed alongside them. The new trading class was experienced in European ways and often secured for their sons elements of a European education.

The emergence of the trading city-states of the Niger Delta represented a social revolution in the eighteenth century. The needs of the overseas trade began to encourage the emergence of monarchical structures beyond the village level. The traditional kinship system gave way to the "house" system, which included both freemen and a large number of slaves needed for trading canoes and caravans from the interior. Strategic and trading settlements were bound by common economic interests into large corporations led by wealthy merchants.

A high proportion of the slaves sold in the Ijaw city-states came from the Niger River delta. The various city-states controlled the waterways to the densely populated homelands of the interior tribes of Ibos and Tiv,* among whom slave raiding was widespread. Local chiefs often sold excess population for the European slave trade; the region was unique in having such an excess supply of labor. In exchange for slaves, the Ijaws and other tribes received supplies of cloth, metals, tools, knives, and later guns.

The suppression of the slave trade, outlawed in the British Empire in the 1830s, was an economic disaster for the Ijaws. Many turned to palm oil and palm kernels to survive, but the prosperity of the slave era never returned. Gold, gum, hides, timber, and other commodities were also exported. Most of Ijawland was incorporated as part of the Oil Rivers Protectorate in 1885 and the Niger Coast Protectorate in 1893, and it became part of the amalgamated British colony and protectorate of Nigeria in 1914.

In 1958, crude oil was discovered in commercial quantity at Oloibiri, in territory claimed by the Ijaws. Oil companies such as Shell, Agip, Elf, and Chevron, in cooperation with successive Nigerian governments and the military, have extracted the oil with little concern for the environment or the people living in the area. Economic exploitation, environmental degradation, and what amounted to internal colonialism by the Nigerian military have resulted. Human-rights abuses and violence quickly eroded the self-sustaining economy of the pre-oil era. Much of the oil wealth was badly mismanaged or unaccounted for.

During the colonial era and after Nigerian independence in 1960, the Ijaws were divided between the Yoruba-dominated Western Region and the Ibo-dominated Eastern Region. When the Ibos seceded in 1967, the Ijaws were divided between two warring factions. Federal troops, often including Ijaw soldiers, invaded the secessionist state of Biafra, often treating the local population as conquerors, although the majority of the Ijaws had resisted secession. Resentment of their treatment by federal troops is still fanned by Ijaw militants.

Muslim groups from northern Nigeria dominated the country for most of the period from the surrender of Biafra in 1970 until 1999. As government became more and more firmly in the hands of the ethnically, religiously, and historically distinct northerners, the Ijaws began to unite. Although they represented the fourth-largest ethnic group in Nigeria, their dispersal in several states and their historical decentralization had previously blocked effective political or cultural mobilization.

The Ijaws lived in abject poverty, without electricity, alongside the modern technology used to extract what they feel is their natural resource. Work in the oil fields or emigration to the burgeoning cities became the only alternatives to staying on the increasingly polluted land. Control of land thought to contain oil became one of the only ways to prosper, leading to violent confrontations between ethnic groups in the delta. The poverty of the inhabitants of the oil-rich delta increasingly became a cause of popular protest. Since 1971, all revenues from oil production have gone to the federal government.

The Ijaws, claiming that the delta was their original homeland and that other tribes had moved into it in modern times, demanded more control over the resources of the region and over development of the oil industry. They also demanded compensation for environmental damage affecting their fishing and farming, and a fair share of oil revenues. For 30 years the Ijaws' oil wealth led only to problems, as the oil companies polluted their land and waterways, and the government did not return to the region enough of the oil revenues either to clean up the damage or promote development in general.

Activists founded the Movement for the Survival of the Ijaw Ethnic Nationality in 1992, but until 1996–97 the Ijaws remained relatively quiet. George Weikezi, the president of the Ijaw Association, has stated that the Ijaws have nothing to show for their membership of the Nigerian federation. The Nigerian government, in 1996, began to divide Nigerian administrative states into smaller units and to move the capitals of some to different cities. These actions led to serious conflicts between communities, who, already concerned about the lack of development of their communities, felt that the loss of local government offices would give them even less access to resources.

In 1998, Nigerian troops were sent to the delta to protect the oil industry against the increasingly militant Ijaws. Troops were airlifted to the city of Warri, the center of the violence and of the Ijaw protests. Demonstrations against the presence of security forces and for a halt to oil production further divided the ethnic groups in the region, leading to raids and reprisal killings.

Ijaw leaders issued on 11 December 1998 the Kaiama Declaration, which demanded the immediate withdrawal from Ijawland of all military forces of the Nigerian state and declared that any oil company that employed the services of the armed forces would be viewed as an enemy of the Ijaw nation. The declaration set out the terms for the self-determination and survival of the Ijaw people, without specifying whether within Nigeria or in a separate state.

In January 1999 the Nigerian military reportedly used helicopters belonging to Chevron Oil Company to attack two Ijaw communities in the western delta. Clashes between Ijaws and Itsekiris just south of Warri reportedly caused nearly 200 deaths. Western and Nigerian oil companies evacuated their personnel from the area as the fighting neared the export terminals. In August 1999, the Nigerian military warned militant Ijaws to stay away from military establishments in order to avoid bloody clashes.

President Olusegun Obasanjo, inaugurated in May 1999 as the first civilian leader of Nigeria in 15 years, met with leaders of the Ijaws, Urhobos, and Itsekiris in June of that year in an effort to end the violent ethnic fighting in Delta state. In an effort to pacify the communities, he created a Special Project Division to plan the development of such services as electrification, environmental protection, sanitation, education, and housing. Ijaw militants rejected his efforts and launched attacks on the Itsekiri, a subgroup of the Yorubas* and the majority population in the city of Warri. The seizure of oil installations and workers seriously disrupted oil production, Nigeria's major economic resource.

New fighting in July–August 1999 between Ijaws and Ilajes in Ondo state left nearly 60 people dead. Fighting between Ijaws and Yoruba groups spread to Lagos in September. In November 1999 government troops attacked the Ijaw town of Odi in Bayelsa state after crowds killed 12 policemen. The troops destroyed much of the town, leaving many dead and injured. The extent of the incident could not be confirmed, as the Nigerian government banned journalists and others from the area. Ijaw activists and human-rights groups accused the military of a pattern of retribution against civilians in the Niger delta. The attack and the so-called massacre inflamed the situation.

The Odi incident led to the widespread mobilization of the Ijaws. Militants issued in January 2000 a statement claiming that "enough is enough" and that the Ijaws must separate from Nigeria. They proposed the creation of a Niger Delta republic, with an Ijaw majority. Independence, they claimed, would enable the Ijaws to benefit from their oil and control the disastrous environmental damage previously allowed by the Nigerian government.

The Ijaw National Congress was founded on 14 September 1999, with its stated aim the liberation of the Ijaws from decades of environmental pollution, corporate violence, unjust socioeconomic structures, and political oppression. During the visit of President Bill Clinton of the United States in August 2000, activists called for the shutdown of all oil and gas production—a gesture meant to prove that they are committed to redressing the massive damage to the regional environment. The Ijaw Youth Council accused President Clinton of aiding and abetting the destruction of lives and property in the Niger delta.

In 1999, Nigerian President Olusegun Obasanjo promised to develop the oil-producing areas when he came to power. He set up a new body, the Niger Delta Development Commission (NDDC), to do this. But so far little has changed for the residents of the area, with unemployment still high and infrastructure poor. Funds may get as far as the state capitals, even local government headquarters, but little filters down to local communities.

The Ijaws shut down Chevron and Shell production sites for most of October 2000, causing the loss of 600,000 barrels per day in production. In November 2000, militants called on Nigeria Agip Oil, a division of Italy's Agip firm, to leave Ijawland immediately or face the wrath of the Ijaw nation. To begin with, Agip was given 21 days to move its operations out of the central Ijaw zone in Bayelsa. The militants also demanded that all Ijaws working for Agip resign with 21 days, to avoid being caught in a cross-fire. The militants' actions were endorsed by 39 Ijaw clans across the delta region, an indication of widespread resentment and anger. The Nigerian government declared a state of emergency in Bayelsa state.

The crisis in the Niger delta continues to be a serious threat to the integrity and unity of the Nigerian state. The creation of more militant groups such as the Niger Delta Volunteer Force, which demands that 70% of all positions in all companies in the Niger delta and 20% shareholding in all oil companies in the delta be reserved for Ijaws. If their demands are not met by an unspecified date, militants threaten to take Ijawland out of Nigeria and to form an independent state to be known as the Niger Delta Republic. The moderate majority, although sympathetic to the separatists, would probably be satisfied with a radical restructuring of the Nigerian state.

Most communities still do not have electricity, transportation and roads are nearly nonexistent, medical care is rudimentary, and health problems connected to environmental damage are growing dramatically. Ironically, gasoline sells for 10 times the official price in the region, because it is so scarce. The damage caused to the region by local pipelines has caused a number of oil spills, which have attracted thousands of people scavenging from burst pipelines. In mid-October 1999, an estimated 700 people were killed in an explosion at such a pipeline break near Warri. The poverty of the Ijaw homeland remains the major cause of the growing militancy. By the end of 2001 the Ijaws had become the most militant and active of the many nations of Nigeria.

Nationalists, in late 2001, declared that the operations of the international oil companies that have colluded with successive military and civilian governments of Nigeria in war of economic exploitation, environmental degradation, and of internal colonialism will no longer go on with impunity. Any oil company that employs the services of the armed forces of the Nigerian State to "protect" its operations will be viewed as an enemy of the Ijaw people.

SELECTED BIBLIOGRAPHY:

Ayomike, J.O.S. *The Ijaw of Warri: A Study in Ethnography.* 1978.
Leis, Philip E. *Enculturation and Socialization in an Ijaw Village.* 1982.
Nnoli, Okwudiba. *Ethnicity and Development in Nigeria.* 1995.
Okonta, Ike, ed. *Where Vultures Feast: Shell, Human Rights, and Oil in the Niger Delta.* 2001.

Ingrians

Inkeri; Inkeroiset; Ingers; Inkeriläinen; Inkeroine; Inkerin Suomalainen; Ingrian Finns; Maaväki; Izhor

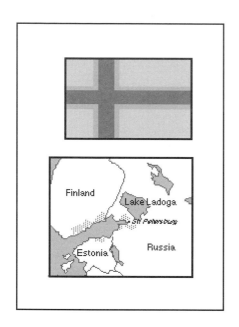

POPULATION: Approximately (2002e) 355,000 Ingrians in northeastern Europe, 85,000 in Russia, and another 20,000 in Estonia and 250,000 in Finland. Outside Europe there are Ingrian communities in the United States and Canada.

THE INGRIAN HOMELAND: The Ingrian homeland lies in northwestern Russia, mostly a flat plain between Lake Ladoga and the Gulf of Finland along the shores of the Neva River and on the east bank of the Gulf of Finland, just north of the St. Petersburg metropolitan area. Lake Ladoga, called Laatokka by the Ingrians, the largest lake in Europe, has abundant fish harvests but is frozen from October to April. The region is used mostly for dairy and truck farming; large herds of hogs and cattle provide produce needed by the over five million urban dwellers of the St. Petersburg area. Ingria has had no official status since 1938; it now forms a nonpolitical district of St. Petersburg Oblast of the Russian Federation. *Region of Ingria (Inkeri):* 1,546 sq. mi.—4,005 sq. km, (2002e) 172,000—Russians 58%, Ingrians 35%, Finns 3%, others 4%. The unofficial capital of Ingria is Zelenogorsk, called Teroki by the Ingrians, (2002e) 24,000. The other major cultural centers are Lomonosov, called Kaaresta by the Ingrians, (2002e) 32,000, on the south shore of the Gulf of Finland; Gatchina, called Hatshina, (2002e) 82,000; and St. Petersburg.

FLAG: The Ingrian national flag, the flag of the former Ingrian republic of North Ingermanland, is a yellow field charged with a blue Scandinavian cross outlined in red.

PEOPLE AND CULTURE: The Ingrians are a Finnic nation, comprising two major divisions—the Ingrians, the descendants of seventeenth-century migrants from Finland; and the Izhor or Izhorians, the original Finnish population of the region, who numbered about 15,000 in 2000. The Ingrians call themselves Inkeri; the Izors are often called Inkerrikko. The Ingrians, part of the East Baltic peoples, are generally fair and with light eyes; they tend to be shorter and stockier than the related Finns or Estonians. Estimates of the total Ingrian populations in the region, including the Izhor on the south shore of the Gulf of Finland, vary greatly, as many have registered as ethnic Russians since the Second World War. A new interest in their language, history, and culture has revitalized the Ingrian nation. Nationalists claim an Ingrian population in the region of over 200,000 and another 400,000 outside Russia, mostly in Finland.

LANGUAGE AND RELIGION: The Ingrian language, Inkerin or Suomen Kieli, is closely related to Finnish; it is partially intelligible to the other Finnish peoples of northwestern Russia, the Karels,* the Veps,* and the Votes.* The Ingrian literary language is identical to Finnish, although the spoken form is different. The language, like Finnish, is written in the Latin alphabet; it is spoken in four major dialects that gradually merge into Karelian. Some scholars list the Ingrian dialects as eastern Finnish dialects. In 1995 the language began to be taught in local schools, replacing the official Russian language.

The majority of the Ingrians and Finns are Protestant Lutherans; a minority are Orthodox. The Lutheran Church, which was allowed to establish new parishes during the 1990s, has become a major center for contact with the Finns of Finland and for rapid reculturation among the Ingrians. Church schools, established as early as 1632, are responsible for the high level of education among the Ingrians, a tradition that continues to the present.

NATIONAL HISTORY: The first permanent settlements on the southern shore of the Gulf of Finland appeared around A.D. 100, when migrating tribes arrived. Finnish tribes from the Volga River basin settled most of northwestern Europe by the eighth century. The tribes gradually separated into a number of separate nations speaking similar languages and with many cultural traits in common. The nomadic Ingrians settled as farmers and fishermen in the flatlands around the gulf and Lake Ladoga to the north. During the tenth and eleventh centuries, some groups broke off from the Ingrians to settle farther south along the Izhora (Inkere) River. In the thirteenth century, Scandinavian monks introduced Christianity to the pagan Ingrians.

The Ingrians, inhabiting the region between the Gulf of Finland, the basin of the Neva River, and Lake Ladoga, were separated from the Finns in the early Middle Ages. From the thirteenth until the late fifteenth centuries, the Ingrians were under the rule of the Slav republic of Great Novgorod. The Ingrians, with their thriving farms and fishing activities, prospered from the trade routes that crossed their homeland. The Novgorodians, more interested in trade than in empire, mostly left the Ingrians to govern themselves and to keep the trade routes to northern Europe safe for Novgorod's traders.

In 1478 Russians from Muscovy, an expanding duchy to the south, overthrew the prosperous Novgorodian republic. Thousands of Ingrians were deported to Russia in 1484–88 to allow colonization of their lands by Russians. Russians, Swedes, and Teutonic Knights contested for control, leaving devastation in their wake. In 1617 the Swedes, under King Gustavus II, conquered the region. During the century of Swedish rule, the Ingrians adopted many Swedish cultural traits and the Swedes' Lutheran religion. Thousands of immigrants from Swedish Finland settled in the eastern Swedish province of Ingermanland around the Gulf of Finland, where they mixed with the indigenous Izhor Ingrians. Between 1656 and 1695, the Ingrian portion of the regional population grew from 41% to 74% of the total.

During the Northern War between Sweden and Russia, the major Swedish fort on the Neva River fell to the forces of Peter II in 1702. The next year Peter, called the Great, began to lay out on the site a new city—St. Petersburg, to be Russia's new capital and its window on the West. The construction of Russia's new capital, called Pietari by the Finnic peoples, brought a massive influx of Slav workers; the city's expansion slowly pushed the native Ingrians westward along the north and south shores of the gulf. Ingria was designated as the province of St. Petersburg in 1710. In 1721 Sweden permanently ceded Ingria to Russian rule. Despite the loss of many of their ancient lands, the Ingrians prospered, supplying the capital with grains and vegetables. In the late eighteenth and early nineteenth centuries, the Ingrians also developed a timber industry, which supplied building materials to the expanding city of St. Petersburg. The growth of the city drew large numbers of Russians; the Ingrians became a minority.

The Russian government's policy of assimilation of minorities succeeded within the expanding urban area in the eighteenth and nineteenth centuries, but it met strong resistance among the large rural Ingrian population. A cultural revival, influenced by the neighboring Finns and Estonians, began to take hold in the 1880s. As a particular result of the Ingrians' Lutheranism and their education in Finnish, a feeling of unity with the Finns of Finland developed. The revival spawned a modest national movement, which gained support following the violence of the 1905 revolution.

There was a steady increase in the Ingrian population in the late nineteenth and early twentieth centuries. The Ingrians grew to 130,413 in 1897, and the Izhorians, counted as a separate national group, numbered 21,700 in 1897 and 26,137 in 1926.

In February 1917, the Ingrians living around the Gulf of Finland enthusiastically welcomed the revolution that overthrew the hated Russian autocracy. Numbering now about 500,000, according to nationalists, the Ingrians in the region petitioned the new Russian government for autonomy within a democratic Russia. More militant nationalists, supported by groups in Finland and Estonia, proposed an independent Ingria around the Gulf of Finland, linking Finland and Estonia. The city of Petrograd (as St. Petersburg was now called) would enjoy autonomous status within the new state.

The Bolsheviks, after taking power in Petrograd in October 1917, promised the Ingrians autonomy within the new Soviet state but instead soon harshly suppressed them, once Soviet power had been consolidated. The many Ingrians who had supported the Bolsheviks, betrayed by the Soviet promise of autonomy, mostly joined the nationalists in opposition to Bolshevik rule. Rebellion spread, with Ingrian rebels taking control of the territory between the new Finnish border, Lake Ladoga, the northern shore of the Gulf of Finland, and the outskirts of Petrograd. The Bolsheviks, hard pressed by the escalating Russian Civil War, were unable to spare troops to deal with the Ingrian rebels until late 1919. On 23 January 1920, threatened by the Red Army, the Ingrian leaders declared the independence of their homeland, which they often called North Ingermanland. Meanwhile, they sent frantic pleas for aid to newly independent Finland. The Finns, in the final months of their own war with the Soviets in the north, could not respond to the appeals, but in late 1920 they negotiated Finnish control of western Ingria, called Ingerinta by the Finns, as part of the peace treaty with the new Soviet Union. The Ingrians left under Soviet rule surrendered to the Red Army in 1921.

The new Soviet government, as part of its nationalities program, created in 1928 a national district called Kuivaisi, Toksova in Russian, for the remaining 115,000 Ingrians. The Ingrians resisted forced collectivization, which was begun the same year. Around 18,000 people were deported from northern Ingria to eastern Karelia, Central Asia, and elsewhere in order to frighten others into accepting collective farms. The Soviet authorities accused the Ingrian Lutheran hierarchy of anti-Soviet activities; all churches and religious societies were forcibly closed, and religious practices forbidden, in 1932. A further 7,000 Ingrians were deported in 1935, and over 20,000 were shipped to Siberia and Central Asia in 1936. Accused of anti-Soviet activities as relations worsened between the Soviet state and Finland in the late 1930s, the entire Ingrian national leadership was purged in 1937; in the same year, cultural activities in the Ingrian language were forbidden. Further punishments included mass deportations and the burning of Ingrian books. In 1938 the Soviet authorities dissolved the Ingrian national district, proscribed the Ingrian nation, and incorporated their homeland into Leningrad (St. Petersburg) Province.

The Soviet Union in 1939 demanded that Finland cede western Ingria and western Karelia—including Finland's fourth-largest city, Viipuri—to Soviet control. The Finnish government refused, relying on the defenses of the Mannerheim Line, which had been constructed across Finnish Ingria. The Red Army during the Winter War of 1940 quickly overran the Mannerheim Line and conquered the region, although the Finns fought fiercely. Forced to give up the territories following the brief war, the defiant Finns later joined the German assault on the Soviet Union in 1941. Finnish troops liberated Ingria in June and July 1941, but the Finns refused to join the German siege of Leningrad, claiming that theirs was a separate war to recover territory taken in 1940. Between 1939 and 1942 at least 13,000 Ingrians died in fighting or during deportations.

The return of the victorious Red Army in 1944 forced the majority of the Ingrians to flee west to Finnish territory. The Ingrians joined a flood of 400,000 Finns, Ingrians, Karels, and others who fled the return of Soviet authority. Thousands of Ingrians, unable to escape, faced deportation to slave labor camps in 1944–45. In 1947 Finland formally ceded the regions west of Leningrad to the Soviet Union. The Soviet authorities demanded that Finland repatriate all former Soviet citizens. Over 55,000 Ingrians were forced to return to the Soviet Union and were scattered across European Russia. Some years after the war, even children of Ingrian descent adopted by Finnish families were reclaimed by the Soviet Union.

During the 1950s over 16,000 of the remaining 140,000 Ingrians were forcibly resettled in Soviet Estonia. Their former homes, in the Narva-Leningrad corridor on the south shore of the Gulf of Finland, were turned over to reliable ethnic Russians, for security reasons. The remaining Ingrians were allowed to return to their homeland, beginning in 1956, but their homes were already occupied by Russian newcomers. The Soviet census of 1959 counted only about 5,000 Ingrians, including 1,062 Izhors, in the region, a decrease of 97% in just 30 years. The 1989 census counted 57,359 Ingrians, but only 820 Izhors. Between 1956 and 1991, when the Soviet Union collapsed, the Ingrians, as far as possible, concealed their ethnic identity, pretending to be Russians.

In the 1950s and 1960s the large refugee Ingrian population mostly assimilated into Finnish society, but most Ingrians retained links with their past and with other Ingrians in Finland. In the 1970s small groups began to form in an effort to keep alive the culture and language in Finland.

In the late 1980s, the era of *glasnost* and *perestroika*, the small Ingrian population in the Soviet Union began to demand the revision of their history, falsified by Soviet historians, particularly the period of their revolt against the Bolsheviks during the Russian Civil War. Many Ingrians, having registered as ethnic Russians during the years of oppression, slowly began to rediscover their past. The Ingrian Cultural Society, in rapidly liberalizing Estonia, was permitted to operate openly from 1989 onward. Cultural groups proliferated, demanding protection for their disappearing culture and for education in their own language, in areas with sizable Ingrian populations.

The liberalization of Soviet life allowed the Ingrians in Russia to reestablish ties to Ingrian populations in the West, particularly the Ingrian population in Finland, the first such contacts since 1944. Language schools, opened with Finnish aid, and thousands of books donated by sympathetic Finnish citizens began to reverse decades of forced isolation and assimilation.

An Ingrian congress held in Tallinn, Estonia, in April 1990, and a second congress convened at Zelenogorsk following the collapse of the Soviet Union endorsed the Ingrians' right to self-determination and to closer ties to Finland. In November 1992 the Ingrians demanded official acknowledgment of their suffering over seven decades of Soviet domination. The Russian government officially rehabilitated the Ingrians in 1993 but has refused to grant nationality status as a separate ethnic group or as an indigenous people. Lutheran congregations have been restored, and national cultural societies have been established in Estonia, Karelia, around St. Petersburg, and in Finland, Sweden, and in other areas with sizable Ingrian immigrant populations.

In 1997, Russian geographers estimated that about 1% of the population of St. Petersburg Oblast, or some 70,000 people, were of Ingrian or Finnish descent. Nationalist and cultural organizations claimed that the Ingrian population was much higher, but until the many Ingrians who registered as ethnic Russians over the last decades feel safe enough to identify themselves as Ingrians, the real population of the region will remain a matter of dispute. Emigration to Finland was the option taken by some 13,000 Ingrians by the mid-1990s, but the majority, with increasing financial and cultural aid from the Finnish government, remain in their historical homeland.

The use of the Ingrian language has been encouraged by annual summer expeditions of Estonian and Ingrian linguists and students from Estonia and Finland to the Ingrian homeland in Russia. The serious interest shown in the Ingrians' language and history has raised the status of their native culture and has helped to begin the reversal of decades of forced assimilation.

SELECTED BIBLIOGRAPHY:

Lehto, Manja Irmeli. *Ingrian Finnish: Dialect Preservation and Change*. 1996.

Nenola, Aili. *Studies in Ingrian Laments*. 1994.

Paasi, Anssi. *Territories, Boundaries and Consciousness: The Changing Geographies of the bibinnish-Russian Boundary*. 1997.

Ylèonen, Kaarina. *Religion and Ethnicity: The Renaissance of the Ingrian Church after the End of Communist Rule*. 1995.

Ingush

Ingus; Ghalghaaj; Galgai; Galghay; Ghalghay; Lamurs; Kist; Nakchi; Nokhchi

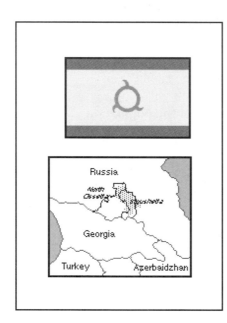

POPULATION: Approximately (2002e) 310,000 Ingush in Russia, concentrated in the Republic of Ingushetia in the North Caucasus region of southern European Russia. Outside Europe there is sizable Ingush population still in the Central Asia republics from which they were deported in 1944.

THE INGUSH HOMELAND: The Ingush homeland lies in the northern Caucasus between Chechenia and North Ossetia in southern European Russia. In the north are the Terek lowlands, and in the south Ingushetia occupies the slopes and northern foothills of the Caucasus Mountains. The Republic of Ingushetia, also called the Galgai Republic, formed part of the Chechen-Ingush Republic until 1992, when it was made a separate republic within the Russian Federation. *Republic of Ingushetia (Ghalghaachie):* 1,451 sq. mi.—3,758 sq. km, (2002e) 489,000—Ingush 80%, Chechens* 9%, Russians 6%, Ossetians* 4%, others 1%. The Ingush capital and major cultural center is Nazran, called Nazranh by the Ingush, (2002e) 121,000. Vladikavkaz, the capital of the Republic of North Ossetia, was long considered the major cultural center of the Ingush, but the majority of the Ingush population was expelled from it in 1992.

FLAG: The Ingush national flag, the official flag of the republic, is a white field with narrow green horizontal stripes at the top and bottom, charged with the centered Ingush national symbol—a red wheel or circle representing the sun.

PEOPLE AND CULTURE: The Ingush are a Caucasian people closely related to the neighboring Chechens; both nations identify themselves as the Nakchuo people. The Ingush call themselves Galgai, or as members of the Galgai tribe of the Nakh nation. The main differences between the Ingush and Chechens stem from their different experiences with Russian colonization. The Ingush are descendants of the western Nakh tribes, mostly the Galgai and Feappi clan federations, who were less hostile to

Russian conquest than were the eastern Chechen tribes. Known for their courage and hospitality, the Ingush are traditionally known for not attacking strangers unless provoked (though blood feuds between clans can be provoked by grievous offenses). The patrilineal families are members of regional clans, which in turn are grouped by dialect and geography into tribal units. Although marriage is not permitted between members of the same clan, partners may be of the same tribe. A very high birthrate raised the Ingush population from 74,000, before their exile in 1944, to 158,000 in 1970. The birthrate, attributed to their Muslim religion, remains high.

LANGUAGE AND RELIGION: The Ingush language forms, along with Chechen, the northeastern or Vienakh group of Caucasian languages. The language is partially intelligible to Chechen speakers, with the eastern dialects gradually blending into the western Chechen dialects. A spoken dialect until the Russian Revolution, Ingush became a literary language in 1923; it is now spoken by 97% of the Ingush as their first language. The Ingush literary language created after the revolution was written first in an Arabic alphabet, then in 1923 in a Latin alphabet, and since 1938 using the Cyrillic script. Ingush and Russian are the official languages of the Republic of Ingushetia.

Nearly the entire Ingush nation is Sunni Muslim, mostly of the Hanafi sect. Many Ingush, unlike their Chechen kin, remained Christian until the nineteenth century, which facilitated relations with the Christian Russians in the eighteenth and early nineteenth centuries. Islam is now an important element in the Ingush identity. The relaxation of restrictions since the collapse of Russian communism in 1991 has led to a revival of Islam, and the building of new mosques, schools, and cultural centers. Prior to the Russian conquest, the majority of the Ingush were pagan or Christian; many then adopted Islam, which they associated with resistance to the Russian occupation of their homeland.

NATIONAL HISTORY: The Ingush are thought to have inhabited the North Caucasus from the seventh century B.C.; they claim descent from the region's early Scythian tribes. The Caucasus Mountain region, often used as an invasion route between Asia and Europe, became a refuge for the early tribal peoples, who sheltered in the high, inaccessible valleys during times of danger. The tribes early developed a warrior society in response to the region's many invaders. Influenced by the Roman culture in the lands to the south in present Turkey, the tribes adopted the Christian religion in the sixth century, but without giving up their warlike culture and traditions.

In the thirteenth century the Mongols overran the lowlands but were unable to take the mountain strongholds of the Caucasian tribes. In the fifteenth century Persians and Turks fought for predominance in the strategic region. In the seventeenth century the Ingush, driven into the mountains by the Mongol invasion, returned to settle their ancestral lands along the Terek River, where they formed close cultural and military ties to the neighboring Chechens. For centuries the Ingush were not distinguished from the larger Chechen population and were often called Western Chechens. Under the influence of the Ottoman Turks many of the Ingush accepted the Islamic religion late in the seventeenth century, but a large minority retained their Christian beliefs well into the nineteenth century.

Increasing Russian interest in the potentially rich area sent Cossack explorers and soldiers to the North Caucasus in the sixteenth century. The Cossacks constructed a string of forts as they moved south, bases for further expansion. In 1784 Vladikavkaz was founded as a fort on the edge of Ingush territory, beginning the Russian expansion in the region. The Ingush rose to drive the invaders from their territory in 1818 but failed to take the Cossack forts.

Joining the region's other Muslim peoples, some of the Ingush clans participated in a great "holy war" against the Russians from 1847 to 1860. The majority took little part in the uprising, but those that remained neutral were often treated by the tsarist authorities just as harshly as the hostile groups. Frequent rebellions and grinding poverty devastated the Ingush culture. By the turn of the century most of the Ingush lived as poor herders in the high valleys, close to mountain strongholds, which the Russian military dared not enter.

The Ingush generally supported their follow Muslims, the Turks, when war began in 1914, but they took little active part in the fighting. With the overthrow of the hated tsarist regime in February 1917, the Ingush believed that at last old wrongs would be righted. Their petitions and pleas ignored, the Ingush swept out of their mountain strongholds to attack the lowland Cossack, Russian, and Ossetian settlements on what they considered their traditional lands. In September 1917 Ingush delegates participated in a newly created autonomous government of North Caucasia, and the Ingush warriors declared *gazava*, holy war, on the Terek Cossacks.

The Bolshevik coup in October 1917 forced the Muslims into an uneasy anti-Bolshevik alliance with the Cossacks, but the alliance soon ended in violent confrontation. In December 1917 the Ingush captured Vladikavkaz but were again driven from the lowlands in the confused fighting and shifting alliances of 1918. Relations between the Ingush and the neighboring Ossetians deteriorated rapidly. The majority of the Ossetians, who, as Christians, had received more privileged treatment under the tsarist government, mostly supported the anti-Bolshevik White Guards. The Ingush, in contrast, reacting to Bolshevik promises to redistribute land, often joined Bolshevik units.

On 11 May 1918, the Muslims of the North Caucasus declared their independence as the Republic of North Caucasia. The Ingush transferred their capital to Nazran after the Cossacks, aided by the Whites, retook

Vladikavkaz in August 1918. With the aid of the Bolshevik forces, the Ingush captured and looted Vladikavkaz in November.

The new Bolshevik rulers, in contrast to the former tsarist authorities, tended to treat all Muslims uniformly. In spite of earlier promises of independence within a federation of Soviet states, the communist authorities attempted to incorporate the Ingush lands into the new Soviet republic. The Ingush, allied to the Chechens, turned on their former allies but were finally defeated in a vicious two-month war. The Ingush homeland was included in the new Mountain Republic, but ethnic conflicts soon led to the breakup of the republic into smaller national units.

A dispute erupted between the Ingush and the Ossetians over the city of Vladikavkaz, which represented the only major urban center of both peoples and the only center of education and industry. In 1924 the authorities set up a separate Ingush region, without Vladikavkaz, which was united with Chechnya to form an autonomous republic 10 years later. During the Stalinist purges of the 1930s, Ingush intellectuals were slaughtered, the language was outlawed, and attempts were made to suppress the Ingush Muslim traditions. In 1937 the Ingush joined a mass Muslim uprising in the region but again suffered defeat and reprisals.

The Russian and Soviet treatment of their nation persuaded some Ingush to support the German invasion during World War II, for which Stalin accused the entire Ingush nation of treason. In January 1944 Soviet soldiers herded the entire population into Nazran and forced them onto cattle cars for deportation to the east. They were dumped at scattered locations across the steppes of northern Kazakhstan, where their language and culture were expected to die out. Between a quarter and half of the deportees perished from the brutal treatment or from disease and hunger in the camps set up on the cold and windy steppes. The dissolved Ingush national region was divided; a zone, known as Prigorodny, was transferred to the neighboring republic of North Ossetia. The region vacated by the Ingush was resettled by ethnic Ossetians.

Supervised by special Committee of State Security (KGB) units, the Ingush survived their exile by clinging to their culture and language, especially their Muslim religion. In 1957 the deported Ingush were rehabilitated and allowed to return to their homes in the officially designated Ingush homeland, including the region now under the control of North Ossetia. Russians and Ossetians refused to vacate the properties they had taken in 1944; in 1958 Christian settlers began attacking the returnees, and three days of violence left many dead and wounded before police could reestablish order. The bitter return sparked the beginning of the modern national movement.

In 1970 the Ingush again put forward claims to their former lands in North Ossetia. They demonstrated in the disputed district of Prigorodny but were driven out by Ossetian police and Russian soldiers. Religion became a part of the Ingush-Ossetian conflict, as the majority of the Ossetians are Orthodox Christians. The influence of Islam in Ingush daily life grew rapidly during the 1970s. In 1975 the Soviet authorities estimated that half the Ingush men belonged to forbidden Sufi brotherhoods, considered hotbeds of dissent and nationalist ideals. To counter underground religious movements, certain mosques were permitted to reopen in Ingushetia, the Ingush homeland, in 1978.

The relaxation of Soviet rule under Mikhail Gorbachev in the late 1980s allowed Ingush nationalism to reemerge. In March 1990, an estimated 10,000 protesters in Nazran demanded Ingush autonomy within Ingushetia's pre-1944 borders. In September 1990 Ingush deportees returning to the region from Kazakhstan clashed, as had happened in 1970, with the Russian and Ossetian inhabitants of Ingush properties confiscated in 1944.

The collapse of the Soviet Union in 1991 fueled a dramatic growth of Ingush nationalism. A new statute in April 1991 restored the national borders that had existed prior to the unconstitutional Soviet policy of deportation and relocation. The statute failed to specify how it was to be implemented and stimulated demands for the immediate return of the Prigorodny region, which accounted for nearly a third of the total Ingush population in the North Caucasus. In July 1991 the parliament of Ingushetia declared the Ingush homeland an autonomous republic within the Russian Federation. Some Ingush groups also laid claim to half the city of Vladikavkaz, the capital of North Ossetia, traditionally the Ingush cultural capital.

The neighboring Chechens declared their independence of Russia, but the Ingush refused all their overtures, fearing Chechen domination. Over 97% of Ingush voters in December 1991 favored the establishment of a separate Ingush state. In January 1992 Ingushetia officially separated from Chechnya, but the region lacked any legitimate government, so the Ingush were not included among the signatories of the Union Treaty in February 1992. On 4 June 1992 the Russian parliament approved the creation of a separate Ingush republic but left the territorial question unresolved.

The return of Prigorodny became the primary nationalist issue. In late October 1992 fighting broke out in the disputed region, and Ingush separatists took control of a sizable part of the territory. In November the Ossetians, aided by Russian troops, drove 60,000 Ingush from Vladikavkaz and the northern districts of North Ossetia into squalid refugee camps in Ingushetia, killing over 300. The involvement of the government troops ended Ingush support for the Moscow government.

Ruslan Aushev, a former Soviet general, became the first popularly elected president of Ingushetia in March 1993, amid rising antigovernment sentiment. In July 1993 the Ingush parliament voted to hold a referendum on the republic's ties to the Russian Federation, and in early 1994, on the

50th anniversary of their deportation, nationalists affirmed the eventual independence of the Ingush nation.

In 1997 the Russian government revoked the status of "free economic zone" that had been granted to Ingushetia on an experimental basis in 1993. The authorities justified the decision by the federal budget's sore need of revenue. The decision came as a bitter blow to the Ingush, who are among the poorest of Russian citizens; their homeland has virtually no industrial infrastructure and has the highest unemployment in Russia. Nearly 150,000 refugees from the conflicts in neighboring Chechnya and North Ossetia were an added burden, with severe shortages of food, housing, and other basic services.

An agreement on the settlement of conflicts and on economic cooperation was signed between the governments of Ingushetia and North Ossetia in early 1996. The Ingush set up a public council to protect the rights of ethnic Ingush still living in North Ossetia. In March 1996, thousands of Ingush refugees demonstrated on the border between the two republics to demand the right to return to their homes. By early 1997, however, only an estimated 10,000 Ingush refugees had returned to their homes in North Ossetia, leaving 45,000 in refugee camps in Ingushetia. Tension rose following an attack by about 1,000 Ossetians on an Ingush refugee camp in the disputed Prigorodny district in July 1997.

In August 1998, nationalists formed a new interregional organization, Zashchita, created to protect the rights and interests of the Ingush nation, including refugees and internally displaced people from North Ossetia. Following new attacks on Ingush in Prigorodny, leaders of Zashchita called for joint Ingush-Ossetian rule of the district, a proposal that was rejected by the North Ossetian leadership. In February 1999 the heads of the Ingush and North Ossetian governments signed an agreement undertaking to return all the refugees and forced migrants to their original homes by the end of the year 2000. The agreement has yet to be fully implemented, a fact noted by the increasingly vocal nationalist groups in Ingushetia.

The unresolved Prigorodny territorial dispute, including the issue of the return of Ingush refugees and the final status of the region, continue as the focus of Ingush nationalist sentiment. Despite Ingush protests, republican authorities have resettled refugees from South Ossetia in the region, denying Ingush refugees' petitions to be allowed to return to their homes. While negotiations on the return of the refugees made some minor progress in 1999–2000, the ultimate status of Prigorodny remains deadlocked.

A new refugee crisis, caused by renewed warfare in neighboring Chechnya in late 1999, added to the unrest and hardship among the Ingush. Ingush leaders, citing the number of refugees in Ingushetia, called on the Russian government to take direct control of Prigorodny and to deploy Russian peacekeepers in the region.

Nationalists in Ingushetia support the creation of a federation of sovereign states in the North Caucasus, but they admit that their first task is to overcome the clan loyalties that have historically divided their small nation. The nationalist movement has been eclipsed by the pressing reality of the Ingush-Ossetian conflict, which carries a high potential for further armed ethnic conflict.

SELECTED BIBLIOGRAPHY:

Conquest, Robert. *The Nation Killers: The Soviet Deportation of Nationalities*. 1970.
Nekrich, Alexander M. *The Punished Peoples*. 1978.
Nichols, Johanna. *The Ingush*. 1997.
O'Ballance, Edgar. *Wars in the Caucasus, 1990–1995*. 1997.

Innus

Montagnais; Montagnars; Moatagnes; Kebiks; Neenoilno; Tshetsiuetineuerno

POPULATION: Approximately (2002e) 23,000 Innu in northeastern Canada, concentrated in the northern parts of the provinces of Quebec and Newfoundland, including the Labrador Peninsula.

THE INNU HOMELAND: The Innu homeland, Nitassinan, lies in northeastern Canada, occupying part of the huge Ungava Peninsula in northern Quebec and the eastern districts of the Labrador dependency of Newfoundland. Nitassinan has no official status; the region claimed by Innu activists forms an unofficial region of Canada, pending the resolution of land claims and negotiations on sovereignty. At present there are nine small reservations in Quebec and one in Labrador. *Innu Land (Nitassinan):* 25,201 sq. mi.—65,270 sq. km, (2002e) 41,000—Québecois* 53%, Innu 40%, Cree* 5%, other

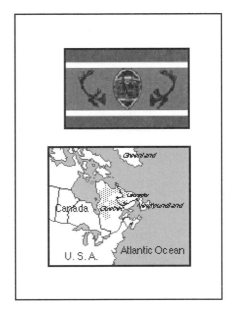

Canadians 2%. The major cultural centers include Goose Bay, called Sheshatshiu in the Innu language, in Labrador, (2002e) 8,000; Shefferville, called Matimekosh, (2002e) 3,000, and Harve Saint-Pierre, called Uepmiskau in the Innu language, in Quebec, (2002e) 2000.

FLAG: The Innu national flag, the flag of the Innu Nation, has horizontal stripes of green, pale blue, green, separated by narrow white stripes, the blue twice the width of the green stripes and bearing two black antlers flanking a centered black Innu drum.

PEOPLE AND CULTURE: The Innu are an indigenous nation comprising three distinct divisions, the Montagnais, the Naskapis, and the Attikamek. The three groups, speaking dialects of the same language and sharing the same culture, represent geographical divisions and their respective adaptations to different environments. The 15,000 Montagnais live along the St. Lawrence between the St. Maurice River and Sept-Îles, the 3,000 Naskapis live east of them in Labrador, and the 5,000 Attikamek live on the upper St. Maurice River north of Montreal. The Attikamek were formerly part of the Montagnais but recently chose to maintain their separate status. Because poor soil and a short growing season make agriculture too risky, most Innu are traditionally hunters and gatherers. The history of colonization severely demoralized the Innu, who now have the world's highest suicide rate and high levels of alcoholism and drug abuse. They are 13 times more likely to kill themselves than anyone else in Canada; nearly a third have attempted suicide.

LANGUAGE AND RELIGION: The Innu speak an Algonquin language called Innu-aimun, with three major dialects that correspond to the three tribal divisions. The language is a Cree language of the Algonquin group of languages. French and English are used as second languages. Innu language use is widespread, except in the southwest, where younger Innu tend to prefer French. In the late twentieth century an Innu dictionary was published, along with other works on the language.

Most Innu are Christians, a majority Roman Catholic. Historically there is no clear separation between the Innu spirituality and civil society. Even today elders are generally respected, both as the civic and religious leaders of the community. To some degree, traditional beliefs associated with hunting and herding have been maintained. The Roman Catholic priests, as a result of early missionary activity, long remained influential in many areas. The Innu see little contradiction between belief in both the Christian God and forest and animal spirits. Attempts by the Catholic Church to regain its former influence by appropriating Innu traditions are welcomed by many Innu elders but often resented by younger Innu leaders, who demand the "decolonizing" of the Innu religion.

NATIONAL HISTORY: According to Innu history, the Innu formed a powerful federation before the arrival of the Europeans in the region in the sixteenth century. Often at war with the Iroquois* to the south, the Innu were forced north about 2,000 years ago and gradually adapted themselves to woodlands and the harsh climate. In their new homeland there was little tribal organization beyond bands of extended families.

The Innu bands learned to use every resource available in the bleak terrain, constructing dwellings of stone and driftwood covered with sod in the winter, and in the summer migrating with their herds of Caribou while living in skin tents supported by wood or whale ribs. The Caribou herds provided shelter, food, clothing, and greatly influenced the Innu culture and traditional way of life. They borrowed many customs and arts from the Inuits,* their only traditional enemies in the region.

European navigators sighted the coast in the late fifteenth century; there were landings by John Cabot, sent by England, in 1498, Corte-Reale of Spain in 1500, and Jacques Cartier of France in 1534. Henry Hudson, who sailed into the huge bay that bears his name in 1610–11, recorded the first European contact with the northern Innu peoples. Samuel Champlain achieved the first contact with the Innu at the mouth of the Saguenay

River, far to the southeast. The French called the Innu bands they met Montagnais, meaning "mountaineers."

The French fur trade concentrated the Innu near the St. Lawrence River in the early seventeenth century, and the southern bands were forced to organize themselves within fixed hunting territories. In 1608 the French founded Quebec in territory claimed by the Innu. Missionaries arrived in the region as early as 1615, bringing Christianity and European contacts with the southern bands, although many of the northern bands were isolated until the 1800s.

The British established a trading post on James Bay in 1668. Encouraged by its success, King Charles II chartered the Hudson's Bay Company in 1670 and granted the company a huge tract of land encompassing Hudson's Bay enormous drainage basin. The land grant included the northern Innu homelands; the native peoples were neither consulted nor considered. In the south the Montagnais came under growing French control. In the 1680s and 1690s the Europeans established treaty relations and alliances with the bands as the competition between the two powers for control of America's rich lands and resources, particularly furs, became a serious and often violent rivalry.

Smallpox, brought to the region by the Europeans, decimated the tribes in the eighteenth century just as the European rivalry turned to war. The Seven Years' War, which began in Europe in 1756, was preceded by two years of fighting in America between the two sides and their native American allies, in a conflict known as the French and Indian War. All the Innu bands came under British rule with the final French defeat in 1763, although little changed in their homeland until the 1840s.

Beaver hats gave way to silk during the 1830s, ending the traditional fur trade that had sustained the Innu for two centuries. Lumber interests moved into the region in the latter half of the nineteenth century, bringing with them increased settlement. The settlers took much of the more fertile land of the Innu homeland while exposing the indigenous peoples to constant epidemics. By 1884, the Innu had declined to 2,000 people.

The Innu heartland became a part of the Northwest Territories in 1869, and a separate territory of Ungava in 1895. In 1912 the Canadian government transferred a part of Ungava to Quebec, and in 1927 the government divided the huge area between Quebec and Labrador. The Innu peoples refused to recognize the partition of their homeland. Successive governments, British, French, and Canadian, simply took possession of the tribal lands and parceled them out to forestry and mining companies.

The Canadian government after World War II decided that the nomadic Innu peoples had to settle. By the 1970s the Innu lived in permanent settlements, partly in response to the government's generous subsidies. Tribal activists, beginning in the 1960s, denounced the subsidies as drains on incentive and desire to work. Nationalists in the 1970s, galvanized by the effectiveness of the Quebec nationalist movement, emerged from a generation that assimilation had nearly robbed them of their language, culture, and way of life.

In the 1980s Innu nationalists launched a campaign to win cultural and linguistic rights, and to press for the resolution of long-standing land claims. A study published in 1984 confirmed that the incidence of suicide in the Nistassine communities was five times the Canadian average and that it particularly affected the young. The demands for the resolution of land claims, paralleling a campaign to return the despairing Nistassine to a more traditional way of life, fueled a powerful cultural and national movement.

In the east, another controversy became a national issue for the entire nation. The Innu opposed the post–World War II establishment of a large NATO base at Goose Bay, a center for flight training, which the Innu claim has decimated their Caribou herds and has greatly affected the way of life of the Innu living around the town and the base. The Canadian government hopes to persuade NATO to choose Goose Bay for a new training center for low-altitude flights, which would raise the number of flights from 7,500 to over 40,000 a year. In 1988, frustrated by government inaction on their grievances, Innu activists invaded the base to publicize their plight and their demands.

Innu nationalism has become closely tied to Quebeçois nationalism. A 1992 Canadian constitutional referendum that would have given native American peoples extensive rights of self-government failed to pass because of the contentious issue of Quebec. Unhappy with the Canadian justice system's attempts to deal with locals, the Innu community on the remote island of Davis Inlet in Labrador evicted a judge, setting off widespread demands for an Innu justice system based on traditional law.

In August 1997, a court placed an injunction on plans to build the world's largest nickel mine in northern Labrador until local courts sorted out land claims by the Innu and Inuits. Innu claims to a large part of Labrador have become a contentious issue, connected to demands for self-government, control of natural resources, and the right to restrict environmentally damaging development.

The resurgence of nationalists in Quebec and their electoral victory in the province in September 1994 stimulated the growth of Innu nationalism. Leaders of the three tribes have reiterated their intention to declare their homeland independent should Quebec secede. In June 1997, during a visit to Sheshatshiu by Queen Elizabeth, the Innu presented a letter detailing their grievances against the Canadian government, which they claimed denied their cultural and territorial rights.

The Canadian government is willing to discuss land rights, but only if the Innu first agree to surrender ownership. In June 1998 the Innu Nation organization put forward a proposal that would involve the creation of two general categories of land. The first category, to be called Innu Land or Nitassinan, would be administered by an Innu government. The second category would be comanaged by the Innu with the governments of Canada and the province.

While the majority of the Innu live in wooden shacks, mostly without plumbing and only wood stoves for heat, government agencies have provided cable television, snowmobiles, and plastic-wrapped goods. The results have been those that too often accompany attempts to reorder traditional societies—including unemployment, poverty, alcoholism, drug addiction, and despair.

International pressure on the Canadian and Quebec governments following reports of despairing Innu youngsters killing themselves in the early 1990s brought more attention to the many problems facing the Innu. International support has helped the Innu to publicize their demands for land rights and autonomy. Government agencies have increased aid, but many Innu reject direct aid, repeating their demands for the right to control their lives and their traditional lands.

The major problems facing the Innu in the first years of the twenty-first century are giant hydroelectric projects in northern Quebec and low-level military training flights over their homeland. The Innu feel powerless to prevent the massive planned mining projects; some have been pressured into discussing financial compensation, though most oppose the mines and hydroelectric dams that, they claim, will destroy their land and culture. Money will not save their small nation. Innu leaders point out that the Innu have never signed any treaty with Great Britain or Canada, nor have they ever given up their right to self-determination.

SELECTED BIBLIOGRAPHY:

Cummings, Peter A. *Canada: Native Land Rights and Northern Development.* 1991.
Fleras, Augie, and Jean Leonard Elliott. *The Nations Within: Aboriginal-State Relations in Canada, the United States and New Zealand.* 1992.
Turner, Lucien M. *Indians and Eskimos in the Quebec-Labrador Peninsula.* 1979.
Wilson, James. *The Two Worlds of the Innu.* 1994.

Inuits

Inupiats; Yupiks, Alutiits; Eskimos

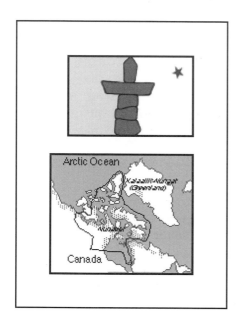

POPULATION: Approximately (2002e) 42,000 Inuits in Canada, concentrated in the northern territory of Nunavut. Other sizable Inuit populations live in Alaska, about 45,000, Greenland, and Siberia. The total Inuit population is estimated at about 100,000 in the Arctic regions of North America and Siberia.

THE INUIT HOMELAND: The Inuit homeland lies in Arctic regions stretching from Siberia through Alaska and Canada to northern Greenland. Nunavut, meaning "Land of the People," or "our land," lies in northern Canada, occupying a huge area north of the Arctic Circle and including a number of large islands in James and Hudson Bays, mostly tundra areas north of the tree line. The islands of Nunavut in the northeast border on Kalaalit-Nunaat, the homeland of the Greenlanders.* Nunavut officially forms a self-governing Inuit homeland within the Canadian federation. *Nunavut*: 849,965 sq. mi.—2,201,400 sq. km, (2002e) 29,000—Inuits 85%, other Canadians 15%. The capital and major cultural center of the Nunavut Inuits is Iqaluit, formerly Frobisher Bay, (2002e) 5,000.

FLAG: The national flag of the Nunavut Inuits is a vertical bicolor of yellow and white, divided by a *unusuk*, a red rock formation in the shape of a man, used as markers on the landscape, and charged with a five-pointed blue star on the upper fly.

PEOPLE AND CULTURE: The Inuit, formerly called Eskimos, a name derived for the Algonquin language and used by the early Europeans in the region, are a native American people living mostly above the Arctic Circle. Their self-designations vary among the languages and dialects, but all, like the ethnic name Inuit, mean simply "the people." The Nunavut Inuit comprise the Baffin, Iqlulik, Caribou, Copper, Netsilik, and Mackenzie Delta bands. The Inuits retain their Asian physical features more than do other indigenous groups in North America. There is little cultural or dialectical variation, as the Inuit all descend from one group, the Thule

Inuit, who migrated across northern America as far east as Greenland, now officially Kalaalit-Nunaat. In recent years the birthrate of the Inuit has increased, with 40% of the population now under the age of 15. Traditional Inuit culture was totally adapted to the extremely cold and icy environment, in which vegetable foods were almost nonexistent, trees were scarce, and fish and sea mammals were the major food sources. Inuit life changed greatly in the twentieth century; snowmobiles mostly replaced dog sleds for land transport, and rifles replaced harpoons for hunting.

LANGUAGE AND RELIGION: The Inuit language belongs to the Inuit-Aleut group of Paleo-Asiatic languages. In Russia the three language varieties are treated as three separate languages, but all belong to the Yupik or Western Inuit group. The Inuits have an extremely rich vocabulary in matters concerning their traditional spheres of life. There is also a unique "spirit language" used by the shamans, retaining many archaic words. The Inuit speak Inuktituk, a language of the Inuit-Aleut group of languages divided into two major dialects—Yupik in south and west of the Yukon River, including the Siberian Inuits; and the Inupiaq, scattered across the whole of the rest of the Arctic, from Alaska to Greenland. The language is called Yupik in south and central Alaska, Inupiaq or Inupiat in North Alaska, and Inuktituk in Canada and Greenland. In Nunavut the six dialects correspond to the major bands in the region. Younger Inuits, particularly in Canada and the United States, often prefer English, which is widely spoken throughout the region.

The majority of the Inuit are Christian, with a minority adhering to traditional beliefs. The Inuits in northern Canada are mostly Anglicans or Roman Catholics, with a Moravian group in northern Labrador. Christian beliefs have largely replaced traditional Inuit religious practices. Many of the traditional Inuit customs and taboos were intended to mollify the souls of hunted animals, such as polar bears, whales, walrus, and seals. The pre-Christian traditions and beliefs, although discouraged for many years, have been revived and are now part of the Inuit reculturation that began in the 1970s.

NATIONAL HISTORY: The ancestors of the Inuit are believed to have crossed into North America from Asia some 4,000 years ago, using a now-disappeared land bridge across the Bering Strait. The Inuits separated from the Aleuts at least 2,000 to 3,000 years ago and spread across a vast territory stretching from northeastern Asia across North America to Greenland. The migrants adjusted to the frozen lands north of the tree line by an adaptation unequaled by any other northern group. The Thule Inuit migrated across the frozen Arctic lands of North America between A.D. 1000 and 1400, with groups leaving the main migration and settling in present-day Alaska, northern Canada, the Canadian Arctic islands, and

Greenland. The fact that the Inuit descend from this one migration gives the various bands a surprising uniformity of culture and language.

Before the arrival of Europeans in the region the Inuit were unaware that other peoples existed, beyond some sub-Arctic Indians with whom they traded. Sir Martin Frobisher in 1576 became the first European to encounter the Inuit of northern Canada. The majority of the Inuit saw Europeans for the first time only in the 1770s, when Russian, Spanish, and English ships explored the Arctic regions and made contact with coastal Inuit bands.

The arrival of Christian missionaries in the late eighteenth century began a century of gradual conversion to various Christian sects. Missionaries introduced various forms of Christianity, including Russian Orthodoxy in Siberia and Alaska. Anglicans, Catholics, and Lutherans were active in Canada and Greenland. The Christians challenged the legitimacy of traditional Inuit beliefs by presenting an alternative to accepted knowledge. Initial converts to Christianity disrupted the solidarity of Inuit societies by separating themselves from the main groups—which were slowly eliminated as the majority adopted the new religion.

Until the mid-nineteenth century the governments in control of Inuit territories mostly ignored the nomadic or seminomadic bands. The Canadian Inuit homeland, included in the Northwestern Territory in 1820, was leased to the Hudson's Bay Company between 1821 and 1869. In 1876 the Canadian government organized the Keewatin District, which gradually lost its southern territories to the provinces of Ontario and Manitoba. In 1895 the Franklin District, including part of the mainland and the Arctic Islands, was organized as a separate territory.

Many Inuits remained isolated until after World War I. The decline of blood feuds and of infanticide led to a steady increase in population during the 1920s and 1930s. The Russian influence in northeastern Siberia made itself felt in the 1930s. The Siberian Inuits in 1935 were resettled away from areas (including Ratmanov Island, in the Bering Sea) near the international border between the Soviet Union and the United States.

The Inuit lifestyle changed very little until the 1950s, when paternalistic national governments began to move the Inuits into government housing projects and built schools and health facilities. Increased education and contacts with the outside world promoted a new political activism in the 1960s.

In 1963 Canadian Inuit nationalists put forward a plan to divide the Northwest Territories and create a self-governing Inuit homeland. The discovery of oil, natural gas, and rare minerals in the region in the 1960s and 1970s added an economic issue to the prior question of land rights. The Inuits, feeling ignored and misunderstood by other Canadians, mobilized in the 1970s to win control of their vast Arctic homeland. Inuit delegations traveled to Ottawa and London seeking support for the creation of a separate homeland, to be called Nunavut.

In 1979 the related Greenlanders were granted home rule by the Danish government and thereby became a model for the Inuits of northern Canada. In 1981 the first commercial airline service was established between Frobisher Bay and Nuuk, the capital of Greenland, strengthening ties between the Inuit communities.

On 14 April 1982, the inhabitants of the Northwest Territories voted four to one to divide the territories so as to create new provinces based on national groups. In 1985, the Canadian government set tentative boundaries, a task complicated by demands for the inclusion of Inuit groups in the northeast Beaufort Sea region, Labrador, and northern Quebec. The campaign to win autonomy politicized the Inuits, with some activists favoring the Greenland-based organization, Inuit Atagatiqüt, which advocates an independent transpolar Inuit state. Support for nationalism increased in 1987–88 as negotiations stalled over land claims and mineral rights.

In September 1989 the Canadian government finally passed the long-delayed Nunavut settlement, the biggest land transfer since the Alaska and Louisiana purchases of the nineteenth century. The agreement gave the Inuit considerable control over mineral development and set aside lands for traditional activities, such as trapping and hunting. In other areas during the 1980s, environmental groups hurt the traditional Inuit economy by successfully campaigning against seal hunting. New restrictions left once-proud Inuit hunters to go to seed on the dole and the bottle.

With few exceptions, the Inuits have no formal organization into such units as clans or tribes, and no regular chiefs. Group identification is usually geographic or dialectical. With modernization, as contacts increase, a sense of belonging to a larger national group has grown. The name "Inuit," originally designating only speakers of the eastern dialects, has been extended to the entire ethnicity. In Alaska many still use the name Eskimo or Inupiat, which means "real people" and is often applied to both Inuit and Inupiaq speakers and to speakers of Yupik dialects.

In 1992 the Nunavut agreement received the necessary voter approval in a referendum. Nunavut, comprising 60% of the Northwest Territories of Canada, was the culmination of 20 years of lobbying by Inuit leaders and activists. The agreement gives the Inuit outright ownership of 18% of the vast territory, most of which will remain Crown land, under joint government and Inuit control. The Inuit won the right to hunt, fish, and trap across the entire area, with special tracts set aside for these activities in areas of mining or other economic activities.

On 1 April 1999 Nunavut, an area three times larger than France, became an autonomous Inuit state within Canada. The new territory gives the 25,000 Nunavut Inuits control of about a quarter of Canada's total territory and an important say in the development of the oil and other natural resources of the region. The 10,000 Inuits of northern Quebec and Labrador, calling their homeland Nunavik, are working for separate autonomy or union with Nunavut.

Inuits from around the Arctic Circle have begun annual meetings to discuss common problems and solutions. Militants from all Inuit regions—in the Russian Federation, the United States, Canada, and Greenland—although still a small minority in each region, continue to demand a sovereign Inuit transpolar state.

SELECTED BIBLIOGRAPHY:

Hamilton, John David. *Arctic Revolution: Social Change in the Northwest Territories 1935–1994.* 1994.
Hancock, Lyn. *Nunavut.* 1997.
Reynolds, Jan. *Frozen Land: Vanishing Cultures.* 1993.
Thompson, Ruth. *The Inuit.* 1996.

Iroquois

Haudenosaunee; Hodinoshone

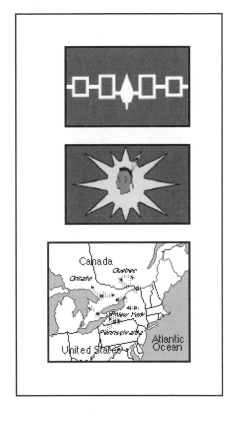

POPULATION: Approximately (2002e) 170,000 Iroquois in northeastern North America, concentrated in New York in the United States, and in southern Ontario and Quebec in Canada. Officially the Iroquois tribes number about 75,000 in Canada and the United States; the remainder are not officially affiliated with tribal governments.

THE IROQUOIS HOMELAND: The Iroquois homeland lies in the eastern United States and Canada, in the area around the Great Lakes. They are now concentrated in about 20 towns and eight reservations in New York, Ontario, and Quebec, with smaller numbers in Wisconsin and Oklahoma. Haudenosaunee, the Iroquois Confederacy, has no official status, though the Iroquois consider their confederacy a sovereign nation that predates both the United States and Canada. Pending the resolution of sovereignty and land claims, the confederacy is confined to 16 reservations in the United States and Canada. The capital and major cultural center of the Iroquois in the United States is Onondaga, Onödageh in the Iroquoian languages, (2002e) 1,200. The capital and major cultural center of the Canadian Iroquois is Grand River, called Gihëgowáhneh, (2002e) 1,000.

FLAG: The Iroquois national flag, the official flag of the confederacy, is a pale blue field bearing a centered white tree, the Tree of Peace, flanked by two white chain links on either side, symbolizing a sacred wampum belt called "Hiawatha's Belt." The flag of the Mohawk Warrior Society is a red field with a Mohawk brave in profile against a yellow sun with twelve rays.

PEOPLE AND CULTURE: The Iroquois, calling themselves and their nation Haudenosaunee or "People of the Longhouse," are a native American people comprising six sovereign nations—Mohawk, Oneida, Onondaga, Cayuga, Seneca, and Tuscarora. The six nations are united by historical, clan, and family ties that cut across tribal lines. Each of the tribes traditionally occupied a geographical and political position within the confederation. The Mohawk (Kahniankehaka), numbering about 37,000, are known as the "keepers of the eastern door," because they were the easternmost member of the league. The Cayuga (Gweugwehono), numbering 4,000, are called the "keepers of the Great Pipe." The Oneida (Onayotekaono), including the Wisconsin Oneida, numbering about 18,000, are called the "stone people." Onondaga (Onundagaono), numbering about 2,000, are the "keepers of the fire" in the center of the confederacy. The Tuscarora (Akotaskororen), about 1,000, joined the confederacy as a nonvoting member in 1722. The Seneca (Nundawaono), about 10,000, are the "keepers of the western door." Culturally the tribes had a matrilineal social structure, with the women owing all property and kinship determined through the mother's line. The modern Iroquois are highly acculturated, most holding jobs in communities surrounding the reservations or in the larger cities.

LANGUAGE AND RELIGION: The Iroquois are mostly bilingual, speaking English and distinct but related languages of the Iroquoian group of the Hokan-Siouan languages. The languages, for the most part mutually intelligible, form, except for Tuscarora, the Five Nations branch of the Northern Iroquoian language group. The dialects are Mohawk-Oneida and Seneca-Onondaga-Cayuga. The Tuscarora speak a dialect (of the Tuscarora-Nottoway branch of Northern Iroquoian languages) that is nearly extinct in the United States. Iroquoian linguistic groups occupy a continuous territory around Lakes Ontario, Huron, and Erie, in present-day New York State and Pennsylvania in the United States, and southern Ontario and Quebec in Canada.

The majority of the Iroquois adhere to their own Longhouse religion, a Quaker-influenced belief that spread through the nations in the nineteenth century. On almost every Iroquois reservation there is a building, called the "Longhouse," that is the center of traditional religious activity. The Longhouse religion is a reformed version of the "Code of Handsome Lake." Handsome Lake was a Seneca prophet whose moral precepts and revelations spread through the confederacy at the beginning of the nineteenth century and aided the Iroquois revitalization that has since enabled them to maintain their ethnic identity and culture.

NATIONAL HISTORY: The Iroquois are believed to have originally inhabited what is now central New York State. Small bands in the eastern woodlands of the land they called Great Turtle Island created a settled society some 1,000 years ago. Men hunted the abundant game, waterfowl, and fish, while others cultivated corn, squash, and other vegetables. Agriculture allowed a new form of society, with large, fortified towns, sophisticated artisans, and a stratified caste system.

The tribes, often warring among themselves, united sometime between

1350 and 1600, although many historians claim that the tribes achieved unification over a thousand years before the generally accepted dates. The general consensus is that a confederacy was formed around 1570. The Peacemaker (Deganawida), the author of confederation, won the support of Hiawatha, an important war chief. They gathered together five warring tribes and planted a white pine, the Tree of Peace, under which tribal leaders buried their weapons of war. The Peacemaker's original instructions form the basis of the oral constitution still honored by the Iroquois nation. The confederacy, guided by the Great Binding Law (Gayanashogowa), became the most sophisticated and powerful north of central Mexico, extending its political sway over a huge area from eastern Canada south to the Carolinas.

The French first came across the confederacy in the St. Lawrence River and the eastern Great Lakes regions. The French called the confederated tribes "Iroquois," probably a corruption of a native epithet. The French, interested in furs, were the allies of the Iroquois' enemies, the Huron and Algonquin. The French gave firearms to these peoples, who drove the Iroquois from the St. Lawrence River. The arrival of the Dutch in 1610 provided the Iroquois a source of firearms with which to counter the French threat. Iroquoian animosity to the French traditionally dates from the participation of Samuel de Champlain in Huron attacks on Iroquois towns in 1609–15. The Iroquois destroyed the Huron confederacy in 1648–50, then launched over a decade of devastating raids on the French settlements of New France. The Iroquois tribes traded beaver pelts to the Dutch and English in exchange for firearms and iron goods.

The tribes of the confederacy probably numbered no more than 20,000 in the mid-seventeenth century. Their inland location protected them from the first epidemics brought by the Europeans, but by 1650 disease, combined with continuing warfare, had cut the Iroquois population by about half. However, through massive adoption of conquered Iroquoian-speaking enemies, including 7,000 Huron, the Iroquois actually increased to about 25,000 by 1660.

The depletion of local beaver populations drove the confederacy to wage war against tribes farther away in order to procure more supplies; the so-called Beaver Wars lasted for 70 years. Between 1648 and 1656 the confederacy dispersed the tribes to the west—the Huron, Tionontati, Neutral, and Erie. At its height in 1680, the confederacy extended west from the north shore of Chesapeake Bay through Kentucky to the junction of the Ohio and Mississippi Rivers and north across lower Michigan, southern Ontario, and southwestern Quebec. By the 1750s, most of the tribes of the Great Lakes region had been subdued, incorporated, or destroyed by the league. The confederacy, strengthened in 1772 by the adhesion of a sixth member, the Tuscarora, played a vital role in the British victory that ended the French and Indian War in 1763.

For 125 years before the American Revolution, the Iroquois blocked European access to the Great Lakes. In the eighteenth century the Six Nations remained the bitter enemies of the French, who were still allied to their traditional enemies, and so gradually became dependent on the British in Albany for European goods. The Iroquois success in maintaining their autonomy in the face of both French and British pressure was a remarkable achievement for a confederation numbering less than 15,000 people.

The outbreak of the War of Independence nearly destroyed the confederacy. A schism developed among the tribes when four of the member nations ultimately joined their traditional British allies, while the Oneida and Tuscarora mostly aided the Americans. During the terrible privations at Valley Forge in the winter of 1777–78, Oneida chief Shenendore brought 3,000 bushels of white corn and even provided an instructor to show the starving Americans how to prepare the food.

The pro-British tribes, led by Chief Joseph Brant, fought for the British at Niagara. Brant's Mohawk warriors decimated several isolated American settlements, drawing upon themselves thereby a horrible revenge. Gen. George Washington in 1779 sent an expedition of 4,000 men to strike at the heart of the confederacy, Onondaga. The Americans destroyed towns, orchards, and crops; their passing completely changed the face of the Iroquois nation. Following the British surrender at Yorktown in 1781, many Iroquois (most of the Mohawk and Cayuga) joined the Loyalists moving north to British Canada. The Onondaga, Seneca, and Tuscarora remained in New York. A generation later, in 1838, many of the Oneida departed for new lands in Wisconsin.

Benjamin Franklin is thought to have modeled parts of the new American constitution on that of the confederacy, which outlined a voluntary association of sovereign nations. In spite of their contributions to American independence, however, the Iroquois found themselves excluded from American life. On 11 November 1794 a treaty, called the Pickering or Canandaigua Treaty, was signed by the chiefs of the Six Nations and representatives of the new United States. It guaranteed forever Iroquois control of much of present-day New York State. The treaty, soon abrogated by American settlers and an unsympathetic government, became the first of 371 treaties signed with the native American nations and subsequently ignored.

The confederacy effectively came to an end in the late eighteenth century. The tribes gradually lost their traditional lands and were forced into ever-dwindling reservations on both sides of the U.S.-Canada border. The nations, mostly desiring peace with their powerful white neighbors, adopted a pacific religion, the Longhouse creed, in the early nineteenth century. Begun among the Seneca and believed to have roots in Quaker ideals, the religion spread rapidly through the scattered remnants of the confederacy.

In the nineteenth century, the Iroquois were forced to adapt to American culture. Many pursued education as the means to survive in the new environment. A Seneca chief, Eli Parker (Donehogawa), educated as a lawyer, served on Gen. U.S. Grant's staff during the Civil War and is believed to have written out the terms of Lee's surrender at Appomattox.

The present urban Iroquois presences in New York, Buffalo, and Montreal largely began in 1896, when Iroquois were hired as laborers during the construction of the Dominion Bridge at Montreal. They showed no fear of heights and rapidly became involved in the construction of many major bridges and skyscrapers constructed in eastern Canada and the United States.

Increased education in the 1920s and 1930s renewed the appreciation of the Iroquois of their unique history and culture. By the early 1950s the revival of the Iroquoian languages and traditions had greatly affected the young. A growing demand for Native American rights and for redress of past injustices merged with the liberation philosophy of the 1960s to produce "Red Power." The militancy of the period marked the beginning of the modern national movement and the end of the patient acceptance of abuses and neglect.

Young lawyers took over the leadership of the nationalist movement in the 1970s and pressed the U.S. and Canadian governments to negotiate the Iroquois land claims, some filed as early as 1946–51 but still pending resolution. Taking the position that the Iroquois Confederacy was a sovereign nation that predated the United States and Canada, tribal lawyers filed numerous court cases attempting to force the governments to honor the treaties signed between sovereign political entities.

In 1974 activists of the Mohawk tribe occupied an abandoned girls' camp near Moss Lake, New York. Called Ganienkeh by the occupants, the area was turned into a self-sufficient agricultural community run by and for the Iroquois according to their own laws, customs, and traditions. The leaders of the groups believed that only by reestablishing their own independent nation could the Iroquois survive.

Iroquois representatives in 1977 presented a petition to the United Nations seeking that body's recognition of Iroquois sovereignty. Passports issued by the Haudenosaunee government have been honored by dozens of countries and are used by Iroquois "Runners,"envoys to other indigenous nations who monitor the situation of indigenous peoples throughout the Americas.

The confederacy, although physically dispersed, remains an important concept in of Iroquois life. It has been responsible for the Iroquois' being able to retain much of their culture and traditions. There is still division, particularly as to whether the council fire belongs with the Six Nations in

Canada or the Onondaga in New York. The state of New York finally returned the sacred wampum belts of the confederacy to the Onondaga in 1989.

Disappointed by government responses to the Iroquois attempts to gain redress by legal means, young militants began to fight for their remaining lands, sparking violent conflicts with state and provincial authorities. "Warrior societies," particularly that of the Mohawk, have become active in seeking redress for land claims and sovereignty. In 1989, members of the Mohawk Warrior Society stated that they no longer recognized the authority of the Council of Chiefs; in 1991 the leader of the society refused to go to the council at Onondaga to seek official recognition. The Grand Council of Grand River in Canada and the Grand Council of Onondaga in New York have not authorized the warrior societies. The societies, some of whose members have been accused of smuggling and drug trafficking, are increasingly seen as disruptive and as a threat to the traditional unity of the Iroquois nations.

The Mohawk Warrior Society was involved in a violent confrontation with Quebec authorities at Oka. The dispute, which began over the extension of a golf course onto land considered a sacred burial ground by the Mohawk, led to a 42-day standoff between Iroquois militants and Quebec police. Although the dispute continued in the late 1990s, most activists have since renounced violence.

The settlement of outstanding land claims is seen as the first step to the recognition of Haudenosaunee as a sovereign nation. Many Iroquois still consider themselves distinct from either Canada or the United States. The majority of the Iroquois resented the extension of American citizenship to all indigenous Americans in 1924, considering themselves already citizens of the oldest living participatory democracy on Earth.

The rapid resurgence of Iroquoian population, a recent phenomenon, has been prompted by renewed national pride as many reclaim their heritages. The 1940 census listed only about 17,000 Iroquois in New York and Canada, but by 1990 over 70,000 were officially affiliated with the tribes, and an estimated 100,000 are culturally and historically tied to the tribes of the confederacy. Since the early 1970s, the unity of the Iroquoian nations has grown increasingly stronger, partly due to the confrontations between Iroquoian activists and the governments of Quebec and New York, episodes that greatly raised Iroquois self-awareness.

SELECTED BIBLIOGRAPHY:

Alfred, Gerald R. *Heeding the Voices of Our Ancestors: Kahnawake Mohawk Politics and the Rise of Native Nationalism.* 1995.
Bial, Raymond. *The Iroquois.* 1998.

Johansen, Bruce E., and Barbara Alice Mann, eds. *Encyclopedia of the Haudenosaunee (Iroquois Confederacy)*. 2000.

Pertusati, Linda. *In Defense of Mohawk Land: Ethnopolitical Conflict in Native North America*. 1997.

Isaaks

Isaaqs; Isaqs; Isxaaqs; Northern Somalis

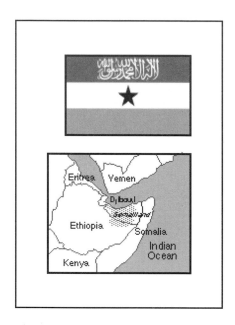

POPULATION: Approximately (2002e) 2,600,000 Isaaks in northeastern Africa, concentrated in the Somaliland Republic and adjacent areas of Ethiopia and Djibouti. Outside the region there are Isaak communities in other parts of Somalia, the United Kingdom, Italy, and the Arabian Peninsula.

THE ISAAK HOMELAND: The Isaak homeland occupies a semi-arid region of coastal lowlands and hilly interior plateaus south of the Gulf of Aden of the Indian Ocean. The homeland straddles the borders of Ethiopia, Djibouti, and the northwestern part of Somalia, now included in the breakaway Republic of Somaliland. Officially the region forms the Somali regions of Woqooyi, Galbeed, Togdheer, Sanaaq, and the western districts of Nugaal. *Somaliland*: 67,936 sq. mi.—175,954 sq. km. (2002e) 2,850,000—Issaks 72%, Gadabursi 14%, Darood 8%, Issa (Dir) 4%, other Northern Somalis 2%. The Isaak capital and major cultural center is Hargeisa, (2002e) 235,000.

FLAG: The Isaak national flag, the official flag of the Republic of Somaliland, is a horizontal tricolor of green, white, and red, bearing a centered five-pointed black star and the *shahada* ("There is no God but God Mohammed is the Prophet of God") in white Arabic script on the green stripe.

PEOPLE AND CULTURE: The Isaaks are a Hamitic people, the largest of the northern clans of the Somali, extending from Somaliland into neighboring areas of Ethiopia and Djibouti. Isaak society is based on kinship ties that emphasize membership in a clan federation genealogically derived from mythical Arab ancestors. It is common for Isaaks to refer to themselves as Arabs. The Isaaks have several subclans, including the Garhajis, further divided into the Idagale and Habr Yunis; and the Habr Awal, divided into the Sa'ad Musa and Isa Musa. Younger Isaaks are the most nationalistic and anti-Mogadishu in their views. While the Isaak clans profess strong allegiance to Islamic unity, their primary loyalties are to self, family, subclan, and clan. The Isaak culture is traditionally was primarily nomadic, centered around herds of camels and other animals. In an area with an average rainfall of less than four inches a year, the Isaaks are consumed with finding water and grazing land for their livestock. Formerly the Isaak diet consisted almost entirely of milk products, but urbanization and modernization have added new staples, including maize meal and rice. About half the Isaaks are still nomads.

LANGUAGE AND RELIGION: The Isaaks speak the Northern Somali dialect of Somali, a Cushitic language of the Hamito-Semitic language group. The language, called Northern Common Somali, has become the national language of the self-proclaimed Somaliland Republic. English, the language of the former colonial administration, is also widely understood and is used as a lingua franca among clans otherwise speaking mutually unintelligible dialects. Clans are genealogically based and cut across dialect lines. Until recent decades Arabic served as the lingua franca and the only literary language. The standard Somali, adopted following independence in 1960, was based on the northern Somali dialects, but since 1991 regional dialects, including the Isaak dialect, have reemerged.

The Isaaks are a Muslim people, most belonging to the orthodox Sunni branch of Islam. In early 2000 the Somaliland administration cracked down on individuals accused of spreading Christianity; around 25 people, mostly Ethiopians working for a Swedish missionary organization, were arrested. The Isaak commitment to Islam has led to the development of legendary claims to origins on the Arabian Peninsula. The Islamic teaching of unity is superseded by clan loyalty and a destructive Somali philosophy of individualism that undermines clan and national unity.

NATIONAL HISTORY: Other than that it was known to the ancient Egyptians as the "Country of Perfumes," little of the region's pre-Islamic history has survived. The Somalis are thought to have separated from the Oromos* before the Christian era. During the first centuries A.D., they migrated in a southeastern direction, finally following the Tana River to the Indian Ocean. Some of the clans turned north to people the northern coast, where they came into contact with Arab and Persian trading communities, from whom they took Islam and a mythological Arabic origin. Interaction over centuries led to the development of a remarkably homogenous Somali culture bound by common traditions, a single language, and the Islamic faith. The emergence of a clan-based society, however, began to divide the Somalis almost as soon as their culture had formed.

By tradition the first Muslims to arrive in the region were refugees who, having fled Mecca with Mohammed in 622 A.D., decided not to continue to Medina with the prophet but turn south to the Red Sea ports and cross the narrow Gulf of Aden to introduce Islam to the northern Somali coast. Muslim Arabs conquerors soon followed, later forming a powerful medieval Muslim sultanate. By the twelfth century, the entire northern Somali coast was Islamized, providing a basis for the extension of Islam to the interior. As the clans moved westward, however, they encountered the forces of resurgent Christian Ethiopia.

The Isaak clan federation was nomadic, although the clan established boundaries for the herding areas of each subclan. There was never a formal political system; councils of clan elders served as an informal government. When the Oromos began migrating into the region in the fourteenth and fifteenth centuries from the southern highlands of Ethiopia, the Isaaks united to resist their encroachment on their grazing lands. Military clashes were common among the many subclans, mostly over land, water, or women.

The Somali sultanate split into small clan states in the seventeenth century. The states mostly came under the rule of Oman, and after 1832 they were administered from Zanzibar. Between the sixteenth and nineteenth centuries the clans participated in the frequent wars between the Muslim peoples and the highland Christian kingdoms of Ethiopia.

Egyptian troops occupied the coastal towns in the 1870s but were withdrawn and replaced by British troops in 1884. Two years later, the British authorities established a protectorate in the northern Somali territory. The remaining Somali lands came under Italian, French, and Ethiopian colonial rule. The Somali clans, ignoring the colonial borders, moved freely across the entire region. Frequent clan wars over water and grazing rights continued well into the twentieth century.

The clans of British Somaliland rebelled in 1901, led by a Muslim religious leader known as the "Mad Mullah," Mohammed bin Abdullah Hassan. The Muslim holy war ended in defeat in 1921, and Hassan fled to Ethiopian-ruled Western Somalia. The focus of Somali nationalism in the 1920s and 1930s remained the reunification of the Somali clans of the Horn of Africa.

In 1936, the Italians defeated and annexed Ethiopia, combining the Somali-populated Ogaden region of Ethiopia with Italian Somaliland. In 1940, following the outbreak of World War II, Italian troops took control of British Somaliland. British forces, operating from Kenya, drove the Italians from all Somali territories in March 1941. The British reestablished the protectorate of British Somaliland and set up military administrations in Italian and Ethiopian Somali zones. Pressed by Somali nationalists, the British presented to the new United Nations a plan for a united Somali trusteeship territory in 1946.

United Nations deliberations continued for five years. The final decision rejected the British proposal, returned the Ogaden region to Ethiopia, and placed former Italian Somaliland under Italian administration as a trust territory. The solution, rejected by Somali nationalists, provoked violence and rioting across the entire Somali region. The Somali nationalists reiterated their demand for a "Greater Somalia," to include British and Italian Somaliland, Ethiopia's Ogaden, French Somaliland, and Kenya's Northwest Province.

British Somaliland was granted independence on 26 June 1960. The new national legislature voted for union with newly independent Italian Somalia to the south. On 1 July 1960 the united Republic of Somalia was proclaimed. The country's first prime minister, Mohammed Ibrahim Egal of the Isaak clan, supported substantial regional autonomy for his homeland in the north. The Isaaks were unhappy with the union, which was mostly dominated by rival southern clans from the beginning.

In 1969 a Supreme Revolutionary Council led by Siad Barre and other members of the central Marehan clan took power in a bloodless coup. The coup's leaders quickly ended regional autonomy within Somalia, demanding also the incorporation of the Somali territories outside the state. Barre ruled Somalia by playing one clan against another and was able to hold off any real threat to this regime until the late 1970s. In 1977 his government launched an invasion of Ethiopia's Somali-inhabited Ogaden. At first successful, the invasion ultimately floundered when resisted by Ethiopia's hastily summoned Soviet and Cuban allies. The defeat greatly weakened Barre's clan-based government.

Refugees from the Ogaden war poured into northern Somalia, most with clan and family ties to the Isaaks. Amid the chaos, northern leaders began to stress clan and tribal ties over pan-Somali nationalism. The increasingly leftist Somali government, dominated by the southern clans, attempted to force the northerners into communist-style collectives. In 1981, with clan conflicts growing, several northern leaders openly espoused separatism and formed the Somali National Movement (SNM). Sporadic SNM attacks against the government began in 1982 and continued throughout the 1980s, in alliance with other opposition groups among the clans of southern Somalia.

In May 1988 the Isaaks, frustrated with Barre's preferential treatment of his own clan and by a sense of economic injustice, began a widespread rebellion across the north. To repel and avenge a SNM offensive, Somali government forces ravaged the Isaak capital, Hargeisa, killing up to 50,000 people. An estimated million people fled the region, either to Isaak regions of neighboring Ethiopia or to other parts of Somalia. Government troops attacked refugee columns and planted thousands of land mines to hinder their flight to Ethiopian territory.

Government reprisals and indiscriminate bombing of northern cities pushed the remaining northern clans to join the separatist revolt. Some 400,000 refugees fled to neighboring countries as towns and villages were pounded to rubble. Weakened themselves by a spreading clan war in the southern provinces, demoralized government troops lost most of the north to a rebel offensive in April and May 1991. The rebel leader, Abdirahman

Ahmed Ali, declared on 18 May 1991 the independence of the territory that formerly had made up the protectorate of British Somaliland. The sovereignty of the region—based on a distinct colonial experience, extreme economic exploitation, and the human suffering of the Somali civil war—was not recognized internationally. The Isaaks dominated the new government, although agreements were reached with most of the other clans in the region.

The world's refusal to grant the breakaway state diplomatic recognition hampered reconstruction and precluded famine aid and development funds. Although the Isaaks were spared the horrors that overtook the southern clans in the 1990s, the peace remained fragile. In January 1992 clan fighting between two Isaak subclans broke out, leaving hundreds dead. In early 1993 clan elders met for four months to work out ways to end the clan conflicts and to keep the chaos and bloodshed of Somalia from spreading to the Somaliland; the elders adopted an elected two-house legislature. They elected Mohammed Ibrahim Egal, the first prime minister of united Somalia in 1960, as president of Somaliland.

In August 1994 the bicameral legislature adopted a separate currency and began to draw up a democratic constitution. The Somaliland legislature again pleaded for recognition, warning of disaster if the world continued to ignore the region. International governments have declined to consider diplomatic recognition so long as the rest of Somalia refuses to agree to its existence. In November 1994, as predicted, violence broke out between rival clan militias and threatened to spread across the devastated republic. Troops loyal to President Egal were attacked by militiamen belonging to rebel groups supported by Mogadishu warlord Mohamed Farah Aydeed. In 1995 Somali forces allied to General Aydeed attempted to enter the area, setting off new fighting as the Isaaks and the allied clans mobilized to defeat the most serious threat to their self-determination. Aydeed died in August 1996, ending outside support for the rebels, and relative peace was established in Somaliland. In October 1996 the UN began repatriating some of the 280,000 refugees still in Ethiopian camps near the Somaliland border.

In November 1997 the government of neighboring Djibouti reportedly officially recognized Somaliland. The Isaaks of Somaliland then opened their first diplomatic mission abroad, in Djibouti's capital. In 1998, President Egal toured Ethiopia, France, and Italy, reinforcing the trend toward "semidiplomatic" recognition, which would allow the country access to bilateral and multilateral financial assistance. Eritrea and Ethiopia exchanged ambassadors with Somaliland, and the United Nations (UN) agreed to give Somaliland observer status.

The celebration in 1998 of eight years of independence included statements by Isaak leaders reaffirming their goal of internationally recognition of the region's independence. Tension rose, however, between the Isaaks and the leaders of the Dulbahanti and Warsangali subclans of the Darod clan in eastern Somaliland, who expressed their desire to rejoin Somalia.

In the late 1990s, the self-proclaimed republic became one of Africa's few success stories, but one that the outside world has been reluctant to help because of the notion that borders are sacred. Although the Isaaks point out that the republic's borders exactly mirror those of the old British protectorate, the world community senses that to recognize a secessionist state could start the unraveling of many of Africa's states within their arbitrary colonial boundaries. In late 1999, the United Nations, United States, and European Union officials discussed the possibility of a special status for the republic, perhaps informal recognition similar to that of the Palestinians* or Kosovars,* which would allow the Isaaks access to international loans and aid.

Isaak sovereignty remains at risk from the occasional fighting by subclans, which could lead to widespread violence, although Egal government has tried to soften rivalries by bringing members of all the subclans into the Somaliland government. It is also threatened by the southern Somali clans, who demand that all of Somalia be reunited, a claim supported by the international community. President Egal suggested in August 1999 that Somaliland be given international status as a distinct political entity, but with the provision that later reunification of Somalia would be possible.

The Isaak diaspora supports five telephone companies and seven airlines, which link the diaspora to the home territory. Remittances from the exile community are estimated at $500 million a year. The remittances and some earning from livestock are almost the only legal revenues.

The leaders of most of the Somali clans met in Djibouti in mid-2000 to work out a system for governing Somalia, which has been without an organized government since 1991, but the Isaaks, reiterating their claims to separate independence, refused to send delegates. Isaak spokesmen pointed to the Hargeisa massacre of 1988 as the reason they can never again assent to rule from faraway Mogadishu. In February 2000, a mass grave containing over 700 bodies, victims of Siad Barre's terror, was found near Berbera and reinforced the determination of the Isaaks to remain free of a reunited Somalia. In August 2000 the Republic of Somalia inaugurated its first president in almost a decade, Abdiqasim Salad Hassan, a member of the Hawiye clan, who claimed to represent all regions of the republic.

After a decade of separation from Somalia, the Isaaks have achieved relative peace in their homeland, a broadly representative government, and promises of a democratic election of future leaders, but the state of Somaliland is still not recognized internationally. Possibility of coal and oil deposits and reports of large deposits of precious stones promise future prosperity. Ethiopia, in early 2001, began to recognize Somaliland passports and Ethiopian Airlines began the first scheduled flights to Hargeisa.

Ethiopian imports through the port of Berbera have increased dramatically and is another source of income.

SELECTED BIBLIOGRAPHY:

Ahmed, Ali Jimale, ed. *The Invention of Somalia.* 1995.
Lewis, Ioan M. *Blood and Bone: The Call of Kinship in Somali Society.* 1994.
Madar, Yusuf Ali. *The Rebirth of the Somaliland Republic.* 1991.
Ricciuti, Edward. *Somalia: A Crisis of Famine and War.* 1999.

Istrians

Istra; Istriots

POPULATION: Approximately (2002e) 412,000 Istrians in south-central Europe, concentrated in the Istrian regions of Croatia and Slovenia. The other sizable Istrian populations are in neighboring regions of Italy.

THE ISTRIAN HOMELAND: The Istrian homeland occupies a heavily wooded, mountainous peninsula projecting into the Adriatic Sea between the Gulfs of Trieste and Rijeka. Lying just south of the Karst Plateau in southwestern Slovenia and northwestern Croatia, Istria is known for its scenery, pleasant climate, good wines, coastal tourist resorts, and beautiful beaches. Istria has no official status; the region forms the Istria district of Croatia and the Koper district of Slovenia. *County of Istria (Istarska Zupanija/Istra):* 11,086 sq. mi.—2,813 sq. km, (2002e) 233,000—Istrians 88%, Italians 8%, other Croats 4%. *District of Koper (Istra):* 325 sq. mi.—842 sq. km, (2002e) 83,000—Istrians 92%, Italians 3%, Friulis, other Slovenes 5%. The Istrian capital and major cultural center is Pulj, also known as Pula, (2002e) 61,000. The major Istrian cultural center in Slovenian Istria is the capital of the region, Koper, called Capodistria in Italian, (2002e) 24,000.

FLAG: The Istrian national flag, the traditional flag of the region and the flag of the national movement, is a horizontal tricolor of yellow, red, and blue. The unofficial flag of the Croat county of Istria is a pale blue field bearing the traditional coat of arms, a yellow goat on a dark blue field. The flag of the Slovene county of Koper is a pale blue field bearing a central yellow sun.

PEOPLE AND CULTURE: The Istrians, referring to themselves as an Istro-Romanic people, constitute a distinct nation that has developed over

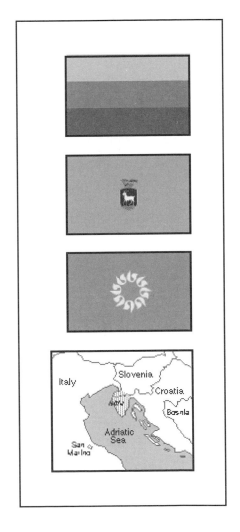

centuries from mixed Slav, Germanic, and Latin elements. Their homeland has a long history as a crossroads of cultures and languages, while the strong sense of a separate Istrian identity has developed mostly since World War II. The Istrian culture, an amalgam of many influences, embraces not only the Istrians but also the Italian and Friuli minorities. Extensive intermarriage, particularly in the decades since the 1950s, has added greatly to the development of a separate Istrian identity. The collapse of Yugoslavia and the subsequent independence of Croatia and Slovenia prompted the mobilization of Istrian national awareness, particularly in Croatia, which was ruled by a xenophobic nationalist regime until early 2000.

LANGUAGE AND RELIGION: The Istrians mostly speak Croat, and Slovene in the northwest. Historically they spoke Istriot, an archaic Romance language of the Italo-Romance group of Italo-Western languages. The language survives, but only about 1,000 people, mostly in the towns of Rovinj and Vodnjan, speak it as their first language. Another language, called Istro-Romanian, more closely related to Romanian, is spoken by less than 1,000 in a few villages in the northeastern part of the peninsula. Many Istrians, estimated at over 100,000, also speak Italian dialects, usually the Istrian dialect of the Venetian language, spoken by the Venetians* of northeastern Italy.

The Istrians are mostly Roman Catholic, but there are Protestant minorities and a small Muslim group. The Catholic religion, after centuries of various governments controlling their homeland, has become an integral part of the culture of the peninsula, one of the few constants in Istrian history.

NATIONAL HISTORY: The ancient Illyrian tribe, the Histri, gave their name to the peninsula. Settlements developed in the region during the Bronze Age. The first mention of the region occurred in the third century B.C., in the writings of the Greek poets Callimachus and Lycophron relating the story of Jason and the Golden Fleece. According to legend, Colcheans chasing Jason and the stolen golden fleece feared to return home when they were unable to recover the treasure, so they settled among the Histri and founded a city, called the City of Refugees—in their language, Polai, later called Pula or Pulj.

The peninsula fell to the invading Romans in 177 B.C. Over several centuries of Roman rule, the Istrians adopted the Roman culture and language. In 46–45 B.C. the region became a Roman colony, with a great spurt in development and construction. Roman towns, complete with elegant buildings, villas, theaters, and public areas, dotted the lush Istrian landscape. The colony backed the losing side in the civil war that divided the empire from 42 to 31 B.C. The victor, Octavian, ordered Pula destroyed and set loose Roman legions to ravage most of the towns and villages on the peninsula.

Due to its advantageous geographical situation, however, the region soon recovered and was rebuilt. Caesar Augustus transformed Pula into an imperial city, and over several centuries monumental works of Roman architecture were constructed, including the sixth-largest amphitheater in the empire, with seating for 23,000 people. Under Augustus most of the peninsula became part of Roman Italy.

Barbarian tribes from the north taking advantage of the collapse of Roman power invaded the region in A.D. 476, destroying much of the Latin structure. Huns and Ostrogoths overran the peninsula, and several decades of anarchy ensued before the rule of the eastern Roman Empire at Byzantium was established. Migrating Slav tribes, the ancestors of the Croats and Slovenes, settled the peninsula and accepted nominal Byzantine rule in the sixth and seventh centuries. The Slavic settlers soon adopted much of the Latin culture that still dominated the peninsula and the surrounding areas.

Istria was divided between several neighboring states following the weakening of Byzantine power in the eighth century. The major powers in Europe, Venice and the Frankish kingdom, vied for authority there. In 788 most of the region was included in the March of Istria, part of Charlemagne's Frankish empire. The southern coast became part of the expanding Venetian state. In the tenth century the duchy of Bavaria gained control of most of the peninsula, which was again split in the thirteenth century between Venice, the dukes of Carinthia, the patriarchs of Aquileia, and the counts of Gorizia.

In the fifteenth century, after centuries of division and shifting borders, the peninsula was once again divided, this time by Austria and Venice; Venice took control of the northwestern districts, and Austria controlled the southeastern districts. The Austrian districts, under Habsburg rule, formed a separate crownland of the Austrian Empire. The northern districts remained under Venetian rule until they too passed to Austria, under the terms of the Treaty of Campoformio in 1797. Under Austrian rule the peninsula formed part of a multi-ethnic region of mixed Italians and Austrians in the coastal towns and Slavic farmers in the rural interior.

The Austrian Empire lost the peninsula to Napoleonic France in 1805. The new French administration added the peninsula to its Illyrian Provinces but allowed a measure of autonomy. In 1815, the peninsula was returned to Austrian rule. The Istrians, after centuries of foreign domination, began to realize that culturally and politically they had more in common with their immediate neighbors—Slav, Italian, or Austrian—than with populations outside their peninsula.

In the late nineteenth century the large Italian-speaking population became the subject of irredentist claims by the newly united Italian kingdom, and a movement to unite the peninsula with Italy gained support among many of the Italian speaking population. In 1915, to entice Italy into the war, the allies promised it Istria and other Italian-speaking Austrian territories.

In the wake of Austria's defeat in World War I, in 1918, a strong movement for separate Istrian independence won widespread support. The prospect of dividing the region, whose peoples had coexisted interdependently for centuries, stimulated the Istrian national movement. In October 1918 the regional parliament at Trieste, the capital of the Austrian crownland, voted to erect an autonomous Republic of Venezia-Giulia under the protection of the new League of Nations; the new Italo-Croat-Slovene state was to include Trieste and its hinterland, the Julian region, as well as the Istrian peninsula.

The fate of the Istrians remained unsettled until 1920, when the entire region was placed under Italian administration. The area's economic and political importance declined rapidly under Italian rule, particularly following the Fascist takeover in 1922. The Fascists instituted programs designed to homogenize the many regional cultures and to eradicate the non-Italian influences. In 1926 the government banned the Slav languages and many of the South Slav traditions. All family names were ordered changed to names agreeable to the Italian Fascist authorities. The Italianization of the peninsula included government-sponsored immigration from Italy's poor and backward south. The growing tension between the peninsula's Italians and Slavs paralleled tension between the Istrian Italians and the culturally and dialectically different newcomers from southern Italy.

World War II exacerbated the peninsula's simmering ethnic and regional problems. Militant pro-Fascist, pro-Allied, Istrian nationalists and Yugoslav-supported communists clashed with rival groups and the Italian army. The peninsula became a battleground. In the spring of 1945, following the German withdrawal, Tito's Yugoslav partisans occupied the peninsula. Thousands of Istrians, both Italian and Slav, real or imagined Fascists, anticommunists, and others opposed to communist Yugoslav rule were rounded up and executed. In an orgy of revenge the partisans tossed the bodies of men, women, and children from the Istrian cliffs into the Adriatic Sea. The Yugoslav communist authorities expelled over 300,000 Italian Istrians between 1945 and 1951.

Communist Yugoslavia received most of Istria in the postwar territorial transfers in 1946; however, the west of the peninsula, due to an ongoing territorial dispute with Italy, became part of the new Free City of Trieste, under United Nations auspices, in 1947. In 1954, after several years of diplomatic wrangling and periodic political crises, the state of Trieste was finally divided by Italy and Yugoslavia. The city and its environs became part of Italy; and the southern zone, including the city of Koper, went to Yugoslavia, which divided it between the republics of Slovenia and Croatia. Istrian opposition to the division of the peninsula between the two Yugoslav republics was one of the reasons that the Treaty of Osimo, which settled the Trieste question, was not ratified by Yugoslavia and Italy until 1975.

The collapse of the communist Yugoslav state in 1991 again divided Istria, this time between the independent republics of Slovenia and Croatia. The new Croatian government, under a resolutely nationalist administration, began to limit local government autonomy, passing laws that threatened Istrian culture. Enjoying excellent inter-ethnic relations in the peninsula, the Croat Istrians rejected the virulent nationalism emanating from Zagreb and began to campaign for closer ties to the neighboring Istrian Slovenes and the Italians.

In 1990, even before the disintegration of Yugoslavia, the Istrians had formed the Istrian Democratic Assembly, a trilingual, tri-ethnic forum that advocated autonomy for the peninsula. Nationalists put forward plans for a transnational autonomy of two sovereign provinces, one in Croatia with its capital at Pula, the other in Slovenia with its capital at Koper. The Croatian Istrians in parliamentary elections in February 1993 firmly rejected Croatia's aggressive nationalism; the Istrian party, the IDS, won 72% of the vote in the county, as opposed to the Croat national party's 16%. The IDS won on a platform of liberal tolerance and the creation of a multi-ethnic region isolated from the chaos and violence of the former Yugoslavia.

A border dispute between Slovenia and Croatia over the Istrian Bay of Pirin fueled Istrian nationalism and demands for a separate transborder Istrian region. However, the bitter territorial dispute was put aside, and an agreement on outside arbitration agreed to, in 1997. The Slovenian and Croatian governments are united in their opposition to the growing Istrian national movement, which threatens their hold on important ports on Croatia and Slovenia's Adriatic coasts.

In 1998 the Croatian ministry of administration denied for the second time approval of a coat of arms and flag for the county of Istria; the designs had been first proposed in 1994. The ruling Croat Democratic Union (HDZ) objected to the inclusion of a crown in the flag and coat of arms, insisting that it meant the Istrians wanted to raise Istria to the level of an autonomous republic within Croatia. Croatian elections in early 2000 ousted the ultranationalist HDZ and replaced it with a moderate, pro-European coalition, including the Istrian political party, the IDS. The election of the new government greatly reduced tension between the Istrian regionalists and the central government in Zagreb, and it has lessened nationalist sentiment. The IDS, also called DDI for its Italian name, Dieta Democratica Istriana, now forms part of the ruling coalition government in Croatia.

In March 2000, the Croatian government declared the major regional bank, the Istarska Banka, bankrupt, setting off protests across the region.

The IDS threatened to leave the ruling government coalition in Zagreb. The president of the Istrian County Assembly, Damir Kajin, declared that the new Croatian government was no better than the near-dictatorship of Franjo Tudjman that ended in 2000. The Istrian political leader, Ivan Jakovfçifa, the president of IDS, threatened that if the bank's problems were not quickly resolved, that the Istrians would seek greater political autonomy.

SELECTED BIBLIOGRAPHY:

Alberi, Dario. *Istria: History, Art, Culture*. 1988.

Bendery, Jill, and Evan Kraft, eds. *Independent Slovenia: Origins, Movements, Prospects*. 1996.

McAdams, Michael C. *Croatia: Myth and Reality*. 1997.

Novak, Bogan C. *Trieste 1941 to 1954: The Ethnic Politics and Ideological Struggle*. 1970.

Jejuvians

Cheju; Chejuans; Jeju; Pukjeju; Pukcheju

POPULATION: Approximately (2002e) 790,000 Jejuvians in Korea, concentrated in the island province of Jeju. Outside their homeland there are Jejuvian communities in Seoul and other large mainland cities, in Japan, in the Unites States, and in Europe.

THE JEJUVIAN HOMELAND: The Jejuvian homeland, the island of Jeju, lies in the East China Sea between the Korean Peninsula and the southern islands of Japan. The island, 60 miles (100 km) southwest of the Korean mainland, has a tropical climate and is a favorite resort, particularly for newlyweds. The island is volcanic in origin and formed around snow-capped Mount Halla, the highest peak in Korea. The island, formerly called Cheju or Quelpart, forms a province of the Republic of Korea (South Korea). *Province of Jeju (Jeju-do):* 706 sq. mi.—1,829 sq. km, (2002e) 551,000—85% Jejuvians, 14% mainland Koreans 1%. The Jejuvian capital and major cultural center is Jeju City, also called Cheju, (2002e) 281,000.

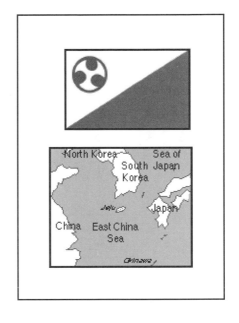

FLAG: The Jejuvian national flag, the official provincial flag, is a bicolor of white and blue divided diagonally. On the upper hoist is a red circle representing the sun with interior wave patterns representing the *samda*, the three abundances: women, wind, and stones, and the *sammu*, the three nonexistent: thieves, beggars, and gates.

PEOPLE AND CULTURE: The Jejuvians are a Korean people whose culture and way of life formed in the relative isolation of their island home. The conditions of nature and resources greatly influenced the ancient Korean culture of Jeju. The unique flora and fauna shaped their outlook and culture, including a unique architecture suited to the milder climate. The most famous domestic animal is the miniature Jeju horses, descended from the sturdy mounts brought to the island by the Mongols in the fourteenth century. The Jejuvians are famous for their strong-minded and independent women who have traditionally enjoyed greater freedom than mainland Korean women.

LANGUAGE AND RELIGION: The Jejuvians speak a unique dialect of the Korean language. The Korean language is spoken in seven main dialects, with the dialectal borders generally corresponding to historical provincial boundaries. All the dialects are mutually intelligible except for the Jejuvian dialect. Due to the physical isolation of the Jejuvians, their dialect has diverged sufficiently to make initial communication with Mainlanders difficult. The mainland dialects have absorbed much more Chinese influence than that of Jeju, where Japanese influences have traditionally been strong. Standard Korean is derived from the language spoken in and around Seoul. English is increasingly spoken as a second language.

The Jejuvians are almost evenly divided between Christian, mostly Protestant, and Buddhists, with smaller numbers of Confucianists and adherents of Chondogyo, an indigenous faith. All Jejuvians beliefs incorporate influences from other religions, with many festivals or ceremonies attended by all religious groups. Pre-Buddhist shamanistic beliefs are still evident. There are a number of practicing *mudang* or female shamans. Lineage groups, like large extended families, are held together by the veneration of common ancestors. Jeju remains the center of shamanism in Korea. Many scholars regard Jejuvian shamanism as less a religion than a medicine in which the spirits are manipulated in order to achieve human ends. There is no notion of salvation, moral, or spiritual perfection.

NATIONAL HISTORY: Until the fourth century B.C., the island was occupied by small pre-agricultural tribal groups, originally migrants from northern Asia. Chinese influence began in the third century B.C., leading to the formation of the Koguryo dynasty, the first unified Korean state. Koguryo was later rivaled by two other mainland state, Paekche and Silla. The three states formed the "Three Kingdoms" period of Korean history. Eventually Silla conquered its rivals and unified the Korean Peninsula.

Silla authority was extended to Jeju in the seventh century A.D. The island often proved a troublesome possession of the Korean monarchs. During the period of Silla rule, Mahayana Buddhism was introduced and the majority of the Jejuvians adopted the new religion. Chinese art forms and cultural influences were important in the formation of the unique Jejuvian culture.

The Silla dynasty gave way to the Koryo dynasty in 918, which, in 1300, divided Jeju into two provinces north and south of Mount Halla. After a period of Mongol domination, the Koryos were replaced by the Yi dynasty in 1392. Yi officials finally took control of Jeju in 1393. Yi influence, which lasted for over 500 years until the Japanese annexation of 1910, saw the development of many socio-cultural patterns that shaped modern Korean culture. The introduction of Confucianism led to the gradual decline of Buddhism. Because of their isolation, the Jejuvians developed a culture and dialect distinct from the homogeneous culture of the Korean mainland. The Jejuvians mostly rejected the pervasive and complex system of social stratification that permeated mainland culture. In 1609 the island was united under a governor sent from the mainland. The island was again divided in 1874, but remained under the administrative authority of the mainland South Cholla provincial government.

Jejuvian introduction to Westerners came with the shipwreck of Dutch sailors on the island in 1653. The sailors, led by Hendrik Hamel, were the objects of great curiosity. They were eventually sent to the Korean capital, Seoul, and escaped by sea in 1666.

One of the distinctive features of Jejuvian culture was the striking rural-urban gap that existed in terms of standards and styles of living. The majority of the islanders were poor farmers and fishermen, with only a small educated minority living in the island's capital. Ambitious youths had to leave the island to live in Seoul in order to progress in government service or the arts.

By 1900, the Yi dynasty and the Korean state had been greatly weakened by incursions from China and Japan and internal discord. In 1904, the Korean kingdom signed an agreement of mutual cooperation with Japan and later in the same year the First Japan-Korea Pact was signed. In June 1906, a mainland revolt against Japanese influence spread to the Jejuvians, but they were defeated by troops sent from nearly Japan. In 1907, Japanese authority increased with the signing of a new pact. On 22 August 1910, the Japanese forced the Korean government to sign the Korea-Japan annexation agreement.

Between 1913 and 1915 several anti-Japanese groups formed on the island, often hiding in the rugged central mountains. Branded bandits, they were hunted down by Korean and Japanese troops. During World War I anti-Japanese activities increased, with guerrilla bands forming in 1919 to fight the Japanese presence on the island. The traditional antagonism between the Jejuvians and the mainland Koreans was submerged in the anticolonial campaign after 1919.

Between 1910 and 1921 the Koreans were not allowed to publish their own newspapers or to organize political or intellectual groups. In the late 1930s, the government reversed the liberalization of the 1920s and began a policy of the total assimilation of the Koreans into Japanese culture.

The Japanese invasion of China in the 1930s brought renewed tensions. In October 1938, the Japanese government decreed that Koreans could serve in the Japanese army. In October 1943, the Japanese authorities decreed a conscription law for Korean students leading to violence in Jeju. In May 1944, dozens of Jejuvian women were detained and forced to work as comfort women for the Japanese military forces.

The Japanese finally surrendered to invading American troops on 15 August 1945. Most Jejuvians supported the proclamation of an independent Korean state, but in September 1945 Korea was divided at the 38 parallel, with communists, supported by China and the Soviet Union in the north, and anti-Communists, including many former collaborators under Japanese rule, in the south.

After liberation from Japanese rule, the Koreans attempted to set up a central government, but chaotic conditions and the isolation of Jeju left the island virtually independent. Democratic people's communes were established in 1945 to fill the power vacuum. From August 1945 to February 1947, the island remained peaceful although increasingly divided between communist, anti-Communist, and regionalist forces.

In March 1947, the anti-Red police of the newly installed South Korean government took a hard line on the people's communes, the self-governing communities controlled by leftist and nationalist forces. In spite of its distance from the mainland, Jeju was increasingly infected by the spreading mainland conflict. Local activists demanded a purge of the police and the elimination of Japanese collaborators in the local government. Jeju was officially under the jurisdiction of the U.S. Army's 59th battalion. Due to logistical problems, their authority extended only to the capital city and several military camps. In August 1946, the island was designated a province and came under the authority of conservative, rightist provincial officials.

The peace on Jeju was shattered on 1 March 1948 when the local police fired on the Jejuvian demonstrators commemorating an uprising against the Japanese on 1 March 1919. Six civilians were killed and many wounded. Hundreds were arrested. The shocked islanders called a general strike. The Korean government, backed by the U.S. military authorities, responded by sending more police. Some 500 strikers and local leaders were arrested. Provincial government officials were dismissed and were replaced by functionaries from the mainland. Unofficial government-armed militias, the Northwest Youth Corps and the Greater East Youth Corps were transported to the island, greatly adding to the tensions and the growing violence.

On 3 April 1948, rebellion against the mainland authorities spread across the island. Jejuvian militias attacked the hated mainland youth corps. Fighting and atrocities by both sides devastated many villages. Initially, the uprising was led by Kim Dal Sam, who organized the leftists on the island. He fled soon after the rebellion began to go to the mainland, where he organized a guerrilla war against the anti-Communist forces who were supported by the United States. He became a national hero in North Korea.

The American navy imposed a complete blockade on the island and provided weapons and advice to the Korean police and army. The victims of the violence lost land, houses, bank accounts, and other properties, which were given to their accusers and the police. All that was needed was "evidence" or a "witness" that collaborated the "communist" sympathy of a targeted victim. The victim would then be arrested, often tortured, and later many were killed. The arresting policeman was entitled to a part of the loot taken from the victim. Many pro-government refugees from North Korea were also settled on the island.

A second phase of the rebellion began in November 1948 when the campaign was intensified. Suppression of the rebellion led to atrocities and massacres. A scorched-earth policy left some districts in ruins. In other areas, the police and youth corps leaders seized the properties of their victims. Many were condemned only because they owned properties coveted by members of the government-backed forces. Thousands of Jejuvians were killed in the so-called anti-Communist crusade. Estimates of the dead are still disputed, but range from 10% of the 1948 island population of 300,000 to nearly half the total. Many Jejuvian activists have settled on a figure corresponding to 26% of the population killed in the fighting and massacres. Activists claim that the U.S. military condoned the violence as an anti-Communist campaign, while some suggest that American soldiers participated.

The rebellion lasted for nearly two years and left the island in ruins. Officially the rebellion continued until 21 September 1954, when the chief of the island police lifted the siege of Mount Hanra. Some 20,000 homes were destroyed, over 100,000 left homeless, and tens of thousands perished. On 9 April 1949, Rhee Syngman, the American-backed president of South Korea, traveled to the island to celebrate his victory over the Jejuvian rebels. The bulk of the army, police, and youth corps members were returned to the mainland. In December 1949, a harsh national security law was passed making communism a crime. However, the law was so comprehensive and vague that it could be used against any opposition group.

When the Korean War broke out in 1950, former rebels and suspected sympathizers were arrested. Massacres of villagers resumed, with police often shooting the inhabitants as suspected communists. Thousands were taken out to sea and drowned. Countless others were buried in mass graves. No police records were retained, so many Jejuvians vanished without a trace. The invasion from North Korea colored subsequent South Korean government attitudes toward internal security. Domestic opposition, especially from the left, was suspect. President Rhee's call for national unity provided political justification for limiting the activities of political opposition or regional groups during the 1950s.

Rhee won a rigged election in 1960. His election triggered widespread student uprisings, including demonstrations by Jejuvian students. He was forced from office by the student groups supported by the South Korean military on 26 April 1960. Korean demands for the truth about civilian massacres by UN troops during the Korean War spurred the Jejuvians to emulate the pro-democracy mainland groups. Activists demanded the truth about the April 1948 "incident" on their island. In May 1961, the government was overthrown in a military coup and a military-supported authoritarian government again clamped down on dissent, leading to the arrest of several leading Jejuvian activists.

For seventeen years, there was no official mention of the Jejuvian massacres until the publication of Hyon Ki Young's novel based on the April 3rd uprising. His fictional story of a massacre on the island moved the Jejuvian people into a new search for the truth. However, this did not last long. Hyon was arrested and the novel's publishers were forcibly shut down. Once again, the Jejuvian massacres were buried. In June 1987, the pro-democracy movement in Korea allowed the Jejuvians to again question the official version of the April 3rd uprising. The first open memorial for the Jejuvian victims was finally held in 1989, but was disrupted by police charges and tear gas.

In spite of continuing political instability, South Korea achieved rapid economic growth, with per capita income rising to 13 times those of North Korea by 1990. Jejuvians were mostly left out of the so-called Korean Miracle, subsisting on agriculture and fishing but remaining, for the most part, poor and underdeveloped until the tourist boom of the 1970s and 1980s.

Disparities in income between different regions of mainland Korea had mostly disappeared by the early 1980s, but the disparity between per capita incomes on Jeju and the mainland remained and even widened. Tourism, fruit production, and fishing remained the only sources of employment for Jejuvian youngsters. Emigration to the mainland or beyond, to the United States or Europe, were the only alternatives.

On 15 April 1991, local provincial autonomy was granted with the establishment of the Provincial Council. In June 1995, more autonomy was allowed with the election of a provincial governor and local functionaries. The April 3rd Special Commission was established by the provincial assembly in 1994. It began to compile a list of the victims of the 1948 suppression and their relatives. Even today many Jejuvians are reluctant to speak, fearing retribution from the police. The truth about the April 3rd uprising and massacres only began to trickle out after the pro-democracy movement that swept Korea in June 1987. The commission published its first report in 1995 with a preliminary list of 14,125 victims, including 610 children under age ten, and 638 people over age 61.

The fiftieth anniversary of the April 3rd uprising in 1998 was marked by widespread demonstrations on the island, but even after 10 years of "openness" in South Korea, few victims stepped forward to point fingers. Although a half century had elapsed since the massacre, only in the 1990s was it possible to access the facts and discuss the incident. In the past, the uprising was passed off as a leftist rebellion, but with greater access to source material, the uprising is now seen as a popular uprising against the brutal government policies and the U.S. military government. The brutal crushing of the uprising, justified as "anti-Communist" is now seen as a holocaust in which between 30,000 and 100,000 people died. Activists continue to demand the return of all properties taken illegally to their rightful owners, that the government publish a list of those responsible, and compensate the victims and their descendants. Many of the island's hotels and tourist firms are owned by members of the youth gangs, police, and army who confiscated properties in the late 1940s.

Resentment of the need to emigrate in order to gain a living became a part of the regionalist-nationalist movement that won support on Jeju in the 1990s. Demands for greater cultural and economic culture were widely supported in the late 1990s, particularly during the economic slow-down after 1997.

The Koreans are among the world's most homogeneous nations, with ethnic minorities a negligible influence. Like the Japanese, the Koreans tend to equate nationality or citizenship with membership in a single homogeneous ethnic group or race. A common language and culture are viewed as important elements in Korean identity. Regional deviations, such as the Jejuvian dialect and culture, were formerly suppressed and still arouse suspicion and distrust. Against this background of ethnic homogeneity, however, significant regional differences exist. Many Jejuvians reject the Korean view of nationality and demand recognition of their unique island culture and teaching and publication in the Jejuvian language.

A sharp decline in the price of tangerines since 2000 contributed to rising economic problems in 2001–2. The government published a plan to create an international center of business and tourism on the island, eventually to create another Hong Kong or Singapore, but encountered widespread opposition from the Jejuvian people, who still distrust outsiders. Many fear that their island will be crowded with golfers and shoppers interested only in seeking bargains in duty-free shops while drowning their unique culture and dialect. Government plans for the development of the island has aroused even more hostility to the mainland.

One in every five Jejuvians lost a family member in the 1948–54 government actions, which continues to fuel anti-government and anti-mainland attitudes. Although few advocate separatism, as claimed by the government, most Jejuvians still want to retain their traditional distance from the mainland and its problems. Demands for greater autonomy are seen by mainland Koreans as separatism or even treason.

SELECTED BIBLIOGRAPHY:

Bedeski, Robert E. *The Transformation of South Korea.* 1994.
Clifford, Mark L. *Troubled Tiger.* 1994.
Eberstadt, Nicholas. *Korea Approaches Reunification.* 1995.
Halliday, Jon, and Bruce Cumings. *Korea: The Unknown War.* 1988.

Jerseians

Jèrriais; Jerseyites

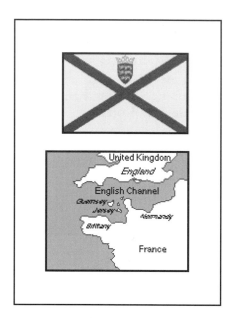

POPULATION: Approximately (2002e) 102,000 Jerseians in Europe, mostly in Jersey, but with a large Jerseian population in the United Kingdom.

THE JERSEIAN HOMELAND: Jersey is an island lying in the English Channel 15 miles west of the Cotentin Peninsula of Normandy in France and southeast of Guernsey. The island, 11 miles long by five miles wide, is the largest of the Channel Islands archipelago, which the Jerseians often call the Norman Islands. A mild subtropical climate, moderate rainfall, and beautiful scenery have contributed to Jersey's popularity as a vacation destination. The soil is generally good, and large quantities of vegetables are grown, particularly tomatoes and early vegetables and fruits for the British market. Cattle raising and dairying—the island has its own breed of Jersey cattle—are important to the economy. Jersey forms a bailiwick, a self-governing dependency of the British crown. The Jersey state is not subject to the British government or parliament unless specifically mentioned in legislation. *Bailiwick of Jersey*: 45 sq. mi.—117 sq. km, (2002e) 89,500—Jerseians 85%, English 7%, Normans* 4%, other British 4%. The Jerseian capital and major cultural center is St. Helier, (2002e) 28,000.

FLAG: The Jerseian national flag, the official flag of the Bailiwick of Jersey, is a white field bearing a red saltaire, and often the Jersey coat of arms above the saltaire, a red shield with three gold lions surmounted by a gold crown.

PEOPLE AND CULTURE: The Jerseians, calling themselves Jèrriais, are descendants of early Norman colonists with admixtures of later French religious refugees, immigrants from Great Britain, and the many other peoples who have settled on the island. There is also an important admixture of Bretons,* inhabitants of the peninsula just to the south. The culture of the islanders is a unique blend of Norman, French, and British elements.

826

Although the majority of the population claim Norman ancestry, modern Jersey culture is basically British, particularly in the urban areas. The islanders, long isolated, retain many traditions and customs that have disappeared on the French mainland.

LANGUAGE AND RELIGION: The Jerseian language, called Channel Island French or Channel Island Norman French, is an archaic dialect related to the Norman dialects spoken on the nearby French mainland. The local dialect, called Jèrriais, is older than modern French; it is not part of the formal educational system, but increasingly language classes and schools are reviving it. The Jerseians fear that without these efforts their unique culture and language will disappear within 50 years. Although French is the official language of the state, the Jèrriais dialect is quite distinct from French and remains the language of daily life in the rural areas of the island.

The majority of the Jerseians are Roman Catholic, with a small Protestant minority. Religion, particularly Roman Catholicism, is an integral part of the island culture and is intricately intertwined with traditional life. The Protestants are primarily English immigrants or the descendants of Protestant refugees from France.

NATIONAL HISTORY: The island of Jersey has been inhabited since ancient times. Ancient stone structures such as cromlechs and menhirs are evidence of early occupation, and prehistoric remains of Paleolithic inhabitants have been found. There is abundant evidence of extensive habitation during the Neolithic and Bronze Ages.

The island was known to the Romans as Caesarea, named for Caesar, the conqueror of Gaul. Included in the Roman province of Gaul, the Celts, called Gauls by the Romans, supplied the first large population to occupy the island. Under Roman rule the Celtic inhabitants adopted the Latin culture and language. Following the collapse of Roman power in the fifth century, the island fell to invading Franks, Germanic tribes moving into the former Roman provinces.

Christianity was brought to the island in the sixth century. Traditionally the island's patron saint, St. Helier, led the conversion of the pagan islanders and was martyred there in A.D. 555. The conversion to Christianity marked the beginning of the development of a distinct culture on the island. Early church documents show that the island was divided into parishes belonging to the diocese of Coutances, on the French mainland.

Vikings, called Norsemen and later Normans, took control of the island in the eighth century. The Norsemen came to the island from the large mainland French territory they had earlier conquered. In A.D. 933, Jersey became a dependency of the duchy of Normandy, and with the Norman conquest in 1066, Jersey was joined to the new Norman kingdom of England. In the early twelfth century, Norman landowners dominated the island, which was divided into three units for tax purposes.

The French seized mainland Normandy in 1117, but the Norman Islands, protected by England's fleet, remained with the Norman-dominated English kingdom. The union with England was made permanent in 1154. In 1204 the island's administration was reorganized, although Norman law and local customs were retained. The French, claiming the islands as historical parts of Normandy, attempted to take control of the island in the fourteenth century, but the English defeated the invasion, and Jersey, with the other Channel Islands, remained an English fief. The English crown's claims to the islands were finally recognized by the French in the Treaty of Bretigny in 1360, but whenever French-English relations soured, French claims to the Channel Islands were pressed. The English used Jersey as a base for its recovery of Normandy in 1417, but the mainland territories were again lost to French control in 1450. The Jerseians remained loyal to the English monarch despite French efforts to regain control of the island during the 1500s.

Although Jersey maintained ties to the English monarchy, the islanders retained their own law, dialects, and Norman-based culture. The island, historically self-governing, remained subject to the English monarchy but was not subject to the English parliament. The Jerseians' personal union with the English crown reinforced their long history of independence and local self-government. By the fifteenth century the island was administered for the English king by a warden, sometimes by a lord. Later the island had its own "captain," in the nineteenth century called a governor.

Feudal customs were retained on Jersey and the smaller Channel Islands as part of their traditional agricultural society. The famous Jersey breed of cattle was developed in the eighteenth century, and dairy farming became a mainstay of the economy. To the present the breed is kept pure by law, which forbids the import of other breeds. The law, in effect since 1789, has allowed the Jerseians to perfect their special breed.

Protestant refugees from religious persecution in France fled to the island in the sixteenth century. The new arrivals easily assimilated themselves into the Norman culture of the island, but many retained their Protestant religion. The French Revolution sent another wave of French refugees to the island. The new refugees reinforced the French culture of the island, and their language, the standard French of the mainland, gradually replaced the island's Norman dialect in the urban areas.

In 1617 it was ruled that justice and civil affairs were aspects of the duties of the bailiff, the king's representative. Through most of the seventeenth century, the De Carterets, seigneurs of St. Ouen, dominated the island. The De Carterets took in the fugitive future English king, Charles II, who stayed on the island from 1646 to 1649. Sir George Carteret was rewarded in 1664 for his support of the Royalists in the English Civil War with a grant of land in North America. His holdings later became the state of New Jersey.

In the eighteenth and nineteenth centuries the Jerseians were divided by feuds, often pitting pro-British against the pro-French islanders. The feuds mostly disappeared following the French defeat at the Battle of Jersey in 1781. At the same time, the islanders prospered from the Newfoundland fisheries, privateering, and smuggling. Later cattle, potatoes, and the tourist trade became important to the local economy.

There was an influx of English from the British mainland after 1830, and many political refugees from the upheavals in Europe settled on the island after 1848. Jersey became a popular Victorian resort and retirement center later in the nineteenth century, due to its subtropical climate, unique foreign culture, and beautiful scenery. English immigrants, attracted to the mild climate and relative ease of life, settled in Jersey permanently, but the government of Jersey carefully controlled the number of new residents. The new arrivals had to meet stringent financial requirements or have skills needed for the local economy in order to remain. Although the Jerseians enjoyed the protection of the Crown, there was considerable anti-English sentiment.

The islanders remained loyal to Britain during World War I, and many Jerseians volunteered to fight in the British military. Jersey was used as a staging area for British troops bound for nearby France. In the postwar era, Jersey became once again a favorite British resort and retirement center. In addition, mainlanders seeking to avoid the high taxes of Great Britain came to the island after World War I to take advantage of the island's liberal tax laws.

In 1940, soon after the beginning of World War II, France fell to the invading Germans, who quickly reached the coast opposite Jersey. Unable to defend the island, the British evacuated all troops and thousands of Jerseians, but they were unable to evacuate the entire civilian population. German troops occupied Jersey on 30 June 1940; the Channel Islands were the only British territory to occupied by enemy troops during the war. The thousands of civilians that had stayed were deported as forced labor in Germany. Many others nearly starved, as the products of the island were taken to feed the German military.

The German surrender in 1944 allowed the Jersey government to return from exile in Britain. During the 1950s the island quickly recovered its earlier prosperity. In the 1960s, Jersey, with its low taxes (and no inheritance tax), became one of Europe's major offshore banking centers. The mild, sunny climate attracted new residents from Britain, bringing a substantial English minority to the population. The island's economy flourished from tourism and early crops for the British market, mainly vegetables and fruits.

In 1958 Jersey began to issue its own currency and stamps, two of the trappings of an independent state, acts that raised new questions about the ultimate status of the island. In 1968 the British government convened a special commission to study the relationship of the island to the United Kingdom. Proposals to join Jersey and Guernsey in cooperative sovereignty were quickly rejected; the traditional enmity between the Jerseians and Guernseians had accelerated as rivalry between their financial activities grew. (The Jerseians claim to dislike the Guernseians even more than they dislike the mainland British.) The islanders lobbied instead for the status quo, preferring to remain a self-governing state, but with the British government taking responsibility for defense and foreign affairs.

Jersey's development as an offshore banking center accelerated following the United Kingdom's entry into the European Economic Community (EEC) in 1973. The island's banking system held some 1.36 billion dollars in 1973, but by 1983 the total had climbed to 24.5 billion dollars, about 80% in foreign currencies. Thousands of foreign firms are registered in St. Helier and are managed by Jerseians. By 2000 financial services accounted for nearly a third of the local economy, tourism for nearly 40%, and the income brought in by wealthy immigrants for some 20%. Fruits and vegetables, grown year-around in greenhouses, remain important exports. The Jersey government has declared a budget surplus every year since World War II.

A census of late August 1989 showed that the island's population had swollen to 82,536. The news was greeted with near hysteria, as it revealed that the psychologically important barrier of 80,000 had been breached. The growth of the population has aggravated the chronic housing shortage, and development is encroaching on the island's green zones. New immigration limits were set in 2000, but the government came under intense pressure to stop immigration completely.

The growth of the population, plus the danger to the island's unique culture and language led to the growth of national and cultural organizations in the 1980s. The largest of the groups, L'Assemblée d'Jèrriais, works to extend the use of the island's Norman dialect in daily life and to preserve its endangered culture. Less moderate Jerseians advocate full independence for the island, with ties to the European Union (EU) similar to those it now has with the British crown. In the 1990s the cultural groups took on many of the aspects of political organizations, as the island has no political parties.

The island seeks to be a conduit for non-European funds into the EU. Its special political and economic status continues within the new European reality, but with respect to the movement of peoples and services. For all practical purposes, Jersey is not part of the EU; it is treated as an outside country.

In 1993 a controversy arose over the extension of Jersey's territorial waters, particularly after a French flotilla violated the new 12-mile limits in March. Boats from both Jersey and Guernsey sailed into the harbor of

Cherbourg on the French coast a few days later to protest the French repudiation of an informal agreement reached by the local fishermen.

The island's financial services industry, loosely regulated and secretive, came under international scrutiny in mid-2000. An international body organized to study the controls and regulations of the world's financial centers named Jersey among the 35 centers that failed to control the laundering of funds, mostly from international drug trafficking and other illegal activities. The Jerseians rejected demands for changes in the state's tax structure. In mid-2000, however, the United Kingdom itself contemplated changing Jersey's tax laws due to the criticism of Jersey's tax system, prompting a renewed debate on independence. Nationalists called for a referendum on independence and a complete break with the British crown. An increasing number of Jerseians view independence as the only way to retain their own tax system.

In late 2001, following the terrorist attacks in the United States, the British government pressed the Jerseian government to review its financial and tax systems to preclude ties to terrorist organizations. The Jerseians again insisted that they maintain rigid standards, but began a review of all accounts that could be tied to illegal activities.

SELECTED BIBLIOGRAPHY:

Balleine, G.R. *The Bailiwick of Jersey.* 1990.
Bunting, Madeleine. *Model Occupation: The Channel Islands under German Rule, 1940–1945.* 1998.
Gardiner, Vince. *The Channel Islands.* 1998.
Hillsdon, Sonia. *Jersey.* 1997.

Jews

Yevrey; Yevry; Evrey; Russian Jews; Yiddishkeit

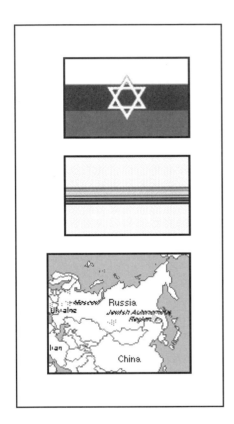

POPULATION: Approximately (2002e) 1,380,000 Jews in Russia and the Commonwealth of Independent States (CIS), where they are counted as a distinct ethnic group. There are about 850,000 in Russia, concentrated in European Russia, 355,000 in Ukraine, 75,000 in Belarus, 50,000 in Kazakhstan, and smaller numbers in other former Soviet republics. Outside the states of the former Soviet Union, there are populations of so-called Russian Jews in the United States, France, the United Kingdom, Canada, Brazil, Australia and New Zealand, Belgium, Mexico, the Netherlands, Turkey, and Israel.

THE JEWISH HOMELAND IN RUSSIA: The Jewish homeland in Russia encompasses a large territory with Jewish populations in many parts of the country. The official homeland lies in the Russian Far East, a mountainous region bordering on China. Lying in the basin of the middle Amur River, the region is mostly level plain. *Jewish Autonomous Oblast/Jewish Republic (Yevreyskaya Autonomnaya Oblast'Jevrejskaja Respublika):* 13,900 sq. mi.—36,001 sq. km, (2002e) 195,000—Russians (mostly Far Easterners*) 78%, Ukrainians 15%, Jews 6%, others 1%. The major Jewish cultural centers in Russia are Moscow and St. Petersburg. The capital of the Jewish Autonomous Oblast is Birobidzhan, (2002e) 77,000.

FLAG: The national flag of the Russian Jews, the flag used by activists, is a horizontal tricolor of white, blue, and red, each stripe separated by a narrow red stripe, bearing a yellow Star of David, outlined in red, centered. The official flag of the Jewish Autonomous Oblast is a white field bearing seven rainbow horizontal stripes centered.

PEOPLE AND CULTURE: The Jews of Russia are considered an ethnic not a religious group. The vast majority of the Jews in Russia and the CIS are Ashkenazic Jews, also called Russian Jews. They are overwhelmingly urban with over 98% living in urban areas, particularly the four cities of Moscow and St. Petersburg in Russia and Kiev and Odessa in Ukraine. Along with being the most urbanized national group, the Jews rank first among all nationalities in educational level and in the number of scientific workers.

LANGUAGE AND RELIGION: The majority of the Jews in the former Soviet Union speak Russian. Yiddish, the Jewish national language in Russia which originated in the High German dialects and which has incorporated additional vocabulary from Hebrew and the Slavic languages, is written in Hebrew letters. The language, widely used before World War II, declined under Stalinist persecution and forced assimilation. About 85% of the Jews in the states of the former Soviet Union regard Russian as their native language, although the former Soviet government and the government of the Russian Federation recognized Yiddish as the national language of the Jews.

The Jews, although considered a nationality rather than a religious minority in the states of the former Soviet Union, are the descendants of the medieval Jews from western and central Europe. After decades of official Soviet atheism, many Jews are secularized—shunning their religious traditions.

NATIONAL HISTORY: The medieval Khazar state was the only Jewish state in the world between the fall of Jerusalem in 67 A.D. and the formation of the modern Israeli state. The Khazars were probably a Turkic people first mentioned in historical chronicles in 627. They moved westward in the late sixth century to settle the region around the Sea of Azov, the Don, the lower Volga, the northern Caucasus, and the Caspian Sea. Arab expansion pushed the Khazars north in 725. The Khazars were traditionally allied to the Byzantines, but the Khazar conversion to Judaism, sometime between 740 and 809 A.D., hastened the end of the alliance.

Judaism, sustained by Jewish scholars invited to settle in the region, was adopted by the Khazar king and the nobility. Scholars differ on the conversion of the vast majority of the Khazars, who are thought to have been Christians, although some scholars believe that most of the population adopted Judaism.

The Khazar state, attacked by the Slavs and the Byzantines, finally disappeared in the eleventh century. The influence of the Jewish Khazars outlasted their national state. The Jews of Kievan Rus' are thought to have descended from the Khazars. Some scholars have argued that the Khazars were the source of Ashkenazic Jewry in Russia, but the claim has not received widespread support.

Ashkenazic Jews, referring to European Jews, developed in western Europe. The expulsion of the Jews from England in 1290, France in 1306 and 1394, many of the German states, and from Spanish and Portuguese territory in 1492–97, led some Jews to migrate east to the expanding Polish-Lithuanian state, which included a large part of Ukraine. There they were welcomed, for economic reasons, as a merchant class. Their language, Yiddish, of German origin, became the daily language of central and eastern European Jews. By 1650, there may have been as many as 1.5 million Jews in the region.

Initially, they were under royal protection and enjoyed considerable internal autonomy although they were concentrated largely in towns and cities. Many lived in small towns called *shtetls*, which came to characterize the eastern European Ashkenazic Jews. Forbidden to own land, many Jews served as estate managers, where they were hated by the peasantry for being responsible for their miserable lives. These early resentments were the seeds of primitive anti-Semitism in eastern Europe and later in the Russian Empire.

The mostly Orthodox peasantry joined the Ukrainian Cossacks in the mid-seventeenth century in a revolt against the Poles and Catholicism, but often targeting the Jewish population. Russian armies swept into the territory following an alliance with the Cossacks in 1654. The Russians killed many thousands, forcibly converted many to Orthodoxy, and drove thousands into exile. The Jewish community declined rapidly following the series of massacres—the Hmelnitsky massacres occurring between 1648 and 1654. Estimates of the numbers of Jews killed in the massacres range from 100,000 to 500,000. The Jews of Poland-Lithuania never recovered from the mass slaughter.

Small numbers of Jews, mostly descendants of the Khazars, lived in the Russian state. They faced the hostility of the Orthodox clergy, but faced less prejudice than Jews in other parts of medieval Europe. By the late fifteenth century, Jews from farther west were barred from entering Russia, although when the Russians acquired part of Ukraine in the 1670s, the Jewish population there was permitted to remain. Some eventually moved to the Russian capital, Moscow, establishing the nucleus of the present Jewish population in the city.

The Jews of Russia were expelled in 1742, but the subsequent incorporation of Polish territory meant that the Russian Empire had the largest Jewish community in the world by the end of the eighteenth century. The ban on Jews remained until the first partition of Poland in 1772. The three partitions of Poland (1772, 1793, and 1795) brought almost one million Ashkenazic Jews into the empire. At first they were allowed to retain the same privileges they had enjoyed in the Polish state. The policy changed at the end of the eighteenth century. Faced with Jewish competition, Russian merchants pressured the government leading to the establishment of the Pale of Settlement, limiting the Jewish population to the newly acquired territories and barring Jews from moving into the traditional Russian territories.

In spite of persecution, the number of Jews in the Russian Empire expanded rapidly during the nineteenth century. The Pale of Settlement remained in force until 1917, with over 90% of Russia's Jews living in the restricted area. The economic ruin of the Jews accelerated in the nineteenth century. A government report in the 1880s stated that the vast majority of the Jews lived from hand to mouth, in poverty, and under very unhygienic conditions.

The Russian state deprived the Jews of the social and religious autonomy they had enjoyed in the Polish-Lithuanian state under the rule of the anti-Semitic Nicholas I. In 1827, a decree ended the Jewish exemption from military service. Jewish recruits were forced to serve for twenty-five years and came under tremendous pressure to convert to Orthodoxy. Many young Jews mutilated themselves to escape military service. The Pale of Settlement was also narrowed with the expulsion of the Jews from Kiev in the late 1820s. Laws were passed forbidding traditional Jewish dress, against women shaving their heads before marriage, and against men wearing the *peies*, the hairlock.

During the reign of Alexander II, in the middle nineteenth century, conditions eased somewhat and privileged Jews were allowed to reside in St. Petersburg and Moscow. Restrictions on Jews with academic degrees were also lifted, allowing them to reside anywhere in the empire. Later artisans, mechanics, and distillers were also allowed to move outside the Pale. Jewish merchants played an important part in the development and marketing of Baku oil in the late nineteenth and early twentieth centuries. Prominent Jews such as Baron Joseph (Yozel) Günzburg, a banker and financier, contributed much to the industrialization and the extension of the railroad network in nineteenth-century Russia.

The situation of the Jews deteriorated under the last Romanov rulers. In 1887, the government introduced strict limits on Jewish education. The authorities also began enforcing residency requirements. Twenty thousand of the 30,000 Jews living in Moscow were expelled in 1891, with only 24- to 48-hours' notice. The last decades of the nineteenth century were also marked by fear for life and property. The pogroms, beatings and riots against Jews and Jewish property, first broke out in 1881, after the assasination of Tsar Alexander II, reaching their height during the pogroms of 1903–6. Led by the Black Hundreds, an officially sanctioned reactionary group composed largely of civil servants, the programs became institutionalized. Government complicity, over the next four decades, led to hundreds of pogroms that worsened during the civil war between 1918 and 1921. An estimated 180,000 to 200,000 Jews were killed in these actions.

The Jews, numbering around 1 million in 1800, had increased to 5.7 million in the 1897 census. According to census figures 93.9% lived in the Pale of Settlement, encompassing Ukraine, Bessarabia, Belarusia, Russian Poland, and Lithuania. The harsh conditions and government suppression prompted a Jewish response—emigration. Between 1881 and 1914, over 1.5 million Jews left the empire, mostly to Canada, the United States, Argentina, and South Africa.

Other Jews responded to oppression by remaining and actively seeking reforms through political action. Jews played an increasingly important role in the revolutionary movement and had a prominent role in the Marxist movement that overthrew the monarchy in 1917. None of the revolutionaries were practicing Jews. Ironically, the tsarist restrictions were lifted and Jews participated in the construction of the Soviet state, but these gains were later obliterated, and attacks on Jewish life and religion in the Soviet Union were resumed.

World War I and the civil war that followed in Russia were calamities for the Jews. The Pale of Settlement was the area where most of the military conflict took place and Jews were killed indiscriminately by Cossacks, the anti-Bolshevik White forces, Ukrainian nationalists, and peasant armies of many ideological basis. Only the Red Army Command prohibited anti-Semitic violence. In addition, the emergence of independent states in Poland, Lithuania, and Latvia, and the annexation of Bessarabia by Romania left large numbers of Russian Jews outside the borders of the new Soviet state. By 1922, the Jewish population of the Soviet Union was less than half of what it had been in the former Russian Empire.

Official Soviet views, laid down by Lenin, were not at first anti-Semitic but were against religion, Zionism, and Jewish cultural autonomy. Lenin opposed all three as divisive—preferring the concept of internationalism, the elimination of the differences among the peoples of the Soviet Union. Hundreds of thousands of Jews were integrated into Soviet cultural and economic life, with many Jews occupying key political positions in the government and the new Communist Party.

The Soviet nationality policy decreed national states within the Soviet state for each of the major national groups. In 1927, a Jewish professor, Boris Brook, arrived in the swampy area between the Bira and Bidzhan Rivers, proof that there was a genuine belief among Jews that a homeland could be created in the Far East. In 1928, a region of the Russian Far East was established as a Jewish colonization area, but it was far from the major Jewish populations in European Russia. Created as an alternative to the lure of the Zionist movement—only about 35,000 Jews migrated to the area—many forcibly deported from European Russia. Others came willingly, with more than 300 families arrived from Argentina, Venezuela, the United States, Germany, Switzerland, and Poland. The region was officially established as an autonomous province in 1934. Although established theoretically as a home for all the Soviet Jews, no mass Jewish migration developed and in Birbidzhan, the so-called Jerusalem on the Amur, Russian and Ukrainian settlers heavily outnumbered the Jews.

After 1930, repression surpassed the ideals of the fledgling Jewish home land in the Soviet Far East. There were many provocations—buildings and homes were burned, and many of the foreign Jewish families were declared spies and were arrested or forced to leave. Many of the Soviet Jews were sent to concentration camps. The 26 Jewish schools, the synagogue, and the library were closed; Hebrew and Yiddish publications were banned.

Although initially the Jews were allowed cultural autonomy, within a few decades, this had been rescinded. The Stalinist purges in the mid- to late 1930s greatly reduced the participation of the Jewish intelligentsia in Soviet political life. Anti-Semitic activity increased during the Stalinist era, particularly after the formation of the state of Israel in 1948, when Jews were suspected of double loyalties.

Adolph Hitler turned on his Soviet ally, Joseph Stalin, and invaded the Soviet Union in June 1941. The invasion was particularly harsh on the large population of Jews in the western provinces. About 2.5 million Soviet Jews were annihilated, often with the collaboration of the local Slav populations who aided the Germans in the Jewish Holocaust. Anti-Semitism also reemerged in areas not under German occupation as propaganda blaming the Jews for the war was widespread and often believed.

The pre-World War I emigration, combined with the independence of Poland after World War I, the horrendous losses of the Holocaust during World War II, and the waves of post-1967 emigration from the Soviet Union, led to the decline of Russian Jewry to less than 1.5 million at the end of the twentieth century. The Jews were the most dispersed nationality in the Soviet Union according to the 1989 Soviet census, although the majority lived in the three Slavic republics, mostly in Europe. The passionate demands for the right to emigrate, in the 1960s and 1970s, spotlighted the continuing anti-Semitism in the Soviet Union. The Jewish population in the Soviet Union declined by about 900,000 between 1959 and 1989 through a low birth rate, intermarriage, concealment of Jewish identity, and emigration.

In spite of increased opportunities for religious activities since 1991, the Jewish religion has been nearly eliminated in the 74 years of Communist rule and the Jews continue to exist as a national minority rather than a religious minority in Russia and the other states of the former Soviet Union. A bid to form a Jewish Republic as a member state of the new Russian Federation was dropped following official opposition in 1991.

The new Russian constitution guarantees the "rights and liberties of persons belonging to ethnic minorities." Since 1993, there has been a marked increase in discrimination and acts against Jews in Russia. Jews continue to face social obstacles, and there are numerous reports of desecration of Jewish cemeteries and bombings of synagogues in the late 1990s. The mostly Christian government of the Jewish Autonomous Oblast openly oppose anti-Semitism and support new attempts to resurrect

Jewish culture in the region, but at the same time many speak of growing Jewish nationalism.

The number of Jews living in the official Jewish Autonomous Oblast in the Far East has dropped from about 25% in the early 1950s, to about 6% in 2000, and the numbers continue to decline as the Jews return to their roots in European Russia or emigrate to Israel. Although the number of Jews living in the territory is dropping, on top of the newly renovated railway station in Birbidzhan is a neon sign with the city's name lit up in Hebrew, highlighting it's status as the official capital of Russian Jewry. The city has Russia's only Yiddish newspaper. A representative of the Israeli embassy in Moscow visits Birbidzhan every month, but support is more moral than financial. Many Jews still believe that an official homeland is an opportunity to recreate the Russian Jews as a nationality, but emigration and the large numbers of secular Jews continue to undermine the effort.

Before the collapse of the Soviet Union, many Jews in Israel and the West believed that once unlimited emigration was allowed, all Jews, except the old and infirm, would leave, effectively ending the Jewish nationality in the former Soviet Union. By 2000, in spite of mass emigration, Russia and Ukraine still have some of the largest Jewish populations in the world.

SELECTED BIBLIOGRAPHY:

Lewin-Epstein, Noah. *Russian Jews on Three Continents: Migration and Resettlement.* 1997.

Pinkus, Benjamin. *The Jews of the Soviet Union: The History of a National Minority.* 1988.

Ro'I, Yaacov. *Jews and Jewish Life in Russia and the Soviet Union.* 1995.

Zipperstein, Steven J. *Imagining Russian Jewry: Memory, History, Identity.* 1999.

Jharkhandis

Adivasis; Mundas; Mundaris; Kherwaris; Khanwars; Kharars; Kharaolis; Kharwaris

POPULATION: Approximately (2002e) 14,500,000 Jharkhandis in northeastern India, concentrated in the Chota Nagpur region of the states of Jharkhand, Orissa, Madya Pradesh, and West Bengal.

THE JHARKHANDI HOMELAND: The Jharkhand homeland occupies the heavily forested Chota Nagpur Plateau and the lowlands of the Bay of Bengal east of the Hooghly River in northeastern India. The word "Jharkhand" means "Forest Land" or "Jungle Country." The Jharkhand region claimed by nationalists forms a number of administrative districts of the northeastern Indian states of Bihar, Orissa, Madya Pradesh, and West Bengal, with an area of over 61,600 sq. mi.—159,500 sq. km. On 15 November 2000, the state of Jharkhand was carved out of the southern districts of the state of Bihar. *Jharkhand (Vananchal)* 28,833 sq. mi.—74,677 sq. km, (2002e) 27,415,000—Biharis 41%, Jharkhandis 38%, other Indians 21%. The Jharkhandi capital and major cultural center is Ranchi, (2002e) 871,000, metropolitan area 964,000. Other important centers are Bo-

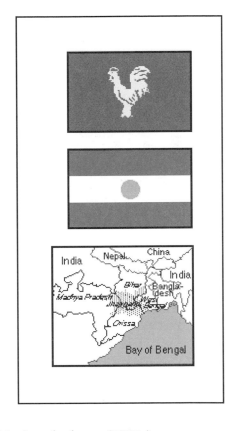

karo, (2002e) 563,000, metropolitan area 855,000, Jamshedpur, (2002e) 516,000, metropolitan area 1,126,000, and Dhanbad (2002e) 213,000, metropolitan area 1,148,000.

FLAG: The Jharkhand national flag, the flag of the Jharkhand Party, is a green field bearing a centered white rooster. The flag of the Chota Nagpur Plateau Praja Parishad has three horizontal stripes of green, white, and green and bears a red disc centered on the white stripe.

PEOPLE AND CULTURE: The Jharkhandis are made up of a number of related tribal peoples. The largest group is the Mundas (Korku, Santhali, Mundari, Bumij, and Ho), who number over nine million. Officially they are included in a category known as "Scheduled Tribes," although they call themselves Jharkhandis or Adivasis, meaning the "original peoples" or "inhabitants." The Jharkhandis also include 5,000,000 Santals, 2,000,000 Mundas, 2,000,000 Oraons, 1,350,000 Ho, 300,000 Kharias, 200,000 Koda, and many smaller groups. Traditional culture includes the institution of girls' and boys' dormitories, an elaborate system of village offices, and a territorial organization into quasi-military confederations. Descent is traced through the paternal line, and youngsters are expected to marry outside the paternal clan. Relegated to the lowest rungs of India's rigid caste system, the Jharkhandi tribes encompass the pre-Dravidian holdovers from ancient India. Although they represent different ethnic communities and languages, the Jharkhandis stress pan-tribal unity and a shared history of marginalization and persecution.

LANGUAGE AND RELIGION: The majority of the Jharkhandis speak languages of the North Munda language group, of which Santhali is the largest. Some of the smaller tribal groups speak Dravidian languages. The next largest are the Mundari and Ho, followed by Korku and Sora. The remaining Munda languages are spoken by small, isolated groups and are little known. Publishing in the Munda languages began in the 1950s, including translations of the Bible. The languages are mostly written in the Devanagari script, mostly in the northern districts, and the Oriya script in the south.

The Jharkhandis are mostly animist, with sizable Christian, Hindu, and Buddhist communities. Traditionally the Jharkhandis worship spirits, some of which they believe cause diseases. Witchcraft and divination are part of their traditional beliefs. Conversion to Christianity and Buddhism in the 1990s has reduced the numbers adhering to the rigid caste system imposed by Hinduism. The Ho are the only tribe in which the majority, about 70%, continue to follow animist beliefs, and the Kharia are the only tribe with a Christian majority. Christianity is also significant among the Mundas and Oraons.

NATIONAL HISTORY: The Munda peoples, believed to have originated in central or southeastern Asia, inhabited large tracts of northern India prior to the ancient Dravidian settlement of India. The tribes, pushed into the less-accessible highland jungles, adopted many Dravidian traditions while retaining their ancient pre-Dravidian languages and cultures. Their territory, difficult to reach and remote from the great centers of Indian civilization, was constantly reduced by the advance and spread of peoples having more elaborate cultures.

Aryan invaders from the Iranian Plateau overran northern India between 1700 and 1200 B.C. The fair, warlike Aryans drove the darker Dravidians into southern India, except for small groups of refugees who fled into Munda territory in the jungled Chota Nagpur Plateau. Successive Aryan kingdoms and empires ignored and avoided the region. The autonomous

Munda and Dravidian tribes retained their own chiefs and rulers under only nominal Aryan rule.

Muslims conquered the region in the twelfth century, and in 1497 the region's small Muslim states came under the rule of the powerful sultanate of Delhi. The tribal peoples, despised and persecuted by the former Hindu majority, enjoyed greater rights under the more tolerant Muslims. Some of the tribal peoples embraced Islam as an escape from the harsh and rigid Hindu caste system.

The tribal peoples, emulating the lowland Hindus, formed small monarchies in the Chota Nagpur Plateau. The small states, later called the Chota Nagpur States, were usually under the nominal rule of larger empires or states. The plateau came under British rule in 1765 as part of the British province of Bengal. Resistance to outside rule provoked several revolts, the most important being the Ho revolt of 1820–27 and the Munda uprising of 1831–32. Many people participated in a general rebellion against British rule in 1857–59. The last Jharkhandi uprising, a reaction in the 1890s to Hindu encroachment on tribal lands, was led by Birsa, a missionary educated Christian and now a Jharkhandi national hero.

Christian missionaries arrived in the area in 1845, leading to major cultural changes. The missionaries won many converts with their message of equality and tolerance. The Jharkhandi survived mostly by subsistence agriculture until the British introduced the use of money and trade crops. British officials and missionaries penetrated previously undisturbed regions. An educated minority, the product of mission schools, gradually took over the leadership of the tribes.

The development of the tribal areas accelerated after coal mining was begun in 1856. The Tata Iron and Steel Factory was established at Jamshedpur in Santali territory in 1907–11. Generally ignored until the discovery of the rich mineral deposits, the region suddenly took on great economic importance. In 1908 the government restricted the Jharkhandi tribes to allotted reserves. Rapid industrialization brought a large influx of Hindu workers. The Jharkhandis moved to the new industrial cities in large numbers in the 1920s and 1930s as the poorest segment of the population. The urbanized Jharkhandis mostly adopted Christianity to escape the violence and discrimination of the Hindu caste system.

Relegated to the least desirable lands and jobs, the Jharkhandis began to organize after World War I. Concerted efforts to maintain their way of life and their traditional lands mobilized the educated elite in interwar period. The early Jharkhand movement was directed at the Hindu newcomers—*dikus* or outsiders—not specifically at the British administration. In 1938 nationalist activists founded the Jharkhand Party to press for pantribal unity and autonomy. In 1947, as Indian independence neared, militants demanded that the British grant separate independence to Jharkhand as a non-Hindu and non-Muslim majority area outside Hindu India and

Muslim Pakistan, but they found little sympathy among the British authorities.

India's independence constitution included provisions for the protection of minority peoples and their lands, but in practice high-caste Hindus controlled large areas, and the Jharkhandis became virtual serfs on land that should have been theirs. The new Indian government established the category of "scheduled tribes" to encompass the diverse tribal groups of the country. Federal policies encouraged education and ensured representation in local governments and in the national parliament. The Jharkhand Party swept the tribal districts in 1949 in the first general elections.

Jharkhandi activists mobilized the tribes in the 1960s, demanding autonomy and the creation of a separate state of Jharkhand. The autonomy movement, gaining wide support in the tribal belt, broke down the remaining tribal barriers. In spite of central government efforts to quell the Jharkhandi movement, it gained strength. Opposition to the autonomy movement by "civilized" Hindus sparked violent ethnic and religious confrontations in 1968–69. In the face of government apathy, activists in Chota Nagpur, which extends into four states, agitated for the separation of their districts from the surrounding states and the creation of a separate Jharkhand state. The nationalization of mines by the Indian government in 1971 was reportedly followed by the wholesale dismissal of 50,000 Jharkhandis and their replacement by outsiders.

Jharkhandi literacy rates are very high for rural India. The legacy of early mission schools and the Jharkhandi willingness to educate both boys and girls, unusual in India, have produced a highly motivated and aware national leadership. Even though they suffer caste and racial discrimination more aggressive and violent than South Africa's former apartheid, until the early 1990s Jharkhandi nationalists conducted a peaceful, reasoned, and articulate campaign to win equal rights for their people. Their moderate demands had little impact until the mid-1990s.

The Indian government until recent years has encouraged the assimilation of the Jharkhandis into the larger Indian society. Constant encroachments upon their lands has made many Jharkhandis landless. In 1986–87 a commission issued a very critical assessment of the inability of the government to address tribal land issues. It stated that economic development policies had done little to halt tribal land alienation or to provide alternative lands in which the tribes could settle.

Young, militant nationalists, claiming that the Jharkhandi condition has steadily worsened since Indian independence in 1947, have formed militias to protect defenseless Jharkhandis against the continuing atrocities heretofore perpetuated with impunity by high-caste Hindus. The movement has adopted the environment as an issue; the Jharkhandis live in one of the world's most polluted regions. Violence continued unabated, with violent deaths highest in Madhya Pradesh in the early 1990s, overtaken by violence in Bihar in the late 1990s. By 1995 Bihar was India's most violent state, with caste violence and increasingly bloody conflicts over land and resources.

The region's mineral wealth and industrial development have been a problem for the Jharkhandis. The area is India's primary source of coal and iron. The Jharkhandis, forming an important part of the industrial workforce in southern Bihar, called a 15-day economic blockade in September 1992. The blockade of southern Bihar's industrial belt was called by the Jharkhand Party and the All Jharkhand Students Union to press their demands for a separate state. The Koel Karo hydroelectric scheme, including a dam that will displace over 50,000 Jharkhandis, became a focus of nationalist sentiment in the late 1990s.

Religious intolerance and violence by high-caste Hindus has greatly reduced the number of Jharkhandi Hindus. In December 1993 an estimated 100,000 Jharkhandis in Bihar participated in a mass conversion to Buddhism. Other Hindus have converted to various Christian sects to escape the rigid and cruel Hindu caste system. Violence against the tribal peoples by high-caste Hindus continues to be the focus of nationalist concerns.

The insecure position of the Jharkhandis with regard to land ownership is compounded by the numerous state and federal forestry laws that have been applied to their traditional lands. Vast areas of tribal territory have been taken for forest reserves, in which tribal peoples have only minimal rights. Since many Jharkhandis are dependent on these areas for their survival, such laws expose them to corrupt local officials, who selectively apply the forestry laws for their own purposes. The creation of forest reserves, denying the tribal concept of landholding, has in many areas also greatly intensified the pressure on tribal lands. Huge tracts of tribal land have been leased by state authorities to timber companies for the extraction of wood and bamboo.

In September 1992, activists threatened to launch a "Quit Jharkhand Movement" if the Bihar state government failed to ensure the passage of the Jharkhand Autonomous Council bill. The Jharkhand movement leaders, Shibu Soreng and Suraj Mandal, called off the threatened agitation in 1993, following progress in the state legislature. The state government of Bihar in August 1995 established a 180-member Provisional Jharkhand Area Autonomous Council. The plan to establish a separate Jharkhand state won more support in 2000. In April 2000, the Bihar legislature passed a bill to turn the mineral-rich districts in southern Bihar into a separate Jharkhand state.

Younger Jharkhandis, objecting to the creation of truncated Jharkhand, demanded that nationalist organizations break off negotiations with state and federal governments and support calls for separation from India. The independence movement represents a small minority, but that could change should the more modest Jharkhandi demands be rejected.

The Indian parliament approved the creation of a separate Jharkhand state in August 2000. The new was greeted with celebrating across the region, but the new state, Jharkhand or Vananchal, to be carved out of Bihar territory only, does not correspond to the territory inhabited by Jharkhandis. Jharkhandi districts in Madhya Pradesh, West Bengal, and Orissa were not included in the legislation, bringing renewed protests from militants, who vow to continue to struggle for a united, democratic Jharkhandi state.

On 15 November 2000, the state of Jharkhand was created in the eighteen southern districts of Bihar. The tribal region in northern Madhya Pradesh was included in the new state of Chattisgarh over the protests of many Jharkhandis who wanted a united Jharkhand to encompass all tribal areas in the region. Nationalists, while welcoming the autonomy of the Jharkhandis in the new state, demanded that the eight Jharkhandi districts of neighboring states be incorporated into an enlarged Jharkhand.

Violence in the region, between Hindus and Tribals, between pro-India and pro-independence groups, and over land and water rights, made Jharkhand second only to Kashmir and Jammu in the number of casualties in 2000–2001. Jharkhandi activists claim that the violence can only be curtailed by the creation of an expanded Jharkhand with the powers and autonomy to address the severe problems faced by the Jharkhandi tribal peoples.

SELECTED BIBLIOGRAPHY:

Devalle, Susana B.C. *Discourses of Ethnicity: Culture and Protest in Jharkhand.* 1994.
Ghosh, Arunabha. *Jharkhand Movement: A Study in the Politics of Regionalism.* 1998.
Kumar, Purushottam. *History and Administration of Tribal Chota Nagpur (Jharkhand).* 1988.
Narayan, S., ed. *Jharkhand Movement: Origin and Evolution.* 1992.

Jummas

Jhummas; Kadeshis; Kaderis; Kaderians

POPULATION: Approximately (2002e) 1,200,000 Jummas in South Asia, with 810,000 Jummas in Bangladesh, concentrated in the Chittagong Hill Tracts in the southeast of the country. There are sizable Jumma communities in the adjacent Indian states of Tripura and Mizoram and in Myanmar.

THE JUMMA HOMELAND: The Jumma homeland occupies a highland region of parallel mountain ranges and long, fertile valleys in southeastern Bangladesh. The Kaptai Dam, constructed in the early 1960s, flooded much of the region's fertile agricultural land. The Jummas have been driven out of many regions by Bengali settlers and by troops of the Bengali army. The Chittagong Hill Tracts were divided in 1989 into three ostensibly autonomous districts, Khagrachari, Rangamati, and Bandarban.

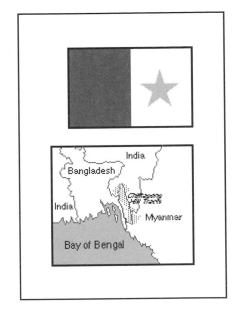

In 1997 an autonomy agreement was signed, but it has yet to be fully implemented. *Chittagong Hill Tracts (CHT) (Kadesh/Kaderia)*: 5,157 sq. mi.—13,361 sq. km, (2002e) 1,255,000—Jummas 51%, Bengalis 48%, other Bangladeshis 1%. The Jumma capital and major cultural center is Rangimati, (2002e) 56,000. The other important center is Kaptai, (2002e) 64,000.

FLAG: The Jumma national flag, the flag of the national movement, is a vertical bicolor of red and white bearing a large yellow five-pointed star centered on the fly.

PEOPLE AND CULTURE: The Jummas, called "Tribals" by the Bengalis, belong to 16 distinct tribes that have intermingled over the centuries, including Chakmas, Marma, Tipperas, Chak, Khyang, Khumi, Mro (Murung/Moorang), Lushai, Bawm and Pankho. The largest of the tribes, the Chakmas, numbering around 600,000, are of mixed, unknown origin and have absorbed more Bengali cultural influences than the smaller tribes. They are historically tied to the Arakanese* of neighboring Myanmar. The related Marma are thought to be of Thai origin. The mainly Hindu Tipperas (Tripuris*) are part of the larger population of adjacent India. The Mro or Moorang, considered the original inhabitants of the Chittagong Hills, are mostly Buddhist, with a substantial animist minority. The other tribes are numerically quite small and are closely allied to the larger tribes. The Chakmas have a strong clan-based organization, while the other Jumma tribes are organized along less formal lines. The Jummas, after centuries of intermingling, can be distinguished from one another more by differences in their dialect, dress, and customs than by tribal cohesion. Only the Chakmas and Marmas display formal tribal organizations, although all groups retain traditional clan distinctions.

LANGUAGE AND RELIGION: The Chakmas have mostly discarded their original Tibeto-Burman language and now speak a variant Bengali dialect. The Chakmas and Marmas have written scripts that are sometimes used in religious teachings. Most Jummas speak some Bengali, but the majority cannot speak, write, or read it. Activists have demanded that the tribal languages be introduced into the primary educational system in the region. Others want three official languages in each of the tribal areas—the indigenous language, English, and Bengali. Each of the languages is further divided into dialects and subdialects. The largest of the languages, Chakma, is spoken in six major dialects, and Tippera counts 36 dialects.

Historically the Jummas observed a complex mixture of animism, Hinduism, and Buddhism, but in the twentieth century the tribes mostly adopted outside religions. The Chakma, Marma, and Mro are mostly Buddhists. The Kuki, Khomoi (Kumi), and some of the Mro are animists. While most of the Lushai (Mizos) and Bawm are Christians, the Tripuris are Hindus. Small numbers of Muslims are also present, particularly among the Marmas. The animists worship gods of fire, water, and the forest; even among the Christians and Buddhists, animist beliefs are still practiced to some degree.

NATIONAL HISTORY: Mountain valleys, inhabited since ancient times, became the refuge of numerous small tribal groups seeking protection in the forested isolation. The Chakma and Marma, led by the Chakma Raja Marekyaja, moved from the Arakan Hills into the Chittagong highlands in the thirteenth century, pushing earlier-arriving tribes into the mountainous jungles. Settled in the fertile valleys, the newcomers called themselves the Khyungtha (Children of the River) and called the dispossessed tribes the Thongtha (Children of the Hills). According to local tradition, the Chakma Raja Marekyaja migrated from Arakan establish his rule and dynasty.

The remote area came under nominal Bengali rule in 1666, but to secure their rule the Bengalis had to fight their way into the hills, valley by valley. The Chakma king, Jallal Khan, established treaty relations with the Bengalis in 1715, but the Bengalis, constantly harassed by tribal warriors, finally ceded the troublesome region to Great Britain in 1760. The British officials, rather than engage in a long and arduous campaign to subdue the tribes, established treaty relations with the Chakma king. The treaties in effect created a tribal preserve called the Chittagong Hill Tracts.

Encroachments by the British, however, led to violence; Chakma warriors fought East India Company troops from 1777 to 1780. In 1787, Chakma king Jan Baksh Khan finally pledged allegiance to the British, who then brought him under direct British rule. The British promised not to intervene in the administration of the region. The tribes of the region were not recognized as British subjects, but as mere tributaries.

Relations between the Chakmas and the British became progressively more cordial nonetheless, and in 1857, during the Great Sepoy Mutiny they sided with the British. under the leadership of Rani Kallendi. On 20 June 1860, the British separated the hill area of Chittagong from Chittagong district and created an independent district called Parbatya Chittagong.

European missionaries arrived in the hills in the 1840s and 1850s. The Christians achieved a degree of success with the smaller pagan groups, but only mission education found favor with the Buddhist and Hindu tribes. An educated minority, the product of the mission schools, gradually brought an end to the endemic tribal feuds and fostered closer relations among the diverse peoples.

An 1881 regulation allowed the tribes of the Hill Tracts to form their own independent police units. The Jummas, particularly the Christian minority, were favored by the British administration over the more numerous Bengalis of the lowlands.

Immigration by Muslim Bengalis from the overcrowded lowlands became a serious problem in the late nineteenth century. The British, responding to tribal appeals, formally designated the region a reserve and prohibited further Bengali settlement in 1900. Continued illegal migration from the overcrowded lowlands provoked serious ethnic clashes and protests over the next decades. In 1935 the authorities declared the region a totally excluded area, with entry for any reason forbidden without specific permission.

Tribal leaders, influenced by the Indian national movement in the late 1930s, organized a campaign to win separate independence for the tribal peoples. Nationalists based their claims on the ethnic, linguistic, and religious differences of the tribal peoples from the majority Bengalis. A council of chiefs formally appealed to the British authorities to prepare the region for independence under British protection. To ensure tribal loyalty during the Japanese advance toward India in World War II, local British officials promised separation should India become independent.

The violent postwar partition of British India into separate Indian and Pakistani states altered British attitudes to independence for minority areas. British plans to add the Hill Tracts to Muslim Pakistan raised protests; many Jummas preferred to unite with secular India. In 1947, over Jumma protests, the British formally joined the Chittagong Hill Tract to Pakistan. The tribes united in rebellion but could not hold areas they captured against the advancing Pakistani troops. To forestall further violence the Pakistani government applied the former British policy: in 1948 the government granted limited autonomy and prohibited Bengali settlement in the region. Several thousand Jummas, however, fearing for their safety, fled to refuge in Indian and Burmese territory.

In 1955 the Pakistani government, in violation of the autonomy statute, took direct control of the district and lifted all immigration restrictions. Funded by well-intentioned international aid agencies, thousands of Bengali Muslims migrated to the area from the densely populated lowlands. Between 1957 and 1962 the Kaptai Hydroelectric Dam was constructed on tribal land, eventually inundating about 40% of it and displacing tens of thousands of Jummas. Over 50,000 Jummas took refuge in India to escape forced relocation by Pakistani troops. In 1962 the Pakistani government greatly reduced tribal control by changing the regulations that governed the region. In 1964 the region's special status was revoked.

The Bengali secession from Pakistan in 1971 obscured the increasing violence between the Bengali immigrants and the Jumma tribes. The Jummas originally supported the Bangladeshi rebellion against Pakistani oppression, but the new government of Bangladesh proved as unsympathetic as the Pakistanis had been. To relieve severe land pressure, the new Bangladeshi government encouraged lowland Bengalis to colonize the underpopulated hill tracts. In 1972, representatives of the Chakma king presented the Bangladeshi government with a petition for the autonomy of the Hill Tracts, but the petition went unanswered.

The Jummas organized guerrilla groups to fight the invasion of government-sponsored colonists in the early 1970s. In 1975 tribal leaders demanded secession and the establishment of a sovereign state. In 1977 the militants of the Shanti Bahini, the Peace Force, attacked government troops in the region. Government attempts to negotiate a solution having failed, the military won broad latitude to combat the rebellion. Brutal reprisals and attacks on undefended villages by Bengali settlers sent a wave of refugees fleeing into India. In March 1980, the local military commander convened a meeting of tribal leaders at a Buddhist temple, where his officers opened fire on the Jumma leaders and civilians, killing nearly 300 people.

In 1984, Bangladeshi delegates to the United Nations Working Group on Indigenous Populations claimed that "Bangladesh has no indigenous population." Moderate tribal leaders, including the Chakma king, formerly favoring dialogue, joined the separatists following the passage of new laws in 1987–88 that made the Bengali language compulsory in education and local administration, and imposed Shari'a, strict Muslim civil law.

Tribal leaders denounced the government for its failure to protect the

Jummas when attacks by Bengali settlers escalated in 1989–90. Massive Bengali immigration, protected by 40,000 government troops, provoked charges of virtual genocide by the beleaguered tribal peoples and many international human-rights groups. By 1990 over 70,000 Jumma refugees had fled into Indian territory, where a reported 10% died of disease and malnutrition in refugee camps.

In April 1992, a Bengali settler was killed, allegedly for the attempted rape of a Jumma woman. In retaliation Bengali settlers and police attacked and destroyed the Chakma village of Logana, killing over 300 and leaving many more injured and displaced. Pressed by international criticism, the Bangladeshi government opened negotiations with the rebel leaders in October 1992. Once again the talks collapsed over Jumma demands for the expulsion of Bengali settlers from their lands. In November 1992 yet another massacre left 90 dead, with yet another weak government response. In spite of continuing violence, large numbers of refugees began returning to the region.

The rapid increase of the Bengali population of the Hill Tracts, growing from just 3% of the total population in 1947 to 45% in 1994, was mostly due to immigration funded by the Pakistani and Bangladeshi governments and international aid agencies. The military presence, increased to protect the Bengali colonists, numbered one military officer for every Jumma in the region by the mid-1990s. A government estimate in 1996 stated that about 8,000 "Tribals," soldiers, and settlers had been killed, but the numbers were disputed by Jumma activists, who insisted that the numbers are much higher.

The renewed rebellion, drawing willing recruits from the estimated 60,000 refugees remaining in camps in India, became a war of survival rather than a fight for rights. After decades of increasing Bengali immigration to their homeland and violence against the indigenous peoples, even the most moderate of the Jumma leaders admitted that cooperation with the government had failed.

In February 1997, the Bangladeshi government and representatives of the Jummas signed the Chittagong Hill Tracts (CHT) peace accord. The accord included an agreement for the disarming of Jumma rebels. In February 1998, over 740 rebels, led by Shanti Bahini leader Jyotindra Bohinpriyo Larma, surrendered their weapons. Larma announced the formal disbandment of the Shanti Bahini military forces. Small militant groups protested against the accord.

At rallies to mark the signing of the CHT agreement in December 1999, Jumma leaders threatened renewed violence if the accord were not fully implemented. The agreement would give the Jummas considerable autonomy and control of tribal lands, but it was opposed by many Bangladeshi nationalists. Strikes and demonstrations delayed implementation of the accord, and genuine autonomy for the Jummas has not yet been achieved.

Increasingly violent confrontations with Bangladeshi soldiers led to several deaths and many injuries in the late 1990s. A conflict that began in October 1999 produced a series of violent clashes with Bangladeshi settlers continuing into the new century. Tribal leaders in early 2000 urged the tribal peoples to have patience and to refrain from violence, but attacks by both sides continue.

Jumma leaders point to the irony of the annual Bangladeshi remembrance of the martyrs of the independence war of 1971 while the Bangladeshi government continues to practice ethnic cleansing of the minority Jumma population, copying the brutal practices of their former Pakistani masters. Statements by Bangladeshi politicians and military leaders confirming that Bangladesh needs the land of the Chittagong Hill Tracts but not the people continue to reflect the Bangladeshi government's attitudes to the plight of the Jummas.

In India, student and militant groups in Arunchal Pradesh State threatened to drive 50,000 Chakmas out of the state and into Bangladesh. The Chakmas had resided in Arunchal Pradesh for over 30 years, but they had never been granted Indian citizenship, only refugee status. The plight of Jumma refugees in many areas of northeastern India underlines the need for an autonomous homeland able to absorb the population groups driven from the area over decades of suppression and violence.

The Bangladeshi government and Jumma leaders remain deadlocked over the formation of a regional council. Several Jummas, including Jyotindra Larma, accuse the government of not adhering to its commitments on dismantling temporary army camps and releasing detained Shanti Bahini rebels. Militants, who claim the Jummas have gained nothing from the 1997 accord, are threatening to restart the war of independence. In December 1998, the government ensured the residence and voting rights of the region's immigrant Bengali population.

Over 50,000 refugees returned to the region from India's Tripura State in May 1999, increasing land pressure and tension between the Jummas and the Bengali settlers. Conflicts over land, water rights, and resources have increased since the accord was signed in December 1997. Jumma demands for the expulsion of Bengali settlers who came to the region after 1950 continue to divide the two groups. The government has consistently refused to resettle the Bengalis, who now form nearly half the region's population.

SELECTED BIBLIOGRAPHY:

Chakma, Biplab. *Chittagong Hill Tracts: In Search of Self-Rule and Autonomy.* 1997.
Mohsin, Amena. *The Politics of Nationalism: The Case of the Chittagong Hill Tracts.* 1989.
Talukdar, S.P. *Chakmas: An Embattled Tribe.* 1994.
Van Shendel, Willem, Wolfgang Mey, and Aditya Kumar Dewan. *The Chittagong Hill Tracts: Living in a Borderland.* 2000.

Jurassians

Jurans; Jurassiens; Rauracians

POPULATION: Approximately (2002e) 190,000 Jurassians in Switzerland, concentrated in the canton of Jura and the northwestern districts of Bern canton. There are Jurassian communities in other parts of Switzerland, particularly in Geneva and Lausanne.

THE JURASSIAN HOMELAND: The Jurassian homeland lies in northwestern Switzerland, comprising the Jura Mountains in the south and the hill region of the Jura Plateau. The region, known for its dense forestation, was called "Jura" from the Gaulish word *juria*, meaning "forest." The entire Jura region is geographically separated by the Jura Mountains from the German-speaking districts of the canton of Bern. The northern Jurassian districts form a canton of the Swiss Confederation. *Canton of Jura (Republic et Canton Jura/Rauracia)*: 323 sq. mi.—836 sq. km, (2002e) 69,000—Jurassians 91%, Bernese 8%, other Swiss 1%. The Jurassian capital and major cultural center is Delémont, (2002e) 11,000. The other important cultural center is Biel, in the Jura region of Bern Canton, called Bienne in French, (2002e) 47,000, urban area 90,000.

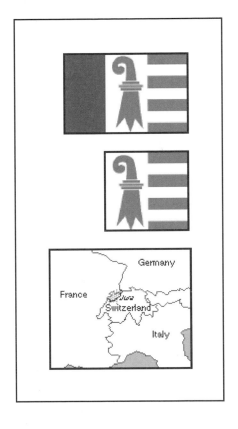

FLAG: The Jurassian national flag, the flag of the national movement, has a vertical blue stripe at the hoist, a center white stripe bearing a bishop's crozier, and seven red and white horizontal stripes on the fly. The flag of Jura canton is square, divided evenly between a white vertical stripe bearing a bishop's crozier and seven red and white stripes representing the seven districts of Jura.

PEOPLE AND CULTURE: The Jurassians are a Latin people, part of the larger population of French-speaking Romands* in western Switzerland. Although considering themselves Romands, there is a strong sense of separate national identity in the region. Their culture evolved in the isolation of their mountain homeland and incorporates both French and Germanic traditions and customs. The Jurassians are known for their independence; traditionally each Jura farmstead collected its own cistern water to ensure that independence.

LANGUAGE AND RELIGION: The Jurassians speak a dialect of French called Jurassic or Jurassian. The dialect, part of the group of dialects called the Romand dialects, is spoken in the mountain regions and is the language of daily life, but standard French is the official language of the region and is taught in schools. Jurassic incorporates many archaic forms and also many borrowings from the German dialects spoken in neighboring regions.

The majority are Roman Catholic, which underlines their desire for separation from predominantly Protestant Bern. Their religion is an integral part of the Jurassian alpine culture; traditionally the year revolved around church holidays that corresponded to the agricultural traditions of the region.

NATIONAL HISTORY: The region was originally inhabited by Celtic peoples, called Gauls by the Romans, who took control of the area in the first century A.D. At the collapse of the Roman Empire in the fourth century, Germanic tribes overran the frontier districts, and the Burgundians* eventually took control of the Jura Mountains area.

The historical towns of the region were first mentioned in historical records of the early eighth century. In 999, the abbacy of Moutier-Grandval, comprising much of the present Jura canton, was given by the king of the Burgundians, Rodolphe II, as a gift to the bishop of Basel. The region became known as the Franches-Montagnes, the Free Mountains, a name acquired in 1384 when the bishop of Basel freed the Jurassians from taxation to encourage the settlement of the remote, isolated mountain area.

The Jura region came under the firm rule of the prince-bishop of Basel in the fourteenth century. For more than 800 years, up to the French Revolution in the late eighteenth century, the prince-bishop remained the ruler of a sovereign state within the Holy Roman Empire. The principality-bishopric retained close ties to the Swiss Confederation after the Treaty of Westphalia in 1648.

The ideas of the French Revolution, which erupted in 1789, quickly spread to the border regions, particularly to the French-speaking areas, such as the Jura. Revolutionaries rose up against the authorities of Basel and on 17 December 1792 proclaimed the Jura independent, as the Rauracian Republic. French soldiers of revolutionary France seized the Jura region in March 1793 and suppressed the republican government. Annexed to the new French republic, the Jura formed the smallest French department in population.

At the end of the Napoleonic Wars, at the Congress of Vienna in 1815, the European powers remapped national borders. They joined the French-speaking Jura region to the German-speaking Swiss canton of Bern, partly to compensate the Bernese for the loss of territory in the cantons of Vaud and Argau. During the nineteenth century Jurassian dissatisfaction with the rest of predominantly Protestant, German-speaking Bern canton continued to mark relations between the Jurassians and the cantonal authorities. The first separatist movement formed in the 1830s and remained a force in the region over the next century. The rise and fall of separatist sentiment often accompanied the political and economic conditions of the region.

A separatist movement emerged in the 1940s as a mass reaction to the domination of the Protestant, German-speaking Bernese and to economic neglect of the region. In 1943 a local artist, Paul Boesch, designed a new flag, which was adopted by the nationalists. The first openly nationalist organization formed in 1947, after the Bern government refused to allocate the position of head of the Department of Public Works to George Moeckli, a French-speaking Jurassian, solely for the reason that he was not a German-speaking Bernese. In 1951 the Bernese cantonal council officially sanctioned the Jurassian flag as a regional emblem, but this gesture did not defuse the growing separatist movement.

The constitution of the Bernese canton of 1950 recognized the Jurassian people living in the seven Jura districts that lay between the Aare River and the French border. The districts, Ajoie, Delémont, Franches-Montagnes, Moutier, Courtelary, La Neuveville, and Laufen, were mostly French-speaking and Roman Catholic, while the minority overall, like the rest of Bern canton, was predominantly German-speaking and Protestant.

The zone known as "historical Jura" encompassed not only the seven districts but also the region around the city of Biel, one of the five officially bilingual cities in Switzerland. Nationalists, led by Roland Béguelin, demanded the inclusion of all of the historical Jura region, including Biel, in a new Jura canton. The separatist dispute escalated into demonstrations and counterdemonstrations, communal clashes, and a small but noticeable wave of terrorist acts. Violent clashes broke out in the region, leaving two people dead and many injured. For democratic, stable Switzerland the separatist violence was a shock.

A plebiscite organized in 1959 approved the separation of the Jurassians from Bern canton, but implementation was delayed due to opposition in many areas of mixed Jurassian and Bernese populations. Another plebiscite in 1974–75 again approved the separation and set a timetable. In 1977 a constitution was accepted, and a year later all the Swiss cantons voted on the creation of Jura Canton. Only three of the seven Jura districts gave majority votes for separation—Porrentruy, Delémont, and Les Franches-Montagnes. The districts of Ajoie, Moutier, Courtelary, La Neuveville, and Laufen, with large German-speaking populations, voted by small minorities to remain part of Bern. In 1979 Jura officially became the 23d canton of the Swiss Confederation. Laufen, the only majority German-speaking Jura district, voted to join neighboring Basel Land Canton. The economy of the new canton improved markedly during the 1980s.

There is considerable bitterness among the Jurassians about the outcome of the vote in the southern districts, and a countervailing resentment among the Bernese that the separatists have not accepted the outcome. It was later learned that the Bernese government used up to 700,000 Swiss francs illegally to oppose the referendum, money that many nationalists claim swayed the votes of many, including in the Moutier district, where the plebiscite was defeated by just 70 votes.

Active separatist organizations continue to operate in both parts of the Jura, and there are frequent clashes with pro-Bern groups. The separatists, closely allied to the Romand nationalists of western Switzerland, are actively pro-European, and many would like to see an independent Jura as a member state of the European Union (EU).

The Jurassians are mostly agricultural or tend cattle and horses; however, watchmaking and precision instruments are important industries. Wildlife, hunted to extinction, has practically disappeared from the entire Jura Mountain region. Dairy herds now feed where wolves, mountain goats, and other animals once roamed.

The Jurassians of the Bernese Jura live in three districts, which continue to form part of Bern Canton. The Laufen district was officially joined to Basel Land in 1992. There is continuing agitation for separation, but the Protestant, German-speaking communities oppose it. Jurassian separatists continue to agitate for the restoration of the unity of all seven districts in a new canton. Nationalists suggest a federation of the two parts of the Jura, with two distinct electoral circles, north and south, each providing equal numbers of deputies to the Jura parliament without regard to the religion or language of the resident population. The six districts of the Jura are estimated to be 72% French-speaking and Roman Catholic, although the German-speaking population is increasing due to immigration from other parts of Bern canton.

The national movement is split between those seeking an expanded canton of the six Jurassian districts within Switzerland, and the more militant wing that works for an independent Jura state within an integrated Europe. The more militant group formed the Jurassian Independence Movement (Mouvement Indépendantiste Jurassien) in 1990. Some activists suggest the name "Republic of Rauracia" for an independent Jura, the name used during the Napoleonic period. Although the separatist movement continues to agitate for complete independence within Europe, the major conflicts are the continued debates between the inhabitants of the historical Jura region, between its component parts, and with the canton of Bern.

The beauty of the Jura has attracted a thriving tourist industry, and especially winter tourism for skiing. The number of holiday resorts and homes bringing outsiders to the region has become a focus of nationalist attention. Rural depopulation and the excesses of modern tourism are seen as threatening the traditional culture and dialect of the Jurassians.

Increased activity in the early 1990s paralleled Switzerland's preparations for the 700th anniversary of the confederation. Nationalists in the city of Moutier in the Bernese Jura adopted in August 1990 the first statutes of separation from the Swiss Confederation. In early 1991 separatists toppled a statue in the capital of Bern, and in August 1991, on the anniversary, they spelled out, by digging up the grass, "Jura libre" (free Jura) in 10-foot-tall letters in the historic Ruetli Meadow. Violence, mostly directed at monuments in the canton of Bern, became a serious problem in the early 1990s. Several bombs exploded—killing just one man, apparently a member of the Belier Party, who was killed when a bomb exploded prematurely in January 1993. Several activists were jailed for bomb attacks in the late 1980s and early 1990s. The police discovered several arms caches; in February 1993, the leader of the Belier Party, Daniel Pape, was arrested, and a cache of 50 grenades was found in his house.

The death of the young separatist in 1993 shocked all the parties involved in the conflict and helped to restart stalled talks. On 24 March 1994, the cantons of Jura and Bern signed an agreement that provided for mutual recognition but stopped short of addressing the nationalist demands for the reunification of the Jura. The agreement was denounced by the nationalists, but a new agreement, negotiated in 1998, remains unsigned by the different parties in 2001. A referendum in Moutier, a district containing one of the major towns of southern Jura, governed by Jurassian nationalists since 1982, held a referendum on joining Jura on 29 November 1998; the referendum failed by 41 votes.

In 1994 a federal commission studied the "Jurassian Question" and in an official document recommended the creation of a second Jura canton to include the six French-speaking districts, but the Bernese government refused to accept the recommendations. Activists in Biel, the largest city of the region, attempted to organize a referendum on joining Jura in 1995 but were blocked by cantonal authorities. Nationalists continue to work for the unification of all the historical Jurassian districts, proposing a bilingual legislature and representation for all religious and linguistic groups in the region.

In March 1995 the first of four plebiscites was held in a small hamlet that wished to secede from Bern and unite with Jura. The other plebiscites followed, slightly changing the boundaries of Jura, but the question of Jurassian reunification remains open, and at the turn of the twenty-first century, the "Jurassian Question" continued unresolved.

The Jurassians are not opposed to the Swiss government but oppose the policies of the German-majority canton of Bern. Continuing communal conflicts between the French-speaking Jurassians and the German-speaking Bernese is complicated by a tangled overlay of religious, linguistic, and regional differences that have left a significant minority of the Jurassians dissatisfied with the political solutions that have been devised to counter each of the six separate Jurassian nationalist movements that have arisen since the 1830s.

In August 2001, a 195-year-old stone, used in Swiss sporting competitions, mysteriously reappeared in Switzerland, 17 years after it was stolen by a group of Jura separatists. The Unspunnen Stone, which takes its name from a castle in the Jura region, used to be the centrepiece of the Alpine Games, when the strongest of Swiss men would compete to see who could throw the 83.5 kg boulder the furthest. The much-respected Unspunnen Stone disappeared from the Interlaken museum in 1984, having been stolen by a group of activists of the Beliers.

In 2001, Jurassian nationalists reiterated their claim to separate sovereignty and membership in the European Union (EU) for a Jurassian republic. The Unspunnen Stone, although returned by the nationalists, can no longer be used in competitions because during its years of captivity it was carefully carved with the circle of stars of the EU.

SELECTED BIBLIOGRAPHY:

Boillat, Pierre. *Jura, Birth of a State*. 1982.
Chauve, Pierre. *Jura*. 1988.
Jenkins, John R.G. *Jura Separatism in Switzerland*. 1983.
Porchat, J. Jacques. *Three Months under the Snow: The Journal of a Young Inhabitant of the Jura*. 1999.

Kabards

Kabardians; Kabardinians; Keberdeï; Kabartai; Qeberdej; Eastern Circassians

POPULATION: Approximately (2002e) 448,000 Kabards in the Russian Federation, concentrated in the Kabardia region of the Kabardino-Balkar Republic in southern European Russia. There are sizable Kabard communities the neighboring Mozdok region of North Ossetia, Stavropol Kray, and Krasnodar Kray, known as the Kuban. The largest Kabard population outside Europe is the estimated 200,000 in Turkey, with smaller groups in western Europe and North America.

THE KABARD HOMELAND: The Kabard homeland lies in the central region of the north slopes of the Caucasus Mountains, occupying the Kabardin Plain and the river valleys on the lower slopes. Kabardia, united with the neighboring region of Balkaria, was made an autonomous area in 1922, soon after the Soviet victory in the Russian Civil War. In 1936 its status was raised to that of an autonomous republic. In 1991 Kabardino-Balkaria became a member state of the newly proclaimed Russian Federation. In 1992 the Kabards and Balkars agreed to the division of the republic into two new republics, but the Russian government has refused to recognize them.

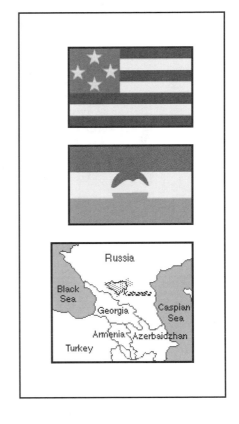

Kabardia, called Kabarda or Qeberdej by the Kabards, comprises the lower foothills and river valleys of the joint republic, leaving the more mountainous south to the Turkic Balkars. *Republic of Kabardia (Respublike Kabarda/Qeberdej)*: 3,876 sq. mi.—10,038 sq. km, (2002e) 653,000—Kabards 61%, Russians and Terek Cossacks* 24%, Ukrainians 9%, Ossetians* 3%, Balkars* 2%, others 1%. The Kabard capital and major cultural center is Nalchik, called Nalshyk by the Kabards, (2002e) 233,000. The center of the Kabards in North Ossetia (Alania) is Mozdok, (2002e) 39,000.

FLAG: The Kabardin national flag, the flag of the nationalist movement adopted for the proposed Kabard republic in 1992, has seven green and white stripes with a light blue canton on the upper hoist bearing four yellow stars in the form of a diamond. The official flag of the Republic of Kabardino-Balkaria is a horizontal tricolor of pale blue, white, and green charged with a centered disk of blue sky, white mountains, and green earth.

PEOPLE AND CULTURE: The Kabards are a Circassian people, one of the three divisions of the Circassians, living in the southern European part of the Russian Federation. The largest of the Circassian nations, the Kabards are a plains people who developed a separate identity in the nineteenth century, an identity that gradually transcended the identities of its subgroups. Kabard society is strongly hierarchical, and there remains a strong tradition of a separate nobility. The Kabards feel superior to surrounding peoples, and this conviction has contributed to the maintenance of the Kabard ethnic identity; there is a powerful tradition against marrying outside the national group. Over 90% of the total Kabard population in Russia lives within the borders of the Kabardino-Balkar Republic.

LANGUAGE AND RELIGION: The language of the Kabards, called Upper or Eastern Circassian, is a North Caucasian language of the Abkhazo-Adygheian group of Ibero-Caucasian languages. Due to the isolation of the Kabard subgroups, the language is spoken in eight dialects—Greater Kabard, Mozdok, Beslan, Baksan, Lesser Kabard, Malka, Beslensi, and Kuban. The Kabard literary language is based on the Greater Kabard dialect, which is spoken around Nalchik. It was developed as a literary language under Soviet rule in 1923–24. Language maintenance is very high, with about 97% speaking Kabard as their first language; Russian is often spoken as a second language. A Kabard literary language was created in 1923–24 on the basis of the Latin alphabet and the Greater Kabard dialect. A Cyrillic-based alphabet was substituted for the Latin in 1936, but in the 1990s support for a reversion to the Latin alphabet grew.

The Kabards are Sunni Muslims, but they were the last of the Circassian nations to be converted, and their ties to Russian Orthodoxy and the Russian culture in general remain strong. A minority of the Kabards, particularly those living around the city of Mozdok, in the neighboring Republic of North Ossetia, remained Christian and adhere to the Armenian Gregorian rite. The Kabards, unlike the neighboring Muslim peoples, have never developed a strong sense of pan-Islamic identity, but their national identity is stronger than theirs.

NATIONAL HISTORY: Scholars believe the Kabards descended from a group of Caucasian tribes, calling themselves Adygey, that originated in the Kuban River basin. Known to the ancient Greeks as Zyukhoy, the Circassians probably settled the region of the north Caucasus before the sixth century B.C. Possibly the earliest representative of the Caucasian peoples, the Circassians populated a wide area north of the Caucasus Mountains that figured prominently in the legends of ancient Greece. The handsome Circassians, valued as slaves, developed a warrior society as protection against frequent invasions and raids by slavers.

Greek monks introduced Christianity to the warlike tribes in the sixth century A.D., but the majority of the Circassian tribes were converted to Orthodox Christianity in the eleventh and twelfth centuries. A common Christian religion facilitated the Circassians' establishment of ties to the Byzantines to the south, and to the opening of trade routes to the early Slav state, Kievan Rus', in the north. The Circassians became widely known for their skill as traders.

At the beginning of the twelfth century, the Circassian tribes began a slow migration from the Kuban to the east. The Mongol invasion in 1241–42 accelerated the eastward migration and weakened the tribes, which came under the authority of the Christian Georgians. To escape Georgian rule, some of the tribes moved farther east, arriving on the left bank of the Terek River by the fourteenth century. There they mixed with the local Alans and eventually became known as Kabards.

In the fifteenth century, the territory on the left bank of the Terek River was known as Greater Kabardia, while the region on the right bank was known as Littler Kabardia. Those Kabards who stayed west of the river became known as Cherkess.*

Early in the sixteenth century the Ottoman Turks and their vassals, the Crimean Tatars,* extended their authority into the Caucasus region. The Kabards, formerly the dominant nation in the region, resented Tatar control, and in 1557 Kabard prince Temryuk petitioned the Russian tsar Ivan IV for protection and reaffirmed the alliance by a marriage between his duaghter and the tsar. In 1561 Kabardia became a Russian protectorate, and the alliance was cemented by Ivan's marriage to a Kabard princess. The Russians between 1563 and 1567 established forts along the Terek River but left the feudal Kabard nobility to dominate the northern Caucasus region until the eighteenth century.

The Russian domination of Kabardia was opposed by the Turks and the Persians. In 1739 the Treaty of Belgrade established Kabardia as a neutral buffer state between the Ottoman territories and the expanding Russian Empire; the territory was annexed by Russia in 1774. Only the Kabardin nobility, noted for wealth and extravagance, integrated itself into tsarist society, becoming part of the tsarist aristocracy. The Kabardin region was included in the Terek province, dominated by the Terek Cossacks, who founded forts throughout the region, including a fort at Nalchik in 1818.

Some of the Kabard clans, influenced by the Turks, adopted the Islamic religion in the seventeenth century. By the early 1800s the majority of the Kabards had adopted Sunni Islam, the Hanafi rite. In the mid-nineteenth century, when a noted religious leader in the North Caucasus, Imam Shamil, led many of the Caucasian nations in a revolt against Russian rule, the Kabards mostly remained neutral. When the Russians had defeated the rebels in the 1860s, around 400,000 Caucasian Muslims left for Turkish territory, although they had remained mostly neutral in the conflict. The mass exodus greatly reduced the Muslim Kabard population in Russia. The Kabards in the Russian Empire numbered only about 90,000 at the turn of the twentieth century.

Many Kabards were openly sympathetic to the Muslim Turks when war broke out in 1914. The overthrow of the tsar in the third year of the war was greeted with enthusiasm. Kabard leaders appealed to the new government for religious freedom, political autonomy, and reunification of the Circassian lands but were ignored. Vehemently opposed to the policies of the Bolsheviks, who took control of the Russian government in October 1917, the Muslims of the region organized an autonomous state called North Caucasia. Threatened by both the Bolsheviks and the anti-Bolshevik White forces, the Muslim leaders declared North Caucasia independent of Russia on 11 May 1918, but the new state collapsed less than a year later, when the Whites took control of the region. The Red Army drove the last of the White forces from Kabardia in early 1920, and established Soviet rule.

The Caucasian peoples accepted a proposal for an autonomous Mountain Republic, with Muslim Sharia law as its basis. In January 1921 the multi-ethnic state was created, but ethnic and territorial conflicts among the national groups quickly arose, and the republic was dissolved after only twenty months. Kabardia was organized as part of an autonomous province, which was extended to include neighboring Balkaria in 1922. The Kabards, unlike other Muslim groups, did not actively resist the imposition of Soviet rule. Their loyalty to Islam was much weaker than that of other Caucasian groups, and they had never developed a strong sense of pan-Islamic identity.

Nalchik, the region's largest city, became an important industrial center under Soviet rule, drawing an influx of non-Kabard industrial workers, mostly ethnic Slavs. The Kabards came under intense pressure to assimilate and to abandon their Muslim religion. Kabard children were taught in Russian, although the Kabards continued to use their own language as their first language. Soviet effort in Kabardia to eradicate religion was not as serious as it was in other Caucasian regions; the Kabards, converted to Islam later than neighboring peoples, were not as intensely Muslim and were considered by the Russian, and the later Soviet, authorities as one of the more loyal of the Caucasian nations.

In World War II, the invading Germans, taking the area during the Caucasus campaign of 1942, offered an alliance to the small Muslim nations and promoted anticommunist solidarity. The Germans closed the hated collective farms and allowed mosques to function. The Kabards' generally pro-Russian tradition, however, and their view that the Germans represented just another in a long series of invaders spared them the brutal deportations suffered by the Balkars and other Muslim peoples following the return of the Soviet authorities in 1943–44.

Ethnic tension, particularly between the Kabards and the Balkars, emerged with the easing of Soviet authority in the late 1980s. The Kabards, forced to share their republic with the Turkic Balkars for most of this century, demanded a separate republic. Ties to the other Circassian peoples, the Adyge and Cherkess, discouraged under tsarist and Soviet rule, were reestablished by calls for the unification of the Circassian peoples.

Demands for change accelerated following the collapse of the Soviet Union in 1991. The government of Kabardino-Balkaria unilaterally upgraded the status of the region to that of a full member in the newly proclaimed Russian Federation. Nationalist sentiment and growing conflicts between the Kabards and the Balkars led to the partition of the republican parliament into its constituent parts in February 1992. In March 1992 the local republican governments signed a new federal treaty regulating relations with Moscow, but Kabard and Balkar demands for separate republics within the Russian Federation were not recognized by the new Russian government.

The Kabards, never having developed any sense of pan-Islamic identity, have been careful to remain outside the many ethnic and regional conflicts in the Caucasus in the 1990s. The growing conflict with the neighboring Balkars, who claim they are dominated by the more numerous Kabards, however, has ignited dormant Kabard nationalism in the early 1990s. In 1994 the Spiritual Board of Muslims and Council of Imams of Kabardino-Balkaria appealed to the Kabards and Balkars not to divide the republic, which would inevitably cause bloodshed and destroy the already weak genetic reserves of the two small nations.

The chairman of the Congress of the Kabardian People, in 1992, announced that it would not pursue a separate republic until the Russian Federation's moratorium on border changes expired in 1995. The president of Kabardino-Balkaria, Valerii Kokov, an ethnic Kabard, suppressed separatism in 1995, but when the Balkars voted to separate from the joint republic in November 1996, the Kabards also increased support for separation and renewed their demands for a separate Kabard republic within the Russian Federation.

The growing influence of radical Islamic groups in the North Caucasus in the early twenty-first century alarmed the moderate Kabard leaders. Many young Kabards, disappointed at the slow pace of change since the collapse of the Soviet Union a decade before, are drawn to Islamic groups as a substitute for the prosperity they feel has been denied them.

SELECTED BIBLIOGRAPHY:

Goldenberg, Suzanne. *Pride of Small Nations: The Caucasus and Post-Soviet Disorder.* 1994.
Olson, James S., ed. *An Ethnohistorical Dictionary of the Russian and Soviet Empires.* 1994.
Smith, Sebastian. *Allah's Mountains.* 1997.
Stavrakis, Peter J. *Beyond the Monolith: The Emergence of Regionalism in Post-Soviet Russia.* 1997.

Kabyles

Kabyle Berbers; Amazigh; Imazighen

POPULATION: Approximately (2002e) 4,800,000 Kabyles in Algeria, concentrated in the Kabylia region on the Mediterranean Sea and the mountainous regions of the Hodna and Aurès Mountains in northeastern Algeria. Outside North Africa, the largest Kabyle community, numbering around 1.5 million, is in France. Population figures are based on unofficial estimates, as Berbers have not been counted separately in Algerian censuses since 1966.

THE KABYLE HOMELAND: The Kabyle homeland lies in northeastern Algeria, occupying the Djurdia Mountains and the coastal plain east of Algiers, and the mountainous regions of the Hodna and Aurès mountains east to the Tunisian border. Most of the lower slopes are covered with oak forests or fig and olive orchards; there are barren regions in the highlands. The Kabyle heartland on the Mediterranean Sea is divided into Great Kabylia and Little Kabylia by the Sahel-Soumman Valley. Kabylia has no official status; the region claimed by nationalists forms the Algerian departments of Batna, Bejaïa, Jijel, Setif, Tebessa, Oum-el-Bouaghi, and Tizi-Ouzou. *Region of Kabylia (Zwawah):* 18,501 sq. mi.—47,918 sq. km, (2002e) 5,926,000—Kabyles (including Shawia) 63%, Arabs 30%, other Algerians 7%. The Kabyle capital and major cultural center is Tizi-Ouzou, called Tizi Wezzu by the Kabyles, (2002e) 247,000. The other major cultural center is Stif, called Asdif, (2002e) 236,000. The major cultural center of the Shawia Berbers is Batnah, called Batna, (2002e) 268,000.

FLAG: The Kabyle national flag is a horizontal tricolor of green, yellow, and pale blue bearing a centered red Z of the Tifinagh alphabet, which is

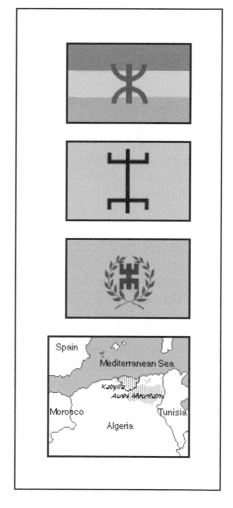

also the symbol for man. The flag of Amazigh national movement is a field of dark yellow bearing a red Tifinagh Z centered. The flag of the cultural movement is a dark yellow field bearing a red Tifinagh Z within a green wreath.

PEOPLE AND CULTURE: The Kabyles, including the Shawia of the Aurès Mountains, are a Berber people more closely related to the peoples of Europe than to the Semitic Arabs. The Shawia number about 1.5 million and are closely related to the lowland Kabyles. Both groups call themselves Amazigh (Free Men) or Kabyles, which means "tribes" and originally was used by the Arabs for all Berbers in North Africa. Often fair and light eyed, the Kabyles have retained a distinctive culture that allows women to be unveiled and affords them great respect and social stature. Village communities still live according to Berber traditions, collectively known as *kanun*, customary law that deals with all questions of property and persons, and the maintenance of the stratified class system. Extended families trace their descent to a single ancestor, preserving thereby a sense of solidarity. An injury to the honor of a family member affects the clan as a whole and demands vengeance. Each community is governed by an assembly of elders called the *djemaa*. The Shawia of the Aurès Mountains are mostly semi-nomadic, partly agricultural, and partly pastoral. Overpopulation, particularly in Greater Kabylia, has forced the Kabyle to emigrate, both to the now mainly Kabyle Mitidja Plain in Algeria and to Europe, particularly France. The shantytowns of Algiers house many Kabyles. To a considerable extent the mountain populations subsist on money sent back by migratory workers. Traditionally the Kabyles of the plains have acted as the only contacts between the mountain tribes and all outsiders. Because many Algerian Arabs have Berber ancestors, the distinguishing national characteristics are linguistic and, to an extent, cultural; they remain based in the Kabyles' passion for independence.

LANGUAGE AND RELIGION: Most Kabyles are trilingual, speaking their own Hamitic language, Tamazight, along with Arabic and French. The language, spoken in several dialects, is written in its own script called Tifinagh and is still being codified. The University of Tizi-Ouzou, one of the centers of Berber education, is the only university in Algeria to still teach in the French language. French remains very important to the Kabyles, as many have lived or worked in France, particularly the Kabyle professional class that dominates in Algiers and other large cities. Kabyle and Shawia are very closely related and are mutually intelligible. They are two of the four major Berber dialects in Algeria. Activists campaign for the right to education in Tamazight and for publications in their own language. Many Berbers are unfamiliar with Arabic and use French as their second language. A Berber Academy was established by exile Kabyles in Paris in 1967 to devise an alphabet for the Berber language.

The majority of the Kabyles are Sunni Muslims, with important Roman

Catholic and Ibadi Muslim minorities. In the more remote mountains many, while nominally Sunni Muslim, have only a rudimentary knowledge of the Koran and other important Islamic texts. Many Berbers believe in the presence of various spirits, *djinns*, which predate Islamic beliefs. Most Kabyle men wear protective amulets containing verses from the Koran. Christian missionaries, responsible for the early development of an educated elite in the region, were expelled following Algerian independence in 1962.

NATIONAL HISTORY: The origins of the Berbers are unclear; waves of migrants—some from Europe, others from sub-Saharan Africa, and others from northeastern Africa—made up the indigenous population of the region in ancient times. Peoples related to the early Europeans were known in North Africa by 3000 B.C., their fair coloring attributed to Celtic migrants from Europe. Some scholars believe their presence in the region dates to at least the fifth century B.C. Ancient Berber civilizations were influenced by Phoenician and later Carthaginian culture. Numidia, approximately coextensive with modern northern Algeria, was drawn into the conflict between Rome and Carthage.

A Roman province from 46 B.C., the region became one of the Roman Empire's major agricultural areas. In the fifth century A.D. incursions by Saharan tribes and an invasion by Germanic Vandals from Europe effectively destroyed Roman civilization in the region. The wanton destruction of the Vandals is recalled by the word coined to describe such actions, "vandalism." Taken under the wing of the Byzantines of the Eastern Roman Empire in the sixth century, most of the Berber inhabitants welcomed Byzantine protection, but Roman civilization failed to revive.

Muslim Arab invaders overran North Africa in the seventh century but suffered one of their rare military defeats at the hands of the Kabyles in A.D. 703. The Arab invasion brought about the Arabization of the lowland cities and most of the coastal zone, but the countryside and mountains remained Berber in culture and language well into the twelfth century. Unable to subdue the fierce Berber tribes, the Arabs formed alliances with individual Kabyle chiefs. The religion they failed to impose by force gradually spread to the Kabyle lands over the next centuries.

The Berber tribes, fleeing the successive invasions, took refuge in the inhospitable environment of the mountains. There they survived, preserving their own languages, traditions, and beliefs, while at the same time they gradually accepted to some extent the Islam of the Arab rulers. The Arabization of the lowlands accelerated during the invasion of Arab nomads from Egypt in the late eleventh century. The Berbers that moved into the Aurès Mountains from the lowland regions of Tunisia during the Arab invasions of the Middle Ages were later known as the Shawia.

The Turks of the Ottoman Empire took Algiers in 1518 but left the Kabyles to rule themselves in return for oaths of loyalty and an annual tribute. In 1705 the Kabyles repudiated Turkish rule and sent their annual tribute to a closer threat, the bey of Algiers, the ruler of one of the nominally independent Muslim states notorious for piracy and the enslavement of Christian captives. Subjected to an American expedition in 1815 and a British bombardment in 1816, the state finally ceased preying on Mediterranean shipping.

The French, claiming that the piracy continued, occupied Algiers in 1830 and rapidly extended their authority to the Algerian lowlands. The Berber tribes, by the late eighteenth century, were limited to the least accessible territories—the high mountains, distant oases, and desert plateaus, where they remain to the present. They opposed French colonial rule despite preferential treatment by the colonial authorities. A French expedition moved into Kabylia in 1833. The force met the fiercest resistance it was to encounter in all of North Africa. The Kabyles, led by Abdu I-Qadir, continued to resist French rule until 1847–50.

The Kabyles rebelled against French rule in 1852, driving the French garrisons from the coastal towns. The French conquest of Kabylia left massive destruction in its wake. To punish the rebels the French authorities confiscated a million acres of prime land, parceling out most to arriving French colonists. Kabyle rebellions broke out in 1876, 1882, and they again met defeat in 1899, but the French required an army of 80,000 to subdue them. The Shawia rebelled against French incursions into the Aurès Mountains in 1879.

The loss of productive farm lands forced thousands of Kabyles to leave their densely populated homeland to search for work in Algiers or the French mainland. Increasing economic competition in the early twentieth century fanned the historical enmity between the Arabs and Berbers. A conflict broke out between the Kabyle and Arab factions of the National Movement for Liberation in the early 1930s. Most of the Kabyle militants were killed, and the anticolonial ideology became exclusively Arab and Islamic. Anti-Arab rioting spread through Kabylia in 1934; only French intervention averted civil war.

The Kabyles of Setif, during the celebrations of victory in Europe in May 1945, rebelled against the French authorities. The rebellion rapidly spread across Kabylia to the Tunisian border but was crushed with unprecedented French savagery. The Kabyles later turned the same brutality against the French during the war of liberation. Harboring an intense hatred of the French authorities, the Kabyles put aside old enmities to form an anti-French alliance with the Arab majority.

The Algerian war of independence, spreading from its cradle in Kabylia in 1954, is now considered one of the most brutal conflicts in recent history. The "Kabyle Smile," a gaping slit throat, became the hallmark of the nationalist forces. Promised autonomy in free Algeria, the Kabyles paid a very high price, losing a tenth of their population before Algeria finally won its independence on 3 July 1962. Refused the promised autonomy, the Kabyles withdrew from the ruling National Liberation Front (FLN) and formed the Socialist Forces Front (FSS), which led a Berber rebellion in September 1963. The last rebel forces were not defeated until 1965. Betrayed by the country the independence of which they had done so much to win, the Kabyles lost even the cultural and linguistic rights they had enjoyed under French rule.

The government, to spread its policy of Arabization, targeted Berber culture, particularly radio and education. Government control of the press excluded any written production in Tamazight. After violent antigovernment demonstrations in 1974, the government began arresting prominent Kabyles and others, often as young as high school students, for crimes as innocent as the possession of a Tifinagh alphabet or a book written in Tamazight. Expulsion from schools, withdrawals of passports, interrogations, and arbitrary detentions were common throughout the 1970s. A new government took power in 1979, but the repressive practices continued.

On 10 March 1980, the students of the University of Tizi-Ouzou invited a Kabyle scholar to lecture on ancient Kabyle poetry. The local authorities prevented the lecture, leading to protests, strikes, and confrontations. On 20 April, military forces assaulted the student-occupied university buildings at dawn, injuring and arresting hundreds of students. Violent antigovernment rioting swept Kabylia, prompting a brutal repression by the military. The brief liberation of the Kabyle homeland, dubbed the "Tamazight Spring," was the most serious threat to the Islamic and Arabic ideology of the Algerian government since independence. The revolt, quickly spreading throughout the Berber region in northeastern Algeria, left a continuing rift between those favoring a secular Algeria and the growing Islamic movement. Anyone showing even a limited interest in Berber languages or culture was labeled by the government an enemy of the Algerian revolution and a threat to the unity of the Algerian state.

Devastated by over two decades of socialist experimentation, Algeria exploded in 1988, and the FLN's domination began to unravel. Belatedly introducing reforms, including legalization of the Berber political parties, the military-backed government found itself under intense pressure by Islamic fundamentalists. Over 200,000 Kabyles demonstrated in Tizi-Ouzou to mark the 10th anniversary of the bloody 1980 riots. In September 1990, a leader of the Islamic fundamentalists called for a *jihad*, a holy war, to be declared against Kabylia to bring it back into the Islamic family "even if a third of its population is exterminated."

In December 1990 the government adopted a law making Arabic the only official language after 1997, with substantial penalties for the users of Berber languages or French. Over 100,000 Kabyles marched in Algiers and many Kabyle cities in defense of their linguistic rights, but the law went into effect.

In 1992 elections the fundamentalist FIS (Islamic Front) looked to win, but a coup replaced the Algerian government and annulled the elections. A state of emergency was imposed to quell spreading fundamentalist unrest. Islamic terrorist groups attacked across the country, murdering and intimidating the population. Berber cultural leaders were often targeted as anti-Islamic and anti-Arabic.

The Kabyles no longer looked for justice in an Algeria that many Kabyles felt is finished as a secular state. The Kabyle's minimum involvement with the military or the Islamic fundamentalists maintained Kabylia as the calmest and least violent region of Algeria, partly due to the mobilization of nationalist self-defense forces. Nationalist militants won some support with their calls for Berber separation from the disintegrating Algerian state.

In January 1994 at least 150,000 Berbers peacefully marched in Tizi-Ouzou to protest Islamic fundamentalist violence and the ruling authorities' failure to protect the population. They also demanded official recognition of their language. Berber villagers in July clashed with Islamic militants in the first fighting between the militants and Berbers since the violence began 30 months before. In August 1994, the U.S. State Department issued a confidential paper that outlined the possibility that Kabylia, where the majority oppose Muslim fundamentalism, would eventually obtain independence while the remainder of Algeria accommodated itself to an Islamic government.

From September 1994 to May 1995 over a million Berber students in the Kabylia region boycotted schools and colleges to demand that their language be taught as an official language. The government negotiated a compromise that would allow limited use of Berber languages in education—a move opposed by the Islamic militants, who oppose all languages other than Arabic and often target authors or musicians using Berber dialects.

In 1996 a majority of Algerians voted in a referendum for a new constitution that banned Islamic organizations, but also those based on language or regions. The murder of the popular Kabyle entertainer Lounes Matoub by Islamic militants led to widespread demonstrations, rioting, and protests against both the militants and the Algerian government. In spite of the demonstrations, the government passed a law generalizing the use of Arabic throughout Algeria on 5 July 1998, ignoring protests by Berber leaders and groups in both Algeria and Europe. The law was imposed on the country's universities, including those in Berber regions, in 2000.

The language conflict continues to drive a wedge between the Berbers and the secular Algerian government. This conflict leaves the Berbers in a very difficult situation, opposing both the Islamic militants and the secular government's Arabization policies. Whichever group finally wins power in Algeria, the Berbers will suffer. The situation eased with the decrease of Islamic violence in late 1999, but tension remains. Foreign commentators continue to speculate on the chances of a civil war and of the partition of Algerian into Arab and Berber states.

The death of an 18-year-old in detention by the gendarmarie in April 2001 began a series of demonstrations and marches that culminated in an estimated 500,000 marching through the major Kabyle cities and Algiers demanding withdrawl of all gendarmes from the region, recognition of their language and culture, and greater economic and educational opportunities. The demonstrations turned violent, when police fired live rounds at protesters. Demands escalated in the face of the authorities' heavy-handed handling of the demonstrations. Protests spread from the Kabyle heartland east of Algiers to the Shawia region to the east and southeast. By early July, protests and demonstrations had spread to most cities and many towns between Algiers and the Tunisian border. The Kabyle Intifada left more than 60 dead between April and July 2001, most killed by security forces trying to quell the uprising.

Thousands of Berber activists gave a lukewarm response to a September 2001 government offer of direct talks after five months of growing unrest. In October, the Algerian government announced that the Berber language would be accepted as an Algerian language and other measures, but were denounced by activists as too little. The Kabyles are still historically mistrusted and are seen as trying to dismember Algeria's hard-won statehood.

SELECTED BIBLIOGRAPHY:

Hanoteau, A. *Kabylia and the Kabyles*. 1976.
Ruedy, John. *Modern Algeria: The Origins and Development of a Nation*. 1992.
Shatzmiller, Maya. *The Berbers and the Islamic States*. 1999.
Zartman, William I., and William Mark Habeeb, eds. *Polity and Society in Contemporary North Africa*. 1993.

Kachins

KaChins; Jingpaws; Jinghphos; Singpos; Singfos; Chingpaws; Chinap'o; Marips; Dashanhua

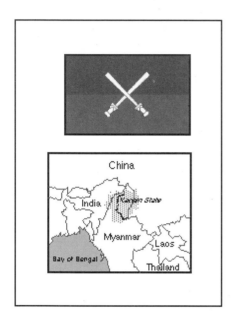

POPULATION: Approximately (2002e) 2,750,000 Kachins in southern Asia, the majority concentrated in northern Myanmar, with about 300,000 in adjacent areas of China's Yunnan province, and 135,000 in Arunchal Pradesh State of India. Exact numbers are difficult to estimate with accuracy due to the lack of systematic development and the pluralism of tribal and ethnic identities in the region.

THE KACHIN HOMELAND: The Kachin homeland lies in northern Myanmar, a mountainous territory in the Himalayan foothills around the upper Irrawaddy River. The heavily forested highlands merge with the Kumon Range to the west. The Kachin homeland, called Kachinland, covers a large area of Myanmar, China, and India. Most of the Kachin (known as Jingpo) in China live in the Dehong Dai-Jingpo Autonomous Prefecture of Yunnan province. The largest Kachin population lives in northern Myanmar, where part of Kachinland forms the state of Kachin. *State of Kachin*: 34,379 sq. mi.—89,042 sq. km. (2002e) 1,323,000—Kachins 88%, Shans* 6%, other Burmese 6%. The Kachin capital and major cultural center is Myitkyana, (2002e) 84,000. The other important cultural center is Banmo, called Bhamo by the Kachins, (2002e) 46,000. The major cultural center of the Chinese Kachins is Tengchong, called Momien by the Kachins, (2002e) 45,000.

FLAG: The Kachin national flag, the flag of the Kachin Independence Organization (KIO), is a horizontal bicolor of red over green bearing two white Kachin swords crossed in the center.

PEOPLE AND CULTURE: The Kachins are a tribal people encompassing a number of distinct groups related by language and culture inhabiting the mountains of northern Myanmar, northeastern India, and adjacent areas of China. "Kachin" refers to the entire cultural group, made up of a number of related tribal groups with differing cultural, linguistic, and political characteristics. The largest of the groups, the Jingpaw, called

870

Jingpo in China, numbering about 700,000, consider themselves the only true Kachins and inhabit an area larger than the territory officially designated as Kachin State. "Jingpaw" is often used to designate the entire cultural group. Other groups forming part of the Kachin nation are the Atsi, Maru (Naingvaw), Lashi, Nung (Rawang), and Lisu (Yawyin). Never under Indian or Chinese cultural influence, the Kachins have not developed the caste distinctions of neighboring peoples and have retained their tribal organizations. Although opium cultivation is not traditional in Kachin culture, the Kachins live in the infamous "Golden Triangle," one of the world's primary opium-producing regions. The drug trade has increasingly influenced the Kachin's indigenous economy and has helped to finance development and opposition to the oppressive government of Myanmar.

LANGUAGE AND RELIGION: The Kachin language forms a group of dialects belonging to the Bodo-Naga-Kachin group of the Tibeto-Burman dialects of the Sino-Tibetan languages. Of the numerous Tibeto-Burman dialects in use by the Kachin peoples, that of the Jingpaw is the most widely distributed. It is an officially recognized minority language of China. Jingpaw, spoken in four major dialects, serves as the lingua franca for a large area, uniting many small tribal groups that speak closely related languages. Other important Kachin dialects are Atsi, Maru, and Lashi. In China the literary language uses a Pinyin alphabet and is based on the Enkun dialect.

Most of the Kachin tribes have retained their traditional religious beliefs, although there is an influential Christian, mostly Baptist, minority making up about 10% of the Kachin population. Traditionally the Kachin religion is a form of animistic ancestor worship, entailing animal sacrifice. Belief in spirits and witchcraft remains widespread, even among the Christian minority.

NATIONAL HISTORY: Small tribal groups moved south from the eastern Tibetan Plateau to settle the present-day Kachin region in probably the eighth century A.D. The numerous tribes, never united under a central authority or controlled by the Burmese kings, often warred among themselves and cooperated only when faced with outside threats. When their homeland was overrun by the Shans, a Thai people, in the thirteenth century, the Kachins retreated to mountain strongholds. Later in the same century they repulsed the invading Mongol hordes.

Traditional Kachin society subsisted on the shifting cultivation of hill rice, supplemented by the proceeds of banditry and feud warfare. Authority in most Kachin tribal areas was held by petty chieftains, who depended on the support of their immediate patrilineal clans.

Ethnic Burmans, the dominant people in the Irrawaddy River basin to the south, moved into the Kachin tribal lands in the seventeenth and eighteenth centuries. Fierce Kachin resistance to the invaders limited Burman rule to the river lowlands. The Chinese, who were pacifying the tribal peoples of Yunnan, sent an army to occupy the Kachin region in 1766. To the dismay of the imperial government, the army withdrew in disorder under ferocious Kachin attacks in 1770. China retained control of only a small eastern Kachin region.

The British, seen as natural allies against the Burmans and Chinese, took control of the lowlands of Upper Burma in 1886, relieving Burman pressure on the tribal territories. The tribal peoples on the northern frontier, never part of the Burmese kingdom, signed separate treaties, as distinct nations, with the British authorities. The British eventually organized the Kachin territory as a protectorate. The British authorities closed an area called the Kachin Hill Tracts to immigration by the lowland Burmans and gave the various tribes considerable autonomy. The last of the tribes submitted to British rule in 1935. Troops recruited from the Kachin tribes, particularly an elite unit known as the Kachin Rifles, became a mainstay of British authority in Burma. In the east the international border with China remained porous; Kachins on both sides ignored the frontier.

The British-imposed peace allowed the creation of Christian missions. For many of the Kachin tribes, the European and American missionaries who ventured into the high mountains and rain forests were the first contact with the outside world. Many of the pagan Kachins accepted the new religion, and many sons of local chiefs were sent to the missionary schools. The Kachins began to advance rapidly, led by a Christian minority educated by the various missionary societies. The Kachins began to form a sense of nation, where before they had only functioned as many separate tribes.

The British allowed the Kachins to retain their own army and administration up to World War II. The Kachins remained loyal to their British allies when war broke out, unlike the majority of the Burmans, who initially supported the Japanese. Guerrilla bands trained by British and American officers parachuted into the region following the Japanese occupation in 1942, wreaked havoc with Japanese communications, and terrified Japanese patrols. The guerrillas, the nucleus of a future Kachin army, gained fame for their valor and tenacity in fighting the Japanese. The Burmans, finding the Japanese harsher masters than the British, switched sides, and by 1944 the Kachin region had been cleared of the invaders.

Immediately after the war the British authorities began preparations for Burmese independence. Convinced that the small protectorates in the northern highlands lacked the resources to become viable independent states, the British urged the creation of a Burmese federation. After long negotiations the Kachins agreed to join the federation, but with a guaranteed right of secession under British protection after 10 years if they felt their interests were not being served.

Chinese troops invaded the Kachin homeland in 1945, at the end of World War II. They left in 1947, but no agreement on the boundary between Burma and China was signed until 1960. Chinese claims to the region, dating from the eighteenth century, are still occasionally pressed, particularly when the Chinese and Myanmar governments are at odds.

The Burmese government, soon after independence in January 1948, abrogated the autonomy agreement and incorporated large tracts of autonomous Kachinland into neighboring provinces. The government then created a truncated Kachin State with only semi-autonomous status, leaving the majority of the Kachin population outside the state's borders. The outraged Kachins rebelled and overran much of northern Burma. In March 1949 the victorious Kachins captured Burma's second city, Mandalay, but their military success produced little result other than to terrify the Burmese troops sent against them. The British, exhausted from World War II, refused to intervene in spite of earlier assurances to the Kachins.

The Burmese army finally counterattacked and drove the Kachins back to their mountains in 1950. Several Kachin factions formed an alliance with the Burmese communists, facilitating the arrival of arms and aid through the Jingpo minority on the Chinese side of the border. The Chinese government in the early 1950s supported the creation of an independent greater Kachin state. In October 1952, the leaders of the Kachins, Karens,* Shans, and the Burmese communists formed an alliance and signed a pact demarcating zones throughout Burma. Other Kachin factions, mostly Christian-led and anticommunist, opposed the communist alliance and turned to the lucrative opium trade to finance a separatist war. Nationalist leaders met leaders of the Jingpo on the Burmese-Chinese border, pledging support and kingship, but in 1958 the Chinese government closed the border and cut all aid to the rebels.

Ten years after Burmese independence, the Kachins formally notified the government of their intention to secede under the 1948 independence agreement. The government retaliated with arrests and military occupation. The establishment of Buddhism as the official state religion in 1961 and the imposition of military rule in 1962 increasingly alienated the Kachins. Kachin state's semi-autonomous status was abolished. Armed with helicopters and sophisticated weapons provided by the United States to fight the drug trade, the Burmese military launched a widespread offensive in 1962. The government soldiers, badly mauled, retreated to a few fortified military garrisons, leaving the Kachins in effective control of the countryside.

The sparsely populated and mountainous heartland of the Kachins, very difficult for the Burmese military to penetrate, remained under only nominal government control throughout the 1970s. In spite of the sometime alliance with the Burmese communists, the nationalist Kachin Independence Organization (KIO) encompassed as many rightists as leftists, and a variety of factions. In the late 1970s, as relations between Burma and China improved, Chinese arms were cut off, and by the early 1980s the Kachins relied heavily on the opium trade to finance their war.

In 1980–81, leaders of the KIO opened negotiations with the Burmese government. The talks were broken off due to the Burmese insistence on a one-party state and the anti-autonomy stance of the government negotiators. In 1982 there were reports that the KIO had spilt between mostly Christian anticommunists and a smaller group of procommunist leftists. In the late 1980s the Christian leadership reasserted its authority and formed an alliance with similar groups among the neighboring Shans fighting the government.

Moderate Kachin leaders, initially favoring an independent Kachinland within a federation of states that would replace Myanmar's brutal military government, mostly joined the separatists following the crushing of the Burmese democracy movement in 1988–90. The Kachins defeated renewed government offensives in 1989 and 1991, and in early 1992 they stopped the largest offensive against them in three decades. Nationalists claimed an area larger than the official Kachin state. The region, called "Greater Kachinland," included Kachin state, the northern districts of Myanmar's Sagaing division, and the Namtu region of Shan State; it covered 61,213 sq. mi. (158,582 sq. km) and had a population of over three million.

During the late 1980s, the Chinese government ceased its support for the Kachin rebels and began to pressure the nationalists to negotiate with the military government. Approached by government leaders seeking negotiations in late 1992, the Kachin nationalists of the Kachin Independence Army (KIA) agreed to a cease-fire, but the armed standoff in the region continued. In 1994 other Kachin groups agreed to a cease-fire with the military government.

Traditionally Kachin nationalists financed their activities through the smuggling of commodities, especially jade. In the 1980s, the effectiveness of opium production in the area drew in many antigovernment Kachin groups. However, the opium trade, increasingly involving groups with little interest in politics and not closely identified with the Kachin nation, is seen by some Kachin leaders as a greater evil than Myanmar's military government.

Fifteen rebel ethnic groups from across Myanmar, including the Kachin Independence Union (KIU), met in territory held by the Karens in January 1997. The groups signed the Mae Tha Raw Hta Agreement, which calls for the establishment of a democratic, federal union in Myanmar. The groups, united in the National Democratic Front (NDF), include several organizations that had signed peace agreements with the military government but had resumed fighting when the agreements brought no gain—

only the same misery, oppression, and poverty they had endured for decades.

Reports of increasing use of slaves to build defenses, roads, and bridges in the frontier regions were published internationally in 1999–2000. Local Kachins were forced to clear land, act as porters for the army, and to provide food and housing for government troops. Refugees from the region claimed that forced laborers were made to march along roads that had been mined by rebels, so as to clear them for the army. Illegal logging, smuggling, and the flourishing drugs industry are often controlled by nationalist groups in the frontier areas but increasingly involve army officers in areas under government control.

Several dozen Kachin refugees who fled from the Hpakant jade mine told of hundreds of thousands of people being used as forced labor in July 1998. The mining area of Kachin state is in disastrous condition, with high numbers of drug addicts, virtual slave labor, and extensive environmental damage. The mines were taken over by the Burmese military following the cease-fire with the major Kachin insurgent groups in 1994. The government refused access or the provision of aid to the inhabitants of the mining region. In December 1998, the Burmese mining authorities and a Chinese company reached an agreement on further prospecting and development of gold and copper deposits in Kachin state.

The military junta, in spite of promises to relinquish control and establish regional states with greater autonomy, maintain its tight political hold on the country. Fighting resumed in the region in 1999, but the larger groups resumed the insurgency in early 2000, citing the situation in the Kachin homeland. According to some reports, 50% of youths in Kachin state are drug addicts. No doctors or medicines are available in the region, and disease is widespread. Documents smuggled out of the country assert that the Burmese military is selling Kachin children to businessmen in China to be used for organ transplants.

The Chinese government has interests in the natural resources of the Kachin region in Myanmar, but also in reopening the World War II "Burma Road" connecting China's Yunnan province to the Indian Ocean. Chinese of Jingpo origins are increasingly used as envoys to the Kachins, with many reportedly becoming rich on smuggling of goods, precious stones, and drugs.

SELECTED BIBLIOGRAPHY:

Armstrong, Ruth M. *The Kachins of Burma*. 1977.

Gilhodes, A. *The Kachin: Religion and Customs*. 1997.

Leach, Edmund Ronald. *Political Systems of Highland Burma: A Study of Kachin Social Structure*. 1986

Wang, Zhusheng. *The Jingpo: Kachin of the Yunnan Plateau*. 1997.

Kadazans

Dusuns; Dusums; Dusurs; Kadayans; Kedayans; Kadasans; Kadazandusun

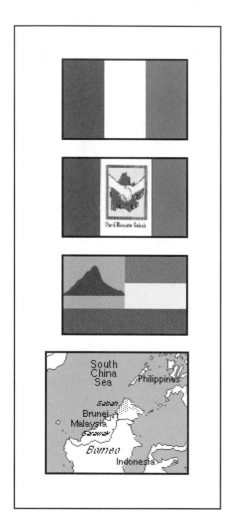

POPULATION: Approximately (2002e) 755,000 Kadazans in Malaysia, concentrated in the state of Sabah in northern Borneo. The name Kadazandusun is often applied to all of Sabah's indigenous peoples who account for about 54% of the total population.

THE KADAZAN HOMELAND: The Kadazan homeland occupies the northwestern tip of the large, mountainous island of Kalimantan, formerly called Borneo in the central Malay Archipelago. Sabah, lying on the South China Sea, is poetically known as the "land beneath the wind," due to a location that protects it from the annual monsoon. The heavily forested upland mountain areas protected the indigenous peoples from outside influences until the early twentieth century. Sabah forms a state of the Federation of Malaysia. *State of Sabah*: 29,545 sq. mi.—76,541 sq. km, (2002e) 2,218,000—Kadazans 34%, Malays 24%, Chinese 22%, Bajaus 12%, Muruts 5%, Bruneis and smaller groups 3%. The Kadazan capital and major cultural center is Kota Kinabalu, (2002e) 217,000. Other important cultural centers are Sandakan, (2002e) 213,000, and Tawau, (2002e) 169,000.

FLAG: The Kadazan flag, the flag of the national movement, is a vertical tricolor of blue, white, and red. The flag of the Kadazan-dominated Parti Beratsu Sabah (PBS) is a vertical tricolor of red, white, and blue bearing a centered square with a map of Sabah, two clasped hands, and the party name on the white. The official flag of Sabah is a horizontal tricolor of blue, white, and red bearing a pale blue canton on the upper hoist, charged with a dark blue silhouette of Mount Kinabalu.

PEOPLE AND CULTURE: The Kadazans, formerly called Dusuns, are the largest of the indigenous peoples of the region. The Kadazans are actually a collection of closely related ethnic and linguistic groups including the Rungus, Lotud, Orang Sungai, Tambanuo, Kuijau, Kimarangan, Sanayou, Minokok, and Tenggera. Other important related groups are the Bajau and Bruneis, who are farmers and fishermen, and the Murut in the higher elevations. Smaller tribal groups live in the interior valleys. Quantifying the Kadazan population in Sabah is a problem of definition, as the overlaying factors of language, religion, and culture produce differing and often contradictory results. In 1963 the name Kadazan was also applied to the Dusun, as there are no major differences between the two groups. The total indigenous population, including about 14 separate tribal groups, numbers over 1,200,000. Ethnically the Kadazans and other indigenous groups are related to the Moros* of the southern Philippines, but historically and religiously they are distinct.

LANGUAGE AND RELIGION: The Kadazans speak a Dusunic language of the Sabah group of the Malayan branch of the Austronesian group of languages. Kadazan comprises 13 major dialects with possibly 30 or more subdialects. The first Kadazan dictionary and grammar was published in 1958. In 1996 an expanded dictionary of the standard Kadazan literary language, based on the coastal dialects, was published, along with Kadazan-Malay and Kadazan-English sections. In 1995 an agreement was reached between rival cultural organizations to call the Kadazan and Dusun languages officially by the new name Kadazandusun; the language is being standardized and eventually will be taught in state schools.

The majority of the Kadazans are Christian, with both Roman Catholic and Protestant congregations, the result of early missionary activity in Borneo. There are also Muslim Kadazans, and a minority are still classed as animists. The Kadazan traditional system of beliefs revolves around their rice planting and harvesting, with female priestesses *(bobohizan)* presiding over the rituals. Many of the customs and traditions of their traditional beliefs have been retained and mixed with the later Christian and Muslim beliefs.

NATIONAL HISTORY: Small, culturally diverse tribes have inhabited the island of Borneo since ancient times. The tribes have a long history of conflict between the coastal and highland peoples. The Kadazan and the related peoples, farmers and fishermen, evolved a society centered on longhouses, with whole villages living under one roof. Muslim sailors and merchants introduced Islam to the pagan coastal peoples in the fourteenth and fifteenth centuries. Powerful Muslim states developed in Brunei and Sulu and in the Philippine Islands to the northeast; the rival sultanates competed for domination of the tribal people of the region.

Historically, the region was under the authority of the Muslim sultanate of Sulu of the Moros. The authority of the Moros goes back to about 1450, when the sultan of Sulu controlled the Sulu Archipelago, the Tawi-

Tawi Islands, the Zamboanga Peninsula, Palawan, and parts of northern Borneo. In 1703, Sabah was formally ceded to the sultanate of Sulu by the sultan of Brunei, in exchange for aid in putting down an internal revolt. English attempts at colonization in the seventeenth and eighteenth centuries failed due to the opposition of the indigenous tribes.

The tribal peoples had little contact with the outside world until the middle of the nineteenth century. An American, Joseph Torrey of Massachusetts, won a concession on the west coast from the sultan of Brunei in 1865, but his American trading company relinquished its claim 10 years later. The British gained control of the area in 1877–79, signing with Sultan Jamalul Alam, the sultan of Sulu, on 23 January 1878, a treaty in which arms to hold off the Spanish were exchanged for a lease on territory in northern Borneo.

In 1881 the British North Borneo Company was granted the right to administer the region. The company's trading activities became steadily more entrenched, and North Borneo became a de facto British protectorate, over the protests of the sultan of Sulu. In 1920, the government of the United States, as the colonial authority in the Philippines, reminded the British government that North Borneo was still part of the sultanate of Sulu, but the message was ignored.

Christian missionaries, Europeans and Americans, established mission stations across northern Borneo between the 1880s and the 1930s. The missionaries, particularly successful with the formerly pagan Kadazan peoples, introduced the new Christians to Western education and ideas. In the 1920s and 1930s an educated, Christian minority took over leadership roles among the Kadazans and began to challenge the traditional domination of the Muslim minority.

In 1941 the British evacuated the region as the Japanese overran Borneo. The remaining British and many Chinese were interned, but the indigenous peoples were forced to perform labor for the Japanese conquerors. Many Kadazans fought with guerrilla groups in the mountains, leading to massacres of civilian populations and other atrocities in reprisal. In 1945, British troops retook the region, reconstituting it as the British colony of North Borneo.

The newly independent Philippines and Indonesia, just after World War II, laid claim to the British colony on historical and ethnic grounds. These external claims to their homeland stimulated the rise of Kadazan nationalism in the 1950s, first assuming organizational form in cultural societies backed by Roman Catholic missionaries. North Borneo nationalism, led by the leaders of the Christian Kadazans, became a potent force as the British moved to decolonize North Borneo. A lack of trained administrators and statesmen and attacks by Indonesian forces, however, convinced the Kadazan leaders that independence was not, at the time, a viable option.

On 22 June 1962, the Philippine government officially registered with Great Britain its claim to North Borneo. Renamed Sabah, the colony joined neighboring Sarawak, the British Malay States, and Singapore in an independent federation in 1963. The residents of Sabah favored joining the federation mainly as a consequence of threatened invasion by Indonesian forces. Refusing to renounce its claim, Indonesia backed guerrilla bands inside Sabah and Muslim rebels operating in Indonesian Borneo. In 1968 the Philippines passed a bill that formally annexed the region but could not press its claim. The conflicting territorial pretensions were finally referred to the United Nations, which settled them in Malaysia's favor. Many Kadazan Christians favored annexation by the Philippines, but the large Muslim Malay population favored Malaysia.

Resentment of Malay domination, especially of the mainland Malays who held most state government offices, again raised the question of independence in the 1970s. The situation was aggravated by increasing tension between the Christian and Muslim populations and by the government's perceived pro-Muslim policies. The refusal of the federal government to recognize Kadazan as an official language in Sabah aggravated matters. In 1975 Sabah's Muslim leaders attempted to secede and to form a federation with the related Moros of the southern Philippines, but they were blocked by the Kadazans and other Christian groups, and by the opposition of the Malaysian government.

The development of extensive petroleum reserves in the late 1970s encouraged Kadazan nationalism as the state's Muslim-dominated government signed away 95% of the state's oil and natural gas revenues and ran up enormous debts on showy prestige projects. The growth of Kadazan nationalism paralleled the Malaysian government's official policy of promoting ethnic Malay interests. The growth of a Kadazan middle class stimulated demands for greater representation in the state government.

In April 1985 a Christian Kadazan, Joseph Pairan Kitingan, became, over strong Muslim opposition, Sabah's first Christian head of state in the federation. The vote was seen as a rejection of Muslim Malay domination and a manifestation of Kadazan nationalism. Allied to the Chinese minority, the new state government made Kadazan and English the official languages and moved to end the Malay domination of the government and economy. In March 1986 Malay rioting broke out and quickly spread to the large refugee Muslim population from the Philippines, prompting Kadazan demands for the expulsion of the Philippine Moros.

Relations between the Kadazan-dominated Sabah government and the Malaysian government deteriorated over Kadazan claims that many of the promises made in 1963 to persuade Sabah to join the federation had not been kept. They also objected to the dominance of West Malaysians instead of Sabahans in the civil service and demanded that half of the royalties from Sabah's oil fields, which produce a fifth of Malaysia's crude oil, be used for development in Sabah.

A 1989 Malaysian government campaign stressing Malay predominance, coupled with growing demands for the creation of an Islamic state in Malaysia, provoked a Kadazan nationalist backlash and stimulated demands for secession from Malaysia. The Muslim-dominated Malaysian federal government, to bolster Muslim influence and continued Muslim preeminence in Sabah, promoted mass immigration of Muslim peoples from neighboring Indonesia and the Philippines. The immigrants numbered an estimated 500,000 in the late 1980s. The growing Muslim domination of the state sparked Kadazan protests and nationalist demonstrations. The government reacted with a wave of arrests of Kadazan nationalist leaders in 1990–91 and reportedly uncovered a secessionist plot in July 1991.

In May 1991 Muslim fundamentalist groups made important gains in mainland Malaysia and greatly increased Muslim influence in the federation government. In the 1990s many Kadazans viewed the Malaysian government as a proselytizing Islamic force, supported by the hundreds of thousands of Muslim refugees from the Philippines settled in the region with government aid, poised to subjugate Sabah's non-Malay majority. The increasing Muslim fundamentalist power in the federation has frightened the Kadazans and stimulated a renewed nationalism. In 1992 Kadazan nationalists denounced the Malaysian government's treatment of Sabah as a colony; it receives only 5% of the revenue from its oil and natural gas, and its once-extensive forests have been nearly logged out.

In 1993, the Kadazan Parti Bersatu Sabah (PBS) formed a coalition with the Muslim-dominated United Sabah National Organization (USNO). The USNO backed Kadazan demands on greater state autonomy and on other issues. By late 1993 Sabah, once Malaysia's richest state, was sliding into stagnation because of its confrontation with the federal government. In February 1994, vowing to defend Sabah's identity and interests, the nationalist coalition led by the Kadazan PBS defeated the Malaysian government's ruling party in Sabah. In late March 1994 the coalition collapsed under Malaysian government pressure, and the country's ruling Malay party took control of the state government. Although no longer part of the Sabah government, Kitingan remained popular among the Kadazans as the *huguan siou*, the paramount leader, of the Kadazan nation.

The political instability in Sabah, coupled with economic recession, deforestation, press censorship, and the drying up of federal development funds, are adding social stress to the tension resulting from the political marginalization of the Christian Kadazan population. The perceived Muslim Malay threat has united the state's Kadazan and Chinese populations in opposition. Should Malaysia replace its beleaguered secular tradition with an Islamic government, Kadazan nationalism, buoyed by oil wealth, will become a potent threat to the future of the Malaysian federation.

The economic downturn in Malaysia in 1997–98 again increased tension in the region, with renewed demands by Kadazan leaders that the estimated 500,000 illegal Muslim residents from the Philippines and Indonesia be repatriated. The Malaysia government instituted an austerity plan for the country and deferred infrastructure programs in Sabah and other states. Concerns about the political stability of Malaysia were compounded in late 1998 when the deputy prime minister, Anwar Ibrahim, was ousted and charged with sexual impropriety, accepting bribes, and compromising national security. The Kadazans viewed the affair as part of the growing authoritarian grip on Malaysia of the prime minister, Dr. Mohamed Mahathir. In 1999 elections, Mahathir's National Front coalition, dominated by the United Malays National Organization, won in state elections by utilizing an organized and well-financed political machine.

In early May 2000, a number of tourists were kidnapped from a resort in Sabah by Moro separatists from the nearby Sulu Archipelago. The Kadazans blamed the periods of Islamic ascendancy in Sabah, when the state government afforded support to the Moro separatists of the Philippines. Sabah is increasingly polarized between a Malay-Muslim group and Kadazan nationalists, led by the Christian majority. The Chinese supply funds and votes to one group or the other. Despite the Kadazan political mobilization of the 1980s and 1990s, the Malay majority of Malaysia retains a firm grip on overall political power.

A major issue of contention is Sabah's large number of illegal immigrants, numbering over 500,000 in 2000. The immigrants, 350,000 from the Philippines, and 150,000 from Indonesia, are nearly all Muslims, which helps the government political party that frequently appeals to Muslim solidarity. The immigrants, comprising nearly a third of the total state population, threaten the Kadazan culture and language by disrupting the demographic balance in the state.

SELECTED BIBLIOGRAPHY:

Kitigan, Jeffrey G. *The Sabah Problem: The Quest for National Unity and Territorial Integration*. 1990.

Noble, Lela Garner. *Philippine Policy toward Sabah: A Claim to Independence*. 1977.

Roff, Margaret Clark. *The Politics of Belonging: Political Change in Sabah and Sarawak*. 1988.

Russell, Sue A. *Conversion, Identity, and Power: The Impact of Christianity on Power Relationships and Social Exchanges*. 1999.

Kalmyks

Khal'mgs; Kalmucks; Kalmuks; Kalmytz; Kalmacks; Qalmaqs; Western Mongols; Volga Oirots; Jazyks; Haljmg

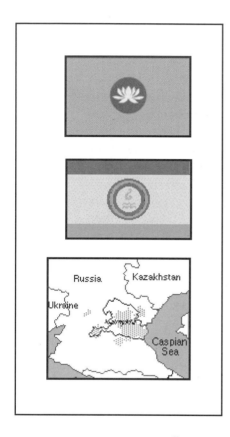

POPULATION: Approximately (2002e) 212,000 Kalmyks in Russia, concentrated in the Kalmyk Republic, a member state of the Russian Federation. Outside Russia there are large Kalmyk populations in Mongolia and China, and smaller groups in Europe, North America, and Taiwan.

THE KALMYK HOMELAND: The Kalmyk homeland lies in southern European Russia, an area of plains and barren steppe south of the Volga River and west of the Caspian Sea. Most of Kalmykia is a sparsely populated, arid semi-desert between the Don and Volga Rivers. The republic has no railroads except one that runs south along the Caspian shore from Astrakhan. In spite of the arid nature of the region, Kalmykia is primarily agricultural. Kalmykia is a member state of the Russian Federation. *Kalmyk Republic (Khal'mg Tangch)*: 29,305 sq. mi.— 75,919 sq. km, (2002e) 313,000—Kalmyks 45%, Russians 26%, Don Cossacks* 8%, Ukrainians 5%, Dargins 4%, Chechens* 3%, Kumyks* 2%, Kazakhs 2%, others 5%. The Kalmyk capital and major cultural center is Elista, called Ëlst in the Kalmyk language, (2002e) 106,000.

FLAG: The Kalmyk national flag, the official flag of the republic, is a yellow field charged with a centered pale blue circle bearing a white lotus flower with nine petals. A flag used by some nationalist organizations, the official flag of the republic in 1992–93, is a yellow field with a narrow pale blue stripe at the top and a narrow pink strip on the bottom and is charged with the Kalmyk national symbol centered, two concentric pink circles around a yellow disc bearing the Kalmyk talisman in the form of a flame in pink above stylized pink waves.

PEOPLE AND CULTURE: The Kalmyks are a branch of the Oirot people of Mongolia, western China, and southeastern Siberia. The descendants of Mongol nomads, the Kalmyks are the only large Buddhist nation in Europe. A long association with the Don Cossacks greatly influenced Kalmyk social life, which developed a strong tribal-military tradition. Since 1991 thousands of ethnic Kalmyks have returned to their homeland from other parts of the former Soviet Union. Oral historical poetry is an important part of Kalmyk culture; it is traditionally recited by local poets to the accompaniment of a two-stringed lute called a *dombr*. At public gatherings, parties, and on holidays poetry, storytelling, and singing are important parts of the festivities.

LANGUAGE AND RELIGION: The language spoken by the Kalmyks belongs to the Oirot or Western branch of the Oirot-Khalka branch of the Mongol languages. The language, often called Western Mongol, which has diverged from other Mongol languages, is spoken in two major dialects in Europe—Torgut (Torgout) and Derbent (Dörböt)—corresponding to the geographic divisions. The Torgut live in southern and eastern Kalmykia, and the Derbent Kalmyk inhabit the northern and western districts. A third division, numerically small, is the Khosheut Kalmyks, the remnant of a much larger group that mostly left the region in 1771. The language was written in the Mongol alphabet until 1931 but was forcibly switched to the Cyrillic alphabet; there is an active campaign to change the language to the Latin or back the original Mongol alphabet. The traditional Mongol script is again being taught in regional schools. Over a third of the Kalmyks speak only their own language, but the majority are bilingual, also speaking the Russian language.

The Kalmyks adhere to the "Yellow Hat" or Gelugpa (Virtuous Way) sect of Mahayana or Northern Buddhism. Commonly called Lamaism, it is also the predominant sect of the Tibetans*; the Dalai Lama is revered as the spiritual head of the Kalmyk nation. The Tibetan language is used in religious services. The Orthodox minority are mostly the descendants of Kalmyks converted to Christianity before the Russian Revolution. Kalmyk Buddhism retains many indigenous and shamanistic elements. Many Kalmyks still depend on shamans to cure the sick by magic and communication with the gods. Shamanistic practices have revived after decades of repression under Soviet rule.

NATIONAL HISTORY: The Kalmyks were among the last Asian migrants to penetrate European territory. A branch of the Oirot Mongols left their homeland in the Altai Mountains of Central Asia in 1636, fleeing the disintegration of the Mongol Empire and growing political and economic pressure from the Chinese, Kazakhs, and Mongols. The Oirot clans moved west, displacing the native Nogais* as they went. The clans, according to Kalmyk tradition, after migrating for 32 years, eventually settled in the lower Volga River basin. The region, which had once formed part of the Astrakhan Khanate, had been incorporated into the Russian Empire in 1556. In 1608 the Kalmyk leaders asked the tsar, Vasilii Shuiskii, for protection against the ravages of the Tatars* and Nogais.

The Oirot clans established an independent khanate, a confederation of tribes ruled by *noyons* (princes) under the ultimate authority of a khan. In 1646 the confederation signed a treaty of allegiance to Tsar Peter I, who charged them to guard Russia's new eastern frontier. Russian protection saved the small nation, and from 1664 to 1771 the Kalmyk homeland formed a frontier khanate in personal allegiance to the Russian tsars.

In the eighteenth century the Mongols adopted the Lamaism brought to the region by missionary monks from Mongolia. Accordingly the Dalai Lama in distant Tibet thereafter appointed the confederation's khans and, traditionally, the Kalmyk khans.

News that their ethnic cousins, the Oirots in Chinese territory, were suffering intense persecution by the Chinese authorities rallied the clans in 1769–70. Catherine II, now Russia's ruler, in the winter of 1771 put aside the 1646 allegiance treaty and attempted to impose direct Russian rule on the clans. Refusing to submit to Christian domination and determined to rescue the Oirots of China, the clans east of the Volga River, led by Khan Ubushi, suddenly undertook a harrowing journey back to their original homeland, over 2,000 miles to the east. Of the 300,000 that departed only a third survived the passage. The majority succumbed to cold, heat, hunger, and attacks by hostile tribes. The Volga River did not freeze in the winter of 1771; unable to cross the raging river, some 60,000 Mongols were forced to stay behind. They came to be called "Kalmyk," from the Turkic word for "remnant."

The Kalmyks formed close political and cultural ties to the Don Cossacks. The Kalmyks took on many of the military attributes of the Cossacks, while retaining their own culture and social structure. Kalmyk society was dominated by the "White Bone" aristocracy; the majority of the population formed the "Black Bone," the commoners. In return for military service and an oath of loyalty to the Russian tsar, the Kalmyks enjoyed broad powers of self-government. From 1803 their loyalty was overseen by a "Guardian of the Kalmyk People" appointed by the Russian monarch.

Government-sponsored immigration by ethnic Russians to the region began a process of bringing the Kalmyk clans under closer Russian authority. In 1806 the authorities limited the Kalmyk pasturelands to the area between the Caspian Sea and 30 kilometers from the Volga River. The tsarist decree severely limited the Kalmyks' nomadic way of life. The Kalmyk herds declined from 2.5 million head in 1803 to one million in 1863, and to only 450,000 at the turn of the twentieth century. Many impoverished Kalmyks were forced off the land to find work as fishermen and salt miners.

Numbering over 200,000 when war began in 1914, the small nation sent warriors who formed elite military units. Released from their oath of loyalty by the overthrow of the tsar in February 1917, the Kalmyk soldiers returned home. A Kalmyk congress convened in March 1917 authorized the formation of a national army from the returning military units and renewed the old alliance with the Don Cossacks. In the wake of the Bolshevik coup in October 1917, the Kalmyks rebelled. Most of the Kalmyk clans supported the anti-Bolshevik Southeastern League, an organization of Cossacks and other non-Russian peoples of the North Caucasus region, although the Kalmyks were divided into pro- and anti-Bolshevik groups.

The Kalmyk congress, dominated by the White Bone aristocracy, voted for secession as the Bolshevik threat increased. On 12 June 1918 the congress declared Kalmykia independent of Russia. The Kalmyks were devastated by heavy fighting during the Russian Civil War; thousands died in battle or of hunger and disease. The advancing Red Army occupied Kalmykia in 1920, creating a Kalmyk Autonomous District. The communists eliminated the White Bone aristocrats and nationalized the Kalmyk herds. Between 1922 and 1925, Kalmyks living in other parts of Russia were forcibly transferred to the autonomous district.

Collectivization of the Kalmyk herds began in the 1920s. The Kalmyks resisted Joseph Stalin's orders; he ordered that all opposition be ruthlessly crushed. Thousands of Kalmyks died in the process, and others joined antigovernment resistance groups. The last Kalmyk guerrilla bands were finally liquidated in 1926. Stalinist purges and antireligious campaigns destroyed the Kalmyk's cultural, political, and religious hierarchy. In 1932 most buildings of Mongol architecture, including temples, schools, and public buildings, were ordered destroyed, along with their contents.

The fervently Buddhist and anticommunist Kalmyks welcomed the German invaders in 1942. Approached as German allies, many Kalmyks enthusiastically joined the Germans' anticommunist crusade. Prince N. Tundutov, the Kalmyk leader during the Russian Civil War, arrived in Elista as head of a new Kalmyk government. The German authorities allowed the reopening of shrines and monasteries. A Kalmyk army, the Kalmyk Banner Organization, fought as German allies, often against Kalmyks fighting with the Red Army.

When the Red Army returned in February 1943, Stalin accused the entire Kalmyk nation of treason and ordered its deportation. Often with only minutes' notice, the Kalmyks, including the families of soldiers fighting in the Red Army, were herded into closed cattle cars and shipped east. Only three Kalmyk families escaped the brutal deportation of the Kalmyk population of Elista. Thousands perished from hunger and thirst on the 22-day journey. Dumped at rail sidings in the Siberian wastes, many more died of disease, exposure, and malnutrition. By 1950 over half the prewar Kalmyk population of 140,000 had perished.

Several thousand Kalmyks escaped the deportation and fled to Western

Europe. Some stayed in Europe, while many families emigrated to the United States, where they settled in New Jersey and Pennsylvania, joining Kalmyks who had fled the new Soviet state between 1917 and 1920. Many of the Kalmyks in Europe were placed in displaced-persons camps in Germany after World War II. In 1952 they were allowed into the United States, where some 2,500 Kalmyks lived in 2000.

The Kalmyks were officially rehabilitated in 1956, three years after Stalin's death. The survivors gradually made their way back to the North Caucasus, the first 6,000 survivors arrived in their former homeland in early 1957. In 1958 their homeland was officially reestablished as an autonomous republic within the Russian Federation, but under strict surveillance, and with a large ethnic Russian presence to ensure stability. The Kalmyk population regained its 1926 level only in the late 1960s. The Kalmyk population grew rapidly during the 1970s and 1980s, reaching a total of 174,000 in 1989.

The Kalmyk homeland today is in a sorry state, for which Soviet economic and agricultural planning is blamed. Ill-conceived irrigation projects left over half the region infertile desert, with another third in a marginal state. In addition, too many sheep, of the wrong type, were grazed in the region in the 1950s. Soviet planners brought in sheep from the Caucasus Mountains. The sheep, famed for their wool, had very sharp hooves, which were perfect for the flinty mountainsides but disastrous for the fertile, yet fragile, grasslands of Kalmykia.

The reforms introduced by Mikhail Gorbachev in 1987 fueled a Kalmyk religious and cultural revival. Renewed ties with the Kalmyk exile community in the United States and Europe, reinforced calls for religious freedom. The exile community in Western Europe, served by five Buddhist temples, numbered only about 1,500, while the over 200,000 Kalmyks in the Soviet Union had only one active temple. Kalmyk scholars, especially at the Kalmyk University in Elista, founded in 1970, protested the genocide of the Stalin era and the falsification of Kalmyk history by Soviet historians. Inspired by the new freedom and by the revival of their Buddhist religion, Kalmyks made nationalism a popular movement. In August 1990, the first *khural* (congress) since World War II convened in Elista; it included delegates from the exile White Bone community. The congress adopted a nationalist platform endorsing the Kalmyk right to self-determination.

The collapse of the Soviet Union in August 1991 provoked a strong Kalmyk nationalist reaction, particularly demands for control of the extensive mineral wealth of their republic. In February and March 1992, the Kalmyks changed the name of the republic to Khal'mg Tangch and unilaterally upgraded the republic's legal status within the Russian Federation. One of the conditions demanded for approving the new Russian federation was Kalmyk control of subsoil resources.

In April 1992, a young Kalmyk millionaire, Kirsan Ilyumzhinov, won the republican presidential elections with a vow to convert Kalmykia into a neutral, Buddhist state. Lapel pins featuring the likeness of the Dalai Lama became as common as the hammer-and-sickle once was. His religious views and his peaceful campaign for Tibetan rights made him the icon of Kalmyk nationalism.

Following the collapse of the Soviet Union, the Dalai Lama sent the republic a *shaddin* (high) lama called Telo Rinpoche, a young American (from Pennsylvania) of Kalmyk ancestry. By 1992 five prayer houses had been opened. An Institute for the Rebirth of the Kalmyk Language and Buddhism was established in Elista, and Buddhist holidays were again celebrated. The Kalmyk University became a center of the Kalmyk renaissance during the 1990s.

The Kalmyks, after decades of Soviet domination, have quickly recovered their culture and language. Their old Mongol script, abolished in 1924, is again being taught in Kalmyk schools. Traditional musical instruments are again being made, with skins and woods brought from Mongolia, and students are being sent to China and Mongolia to learn to play them. There is talk of bringing sheep and cattle from Xinjiang to restore the breeds that arrived with the first Kalmyk settlers.

The Kalmyk leader, Kirsan Ilyumzhinov, in November 1998 set off a crisis in Russia when he demanded greater autonomy for his small nation. He threatened to withhold tax revenues, arguing that while the Kalmyks paid heavy taxes to the federal government, they got nothing in return. More radical nationalists, opposed to Ilyumzhinov, pressed for secession from the Russian Federation. The crisis deepened as other discontented ethnic groups gave the Kalmyks their support. The crisis ended with several agreements on finances and cultural subsidies, but the underlying animosity of the Kalmyks for the Russians, which dates from the Stalinist era, remains a potent force.

President Kirsan Ilyumzhinov has established a Soviet-style personality cult. He is an enthusiastic chess player and is president of the International Chess Federation. Irregularities in the use of budget funds in Kalmykia between 1998 and 2000 included millions of rubles used for preparations for the World Chess Olympiad in Elista in 1998 and on a new stadium for the local football club has prodded the development of a nationalist opposition. Harsh living conditions and suppression of the opposition in the republic, including rigged local elections, added to the tension in 2000–2001. The leading opposition newspaper is printed outside the repeublic, in Stavtopol Kray, and is sold without government permission within the republic. Repression increased in 2001 as the 2002 Kalmyk presidential elections neared. Increasingly seen as a puppet of the Russian government, Ilyumzhinov, once proclaimed as the Kalmyk leader, has lost the support of much of the Kalmyk population.

SELECTED BIBLIOGRAPHY:

Halovic, S. *The Mongols of the West.* 1997.
Khodarkovsky, Michael. *Where Two Worlds Met: The Russian State and the Kalmyk Nomads, 1600–1771.* 1992.
Nekrich, Alexander. *The Punished Peoples.* 1978.
Rubel, P. *The Kalmyk Mongols.* 1997.

Kanaks

Kanakis; New Caledonia Melanesians

POPULATION: Approximately (2002e) 96,000 Kanaks in the South Pacific, mainly in the French Territory of New Caledonia. Outside the region there are Kanaks in French Polynesia, France, and Australia.

THE KANAK HOMELAND: The Kanak homeland lies in the southwestern Pacific Ocean 750 miles (1,207 km) northeast of Australia. The archipelago comprises the cigar-shaped main island of New Caledonia, the Loyalty Islands, the Isle of Pines, and a number of smaller islands and islets. The islands, called Kanaky or Kanaki by the Kanaks, form the French overseas territory of New Caledonia. The territory is divided into three provinces—North (Nord), Loyalty Islands (Iles Louyate), and South (Sud). The first two constitute an autonomous Kanak region. *Territory of New Caledonia (Kanaky)*: 7,367 sq. mi.—19,085 sq. km, (2002e) 219,000—Kanaks 44%, French (Caldoches) 34%, Wallisians and Futunans* 9%, Tahitians* 4%, Javanese 3%, Vietnamese 2%, Chinese 2%, others 2%. The Kanak capital and major cultural center is Nouméa, called Numea by the Kanaks, (2002e) 85,000, urban area 134,000. Other important cultural centers are Wé in the Loyalty Islands Province, (2002e) 11,000, and Houailu, in North Province, (2002e) 5,000.

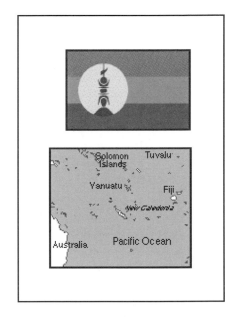

FLAG: The Kanak national flag, the flag of the national movement, is a horizontal tricolor of blue, red, and green charged with a large yellow disc representing the sun bearing a stylized black totem.

PEOPLE AND CULTURE: The Kanak, or Kanaka, are a Melanesian people of mixed Melanesian and Polynesian background. They form part of the large Melanesian population of the Pacific islands region known as Melanesia. Kanak identity is based on an extensive clan system, a network of family alliances, and specific traditional land rights. Village leaders retain considerable influence and are the ultimate authority in the more remote regions and islands. The Kanak population is widely believed to have declined rapidly in the nineteenth century from violence, forced labor, and disease. In the twentieth century the Kanak population remained fairly stable up to 1939, but more than doubled in the years since World War II. Although the birth rate is now fairly high, infant mortality is also high and life expectancy is relatively low.

LANGUAGE AND RELIGION: The Kanaks speak about 30 distinct dialects, each with its own place-names and and words for the flora and fauna. French is the only official language and is the only language taught in the territorial schools. The Kanak speak a western Melanesian variant of the Melanesian branch of the Malayo-Polynesian language group. The majority also speak French, the language of government and of the large European minority, and at least one other of the many Melanesian dialects. Nationalists are working on the development of a standard dialect that will become the national and literary language and will bridge the differences between the many island dialects.

The majority of the Kanaks are Christians, mostly Roman Catholic, although a number of Protestant denominations are represented. Two local Protestant churches, the Evangelical Church in New Caledonia and the Loyalty Islands and the Free Evangelical Church, are the major non-Catholic denominations and are almost exclusively Kanak in membership. The traditional Kanak beliefs, derived from the ancient Melanesian religious tradition, retain considerable influence.

NATIONAL HISTORY: Melanesians settled the islands more than 3,000 years ago but remained isolated except for occasional Polynesian voyagers and a later Polynesian migration from the east. The various groups evolved a segmented, tribal society. Numerous small tribes, each with its own dialect and culture, jealously maintained tribal territories and often warred among themselves.

Lying east of the sea routes taken by early European explorers, the islands remained unknown to the Europeans until 1774. British captain James Cook called the mountainous main island New Caledonia, the poetic name for Scotland, and named the entire group the Loyalty Islands. Cook was followed by a French navigator, Antoine de Bruni, in 1793, but the fierce Kanaks discouraged exploration or colonization. Sandalwood traders from Australia introduced the islanders to the use of iron in 1841. A French military expedition finally subdued the tribes in 1853; France formally annexed the islands in 1864.

The French authorities, ignoring the indigenous population, considered the islands virtually uninhabited and made the entire archipelago a penal colony. New Caledonia's isolation allowed a penal system considerably less harsh than similar establishments in French Guiana in South America. In 1894 the French disbanded the penal colony, and the prisoners either returned to France or settled in the islands. A naval base established at Nouméa gave the French an important military presence in the western South Pacific. European diseases, however, decimated the Kanak population.

A Protestant mission from the London Missionary Society was established in the Loyalty Islands in 1841, and a Catholic mission was set up on the main island with the aid of the French navy in 1843. The Protestant and Roman Catholic missionaries introduced Western-style education, leading to the creation of an educated minority by the later nineteenth century.

The Kanak population, unsuited to plantation agriculture, continued to be generally ignored by the French authorities. More pliable workers from other French colonies were imported to work the plantations. By 1900 the non-Kanak population had grown to form a quarter of the total. The discovery of rich nickel deposits brought an influx of workers from France and reinforced the European domination of the islands. Nouméa grew rapidly; the large European minority enjoyed fine restaurants, clubs, theaters, and branches of famous Paris shops.

The Kanak, excluded from the colony's political and economic life, retained their traditional village society. The colony's two largest population groups lived distinctly separate lives, but from the time of colonial settlement until as late as 1917 Kanak uprisings were common, and the French settlers and authorities lived in constant fear of spontaneous revolts. An insurrection of 1856–59 near Nouméa and an uprising of 1878–79 seriously threatened the French hold on the territory. Kanak grievances focused on the confiscation of Melanesian lands, foraging by settlers' cattle in Kanak produce gardens, and a head tax imposed by the colonial government in 1899.

The French authorities suppressed each uprising by destroying entire villages and crops, demanding unconditional surrender, The insurgents were often punished by deportation, execution, or the confiscation of their lands. By the end of the nineteenth century, large areas of Kanak land had been taken and the inhabitants relegated to reserves. Forced labor, limitations on movement, and curfews were imposed and became the basis of a system of administration codified in 1887 as the *indigénat*, the native regulations. Serious revolts in 1917 and 1922 were brutally suppressed. Although the Kanaks had no political rights, they were forcibly conscripted during both world wars.

The head tax had been levied on male Kanaks to oblige them to take employment with the European settlers or the government. Like the *indigénat*, the head tax remained in force until 1946. Between 1864 and 1939, some 60,000 indentured labors and convicts constructed public works, worked the plantations, and performed domestic service. To augment the European population, emigration from nearby Australia and New Zealand was encouraged, and two later waves of settlers in the 1890s and 1920s were granted government funds to establish coffee and cotton industries.

In 1936 the Kanaks numbered 29,000, while the growing European population counted about 15,000; the survival of the indigenous Kanaks was in serious question.

Kanak resentment of French privilege swelled in the 1950s as European migration increased and related Melanesian peoples moved toward independence in Fiji, Vanuatu, and other islands. Nationalist groups began to demand Kanak autonomy and redress for a century of neglect. Embarrassed by Kanak poverty, many of the "Caldoches," French settlers, supported the Kanak demands. The interests of the powerful Société Nickel prevailed, however, and the demands were ignored, economic concerns taking precedence over Kanak appeals for equality. Nonetheless, French citizenship was extended to all, regardless of ethnic origin, in 1953. In 1958 the voters of the islands, mostly French, approved a proposal to remain a French territory.

In the early 1970s, for the first time, the Kanaks became a minority in their own homeland, although they remained the largest single national group. Pro-independence, pro-autonomy, and pro-French groups all campaigned for Kanak support. In 1978 rioting swept the main island, the most serious disturbances in the colony's history. Nationalists, supported by the mostly Caldoche local government council, demanded immediate independence. A pro-independence front took 35% of the vote in elections for a territorial assembly in 1979. The authorities dismissed the regional government and sent troops to restore order. The French socialists, making vague promises of autonomy, won 60% of the Kanak vote in 1981, but government inaction in the months that followed rekindled militant Kanak nationalism.

Pro-independence Kanak and Caldoche parties won a majority in the territorial assembly in 1982. The assembly voted to set 24 September 1983 for independence, exactly 130 years after the French occupation. In July 1983 serious violence between pro-independence and pro-French groups spread across the main island. The French authorities seized on the violence as a pretext not to grant independence on the designated day.

New elections for an autonomous regional government in 1984, boycotted by nationalists, returned a pro-French faction to power. When a French settler was shot in his farmhouse, anti-independence forces killed some 20 Kanak activists. Serious disturbances broke out across the main island, forcing many settlers to abandon outlying farms and towns for the relative safety of Nouméa. Swift action by the French police and military, augmented by reserves from Europe, narrowly averted civil war. Melanesian states in the Pacific gave their support to the Kanaks against the French, already unpopular for their nuclear tests in French Polynesia. In 1986 the French authorities held a referendum, boycotted by the nationalists, which produced a large majority in favor of continued ties to France

Individuals charged with the ambush of 10 Kanak activists were acquitted in October 1987.

Separatist violence once again erupted in April 1988, after two years of relative calm. After several gendarmes were taken hostage, there was a settler attack on Ouvéa, where 19 Kanaks were killed, allegedly after surrendering. Gun battles between Kanak separatists and the French police spread even to the suburbs of Nouméa.

Kanak leaders agreed to negotiate and finally accepted a compromise in 1988, the Matignon Accord. The Kanak gained greater participation in the regional government, autonomy for the two Kanak-majority provinces, and a massive aid package designed to raise the Melanesian standard of living to the European level. The question of independence was postponed for 10 years. The compromise ended the separatist violence and avoided a civil war that would probably have ended with the partition of the territory. In April 1990, Kanak nationalists announced the purchase of the island's largest nickel mine from its French owner.

Territorial elections in October 1996 brought a new, centrist party to prominence, as the balance of power shifted between the pro-French and the pro-independence groups. The group, "A New Caledonia for All," aligned itself with the independence parties to form a government.

A referendum on independence was organized in 1998, 10 years after the signing of the Matignon Accord. The Kanaks, as a minority, were uncertain of support from other ethnic groups, so the outcome of the referendum was far from certain. On 21 April 1998, before the planned referendum, an agreement was announced between the pro-independence FLNKS, the pro-French groups, and the French government that would give the territory greater autonomy and a New Caledonian citizenship. The agreement was put to a vote in the territory on 8 November 1998 and was adopted by a 72% majority. The adoption of the new accord set in motion a process of peaceful decolonization. The agreement provided for wide-ranging autonomy between 2000 and 2014; the inhabitants of the territory would then vote on such issues as political independence, a separate currency, their own defense, and foreign affairs.

In June 1999, the territory's first elected government took power, with both the Kanaks and anti-independent settlers claiming that the 1998 agreement as a victory. The Kanaks and a minority of the Europeans who favor independence claim that the Nouméa agreement will lead inexorably to statehood, while the pro-French forces see the agreement as providing for an indefinite "associated autonomy." The most likely outcome is continued political squabbling and perhaps yet another round of violence. Independence would mean the end of the French subsidies, estimated at about $880 million in 1999–2000.

Both groups agree on the need to develop the economy quickly. Kanak leaders are carefully monitoring the fulfillment of the French promise to raise Kanak living standards to the level of opulent Nouméa, a daunting task even without the opposition of the majority of the French settler population. New Caledonia is one of the world's largest producers of nickel, but in 1999 prices for the metal hit a 12-year low, reflecting the declining demand for steel. The Kanaks want to develop their other resources, notably tourism and fishing. The pro-French settlers argue that a prosperous economy will benefit all the territory's inhabitants and will make the Kanaks see the folly of independence. The Kanaks point out that a viable, healthy economy is a precondition of statehood and will give the Kanaks the confidence to cut their remaining ties to France.

SELECTED BIBLIOGRAPHY:

Aldrich, Robert. *France and the South Pacific since 1940.* 1994.
Connell, John. *New Caledonia or Independent Kanaky?* 1989.
Logan, Leanne, and Geert Cole. *New Caledonia.* 1997.
Spencer, Michael, ed. *New Caledonia: Issues in Nationalism and Dependency.* 1988.

Kanuris

Kanowris; Kanouris; Kanourys; Kole; Siratas; Bornouans; Beri-beri

POPULATION: Approximately (2002e) 6,135,000 Kanuris in the Lake Chad basin of north-central Africa. The majority, numbering 4.9 million, live in northeastern Nigeria in the states of Borno and Yobe. Other sizable populations are the 675,000 in adjacent areas of Chad, 525,000 in Niger, and 75,000 in Cameroon. Outside the Lake Chad basin the largest community, about 20,000, are in western Sudan.

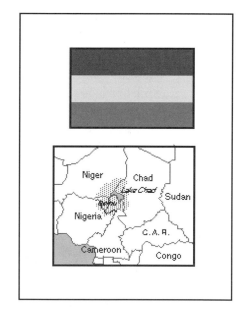

THE KANURI HOMELAND: The Kanuri homeland occupies the plains in the huge, shallow basin of Lake Chad in west-central Africa. The basin is lined with clay and sand sedments; it is rimmed by the Oubangui Plateau to the south and the vast Biu Plateau to the west. The lake is surrounded by the *firki*, the black cotton swamps and marshy areas that are impassable during the rainy season. Most of the Kanuris, about two-thirds, live in small villages, although urbanization is accelerating. Kanem, in Chad, forms the prefectures of Kanem and Lac. *Kanem*: 52,834 sq. mi.—136,840 sq. km, (2002e) 602,000—Kanembu 89%, Baguirmi 7%, other Chadians 4%. Bornu, the Kanuri heartland, lies in northeastern Nigeria, making up the states of Borno and Yobe, the latter separated from Borno in 1991. *Bornu (Borno-Yobe/Kanowra)*: 46,636 sq. mi.—120,818 sq. km, (2002e) 6,858,000—Kanuris 71%, Fulanis 11%, Hausas* 6%, Margis 3%, Shuwa Arabs 3%, other Nigerians, 6%. The Kanuri capital and major cultural center is Maiduguri, often called Yerwa, (2002e) 983,000. The other important center in Nigeria is Damaturu, the capital of Yobe, (2002e) 225,000. The major cultural centers of the Kanembu Kanuris in Chad are Mao, (2002e) 17,000, and Bol (2002e) 10,000. The center of the Manga Kanuris of Niger is Diffa, (2002e) 23,000.

FLAG: The Kanuri national flag, the flag of the national movement, is a horizontal tricolor of blue, yellow, and green, representing the sky, the land, and the water of Lake Chad.

PEOPLE AND CULTURE: The Kanuris are thought to be descended from early Berber tribes, with later admixtures of Arabs, black Africans and other Saharan peoples. Often quite fair, the Kanuris prize light skin color and Arabic facial features. The name of Bornu, the traditional Kanuri heartland in northeastern Nigeria, is said to mean "Home of the Berbers." The Kanuris, calling themselves Kanowri, form a cluster of 11 closely related groups in five countries. The major ethnic divisions are the Yerwa, Manga, and Kanembu, each having a number of subgroups. The Kanuris are more closely related to the peoples of North Africa than to the inhabitants of the neighboring areas in central Africa. The Muslim Kanuris are united by culture, language, and over a thousand years of shared history. Although the Kanuris no longer control the great wealth generated by the caravan routes, the royal and aristocratic classes are still highly respected and dominate Kanuri society. The Kanuri language, culture, and history are distinctive and unique in Africa, including Islamic law and politics, extended households, and rural-urban distinctions. Kanuri cultural identity remains very strong in all areas, as exemplified by a complex cuisine, the hairstyles of the Kanuri women, and the identification with ruling dynasties, whose names and exploits are known to all. Kanuri society is stratified into several distinct classes. "Beri-beri," the Hausa name for the Kanuri nation, is considered derogatory. About a quarter of the Kanuris are urban, living in towns of 10,000 or more population.

LANGUAGE AND RELIGION: The Kanuri language is classified as belonging to the Saharan branch of the Nilo-Saharan language family. Over many centuries the language has added borrowings from Arabic, Hausa, and other neighboring languages. The language is divided into several closely related dialects—Kanembu in the north and east, Manga in the west and northwest, and Yerwa the southwest and south—each further divided into numerous subdialects. The language is written in the Ajami script, a modified Arabic alphabet. The literary language is based on the dialect spoken around Maiduguri. Kanuri is of the few languages of sub-Saharan Africa to have developed a precolonial literary tradition. The language has the largest number of speakers in the Nilo-Saharan language group, which stretches from northeastern Nigeria to central Sudan. Most Kanuris speak Arabic or Hausa as a second language, and most Kanuris in Nigeria can speak some Hausa.

The Kanuris are mostly Sunni Muslims but retain many pre-Islamic traditions and customs. Birth, naming, marriage, death, and burial all have their ceremonies, which involve traditional rituals and readings from the Koran. The majority of the Kanuris adhere to the Malikite code of Islamic law. Traditional and Islamic holidays mark the days of the year and give Kanuri life meaning and structure. Some superstitions are also still practiced. Charms and amulets are worn; charms ensure successful pregnancies and keep the ghosts of the dead from haunting descendants. In August 2000 Islamic Shari'a law was adopted in Borno state.

NATIONAL HISTORY: The Chad basin contains the earliest evidence of hominid occupation yet found in western Africa, and most scholars believe that the region has been continuously settled since 500 B.C. Pastoral Berbers, driven from North Africa by the Arab invasion, occupied the region around Lake Chad in, probably, the late seventh century A.D. The Berbers later absorbed migrants from the area of the upper Nile River. A number of walled city-states existed east of the lake in the eighth century. According to Kanuri tradition, Sef ibn Dhi Yazan, the son of Dhu Yazan of Yemen, came to Kanem in the ninth century and assumed leadership of the Magoumi clan. He eventually extended his control to the various city-states of the region. The dynasty he founded in Kanem took his name—the Sefwa or Sayfwa dynasty. The leaders adopted the title *mai*, or king, and their subjects regarded them as divine.

Islam was brought to the region by Arab invaders and immigrants during the tenth century. Toward the end of the eleventh century, the Sefwa Mai Humai converted to Islam. Islam offered the Sefwa kings new ideas from Arabia and the Mediterranean, and it established Arabic as the language of administration. Many Kanuris resisted the new religion in favor of traditional beliefs and practices, leading to serious division among the peoples of the region.

Kanem became a center of Muslim learning and for the spread of Islam, eventually controlling all of the territory around Lake Chad. Its expansion peaked during the long reign of Mai Dunama Dabbalemi, from 1221–59. Dabbalemi devised a system whereby military commanders held authority over the peoples they conquered. This system helped to extend Kanem's borders across much of central Africa.

By tradition the region of Bornu, west of the lake, was bestowed on the Sefwa heir to rule during his apprenticeship. In 1386, however, Kanem fell to nomadic invaders, and the center of the state shifted west to Bornu; thousands of Kanembu refugees followed Mai Umar Idrismi there. Over time, the mixture of the Kanembu and the Bornu peoples created a new Kanuri nation and language. From Bornu the resurgent Kanuri in time reconquered Kanem and created a powerful empire known as Kanem-Bornu. At the height of its power, in the sixteenth and seventeenth centuries, the Sefwa dynasty of Kanem-Bornu ruled vast territories in present-day Nigeria, Niger, Chad, Cameroon, and Sudan.

Kanem-Bornu reached the height of its power under Mai Idris Aluma in the late sixteenth century. Idris Aluma is credited with acquiring firearms from the Turks in North Africa. He is revered as a national hero and remembered for his military skills, administrative reforms, and Islamic piety. One Kanuri epic poem extols his victories in 330 wars and more than 1,000 battles. His innovations included fortified military camps, a scorched-earth tactic wherein soldiers burned everything in their path, and the use of armor for both horses and riders. Aluma introduced a number of legal and administrative reforms based on Islamic law and sponsored the construction of many mosques.

The Kanuri empire, straddling the major caravan routes between western Africa and the Mediterranean coast, grew rich on trade, particularly slaves shipped north to the Mediterranean. Muslims were forbidden to take other Muslims as slaves—one of the reasons for the rapid spread of Islam in sub-Saharan Africa during the eighteenth and nineteenth centuries.

Muslim Fulani, having conquered the states of the Hausas to the west, invaded the declining Kanuri empire in 1809. The Kanuri turned back the invasion, but two years later the empire collapsed in a civil war begun by Kanembu warriors who had come to Bornu to fight the Fulani. In 1814 the Sefwa ruler regained control of Bornu and the western territories, and built a new capital at Kukwa, in present-day Nigeria. The resurgent Kanuri emirate was visited by a British expedition in 1823. Impressed by the sophisticated state, the British established formal diplomatic relations with Kanem-Bornu in the 1830s.

Civil war again erupted in 1835 and culminated with the overthrow of the Sefwa dynasty in 1846. The sense of continuity, so important to the Kanuri, was not lost with the succession of a new dynasty; however, a series of weak rulers in the late nineteenth century seriously undermined the state.

In 1890 the Kanuri king, threatened by the "Napoleon of Africa"— Rabeh Zobier, a Sudanese ex-slave turned conqueror—appealed to the European powers for assistance. While the Europeans negotiated for advantage, Rabeh advanced and in 1893 destroyed the Kanuri capital, Kukwa, a city of 60,000 inhabitants. After consolidating his control of Kanem-Bornu, Rabeh founded a new capital at Dikwa in Bornu. Rabeh's empire expanded into areas claimed by the European powers and finally met defeat at the hands of a multinational European military force in 1900. In 1902 the European powers divided the empire's territories. The British took Bornu and added it to British Nigeria, the French absorbed Kanem into French Equatorial Africa, and the Germans added most of the Dikwa region to their colony of Kamerun.

Bornu formed a part of the region of Northern Nigeria, a region dominated by the more numerous Hausa-Fulani peoples. The British abolished slavery and took control of all decision making, but they left most of the traditional social system intact. The region became the center of growing Kanuri nationalism in the 1950s. Neglected by the regional government, Bornu remained underdeveloped. Its economy the least developed and the literacy rate the lowest in all of Nigeria. Fearing domination by the Hausa-Fulani in a projected independent Nigeria, nationalists formed the Bornu Youth Movement (BYM) in 1954. Initial aims included separation from

Nigeria's Northern Region, but more radical views included the reunification of the Kanuri-populated territories of the former Kanem-Bornu empire.

Nigeria, granted independence in 1960, emerged as an unstable confederation of three regions, with Bornu included in the Hausa-Fulani-dominated Northern Region. In an effort to integrate the independence-minded Kanuri into the new state, the government constructed a railroad to Maiduguri in 1964. The Kanuris mainly supported local politicians, and the majority rejected the pan-Islamic movement supported by the Hausas and Fulanis of Northern Nigeria.

The Kanuri were gradually drawn into the growing interethnic conflicts in Nigeria of the 1960s. When rioting against the southern Ibos* erupted in the Hausa states in May and June 1966, Bornu, however, remained calm. The military coup of July 1966 led to an exodus of Kanuris from Lagos and southern Nigeria and also from Kaduna, the capital of Northern Nigeria. Kanuri nationalist agitation, only temporarily interrupted by the secession of Biafra and the civil war of 1967–70, continued to dominate regional politics.

The Nigerian government attempted to satisfy the country's numerous ethnic groups by dividing the regions into ethnic states. A Kanuri state, called Borno, created in 1976, only whetted nationalist appetites. In November 1976 mass demonstrations erupted, demanding immediate independence. Hundreds of armed men tried to force the new Borno state government to establish a separatist Kanuri government. The nationalists outlined a plan for the independence of "Greater Kanowra," which would eventually include historical Bornu in Nigeria, plus the prefectures of Lac and Kanem of Chad, the southern districts of Diffa and Zinder departments of Niger, and the northern districts of Extrême Nord Province of Cameroon. The region claimed by the militants had an area of 205,529 sq. mi. (532,460 sq. km) and a population of over nine million. The uprising, crushed by Nigerian troops, was ultimately blamed on Kanuris from outside Nigeria, particularly the numerous Kanembu refugees from the east who had fled Chad's civil war.

Muslim fundamentalism spread through the region in the early 1980s, with serious religious rioting in 1982–83. Muslim extremists followers of Alhaji Mohammadu Marwa, the self-proclaimed prophet of Islam, rioted in Maiduguri, leaving hundreds dead and much of the city devastated. Rioting again broke out in 1983, and there were reports that nationalists were using the upheavals to pressure the Nigerian government for larger subsidies. The disturbances, with nationalist overtones, continued sporadically until 1989.

The end of the Cold War, the reunification of Germany, and Africa's slow turn toward multiparty democracy fueled a resurgence of Kanuri nationalism in 1991–92. In March 1992, protests paralyzed Maiduguri when the Nigerian government attempted to send jailed Kanembus back to Chad, where they faced persecution. The protests marked the beginning of a new militancy and unity among the divided Kanuri, whose strong sense of identity has not been diminished by partition or the imposition of artificial international borders.

The Kanuri homeland, the former Bornu emirate, is viewed by the Kanuris as a political entity, and its present political disunion a result of colonialism. Kanuri identity is still largely based on precolonial values, traditions, and ideology. The *shehu*, the Kanuri king, remains both the political and religious leader of all the Kanuris. Social organization emphasizes the importance of the nuclear family and the supremacy of the father figure, which is extended through the social hierarchy to the *shehu*.

In 1998–99, many Kanembu refugees from Chad began to return from Nigeria. The voters in Chad approved a new constitution for the country in 1996, and with relative peace many refugees felt able to return to their traditional homeland on the eastern and northern shores of shrinking Lake Chad. Ties among the various Kanuri groups, although divided by international borders, remained strong due to family and kinship ties.

The Kanuris continue to categorize the population of their homeland in three classes with themselves at the top, the non-Kanuris in the middle, and at the bottom the tribes from which they formerly took slaves. The Kanuri ethnic identity, reinforced by their physical differences from the surrounding peoples, remains the focus of Kanuri loyalty. They have survived upheavals, wars, economic recessions, conquests, colonization, and combination of the tribal elites of newly independent African states without losing their special identity.

SELECTED BIBLIOGRAPHY:

Asiwaju, A.T. *Partitioned Africans: Ethnic Relations across Africa's International Borders.* 1985.
Benton, P.A. *Languages and People of Bornu.* 1968.
Cohen, Ronald. *The Kanuri of Borno.* 1987.
Koslow, Philip. *Kanem-Borno: 1,000 Years of Splendor.* 1995.

Karabakhis

Karabachis; Artsakhis; Artsakh Armenians; Eastern Armenians; Azeri Armenians

POPULATION: Approximately (2002e) 223,000 Karabakhis in the Caucasus region, mostly concentrated in the Nagorno Karabakh region, called Artsakh by the Armenians, of Azerbaijan. Other large Karabakhi communities live in Armenia, mainly in Yerevan, Russia, western Europe, and North America.

THE KARABAKHI HOMELAND: The Karabakhi homeland, officially called Nagorno-Karabakh, occupies a mountainous region around the valley of the Kura River in western Azerbaijan. The environment varies from flat plains in the valleys of the Kura River to the peaks of the Karabakh Range. The section is separated from the Republic of Armenia by some 15 miles of Azeri territory, which has been under Karabakhi and Armenian occupation since 1993. Nagorno-Karabakh was declared independent as the Republic of Artsakh in January 1992. Artsakh's status remains unsettled. Officially the area forms an autonomous district of the Republic of Azerbaidzhan. *Republic of Artsakh (Nagorno-Karabakh):* 1,699 sq. mi.—4,402 sq. km, (2002e) 203,000—Karabakhis (Karabakhi Armenians) 93%, Assyrians* 5%, Greeks, Kurds* 2%. The capital and major cultural center of the Karabakhis is Stepanakert, called Xankändi by the Azeris, (2002e) 63,000.

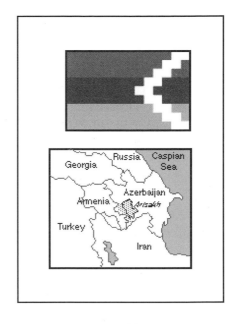

FLAG: The flag of the Karabakhis, the official flag of the breakaway republic, is a horizontal tricolor of red, blue, and orange with a white, step triangle on the fly.

PEOPLE AND CULTURE: The Karabakhis are a division of the ancient Armenian nation, which forms a separate branch of the Caucasian peoples. The Karabakhis, also known as Artsakhis or Eastern Armenians, are a mountain people, ethnically and culturally part of the larger Armenian nation, but separated by centuries of history. Their highland culture, based on their long isolation, incorporates many Azeri, Persian, and Turkish influences not found in Armenia proper. Many Karabakhis, while acknowl-

901

edging their position as part of the larger Armenian nation, like to stress their distinct history and dialect as the basis of their small national group. Relations between the Karabakhis and the Armenians of the Armenian heartland in the Republic of Armenia are not always cordial. Armenians always called the Karabakhis in Azerbaijan Shurtvats, meaning turned upside down or stupid.

LANGUAGE AND RELIGION: The most easterly of the traditional Armenian groups, the Karabakhis speak a dialect of Armenian, the only surviving example of the Thraco-Phrygian group of the Indo-European languages. The language has developed from a very early form of Indo-European and the alphabet developed around A.D. 400. The uniqueness of the alphabet and language, along with the Armenian religion, have allowed the culture to survive for 3,000 years in the face of near constant occupation and foreign rule.

The majority of the Karabakhis adhere to the independent Armenian Orthodox religion, with a small minority, called Khemsils, who practice a form of Sunni Islam. The religion, an integral part of the Karabakh highland culture, is one of the major features of the area. The Karabakhis tend to be more conservative and religious than the Armenians of Armenia proper, having embraced their religion in the face of centuries of Muslim threats and pressure.

NATIONAL HISTORY: According to Armenian legends, Noah's Ark landed on Mount Ararat, the symbol of Armenian nationhood, and the Armenians claim descent from Noah through Haik, and call their historic homeland Haikakan. Known to the world as a separate people since very ancient times, the Armenian nation was the first to adopt Christianity as the national religion in A.D. 303, with their independent church established in 491. Sovereign Armenian states, with varying borders are always prey to stronger neighbors, have existed for only short periods during their long history.

The Karabakh highland region was separated from Armenia proper in 387, during the division of the Armenian kingdom. In the seventh century Karabakh fell to the invading Arabs, remaining under Muslim Arab rule for three centuries. In the eleventh century Karabakh came under the rule of the Bagratid kings of Georgia, who held it until the Mongol Invasion in the thirteenth century.

After repeated rebellions, independence, and reconquest, the last of the Armenian kingdoms was conquered by the Arab Mamelukes in 1375. The only remaining autonomous pockets of Armenians were in Karabakh and Zangezour, both in eastern Armenia. The Ottoman Turks conquered western Armenia in the fifteenth century, while the Persians took control of the eastern territories. In 1603, Shah Abbas of Persia allowed local rule in Karabakh under five *meliks* or kings. These five small states were later joined, but not supplanted, by a Muslim khanate, which survived until the

Russian conquest. Suffering persecution and discrimination under Muslim rule, the Karabakhis welcomed the advance of the Christian Russians into the Transcaucasus. In 1813, the Russians took the area and in 1828 it was incorporated into the Russian Empire as Nagorno-Karabakh (Highland Karabakh).

Nagorno-Karabakh formed part of Russian Armenia, where the Armenian national movement was founded in 1840. Demands for the unification of the Armenian lands under Russian, Persian, and Turkish rule fueled the national movement in the nineteenth century. In Turkey, Armenian nationalism sparked stern countermeasures, including horrible massacres and deportations that began in the 1890s and continued up to World War I. The political mobilization of the Armenians also worried the Russian authorities. One of their responses was to provoke a conflict between Armenians and Azeris, the so-called Tatar-Armenian war of 1905–7.

Divided Armenia became a battleground when war began in 1914, the vast majority of the Armenians supporting Christian Russia. Thousands of refugees, fleeing renewed massacres and deportation in Ottoman territory during the war, settled in the mountainous Karabakh area away from the front lines and under the protection of the Christian Russians.

Revolution in Russia in 1917 led to the collapse of civil government. A local government, the Assembly of Karabagh Armenians, took control of the highland region, which was immediately disputed by Azeri and Armenian nationalists. The independence of the Transcaucasian states of Armenia and Azerbaidzhan in 1918 intensified the conflict. Attempts at a federation to include Armenia, Azerbaidzhan, and Georgia failed due to the bitter rivalries between Armenia and Azerbaidzhan, particularly rival claims to the Karabakh region. The region, at the end of the Russian Civil War, fell to the victorious Red Army and was incorporated into the new Soviet Union.

At first, the Soviets returned Nagorno-Karabakh to Armenia, but in 1921 the authorities arbitrarily redrew the Caucasian borders, leaving traditionally Armenian territories, Karabakh, Ganja, and Nakichevan to Azerbaijan. In 1923, Stalin placed the region under the control of Soviet Azerbaidzhan as an autonomous province cut off from Armenia by Azeri territory. To justify its control over the region, the Azeri government produced evidence that an Azeri khanate had occupied the region prior to the Russian takeover in 1813.

Throughout the period of Soviet rule, the question of Karabakh remained an issue of Armenian nationalism. Tensions rose in the early 1960s, and in 1968 clashes broke out between Karabakhis and Azeris in Stepanakert, the capital of the enclave. Nagorno-Karabakh had an Armenian-speaking majority of 74% in 1979, but received no Armenian language television and had no Armenian institutions of higher learning. As early as

1974 Armenian nationalists were calling for the unification of the Armenian lands.

Decades of Soviet rule tended to blunt the antagonism between the Armenians and Azeris, but in the more relaxed atmosphere of the late 1980s the Karabakhis began to call for reunification with Armenia and an end to the Azeri domination of their homeland. In early 1988, mass demonstrations erupted in Nagorno-Karabakh and Armenia in support of demands for the transfer of the enclave to Armenian control. In February 1988, the Soviet government refused to consider a transfer of sovereignty, but responded with proposals for economic and political development schemes in the enclave. Unsatisfied, on 12 July 1988, the parliament of Nagorno-Karabakh voted to secede from Azerbaidzhan, a move denounced by both the Azeri and Soviet governments.

To most Armenians, Karabakh was the most vital issue of the *glasnost* era. To the Armenians, Azeri control of Karabakh represented the continuing subjugation of Armenians by Turks. Armenians tend to see Azeris as ethnic Turks, who were responsible for the Armenian genocide during World War I. Ethnic tensions escalated rapidly and in November 1988 turned deadly when ethnic clashes left 19 dead in the first open ethnic conflict in the Soviet Union since the end of strict Soviet control. In early 1989, the Soviet government changed the status of the enclave and placed it under direct rule from Moscow, a move that satisfied neither side; after several months Nagorno-Karabakh returned to Azeri control as fighting intensified in the region. On 1 December 1989, the Armenian government declared the region part of a unified Armenian republic.

The Azeri military subjected Stepanakert to months of bombardment in 1991 but failed to defeat the local militia, augmented by volunteers from Armenia. On 30 August 1991, Azerbaijan, including Nagorno-Karabakh, was declared an independent republic, followed by Armenian independence in September. The independence of the two republics intensified the conflict over the Nagorno-Karabakh enclave and fighting spread across a long front from Stepanakert to the Armenian border.

By late 1991, the Karabakhis had taken control of the enclave, and in December the last of the former Soviet troops withdrew. A referendum in Nagorno-Karabakh on 10 December 1991 showed overwhelming support, some 99%, for separation from Azerbaidzhan and on 6 January 1992 the enclave's leaders declared Artsakh an independent republic. Serious fighting engulfed the region as the Azeris attacked, forcing the inhabitants to live in shelters and cellars during intense shelling. An economic blockade was imposed and most contact with Armenia was cut. Supplies were flown in by a hazardous helicopter airlift from Yerevan, the capital of the new Armenian republic.

In 1993, Armenian and Karabakhi forces overran the Azeri territories that divided the enclave from Armenia, driving over 600,000 Azeri refugees from the area and taking control of the important land corridors that connect the beleaguered enclave to its only source of aid and supplies in Armenia. The Karabakhi forces looted and burned the Azeri villages, making the return of Azeri refugees very difficult. In 1994, a cease-fire was negotiated, which is still being observed. The fighting that ended in 1994 took more than 35,000 lives and left hundreds of thousand injured and homeless.

The war between the Karabakhis, aided by the Republic of Armenia, and the Azeris has continued sporadically since 1988. Talks over ending the conflict have floundered as the Azeri government refuses to negotiate with the government of Nagorno-Karabakh. The Azeris continue to demand the return of all territory in both Nagorno-Karabakh and the surrounding occupied territories as a precondition to negotiations, which the Karabakhis have refused. The conflict remains a stalemate of fruitless negotiations and intermittent shelling. There seems to be little common ground for a compromise and the Karabakhis want to use their territorial gains to secure their independence and to maintain their links to Armenia. In 1997, the Armenians began construction of an asphalt road straight through to Stepanakert. The conflict still threatens to destabilize the region between the Black Sea and the Caspian Sea.

On the surface, Karabakh and Armenia are now inseparable. They use the same currency and traffic flows back and forth, often carrying Armenian soldiers doing military service. However, the dour highlanders of Karabakh, with their own government, their own army, their own politics, and speaking in their thick accents, have demonstrated that they will not be pushed around by their cousins in Yerevan. Since 1995, the Armenian government has accepted the wishes of the Karabakhis to be independent. The situation, in 2002, is one of no peace, but no war while the Karabakhis and the Armenians control over 20% of Azerbaijan's national territory, having displaced about 1 million Azeri refugees, who were forced out or fled the area.

In 2000 the military stalemate continued in the region, but a return to war recedes with each passing year. An economic upturn in both Armenia and Azerbaijan would be threatened by renewed violence, but negotiations on the Nagorno-Karabakh issue again broke down in late 2000. The Karabakhis continue to reject any agreement that would compromise their bid for independence from Muslim Azerbaijan.

The foreign minister of Karabakh, Naira Melkumian, visited Vienna in July 2000 to attend a meeting of the Organization of Security and Co-operation in Europe (OSCE), which was attempting to overcome the deadlock in the peace process in Nagorno-Karabakh. The OSCE was holding a three-day extended session to evaluate the results of visits to both Azerbaijan and Armenia. Melkumian reiterated the view that the problem would not be settled immediately, but that negotiations must continue or war would again break out.

The dispute over Nagorno-Karabakh saps the strength of both Armenia and Azerbaijan, but a negotiated settlement is difficult. The Armenians refuse to abandon the Karabakhis after supporting their bid for independence from Azerbaijan since 1988. The Azeris, with more than 500,000 of their people from Nagorno-Karabakh and western Azerbaijan in refugee camps, has refused to discuss any settlement other than a return to the Soviet-era borders. Talks between the parties resumed in June 2000 in Moscow, and in July 2000 in Yalta and New York. The talks continued in Moscow, but again broke down in November 2000.

The Karabakhis continue to dismiss any plan or suggestion that would put their homeland under direct Azeri control. Most support a proposal advanced in late 1998 on the creation by Azerbaijan and the unrecognized Artsakh Republic of a "common state." The Azeris have already rejected that proposal, because of economic and political aversion to it, along with others put forward during negotiations in 2000.

In April 2001, the first meeting between the presidents of Azerbaijan and Armenia took place in the United States, giving new hope to a peaceful settlement to the long-running territorial dispute. The Karabakhis protested their lack of representation at the meeting, but relied on the Armenians to look after their interests. The main parts of the agreement would return 6 of the 7 regions they took from the Azeris during the long series of skirmishes and battles, while Karabakh and the adjacent Lachin region that connects it to Armenia would be granted the status of an autonomous republic within Azerbaijan.

SELECTED BIBLIOGRAPHY:

Denber, Rachel, and Robert Goldman. *Bloodshed in the Caucasus: Escalation of the Armed Conflict in Nagorno Karabakh*. 1992.

Khorenats'i, Moses. *History of the Armenians*. 1978.

Lang, David Marshall. *The Armenians*. 1988.

Walker, Christopher. *Armenia: The Survival of a Nation*. 1990.

Karachais

Karachays; Karachevs; Karacaylars; Qarachaili; Kiarchal; Alans

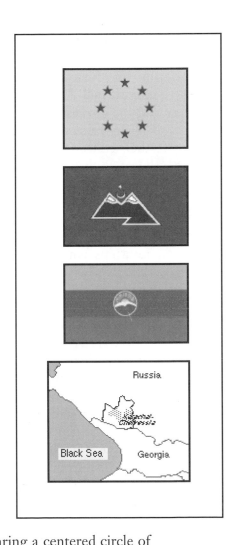

POPULATION: Approximately (2002e) 164,000 Karachais in Russia, mostly living in the Karachai region of the Karachai-Cherkess Republic, a member state of the Russian Federation. Outside Russia there are Karachai populations in Turkey, Western Europe, Central Asia, and North America.

THE KARACHAI HOMELAND: The Karachai homeland lies in southern European Russia, a rugged area of foothills and canyons in the northwestern part of the North Caucasus highlands. The region is rugged and mountainous, except the regions traversed by the valleys of the upper Kuban River and its tributaries, the Taberda, Zelenchuk, and Aksut. The Karachais' highland valleys are called the Dombai. The region has no official status but forms the southern districts, known as Karachai, of the Karachai-Cherkess Republic. The division of the republic has not been recognized by the Russian government. *Karachai Republic (Qarachaj Respublika)*: 3,821 sq. mi.—9,896 sq. km, (2002e) 205,000—Karachais 80%, Nogais* 10%, Russians and Kuban Cossacks* 6%, Cherkess* 2%, Ukrainians 1%, others 1%. The Karachai capital and major cultural center is Karachayevsk, called Qarachajscahar by the Karachais, (2002e) 22,000.

FLAG: The Karachai national flag, the flag of the unrecognized republic, is a yellow field bearing a centered circle of eight red five-pointed stars. The flag of the major nationalist organization, the Congress of Muslims of Karachay, is a blue field bearing two centered black mountains, white-capped and outlined in yellow, below a yellow crescent moon and five-pointed yellow star. The flag of the Republic of Karachai-Cherkess is a horizontal tricolor of blue, green, and red bearing a centered yellow circle around a white-capped mountain below a rising yellow sun with 13 yellow rays.

PEOPLE AND CULTURE: The Karachai are a Turkic people who have traditionally inhabited the Dombai since time immemorial. The origin of their name is disputed; some scholars believe that it means "people living near a mighty river," since *kara* means "strong" or "mighty," while *chay* is "water," "drink," or "river." Others think the name comes from Karcha, the legendary ancestor of all the Karachai. The Karachais are believed to be descended from tribes settled in the region since the Bronze Age, with later admixtures of Alans, Bulgars, and Kipchaks. The Kuban Bulgars and Kipchak tribes were driven into the Caucasus Mountains by the Mongols in the thirteenth century. The Karachais, until World War II, did not have a well-developed sense of nationhood, due to the geographic isolation of the dozens of tribes that make up the Karachai nation. Patriarchal clan loyalty remained more important than the sense of being Karachais until their collective deportation in 1943. The four clan groups are the Adurkhay, Budian, Nawruz, and Trama; loyalty to one of them remains a prominent feature of Karachai society. Each family is still led by a family council, which consists of the men of the oldest generation and the eldest woman. The senior woman plays a significant role in upholding the family pride and honor, as hospitality is extremely important to Karachai relationships. An estimated 62% of the Karachais live in rural areas.

LANGUAGE AND RELIGION: The Karachai language, the Karachai dialect of the Karachai-Balkar language, is Ponto-Caspian language of the western Turkic language group. The two languages are nearly identical and share a literary language. It is spoken as the first language by about 97% of the Karachai population, and its use remains very high and a matter of pride. Many Karachais speak Russian as a second language, with smaller numbers speaking Turkish or other Caucasian languages.

Sunni Islam of the Hanafi school is the official religion of the Karachais, and each village has its own mosque, but the Karachais remain less devout than some neighboring peoples and have not experienced the fervent Islamic revivals that other Muslim peoples have undergone in recent years. Forbidden from openly practicing their Islamic religion for many decades, they often conducted religious ceremonies and funerals secretly, but a large portion of the population embraced secularism. Karachai women enjoy greater independence than those of most Muslim peoples, and the traditional dietary restrictions, including the eating of pork, are not generally observed. Many traditional pagan beliefs have been intermingled with their religious rituals. The Karachais believe in evil spirits and often perform pagan sacrifices and rituals. Many Karachais, even atheists, observe the major Islamic festivals such as Ramadan and Eid. In 1999–2000 Wahhabite fundamentalists were active in the region, reportedly arming and preparing for battle against secular civil authorities and the moderate religious leaders.

NATIONAL HISTORY: The origins of the Karachais are unknown. There are many theories, but according to Karachai legend, they are descended from the ancient inhabitants of the Dombai. Archeologists have found bronze and iron tools and gold ornaments dating back to the first millennium B.C. They had a highly developed culture and extensive ties to many parts of the Mediterranean and Asia. The culture of the region, known as the Koban culture, is still mostly a mystery, with little known of the region before the coming of the steppe and nomad tribes who intermingled with the local inhabitants.

Alans controlled the area from the first to the fourteenth centuries, while Bulgars and Kipchaks also migrated to the region, mostly during the Mongol invasions of the lowlands. The mixture of the Kipchaks, Bulgars, and Alans in the twelfth century is considered the beginning of the distinct Karachai nation. Kipchak tribes from the Crimean Peninsula, driven from that territory during upheavals in the fourteenth century and migrating south along the shore of the Black Sea, mixed extensively with the earlier Cherkess, and finally settled in the mountains, where they merged with the local tribes. The tribes were converted to Christianity in the tenth century; there are Alan churches in the region dating from the tenth and eleventh centuries.

The Karachai clans became vassals in the sixteenth century of the Kabards,* who introduced Islam. The Karachais attribute their conversion to Ishak Efendi, an eighteenth-century Kabard mullah. In the seventeenth century, the Ottoman Turks began to exert influence in the region through their vassals the Crimean Tatars.* The Karachais resisted Turkish and Tatar encroachments on their territory, but in 1733 the Karachai homeland came under direct Turkish rule.

Russians expanded into the territory of the declining Ottoman Empire in the eighteenth century and reached the Dombai in 1774. The Russians took control of the Karachai region in 1828 and in 1829 forced the Ottoman Turks to cede the Caucasian territories. Resistance to Christian Russian rule erupted in a long and savage guerrilla war that continued until 1864. Thousands of Karachai-Balkar moved south to Turkish territory. Those that remained under Russian rule took up arms against the tsarist authorities at every opportunity. Many more left the region after a land reform of the 1870s gave much Karachai land to tsarist officials.

The Muslims of the Russian Empire, their loyalty suspect, were exempted from military duty when World War I began in 1914. Though a majority of the Muslim peoples openly favored Muslim Turkey, the Russian government, desperate for manpower, began conscripting Muslims in 1916. Muslim labor units sent to the front came into contact with new revolutionary and nationalist ideas, which took hold as Russia slipped into chaos. The Karachai and Balkar conscripts deserted and returned home after the revolution of February 1917. As civil government collapsed, a Karachai-Balkar national committee took control of the Karachai and Balkaria. The national committee gave its support to Russia's new Provisional Government, which vaguely promised autonomy for Russia's minority peoples.

The Karachais and the Islamic peoples of the North Caucasus attempted to unite in cooperative independence out of opposition to the antireligious stance of the Bolsheviks, who took power in Russia in October 1917. Threatened by local Bolsheviks and rival political groups, the Karachai-Balkar leaders declared Karachai-Balkaria an autonomous state on 18 May 1918. Forced into an alliance with the White forces fighting the Bolsheviks in the expanding Russian Civil War, the Karachai withdrew to mountain strongholds when the White resistance collapsed in 1920.

A detachment of the Ninth Soviet Army invaded the region in support of an uprising by local Bolsheviks, mostly ethnic Russians. The Soviets overthrew the separatist government, whose members they called "bourgeois nationalist exploiters." The new Soviet government, bent on destroying any sense of North Caucasus unity or resistance, separated the related Karachais and Balkars as part of a divide-and-conquer strategy. A separate Karachai national territory was created in 1920.

The religious life of the Karachais also came under attack; most mosques and religious schools forcibly closed during the collectivization of the region. Karachai resistance to collectivization led in 1930 to open rebellion, which was brutally crushed. Over 3,000 rebels were executed. The extent of continued opposition to Soviet collectivization and the Soviet's antireligious programs was shown by a purge of over 1,500 Karachai Communist Party members for "counterrevolutionary" activities.

During World War II, a German offensive drove into the Caucasus in mid-1942. The invaders were welcomed by many Karachais as liberators from hated Soviet rule, and thousands of volunteers joined the Turkish League, an anticommunist military unit fighting as an ally of the Germans. Encouraged by the occupation forces, Karachai nationalists convened a committee and formed a national government, under Kadi Kairamukov. Supported by the Germans, the national committee declared the region, including Balkaria, independent of the Soviet Union on 11 August 1942. The new government moved to restore the region's traditional social and religious structure, opening mosques and decollectivizing rural life.

Horrified by German brutality, however, the republican government increasingly distanced itself from German sponsorship and attempted to create a neutral state allied to Turkey. By early 1943 over a dozen guerrilla bands had taken up arms against the German occupation force. Karachai supporters of the pro-German separatist government often faced other Karachais fighting with the guerrilla groups in the mountains.

The sovereign Karachai-Balkar state collapsed with the Soviet reconquest of the North Caucasus in October 1943. Joseph Stalin, the Soviet dictator, accused the entire Karachai nation of treason and participation in Nazi atrocities. In November 1943 the 75,000 Karachais, including the families of thousands of soldiers fighting with the Red Army, were shipped east in closed cattle cars. The Soviet guards dumped the deportees in the Central Asian wastes, often without provisions or shelter. Thousands of Karachais perished from exposure, hunger, and disease. In 1956 the survivors were officially rehabilitated and returned to their Caucasian homes. In 1957 the Karachai-Cherkess Autonomous Oblast was reestablished. All contact between the Karachais and Balkars, except cultural exchanges, was forbidden.

A serious nuclear accident at a local power plant in 1964 contaminated the waters of Lake Karachay and forced the evacuation of tens of thousands of people from the region. The incident, now thought to have been considerably worse than the 1986 Chernobyl accident, was covered up; little news of it leaked out to the West. In 2000, about 10,000 families evacuated from the contaminated area were still living in makeshift housing built over 35 years ago. Work on filling in radioactive Lake Karachay was suspended in November 1998 due to lack of funds.

The Soviet liberalization of the late 1980s slowly penetrated the Caucasus Mountains. The Karachais began to mobilize, but due to their somewhat weak collective identity, they were slow to develop a modern nationalist movement. Following the disintegration of the Soviet Union in 1991, the leaders of the autonomous province they shared with the Cherkess unilaterally declared the region a full republic of the newly constituted Russian Federation. The change in the region's status, recognized by the government in Moscow, allowed the numerically superior and increasingly nationalistic Karachais to dominate it. Renewed contact with the closely related Balkars, forbidden for over three decades, aided the cultural and national revival of the small nation.

The Soviet collapse also stimulated demands for separation from the hybrid region, Karachai-Cherkessia, into which they had been forced under communist rule. In November 1991 Karachai nationalists rallied in the city of Karachayevsk demanding the restoration of autonomy for the Karachai republic lost during the Stalinist era, as part of the "complete rehabilitation" of the Karachai nation. The loss of power in the joint republic to an alliance of the Cherkess, Abaza,* Russians, and Cossacks stimulated the growth of Karachai nationalism.

In 1992 the Karachai leaders unilaterally withdrew their territory from the joint republic, a move that the Russian authorities have not recognized. Demands for the official unification of Karachai and Balkaria have so far been ignored by the Russian authorities, which has raised tension in the region, one of the least Russified areas of the North Caucasus. In July

1992, a congress of Karachai peoples held in Karachayevsk again called for a restoration of Karachi autonomy.

In October 1993, in official ceremonies and speeches, the Karachais marked the 50th anniversary of their deportation to Central Asia. Karachai leaders reiterated their demands for a separate Karachai state within the Russian Federation.

The Karachai perceive themselves as the victims of prejudicial treatment, particularly in respect to the job market and universities. They have been blocked from assuming socially or politically sensitive positions in their homeland. Karachai nationalists claim they will remain disenfranchised until they secure their separate autonomous state and achieve "complete rehabilitation" after the punishments in the Stalinist era.

In late 1993, the Russian government agreed to support the social and economic development of the Karachai nation. Negotiations were begun on restitution payments for individuals deported by Stalin in 1943. In mid-1994, an additional decree was issued on measures supporting the economic and cultural rehabilitation of the Karachais. Karachai officials negotiated agreements aimed at defusing growing political and ethnic tension in the region, in party by the formation of local and republican-level representative bodies.

The growth of Karachai nationalism increased conflict with the other national groups in the republic. In 1995 Cossacks in the region announced that they were forming a militia as a self-defense measure against armed gangs of Ingush,* Kabards, and Karachais, though violent ethnic conflict in the republic has been at a low level.

The Russian, Cossack, and Cherkess populations, in 1997, demanded the return of the Karachai-Cherkess Republic to the administrative control of Stavropol Kray as it had been prior to the Soviet collapse in 1991. The demand, which would place the Karachais once again under the Russian-dominated provincial government, has been vigorously resisted and is blamed for an increase in Karachai nationalism. Anti-Russian sentiment, always strong among the Karachais, remains an important part of the Karachai national movement.

Elections for the head of the government of the Republic of Karachay-Cherkessia were declared invalid in mid-1999 following serious clashes between supporters of the Karachai candidate, Gen. Vladimir Semenov, and the candidate supported by the Cherkess and Abaza in the republic, Stanislav Derev. The election hinged on the demands by the non-Karachai groups for a return of the republic to the authority of Stavropol Kray, of which it formed part until 1991. The Karachai candidate, Semenov, was finally declared head of state, but the decision set off serious clashes across the republic and renewed demands for the separation of the Cherkess and Abaza regions.

Violent confrontations between Karachais and Cossacks over land rights and Karachai demands for a separate national state began in February 2001 and continued sporadically throughout the year. Nationalists claim the growing violence in the republic can only be remedied by allowing the national groups to separate.

SELECTED BIBLIOGRAPHY:

Conquest, Robert. *The Nation Killers.* 1970.
Cornell, Svante E. *Small Nations and Great Powers: A Study of Ethnopolitical Conflict in the Caucasus.* 1999.
Smith, Sebastian. *Allah's Mountains.* 1997.
Tutuncu, Mehmet, ed. *The Turkic Peoples of the Caucasus.* 2001.

Karaims

Karaites; Karailar; Qara'im; Karajlars; Karaits; Karaylarin; Karaimi; Karaim Tatars

POPULATION: Approximately (2002e) 12,000 Karaims in eastern Europe, with another 4,000 in western Europe. Outside Europe there is a sizable community numbering over 15,000 in Israel, 5,000 in the United States, and smaller groups in Egypt, Turkey, and other parts of the Middle East. The total population of Karaims is difficult to estimate due to assimilation, a lack of census material, and the practice of registering as ethnic Russians or other groups for survival during the decades of Soviet rule. Traditional Karaim law forbids their being counted in census. Estimates of the total world population of Karaims ranges from just 8,000 to over 50,000.

THE KARAIM HOMELAND: The Karaim homeland lies in the countries of the former Soviet Union, concentrated in Lithuania, Crimea in the Ukraine, and in Russia. The major Karaim cultural centers are Trakai, called Trox by the Karaims, in Lithuania, and Halich, called Galich, near Lviv in Ukraine. There is also a sizable Karaim community in Vilnius, the Lithuanian capital.

FLAG: The flag of the Lithuanian Karaims is a white field bearing the Karaim coat-of-arms centered and two narrow pale blue stripes at the top and bottom.

PEOPLE AND CULTURE: The Karaims are an ethnoreligious group who call themselves by a Turkic name, Karajlar. In English they are often called Karaites. The question of the Jewishness of the Karaites divides the originally Arabic-speaking Karaites in Israel and California, who call themselves Karaite Jews, from their kin in Eastern Europe, and in the eastern United States, who call themselves Karaims and stress the independent national character of their community. Besides being a national minority, the Karaims represent an independent religion that separated from Judaism in the ninth century. The majority of the Karaims, estimated at 97%, live in big cities and their culture is now little different from the neighboring groups, but a revival that has taken hold since the collapse of the Soviet Union has ended the cultural and linguistic decline that seemed to spell the extinction of the small nation.

LANGUAGE AND RELIGION: The Karaim language is a Ponto-Caspian dialect of the western group of Turkic languages. Due to the dispersion of the small Karaim nation, the language is spoken in four major dialects, Eastern Karaim, Northwestern Karaim, Trakay, and Galits. Eastern Karaim is thought to be extinct. The spoken language is close to the languages spoken by the Karachais* and Kumyks.* The literary language is based on the Northwestern dialect. The Indo-European languages, Polish, Russian, and Lithuanian, have left deep vestiges in the vernacular Karaim spoken by the multilingual Karaims. Especially during the Soviet period, when no instruction was available in the national language, most Karaims adopted the language of neighboring peoples. Until the national revival of the 1990s, about 16% of the Karaims in Lithuania and Ukraine spoke Lithuanian as their first language, and another 12% spoke Russian. The Crimean Karaims, by the end of the nineteenth century, had mostly adopted the Crimean Tatar language and many had assimilated although they retained their religion. The written language now uses the Latin alphabet, as the Cyrillic used during the Soviet period evokes negative memories of oppression and forced Russification. In 1993, the Cyrillic characters used in Russia and Ukraine were replaced with the "European" alphabet.

Karaism is a religion based on Judaism in the same way as Christianity is an independent religion with a Jewish background. They are considered by some as a sect of Judaism as their religion is based exclusively on the Old Testament, but most Karaims see themselves as distinct from the Jews.* Karaism is claimed as the original form of Judaism that denies the human additions to the Torah such as the Rabbinical oral Talmud and the principle that rabbis are the sole authorities for interpreting the Bible. Karaims call other Jews by the name Rabbinites and see them somewhat as Roman Catholics view Protestants. The majority of the Karaims had been without religious education for the long decades of Soviet rule but the religion has revived since 1990–91.

NATIONAL HISTORY: The ancient Jews adopted monotheism as a belief system based on their sacred writings. Over many centuries many sects arose, most based on additional teachings other than the Bible, including the majority of the present Jewish population that descended from the ancient Pharisees.

In the seventh century A.D., Muslims overran the Middle East. They had little interest in converting the Jews, who were called people of the book. The Jews were given autonomy under a system called the Exilarchate. The Muslim authorities empowered the rabbis and gave them full authority over other Jews, but many resisted the imposition of the Talmud and other writings that developed in Babylon and were revered as sacred writings.

The Karaite reformation movement arose among the Jews of Mesopotamia in the eighth century A.D. The leader of the movement, Anan ben David, preached a return to the written word of the Hebrew Bible, the Old Testament. He also spoke against the oral laws so highly esteemed by Rabbinate Jews and favored replacing the Talmud and other traditional teachings solely with the Bible and its literal commandments. He lobbied the Muslim Caliphate to establish a second Exilarchate for those who rejected the Talmud. The Muslim authorities granted Anan and his followers the religious freedom to practice Judaism in their own way. He and his followers became known as Ananites, but at his death his followers merged with other anti-Talmudic groups and eventually took the name Karaims. From the eighth to the tenth centuries the Karaims were subjected to the rule of the Jewish Khazars.

The Karaite movement never became a mass movement among the Jews of the region, but a number of Turkic tribes on the shores of the Black Sea converted to Karaimism not later than the twelfth century. The tribes, the ancestors of the modern Karaims, settled in Ukraine and the Crimea. Later they settled the borderlands between Lithuania-Poland and Russia. In their communities the Karaims retained their reformed Jewish faith, Hebrew as the language of their religion, and their Turkic language, called Karaim, as the language of daily life. In the ninth century, the neighboring peoples also began calling them Karaims, a Hebrew plural meaning "readers" or "experts," and the name was adopted as an ethnic designation.

Grand Duke Witold of Lithuania defeated the Tatars in 1392 and among the prisoners he took back to Lithuania were 330 Karaim families, who were settled at Traki. The Karaims spread from there to other towns in Lithuania, Poland, and Ukraine. The majority of the Karaims remained in the mountainous central part of the Crimea, where they had settled before the twelfth century Mongol invasion. They lived mostly near the Crimean Tatar capital, Bakhchisarai, in an autonomous fortified town called Chufut Kale (Jews' Castle). Resettlement of Karaims from the Crimea to Lithuania and Ukraine continued in the fifteenth and sixteenth centuries.

In the Middle Ages, the Karaims adopted a biblical year that began with the ripeness of the barley crop in Israel. The Rabbinical Jewish calendar had originally followed this practice, but around the ninth century they adopted a calendar that was far less accurate. This often caused a variation of a month between the Karaim and Jewish calendars. The modern Seventh Day Adventists based their religious calendar on that of the Karaims.

In 1495, the Karaims and the Jews were driven out of Lithuania by Grand Prince Alexander. The Karaims were initially allowed to remain in Poland, but when Alexander became king of Poland in 1503 they were sent back to Lithuania. From Lithuania many Karaims settled in western Ukraine and in 1692 a Karaim settlement was established near Lviv. The first Karaim publication, a prayer book, was published in Venice in 1528.

As a result of the partitions of Poland in 1772, 1793, and 1795, most of the Karaims of eastern Europe came under the Russian government. In the middle nineteenth century, when ethnic and social conflicts swept the Russian Empire, an ethnic and linguistic awareness was awakened and felt to be important. A definite distinction was made between the Karaims and the Jews in order to gain the civil rights denied the Russian Jews. The National Karaite Movement, in 1863, achieved their exemption from all the civil disabilities of the Jews and they enjoyed the same privileges as Christians in the Russian Empire.

According to the Russian census of 1897, there were about 13,000 Karaims in tsarist Russia. At the time, other communities lived in Austrian Galicia and in western Europe. The Karaims were scattered across the western part of the Russian Empire, in the Crimean, Lithuania, Ukraine, and in the major cities of Moscow, St. Petersburg, Kiev, and Odessa. Outside continental Europe there were communities in the Ottoman Empire, Egypt, and Jerusalem.

At the end of the nineteenth century, an alphabet of Latin characters was devised to replace the Hebrew letters of the traditional Karaim language. In Russia, the first Karaim publications in the Cyrillic alphabet appeared in the first years of the century, while in Lithuania the Karaims adapted the principals of the Lithuanian alphabet for their national language.

In the early nineteenth century many of the Crimean Karaims migrated to the big cities in southern Russia. By 1900, there were Karaims scattered all over western Russia, mostly in the big industrial and trading centers. Early in the twentieth century some Karaims from Russia settled in France and others emigrated to the United States. During and after World War I and the Russian Revolution, when Jews were often singled out or suffered pogroms, many more fled to western Europe. The scattered Karaim communities tried to maintain contact, even over the long distances between the diaspora groups.

After World War I, the Karaims in western Ukraine and Lithuania came under Polish rule. The change in their political situation brought about a cultural and political renaissance. A number of Karaim books of history, fiction, and the arts were published in Lutsk, in Ukraine, and a grammar and dictionary of the Ukrainian and Lithuanian dialects of Karaim were published. The Karaim language was separated from Hebrew influences, and an effort was made to translate the whole liturgy into their Turkic language.

The first Crimean Karaim Community Congress was held in 1924 amid great controversy as to the mother tongue of the Karaims, Turkic Karaim,

Tatar, or Hebrew. The latter was referred to as the ancient Karaim language in the notes from the congress. The Karaims of the diaspora have always had a more positive attitude to their own Turkic language, which survived in the northern provinces of Russia, western Europe, and the Middle East.

The Germans overran most of the western Soviet Union in 1941–42, including the Crimean Peninsula. The Karaims, originally singled out for special treatment, were later judged not to be Jews and the majority survived. The Karaims in southern France came under the control of the collaborationist French government in Vichy. The local Commissariat General aux Questions Juives decided to regard the Karaims as Jews and marked them for special treatment and eventual deportation to eastern Europe. It was German pressure that forced the French to retract their policy in regards to the French Karaims, who then survived the war and the Holocaust.

The Karaims of Lutsk, in western Ukraine, reportedly cooperated with the Nazis during the war, and acted as a liaison between the Nazi authorities and the Judenrat, the Jewish authorities in the Lutsk ghetto. They were accused of helping the Nazis to exterminate the local Jewish population during the liquidation of the Lutsk ghetto in August 1942.

After the war, Karaims arrived in western Europe and from 1950 onward, many emigrated from Egypt and other parts of the Middle East. Some of the Karaims later migrated to the United States, mostly settling in the eastern states around New York City. Others assimilated into the Jewish population in Paris and other western European cities.

The communist regime strongly oppressed all Karaim national and religious activities. During the Stalinist era, from the 1920s to the early 1950s, a majority of the Karaims attempted to hide their religious and national background. Those that could registered as ethnic Russians or Ukrainians or Lithuanians, any nationality that suffered less oppression than the Jews and other religious-ethnic minorities. An attempt was made to develop a secular, non-religious Karaim nation, with an ethnic culture of its own.

During several decades the *kenesa* in Trakai, Lithuania, was the only Karaim religious building open in the Soviet Union. Religious instruction and topics were forbidden, and religious literature was represented by a number of old books published in pre-Soviet times. As a result, very few Karaims learned the content of Karaim theology, seeing themselves as just a national minority or trying to distance themselves from their past in order to survive in the Soviet world.

Soviet ideology gradually collapsed at the end of the 1980s, allowing the Karaims to finally reestablish contact among the scattered communities. Several cultural organizations were established with their objectives the awakening of national consciousness, the cultivation of the national language, and the reorganization of their religious life. The obstacles to the revival were many, particularly effecting a renaissance among a nation that has almost completely forgotten its cultural patrimony. The first post-World War II convention of the Karaim nation took place in Pieniezno, Poland, in April 1987.

Among the Karaims, a knowledge of one's nationality had been kept alive by the internal passports on which the nationality of each Soviet citizen was indicated. The Karaim awakening implied giving intellectual and educational substance to the appellation Karaite or Karaim. Activists organized meetings, celebrations, academic conferences, exhibitions, and performing and study groups that established a bridge between the traditional life of the past and the opportunity provided by the restored cultural freedom. At first, activities remained concentrated among a quite small nucleus of enthusiastic nationalists. Gradually, as Soviet controls disappeared, others began to take an interest in their unique culture and history, including many of those who had assimilated into the Russian or Ukrainian nationality.

Several national conferences, in Trakai and Vilnius in 1989 and in Simferopol in the Crimea in 1995, were held to invite the scattered Karaims from other parts of the former Soviet Union to return to their national and religious beliefs, but results were quite meager. Assimilation and secularization had proceeded to such an extent that the idealistic calls to national reawakening did not affect the majority. Only after 1995, when the memories of Soviet oppression began to fade, did many Karaims feel able to reveal their nationality and to join the rebirth of the Karaim nation. The rebirth, particularly in Lithuania, involved restoring ties with the Karaites in Israel, the United States, and Turkey.

One important factor that had contributed to the preservation of the Karaim religion is one similar to an early Protestant principle, the *kenesa* service is in the Karaim national language instead of the traditional holy tongue, Hebrew. The change began over the last century, but has accelerated since the collapse of the Soviet Union. The two tablets of traditional Jewish law that embellish the altars of synagogues are also written in the Karaim language in the new or reconstructed religious meeting houses.

In 1995, the Lithuanian parliament passed a law on religious communities that granted communities the rights to community properties and made the religious groups eligible for financial assistance from the state. The Karaims were listed, along with the Jews, Orthodox and Roman Catholic Christians, Old Believers, and other groups as a recognized religious group. The president of the Lithuanian Karaims is also their religious leader.

The Karaims are often mistaken for Jews, both ethnically and religiously, but they have been a separate nation for over six centuries and maintain their distinct culture and religion even in the Jewish homeland in Israel. The hostile attitude of the surrounding world fostered a sense of unity that remains throughout the Karaim diaspora, although in the United States many have assimilated into Jewish communities. The reculturalation of the 1990s has strengthened the ties between the scattered Karaim communities and the resulting sense of national identity. Young Karaims, particularly in the United States and the Crimea, are trying to revive the language although native speakers are rare and learning the language from books is a slow process.

In 1997, the Karaim community in Lithuania celebrated the six-hundredth anniversary of its foundation in the Baltic region. This last, relatively intact Karaim community in eastern Europe is recognized as a national minority by the Lithuanian government.

SELECTED BIBLIOGRAPHY:

Kobeckaite, Halina. *The Status and Treatment of National Minorities in the Republic of Lithuania*. 1991.
Miller, Philip E. *Karaite Separatism in Nineteenth-Century Russia*. 1993.
Schur, Nathan. *The Karaite Encyclopedia*. 1995.
Szyszman, Simon. *The Karaites of Europe*. 1989.

Karakalpaks

Kara-Kalpaks; Karakalpakians; Qaraqalpaqs; Qoraqalpogs; Tudzits; Tchornis; Karaklobuks

POPULATION: Approximately (2002e) 623,000 Karakalpaks in Central Asia, concentrated in the Karakalpak Autonomous Republic in Uzbekistan and adjacent areas of Kazakhstan and Turkmenistan. There are small Karakalpak communities in Tashkent and other parts of Uzbekistan, as well as in Afghanistan and Kyrgyzstan.

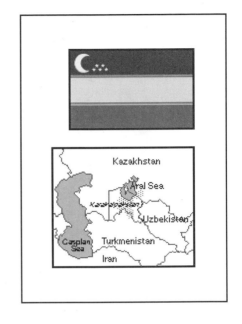

THE KARAKALPAK HOMELAND: The Karakalpak homeland lies in Central Asia, south of the Aral Sea. The region includes the western half of the Kyzyl-Kum Desert, a vast plain of shifting sands. In the central districts lie the valley and delta of the Amu Darya River, a low-lying area intersected by many streams and canals. On the west the homeland includes the southeastern part of the Ust-Yurt Plateau. Karakalpakstan forms an autonomous republic within the Republic of Uzbekistan. *Republic of Karakalpakstan (Qaraqalpaqstan Respublikasy/Korakalpogiston)*: 63,938 sq. mi.—165,642 sq. km, (2002e) 1,634,000—Karakalpaks 34%, Uzbeks 28%, Kazakhs 27%, Russians 4%, Turkmens 4%, Tatars 1%, others 2%. The Karakalpak capital and major cultural center is Nukus, called Nökis by the Karakalpaks, (2002e) 252,000. The other important cultural center is Hücayli, called Khodzheyli, (2002e) 79,000.

FLAG: The Karakalpak national flag, the flag of the autonomous republic, is a horizontal tricolor of blue, yellow, and green, the colors separated by narrow red and white stripes, charged with a white crescent moon and 5 five-pointed white stars on the upper hoist.

PEOPLE AND CULTURE: The Karakalpaks are a Central Asian people of obscure, mixed origins. They include in their ancestry Oghuz and Kipchak Turks, Mongols, and Iranians; they developed as a separate people in the fifteenth century. Their name, Karakalpak, means "black cap" or "black hat." The Karakalpaks are closely related to the neighboring Kazakhs, although unlike the Kazakhs they are physically more Turkic than

921

Mongol. The status of women, more advanced in the region than in the rest of Uzbekistan, is considered one of their few positive legacies of the communist era. Even though the Karakalpaks' sense of separate identity is well developed, their status as a Kazakh subgroup or a separate ethnic group is still debated. In 1999–2000 over 30% of the Karakalpaks lived in cities and towns, which reduced the high birth rate, but large families remain the Karakalpak ideal. Formerly a large number of Karakalpaks worked as fishermen in the Aral Sea, but the majority are now agriculturists.

LANGUAGE AND RELIGION: Their language, of the West Turkic (Kipchak) language group, is classed by some scholars as a dialect of Kazakh, although it developed as a separate literary language after the Russian Revolution. The language is spoken by a very high number as a first language, an estimated 96% of the total Karakalpak population. The language is spoken in two major dialects, Northeastern Karakalpak and Southeastern Karakalpak, and a number of subdialects. Many Karakalpaks speak Uzbek or Russian as a second language. The Latin alphabet has been adopted, but the Russian Cyrillic alphabet is still widely used.

The Karakalpaks are Sunni Muslims of the Hanafite branch, which promotes political conformity. There are also many members of the Sufi sect of Islam. Many pre-Islamic rituals have survived, particularly an altered mental state induced by frenzied dancing and chanting. In 1998 an estimated 78% were practicing Muslims, 19% were nonreligious or nonpracticing Muslims, and about 3% claimed to be atheists. There is a small Christian minority, mostly belonging to evangelical Protestant sects. Portions of the Bible were translated into Karakalpak in 1996.

NATIONAL HISTORY: The fertile lands around the Aral Sea, originally inhabited by Caucasian peoples, came under the domination of the Oghuz Turks from Mongolia in the seventh century. The Turkic invaders absorbed the settled Caucasians, and their Turkic language and culture supplanted the Caucasian's original culture. In the eighth century Arab invaders overran the region and converted the inhabitants to Islam. The Aral Sea area later fell to the Seljuk Turks; a faction of the Karakalpaks joined the Seljuks in their invasions to the south and west. In the thirteenth century the Karakalpaks came under the rule of the great Mongol empire.

According to their national tradition, the Karakalpaks, the Black Caps, split from the Mongol-Turkic Golden Horde to emerge as a separate people in the fifteenth century. They were virtually independent but remained divided along tribal lines. Their independence lasted only for a few years before they became subject to the Dzungarians (later called the Hui*), the Bukharans, and the Kazakhs. The Dzungarian invasion split the tribes, as the Karakalpaks fled in two directions. One group, the "upper Karakalpaks," settled along the Syr Darya River east to the Fergana Valley. The other, the "lower Karakalpaks," moved closer to the Aral Sea. Sixteenth-century chronicles mention the Karakalpaks as a pastoral nomadic people in the valley of the Syr Darya River east of the Aral Sea, subjects of the emirate of Bukhara. Under pressure from the Kazakhs to the north and the Bukharans to the east, between the sixteenth and eighteenth centuries the Karakalpak tribes moved southwest to settle the Amu Darya basin south of the Aral Sea, an area loosely controlled by the Uzbek khanate of Khiva.

Russian and Cossack explorers first came across the Karakalpaks in the seventeenth century while traveling through the Uzbek-dominantd Central Asian states. The states repulsed early attempts to extend Russian rule to the region; however, the Russians returned in force in the nineteenth century. Between 1865 and 1876 nearly all of Central Asia came under Russian control. The Russians annexed the western districts of Karakalpakstan outright in 1873, while the districts east of the Amu Darya River remained under the rule of the Khiva, a nominally independent Russian protectorate.

The Karakalpak nomads, except for the loss of favored grazing lands, felt little of the effect of Russian rule until World War I. In June 1916, in desperate need of manpower the tsarist authorities began to conscript Central Asians into labor battalions. Resistance to conscription provoked serious incidents and a widespread rebellion in August 1916. Fearing Russian reprisals, many Karakalpaks took shelter in the marshes in the Amu Darya delta. The Central Asian rebellion forced the tsarist government to withdraw badly needed troops from the front, where the war was already going badly. Confrontations between the Muslim rebels and the Russian military units ended when the news of the Russian Revolution of February 1917 reached the area.

The Karakalpak leaders, as civil government collapsed, attempted to establish the instruments of self-rule. They sent delegates to a conference of Central Asian peoples. Several rival governments established in Central Asia contested for control of Karakalpak territory south of the Aral Sea. In 1918 the Russian Civil War spread to Central Asia, bringing chaos. The Karakalpaks opposed the antireligious rhetoric of the Bolsheviks and generally allied themselves to the anti-Bolshevik White forces in the region. The defeat of the Whites left the region open to Soviet occupation in 1920.

The Soviets dissolved the traditional state borders and divided Central Asia into ethnic states in 1924. A Karakalpak autonomous region created in May 1925 was transferred in 1930 to the Russian Federation; in 1932 the Soviet authorities upgraded its status to that of an autonomous republic. Four years later the Soviets again transferred the Karakalpak region, to the authority of the Uzbek Soviet Socialist Republic.

The former nomads, in spite of the political confusion and the repression of their Muslim religion, made great strides in education and culture, and developed a strong sense of their separate national identity. After centuries of Uzbek, then Russian domination, the cultural freedom allowed by the Soviet authorities in the 1920s produced a Karakalpak literary language and a cultural revival that continued until the repression of the Stalinist era.

After Stalin's death in 1953, Soviet authorities developed the region as a major producer of cotton, to the exclusion of the traditional agricultural and pastoral products. The Amu Darya River, one of the major sources of regional water, was diverted for cotton irrigation in 1962. The river rapidly became heavily polluted with chemical fertilizers. With its main feeder rivers diverted, the Aral Sea began to shrink rapidly, an ecological disaster mostly hidden from the world until the liberalization introduced in the Soviet Union in 1987.

Karakalpak nationalists, with a strong environmental faction, began to organize in 1989 as the reforms introduced by Mikhail Gorbachev reached their homeland. Revelations of the extent of health problems caused by the massive use of chemical fertilizers in cotton production over decades both shocked and galvanized the nationalists. Karakalpak activists condemned the bureaucrats of the Uzbek government; they demanded separation and the creation of an autonomous Karakalpak republic within the Soviet Union. In 1990 the Karakalpak government declared the republic a sovereign state.

Uzbekistan became an independent country with the disintegration of the Soviet Union in August 1991. The new Uzbek national government, dominated by ex-communists turned Uzbek nationalists, moved to crush the Karakalpak national movement. In late 1991 serious ethnic violence erupted. Disputes over water and land rights became national issues, and nationalists gained widespread support. Rival factions developed within the national movement, some calling for a federal relationship with Uzbekistan, while a more radical faction advocated declaring independence before negotiating with neighboring Central Asian states.

The Karakalpaks, although the smallest of the Central Asian peoples, have a sense of identity as strong as those of the larger neighboring Central Asian nations. In January 1994, ignoring Uzbek government pressure, the Karakalpaks announced plans to introduce the Latin alphabet. The change would give them access to Turkish newspapers and television, and would help to end their dependence on the largesse of the Uzbek government.

The disastrous depletion of the flow of the two historic rivers, the Sry Darya and Amu Darya, has drastically changed the Aral Sea and greatly altered the delta of the Amu Darya. Most streams of the delta have dried up; the Aral Sea, formerly the fourth-largest inland sea in the world, has lost more than three-fifths of its water and some two-fifths of its area since 1960. In some places the sea's shoreline has receded more than 75 miles (120 km). The diversion of the rivers resulted in intense salinization of the sea, which also suffers tremendous pollution from insecticides and chem-cals dumped into it during the past several decades. This chemical pollution and the decline in water level have doomed the once-flourishing fishing industry and contaminated wide areas around the sea with salty, lethal dust. The pollutants have poisoned vegetables and drinking water, and they have seriously harmed the health and livelihood of the Karakalpaks around the southern shores of the sea.

The poisoning of the Aral Sea has become a major focus of Karakalpak nationalism. Their expectations that the Soviet era ecological disaster would be addressed following the collapse of the Soviet Union in 1991 have been disappointed. The Uzbek government, desperate for export crops, has continued to divert the rivers for cotton production and has consistently ignored Karakalpak concerns. The resulting depopulation of many areas of the Karakalpak homeland is seen as a serious threat to the small nation. An estimated 66% of all Karakalpaks have hepatitis, typhoid, or throat cancer due to of the heavy pollution. One out of every 10 Karakalpak babies dies before its first birthday, and 85% of all children have long-term medical conditions. Biological testing on the islands in the Aral Sea has put the region at risk of man-made epidemics. The Karakalpaks charge that the Uzbek government, while ignoring their plight, continues to reserve funds for the development of the eastern part of the country.

The Uzbek government, still controlled by elderly ex-communist bureaucrats of the Soviet era and authoritarian president Islam Karimov, continue to discourage any sign of activism in Karakalpakstan. Nationalist organizations, some operating from neighboring Kazakhstan, are banned, and their members are often arrested. The desire of the Karakalpaks to take their place as an independent Central Asian nation has been suppressed, but changes to the aging government in Tashkent could again ignite the nationalist issue in the region.

Most Karakalpaks agree with the government on at least one important point, that all measures must be taken against a takeover by Islamic fundamentalism. Militant Islamists, known as Wahhabis, formerly active in Karakalpakstan, are fiercely suppressed and have either gone underground or fled to Afghanistan. During the broad waves of anti-Islamic repression in 1992 and 1998, a full beard was enough to get a man arrested.

The terrorist attacks on the United States in September 2001 led to an alliance against Islamic terrorists. The Uzbek government, charging that Kalpak nationalists harbored terrorists, cracked down on all dissident groups in the region. Karakalpak spokesmen for legal political parties and even illegal nationalist groups now keep an unmistakable distance from the Islamists.

SELECTED BIBLIOGRAPHY:

Glantz, Michael H. *Creeping Enviornmental Problems and Sustainable Development in the Aral Sea Basin.* 1999.

Karakalpaks

Hostler, Charles Warren. *The Turks of Central Asia.* 1993.

Karimov, I.A. *Uzbekistan on the Threshold of the Twenty-first Century: Challenges to Stability and Progress.* 1998.

Thubron, Colin. *The Lost Heart of Asia.* 1994.

Karels

Karelians; Karjala; Korela; Karyalainen; Karjaliset; Karjalazhet; Karjalaised; Karjalazed

POPULATION: Approximately (2002e) 505,000 Karels in northern Europe, concentrated in the Karelian Republic in Russia, but with a large Karel population in Finland, particularly in Kuopio and Oulu Provinces, and a small community in Sweden. Other Karel populations are in the Russian regions of Tver, Murmansk, St. Petersburg, Arkhangelsk, Moscow, and Kemerov.

THE KARELIAN HOMELAND: The Karel homeland lies in northwestern European Russia, extending from the Finnish border east to the White Sea. Most of the region forms part of the Karelian Plateau, a broad, flat, and swampy plain with mountains in the west. Heavily forested Karelia is rich in minerals and water resources, with over 50,000 lakes. The traditional territory of the Karels is now divided. The largest part forms the Republic of Karelia, a member state of the Russian Federation. Historical Karelia also includes Western Karelia, transferred to Leningrad (St. Petersburg) Oblast in 1946, and Northern Karelia, which was transferred to Murmansk Oblast in 1938. *Republic of Karelia (Karjal/Karjala)*: 66,567 sq. mi.—172,466 sq. km, (2002e) 756,000—Russians 55%, Karels 26%, Belarussians 6%, Finns 6%, Ukrainians 2%, Veps* 2%, Ingrians* 2%, others 1%. The Karelian capital and major cultural center is Petrozavodsk, called Petroskoi in Karelian, (2002e) 282,000. The major cultural centers of Western Karelia and Northern Karelia are Vyborg, Viipuri in Karelian, (2002e) 79,000, and Kandalaksha, Kaananlahti in Karelian, (2002e) 45,000.

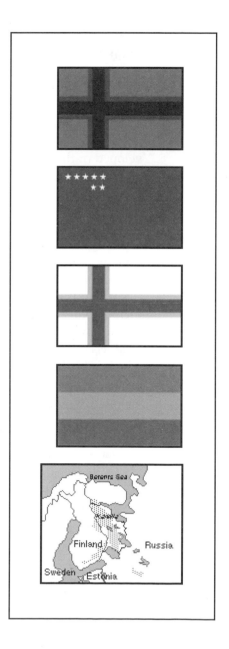

FLAG: The Karelian national flag, the traditional flag of the Karelian nation, is a pale green field bearing a black Scandinavian cross outlined in red. The flag of the national movement is a blue field bearing seven white stars representing the "Big Dipper" on the upper hoist. The flag of the Karels in Finland is a white field bearing a blue Scandinavian cross outlined in yellow. The official flag of the Karelian Republic is a horizontal tricolor of red, blue, and green.

PEOPLE AND CULTURE: The Karels are a Finnic nation, descendants of a collection of tribal peoples who migrated from the Volga River region. The Karels, closely related to the Finns, are the descendants of the early Finnish peoples most influenced by contact with the Slavs. The Karel nation is made up of two major divisions, the Karels and the Olonets (or Anus). The actual number of ethnic Karels in the Russian Federation is a matter of dispute. Official records count about 140,000 Karels, but during the Soviet era many Karels registered as ethnic Russians to escape oppression. A movement to restore the Karelian language and culture developed in the late-Soviet period, and by the late 1990s thousands of Karels had again assumed the Karelian nationality. Over the centuries the Karelians have become dispersed over a wide territory and now constitute several distinct subgroups. The largest are the North Karels, in Karelia and Murmansk; the South Karels, in the Tver, Novgorod, and St. Petersburg Oblasts; the Olonets, calling themselves Liüdi or Liügi, between Lake Ladoga and Onega; and the Ludics, in the central and southern districts of Karelia. In the 1960s, the Karels of Tver, Novgorod, and St. Petersburg (Leningrad) Oblasts numbered between 90,000 and 100,000 but were not included in subsequent official records. The Valdai Karels of the Novgorod region and the Tikhvin Karels of the St. Petersburg region were considered assimilated, but during the 1990s a reculturation took hold; Karels who spoke Russian as their first language took a new interest in their culture and language. The Karels in Finland, although Finnicized, strongly support the cultural movement.

LANGUAGE AND RELIGION: The language of the Karels belongs to the Finnic branch of the Uralic languages of northwestern Eurasia. The language, nearly identical in its written form to Finnish, is spoken in two major dialects, Karelian and Olonets. The Karelian dialect is further divided into three distinct subdialects, all of which have been influenced by Russian. Karels in the southern districts are called Livviki and speak the Livvi dialect. The Karels in the center, the Karels proper, speak Karjala; the Lyydidi, who inhabit districts in the south and southwest, speak the Lyydiki dialect. The 10,000 Ludians, a small, closely related group, speak their own dialect called Ludic, which is sometimes regarded as a separate language. The northern dialects blend into the northeastern Finnish dialects. Unlike most ethnic minorities in the former USSR, the Karels had been allowed to retain the Latin alphabet. Until the 1990s, the Karel formed the largest national minority in Russia that did not have its own literary language, which is considered one of the reasons that the Karels assimilated at a rapid rate. A literary language has been created, in the Latin alphabet. It is used in both the northern and Tver Karelian communities; it has been introduced into the school curriculum, and textbooks and other literature have been produced. During the Soviet era many Karels assimilated or were forced to adopt the Russian nationality; by 1989, 56% of urban ethnic Karelians and 35% of rural ethnic Karelians considered Russian their first language.

The Russian influence on Karel society is most pronounced in religion. The Karels are mostly Russian Orthodox, while the Finns and Ingrians to the west are Lutherans. The historical boundary between Finland and Karelia reflected the religious boundary between the two Finnish nations until the twentieth century.

NATIONAL HISTORY: Nomadic tribal peoples from the Volga River basin west of the Ural Mountains settled the forested Karelian Plateau probably in the eighth century, driving the earlier Samis* or Lapps farther to the north. The tribes that settled near Lakes Ladoga and Onega expanded north along the Dvina River to the White Sea and into Finnish Karelia and Savo. Mentioned in Scandinavian writings of the eighth century and in European and Russian chronicles of the ninth century, the Karels were known as a separate northern people living in the forests between the Baltic and White Seas and around Lakes Ladoga and Onega. The Karel tribes never unified but lived in autonomous groups, with few ties beyond the clan level.

From the ninth to the twelfth centuries, the southern clans were under the authority of the Kievan Rus' principality. In 1216, the pope confirmed Swedish title to much of Finland, and also to mission territories in the east and north. In 1323, a treaty divided Karelia between the Swedes and the Novgorodians. The eastern Karels mostly came under the rule of the Slav republic of Novgorod, and many adopted Orthodox Christianity. Traditionally the Karels worked as farmers, fishermen, or timber cutters. In 1478 the expanding Russian empire took control of Novgorod and its territories, including Eastern Karelia.

The Swedes, expanding their empire to the east, conquered the Finns, but the fierce Karels stopped the Swedish advance to the east for a time. Eventually, in the fifteenth century, the Swedes gained control of Western Karelia, but Slavs from the Republic of Great Novgorod maintained control of Eastern Karelia. The Karels were freed by the Russian conquest of Novgorod in 1478 and formed a separate confederation, which developed into a strong medieval state with a vigorous culture. The Karelian folktales and songs of this period are the source of the Finnish national epic, the *Kalevala*, considered part of the national heritage of both peoples. The influence of the Slavs extended to religion, most Karels converting to Orthodoxy.

Swedish forces finally conquered the Karel state in 1617, but they kept the newly conquered region separate from Western Karelia. Thousands of Karels, evicted from their lands or fleeing the imposition of feudal taxes and the Lutheran faith, left the northwestern shores of Lake Ladoga for North Karelia, and another large group moved south to the Valdai Hills in central Russia. The Karel migration from their war-torn homeland had already begun in the late sixteenth century, but became extensive in the first half of the seventeenth century. An estimated 25,000 to 30,000 people left the region, a very large migration for that time. The Russian government supported the Orthodox Karelian exodus with financial assistance.

The Russians, during the Northern War, took Karelia from the Swedes; the annexation was formalized by the Treaty of Nystad in 1721. Western Karelia, Finland, and the Aland Islands were ceded by Sweden to Russia during the Napoleonic Wars, at the conclusion of yet another Swedish-Russian war in 1809. The two Karelian regions remained divided by Russia's internal political borders. Eastern Karelia, poor and underdeveloped, became known as a place of exile for tsarist political prisoners and common criminals. Western Karelia, closely associated with Finland, was more developed.

The Finnic people's experiences at the hands of both the Swedes and the Russians stimulated a sense of nationalism. Influenced by the Finns, the Karels experienced a national and cultural revival in the late nineteenth century. In 1899 the tsarist authorities clamped down and imposed new restrictions on education and publishing in the Karel language. Finnish nationalist literature, smuggled across the border, supported the growth of an underground nationalist movement. The Russian authorities countered with increased pressure to assimilate.

Karel soldiers fought in the Russian army during World War I, but in February 1917 the overthrow of the tsarist autocracy threw Karelia into chaos; prisoners and political exiles were suddenly free to roam the region. Karel military units, deserting the front, took control of Karelia as civil government collapsed. On 17 March 1918, Karel leaders convened a congress at the town of Uhtua. The delegates voted to separate from the collapsing Russian empire and called for union with Finland.

The Karels were soon, however, caught up in the Russian Civil War. Protected by Finnish troops and British forces landed to support the Whites, the Karel forces opposed the Bolsheviks in the spreading conflict. The Karel leaders declared their homeland an autonomous state in May 1919. In July, a conference of Karel delegates appointed a committee to act as a provisional government of Eastern Karelia. The committee organized the first Eastern Karelian Diet, elected by universal suffrage and made up of representatives of the twelve parishes of White Sea Karelia.

On 22 March 1920 the diet voted for independence from Russia. The second Eastern Karelian Diet, meeting in June 1920, voted to create an army and to mobilize, but the Red Army invaded the region; the Karelian government mostly fled to Finland. The region became the refuge for many Finnish communists, defeated in the Finnish civil war.

In early 1921, the Karels rebelled and drove the Soviets from the region. On 21 April the rebels proclaimed the independence of the Republic of Eastern Karelia (Itä Karjala) and created a democratic government that invited participation by the area's many national groups. The Finns, exhausted by war and attempting to maintain peace with their giant Soviet neighbor, were unable to respond to the Karel's frantic appeals for military aid when the region was overrun by the new Red Army.

Karelia was organized as an autonomous province and in 1923 was raised to the status of an autonomous republic within the Soviet Russian Federation. Another autonomous region was created for the Tver Karelians, farther south. A Karel literary language was attempted, but the Soviet authorities decided to use the Finnish language as the literary language in the northern districts and Russian in the southern districts, where most Karels were bilingual.

The culture of the regions was predominantly Karelian, with a great amount of Finnish influence. Joseph Stalin, to break the Finnish cultural domination, began a cruel purge. In 1935 the leaders of the autonomous republic were accused of nationalist tendencies and were eliminated, most of them ending up in labor camps in Siberia. By 1938, every trace of Finnish had been banned within the Karelian republic, and the Latin script had been forcibly replaced by the Russian Cyrillic alphabet. In 1939 the Tver Karelian autonomous region was liquidated, its leaders killed or deported, and its records and all books in Karelian or Finnish destroyed.

In the late 1930s the Stalinist government became increasingly aggressive against the small Baltic Sea republics that had seceded during the Russian Civil War. In late 1939 the Soviet government demanded the cession of Western Karelia from Finland as part of a plan to reunite the Karels under Soviet rule. The ensuing conflict, the Winter War, ended with Finnish defeat in 1940. The Soviets added Finnish Karelia to the Karelo-Finnish Soviet Socialist Republic, which then was joined to the Soviet Union as the twelfth constituent republic. Tens of thousands of Karels and Finns fled west to escape Soviet domination. The 1939 Soviet census counted 253,000 Karels, but by 1959 that number had dropped to 167,000 as ethnic Karels sought to hide their nationality by registering as ethnic Russians and assimilating into Russian culture.

The Finns, unreconciled to the loss of Western Karelia, joined the German assault on the Soviet state in June 1941. Finnish troops liberated all of Karelia, but declaring that theirs was a separate conflict refused to join further German offensives, particularly the attack on Leningrad. Defeated in 1944, the Finnish troops withdrew, accompanied by over 400,000 Karels and Finns civilians fleeing the Soviet advance. The Soviet authorities again divided the Karel lands in 1945–46, transferring the western districts to Leningrad Oblast and returning Northern Karelia to Murmansk Oblast. In 1956, on the grounds that the Karels formed only a minority in the republic, the Soviet government downgraded Karelia's status to an autonomous republic within the Russian Federation.

In the 1960s and 1970s the Karels, deprived of their autonomy and pressured by the Soviet government, assimilated into the neighboring Russian community. Many adopted Russian identity to escape linguistic and cultural pressure and the limits placed on the non-Russian national groups.

In the late 1980s, Mikhail Gorbachev introduced reforms to the creaking Soviet system. In May 1988 the administration officially acknowledged the campaign of terrorism launched against the Karels by Stalin. Renewed contact with the Finns and the large Karel exile population spurred a rapid growth of national sentiment. In June 1991, the first Karel congress in 70 years, at Olonets on Lake Ladoga, brought together representatives of the exile Karel population, representatives of the autonomous republic, and delegates from the Tver Karels. A 50-member executive committee was elected to introduce a bill proposing sovereign Karel territories, areas where the Karel language and culture could be preserved.

The nationalist mobilization accelerated after the disintegration of the Soviet Union in August 1991. In November 1992 representatives of the Karels demanded legal recognition as a "repressed nation" that had suffered disproportionately during 70 years of Soviet communist rule. Democracy in Russia allowed the Karels to reestablish close cultural ties to neighboring Finland, which began to finance cultural and economic development in Karelia.

Karel cultural and nationalist groups in the 1990s campaigned for the partition of Karelia so as to provide for a Karel-majority homeland; they denied, however, accusations that they wished to unite with neighboring Finland. The large exile population in Finland supports the exile Karels' right to return to their homeland, particularly the region of Western Karelia, ceded to the Soviet Union at the end of the Winter War in 1940. Karel nationalists—whose own homeland is dismal and poor, even by low Russian standards—look to wealthy Finland. The Karels have finally been freed of communist rule but now fear their homeland will become a backward dependency of the Russian Federation. Nationalists vow that Karelia will not return to the status of a colonial outpost of a new Russian empire.

The language issue also continues to cause friction, as Finnish, not Karel, is the second official language of the republic. There are now a serious campaign to revive the Karel language and culture. The campaign has been directed by the Union of the Karelian People (Karjalan Rahvahan Liitto). The main arguments against Kalelian are that it is still a spoken but not well-developed literary language and that it has two different unintelligible dialects. A dictionary of the Olonets dialect was published in 1990, and thereafter a Tver Karelian dictionary. A dictionary of the Karelian language in several volumes is being compiled in Finland. The de-Russification of the language, especially in the southern dialects, has become a nationalist issue.

SELECTED BIBLIOGRAPHY:

Levinson, David. *Ethnic Groups Worldwide*. 1998.

Mouritz-Cen, Hans. *Bordering Russia: Theory and Prospects for Europe's Baltic Rim*. 1998.

Puuronen, Vesa, and Pentti Sinisalo. *Youth in a Changing Karelia: A Comparative Study of Everyday Life, Future Orientations and Political Culture in North-West Russia*. 2000.

Rizzardo, Rene. *Cultural Policy and Regional Identity in Finland: North Karelia between Tradition and Modernity*. 1987.

Karennis

Karennyis; Kayahs; Kayays; Red Karens

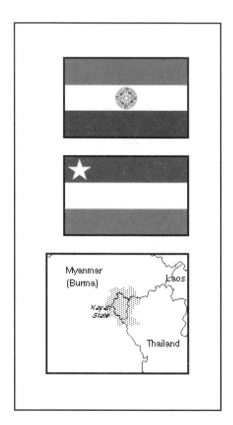

POPULATION: Approximately (2002e) 755,000 Karennis in southeastern Asia, concentrated in Kayah State and surrounding districts in eastern Myanmar, and about 200,000 in adjacent areas of neighboring Thailand. There are Karenni communities in India, the United Kingdom, and the United States.

THE KARENNI HOMELAND: The Karenni homeland lies in eastern Myanmar, a rugged highland region occupying part of the southern Shan Plateau on the Thai border. The Karenni mountains are traversed by the basin of the Upper Salween River and its tributaries just north of the Thai border. The region is made up of three small, formerly independent states—Kantarawadi, Bawlake, and Kyebogyi—that were consolidated in Karenni state in 1947. The state was enlarged and renamed Kayah in 1952 Kayah State is a nominally autonomous state of the Federation of Myanmar. *State of Kayah* 4,519 sq. mi.—11,704 sq. km, (2002e) 243,000—Karennis 85%, Shans* 7%, Karens* 5%, other Burmese 3%. The Karenni capital and major cultural center is Loikaw, (2002e) 17,000. The center of the Thai Karennis is Mae Hong Son, (2002e) 7,000.

FLAG: The Karenni national flag, the flag of the national movement, is a horizontal tricolor of red, white, and pale blue, bearing a centered disc representing the top of a Karenni frog drum. The flag of the Karenni National Progressive Party, the largest of the nationalist groups, is a horizontal tricolor of blue, white, and red, bearing a white five-pointed star on the upper hoist.

PEOPLE AND CULTURE: The Karennis, or Red Karen, are a tribal people of Thai-Chinese background. They are believed, with the Mons,* to be the indigenous population of present Myanmar, predating the Burman invasion of the region. The Karennis comprise four major divisions—

the Bre, Padaung, Yinbaw, and Zayein. Although ethnically and linguistically Karen, the Karennis have developed their own national identity. The Karennis having been less assimilated than the related Karens, their culture has been less influenced by the Burmans and has more Thai and Shan influences. Most of the Karennis are subsistence hill farmers or work in the region's mines, which provide much of the wealth coveted by the Burmese military government.

LANGUAGE AND RELIGION: The Karenni language is a Karen language of the Sgaw-Bghai group of Sino-Tibetan languages. The language, called Kayahli, forms a continuous chain of dialects from northwestern Thailand to west of the Salween River basin. The language is spoken in two major dialects—Eastern Karenni, spoken in Thailand and east of the Salween River in Myanmar; and Western Karenni, spoken west of the Salween River. Speakers of Eastern Karenni, mostly in Thailand, have difficulty understanding speakers of Western Karenni. The literacy rate among the Thai Karennis is between 50 and 75%, but in Myanmar it is estimated at less than 15%. Many Karennis speak English as their second language, as the result of decades of missionary activity in the region.

A majority of the Karennis are believed to be Christian, estimated at about 65% of the total population. Most of the Christians are Roman Catholic, with a substantial Protestant, mostly Baptist minority. For many years foreign missionaries and religions have been prohibited, but religion remains a central part of the Karenni culture. The non-Christian Karennis are animist or Theravada Buddhists, particularly among the Thai Karennis.

NATIONAL HISTORY: The Karennis arrived in their present homeland from southwestern China, traditionally in the fifth century B.C. Differentiated by the color of their cloaks, the "Red Karens" slowly separated from the larger Black Karen population to the south when they moved into the mountainous Shan Plateau. Influenced by the neighboring Shans, a Thai people, the Karennis erected small, independent states ruled by princes, and they adopted many Shan cultural traits.

The Karennis retained close ties to the neighboring Karens, and the two peoples often cooperated when threatened by invaders, especially the warlike Burmans, who conquered the lowlands in the eleventh century. In the thirteenth century, the Karenni states became vassals of the Shans, who ruled most of Burma until their defeat by the resurgent Burmans in 1586.

The five small Karenni principalities, protected by a long military tradition, maintained their independence against repeated Burman offensives in the sixteenth and seventeenth centuries and against a Thai incursion in the eighteenth century. The Karenni states, through royal marriages, were later reduced from five to three, Kantarawadi, Bawlake, and Kyebogyi. The small states grew rich from the sale of precious stones from their mines.

Europeans, drawn by the fabulous gems, visited the region in the eighteenth century. The Karennis were first contacted by the British authorities after the First Anglo-Burmese War in 1826. Sustained contact with Europeans began with the British annexation of the lowlands in 1852. Never part of the Burman kingdom, the Karenni principalities established direct treaty relations with the British authorities and accepted British residents attached to the courts of the Karenni princes. An agreement signed on 21 June 1875 recognized Karenni independence under British protection and provided for full independence should the protectorate agreement be terminated. In 1881 the Karenni states officially became part of the British Empire.

European missionaries arrived in the Karenni states in the 1870s and 1880s. The mainly pagan Karennis were receptive to Christianity, and many converted. Western education in missionary schools, provided mostly for the sons of the nobility, produced an educated group that later took over the political leadership of the Karennis from the traditional princes. While the missionary-educated elite became politically active and espoused Western ideas of freedom of speech, human rights, and freedom of religion, the majority of the Karennis retained their traditional beliefs and loyalty to the Karenni princes.

The British authorities recruited many Karennis, renowned as warriors, into the colonial forces. Karenni troops were often used to control the majority Burman population, creating an enmity that continues to the present. The Karenni soldiers, taught Western military tactics and discipline, were known for their loyalty and tenacity.

The ethnic Burmans, allied to the invading Japanese, drove the British from Burma in 1942. Declared independent under Japanese protection, the new Burman state laid claim to the Karenni principalities. Burman and Japanese troops occupied the Karenni principalities, while many Karennis, particularly the British-trained soldiers, retreated to the mountains to form guerrilla groups. The guerrillas, trained by Allied officers parachuted into the highland jungles, terrorized the Burman and Japanese units sent against them. The Burmans, disillusioned with their Japanese allies, changed sides in 1943 and aided the return of the British forces. No longer essential to the war effort, the Karennis were mostly ignored.

The British began to prepare Burma for independence at the end of the war and pressed the small British protectorates on the borders to join a proposed federation. The Karennis, expecting the British to honor the terms of the 1875 agreement, which had never been nullified, rejected the Burmese federation and notified the British of their wish for separate independence. The British authorities, believing that the Karenni region was too small for separate independence, refused the honor the agreement. Their refusal and the insistence that the Karennis join Burma provoked a Karenni uprising that spread following Burmese independence in 1948. The small Karenni states were officially joined in a new state called Kayah, which was joined to the new Burmese federation.

The Burmese government finally crushed the Karenni rebellion in 1950. Determined to separate the Karennis from the Karen insurgency to the south, the government granted the Karenni states semiautonomous status in 1952. Seven years later the authorities deposed the Karenni princes and forced them to renounce their rights and privileges. The outraged Karennis resumed their rebellion in 1959 and renewed their traditional alliance with the Karen groups fighting the government.

The Karenni rebels allied themselves to the Karens, Mons, and Burmese communists in 1971. Supplied with arms by the communists, the Karennis gained successes against the government troops, but in 1975 the government announced the defeat of the Karenni forces. The Karennis joined other ethnic nationalist groups to form the Federal National Democratic Front (FNDF)—its stated aim the overthrow of the Burmese military government and the establishment of a federation of independent states.

The State Law and Order Restoration Council (SLORC), the ruling military junta, began to carry out a population transfer program in Kayah in 1976. The relocations, carried out in areas of heavy rebel activity, were designed to deny the aid and support of the civilian population to the antigovernment and separatist groups operating in Kayah state. The forced relocations alienated many of the Karenni farmers, who were separated from their ancestral lands.

Karenni support for the democracy movement, which the government brutally crushed in 1990, reaffirmed Karenni determination to separate from Burma. The destruction of the democracy movement, and with it the possibility of democracy within a new federation that would replace the hated military junta, marked a new phase in the Karennis' fight for self-rule. Burmese government agreements with economic interests in neighboring Thailand to log the Karennis' forests and exploit the region's mineral wealth alienated even the most moderate Karennis and made negotiations more difficult.

The Karennis, claiming that they never agreed to inclusion in Burma, have fought for decades to secure the independence guaranteed by the 1875 agreement. The brutal military government of Burma, renamed Myanmar, has only reinforced the Karenni desire for separation. The Karenni leaders believe their abundant timber and mineral wealth forms a viable economic base; they assert that the war is no longer just about freedom but about the survival of the Karenni nation. The growing Karenni diaspora supports the national movement with financial aid and weapons purchased in Thailand and smuggled across the border.

The Burmese military in March 1992 relocated the inhabitants of 57 Karenni villages to sites in northwest Kayah State where they could be more easily controlled. Many others were forced to work on the Aunban-Loikaw railway or as porters for the military. In December 1994, after a two-year lull, fighting again erupted in the region. The Karenni leaders, citing new border restrictions, accused the neighboring Thai government of backing the offensive by Myanmar's military junta in order to win lucrative logging and mining concessions.

The 1,400-strong Kayah New Land Party (KNLP) finally agreed to a cease-fire in July 1994, the 12th rebel group in Myanmar to do so. Other Karenni nationalist groups in March 1995 agreed to a cease-fire with the government, but the agreements disintegrated by June when heavy fighting resumed. The most recent cease-fire talks broke down in May 1998 in Yangon (Rangoon) when attacks on government troops occurred near Loikaw.

Myanmar became a full member of the Association of Southeast Asian Nations (ASEAN) in July 1997. The other ASEAN members argued that membership for Myanmar would encourage the military government to improve its human rights record, but the opposite proved true. Stepped-up repression, forced relocations, and the use of forced labor occurred in several of the ethnic states, particularly Kayah.

During the first half of 1996, the Myanmar armed forces began a massive relocation of civilians as part of a counterinsurgency strategy in Kayah State. Between 20,000 and 30,000 Karennis were forced from their home villages into designated relocation sites, where there was inadequate food, water, or sanitary facilities. Hundreds died of treatable diseases, and many thousands fled into Thai territory. Others hid in the heavy forests in an attempt to live outside the control of the oppressive military government. The government initiated the forcible relocations in an area where rebel groups were active and where mountain villages were difficult to control. The Myanmar government refused to allow international humanitarian organizations access to the relocation sites.

Several Karenni groups joined other ethnic insurgents to coordinate armed resistance to the Burmese military junta in 1997. The group, mostly led by exile leaders, attempted to end long-standing feuds between different nationalist organizations, to organize a popular front to oppose the brutal junta, and to work for the replacement of the military government by a democratic federation of autonomous states.

In 2000–2002, refugees arriving in Thailand reported widespread incidents of forced labor and portering, arbitrary arrests, and torture. The Karennis, particularly those in relocation centers, became in effect an unwilling pool of labor that the military drew on for work on military bases, building roads, and clearing land. Reports of forced labor involving men, women, and children over 12 years old increased after 1998. Massive human-rights violations, including rape, forced population movements, and slave labor, occurred as part of the government's counterinsurgency campaign against the Karenni separatists of the Karenni National Progressive Party (KNPP) and other groups, who have been fighting for a free and independent Karenni state for over half a century.

SELECTED BIBLIOGRAPHY:

Bernard, Patrick. *Karennis: Fighters of the Golden Triangle.* 1997.
Chapman, Dean. *Karenni.* 1999.
Lintner, Bertil. *Land of Jade: A Journey through Insurgent Burma.* 1990.
Smith, Martin. *Burma, Insurgency and the Politics of Ethnicity.* 1988.

Karens

Kawthules; Kawthooleis; Sg'au; Sgaws; Kariang; Yang

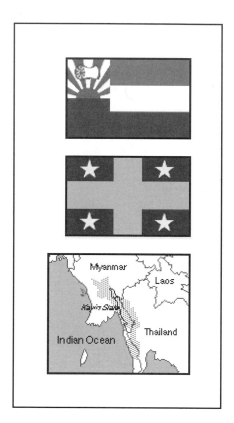

POPULATION: Approximately (2002e) 4,400,000 Karens in southeastern Asia, concentrated in southern Myanmar and northwestern Thailand, where about 400,000 Karens live. There may be as many as 500,000 Karens living illegally in Thailand in addition to those in the refugee camps and the 100,000 refugee Karens along the border. Nationalists claim a national population of over eight million Karens in southeastern Myanmar and northwestern Thailand.

THE KAREN HOMELAND: The Karen homeland, called Kawthoolei, meaning "Land of Flowers" in the Karen languages, lies in southeastern Myanmar and northwestern Thailand. The traditional Karen homeland includes much of southern Myanmar, including the lower Irrawaddy River basin and the densely forested mountains of the Pegu Yoma Mountains in Kayin State and Tanintharyi (Tenasserim) Division. The Karen homeland is divided between Kayin State, Toungoo and Prome Districts of Pegu Division, and the mountainous eastern strip of Tenasserim Division of the Union of Myanmar. The former Karen state, renamed Kayin in June 1989, covers the highland region in the southeast of the traditional Karen homeland. *State of Kayin (Kawthoolei)*: 11,731 sq. mi.—30,383 sq. km, (2002e) 1,527,000—Karens 78%, Burmans 16%, Shans* 3%, Mons* 2%, others 1%. The Karen capital and major cultural center is Toungoo, called Taungthu by the Karens, (2002e) 108,000, the center of the lowland Karens. Other important cultural centers are Paan, called Hpa'an by the Karens, (2002e) 9,000, the capital of Kayin State, and Thabaw, in Tenasserim Division.

FLAG: The Kawthoolei flag, the flag of the national movement and of the Karen National Union (KNU), is a horizontal tricolor of red, white,

940

and blue bearing a vertical blue stripe at the hoist charged with a rising red sun surmounted by a golden Karen drum. The flag of the Karen National Association (KNA) is a blue field bearing a broad red cross dividing the field into four quadrants, each with a white five-pointed star.

PEOPLE AND CULTURE: The Karens are a people of mixed Thai, Chinese, and Malay ancestry encompassing three main divisions—the Sgaw in the hills and upper valleys of the east and southeast, the Bwe in the more remote mountain valleys, and the Pwo, the lowland Karen dispersed among other ethnic groups in the center and west. They are not a unitary group in any ethnic sense, differing linguistically, religiously, and economically. Collectively the Karen tribes form the second largest of the non-Burman national groups in Myanmar, after the Shans. Most lowland Pwo Karens live in the river valleys and build their houses on stilts to prevent flooding during the rainy season. Significant numbers of ethnic Karens in the Irrawaddy region and in Yangon (Rangoon) have partially assimilated into the majority culture and have established ties to the neighboring Burmans.

LANGUAGE AND RELIGION: The Karen language comprises a group of related dialects usually divided into three broad groups: Northern, including Taungthu; Central, including Bwe and Geba; and Southern, including Pwo and Sgaw. There are numerous subdialects based on geography and clan groups. Only Pwo (Pho) and Sgaw are literary languages. Most scholars believe that the Karen languages are related to the Tibeto-Burman group of the Sino-Tibetan language family, but the relationships do not appear to be close. The Karen dialects have been greatly influenced by the Tai and Austro-Asiatic language groups.

The majority of the Karens are Buddhists or adhere to traditional beliefs, with a large and important Christian minority, mostly Baptist, as well as a sizable Muslim population. American Baptist missionaries set up the first mission stations in most Karen regions in the nineteenth century; much of the military and cultural elite is drawn from the Christian community.

NATIONAL HISTORY: According to legend, the Karens originated in an area north of ancient Babylon and passed through the Gobi Desert, called the River of Sand, 4,500 years ago. The tradition claims that the Karens arrived in their present homeland by way of China in the fifth century B.C. An early Karen state, a federation of tribes called Thowanabonmi, flourished in the area until its destruction by invading Burmans in 1044. Abandoning the lowlands to the invaders, many of the Karen tribes retreated to strongholds in the mountains.

Nearly constant war with Burmans forced the Karens to develop a strong military tradition and a resolute sense of independence. Fierce Karen warriors repulsed the Mongols in the thirteenth century and defeated Burman offensives in the sixteenth and seventeenth centuries. The passionately independent Karen tribes, resisting all invaders of their mountain homeland, retained a precarious freedom that was constantly threatened by Burman and Thai incursions.

The British conquest of Burma, beginning in 1826, eased Burman military pressure on the highland Karens. Tribal chiefs and elders, welcoming the British as valuable allies, signed military and political agreements and provided willing recruits to Britain's colonial army. The autonomous tribes remained mostly self-governing under nominal British rule and most were not included in the Burmese territories. Traditional leaders retained a degree of political control.

A Karen legend that their true religion would arrive with light-skinned strangers facilitated the establishment of European and American missions in their homeland in the 1870s and 1880s. Mission schools introduced the tribes to modern education and facilitated communication among the far-flung Karen clans. The Karens became the first people in the region to evolve an educated, Christian leadership. Western ideas, particularly those of culture and nation, stimulated the growth of national sentiment among the disparate tribes. The first Karen cultural organization formed in 1881, the forerunner of the later Karen separatist movement.

The Karens, considered outstanding soldiers, provided over half the recruits to the British colonial army in Burma in the 1930s. The Karens were increasingly used to contain a growing Burman nationalist movement; as a result, the ancient enmity between the two peoples deepened, and frequent violent confrontations occurred, particularly in the lowlands, where the two peoples lived interspersed.

In 1941 the Burmans, promised independence, supported the Japanese invasion. To counter the Japanese advance, the British ensured Karen loyalty with a parallel promise of eventual Karen independence. Less dependent on Karen support after the Burmans switched sides in 1944, the British changed tactics and began to support Burman demands for the inclusion of the non-Burman areas in an independent state.

A Karen delegation traveled to London in 1946 to discuss the details of the promised independence. Disappointed by the British support of a Burman state to include all of the British territories in the region, the Karens initially refused to discuss inclusion. Under intense British pressure they finally negotiated an agreement that provided for a large degree of autonomy within Burma and the right to secede if they wished, under British protection, after 10 years.

The Union of Burma's first president, Aung San, died at the hands of opponents soon after independence in 1948. Burma's new leaders rejected the independence constitution and refused to grant Karen autonomy. Their appeals to the British government ignored, the Karen nationalists led a widespread revolt. Quickly overrunning most of south-central Burma, the rebel army laid siege to the Burmese capital, Rangoon. The Burmese government leaders, U Nu and Nu Win, agreed to negotiations, but once in the city the entire Karen delegation was murdered.

The leaderless Karen rebellion began to collapse, and the rebels fell back under heavy attacks. New Karen leaders, disavowing earlier demands for autonomy, declared the independence of the Republic of Kawthoolei on 14 June 1949. They created a new national capital at Toungoo, the center of lowland Karen culture. Overrun by government troops in March 1950, the Karen nationalists once again retreated to their mountains. Their new capital at Papun in the highlands was captured in 1955.

A number of nationalist organizations emerged during the decades of insurgency after 1949, the proliferation reflecting the Karen's religious, political, and regional differences. The rebels, controlling a region with 75% of the world's remaining teak resources, long depended on modest logging operations to finance their separatist war. Logging concessions sold to Thai officials by the Burmese military government devastated the forests, and some of the Karen organizations turned to the drug trade for revenue.

Antigovernment Karen groups remained active, particularly in the mountainous regions, throughout the period from 1948 to the late 1980s. In 1976 a number of national groups formed the National Democratic Front, aiming to create a federation of independent states. In 1984 the first refugee camps were set up in Thailand under the de facto control of Karen nationalist leaders. The Thais, at that time opposed to the Burmese military government, allowed the Karens to cross the border freely and provided goods and protection for Karen refugees fleeing government military operations.

A strong prodemocracy movement swept Burma in 1988, but a military junta, calling itself the State Law and Order Restoration Council (SLORC), took power and brutally crushed it. Many ethnic Karens, particularly those living in the lowlands, supported the democracy movement, which had promised autonomy and cultural rights. The SLORC consolidated its hold on Burma, which it renamed Myanmar, by negotiating cease-fires with some ethnic nationalist groups and attacking others militarily.

Myanmar's military government, considered one of the most brutal of the world's surviving dictatorships, launched the largest offensive against the Karens in over a decade in early 1992; it saw the Karens, harboring many Burman opponents of the government, as the greatest threat to the military regime and the key to the country's other ethnic insurgencies. In April 1992, the military junta declared a unilateral cease-fire with all ethnic rebel groups and offered peace talks, which seriously divided the Christian and Buddhist factions of the Karen nationalist groups. Buddhists in the Karen National Union (KNU) defected and formed the Democratic Kayin Buddhist Army (DKBA), which opened negotiations with the government and formed a military alliance against the Christian-led KNU. The leaders of the DKBA charged that Buddhists had been discriminated against by the Christian leadership of the KNU.

In January 1994 several Karen groups, lulled by the government cease-fire, announced their intention to open a dialogue with the government. The decision opened a rift between the various Karen factions and revealed continuing religious and regional divisions. In December 1994, disregarding its own cease-fire, the government sought to take advantage of the Karen rift by launching a strong offensive against the Karen mountain strongholds. The offensive reunited the Karen leadership and reopened the long separatist war.

The Karen leaders denounced Thai involvement in the conflict. The Thai government, interested in lucrative ties to the military junta in Rangoon, closed the border and cracked down on Karen nationalist and refugee organizations operating in Thailand. In March 1997, the Thais began to repatriate forcibly some of the 100,000 Karen refugees, who faced reprisals in Myanmar.

Government troops and Buddhist Karens overran the Karen National Union (KNU) headquarters at Manerplaw on the Thai border in February 1995. The fall of the separatist capital sent some 15,000 refugees fleeing across the Thai border. The fall of Manerplaw freed the Karen fighters of the KNU from defending a fixed position, allowing them to return to the hit-and-run tactics favored by the guerrilla forces. Peace talks initiated by the SLORC collapsed in January 1997, followed by a renewed government offensive against Karens along the Thai border.

Government troops swept through the lowland Toungoo, Nyaunglebin, and Thaton Districts in 1995, burning and looting Karen villages, and conscripting civilians as laborers or porters. The tactics used to terrorize the civilian Karen population in the lowlands seemed random, as most lowland Karens had carefully remained neutral since the widespread Karen revolt since the late 1940s.

Karen nationalist leaders, in 1997–99, held meetings with other ethnic groups who felt betrayed by the government's duplicity since the cease-fire agreements of the early 1990s. The meetings aimed at rekindling a united front against the junta and voiced support for the opposition democratic leader of Myanmar, Aung San Suu Kyi. In June 1997, the leader of the Karen National Union, Bo Mya, rejected a new invitation from the ruling military junta to visit Yangon (Rangoon) for a new round of talks aimed at securing a cease-fire agreement.

In August 1997, the Burmese military burned 178 Karen villages, killing 83 civilians, in a bid to cut off support to the KNU. Some 46,000 civilians were left homeless or were forced to relocate in four districts in Karen

State and Pegu Division. Many crossed into Thai territory to join the thousands of refugees already there.

Fighting between nationalist Karen groups and the progovernment DKBA escalated in 1998. Attacks on Karen refugee camps in Thailand by the DKBA led to international condemnation and greater financial support for groups working with the refugees.

The State Law and Order Restoration Council changed its name in November 1997 to State Peace and Development Council (SPDC) in an effort to reduce the negative image of the military junta. Several SLORC officials alleged to be involved in large-scale corruption were sidelined, but otherwise government policies, particularly those involving antigovernment ethnic groups, remained unchanged. Slavery, forced labor, relocation, and arbitrary killings continued unabated.

Twenty-three ethnic and political groups met in Karen territory in December 1998 to attend a seminar on national solidarity. The delegates reaffirmed their support for the replacement of the brutal military government of Myanmar with a democratic federation of sovereign states. In April 1999, delegations from 15 ethnic groups met to consolidate their power and prepare guerrilla troops to fight the government.

In late January 2000, rebels of a Karen splinter group called God's Army took control of a hospital in western Thailand, demanding that the Thais open their border to Karen refugees fleeing the Burmese army and to wounded Karen fighters seeking medical assistance. Thai soldiers routed the Karens holding the hospital, but the Karen demands that the border be reopened to refugees remains a sensitive issue, particularly among the Thai Karen population.

The estimated 100,000 Karens in the refugee camps in Thailand are increasingly at risk. The mainly Christian Karens are being helped by Christian aid organizations, but in January 2000, after the attack by God's Army, the attitude of the Thai government hardened. Movement of the refugees was forbidden, even to leave a camp for work. Repatriation of the Karen refugees to Myanmar increased. For the refugees, the major hope for the future is a change of government in Yangon.

In early 2000 reports coming out of closed Myanmar told of a renewed government policy involving killing Karen civilians at random, in an apparent effort to terrorize villagers into severing their alleged connections with rebel soldiers. The government continues earlier policies of forcibly relocating Karen villagers to sites controlled by the military and of conscripting Karen civilians for unpaid labor. The Karens, who have fought for over a half-century for self-determination, one of the longest continuing insurgencies in modern history, continue to struggle for a more basic aim, their national survival.

SELECTED BIBLIOGRAPHY:

Fisher, Frederick. *Myanmar*. 2000.
Gall, Timothy L. *Worldmark Encyclopedia of Culture and Daily Life*. 1998.
Lintner, Bertil. *Land of Jade: A Journey through Insurgent Burma*. 1990.
Smith, Martin. *Burma, Insurgency and the Politics of Ethnicity*. 1988.

Kasaians

Luba-Kasai; Luba-Lulua; Western Lubas

POPULATION: Approximately (2002e) 11,500,000 Kasaians in Congo, concentrated in the southern provinces of Kasai and Katanga. Outside Congo there are Kasaian populations, known by the names of subtribes, in Angola and Zambia.

THE KASAIAN HOMELAND: The Kasaian homeland occupies the heavily wooded basin of the Kasai River and its tributaries in south-central Congo, a region of rain forests and lowlands. Kasai forms two provinces, Kasai-Occidental and Kasai-Oriental, of the Democratic Republic of Congo. *Kasai*: 125,500 sq. mi.—325,045 sq. km, (2002e) 9,715,000—Kasaians (Lubas and Luluas and subgroups) 83%, Tetelas 8%, Lundas 5%, other Congolese 4%. The capital and major cultural center of the Luba-Kasai is Mbuji-Mayi, (2002e) 896,000, metropolican area 1,043,000, the capital of Kasai-Oriental. The capital and major cultural center of the Lulua is Kananga, (2002e) 536,000, the capital of Kasai-Occidental.

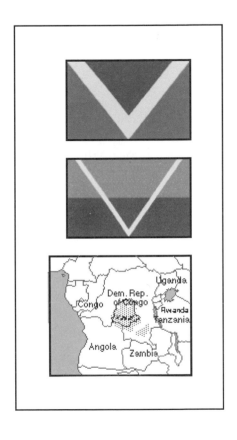

FLAG: The Kasaian national flag, the flag of the former republic, is a green field bearing a large red triangle in the center, point down, outlined in yellow. The flag of the national movement is a horizontal bicolor of red over green bearing a large yellow V centered.

PEOPLE AND CULTURE: The Kasaians comprise the Luba and Lulua tribes and their subtribes. The two peoples are part of the same nation and formed one tribe until the seventeenth century. Their origins are traced to an area east of the Kasai River around the headquarters of the Lualaba River, from which they spread over a large area. Although they remain separate, the Luba centered on Mbuji-Mayi and the Lulua on Kananga have greatly increased ties and cooperation since the chaos of the 1960s. The Kasaians are a patrilineal people, with descent through the male line, except the Hemba subgroup in the east, which is matrilineal. Kasaian society is traditionally divided into castes, including nobles, warriors, freemen, foreigners, and slaves. Chiefs are chosen from the noble class. Individual communities are fairly independent.

LANGUAGE AND RELIGION: The language of the Kasaians, called Tshiluba or Luba-Lulua, is a Bantu language of the Benue-Niger language group. It is spoken in seven major dialects—Luba-Kasai, Lulua, Luntu, Binji, Mputu, North Kete, and Songye, as well as a number of subdialects. There are significant dialectal differences between the Lubas or Eastern Kasaians and the Bena Lulua or Western Kasaians. The language is loosely related to Luba-Katanga, spoken by the Katangans* to the southeast. French is widely spoken as a second language and is to a considerable extent the lingua franca of the Kasai region.

The majority of the Kasaians are nominally Christians, mainly Roman Catholic. Traditional beliefs are based on a supreme being who is either a sky or earth god. Ancestor spirits are also worshipped. The ancestors, both mythic and recent, are honored at shrines, while nature spirits are believed to inhabit trees, mountains, and other elements of nature. There are various religious practices that focus on fertility, the protection of children, and ensuring good crops and successful hunts.

NATIONAL HISTORY: Bantu peoples settled their present region before the fifth century A.D., establishing numerous small clan and tribal states. In the eighth and ninth centuries an elaborate culture evolved, based on mining and on trade, mostly in slaves and ivory. A local chief, Kongolo, began to expand his territory by conquering neighboring chiefdoms in the early fifteenth century. Kongolo's son, Kalala Ilunga, completed the unification of the Luba kingdom. The powerful Luba state controlled extensive territories in what are now Congo, Zambia, and Angola, including a number of tributary states.

The early kingdoms of the region maintained relations with the Portuguese in Angola, who supplied cloth and other goods in return for slaves and ivory. Around 1600 the Luba kingdom fell to the Lunda kingdom of Katanga; it soon broke away, only to disintegrate through internal dissension and civil war. Attacks by the Luba-Katanga drove many Lubas to migrate northwest, from where they established new kingdoms. The Luba tribe split following a territorial dispute. The Lulua subtribe in the north organized as a separate tribe. A number of small successor states were visited by European explorers in the 1850s and 1860s. The Europeans reported a decayed empire rich in diamonds and other valuable minerals.

The Belgians, extending their territorial holdings east from the Congo River, penetrated the region in the 1870s and 1880s. In 1885 the Belgians formally laid claim to the Kasaian homeland. Mining companies quickly formed to exploit the rich diamond and mineral deposits. In 1895 a widespread revolt of African troops against the Belgians in Kasai seriously threatened the European hold on the region. In 1908, in response to international criticism of its treatment of the African population, Belgium annexed the area, which had been a personal concession of the king, as the Belgian Congo.

The Lubas readily adapted to European culture and education. Expanding throughout most of the Kasai region in the 1920s and 1930s, the Luba began to move into the Lulua territory. The Luba rapidly became the largest ethnic group in the Lulua's traditional capital, Luluabourg, later renamed Kananga. While the Lulua remained a mostly rural people, the Luba urbanized and moved into the local administration. The Kasaians, now called Luba-Kasai, began migrating to neighboring Katanga to work on the Belgian farms and in the growing industries.

Production of goods and minerals was greatly increased to aid the Belgian war effort during World War II. The urbanization of the Kasaians accelerated and brought large-scale social and economic change. Demands for political reform and greater local control of mineral wealth began in the postwar era. Legal reforms were enacted permitting Africans to own land and to participate, in limited ways, in politics.

Elections for local city councils in 1957 gave the peoples of the Belgium Congo their first taste of democracy. Long prohibited, political parties quickly formed, many based on tribal and regional loyalties. Anticipation of Belgium's announced intention to grant independence to the Congo reactivated old tribal and regional rivalries.

The Congolese National Movement (MNC), based in Kasai, emerged as an important factor in the independence movement. In July 1959 the MNC split into two rival organizations. One faction was led by Patrice Lumumba, an ethnic Tetela from northern Kasai, and was largely supported by the Luluas. The other faction was headed by Albert Kalonji, a Luba-Kasai. This more moderate wing, known as MNC-Kalonji, drew support from the Luba-Kasai in the south and west of Kasai.

Violence between the Luba and Lulua escalated rapidly as chaos overtook the huge Congo territory. Over a million Luba fled back to their homeland in southern Kasai in 1959–60. With the Congo government unable or unwilling to protect them, the Luba increasingly espoused demands for separation. The Luba nationalist leader, Albert Kalonji, proposed a federation of autonomous states in the Congo, but the Belgian authorities ignored the suggestion in their haste to grant independence to a unified Congo state.

In May 1960, in national legislative elections, MNC-Lumumba won the largest number of votes, and the Belgian authorities named Lumumba prime minister. On 30 June 1960 Congo received its independence amid growing turmoil and violence. In Kasai, armed Luluas launched attacks on Luba areas and overran Luluabourg, setting off a bloody civil war in the province. The Belgian military intervened only to rescue endangered Europeans. Encouraged by the secession of neighboring Katanga, Albert Kalonji declared the independence of the Republic of South Kasai on 9 August 1960. Backed by the Belgian mining companies and Belgian volunteers, the Lubas retook Luluabourg and consolidated their hold on the province. Lumumba used loyal military forces to launch a major offensive against both Katanga and Kasai secessionists. The troops never reached Katanga, but their attack on Kasai led to a large-scale massacre of the Luba population.

In September 1960, amid infighting between the new country's leaders, the chief of staff of the military, Mobutu Sese Seko, stepped in and assumed power, retaining the facade of a civilian government. In January 1961 Lumumba was assassinated, further alienating his Lulua supporters. Soldiers of the reorganized central Congolese government invaded the breakaway Kasaian state in December 1961. The Congolese were driven back but returned in September 1962. Thousands died in the pacification of South Kasai in the spring of 1963. Refugees fleeing into Angola formed antigovernment groups that continued to harass the border region for several years.

Mobutu seized power in a military coup and was installed as Congo's president in 1965, receiving the support of the West as an anticommunist ally in central Africa. Fears that the resources of the huge country would fall into the hands of the Soviet Union led to widespread Western support in spite of massive corruption and repression. The French government became the main aid and financial supporter, while the United States provided military and logistic aid. Mobutu established a one-party dictatorship that allowed little dissent or opposition. Over the next decades the Mobutu regime systematically looted the once rich country, which Mobutu renamed Zaire in 1971. Mobutu tried to create a specific nationalism based on loyalty to the Zairean state in the place of regional nationalism, and to downplay ethnic differences and loyalties, but regionalism, nationalism and ethnic rivalries remained strong. Mobutu seized hundreds of foreign-owned businesses and gave them to his cronies, who promptly brought them to ruin.

Kasaian nationalism resumed in the early 1970s, driven by the declining economy and massive government corruption. By 1976, when Mobutu reversed the nationalization of foreign-owned firms, incomes and development in the region had fallen to less than half of what they had been in the secession period; the economy was in ruins. Revenues from Kasai's industrial diamonds, some 90% of the world's total, disappeared or were stolen, while no new roads, construction, or maintenance had been undertaken for over three decades.

The end of the Cold War greatly reduced the West's automatic support of Mobutu; his former allies rapidly reduced military aid and demanded political and economic reforms. Mobutu's loosening hold on the huge country fueled the rapid growth of regional and national sentiments.

The resurgent nationalism in neighboring Katanga was manifested in ethnic violence in 1990, when Katangans turned on the Kasaian minority. Many of the Kasaians living in Katanga were educated city dwellers, easy targets for Katangan mobs. Violent attacks on the Kasaians forced thousands to flee back to Kasai, the refugees provoking a rapid increase in Kasaian nationalism. Renewed attacks in Katanga in 1992–95 left thousands of Kasaian dead and injured, swelling the refugee population to over 100,000.

The Kasaian peoples, the Luba and Lulua, renewed their ties in the face of the common threat, and both peoples supported the growing national movement. The revival of ethnic rivalries, fanned by the Mobutu regime, which claimed that only President Mobutu could hold the country together, renewed the Kasaian nostalgia for the pre-independence peace and security of the Belgian colonial period. The Kasaians' shared poverty in a region that should be one of Africa's most prosperous became the prime movement in the reconciliation of the Luba and Lulua.

In 1990 the Zairean government legalized political opposition, at the insistence of the international aid donors. One opposition leader, Etienne Tshisekedi, a Kasaian, formed the Union of Federalists and Independent Republicans. Several of Tshisekedi's former allies deserted the opposition to form an alliance with Mobutu—in order, they declared, to prevent a dictatorship by the Kasaians. One of these men, Gabriel Kyungu wa Kumwanza, became governor of neighboring Katanga. Attacks on Kasaians in Katanga became more frequent, and over 100,00 Kasaians who had lived in Katanga for generations returned to the Kasaian heartland. Fighting between the Katangans and the Luba-Kasai led to large-scale expulsions of Kasaians from Katanga between 1992–95. Thousands died in ethnic clashes and in concentration camps.

Tshisekedi was named prime minister of Zaire in 1992. The Kasaians demonstrated in triumph, but violence again broke out in Katanga, and mass expulsions of Kasaians resumed. Mobutu (as president and head of state) attempted to dismiss Tshisekedi just a week after his appointment, leading to renewed crisis. Two assassination attempts on Tshisekedi by Mobutu's private militia in 1994 caused rioting in Kasai and calls for autonomy under a sovereign government led by Tshisekedi. The renewed violence and "ethnic cleansing" of the 1990s revived the Kasaian nationalist sentiment and calls for independence of the early 1960s. In June 1995, leaders of the Zairean government announced that the secession of Kasai or Katanga or any other province would not be accepted peacefully.

The Mobutu regime mostly ignored the provinces as the structures of statehood vanished in the 1980s and 1990s. The Kasaians developed their own local power center, virtually autonomous of the Kinshasa government,

600 miles (1,000 km) to the west. The Kasaian political groups and the mining companies collaborated to reverse, at least in Kasai, the national slide toward economic collapse. The industrious Kasaians describe themselves as the "the Jews of Congo," and there are Kasaians in many parts of the huge country, giving the Kasaians the support of a large diaspora. The output of diamonds continued to grow until civil war began in 1997.

An attempt in October 1996 to expel ethnic Rwandan Tutsis from eastern Zaire sparked a revolt by the Tutsi minority there. The governments of Uganda and Rwanda, seeking to clear out the bases of rebels operating from inside Zaire, put Laurent Kabila, a Katangan, at the head of a mainly Tutsi rebel army. The rebels, gaining recruits from many ethnic groups willing to help oust Mobutu, overran most of Kasai in April 1997, effectively ending the de facto autonomous state that had operated in Kasai in recent years. Kabila then gave the population of eastern Kasai province an opportunity to elect their own leader. They chose an ally of Etienne Tshisekedi, Jean Mbuyi Mulomba, the president of the local Kasaian political party. Mulomba promptly declared that Kasai had already been freed; it did not need liberating again. After mid-1997 the Kabila government tried to depose him.

Kabila's forces finally forced Mobutu Sese Seko from power and took control over much of the country, including Kinshasa in May 1997, but differences with his Rwandan sponsors led to renewed fighting in August 1998 with newly organized rebel groups backed by Rwanda. Kabila declared himself president and took office on 29 May 1997. He restored the original name of the country, Congo. In June 1997, Tshisekedi was arrested by security agents, raising tension among the increasingly anti-Kabila Kasaians.

In July 1997, four generals in exile in South Africa announced that they would fight for the secession of Katanga and Kasai. The generals, funding their separatist campaign from the sale of cobalt illegally shipped out of Zaire before Kabila's takeover, gathered considerable support among the dissatisfied Kasaians. In September 1997, Mobutu Sese Seko died in exile in Morocco, and many of his loyalists joined the growing numbers calling for the secession of the southern provinces.

The Kasaians originally supported Kabila, hoping for an end to years of poverty and decline under the corrupt rule of the Mobutu regime. By May 1998, a year after assuming power, Kabila's government had proven just as corrupt and repressive as the former one; dreams of democracy and Kasaian autonomy quickly faded, and ethnic tension abounded. Mining investment in Kasai had slowed to almost nil, because the new government had broken earlier promises, making investors leery.

The Congo conflict drew in many of the countries of central Africa and became the most dangerous war in the region since the decolonization of the 1960s. Congo collapsed as a nation-state; plans for international peacekeepers and an imposed peace will probably not end the conflict. The Kasaians will continue to seek peace and prosperity in autonomy.

In April 2000, the Kabila government confiscated a 257-carat diamond from a group of traders in Mabuji-Mayi. The gem, the third largest ever found in Congo, had been bought by the traders, who had pooled their funds to finance the deal. The confiscation brought greater economic problems to the region, as it left the traders without funds to buy other diamonds coming onto the market. The Kasaians, calling the confiscation outright theft, participated in mass demonstrations, which turned into nationalist, antigovernment forums.

Laurent Kabila was shot in an argument in January 2001. His death, and his succession by his son, brought new instability to the Congolese state. Rebel groups stepped up their activities, and Kasaian leaders called for the replacement of the wrecked Congo state with a loose federation of autonomous states that would bring an end to the devastating civil war.

SELECTED BIBLIOGRAPHY:

Heale, Jay. *Democratic Republic of the Congo*. 1999.
Roberts, Mary Nooter, and Allen F. Roberts. *Luba*. 1998.
Schuyler, Philippa. *Who Killed the Congo?* 1962.
Wormersley, Harold. *Legends and History of the Luba*. 1984.

Kashmiris

Keshur; Pogulis; Kaschemiris; Cashmiris; Cashmeerees; Kacmiris

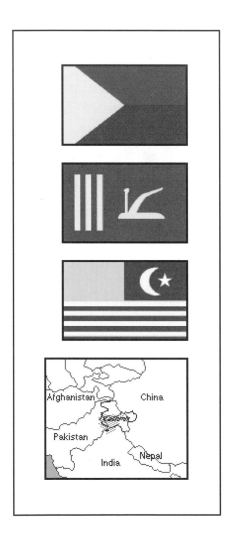

POPULATION: Approximately (2002e) 8,050,000 Kashmiris in South Asia, concentrated in the Jammu and Kashmir State of India, with a Kashmiri population of 5,663,000; and in the Azad Kashmir under Pakistani control, with a Kashmiri population of 3,015,000. There is a large Kashmiri refugee population in neighboring Pakistan. Outside the subcontinent the largest Kashmiri community, numbering about 150,000, is in the United Kingdom.

THE KASHMIRI HOMELAND: The Kashmiri homeland lies in the Vale of Kashmir, the basin of the Jhelum River, in the foothills of the Himalayas. The Pakistani zone forms a quasi-state called Azad (free) Kashmir, which has its own government and is regarded by Pakistan as a sovereign state. It consists of an arc-shaped territory bordering Indian Kashmir. Historical Jammu and Kashmir, 90% of which is mountainous, has a territory of 85,806 sq. mi.—222,236 sq. km—and is currently divided between India, Pakistan, and China, which occupied a sparsely populated part of Indian Kashmir in 1962. Historical Kashmir, with a population of over 10 million, is divided between the Indian state of Jammu and Kashmir and Pakistani Kashmir, encompassing Azad Kashmir, the districts of Muzaffarabad, Kotli, Mirpur, and part of Punch, and the Northern Areas (Gilgit and Baltistan). *State of Jammu and Kashmir*: 53,665 sq. mi.—138,992 sq. km, (2002e) 10,296,000—Kashmiris 55%, Paharis 24%, Dogris 7%, Punjabis 2%, other Indians 12%. *Azad Kashmir*: 4,494 sq. mi.—11,531 sq. km, (2002e) 3,351,000—Kashmiris 90%, Punchis 8%, other Pakistanis 2%. The Kashmiri capital and major cultural center is Srinagar,

954

(2002e) 1,094,000. The capital and major cultural center of Azad Kashmir is Muzaffarabad, (2002e) 40,000.

FLAG: The Kashmiri national flag, the flag of the national movement and of the Jammu and Kashmir Liberation Front (JKLF), is a horizontal bicolor of green over red with a white triangle at the hoist. The flag of the Indian state of Jammu and Kashmir is a red field bearing a centered, stylized white swan and three white stripes. The flag of Azad Kashmir is a green field bearing four narrow white stripes on the bottom, an orange canton on the upper hoist, and a white crescent moon and a white five-pointed star on the upper fly.

PEOPLE AND CULTURE: The Kashmiris are the descendants of Indo-Aryan people; many of them tall and fair, they more closely resemble the peoples of Central Asia than those of India or Pakistan. Believed to have originated in Central Asia, the Kashmiri culture retains many ancient customs and traditions, brought to the region by the original settlers; the survivals have combined with later Indian and Muslim influences. The majority of the Kashmiris are rural, with only about 20% living in urban areas. Extended families commonly live together in family compounds or villages. The Kashmiris are known for their hospitality, which is a cultural obligation and tradition. The Muslim religion has always formed an integral part of the Kashmiri culture and has become even more important since the outbreak of violence in the late 1980s.

LANGUAGE AND RELIGION: The Kashmiris speak Kashmir, a Dardic or Central Asian language of the Indo-Iranian language group. The language is written in the Persian script. The literacy rate, after more than a decade of violence, is now below the average in India, and it continues to fall as schools remain closed or curtailed. The Kashmiri language is spoken in 13 dialects; the literary language is based on the Standard Kashmiri or Kashtawari dialect. The southern dialects of Kashmiri form a linguistic bridge to Punjabi. Urdu, the language of many of India's Muslims, is spoken by many Kashmiris and is often considered more prestigious than Kashmiri. English is also spoken as a second language. Kashmiri literature can be traced to the fifteenth century, and poetry remains an important part of modern literature.

The majority of the Kashmiris are Sunni Muslims, with a small Shi'a Muslim minority. In the Kashmiri heartland, the Vale of Kashmir, the population is 98% Muslim. The religion as once practiced by the Kashmiris was more tolerant and less militant than in most Muslim groups, but the religious aspect of the present conflict has polarized religious sentiment, and a strain of intolerant fundamentalism is now evident among many Kashmiri nationalists. There are small Kashmiri Hindu and Christian communities.

NATIONAL HISTORY: The Vale of Kashmir region, first mentioned in ancient chronicles as part of the Buddhist Mauryan state in about 200

B.C., mostly converted to Hinduism under later rulers. Lying at the confluence of several ancient empires, the region knew many conquerors from Central Asia, Mongolia, and Iran. The smaller ethnic groups survived only in inaccessible mountain valleys. In the second century A.D. Kashmir was annexed by Emperor Kunishka, who made it part of the Kushan Empire.

Aryan Muslim tribes, moving south from Central Asia, conquered the Kashmir region in the fourteenth century. Their Islamic religion rapidly spread across the area to most of Kashmir's earlier inhabitants. An independent Muslim sultanate, created in the mid-fourteenth century and centered in the Vale of Kashmir, experienced a great flowering, a golden age, under the rule of Sultan Zain-al-Abadin; this period, lasting from 1420 to 1470, is known as the "Budshah." Kashmir's independence lasted until its conquest by the Mogul Empire in 1586. Reestablished at the collapse of the lowland Moguls in 1751, the Kashmiri state soon fell to invading Pushtuns* from Afghanistan. From 1756 the Kashmiris retained considerable autonomy under loose Pushtun rule.

The Sikhs* conquered the Vale of Kashmir in 1819. The Sikhs set up a Hindu Dogra, from a non-Kashmiri minority group, Gulab Singh, as the ruler of Jammu in 1820 but retained the rest of Kashmir under direct Sikh control. Continued Sikh incursions into British territory provoked the First Sikh War in 1846. The victorious British deposed the Sikh rulers and sold the conquered Kashmir area to Gulab Singh of Jammu, who had remained carefully neutral during the conflict. This allowed the British to create a buffer between the colony in India and China and Russia, without having to deal with the financial or administrative responsibilities. In 1885 the British installed a "resident" in Srinagar to oversee relations between Kashmir and British India.

The rule of Gulab Singh's descendants, the Hindu Dogra rajas of Kashmir, became increasingly despotic in the early twentieth century. The growing Muslim discontent and resentment of their Hindu ruler finally erupted in open rebellion in 1931. Forced to make concessions, the raja legalized political parties and in 1934 granted a legislative assembly.

In 1939 the Muslims, led by Muhammad Abdullah, called the "Lion of Kashmir," formed the Kashmir National Conference. The formation of the political party is considered the inception of modern Kashmiri nationalism. Inspired by Mahatma Gandhi's movement in India, the Kashmiris began to agitate against Hindu domination.

The British authorities at the end of World War II began preparations to grant independence to the two divisions of British India, Hindu-dominated India and Muslim Pakistan. Kashmir's Hindu majaraja, Hari Singh, imprisoned Muhammad Abdullah for leading a pro-Pakistani campaign and refused to cede his state to either India or Pakistan. Faced with a widespread Muslim uprising, the raja released Abdullah, who kept Kashmir calm as violence and massacres flared in many other areas of India and Pakistan during the political partition of British India.

Pushtun Muslim tribesmen from Pakistan invaded, and a pro-independence uprising erupted within the state. On 4 October 1947 a provisional government deposed the raja and declared the independence of the Republic of Azad-Kashmir (Free Kashmir). Maharaja Hari Singh fled to Delhi, where he signed a treaty of cession to India on 17 October 1947. Indian troops, airlifted into the Vale of Kashmir 10 days later, confronted the Muslim rebels and the invading Pakistani troops. The Indians suppressed the separatist government, and in 1948 a United Nations cease-fire effectively partitioned Kashmir between India and Pakistan, but only as a temporary measure until a referendum could be organized to decide Kashmir's future. In January 1949, the UN Commission for India and Pakistan passed a resolution mandating a plebiscite of the Kashmiri people.

The Indian government rejected the plan for a referendum and organized Indian-occupied Kashmir as the State of Jammu and Kashmir, the only Indian state with a Muslim majority. The Kashmiris were thus denied free and open elections. Advocates of Kashmiri self-determination were severely suppressed, but many Kashmiris believed secular India would protect their distinct identity better than avowedly Islamic Pakistan.

Muhammad Abdullah, continuing to demand a referendum on independence, spent years in Indian prisons. Released in 1964, he denounced India's authority in the state as illegal. In response, the Indian government replaced Kashmir's local administration with Indian civil servants. Tension in the region sparked another inconclusive war with Pakistan in 1965; a Pakistani invasion failed to win popular Kashmiri support for union with Pakistan. After the war, Kashmiri resistance to Indian rule became more militant. The Indian authorities responded with strict censorship, curfews, and the arrest of virtually all supporters of Kashmiri self-determination.

Fighting again erupted in Kashmir in 1971, when Indian and Pakistan fought a war over the secession of East Pakistan, later called Bangladesh. Pakistan, significantly weakened by the secession of Bangladesh, was less able to challenge Indian control of Kashmir. The fighting ended with a new cease-fire line drawn across Kashmir in July 1972.

Muhammad Abdullah died in 1982, but his National Conference Party, led by his son Farooq, won state elections in 1983. Years of Indian misrule had alienated most Kashmiris, but movement toward secession ended with the imposition of direct rule from New Delhi in 1984; the disbanding of the nationalist Kashmiri government marked a rapid upsurge of nationalist sentiment. Widespread protests erupted across the state.

Kashmiri Muslims set off a series of bombs, arson attacks, and strikes. The Indian government responded with military actions that often targeted the civilian population. In 1988 a widespread Muslim rebellion began in the state, led by the JKLF. By 1992 at least three separate nationalist organizations were active in the region. The separatist Kashmiris soon split into two rival groups, pro-independence and pro-Pakistan, which often fought among themselves. The proliferation of groups of varying ideological and religious factions ultimately had adverse effects on the Kashmir national movement. The Indian government stationed a large number of troops and imposed strict curfews and press regulations. Indian security forces, in 1992, were accused by human rights organizations of a campaign of terror against the Kashmiri civilian population.

Pro-independence sentiment spread to Pakistani Kashmir. The mounting tension in the region, and Pakistani support of the pro-Pakistani Kashmiri groups, brought India and Pakistan close to war in 1990. Attempts by Kashmiri nationalists in Pakistani Kashmir to march across the cease-fire line in an effort to reunify their homeland ended in violent confrontations with Pakistani troops in early 1992, leaving 18 dead and over 350 injured. The violence fueled a rise of pro-independence feeling in the Pakistani zone.

In May 1994, the Pakistani government accused the Indians of attacking Kashmiris in Azad Kashmir; the clashes between Indian and Pakistani troops escalated. The Indian government accused Pakistan of supporting the Kashmiri separatists; India suspected Pakistan of arming, training, and logistically supporting the militants.

The rivalries between the various groups active in the region led to violent confrontations between pro-Pakistani and pro-independence advocates throughout the 1990s. Killings and attacks on the leaders of nationalist organizations were routinely carried out by rivals and the Indian security forces.

The Jammu and Kashmir Liberation Front offered in 1994 to give up the violent campaign for independence if the Indian government would agree to talks. The Indian government proposed regional elections. The separatist groups almost unanimously rejected the elections, declaring that only a plebiscite on secession will be accepted.

In May and June 1999, Indian and Pakistani forces clashed in the mountainous region along the cease-fire line after infiltrators from Pakistan entered Indian-held territory. The conflict, which brought international intervention by U.S. president William Clinton, nearly escalated into yet another Indian-Pakistani war—a prospect that is more dangerous than in the past, because both India and Pakistan now possess nuclear weapons. International leaders called on both India and Pakistan to settle the Kashmir issue and the seemingly endless cycle of violence in the region that had left between 25,000 and 70,000 dead by 1998.

The JKLF claims that historical Kashmir is an indivisible political entity and that no part of the region is constitutionally part of India, Pakistan, or China. To the nationalists, the Kashmir issue is not a territorial dispute between India and Pakistan but concerns the right of the Kashmiri nation to self-determination. They advocate the reunification of Jammu and Kashmir as a fully independent, democratic state.

The Indian government, in an attempt to crush the rebellion, has given broad powers to the Indian military, powers that have led to widespread abuses of human rights and to a brutal repression. The Indian excesses have alienated even moderate Kashmiris and have generally polarized Kashmiri opinion in favor of a united republic independent of both India and Pakistan. In late 1999, the government offered to begin talks with the Kashmiri nationalists, but on the condition that Kashmir remain part of India.

Farooq Abdullah is the highest elected Kashmiri state official and increasingly supports a return to the autonomy that Kashmir enjoyed in the first years of Indian independence. Abdullah's prestige as the son of the "Lion of Kashmir" makes him the only Kashmiri politician able to unite many of the disparate groups active in the region. Farooq Abdullah has become the spokesman for the Kashmiri desire for *azaadi*, the distancing of the Vale of Kashmir from both India and Pakistan.

Many scholars believe that the historical state of Jammu and Kashmir comprises a number of different units that should be allowed to exercise the right to self-determination separately, with full or limited independence for the Kashmiri homeland in the Vale of Kashmir one possible option. The opposition of the non-Kashmiris of the state, particularly the mainly Buddhist Ladakhis* and the Shi'a Balawaris,* to an autonomous Kashmiri state remains a major complication to an overall settlement of the conflict.

In June 2000, the provincial assembly of Indian Jammu and Kashmir, dominated by the National Conference Party, approved a plan to implement autonomy, opening a bitter conflict with the Indian national government. Members of the state government supported the motion as a first step back to the former arrangement. The motion approved a return to the pre-1953 status, when Jammu and Kashmir had its own president and prime minister. Until 1953, when the Indian government abolished the state's special status, all state activities except defense, foreign affairs, and telecommunications were under local control. The Indian government, dominated by Hindu nationalists, is bitterly opposed to granting autonomy to the Kashmiris, as are the Buddhist and Hindu inhabitants of Jammu and Kashmir, who see it as a first step to secession.

In July 2001, the leaders of Pakistan and India met for the first time, but the dispute over Kashmir was not broached. In the wake of the terrorist attacks in the United States in September 2001, several Kashmiri groups were listed by the United States as terrorist organizations.

SELECTED BIBLIOGRAPHY:

Ganguly, Sumit. *The Crisis in Kashmir: Portents of War, Hopes of Peace.* 1997.
Lamb, Alastair. *Kashmir: A Disputed Legacy, 1846–1990.* 1991.
Schfield, Victoria. *Kashmir in Conflict: India, Pakistan and the Unfinished War.* 2000.
Thomas, Raju G.C. *Perspectives on Kashmir: The Roots of Conflict in South Asia.* 1992.

Kashubians

Kashubs; Kaszébé; Kaszubes; Kazubs; Kaszubi; Kaszubians; Kaschuben; Cassubians; Cashubians

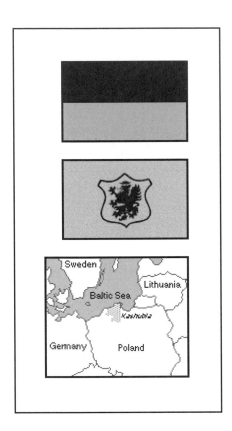

POPULATION: Approximately (2002e) 250,000 Kashubians in north-central Europe concentrated in Gulf of Gdansk region of northeastern Poland. The largest concentrations outside Poland are in Germany, the United States, Canada; with smaller numbers live in Brazil, Argentina, and Australia.

THE KASHUBIAN HOMELAND: The Kashubian homeland lies in the lowlands of northeastern Poland, mostly in the delta of the Vistula River and the coastal plains around the Gulf of Gdansk. Traditionally Kashubia occupies a triangular-shaped area directly south of the Baltic Sea and between the Odra (Oder) and the Wisla (Vistula) Rivers. The region, west and northwest of Gdansk, is included in the Polish provinces of Bydgoszcz, Gdansk, and Slupsk comprising all or parts of the districts of Puck, Wejherowo, Kartuzy, Koscierznya, Bytow, Chojnice, Czluchow, Lebork, Starogard Gdanski, and Tuchola. Kashubia is one of the most scenic parts of Poland, with sandy beaches, the picturesque and unusually narrow Hel Peninsula, and the numerous lakes found in the Kashubian Lake District, the "Kashubian Switzerland," to the south. Historically the Kashubian region is divided into western and eastern parts, the border running along the Slupia River southward to the town of Szczecinek. The region of Kashubia, called Kaszuby by the Kashubians, also Region Kaszubski, has no official status in Poland, but it constitutes a historical region and is considered the homeland by the Kashubian nation. The region has a large Polish majority. The Kashub capital and major cultural center is Kartuzy, (2002e) 12,000. Other important cultural centers are Chojnice, (2002e) 40,000, and Lebork, (2002e) 37,000.

FLAG: The Kashubian national flag, the unofficial flag of the Kashubian region, is a horizontal bicolor of black over yellow. The regional flag is yellow field bearing the Kashubian coat of arms, a black lion rampant on a yellow background centered.

PEOPLE AND CULTURE: The Kashubs, or Kashubians, are called Kaszubi by Poles but call themselves Kasz'b'. Traditionally the Kashubs are the last remnants of the ancient Slavic Pomeranians, whose name in the West Slavic dialect, Pomorze, means "along the sea." Traditionally the Kashubians' main occupation was fishing, which was carried out by teams, usually members of a single family, called a *mazoperia*. Before each fishing expedition, prayers for a safe return are offered to the Madonna of Swarzewo, the patroness of Kashubian fishermen. The modern Kashubians are still mostly fishermen, both along the Baltic Sea and in the lake region. A minority are industrial workers in the large cities of Gdansk, Gdynia, and Slupsk. The culture of the Kashubians has been influenced by the region's many rulers, particularly the Germans and Swedes. The culture, which has enjoyed new interest in the last decade, includes a distinct musical tradition. The traditional Kashubian *kapela*, a band of musicians, was resurrected as part of the overall cultural revival of the 1990s.

LANGUAGE AND RELIGION: The Kashubian language is a West Slavic language related to Polish. It is often called the Pomeranian dialect of Polish, but the language is distinct and has been heavily Germanized. Under communist rule Kashubian was treated as a dialect of Polish, though it had evolved as a separate West Slavic language. The number of speakers is thought to surpass 200,000, although the language of daily life is primarily the Pomeranian variant of Polish. Kashubian is spoken in two distinct dialects, Kashubian Proper and Slovincian; there are transitional dialects between Kashubian Proper, Slovincian, and Polish. Since the late 1980s, efforts have been made to revive the language. The Kashubian language differs greatly from literary Polish; however, with Polish (and Sorbian, spoken in Saxony in Germany) it belongs to the Lechitian subgroup of West Slavic languages. The first Kashubian schools in almost 50 years were opened in 1991, and a number of press titles in the language were published after 1992.

Roman Catholicism, the religion of the Kashubians, is an integral part of their culture. The Catholic Church promotes the Kashubian language in church services; a Kashubian translation of the New Testament was published in 1992. Church services often play large roles in the traditional occupation of fishing; annual religious festivals and celebrations reflect the rhythms of the fishing year.

NATIONAL HISTORY: The ancestors of the Slavs are thought to have been Neolithic tribes who occupied the Polesie Marshes in western Ukraine. By the sixth century Slavic tribes, including the Kashubs, had settled the coast of the Baltic Sea and occupied the inland territories. Sedentary fishermen and farmers, the Kashubs adopted a loosely democratic social organization.

In the tenth century, the Polians (dwellers of the fields), later known as Poles, led by their chief, Boleslaus I, conquered the Slavic tribes that inhabited Pomerania. The Poles' conversion to Christianity brought missionaries among the conquered tribes. In the eleventh century the Kashubians of Pomerania threw off Polish rule and created an independent duchy. In the twelfth century, the Poles again overran Pomerania. At the death of Boleslaus III in 1138, the Polish kingdom broke up; the Kashubians regained their independence in 1227.

Pomerelia, as eastern Pomerania, the Kashubian homeland, was retaken by the Poles in 1295. Germans known as "Teutonic Knights" gained a foothold in the region, and in 1308 the 10,000 inhabitants of Gdansk, mostly Kashubians, were massacred and replaced with ethnic Germans, beginning the history of German Danzig. By 1309 all of Kashubia had fallen to the German knights. The Poles defeated the Germans at Tannenberg in 1410 and began the reconquest of the region around the Gulf of Gdansk. In 1454 the entire Kashubian territory was incorporated into the Polish kingdom.

In 1466 the city of Gdansk, with its large German population, was granted the status of an autonomous city under Polish protection. The Kashubians, the original inhabitants, were reduced to a small minority by the beginning to the sixteenth century. The city became one of the leading cities of the Hanseatic League. In 1576 the city withstood a long Polish siege and preserved its special privileges.

The Kashubian homeland, although overrun by foreign armies several times during the wars of the fifteenth and sixteenth centuries, remained an integral part of the Polish kingdom except for areas incorporated into the Swedish kingdom. Mostly peasant farmers and fishermen, the Kashubians had been reduced to virtual serfdom by the sixteenth century under both Polish and Swedish rule. Many began to assimilate themselves into the Polish culture and language, particularly those living in the large city of Gdansk, where both the Kashubians and the Poles were less numerous than the German population.

The Poles lost Kashubia to Prussia during the first partition of the Polish kingdom in 1772. The region formed part of the Prussian province of West Prussia, with Gdansk as its capital. Under Prussian rule the Kashubians were subjected to intense Germanization. Danzig, with its surrounding area, became a German stronghold and cultural center. At the end of the Napoleonic Wars, the Congress of Vienna created a small Polish kingdom, including eastern Kashubia, in personal union with the Russian tsar. Under different political systems and influences, the western Kashubians partly Germanized, while those to the east clung to their Slavic language and culture.

The Kashubians participated in the Polish national revival that began in the 1820s. The revival, which helped to unite the various regional Polish groups, began as an anti-German and anti-Russian mass movement. Thousands of Kashubians joined the general uprising against Russian rule in 1830. With Polish defeat in 1831, their homeland, except for the region under Prussian rule, became part of the Russian Empire. Further violence broke out in Prussian Poland in 1848, and in Russian Poland in 1863.

Poor, sandy soil made farming difficult in Kashubia, and the returns from fishing were always unpredictable. Partition and political instability added to the grinding poverty. Many Kashubians chose to leave their homeland and emigrate to Canada and the United States. The largest wave of immigration took place between 1859 and 1898. Kashubian colonies were established in New World, where the old customs, traditions, and language were preserved alongside the new culture and their new language, English.

Germany's defeat in World War I allowed the Poles to resurrect their independent state. The 1919 peace treaty gave Poland part of eastern Kashubia, but in spite of Polish claims, German-populated Danzig, with its Kashubian hinterland, was made a separate free state under the protection of the new League of Nations. The city-state joined the Polish Customs Union and served as Poland's primary outlet to the sea, but the Poles, preferring their own port, constructed a new one at Gdynia, a small Kashubian village north of Danzig. In 1930 the city of Danzig, which was 95% German-speaking, had a population of 259,000, while the Free State of Danzig had population of 407,000, including many Germanized Kashubians.

The process of industrialization and modernization of Poland in the interwar period almost annihilated the ancient folk culture of the Kashubians. Many rural Kashubians, seeking employment, moved to cities, particularly Gdynia and Danzig (Gdansk).

The rise of the Nazis in Germany during the 1930s was paralleled by the increase in Nazi activity in Danzig. In November 1937, the Nazis obtained a two-thirds majority in the Danzig legislature. The Poles and Kashubians living in the state suffered increased repression as totalitarian rule was extended. In March 1939, Nazi Germany made extensive demands on Poland as regards Danzig and Pomerania, but Poland's alliance with France and the United Kingdom induced the German government to back down.

However, on 1 September 1939, without a declaration of war, the Germans invaded Poland. The Kashubians suffered tremendous losses of life and property in the war; many, particularly those able to speak German, were sent to labor camps in Germany. The last German troops were expelled from Poland in 1945 by Soviet troops. Many Germanized Kashubians also left for Germany, including the mother of Günter Grass, modern Germany's most celebrated writer.

The most immediate consequence of World War II for the region was what was called the return of Poland to its "ethnic borders," ordered by the Allied powers. With the conclusion of peace, the Soviet authorities encouraged the Poles to expel the German population of the Gdansk region, which included many Germanized Kashubians, but Kashubia was once again reunited. Poland was officially proclaimed a mono-ethnic state, with no national minorities. The idea of a homogenous population, part of the ideology imposed by Poland's new communist rulers, was pursued in spite of the existence within the country of some 20 self-identified ethnic groups. After 1945 the authoritarian government promoted research on, preservation of, and promotion of the Kashub culture, but only as a local subgroup of the Polish nation. Dance troops and *kapelas* were organized to preserve the distinct Kashubian musical heritage.

On Easter in 1949, local priests had to read a decree banning the use of the Kashubian language even in family settings and private conversations, and the wearing of their distinctive national costumes. Education and official publications in the Kashubian language were prohibited. In the 1960s and 1970s all forms of Kashubian self-government and cultural autonomy were gradually limited, and official institutions eliminated all vestiges of Kashubian place-names.

The end of communism in Poland began in the 1980s in the workers' unions of shipyards in Gdansk. In 1989 an accord between the unions and the government opened the way for democratic government in Poland. The collapse of the Polish communist regime and its replacement with a democratically elected government finally allowed the Kashubians to begin to reclaim their ethnic identity. The long Kashubian silence was finally ended in 1991 with the foundation of the first Kashubian primary and secondary schools since World War II.

The return of democracy sparked a Kashubian revival in the 1990s. Activists promoting the revival of the language began regular television programming in Kashubian and offered video courses for learning and speaking the language. The newly formed cultural and national organizations sponsored academic research embracing sociological, historical, linguistic, and literary studies related to the Kashubian nation. A Kashubian congress was held in Gdansk in June 1992 to discuss the future of the Kashubians. Subsequent congresses focused on regional economic development and reestablishing ties to the Kashubian populations in Germany, the United States, and Canada.

In the late 1990s the Kashubian region was the only region of Poland where a "battle of the languages" actually took place. A very strong regional movement promoted the upgrading of the linguistic status of Kashubian. Under the communists Kashubian had been officially declared a local dialect of Polish. Kashubian nationalists look forward to Poland's entry in the European Union, where its regional status is an accepted fact. In postcommunist Poland, however, many politicians are overtly nationalist and openly reject the very idea of minority rights. The cultural revival has sparked a parallel national movement aimed at winning political autonomy for the region, under the slogan, *Nigde do zgube nie przinda Kaszebe*, "The Kashubians will never perish."

SELECTED BIBLIOGRAPHY:

Erdmans, Mary Patrice. *Opposite Poles: Immigrants and Ethnics in Polish Chicago.* 1998.

Guuenwald, Myron E. *Pomeranians: The Persistent Pioneers.* 1987.

Wandycz, Piotr S. *The Lands of Partitioned Poland, 1795–1918.* 1993.

Zamoyski, Adam. *The Polish Way: A Thousand-Year History of the Poles and Their Culture.* 1993.

Katangans

Katangais; Katangese; Shabans; Lundas; Lunda-Yeke

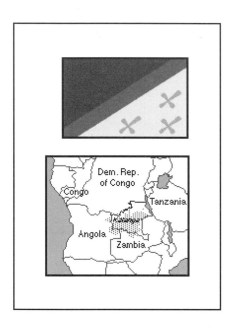

POPULATION: Approximately (2002e) 5,356,000 Katangans in the Democratic Republic of Congo, concentrated in Katanga Province, but with sizable communities in other parts of the country, particularly in the capital Kinshasa. Another two million belonging to groups related to the Katangans (Lundas) live in neighboring parts of Angola and Zambia.

THE KATANGAN HOMELAND: The Katangan homeland lies in southeastern Congo, a forested region traversed by the Lomami and Lualuaba Rivers, tributaries of the Congo River. Much of the region lies in the elevated Shaba Plateau, rising to the Mitumba Mountains west of Lake Tanganyika. Katanga forms a province of the Democratic Republic of the Congo. *Province of Katanga*: 191,845 sq. mi.—496,878 sq. km, (2002e) 4,308,000—Katangans (Lundas) 76%, Lubas (including Kasaians* or Luba-Kasai) 15%, Yekes 6%, Tabwas 2%, other Congolese 1%. The Katangan capital and major cultural center is Lubumbashi, (2002e) 1,073,000, metropolitan area 1,219,000. The other important cultural center is Kolwezi, (2002e) 797,000.

FLAG: The Katangan national flag, the flag of the former republic, is a diagonal bicolor of red over white divided by a green stripe lower hoist to upper fly, charged with three red-brown crosses representing the old form of smelted copper on the white triangle at the lower fly.

PEOPLE AND CULTURE: The Katangans, comprising the large number of tribal groups collectively called Lundas or Lunda-Yeke, are a Bantu people. The Katangans formed part of the more numerous Luba peoples until the seventeenth century. The Lundas and the closely related Yekes feel they are the only authentic Katangans and are highly resentful of the Luba-Kasai, the Kasaians, who migrated to the region under Belgian rule. The Lundas are made up of a number of tribal groups related by language and culture, including the Lunda Musokantanda, Kazembe, Shinje, Kanoogesha, Ndembu, Luvale, Chokwe, Luchazi, Songo, and Mbunda. Most

966

of the tribes represent groups that broke away from the historical Lunda kingdom. Descent systems differ; the southern groups are matrilineal, but most of the northern groups are patrilineal. Economic pursuits are dictated by the regions in which they live—Katangans are fishermen, farmers, and urban workers. By 1999 the Katangan purchasing power had collapsed to a quarter of what it had been during the 1950s.

LANGUAGE AND RELIGION: The Katangans, also called Lundas or Lunda-Yeke, speak a language of the Salampasu-Ndembo group of Benue-Congo languages. Lunda proper is spoken in three major dialects—Ndembu, Kalunda, and Kambove—while the peoples of the greater Lunda cultural group speak a number of related mutually intelligible languages, including Ruund or Northern Lunda, Yeke, Chokwe, Luchazi, and Tabwa. Swahili, often called Congo Swahili, is the lingua franca of the region, spoken by most people in Katanga and in neighboring areas. Most Katangans speak the Lualaba dialect of Swahili and many also speak French.

Most Katangans are Christians, mostly Roman Catholic, as the result of nineteenth-century missionary activity. Traditional religious beliefs are based on a supreme being called Nzambi, who is either a sky or an earth god. The worship of ancestors is also widespread, and ancestors are called upon to intercede with the deity. Pre-Christian traditions remain strong in the region. Belief in oracles and divination remains powerful.

NATIONAL HISTORY: Little is known of the region's ancient history or of the early Bantu peoples, probably from present Uganda and Kenya, who settled the Shaba Plateau. The first known records are of small Luba states that formed in the area in the eleventh and twelfth centuries. In the sixteenth century a number of states united to form a powerful Lunda empire. According to tradition, the Lunda kingdom was founded by the brother of the reigning Luba king in the seventeenth century. By the eighteenth century, the Lundas expanded into Luba territory, setting off a series of wars.

The Lunda empire consisted of a central core, a ring of provinces closely tied to the capital; an outer ring of provinces that paid tribute but were otherwise sovereign; and an outer fringe of independent kingdoms that shared the Lunda culture. The boundaries of the Lunda empire were only loosely defined. The empire traded with the Portuguese on the Atlantic from about 1650, trading ivory and slaves for firearms, cloth, and iron goods.

Constant war with a rival Luba state, Murato Yanvo, blocked Lunda expansion to the north, but in the south the Lunda controlled vast territories in present-day Congo, Zambia, and Angola. The Lunda empire, one of the most powerful in sub-Saharan Africa, drew its wealth from copper, mostly mined by Swahili Muslims from Africa's east coast. Lunda influence extended from Lake Tanganyika to the Atlantic Ocean.

In the eighteenth and nineteenth centuries, the Lunda empire was divided into several sections, each controlled by a different monarch. Continuous wars, migrations, and internal disputes eventually split the empire, and numerous autonomous chiefdoms replaced the imperial authority. The Yeke, often considered a subgroup of the Lundas, established a kingdom in the middle of the nineteenth century, but it lasted for only 30 years. The Yeke influence on Lunda culture and trading remained strong throughout the century.

In the 1850s a local chief, M'siri, began to expand his territory by conquering neighboring tribes, including a chiefdom called Katanga, whose name he took for his new kingdom. A large tribal migration moved into his kingdom in the 1880s; the turmoil caused by the migration gave Europeans an opportunity to begin acquiring influence in the kingdom. Portuguese troops arrived from Angola in 1884. On 31 December 1891, a European colonialist assassinated M'siri, and his kingdom rapidly disintegrated. Belgians from the Congo Free State sent troops into the region in 1898; the Lunda homeland was partitioned between Portugal and Belgium. The Belgians quickly took control of Katanga, the last part of present-day Congo to come under Belgian rule. Guerrilla warfare against the Belgians continued until 1909, when the rebel leaders were captured and executed.

In 1908, in response to growing criticism of its treatment of the African population, Belgium annexed what became known as the Belgian Congo. In 1910 the Belgian authorities set up the Katanga Company to exploit the rich mineral deposits; simultaneously, they separated Katanga's colonial administration from the Belgian Congo, an action that became the basis of later Katangan separatism.

During World War II, the production of minerals was greatly increased to finance the Belgian war effort. Industrialized in the early 1950s, the region flourished as one of sub-Saharan Africa's most advanced areas. Thousands of rural Katangans migrated to the growing industrial cities. The inhabitants, both European and African, enjoyed one of Africa's highest standards of living.

Ethnic Lubas, called Luba-Kasai or Kasaians to differentiate them from the Luba-Katanga in northern Katanga, migrated to the region in large numbers to work in the European-owned mines. Over time the better-educated Kasaians also became in large part the administrative and professional class, a development that fueled the resentment of the Lundas and Yekes and related groups, who described themselves as only "authentic Katangans."

The Belgian government, under international pressure, lifted in 1957 a long-standing ban on political parties and allowed Africans to vote in elections for local councils. The Kasaians, though considered outsiders or immigrants, scored another victory by winning the majority of urban council seats in the region, further alienating the Katangans.

Moise Tsombe, with a European cofounder, organized the Confederation of Tribal Associations of Katanga (Conakat), which quickly became the party of Katangan nationalism, with the support of the Lundas, the European minority, and the mining companies. In 1960 Conakat won control of the provincial assembly. The only large opposition group arose among the Luba tribe in the north, the Association of the Baluba People of Katanga (Balubakat). A strong anti-Kasaian strain emerged as an expression of Katangan nationalism, along with demands for the expulsion of the largely urbanized Kasaians from the region.

To the accompaniment of widespread violence and chaos, the unprepared Belgian Congo gained independence on 30 June 1960. The new state rapidly disintegrated along tribal and regional lines. Supported by the Europeans and the majority Lundas, Tsombe declared Katanga independent on 11 July 1960. Protected by its Belgian-officered and supplied army, Katanga remained calm as most of the Congo dissolved in civil war. For a time Katanga continued as before—the administration functioned, the mines produced, and industries boomed. The only jarring note came from a growing Luba rebellion in the northern districts.

In September 1960, the president and prime minister of the new Congolese government quarreled and attempted to dismiss each other. Mobutu Sese Seko, the chief of the military staff, stepped in and assumed power. He quickly won the support of Belgium and the other Western powers with his anticommunist rhetoric and willingness to hold the vast and wealthy country together with Western military aid and advice.

Katanga, with only 13% of the Congo's population, produced 60% of the export revenues, funds badly needed by the Congolese government. An appeal to the United Nations, supported by other African states, brought the dispatch of UN troops. A United Nations attempt to disarm the Katangans failed, and fighting broke out in the border areas. The UN troops invaded Katanga in December 1961. Katanga's former tranquility collapsed into anarchy as fighting spread. Luba rebels launched a campaign of terror against the Katangans and Europeans in the southern cities. The terrorist campaign of murder, rape, and looting provoking a flood of terrified refugees.

Belgium and its Western allies, supporting Mobutu as a "reliable" man, used UN troops to force an end to the Katangan secession in 1963. Tsombe was arrested and exiled, and Katanga was forcibly reintegrated into Mobutu's republic. In July 1964, Tsombe was recalled from exile and was appointed prime minister in an effort to reconcile the Katangans. In 1965 Mobutu officially seized power and named himself president of the country. Two years later, he created the Popular Revolutionary Party, which became the sole legitimate political party.

Although Mobutu installed a corrupt, undemocratic regime that virtually ended all progress in the country, he was supported by the Western powers as a bulwark against communist influence in central Africa. In 1972, to break with the past, Mobutu renamed the Democratic Republic of Congo the Republic of Zaire. The province of Katanga was renamed Shaba, the Swahili word for copper. Mobutu tried to create a Zairian nationalism based on loyalty to the state rather than tribal or regional loyalties, but in this he was unsuccessful.

In 1968 Katangan refugees living among the ethnic Lundas in neighboring Angola formed the nationalist Congolese National Liberation Front (FLNC), with its aim the resurrection of the independent Katangan state. In March 1977, FLNC rebels invaded the region from Angola but were eventually defeated by government troops aided by France and Belgium (which sent troops) and the United States (which provided arms). Morocco and Egypt supplied combat troops and pilots. The Katangans again invaded in May 1978, this time from Zambia, and were again defeated with the help of French and Belgian troops and U.S. logistics, but not before some 200 Belgian residents had been massacred in the city of Kolwezi.

President Mobutu, propped up by Western governments, systematically plundered the country. The Katangans, whose homeland provided the bulk of Congo's annual revenues before 1997, remained under the control of all-pervasive and brutal state security forces. The Katangans greatly resented the diversion of profits from their resources for development projects in Kinshasa and Mobutu's home region in northern Zaire. Living in what should have been one of Africa's most prosperous areas, most Katangans suffered abject poverty, unemployment, and despair, while Mobutu and his cronies stashed billions of dollars outside the country.

In 1990, President Mobutu, under Western pressure, announced that he would allow democratic elections under a multiparty system. On 11 May 1990, students were massacred by Mobutu's elite forces after pro-autonomy demonstrations at Lubumbashi University. Mobutu recognized the FLNC as a political party, and about half the 15,000 exiled Katangan rebels laid down their arms and returned to Zaire, while others, mistrusting Mobutu, remained in exile in Angola and Zambia.

Three politicians from the region led a democratic movement in the southern provinces, the Union of Federalists and Independent Republicans (UFERI)—Etienne Tshisekedi, a Kasaian, and Nguz Karl-i-Bond and Gabriel Kyungu, native Katangans. For some months they were united in opposition to the Mobutu government, but Mobutu persuaded the Katangans to join his government, appointing Karl-i-Bond prime minister and Kyunga governor of Shaba, the first native Katangan to hold the post. Karl-i-Bond and Kyungu turned their criticism of Mobutu to the so-called enemy within, the Kasaian population in Shaba. In August 1992 Kyungu restored the forbidden name, Katanga, and announced his aim of eventual independence.

In October 1992, Kyungu announced that the Katangans and Kasaians could not live side by side in Katanga. Militant Katangans drove tens of thousands of immigrant Kasaians from their homes, with covert government support. Thousands were massacred, while over 250,000, after generations of living in Katanga, fled to neighboring Kasai. In December 1993 the Katangan government declared the political and economic autonomy of Katanga and continued the brutal "ethnic cleansing" of the Kasaians. Many analysts believe that Mobutu secretly encouraged the violence to emphasize to the world that only his central government could hold the huge country together.

Relations between Kyungu and Mobutu soured over growing demands for Katangan autonomy and greater control of the region's natural resources. In 1994, the Katangan provincial parliament created a charter outlining the powers of the regional parliament; it was rejected by the central government. In May 1995, Governor Kyungu was suspended by Mobutu for allegedly storing weapons, and later placed under arrest. Incidents between the army and Katangan nationalists increased in violence in 1995–96. In June 1995, a Mobutu spokesman warned that the government would not accept the secession of Katanga or any other province.

Joseph Tsombe, the son of Moise Tsombe, the 1960s secessionist leader, played a major role in the autonomy movement as the leader of the Lundas and Yekes, the native Katangans. Secessionist sentiment continued to grow as Zaire moved from crisis to crisis. By 1995, Katangan incomes were only about 40% of the secessionist period in the early 1960s. Economic hardships fueled the growing nationalist movement. In July 1995, nationalists demanded that the government grant widespread autonomy and allow Katanga to keep 70% of the mining revenues, leaving the central government responsible only for foreign affairs and national security.

A Tutsi rebellion in Kivu, to the north, quickly spread across eastern Zaire. Laurent Kabila, an ethnic Luba from northern Katanga and a long-time Marxist, became the leader of the rebellion, which became a mass anti-Mobutu movement in 1996. Kabila, after reassuring the foreign mining companies, received Western support as his forces moved into Katanga in January 1997. Many of the Katangan nationalist exiles in Angola joined the anti-Mobutu campaign. Mobutu reinstated Kyungu as governor of Katanga in a bid to divide the loyalty of his opponents, but in April 1997 the rebels took control of Lubumbashi.

An alliance of four political parties in the east of Congo, including a Katangan nationalist party led by André Kisase, was announced in October 1996. Kisase was the only regional leader to challenge Kabila. He later died in mysterious circumstances. Kisase represented the old Katangan movement, no longer openly separatist but seeking autonomy for the region.

Mobutu was overthrown in May 1997, and Laurent Kabila declared himself president. He restored the earlier name of the country and promised a democratic revolution, but he named his cousin, Gaetan Kajudji, as the interim governor of Katanga. The angry Katangans withdrew their support from Kabila's government. Four generals, from their exile in South Africa, announced that they would lead the fight for the secession of Katanga and neighboring Kasai. Many Katangans, including soldiers formerly allied to Kabila's forces, fled to neighboring Angola to join the long-standing Katangan exile community. In November 1997, some 300 nationalist leaders and army officers were imprisoned for demanding the autonomy promised during the anti-Mobutu campaign. Conflict between Luvales and Lundas in northern Zambia in August 1998 left hundreds homeless and threatened to spill across the border into Katanga.

The fragmentation of the Democratic Republic of Congo fueled the creation of local armies rooted in local tribes. During the civil war, Tutsis were targeted and retaliated by murdering Katangans. By late 1999, rebel forces allied to the Tutsis held the northern districts of Katanga.

Rebel groups in several parts of Congo, backed by Uganda and Rwanda, became active in the eastern provinces, while Angola, Namibia, and Zimbabwe sent troops to support the Kabila government, which lost most of its Western backing. The widening conflict in the country, a war increasingly drawing in the neighboring African countries, forced many Katangans into exile. The nationalist movement mostly went underground as fighting flared in the region in 1998–99. As the Congo again descended into chaos and war, Katangan groups prepared for armed struggle against the Kabila government in 2000.

The death of Laurent Kabila in January 2001 increased the instability in the country, with many regional leaders calling for elections. Katangan leaders, with half their homeland under rebel control, demanded that Katangan soldiers fighting in other areas of the country be returned to Katanga, and they again called for devolution of power to allow the local government to deal with the growing chaos and violence.

SELECTED BIBLIOGRAPHY:

Bustin, Edouard. *Lunda under Belgian Rule: The Politics of Ethnicity*. 1975.
Gerard-Libois, Jules. *Katanga Secession*. 1967.
Heale, Jay. *Democratic Republic of the Congo*. 1999.
Hochschild, Adam. *King Leopold's Ghost*. 1999.

Kewris

Kuwris; Chamamas; Southern Mauritanians

POPULATION: Approximately (2002e) 755,000 Kewris in Mauritania, concentrated in the southern administrative regions in the basin of the Senegal River Valley. Outside the valley, there are Kewri communities in Nouakchott, the Mauritanian capital, other areas of the country, and about 40,000 in Senegal. There are Kewri communities in Mali, France, and the United States. Activists claim a Kewri population of over 1.5 million, including 200,000 refugees living in Senegal and Mali.

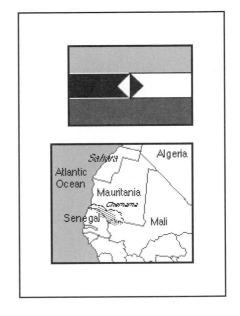

THE KEWRI HOMELAND: The Kewri homeland, called the Chemama, lies in the fertile lowlands in the valley of the Senegal River, an area of semi-tropical savanna in northwestern Africa. The narrow belt of land north of the river ranges from 16 to 30 kilometers wide in most areas, although it is wider in the Guidimaka Region. By the late 1980s, desertification had reached the northern bank of the river in some parts of the valley. The Chemama forms the Mauritanian administrative regions of Guidimaka, Gorgol, and the southern districts of Hodh, Assaba, Brakna, and Trarza. *Chemama:* 19,884 sq. mi.—51,500 sq. km, (2002e) 1,097,000—Kewris 67%, Maures 31%, other Mauritanians, Senegalese 2%. The Kewri capital and major cultural center is Kayhaydi, called Kaédi by the Kewris, (2002e) 52,000. The other important cultural center is Rusu, called Rosso, (2002e) 47,000.

FLAG: The Kewri national flag, the flag of the Forces de Libération Africaine de Mauritanie (African Liberation Forces of Mauritania), has three horizontal stripes of yellow, mixed black and white, and green. The black and white stripe is divided in the center with the white half, outlined in black, on the hoist, and the white, outlined in black, on the fly, with two opposing triangles, countercolored, in the center.

PEOPLE AND CULTURE: The Kewris are the black African inhabitants of the largely Arab and Berber state of Mauritania. The Kewris include several ethnic groups, the Pulaar, also called Peul or Tukolars, the Wolofs, the Soninke, and the Bambara. These four groups have become closely related over centuries. The majority are farmers, although urbanization has accelerated since the late 1980s. The Kewris, although separated by hundreds of years of history, are ethnically and linguistically related to the peoples of Senegal on the south side of the Senegal River, particularly the Wolof and Pulaar. Historically the black African peoples were dominated by Berber and later Arab groups. The Kewris share a common history, and a kinship system in which family is preserved by social interaction, shared religious observances, and rituals celebrating the stages of life. Traits borrowed from the Berber-Arab Maures, who dominate society in Mauritania, include strong influences on the African dialects and caste and lineage differences, which determines one's place in the Kewri culture. Social stratification is fairly rigid, intermarriage across tribal boundaries at the same stratum being far more common than intermarriage across strata. Modernization has led to a gradual decline in the importance of the caste system, but loyalty to lineage and regional identity outweighs allegiances to state or national institutions. Descent is patrilineal and the basic social unit is the extended family. Slavery is still practiced, both by the Maures and the Kewri peoples influenced by Maure culture. Slavery has traditionally freed Kewri women from domestic chores; they still dominate the markets and most retail activity.

LANGUAGE AND RELIGION: The Kewris speak related languages of the Fula-Wolof and Soninke-Bobo groups of the Niger-Congo languages, Pulaar, Wolof, and Soninke. Arabic and French are the country's official languages, which is a great disadvantage to the Kewris who study in their own languages in primary school, but switch to Arabic, the language of instruction in all secondary schools. Kewris argue that the use of Arabic in secondary school has been an effort on the part of the Maures to block Kewri advancement. Arabic is also the language of religion, but without a strong knowledge of Arabic it is difficult for Kewris to advance in social importance in the reigious sphere. Literacy is estimated at about 38%.

The Kewris are mostly Muslims, adhereing to the Malekite Rite, one of the four major Sunni Muslim schools. Many belong to the Tijaniya and Quadiriya brotherhoods, which are subgroups of the Malekites. Many pre-Islamic courtship and death rites have been retained and incorporated into the Muslim belief system. Most believe in divination and supernatural power *(baraka)* associated with Islamic holy men.

NATIONAL HISTORY: Archaeological evidence suggests that Berbers and black Africans lived in relative peace until the spread of the desert drove the Berbers southward beginning in the third century A.D. Seeking pastures for their herds, the Berbers drove the black tribes south from the grasslands into the lowlands along the Senegal River. A Berber tribal confederation, the Sanhadja Confederation, which reached its height in the eighth century, dominated the territory north of the Senegal River. Arabs moving south from the newly conquered North Africa settled among the Berbers in the eighth and ninth centuries pushing many Berbers further south into the black tribal territories. By the sixteenth century, most blacks had been pushed to the Senegal River. Those remaining in the north became slaves.

In the tenth century, the Berbers and Arabs succumbed to invasions from the south by the forces of the Kingdom of Ghana. From the tenth through the fifteenth centuries black African empires, Ghana, Mali, and Songhai, brought their political structure and cultural influence to the region, particularly to the black tribes living on both sides of the Sengal River.

The Islamization of the Pulaar, Soninkes, Wolofs, and Bambara was a gradual process that began slowly through contacts with Berber and Arab merchants engaged in the important caravan trade. The tribal peoples mostly adopted Islam because the Koran, the Islamic holy book, prohibits the enslavement of fellow Muslims. Arab traders brought slavery to Mauritania as early as the fifteenth century. The caste structure and racial divide perpetuated the role of slavery over the centuries both as an economic system and as a means of perpetuating the dominance of local Maure leaders.

European contact began in the fifteenth century. The trade in gum arabic, which was produced in the Senegal River Valley, attracted several European powers. Four French companies enjoyed a French-government monoply of the Senegal River trade from 1659 to 1798. Trading posts established at the mouth of the river were soon engaged in the slave trade. Berber and Arab slavers raided the black tribes for slaves to sell to the Europeans. Many of the Kewri tribal peoples also engaged in the slave trade. French sovereignty over the Senegal River and the coastal zones was recognized by the Congress of Vienna in 1815.

French penetration beyond the coast began in earnest in the mid-1800s. The territory north of the Senegal River was claimed as a protectorate in 1903. In 1920, Mauritania became a French colony. The French occupation led to the return of sedentary farmers of black African origin across the Senegal River into southern Mauritania, an area from which they had fled or been expelled by warring Maure nomads in previous centuries.

Mauritania was economically, politically, and administratively dependent on Senegal. The Kewri tribes, more amenable to French rule than the nomadic Maure tribes to the north, were recruited into the colonial administration and military, further separating them from the Arab-Berber majority.

After World War II, the French introduced administrative decentralization and increased local autonomy. A series of social and political reforms to the French colonial system allowed increased authority of elected officials in 1957, giving the Maure majority a dominate role. Mauritania entered the French Community in 1958 as an autonomous, but not fully sovereign state.

The nationalistic fervor that swept French West Africa in the 1950s was largely absent from the Maure regions of Mauritania, but in the south, the Kewris supported the idea of a Mali Federation to include Senegal, Mali, and Chemama. The Kewris rejected inclusion in the Maure-dominated Mauritania. Their protests and pleas were ignored by the French.

The French, seeking to retain control of neighboring Algeria, favored Maure control of Mauritania. In order to ensure that the Maures controlled the country, the French went so far as to publically warn the Maure leaders that if they did not mobilize themselves politically that the black Kewris were going to win the 1958 elections and thereby seize power. The Maures won the 1958 elections and declared the Islamic Republic of Mauritania within the French Community, and later declared full independence in 1960. Outside the Chemama region the level of political and economic development was, at best, embryonic, but the Maure majority in Mauritania effectively excluded the Kewris from government.

For the Kewris, independence in Mauritania was a transition from colonial rule to Arab domination and misrule. Local and regional governments in all Kewri areas were put under aggressive Maure prefects and governors. Differences over linguistic and racial issues subsequently caused strikes and demonstrations by trade unionists and students in 1968–69 and 1971. All demonstrations were harshly repressed by the government, which in 1966 had banned discussion of racial problems.

Mauritania's post-independence history was dominated by regional politics. The first years of independence, under Moktar Ould Daddah, a Maure, emphasized the country's Arab heritage. The Kewris, who largely made up the civil service during the colonial period, were excluded and alienated. His government sought to eliminate the friction that resulted from economic, political, and social differences that could impede the attainment of national unity. Closer ties to Morocco and other Arab states made the Senegal River both a physical and political barrier between the Kewris and the related peoples in Senegal and Mali.

The Mauritanian government, along with Morocco, occupied the former Spanish colony of Western Sahara in 1975. Opposed by the Sahrawis,* they became involved in the war that spread across the disputed territory. Economically the war, which coincided with a period of severe drought, forced Mauritania to become more dependent on foreign aid, particularly from conservative Arab countries. The war and the increasing economic problems led to a military coup d'état in July 1978. In 1980, the Mauritanian government was the last in the world to outlaw slavery, although the abolition was the third since 1960.

Before the drought of the 1970s and 1980s, there were no serious problems over land ownership. The different ethnic communities stayed in and around their traditional areas. The Maures led their nomadic life style in the north while the Kewris continued their mainly sedentary life along the Senegal River. However, the drought, which severely reduced the productive capacity of the northern regions of the country, forced many Maures to move towards the south. The migration was encouraged by the government. Competition between the traditional owners, on the one hand, and the Maure internal refugees and their government, on the other, over land led to violence.

Successive military governments became increasingly repressive. Ethnic conflicts between the Maures and the Kewris became more pronounced. The military dealt harshly with dissidents, forcing many Kewri leaders to flee to Senegal or France. Among the Kewris there was a growing fear of Arabization of the country, which was exacerbated by Mauritania's close ties to Iraq and other Arab countries. Land reform laws introduced in 1983 and 1988 were used as a legal cover up to confiscate Kewri farm lands along the Senegal River. Tens of thousands of Kewris were ordered deported to Senegal or Mali and their lands were immediately distributed to Maure business men or settlers from the north.

Kewri activists organized the Forces de Libération Africaine de Mauritania (African Liberation Force or FLAM) in 1983. FLAM opposed the repressive policies of the Mauritanian government. At first it advocated a separate state for the Kewri, but it later toned down its rhetoric. FLAM leaders, in 1986, issued an "Oppressed Black" manifesto in 1986, which called for Kewri liberation. The leaders of the group supported an attempted coup in 1987, which was followed by severe reprisals against the Kewri population.

The conflict escalated until finally a land dispute between Maures and Kewris along the Senegal River led to violence in 1989. The Senegal government backed the Kewris. Relations between the neighboring states worsened as rioting broke out in both capitals and in cities in Chemama. Hundreds of people were killed and the two governments expelled tens of thousands of each other's citizens. Maure activists attacked Kewri villages. Some Kewris claim that up to 3,000 were killed in massacres. Thousands of Kewris fled or were expelled before the two states broke diplomatic relations and closed the international border at the Senegal River. The Maures forced over 70,000 Kewris across the river, claiming they were Senegalese nationals rather than Mauritanian citizens.

Faced with the internal crisis and the cut-off of military and development aid, the Mauritanian government implemented reforms in 1991, including the legalization of political parties. A civilian government, dominated by the Maures, was inaugurated in 1992, but little changed for the Kewris. In May 1993, the government granted a general amnesty to those responsible for the mass killings and disappearances of Kewris during the 1989–90 upheavals.

FLAM suspended its armed struggle in July 1991 in response to the government's general amnesty and the promulgation of a new constitution that promised equal rights, but in 1992 renewed its antigovernment military campaign. In early 1995 the group split, with the majority favoring a federal system of autonomous states in Mauritania. A smaller faction supported the secession of the Kewri region and federation with neighboring Senegal.

Successive rounds of legislative and presidential elections since 1996 returned the ruling Maure poltical party. Although the ethnic violence of the late 1980s and early 1990s subsided, social, political, and economic conflicts between Maures and Kewris, centering on language, radical religious beliefs, land tenure, and other issues continue to challenge Kewri participation in the Mauritanian administration. Located on the cultural and racial divide between black and Arab Africa, the Maure-dominated Mauritanian government's approach to the divide is to deny the African identity and to stress the Arab-Berber identity with intolerance and repression. The alienation of the Kewris continues to fuel nationalist and separatist sentiment.

In the mid-1990s, the rise of Islamic radicalism that stressed Arab solidarity was embraced by many Maures, particularly the poorest segment of society. FLAM, led by Samba Thiam, opposes religious fundamentalism as opposed to Kewri interests. Religious tensions have become part of the racial and linguistic conflict.

During the 1990s, an estimated 30,000 Kewris gradually returned to Mauritania. An estimated 40,000 remained in Senegal in 2000. Many Kewris have indicated that they will not accept repatriation until the Mauritanian government guarantees their citizenship and reimburses them for lost property. Others prefer to remain in Senegal because of security, ethnic, family, or economic ties. In 2000, the Mauritanian government agreed to implement an assistance program that is designed to facilitate the reintegration of the returning refugees.

Increased desertification is pushing wealthy Maures to buy up or simply take over what historically have been black lands. Recent efforts by neighboring Senegal to divert part of the Senegal River for agricultural purposes has further exacerbated tensions. The Kewris increasingly view their future in a united Mauritania as more difficult than separation. The majority would probably be content with regional autonomy and linguistic and cultural rights, but a growing number are pessimistic about Maure willingness to compromise.

SELECTED BIBLIOGRAPHY:

Baduel, Pierre Robert. *Mauritania between Arab and African.* 1989.
Diallo, Garba. *Mauritania—The other Apartheid.* 1993.
Gerteiny, A.G. *Historical Dictionary of Mauritania.* 1981.
Nnoli, Okwudiba, ed. *Ethnic Conflicts in Africa.* 1998.

Khakass

Khakass-Shor; Khakassians; Khakas; Khaas; Tadar; Yenisei Tatars; Abakan Tatars; Khorray

POPULATION: Approximately (2002e) 127,000 Khakass in Siberia, concentrated in the Khakass Republic in south-central Siberia near the geographic center of Asia. The Khakass nation included two subgroups divided during the Soviet era—the Shors, numbering over 20,000, and the Chulyms, numbering about 17,000. There are smaller Khakass populations in the neighboring Tuvan Republic and Krasnoyarsk Territory, as well as in China.

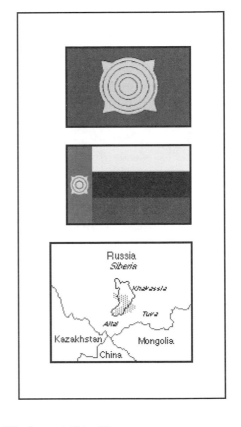

THE KHAKASS HOMELAND: The Khakass homeland lies in south-central Siberia, a region occupying the middle reaches of the Yenisei River basin and the upper reaches of the tributaries of the Yenisei, the Abakan and the Chulym. The northern and eastern parts of the region are flat steppe, the Abakan Steppe, while the southern and western regions are mountainous. Although the Khakass have steadily increased in numbers since the 1960s, they remain a minority in their traditional territory. Khakassia forms a republic, a member state of the Russian Federation. *Republic of Khakassia (Xakasskaj Respublika/Hakasiya)*: 23,900 sq. mi.—61,901 sq. km, (2002e) 577,000—Russians 70%, Khakass 14%, Germans 2%, Ukrainians 2%, Belarussians 2%, Tuvans* 1%, others 9%. The Khakass capital and major cultural center is Abakan, (2002e) 172,000.

FLAG: The Khakass flag, the flag of the national movement, is a green field bearing a centered Khakass sun symbol. The flag of the Khakass Republic is a horizontal tricolor of white, blue, and red with a broad horizontal green stripe at the hoist bearing the Khakass sun symbol.

PEOPLE AND CULTURE: The Khakass are of mixed Turkic and Mongol background, physically resembling the Mongols but linguistically and culturally closer to the Turkic peoples. They are divided into seven divisions or tribes: Kacha, Sagai, Kyzyl, Teltir, Koibal, Shor, and Chulym.

Each of the tribal divisions is further divided into subgroups and clans. The Shor and Chulym, because of their geographic locations, were designated as separate peoples during the Soviet era. The tribes are the result of fusion of many clans and groups; loyalty to the tribe or clan remains strong. The educational and cultural level of the Khakass is quite high. The name "Khakass" was not used until 1923, when the Soviet authorities decided to use the name for the related tribal groups of the region. Khakass identity, although strengthened since the collapse of Soviet power in 1991, remains focused on clan and family systems. Assimilation, particularly intermarriage with Slavs, is increasing, primarily among the urbanized Khakass.

LANGUAGE AND RELIGION: The Khakass speak a Uighur-Oguz language of the eastern Hun branch of the Turkic languages. The language is spoken in seven primary dialects—Kacha, Sagai, Kyzyl, Katchin, Kamassian, Chulym, and Shor—and a number of subdialects. Thought to have evolved from the ancient Uighur language, the Khakass language remained an aggregation of different tribal dialects until it evolved as a standardized language under Soviet rule in the twentieth century. A new Cyrillic alphabet was introduced in 1924, and a new written language based on the Katchin dialect was introduced. The structure and basic vocabulary of the language are of Turkic-Tatar origin. The modern language has many loanwords from Mongol and Russian, particularly those pertaining to technical, administrative, and ideological subjects. The modern literary language, based on the Sagai dialect, has played an important part in the standardization of the language. The first Khakass-Russian dictionary was published in 1961. Most Khakass are bilingual in Russian.

The Khakass peoples are mostly Orthodox Christian but retain their pre-Christian beliefs, a mixture of shamanism and Buddhism. Most still worship fire and milk, and they continue to respect the wisdom of the traditional shamans. Their beliefs in spirits inhabiting all of nature and meddling in people's lives have become one with their Orthodox beliefs. Shamanism not only outlasted the Soviets, but renewed itself and has become an integral part of the Khakass cultural revival.

NATIONAL HISTORY: As early as the Paleolithic period, pastoral nomads, hunters, and fishermen inhabited the Yenisei Basin, which was first mentioned in the early fifth century A.D. in Chinese records as a region inhabited by nomadic tribes. The indigenous peoples, tribes of Samoyedic or Kettic origin, inhabited areas as far west as the Kuznetsk Basin. The region was overrun and settled by migrating Turkic peoples; a Turkic khanate dominated them from the sixth to the eighth centuries, strengthening the influence of the Altaic and Uighur tribes over a wide region. The tribal peoples gradually adopted the language and many of the cultural traits of their Turkic rulers. The Yenisei tribes, the ancestors of the modern Khakass, formed tribal groups in the eighth and ninth centuries.

The expanding Mongol empire absorbed the tribal lands of the Yenisei Valley, called Khongoray, in 1207. The Khakass tribes remained under nominal Mongol rule for over two centuries. Even after the dissolution of the Golden Horde, the region was subject to periodic Mongol incursions. A powerful tribal federation, dominated by the Altai Oirot tribe to the south, formed in the sixteenth century and eventually extended its sway over the Yenisei Basin.

Slavic Cossacks, the vanguard of Russian expansion, began to penetrate the federation and by the late sixteenth century regularly collected a fur tax from the northern tribes. Drawn to the rich copper mines of the Yenisei River valley, the Russians extended their rule to Khakassia in the seventeenth century. The nomadic tribes were unable to unify in the face of the new threat, and they were each defeated in turn. In 1621 a fort was established at Meletsk to ensure Russian control of the Yenisei River basin. Control of the growing trade in furs and animal products allowed the Russians to extend their influence among the southern mountain tribes over the next century. The tribal peoples were called Tatars by the Russians and were referred to as "Tadar" by the neighboring Turkic peoples.

The influx of Russian settlers into the valleys of the Yenisei and upper Tom' Rivers in the late eighteenth and early nineteenth centuries changed the economic life of the region. Russian officials forced the tribes to pay the *yasak* fur tax. The tax was often so high that many clans left their homes and headed into the forests to hunt sable and other fur-bearing animals. The Khakass and other groups developed feelings of intense hatred for the Russians who had disrupted and dramatically changed their lives.

The tribal leaders, pressed by the Mongol attacks, turned to the Russians for protection. In 1727 the Russians proclaimed a protectorate over Khongoray, bringing stability to the region. The Russians established a civil government, collected taxes in the form of furs, and occasionally put down uprisings but generally left the nomadic tribes to govern themselves, under their traditional rulers. The Khakass areas were divided into counties, each governed by a local prince. The princes were supported by Cossacks in collecting the fur tax and in maintaining order.

The process of the evolution of the Khakass nation began in the late seventeenth century. The Kacha and Kyzyl tribes developed from a fusion of Kets and Uighurs*; the Beltir tribe is closely related to the Tuvans to the east; while the Sagai and Koibal have a complex ethnic background and are close to the Shors and Chulyms. A code of laws governing non-Russian peoples was published and applied in 1822. The code governed the administrative divisions, taxes and tributes, and legal status of the tribes.

The constant debt owed the Russian authorities in the form of the unpopular fur tax, the large numbers of Slavic settlers, the despotism of the

Russian bureaucrats, Christianization, and Russification greatly decreased the self-confidence and independence of the Khakass tribes. In 1876, missionaries not knowing the local language simultaneously baptized 3,000 Khakass, naming all the men Vladimir and all the women Maria. Officially the Khakass were converted to Orthodox Christianity, but their traditional religion, a fusion of shamanistic and Buddhist beliefs, remained an important part of their culture. Although Christian missionaries made superficial conversions, what ultimately emerged was an eclectic fusion of folk beliefs and Christian doctrine.

The completion of the Trans-Siberian railway, extended through the area in the 1890s, brought increasing numbers of Slavic settlers. The Khakass were increasingly marginalized; their best agricultural lands were seized by the colonists, and government functionaries demanded more and more furs as taxes and tribute, up to six sable furs per person.

The Khakass began to stir in 1905, demanding a return of their traditional autonomy. In 1911 the related people of Tannu Tuva declared their independence as revolution swept the Manchus from power in China. The declaration greatly affected the growth of Khakass identity and leading to the first attempts to unite the related tribes.

Virtually untouched by World War I, the Khakass tribes were left effectively independent as Russian civil government collapsed in the wake of the Russian Revolution in February 1917. United for the first time, the tribes organized to resist attempts by local Bolsheviks to take power as chaos and civil war spread throughout the disintegrating Russian Empire. In spite of valiant resistance, the tribes were brought under Soviet rule by 1920.

The Kuznetz Basin, with some of the world's richest deposits of iron ore and coal, which Soviet industry desperately needed, was flooded by immigrants from European Russia. In 1923 the Soviet government created the Khakass National Okrug and a separate autonomous county for the Shors of the Kuznetz Basin in 1929. In 1924 the Khakass constituted 75% of the okrug population. Cooperatives and collective farms were formed, and the nomadic clans were forced to settle on designated lands. The Khakass region was upgraded to an autonomous province within Krasnoyarsk Territory in 1930. The Shor region, called the Mountain Shor Autonomous County, was dissolved in 1939 following the massive development and colonization of the Kuznetsk Basin. The Slavic settlers established themselves in towns, relegating the Khakass to rural poverty. Those Khakass who migrated to the towns were faced with the condescending attitude of the Russians to people they called "blacks." Everyday life came to the dominated by Russian culture, and the importance and the prestige of the Russian language was constantly highlighted.

The Soviet government's antireligious campaign included traditional beliefs. Shamans were forbidden to exercise their rituals, and their attributes, such as magical potions and powders, and holy objects were confiscated and destroyed. Militant atheists also fiercely attacked the veneer of Christianity.

The small nomadic nation, devastated by war and divided and forced to settle and collectivize in the 1930s, began to decline rapidly in population. Alcohol abuse became a major social problem, as pressure increased to embrace a universal Soviet culture. A modest national revival took hold in the relaxation following Stalin's death in 1953, a revival that began to reverse the long Khakass decline. In the 1960s the Khakass nation again began to increase in numbers.

The liberalization of the late 1980s prompted Khakass demands for reunification and an end to the artificial divisions imposed by Stalin. The collapse of the Soviet Union began to reverse the forced assimilation of the decades of authoritarian rule. Various cultural groups became active, working for reforms and to promote Khakass cultural institutions and the Khakass language. Younger, more militant activists demanded full independence and measures to ensure that ethnic Khakass occupied the leading political posts. There are reports of attempts to form special Khakass militias, countered by the formation of military units by local Slavs, particularly those claiming Cossack background.

Social apathy, alcoholism, drug abuse, and such afflictions as tuberculosis and venereal diseases became calamities for the Khakass nation at the end of the twentieth century. Activists became increasingly convinced that only the reforming of Khakass society, including the effective growth of national consciousness, could ensure the survival of the nation. In 1989 the first social-political Khakass organization, called Tun, was formed and began to unite the scattered Khakass clans. In 1990 the first congress of the Khakass nation was formed. Following the dissolution of the Soviet Union, schools and classes teaching the Khakass language appeared.

A special feature of the Khakass revival at the end of the 1990s was a return to the spiritual origins of the nation. In 1997 Khakass religious and cultural leaders put Khurtuiakh Tas, a fertility deity represented by a huge stone figure put in the museum in Abakan by the Soviet authorities, back in its former place. For thousands of years she had been the protector of the Khakass.

The Khakass' ancient shamanism, closely tied to the culture, was officially accepted by the leaders of the small nation in late 2000, as a parallel spiritual asset alongside Christianity. The problems of alcoholism, poverty, and the loss of culture that plagued the Khakass during the Soviet era began to disappear during the cultural revival of the 1990s. The census results of the 1999 Russian census, released in 2001 confirmed the reversal of the long Khakass decline.

SELECTED BIBLIOGRAPHY:

Anzhiganova, Larissa. *Renaissance of a Culture: How Khakass Shamanism Survived and Flourishes Today*. 1998.

Butanaev, V. *Traditional Khakass Culture and Way of Life*. 1996.

Olson, James S. *An Ethnological Dictionary of the Russian and Soviet Empires*. 1994.

Thomas, Nicholas, and Caroline Humphrey, eds. *Shamanism, History, and the State*. 1994.

Khasis

Kahasis; Khasiyas; Khuchias; Kassis; Khasas; Khashis; Jaintias; Hynniew Trep

POPULATION: Approximately (2002e) 1,185,000 Khasis in northeastern India and northern Bangladesh. The majority inhabit the Khasi and Jaintia Hills in western Meghalaya state. About 120,000 live in adjacent areas of Bangladesh.

THE KHASI HOMELAND: The Khasi homeland lies in northeastern India, occupying a mountainous region south of the Assam Plain. The rugged terrain of the hilly tablelands has contributed to the differences in culture, dialect, economy, social life, and political organization of the Khasis. Transportation problems have slowed development; access is possible only by a highway from Gauhati in Assam to Shillong. The region forms the administrative districts of West Khasi Hills, East Khasi Hills, Jaintia Hills, and Ri-Bhoi of India's Meghalaya state. *United Khasi-Jaintia Hills District (Khasiland/Ri Hynniewtrep)*: 5,554 sq. mi.—14,385 sq. km, (2002e) 1,521,000—Khasis 88%, Garos (Bodos*) 8%, Assamese 2%, other Indians 2%. The Khasi capital and major cultural center is Shillong, called Yeddo by the Khasis, (2002e) 166,000.

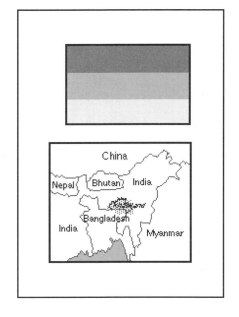

FLAG: The Khasi national flag, the flag of the national movement, is a horizontal tricolor of red, pale blue, and yellow.

PEOPLE AND CULTURE: The Khasis are closely related, matriarchal tribal peoples known to be one of the earliest ethnic group of settlers in the Indian sub-continent, belonging to the Proto-Austroloid Mon-Khmer race. The major divisions are based on geography and reflect the rugged terrain of the region; they include the Khasis, Jaintias, Bhoi, War, Pnars, and Lynngam. These groups are themselves divided into numerous clans. Collectively the Khasis call themselves Hynniewtrep. In the seclusion of their hills, the Khasis have maintained their cultural identity intact. Many scholars theorize that the Khasis originated in Southeast Asia. They have a matrilineal social system, with inheritance going to the youngest daughter. When children are born they take the surname of the mother. In the late 1990s, a serious controversy arose over the ancient matriarchal system. Khasi men, claiming that they had been reduced to breeding bulls or babysitters, wanted to change the inheritance and lineage customs that make women the dominant force in Khasi society.

LANGUAGE AND RELIGION: The Khasi language is a Mon-Khmer language of the Northern Mon-Khmer group. The language is spoken in six major dialects—Bhoi-Khasi, Jaintia, Lyng-Ngam, Nongtung, Cherrapunji, and War. The most important of the dialects is Jaintia; its name is often applied to the eastern Khasis. The Khasis are the only nation in India speaking a Mon-Khmer language, more commonly found in Southeast Asia. Writing was introduced by Methodist missionaries, who applied the Latin alphabet to the Cherrapunji dialect in 1842.

The majority of the Khasis, estimated at 67% of the total population, are nominally Christians. Most nonetheless continue to adhere to a traditional religion called Seng Khasi, which teaches that God, known as Blei Trai Kynrad, is everywhere and should not be represented in any special form or worshipped in special buildings. They believe that all nature is a temple. They revere trees, groves, forests, and rivers as manifestations of deities or places in which God resides. The Jaintia in the east share the same religious tradition but have been more influenced by Hinduism. Increasing missionaries of evangelical Protestant sects have been active, a development resented by both the Christian and the animist Khasis. Animistic forms of Hinduism are also practiced.

NATIONAL HISTORY: The Khasis, thought to have migrated to the region over 2,000 years ago, inhabited a much larger area in ancient times. They retreated to the mountains to escape successive waves of invaders in the lowland plains. Protected in mountain strongholds, the Khasis developed elaborate and unique cultures and ways of living. The western Khasis eventually created 25 small states in the highlands. Apart from accounts of the more important Khasi principalities in the chronicles of neighboring peoples, little is known of their history before the British period. The various Khasi groups all claim descent from the legendary first Khasi "Ki Hynniew Trep."

The tribal peoples retained their independence during the period of state consolidation in northern India by paying tribute to the Gupta emperors. Never united under a central authority, the various Khasi states often warred among themselves. Assamese kings asserted influence in the hill states in the twelfth century; the Assamese influence was later challenged by Tibetans, Burmans, and Bengalis.

British Methodist missionaries moved into the Khasi Hill Tracts in 1832. They were soon followed by Unitarians, Seventh-Day Adventists, Roman Catholics, and others. Many of the Khasis, already accustomed to a monotheistic belief system, adopted the Christian religion, but most retained their traditional beliefs and customs.

Overrun by invading Burmans in 1822, the region came under British rule following the first Anglo-Burman War in 1826. The British desire to build a road through the region in order to link Bengal and Assam led to a treaty with the ruler, the *syiem*, of the Khasi principality of Nonkhlaw in 1827. Opponents of the treaty persuaded the *syiem* to repudiate it in 1829. A subsequent attack on a British column led to full-scale military operations against the Khasi states. By the mid-1830s, most of the local rulers had submitted to British rule.

The Khasis, under the nominal rule of the British government of Assam, retained considerable self-rule in their mountains, with only occasional British incursions to settle disputes or to subdue periodic rebellions. The British effectively blocked immigration into the more abundant hill lands by the Bengalis of the overcrowded lowlands to the south.

Christian missionaries returned to the hill tracts in the early twentieth century, and many tribal people adopted the new religion to avoid absorption into India's rigid caste system, which relegated tribal peoples to the despised lower castes. Younger tribal leaders, educated in mission schools and better able to protect the interests of the tribes, moved into leadership positions in the 1930s and 1940s.

On the eve of Indian independence in 1947, Khasi and Garo leaders began a campaign for the separation of the hill tracts from Hindu-dominated Assam and for the creation of a new tribal state in the region. Ignored in the chaos of partition and independence, a small part of the hill tracts became Pakistani territory, while India retained control of the remainder as part of the state of Assam. Although included in Assam, the peoples of the hill tracts retained a great deal of autonomy.

Conflict and violence between the Hindu Assamese and the tribal peoples increased during the 1950s. Leaders of the five major Khasi and Garo tribes formed the Assam Hill Tribal Union to press for separation from Assam. In 1960, following the introduction of Assamese as the official language, the tribal leaders formed a coalition of nationalist and cultural groups, the All-Party Hill Leaders Conference, and demanded the self-government and unification of the non-Indian regions of southwestern Assam. In late 1963 thousands of their kinsmen, fleeing Pakistani troops, crossed the Indian border and were allowed to stay. The Indian government, aware of the propaganda possibilities, announced that the mostly Christian tribesmen preferred secular India to Muslim Pakistan.

Hoping that autonomy would preempt the increasing calls for armed rebellion in the region, in 1969 the Indian government issued a decree that created within Assam an autonomous state called Meghalaya, meaning the "Abode of the Clouds." In 1972, following renewed demonstrations and pressure from tribal leaders, the government finally separated Meghalaya from Assam and made the tribal region a full state of the Indian union. Since its inception most of the state's chief ministers have been

Garos, creating a feeling among the Khasis that they have been ruled by the rival Garos.

The new state government in 1974 demanded greater autonomous power and also restrictions on immigration of lowland peoples. Fears of being swamped by immigrants incited a rapid expansion of nationalist sentiment in the 1980s. In 1986 over 10,000 illegal aliens fled the state during nationalist demonstrations and anti-immigrant violence. In 1987 the Indian government restricted nontribal individuals from running for office in the state, but it stopped short of meeting nationalist demands for a ban on all settlement from outside the state.

Relations between the Khasis and Garos deteriorated during the 1980s. Demands for greater Khasi participation in state and local governments set off a series of often violent conflicts between the two groups. Nationalists on both sides began agitation for the division of Meghalaya into two new states, one for the Khasi-Jaintias and one for the Garos.

Pope John Paul II visited Shillong in 1986, 200 years after the first missionaries braved headhunters and other obstacles to bring their teachings to the isolated hill tribes. Over 200,000 people attended an outdoor mass. Many Khasis traveled for many days to attend the event.

A rebellion by the Bodos in neighboring districts of Assam in 1989 dramatically increased tension in Meghalaya. The Garos, part of the larger Bodo population of neighboring Assam, stepped up demands for a separate state or inclusion in a proposed Bodo state to be carved out of Assam. The violent Bodo campaign for autonomy or independence often spilled into Meghalaya, further straining relations between the Khasis and Garos. The rise of Hindu militancy in the early 1990s further alarmed the tribal leaders and brought renewed demands for protection. In October 1991, after serious nationalist disturbances, the Indian government suspended the government and placed the state under direct rule from New Delhi.

An incident that refuses to go away is the bloody Durga Puja celebrations in 1992. It was the time when the Hindus in Meghalaya don their best to go and celebrate. The Federation of Khasi, Jaintia, and Garo People, a pressure group of tribals, called for a road blockade. Rioting broke out and fighting between tribal peoples and Hindus left several dead and many injured. Since that time the Khasis and smaller Hynniewtrep peoples have moved to areas separate from that inhabited by Hindus in a voluntary segregation.

In the 1990s, militant groups based in Khasi villages and towns in Bangladesh began a campaign to win full independence for the Khasi nation. Their support was not widespread, but an increasingly violent campaign for independence seriously disrupted the region. In November 1999, militants led by the Khasi Students' Union (KSU) called on Khasi women to stop wearing saris and other foreign clothing that erode the traditional Khasi culture and traditional modes of dress. In another move, KSU acivists began to search for and deport all illegal immigrants. In August 2000, after gun battles between militants and police, a curfew was imposed n Shillong, and security forces were brought in to aid the local police. Suspected militant bases in the hills were raided, and several leaders of the Khasi nationalist movement were arrested.

In January 2000, during a visit to Meghalaya of Indian prime minister Atal Behari Vajpayee, leaders of the Hill State People's Democratic Party submitted a memorandum urging the creation of a separate Khasi state within India. Another delegation, representing a federation of the 25 Khasi states also urged the prime minister to resolve the issue by supporting the division of Meghalaya into two autonomous states. The Khasis, with one of India's highest literacy rates, the result of over 200 years of missionary activity, have produced an articulate leadership determined to protect their small nation, even at the expense of India's national unity.

Since the late eighties, numerous cycles of ethnic cleansing have pockmarked the state. Nepalis, Bengalis, and Marwaris have all been a target of attack. Nepalis are largely illegal migrants and work as labourers and housemaids. Bengalis have a large share of jobs and work as clerks and office managers. Marwaris control business activity. In April 2001, bowing to growing pressure from nationalist, student, and cultural groups, the Meghalaya government banned the sale of land to non-indigenous peoples. The insurgency spread in 2001 as violence erupted in several areas. Demands for a separate Hynniewtrep state has widespread support, while independence is supported by a small, but growing, militant minority.

SELECTED BIBLIOGRAPHY:

Giri, Helen. *The Khasis under British Rule, 1824–1947*. 1998.
Karna, M.N., L.S. Gassah, and C.J. Thomas. *Power to People in Meghalaya*. 1998.
Rana, B.S. *The People of Meghalaya*. 1989.
Synrem, H. Kelian. *Revivalism in Khasi Society*. 1992.

Khmer Krom

Krom; Southern Khmer; Viet Goc Khmer (Vietnamese Khmer); Viet Goc Mien; Khome; Kho Me; Cu Tho; Cur Cul

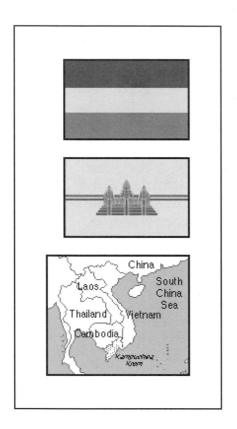

POPULATION: Approximately 7,000,000 Khmer Krom in Vietnam (only about 1,000,000 acknowledged by the Vietnamese government) concentrated in the southern provinces formerly known as Cochin China. About 80% live in the Mekong delta, with smaller numbers in other parts of southern Vietnam. Some estimates of the Khmer Krom population are as low as 700,000, but activists, many scientists and journalists claim a Khmer Krom population of at least seven and up to 12 million in Vietnam. Outside Cochin China, there are an estimated 1.2 million Khmer Krom in Cambodia with smaller communities numbering a total of over 45,0000 in Europe, North America, Australia, and other countries of Southeast Asia.

THE KHMER KROM HOMELAND: The Khmer Krom homeland, Kampuchea Krom lies in Southeast Asia, occupying the Delta of the Mekong River in southern Vietnam. The region, historically known as Cochin China formed a separate French colony until 1949 Kampuchea Krom means "Cambodia below" or Southern Cambodia. Cochin China lies between Cambodia on the north, the Gulf of Siam, and the South China Sea. Most of the territory is low-lying rice lands in the fertile river Delta one of the world's great rice-growing regions. In the northeast the southern spurs of the Annamese Cordillera form a rugged upland. *Cochin China (Kampuchea Krom)*: 29,974 sq. mi.—77,633 sq. km, (2002e) 24,650,000—South Vietnamese* 53%, Khmer Krom 28%, Chinese 14%, Montagnards,* Chams,* other Vietnamese 5%. The Khmer Krom capital and major cultural center is Can Tho, called Prek Rusey by the Khmer Krom (2002e) 247,000. The other important cultural centers are Rach Gia, called Kramour Sar, (2002e) 192,000, and Saigon/Ho Chi Minh City, called Prei Nokor.

FLAG: The Khmer Krom national flag, the flag of the national movement, is a horizontal tricolor of blue, yellow, and red. The former flag of the Cochin China era is a yellow field bearing a red Khmer Krom pagoda centered and two narrow red horizontal stripes.

PEOPLE AND CULTURE: The Khmer Krom are a Khmer people closely related to the Cambodians. Originally part of the Cambodian nation, the Khmer Krom were separated from the Cambodians in the eighteenth century. The majority of the Khmer Krom live in rural areas, although urbanization has accelerated since the 1980s. They have a long tradition of wet-rice cultivation and are experts in irrigation techniques and land upkeep. Khmer Krom culture is closely tied to religion. In the large pagodas there are various teams of drums, trumpets, and *ghe ngo* (a kind of small boat used for boat racing). Traditional festivals are very important, including the Chon cho nam tho may (New Year festival), and Buddha's birthday. The Khmer Krom are considered, by the Vietnamese, to be culturally more developed than most of the other minority groups in Vietnam, but less so than the Vietnamese.

LANGUAGE AND RELIGION: The Khmer Krom speak the southern dialect of Khmer or Cambodian, a Mon-Khmer language of the Austro-Asiatic language group. The dialect retains many antiquated words and forms no longer in use in Cambodia; it has many words borrowed from Vietnamese, Cham, and French. Accents, particularly, separate the speakers of Khmer Krom and Khmer Ler or northern Cambodian. Administration and education are in the Vietnamese language. Very few Khmer Krom are selected for higher education. No Khmer publications are allowed unless they serve government policy or propaganda. The language is taught in Khmer Krom Buddhist temples, although it is officially forbidden. The Khmer spoken in Cambodia is based on the Phnom Penh dialect and is quite different from the Khmer Krom dialect. The Khmer script evolved from Pallava, a variant of the Davanagari script used in India.

Approximately 95% of the Khmer Krom are Buddhists. They practice Hinayana (Southern School) Buddhism, whereas most Vietnamese practice Mahayana (Northern School) Buddhism or Christianity. There are more than 500 Hinayana temples and over 10,000 monks throughout the region. Some of the temples were erected many centuries ago, but of the estimated 700 in existence in 1900, about 200 have since been destroyed. Many religious practices and beliefs can be traced to the region's former Brahmanism and even its pre-Brahman beliefs. Many young Khmer Krom serve as monks, which provides access to more education and fulfills a long religious tradition. Monks often teach the people to read and write in exchange for labor.

NATIONAL HISTORY: The Funan Empire was established in the region of the upper Mekong River in the first century A.D. By the third century, the Funanese had conquered the neighboring states and expended their sway to the vast Delta of the lower Mekong River. In the fourth century, according to Chinese records, an Indian Brahman extended his rule over Funan, introducing Hindu customs, Indian laws, and the alphabet in use in central India. Khmers from the rival Chen-la state to the north overran Funan to establish the Khmer Empire in the sixth century.

The empire divided in the eighth century, but was reunited under Jayavarman II in the early ninth century. A new capital was established at Angkor, beginning a golden age of Khmer culture and power. The empire controlled the valleys of the lower Menam River in present Thailand, Cambodia, the Mekong Delta, called Southern Cambodia or Kampuchea Krom, and parts of Laos.

Indian culture and religion largely influenced the Khmer civilization. Buddhism flourished alongside the worship of Shiva and other Hindu gods. Both religions included the cult of the deified king. Many foreign scholars and artists, mostly from India, were attracted to the brilliant court at Angkor. Sanskrit literature flourished with royal patronage. In the Mekong Delta a second great Khmer center, Prei Nokor, became the trading center of the empire.

The Khmers fought repeated wars against the Annamese (Vietnamese) and Chams. In 1177, the Chams sailed up the Mekong, defeated the Cambodians and sacked the Khmer capital, Angkor. The Mongols overran the region in 1282. After the establishment of a strong Thai kingdom about 1350, the Khmer lands were under constant pressure from the east and north and Khmer power declined. In 1434, after the Thai capture of Angkor, the Khmer capital was transferred to Phnom Penh; this event marked the end of the brilliant Khmer civilization.

The Vietnamese, originating in the Red River region of present northern Vietnam, began to expand south into Cham territory in the tenth century. In the seventeenth century the Viet, after hundreds of years of trying, finally defeated the Chams and expanded their borders south to Kampuchea Krom. In 1698, the Vietnamese occupied Prei Nokor, which they renamed Sai Gon. They called their expanded state Dai Viet (Great Vietnam). Thousands of Cham refugees fled south to Khmer territory. All Vietnamese rulers continued the policy of territorial expansion. At times the Vietnamese used conquest, at other times they married into the nobility of the targeted territory. Assault troops of orphans raised by the state were always ready for war.

The first Europeans to visit the coast were the Portuguese in 1535. They were followed by Dutch, French, and English traders and adventurers. Missionaries established stations in the Mekong delta, winning some converts to Roman Catholicism, but more importantly introducing the local Khmer Krom to European-style education.

The Vietnamese settlers began to move into the territory as early as 1623, during the reign of the Khmer king, Chey Chetha II. The Annamese

Vietnamese gradually infiltrated the region through the mouths of the Mekong, increasing their commercial influence until they took control of the region in the eighteenth century. Hundreds of thousands fled the Vietnamese to settle in the Cambodian kingdom. The Cambodian kingdom became a protectorate of the Vietnamese kingdom, Annam, in 1807, but soon threw off Vietnamese domination.

During the rule of the Annamese King Gia Long, thousands of Khmer Krom were forced to dig a canal named Chum Nik Prek Teng, from the Bassac River to the Gulf of Siam. During this forced labor, from 1813 to 1820, thousands of Khmer Krom died. In the 1840s, the Khmer Krom were forced to assimilate, to abandon their culture and language. A Khmer Krom uprising was put down with great severity. The refusal of the Cambodian king, Ang Doung, to come to their aid began the separation of the Khmer Krom as a separate people.

Another Khmer Krom uprising, under the command of Sena Sous, threatened the Vietnamese hold on the region in 1859. After three years of fighting, the Khmer Krom, having defeated the troops sent against them, began to collapse following the murder of Sena Sous by a Vietnamese spy. The upheaval allowed the Europeans to extend their influence, particularly the French, who were welcomed as liberators from Vietnamese oppression.

The persecution of Christian converts was a factor prompting the French intervention in the mid-nineteenth century. They took control of Saigon in 1859. After a period of warfare, the Annamese state ceded eastern Cochin China to French rule in 1862. The remainder, including the Mekong delta, was ceded to France in 1867.

Cochin China was organized as a colony, whereas the other territories of French Indochina, Cambodia, Tonkin, and Annam, were declared protectorates, so that French influence was strongest in Cochin China. The French authorities favored the majority Vietnamese who filled the lower rungs of the colonial government, the police, and worked as translators, interpreters, and soldiers. The Khmer Krom were relegated to labor, mostly agriculture in the rice lands. The French territories of Cochin China, Annam, Tonkin, and Cambodia were united for administration in 1887.

Invading Japanese took control of French Indochina on 9 March 1945. They established an administration for the different territories, often aided by pro-Vichy French. Fighting in the area led to massacres by Vietminh forces, reported by Khmer Krom activists as eliminating about 200,000 people.

On 17 April 1945, before the French could reestablish their authority, the Vietnamese declared the independence of the Empire of Annam in central Vietnam. In June, the Vietnamese emperor, Bao Dai, declared that he wanted to unify the historical Vietnamese lands of Tonkin, Annam, and

Cochin China. The inclusion of Cochin China was protested by the Cambodians and the Khmer Krom. Fighting broke out between armed Khmer Krom and Vietnamese. The retreating Japanese turned Cochin China over to Annamese control in August.

Between December 1945 and January 1946, many Khmer Krom rejected Vietnamese authority and fought against the forces of the Vietminh, the Vietnamese nationalists. Hundreds of Khmer Krom villagers were killed and their bodies thrown into rivers. Many Khmer Krom fled the countryside for the relative safety of Saigon and other cities under French control.

A Chinese-supported communist rebellion in northern Vietnam, led by Ho Chi Minh, portrayed itself as a nationalist crusade against the colonial authority. The French, in an effort to counter growing communist influence, reinstated the Annamese emperor, Bao Dai, ousted during the war, but supported by the Japanese until the puppet Vietnamese government collapsed in 1945. French troops, supported by British troops in southern Vietnam and Cochin China, attempted to reassert their authority. Communist guerrillas and Chinese troops took control of the north.

In March 1946, an agreement allowed Vietnam independent autonomy within the French Indochina federation and the French Union, a grouping of France and its possession. Differences immediately arose over Cochin China. The French, backed by the Khmer Krom, favored a separate republic in Cochin China. Fighting broke out in November 1946. The Vietnamese nationalists often targeted the Khmer Krom, seen as opposing Vietnamese unification. The long and bloody conflict became part of the war called the French Indochina War of 1946–54.

The French National Assembly met in Paris to decide the fate of Cochin China on 21 May 1949. The decision was to place the territory under Vietnamese control with certain rights for the Khmer Krom (the Deferre Motion) despite a strong opposition from a Khmer Krom and Cambodian delegation attending the session. The Cambodians and the majority of the Khmer Krom favored the reunification of the historic Cambodia, which included Cochin China.

On 4 June 1949, Cochin China was transferred to Vietnam by the French government without the consent of the inhabitants. In a lavish ceremony the French formally gave the region to Emperor Bao Dai. The four Khmer Krom provinces of Do Nai, Long Ho, Mot Chrouk, and Pream, were abolished and divided into 21 Vietnamese provinces.

An agreement, signed by the French authorities and the Vietnamese granted Vietnam independence within the French Union in December 1949; however, the communists, in control of the north, established a rival government effectively partitioning Vietnam into two distinct territories. Western governments generally supported the government established in the south. The Soviet Union, the People's Republic of China, and other communist states recognized the rival government led by Ho Chi Minh.

The Khmer Krom and their protests, demonstrations, and appeals to the new United Nations were ignored. In February 1950, the French government formally asked the United States to aid the Bao Dai government. By 1954, the United States was paying around 80% of the French war costs.

The Ho Chi Minh government, following socialist doctrine, allowed the minorities in its territory to exercise limited autonomy in special zones. The government in the south established a centralized regime that prohibited minority rights and pressed assimilation. In 1954, the French were defeated by the communists and nationalists. As a temporary measure, Vietnamese territory was divided at the seventeenth parallel. Nearly a million Vietnamese fled the north, with most resettled among the Khmer Krom in the Mekong delta.

The American involvement grew as Ho Chi Minh gained support in both North and South Vietnam. Seeking allies among the non-Vietnamese groups, the Americans formed close relationships with the Montagnards* in the highlands and the Khmer Krom. The small allied nations fought beside the Americans until the cease-fire of 1973. During the war, they were loyal allies and fought with great distinction with the U.S. Special Forces and in a dangerous, experimental unit, the Mobile Guerilla Force. Their anti-communist stance and their alliance with the American forces eased the discrimination the Khmer Krom had suffered. In 1975, ignoring the cease-fire agreement, the North Vietnamese invaded and overran South Vietnam.

Thousands of Khmer Krom, accused of collaboration, were sent to reeducation camps by the victorious communists. Political leaders, teachers, and students who were thought to oppose the communist government were targeted. The Khmer language was prohibited, religion curtailed, and many lost their lands. Assimilation became official policy. Using Khmer or Khmer Krom as a national or ethnic designation was punishable by a prison term. All Khmer Krom were called Vietnamese of Khmer origin. Many fled to Cambodia or escaped in small boats. A large number of the Khmer Krom refugees eventually settled in the United States, Australia, or France.

In 1976, a group of Khmer Krom rebelled against communist rule. The revolt, possibly encouraged by the government, gave the communist authorities a reason to eleminate Khmer Krom from the government and the armed forces. Any leaders who had supported the uprising were imprisoned. Thousands of fearful Khmer Krom fled to Cambodia. In 1986, Kim Toc Chuong, the Buddhist patriarch of Tra Vinh Province, and 21 other Khmer Krom religious leaders, some implicated in the 1976 revolt, were reportedly murdered by security forces. The men are now venerated as martyrs.

Vietnamese troops invaded and occupied neighboring Cambodia in 1979, partly to remove the murderous Khmer Rouge government, which had murdered millions, including up to 150,000 Khmer Krom. From 1979 until 1993, when the Vietnamese withdrew, another 20,000 Khmer Krom in Cambodia died in labor camps, detention, or in other violent ways.

The Khmer Krom, suspect and suffering discrimination, attempted to blend into Vietnamese society. Not counted as ethnic Khmer Krom in official census, they claimed Vietnamese identity to escape persecution. The majority lived in rural areas with few contacts with government officials. Urbanized Khmer Krom were particularly careful not to draw attention. Violations of human rights became the official policy for dealing with non-Vietnamese in Vietnam. Racial and cultural discrimination continued as part of an unrelenting policy of assimilation in the 1980s and 1990s.

A four-member delegation traveled to Geneva, Switzerland in 1999 to present the Khmer Krom grievances to the United Nations High Commissioner for Human Rights. The visit to Geneva, undertaken prior to a planned visit to Vietnam by a UN delegation, implored the world body to take appropriate action to stop the gross violation of the human rights of the Khmer Krom nation. The Vietnamese government prevented the UN representative from seeing Khmer Krom political or religious leaders. Another group of activists demonstrated in New Zealand during the Asia Pacific Economic Cooperation conference attended by 21 heads of state including the U.S. president and the prime minister of Vietnam.

More than 1,500 Buddhist monks gathered in Phnom Penh in June 2001 to appeal for increased human rights for the Khmer Krom. The demonstration, held on the 52nd anniversary of the transfer of the territory to Vietnam, marked a new relationship between the Cambodians and the Khmer Krom, who share their language and ancestry but have been separated by history. Activists demanded a French apology for the illegal transfer of their homeland to Vietnam and the Vietnam government for accepting the transfer. They also sought UN and international governments to condemn the illegal act.

In July 2001, the Khmer Krom, represented by the Khmer Kampuchea Krom Federation, joined the UNPO. Activists demanded autonomy within Vietnam as a first step to the rebirth of Khmer Krom sovereignty. The nation, almost unknown outside Cambodia and Vietnam, has begun a program to let the world know of their plight.

SELECTED BIBLIOGRAPHY:

Nguyen-Vo, Thu-Huong. *Khmer-Viet Relations and the Third Indochina Conflict*. 1988.

Smith-Hefner, Nancy Joan. *Khmer American: Identity and Moral Education in a Diasporic Community*. 1999.

Taylor, Philip. *Fragments of the Present: Searching for Modernity in Vietnam's South*. 2000.

Zephir, Thierry. *Khmer: The Lost Empire of Cambodia*. 1998.

Kodavas

Kodagus; Coorgs

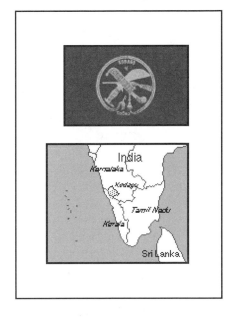

POPULATION: Approximately (2002e) 159,000 Kodavas in southern India, concentrated in Kodagu District of the Indian state of Karnataka, with smaller communities in neighboring districts of Karnataka and in adjacent areas of the state of Kerala.

THE KODAVA HOMELAND: The Kodava homeland, called Kodavu in the Kodava language, lies in southwestern India, at the southern end of the Western Ghats. Kodavu (or Kodagu) means "higher forest land" in the Kanrese language; the name was changed to Coorg by the British. The region is a rugged, hilly, and thickly forested district in the southern part of the Indian state of Karnataka. *District of Kodagu (Kodavu)*: 1,587 sq. mi.—4,110 sq. km, (2002e) 528,000—Kanarese 46%, Kodavas 25%, Tamils* 11%, Malayalis* 9%, other Indians 9%. The Kodava capital and major cultural center is Mercara, called Madikeri by the Kodavas, (2002e) 33,000.

FLAG: The Kodava national flag, the flag of the national movement, is a black field bearing the traditional seal of Coorg, two crossed swords over a rifle surrounded by chains.

PEOPLE AND CULTURE: The Kodavas are a rugged, athletic, and previously warlike people who are proud of their unique ancestry. They see themselves as a lost Aryan nation. Unlike Dravidian peoples of southern India, the Kodavas are tall and fair. The Kodavas have one of the lowest population growth rates in the world. Traditionally the Kodavas are a patrilineal people; women were responsible for the family and bore the brunt of labor on village farms. Kodava houses are raised off the ground and are always built facing the east. A large portion of adult males are soldiers, serving in the Indian military and preserving their tradition as warriors. Even today, male births and deaths are celebrated with gun salutes. Because of their martial tradition, the Indian constitution permits them to carry guns without licenses.

LANGUAGE AND RELIGION: The language spoken by the Kodavas called Kodagu, is a Dravidian language belonging the Southern Dravidian group. Literacy is very high, estimated at 98%, one of the highest rates in India. Kanarese, a related Dravidian language, is the official language of Karnataka, and most Kodavas are able to communicate in it. English is widely spoken as a second or third language, and it is proposed as the official language of the restored Coorg state. The Kodava greeting "Enne ray" bears a striking resemblance to the Greek greeting "Ella ray," which some Kodavas claim validates their tradition that they are the descendants of soldiers that came to India with Alexander the Great.

The Kodavas are Hindus, and as a warrior group they are members of the high Kshatriya caste. They are known to be more liberal and independent than other Hindus, particularly in relation to marriage, divorce and ceremonies: the Kodavas are the only Hindus in India who do not require marriage dowries, and they observe their own festivals but do not generally celebrate any other Hindu festivals. The Kodavas strictly observe the caste hierarchy and do not generally form relationships with people of other castes. The Hindu observances of the Kodavas retain many pre-Hindu elements, including ancestor worship, particularly of the first member of their family, known as the *karanova*. They believe that by worshipping their ancestor *karanova* they worship God directly. An estimated 95% consider themselves Hindus, while 4% adhere to their ancestral beliefs. There are small Christian and Muslim minorities.

NATIONAL HISTORY: According to Kodava legends their origins began with Chandravarma, the youngest son of King Siddhartha of Matsya who came to the region on a pilgrimage to the origin of the River Kaveri. He settled and had eleven sons, and each son had over a hundred sons. All the grandsons of Chandravarma bathed in the river, becoming the Kodavas. Today the river, the Cauvery, is still worshipped; the Kodavas call themselves the "children of Cauvery."

Scholars believe the Kodavas evolved from a synthesis of peoples, originally settlers from the eastern Arabian Peninsula in the fifth century B.C. They took local women in marriage. Later Scythian Greeks in the army of Alexander the Great settled in the region after he abandoned his northwestern Indian campaign in 327 B.C. Welcomed by the earlier inhabitants the Greeks intermarried. In the isolated highlands, the fusion of peoples produced a tall, fair people unique in southern India.

The region, called Kodavu, formed an independent kingdom from the ninth century. The remote region, inaccessible during the monsoon, began to prosper from the salt trade through the mountains from the Kerala coast to the great cities to the east. The Kodavas' growing wealth attracted many invaders, but the fierce mountain fighters repulsed them all but the most determined.

The earliest written record of Kodavas is an inscription by a Chengalva king, thanking the Kodavas for their contribution to some local battle. It has been dated to be from around 1050 A.D., when the Chengalvas were vassals of the Cholas. Historical inscriptions show that the region was nominally included in the kingdom of the Gangas in the ninth and tenth centuries, then under the rule of the Cholas in the eleventh century. The early peoples took the name Kodava, meaning "blessed by Godmother Kaveri (Cauvery)." The Kodava kingdom, under the Chengalva dynasty, was tributary to the empires that controlled the region but remained mostly independent until the fourteenth century, when the Hoysalas took control of the Western Ghats. Known as the "little nation of warriors," the Kodavas were widely known for their courage, honor, and loyalty.

In the sixteenth century the Hindu religion superseded the animist beliefs that had evolved over the 2,000-year history of the Kodavas. The caste system, rigidly adhered to in other parts of India, was mostly rejected, although as warriors the Kodavas were accepted as upper-caste. A Hindu dynasty, the Kannadigas, ruled almost continuously from 1633 until it was overthrown by the British in 1834. The kingdom comprised 12 principalities.

Because of its rugged terrain, Coorg was sometimes referred to as the "Switzerland of India" by the British. The rajas of Coorg and local Kodava headmen deliberately kept the hill country devoid of roads, allowing only the narrowest of jungle trails between towns, thus making the highlands impregnable against anyone unfamiliar with the territory. Between 1780 and 1789 the kingdom came under the control of the Muslim rulers of Mysore, who conquered almost all of southern India.

The isolation of the region allowed the rajas to become increasingly oppressive. Raja Chikaveera Rajendra in the early nineteenth century ruled through terror. Paranoid about assassination, he executed anyone who defied his authority. By the time he had been on the throne for several years, his ruthless rule and profligate spending had reduced the cohesive little state into insolvency, political instability, and terror. Ministers and local merchants began writing in secret to the British resident of neighboring Mysore, which had been annexed by the British a few years before on the pretext of removing a similarly abusive ruler. In 1834 the British deposed the raja and declared Coorg a protected state under a governor chosen from among the Kodavas. In return for cooperation and military service, the British allowed the Kodava state to retain nominal independence. From 1834 to 1857, Coorg was ruled by a commissioner responsible to the British East India Company. In 1857 it came under the direct rule of the British raj.

The British made the former kingdom a "chief commissioner's province," the first to be permitted to have a legislative body in 1924. British influence brought Western education and ideas, which were readily accepted. The Kodavas, recruited into the British colonial army, produced many fine officers and generals. Because of their unique history and physical appearance, they were the subject of study by British scholars. Sir Erskine Perry, an author and anthropologist, wrote of the Kodavas that they "have no resemblance to any races of south India."

Traditionally every Kodava village was self-sufficient, with its own artisans, workers, and administrators. Under British rule this began to break down, as the Kodavas were forced to seek employment on coffee plantations or other types of agricultural labor. The need for labor meant importing Tamils, Malayalis, and other non-Kodavas to the region, setting off outbreaks of violence in the 1920s and 1930s.

The state was administered by the chief commissioner of Mysore from 1881 until Indian independence in 1947. From 1952 to 1956 Coorg formed a separate state, a "Part C" state under the Indian constitution, with two parliamentary seats in the national legislature. Coorg was considered a model state both under British rule and within the Indian union in the early 1950s. It was well administered and financially sound. In 1956 the Indian government reorganized all the states along linguistic lines, uniting Coorg, with its Kanarese-speaking majority, with the new Kanarese-language state of Mysore, later renamed Karnataka. The majority Kanarese of Karnataka relegated Kodagu to the status of a remote backwater, neglected by state ministries and useful only for the oranges and coffee it exported.

The neglect continued during the 1960s and 1970s, sparking a national movement beginning in the late 1970s. National sentiment was paralleled by a reculturation, a new appreciation for the Kodavas' unique history, language, and culture. The national movement looked back on a long history of independence and later separate status under British rule.

The deforestation of the Western Ghats added a strong environmental element to the growing Kodava national movement. The native forests were threatened with extinction due to illegal logging and encroachments. The region was about 80% forested in 1971, but only 38% in 1991.

The lack of roads, and the poor condition of the few that exist, has hampered economic development, and safe drinking water is available only in some districts, though Kodagu, due to its abundant coffee, is the highest-revenue-earning and tax-paying district in Karnataka state. The district has no railhead.

In November 1997, Kodava leaders, with widespread backing in the district, demanded separation from Karnataka and the restoration of the separate status that disappeared in 1956. Activists blame the Karnataka government for neglecting the region and forcing the Kodavas to support separatism. The demand for the restoration of Kodagu statehood was supported by a mass rally in Madikeri on 21 November 1997. Activists have collected tens of thousands of signatures in favor of submitting a memorandum to the Indian president. A general strike and peaceful demonstrations in December showed that the nationalists had the support of the majority of the Kodavas.

Thousands of men who had served in the Indian army formed a militant faction of the nationalist movement in the 1990s. Their grievances included low pensions and a lack of rehabilitation programs for ex-service men. Militant activists in late 1998 called for a declaration of independence before beginning negotiations with either the Indian or Karnataka governments.

In March 2000, the leader of the nationalist Kodagu Rajya Mukthi Morcha (KRMM) appealed to the president of India to classify the Kodavas as a nonreligious racial minority, which would allow them to enjoy political reservation, guaranteed representation in government bodies, and other benefits allowed to minorities. Nationalists claimed that in spite of the unwarranted aggression by the successive governments of Karnataka, the Kodavas had successfully maintained their distinct national identity. The Kodava nationalist favor small states as an antidote to the unwieldy and cumbersome linguistic state of Karnataka.

In 1997–98, opponents of Kodagu statehood attempted to incite the Tamils and Malayalis, who form the major part of the labor force on the orange and coffee estates. Nationalist assurances that there would be no expulsions after statehood reassured the minority communities that they would be welcome and would prosper in a sovereign Kodagu.

The Kodavas also demanded a separate seat in the national legislature in New Delhi, a privilege that had ended in 1964. In March 2000, activists of the KRMM demonstrated in Madikeri against government plans to delimit parliamentary constituencies on the basis of census results without addressing Kodava demands for a separate constituency. In September 1999, the nationalists called off an election boycott but urged their supporters to vote only for local candidates who supported the restoration of statehood.

The loss of local control since 1956 has seriously threatened the language and culture of the region. In the late 1990s a concerted effort was under way to revive the Kodava culture. The decline of the distinctive culture is seen as a manner of conquest. The Kodavas argue that their nation has never been conquered, and that is the basis of the modern nationalist movement.

Talks between representatives of the states of Karnataka and Tamil Nadu, in January 2001, were begun in an effort to end a long-standing conflict over how to share the water of the Cauvery River. Kodava activists organized protests against the talks, which they claim will deprive them of a major resource and that access to the river violates local religious beliefs.

SELECTED BIBLIOGRAPHY:

Cariappa, P. *The Coorgs and Their Origins.* 1981.
Isaac, Jeanette. *Coorg: The Land of the Kodavas.* 1995.
Ponnappa, Kongetira. *A Study of the Origins of the Coorgs.* 1997.
Srinivas, M.N. *Religion and Society among the Coorgs of South India.* 1989.

Komis

Komi Morts; Komi-Mores; Komi-Zyrians; Komi Zyranes; Zyrians; Zyryans; Northern Komis

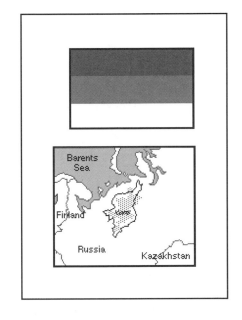

POPULATION: Approximately (2002e) 395,000 Komis in northwestern Russia, concentrated in the Komi Republic in the northeastern part of European Russia, with smaller communities in Arkhangelsk, Sverdlovsk, Murmansk, Omsk, and Tyumen Oblasts, and the Nenets, Yamalo-Nenets, and Khanty-Mansi autonomous regions.

THE KOMI HOMELAND: The Komi homeland lies in northeastern European Russia, occupying the basins of the Pechora, Vychegda, and Kama Rivers and the upper reaches of the Mezen River, a region partly above the Arctic Circle. The population is denser and more assimilated in the southern districts. An estimated 15,000 Komi live in the Nenets region above the Arctic Circle, which was administratively separated from the Komi homeland in 1929. The majority of the Komi homeland forms a member state of the Russian Federation. *Komi Republic (Komi Republika/Komi Mu)*: 160,579 sq. mi.—415,900 sq. km, (2002e) 1,109,000—Russians 51%, Komis 33%, Ukrainians 10%, Belarussians 3%, Nenets* 1%, Tatars* 1%, others 1%. The Komi capital and major cultural center is the city of Syktyvkar, called Syktylsajas by the Komis, (2002e) 229,000. The other important cultural center is Uhta, (2002e) 95,000.

FLAG: The Komi national flag, the official flag of the Komi Republic, is a horizontal tricolor of blue, green, and white.

PEOPLE AND CULTURE: The Komis belong to the Permian branch of the Finno-Ugric peoples. The Komi national group, the most advanced of the northern peoples of the Russian Federation, is divided into eight ethnographic groups based on geography. One group is the Izhmi, who migrated to the Kola Peninsula and the Ob River basin in western Siberia in the nineteenth century. The Izhmi mixed with the Nenets and are the only Komi group whose primary activity is reindeer herding. The Yazua live in Perm Oblast, south of the Komi Republic. Economic activities vary from region to region. The majority of the Komis work in farming, timber, and as traders or cattle or reindeer herders.

LANGUAGE AND RELIGION: The language of the Komis is a Permic language of the Finno-Permian group of Finno-Ugric languages. Komi is spoken in three major dialects, Pechora, Udor, and Verkhne-Vyshegod. Seven subdialects are divided into two major groups: Northern or Zyran and Eastern or Yazva. The literary language is based on Zyran and Yazva—more accurately, it is a transition dialect to Komi-Permyak. The Komi reculturation is evident in language figures. In 1989, 42.8% of the Komis living in the republic reported Russian as their first language; by 1994 this percentage had dropped to 26.3%. The reculturation of the 1990s is largely based on language, but de-Russification of the culture is also stressed. School instruction in the Komi language was introduced in 1994–95.

The Komis are mostly Russian Orthodox, but their religious traditions are laced with the shamanistic traditions of their pre-Christian heritage. A substantial number of the Komi Orthodox population are Old Believers, who adopted their religious beliefs from the Russian Old Believers who settled in the region to escape persecution by the Orthodox authorities.

NATIONAL HISTORY: The Permian peoples are descended from ancestors who originally inhabited the middle and upper Kama River area. During the first millennium before the Christian era, the Permians split into two major groups, the Komis and the Udmurts. Around 500 A.D., the Komi group again split, some of the clans migrating to the Vychegda Basin. The migrants, settling in the colder north, mixed with local peoples and began the development of a separate nation. The clans left behind in the Kama Basin became known as Permyaks* or Komi-Permyaks.

The Komi came under the rule of the Slavic republic of Great Novgorod in the thirteenth century; they were called Perms by their neighbors. Novgorodian fur traders used their rivers to travel across the Urals into Siberia. When overhunting diminished the Komis' wealth of furs and easier, shorter routes to Siberia were discovered, the area declined in importance.

Formerly practicing a form of ancestor worship, the Komi converted to the Orthodox Christianity introduced to the clans by Saint Stephen in the 1360s and 1370s. Saint Stephen of Perm, the Komis' patron saint, is called the "Enlightener of the Komi" and is revered for opening the Komi homeland to the world outside. He not only converted many to Orthodox Christianity but also constructed an alphabet for the Komi language and translated parts of the Bible.

In the mid-1500s, the Komis began another migration, moving deeper into the upper Vychegda and Pechora River basins. The Russians of the rival Muscovite duchy began to penetrate Novgorodian territory in 1450 and finally conquered Novgorod between 1471 and 1478.

The Komis were subjected to prejudice and a harsh colonial regime.

The Russians suppressed the Komi languages and culture and forced their assimilation. The Russians encouraged their Orthodox faith, although Old Believers often suffered. In the mid-sixteenth century, to escape harsh Russian rule, many Komi clans again migrated, moving deeper into the upper Vychegda and Pechora River basins.

In the eighteenth century, the authorities opened the southern Komi districts to Slavic colonization, setting aside the forest and Arctic zones as places of exile for criminals and tsarist political prisoners. Syktyvkar was founded as the center of Russian colonization and of the exploitation of the region's forest and mineral resources. The abolition of serfdom in Russia in 1861 led to a massive influx of freed serfs into the region. The Komis rebelled several times against harsh tsarist rule and the growing number of foreigners settling in their homeland.

Major trade routes developed across the Komi homeland from Archangel to the Viatka-Kama Basin and on to Siberia. The Komis earned a reputation as shrewd traders in the isolated settlements north of the Arctic Circle. By the nineteenth century, industries were established in the region. The Komis took to reindeer breeding late in the nineteenth century, especially the clans living in the northern reaches of the homeland.

Komi resentment of the Slav colonists, who appropriated the best lands, led to violent confrontations in the 1870s and 1880s. The treatment of the Komis by the growing Russian population in their territory triggered a national revival. A Komi cultural movement in the late nineteenth century, emphasized their language, particularly the distinguished tradition of oral epics and folk literature. The revival began to reverse centuries of forced assimilation. A parallel movement, heavily influenced by the attitudes and ideals of the large population of political exiles in the region, evolved Komi national sentiment, antigovernment and anti-Russian.

The outbreak of World War I reinforced the growing antitsarist movement. Many young Komis took refuge in the forests to escape conscription. The overthrow of the tsar in February 1917 raised Komi expectations that the abuses and wrongs of the past would finally be addressed. A Komi congress in the summer on 1917 voted for autonomy in a new democratic Russia and sent a formal petition to the Provisional Government.

The Bolshevik coup in October 1917 swept away the remaining Russian authority in the region. Left virtually independent, the Komi leaders began to organize institutions of self-rule, but early in 1918 Bolshevik troops of the new Soviet government invaded the region.

Allied Anglo-American interventionist forces that had landed at Arkhangelsk drove the Bolsheviks from the Komi region in May and June 1918. The interventionists encouraged the Komis to organize a national state to combat Bolshevik influence in the region. Aided by the numerous freed political prisoners and members of the foreign interventionist forces, the Komis created a number of cultural and governmental institutions. In

1919 the interventionist forces withdrew from the region, opening the way for the Soviet reoccupation of the Komi state.

In 1918, a Komi national school was created, and in the 1920s and 1930s the Soviet authorities encouraged the Komis to develop in the fields of literature, music, and folklore. On the other hand, especially during the collectivization of the Komi lands in 1928–32, the Komis' traditional culture and way of life were partially destroyed by forced Sovietization. Industrialization required that many of the Komis to settle in newly constructed cities, where they were put to work in factories. Many non-Komis were also resettled in the region.

The Soviet authorities created an autonomous province, as part of their early nationalities policies, for the Komis in 1921. The province was raised to the status of an autonomous republic within the Russian Federation in 1936, but the illusion of autonomy was overshadowed by increasing Soviet oppression.

During the Stalinist purges of the 1930s, the mental and physical destruction of the Komi intellectual class was completed. Accused of armed bourgeois nationalism, cultural and political leaders were liquidated with great brutality. The murder of the Komi leadership marked the beginning of the intense Russification of the general Komi population.

To disseminate information over the large territory, the Soviet authorities devised a new Komi alphabet to fit their Permian language. In 1923 the Komis and Permyaks were officially recognized as two distinct nations; two dialectal forms were established, with different writing standards. The alphabet, using mixed Latin and Cyrillic characters, was used in printing after 1920, but in 1938 the authorities eliminated the distinctive Komi alphabet and substituted Russian Cyrillic.

The Slav population of the region, only 7% of the total in 1926, expanded rapidly during the Stalinist years. The Gulag, a vast chain of prison-labor camps built to exploit the high-quality coal discovered in the Pechora Basin and to provide labor for the construction of logging roads and mills, swallowed up thousands of prisoners. The Pechora Basin had been sparsely inhabited. Northern Zyria, a region so forbidding that it had been rejected as a place of exile by Tsar Nicholas I, had by the mid-1930s a population of over 100,000, mostly prisoners.

The severity of the climate and the relative inaccessibility of the region kept the Komis culturally isolated until after World War II. The Komi homeland gained new importance during the course of the war as threatened industries and populations were shifted east and north from provinces overrun by the Germans. In 1943, the Vorkuta-Kotlas Railway was completed across the region, entirely built by slave labor. The opening of the rail link allowed the exploitation of the oil fields discovered in the Pechora and Ukhta regions, and a period of spectacular growth began. The population of the Komi region quadrupled between 1939 and 1949. By the end of World War II the Komi population formed only a large minority in their homeland.

Purges ordered by Joseph Stalin during the late 1940s and early 1950s once again eliminated the cultural and political leadership of the Komis; education in the Komi language was forbidden. Ethnic Slavs filled nearly all the positions in the local government and Communist Party hierarchies. In the 1960s, the region became more important economically as minerals began to be exploited. Rapid industrialization forced many Komis to settle in the growing industrial and mining cities, where they could find work in the new mills, factories, and mines. There was a massive immigration of ethnic Russians to the Komi territories between 1950 and 1960 as the vast natural resources of the region were ruthlessly exploited. The newcomers were encouraged to settle in the northern districts by offers of higher salaries and other benefits.

The Soviet reforms introduced by Mikhail Gorbachev in the late 1980s had an immediate impact on the region. The relaxation of strict controls provoked massive strikes in 1989–90 by the region's coal miners to punctuate demands for higher pay and better working conditions. The strikes and disturbances by miners, already handsomely paid by Komi standards, loosed a torrent of Komi grievances and demands that Komi mistreatment be addressed by the republic's chamber of deputies. Economic demands gave way to political demands, including calls for the reunification of the Komi lands divided by Stalin between 1925 and 1929. On 29 August 1990, the leaders of the republic declared Komi a sovereign state.

The disintegration of the Soviet state in August 1991 fueled a dramatic increase in the Komis' national awareness. The republican government in November 1991 unilaterally declared Komi a constituent republic of the renewed Russian Federation and reiterated an earlier demand for the reunification of the Komi homeland into one state.

Several Komi national organizations formed mostly since 1991 demanded local control of the region's vast mineral resources and a larger share of the revenues earned for local development projects. Economic demands have grown since the economic collapse of the Russian economy in 1998. The coal reserves in the Komi homeland would give the region a valuable commodity to trade for basic needs.

Since 1993 the Komi nationalists have waged a nonviolent war of symbols. Denouncing the new Russian flag as a symbol of colonialism, as offensive as the red banner of the communists, nationalists routinely tear it down and raise the banner of Komi nationalism in its place. The Komi flag, representing the nationalist's aspirations and demands for unification, has come to symbolize the Komis' contention that their natural resources would sustain their small nation through the hard economic times ahead. The Komi Republic was the first Finno-Ugrian region in Russia to adopt officially a Finnic language.

The Komi rebirth that began during the late Soviet era accelerated in the post-Soviet period. During the Soviet period some Komi traditions were lost, but a literary culture developed. Komi literature had been published in the eighteenth and nineteenth centuries, but alphabet reforms and mass education during the Soviet period generated a literary renaissance, which continues to the present. Organized movements to revive the Komi languages, traditions, and religious practices developed in the late Soviet period but became a mass cultural movement after 1991.

In the late 1990s, the Komis attempted to create a technical and political support for their national revival through the creation of a national elite. A newly created Finno-Ugrian Faculty at the University of Syktyvkar became the focus of the reculturation. The former Soviet Komi leadership, mostly non-Komi or assimilated Komis who spoke Russian as their first language, gave way to a nationalist leadership, but the national renewal still suffers from decades of official opposition. In 1996, an agreement on Komi national self-determination was signed between the Russian Federation and the Komi Republic.

In the years after the collapse of the Soviet state, the ecological problems resulting from Soviet industrialization became evident, making the traditional Komi way of life ever more difficult. Massive oil spills and fires caused by pollution devastated vast areas of the Komi homeland. The growing nationalist movement has a strong environmentalist faction demanding redress for the mistakes of the Soviet era.

The emigration of many Russians from the republic due to the increasing economic problems, particularly in the northern districts, has increased the Komi share of the republic's population and has allowed the Komis greater influence in the republic's decision making. The national movement, advocating the "de-Russification" of the Komi homeland, supports the republican government.

SELECTED BIBLIOGRAPHY:

Olson, James S. *An Ethnohistorical Dictionary of the Russian and Soviet Empires*. 1994.
Slezkine, Yuri. *Arctic Mirrors: Russia and the Small Peoples of the North*. 1994.
Taagepera, Rein. *The Finno-Ugric Republics and the Russian State*. 1999.
Warhola, James W. *Politicized Ethnicity in the Russian Federation: Dilemmas of State Formation*. 1996.

Kongos

Bacongos; Bakongos; Musicongos; Congos; Koongos

POPULATION: Approximately (2002e) 11,560,000 Kongos in west-central Africa, concentrated in the western part of the Congo River basin in Angola (1,795,000), Republic of Congo (1,530,000), and Democratic Republic of Congo (8,235,000). Other communities live in Luanda, the Angolan capital, and in Europe, principally in Portugal and France.

THE KONGO HOMELAND: The Kongo homeland lies in west-central Africa, occupying the basin of the lower Congo (Zaire) River. The lowland region stretches along the Atlantic Ocean, rising in Angola to inland plateaus of open grassland and brush. The Kongo homeland has no official status and is divided between three countries. The traditional Kongo territory makes up Central Congo, the provinces of Bas-Congo, Kinshasa, and Bandundu of the Democratic Republic of Congo; South Congo, the provinces of Cabinda, Uige, and Zaire of Angola; and North Congo, the regions of Kouilou, Niari, Lékoumo, Bouenza, Pool; and the commune of Brazzaville of the Republic of Congo. *Central Congo:* 138,821 sq. mi.— 359,544 sq. km, (2002e) 17,569,000—Kongos 66%, Bambalas 18%, Mongos 10%, Kasaians* 4%, other Congolese 2%. *South Congo:* 40,964 sq. mi.—106,096 sq. km, (2002e) 1,580,000— Kongos (including Cabindans*) 86%, Ovimbundus 10%, other Angolans 4%. *North Congo:* 41,276 sq. mi.—106,905 sq. km, (2002e) 2,734,000—Kongos 52%, Tekes 17%, Mbochis 12%, Mbetes 5%, other Congolese 14%. The capital and major cultural center of the central Kongos is Kinshasa, (2002e) 6,269,000. The capital and major cultural center of the northern Kongos is Brazzaville, called Ntámo, (2002e) 1,131,000. The Kinshasa-Brazzaville metropolitan area has a population of 8,529,000. The major cultural center of the south Kongos is M'banza Congo, (2002e) 62,000, the traditional capital of the Kongos.

FLAG: The Kongo national flag, the flag of the national movement, is a horizontal tricolor of red, white, and yellow, charged with a centered white star outlined in black. The flag of the pan-Kongo movement, is a horizontal tricolor of white, red, and yellow. The flag of the Kongos in Angola, the flag of the FNLA, has diagonal stripes of white, red, and yellow, bearing a centered five-pointed white star.

PEOPLE AND CULTURE: Kongo is a generic name; officially "Bakongo" refers to the people, "Kikongo" to the language, and "Musikongo" to the homeland. The Kongos are a Bantu people divided among twelve distinct clans spread across parts of Zaire, Angola, and Congo. Historically the Kongos were a united people, the descendants of the medieval Kongo empire; today, due to the geographic range of settlement, there is wide variations in culture and language among the various Kongo groups. The main characteristic of modern Kongo culture is fragmentation; nearly every village is independent of its neighbors. The clan system remains important in Kongo culture. Often called "houses," the clans are based on matrilineal descent. Authority within the clans is shared with persons both inside and outside the house, in a complex fashion. The influence of early Roman Catholic and Protestant missions, which placed particular emphasis on the traditions of the Kongos, created a complex interaction of myth, competition, and ambition that continues to the present. Traditionally fishing, hunting, and farming occupied the majority, but by the 1970s over half the Kongos were urban dwellers, particularly in the cities of Kinshasa and Brazzaville.

LANGUAGE AND RELIGION: All of the clans speak dialects of Kikongo, a language of the Bantu group of the Benue-Congo branch of Niger-Congo languages. Because of the size of the Kongo population and the territorial range of the language, much dialectical variation has developed, to the point that some dialects are barely mutually intelligible. The major dialects are South Kongo, Central Kongo, West Kongo or Fiote, Bwende, Laadi, East Kongo, Southeast Kongo, and Nzamba. In Angola the San Salvador dialect has been heavily influenced by Portuguese. Most Kongos speak at least some French or Portuguese.

The majority of the Kongos are nominally Christians, mostly Roman Catholic. Protestant denominations, including Baptists, Methodists, and Congregationalists, claim adherence among over 20%, a share that is growing rapidly. Even the most devout Christians still adhere to many of the beliefs and traditions of their ancient African religion. In the central region a prophetic nationalist religion called Kimbanguism, which merges traditional beliefs and rituals with Christianity, has many adherents. Traditional beliefs embody the concepts of monotheism, animism, and spirit and ancestor worship. Witchcraft and sorcery are in use, in varying degrees. Many Kongos maintain ancestral shrines in their homes where families pray for the intercession of the dead. A strong prophetic and messianic tradition among the Kongos has given rise to various nativistic political-religious movements.

NATIONAL HISTORY: The basin of the Congo River was originally inhabited by pygmy peoples. Bantu peoples settled the region in successive waves in the seventh and eighth centuries A.D. The migrants are believed to have originated in the highland lakes region to the northeast or in present Nigeria. The Bantus created a number of small, autonomous chiefdoms or states in the lower Congo Basin. In the thirteenth century a number of the small Kongo states united themselves under a paramount king called the *manikongo*.

The united Kongo state eventually expanded to incorporate twelve related clans or tribes living in six provinces south of the Congo River and three tributary states north of the river. The Kongo kingdom, based on tropical agriculture, evolved a sophisticated state system, an efficient bureaucracy, and an advanced culture. The Kongos established trade links with the huge Congo River basin.

The Kongo territory was visited by Portuguese explorer Diogo Cao in 1482. The Kongos welcomed the strangers and allowed the Portuguese to establish trading posts. In 1483 the reigning king, Nzinga Knuwu, sought the aid of the powerful newcomers against a rebellion. The king allowed missionaries, artisans, and soldiers to reside in his capital city from 1491 onward. By 1500 the *manikongo* and most of his court had adopted Catholicism and regularly exchanged emissaries with Portugal and the Vatican. The pope consecrated history's first black bishop, a member of the Kongo royal family, in 1520.

The Portuguese, having established a foothold in the kingdom, turned to the lucrative slave trade. By the 1570s, the Portuguese had turned their attention farther south, where slaves were more readily available. The slave trade spelled disaster for the Kongo kingdom and its formerly peaceful inhabitants. Raids on surrounding peoples for slaves to sell to the Europeans disrupted a wide area of the Congo Basin.

In 1665 Portuguese adventurers, believing stories that gold was to be found, invaded the declining kingdom. The kingdom quickly disintegrated into a number of small warring states only loosely loyal to the *manikongo*. The small Kongo states were easy prey for the encroaching European powers. By the mid-eighteenth century the kingdom consisted of six provinces, three in Central Congo and three in Angola. The tributary states of Bungu, Mgoy Kakongo, and Loango lay to the north of the Congo River.

In 1878, King Leopold of Belgium, believing that his country needed colonies, engaged the explorer Henry M. Stanley to establish Belgian claims in the region of the Congo River. The French, alarmed by Stanley's activities, established treaty relations with the Kongo tributary states north of the river, founded Brazzaville, and established a protectorate in 1882. The Portuguese continued to recognize the Kongo kingdom until 1884, when by treachery they gained control of the southern provinces. The Berlin Conference of 1885 partitioned the Kongo kingdom along arbitrary lines. The colonial partition of the Kongo lands eventually gave Portugal the region south of the Congo River and the enclave of Cabinda to the north, the Belgians took the northern part of the kingdom with an outlet to the sea between Cabinda and Portuguese Angola, and the former tributary states to the north came under permanent French control.

By the early 1900s, all of the Kongo peoples, even those of the formerly tributary kingdoms, were claiming descent from the old kingdom. In 1907 the Portuguese completed the reconquest of the southern area, but in 1914 another revolt broke out; it continued until 1917. In 1921 a Kongo prophet, Simon Kimbangu, began a religious-nationalist movement in the Belgian Congo that rapidly gained support in all three colonies. The Europeans saw the movement as a threat to the colonial authorities and banned it. Kimbangu was ultimately arrested and exiled, but the cultural reawakening he had started continued to grow, and the exiled prophet became a powerful symbol of Kongo irredentist nationalism.

Primary schooling in the 1920s and 1930s was largely in the hands of religious groups. Missionary schools educated mainly the sons of chiefs, who formed an elite group in all three territories. Politically, the educated minority began to demand participation in the colonial administrative process in the early 1930s, with a more militant minority planning for the reunification of the traditional Kongo territories in one political unit.

Nationalists in the Belgian sector formed in the late 1940s the Association for the Maintenance, Unity, and Expansion of the Kikongo Language (ABAKO), a Kongo cultural organization that quickly became the major political force among the Belgian Kongos. In 1954 ABAKO, led by Joseph Kasavubu, demanded autonomy for the Kongo regions of the Belgian Congo. In 1958 ABAKO announced its support for the reconstitution of the old Kongo kingdom within its historical borders. ABAKO concentrated on the past splendors of the Kongo kingdom and on the culture and language of the Kongo people. Its proclaimed objective was the reconstruction of the Kongo state; many members advocated secession as the quickest way of achieving this goal.

A speech by French president Charles de Gaulle in Brazzaville in August 1958, in which he declared that whoever wanted independence would have it, fired Kongo nationalism in all three colonies. Joseph Kasavubu and Abbé Fulbert Yolou, later the first president of the former French Congo, called for a reunited Kongo state, but the European authorities in all three colonies vehemently rejected resurgent Kongo nationalism. Ethnic rivalries in French Congo led to severe rioting in Brazzaville in 1959.

The prospect of independence made the Kongo the largest single group to define themselves in ethnic terms for political purposes and one of the few to develop an articulate national ideology. ABAKO leaders in June 1959 sent the Belgian government a detailed plan for an independent Republic of Central Kongo, including within its proposed limits the mostly Kongo capital of Belgian Congo, Leopoldville (Kinshasa). It threatened to declare Central Congo independent by the end of 1959. The plan was rejected, and in October 1959 ABAKO began a campaign to undermine Belgium's authority. The Belgian authorities instead hastily granted independence to the entire Belgian Congo as the Democratic Republic of Congo on 30 June 1960. In the first Congolese elections ABAKO won a sweeping victory in the Kongo-populated areas, and Joseph Kasavubu became the first president of the already rapidly disintegrating republic.

Kongo nationalists led by Holden Roberto in northern Angola founded the first political party in 1954 of which the goal was to reunify the Kongo people divided by colonization. The party led a violent rebellion against the Portuguese in 1961, the first open rebellion against the colonial authorities in the post–World War II era. In 1962, the party assumed an Angolan nationalist orientation and was renamed the National Front for the Liberation of Angola (FLNA); it now demanded immediate independence. Attacks on European settlers killed over 700 people, but massive Portuguese reprisals left over 20,000 Kongos dead. An estimated 130,000 Kongo refugees took refuge in the territory of the newly independent Democratic Republic of Congo. In 1963, Jonas Savimbi broke with the FLNA to found UNITA, the National Union for the Total Independence of Angola, which drew support from the Ovimbundus and some Kongos.

The Congolese civil war ended the first attempt at democratic government and eventually led to the dictatorship of Mobutu Sese Seko. His rule, known for corruption and nepotism, reduced the Kongos, except those associated with the government, to abject poverty. In January 1964 a rebellion broke out among the Kongos in the Kwilu region of the country, continuing until the rebels were finally defeated in December 1965. By the 1970s, average incomes in the Kongo provinces, except Kinshasa, had fallen to less than half of those of the pre-independence period.

The French Congo, granted independence in August 1960, became a republic dominated by the dominant Kongo ethnic group. Abbé Fulbert Yolou, a Catholic cleric and Kongo nationalist, became the first president, pledging support for Kongo unity. A coup in 1963 overthrew his government and replaced it with a government dominated by non-Kongo tribal groups in northern Congo, particularly the M'bochi. Severe ethnic fighting spread across the region in 1963–64.

In 1961, as violence spread across the huge region, nationalists from the three regions petitioned the United Nations Committee on Decolonization for the creation of a separate Kongo state, but without success. On 9

September 1962, King Pedro VIII was enthroned at Sao Salvador (M'Banza Congo) as the king of all the Kongo people.

Kimbanguism, officially the Church of Christ on Earth by the Prophet Simon Kimbangu, revived in the 1960s. Many Kongos embraced the faith as part of their cultural revival. In 1969, it was the first independent African church admitted to the World Council of Churches.

Portuguese control of Angola began to crumble in 1974. The rapid retreat of the colonial power left behind a three-way civil war fought by armies based on the major ethnic groups. The Kongos, led by Holden Roberto's FNLA, were initially supported by neighboring Zaire, South Africa, and the United States. Western aid was countered by massive Soviet support, and Cuban troops landed to aid the Marxist Popular Movement for the Liberation of Angola (MPLA) of the Ovimbundu people of central Angola. Following Angola's independence in November 1975, the victorious MPLA gained international recognition. The United States and South Africa ended direct aid; the FNLA was soon defeated and partially absorbed into the remaining opposition group, UNITA, originally based among the Mbundu people. The Marxist government launched a campaign against the Kongos in northern Angola in 1980.

The civil war in Congo (later renamed Zaire), the leftist takeover of Congo-Brazzaville, and the Kongo defeat in the Angolan civil war in the 1970s ended the initial postcolonial spurt of Kongo nationalism. Dominated by rival tribes or vicious dictatorships, the Kongo sought only to survive the upheavals and violence of the postcolonial period. Kongo cultural identity only began to revive in the late 1980s.

In October 1992, elections were held in Angola with Holden Roberto, returned from exile, running for president. His FNLA won only 2.5% of the votes; the remainder were mostly split between the government and the main opposition party, UNITA. The Kongos of northern Angola remained opposed to the government, but most supported UNITA as the only viable opposition group in the country. The elections set off a new round of violence in Angola, in which Ovimbundus and Kongos were targeted by government forces. On 22 January 1993, the military, national police, and Mbundu civilians massacred Kongos in several cities, reportedly in a deliberate attempt to destroy the cohesion of the Kongos. The number of dead was estimated at between 4,000 and 6,000, on the day since called "bloody Friday."

The traditional Kongo homeland could be one of the most prosperous regions of Africa, but instead it presents one of its worst humanitarian crises. If the economic and cultural recovery of the Kongo peoples is to begin, the area needs peace. Civil wars in Angola and Democratic Republic of Congo and chronic ethnic and political conflicts in Republic of Congo both retarded the prospects, and fueled the growth, of Kongo nationalism in the late 1990s. The former unity and prosperity of the Kongo kingdom has become the focus for ethnic loyalty and the basis of reawakening Kongo nationalism, but colonial division and domination by rival tribes remain the realities.

The Republic of Congo was ruled as a one-party Marxist state from 1979 to 1992 by President Denis Sassou-Nguesso, a northerner. Free elections held in 1992 resulted in a victory by Pascal Lissouba, an ethnic Kongo from the south. Sassou-Nguesso retired to his home region in the north until new elections were scheduled in 1997. He then returned to Brazzaville, accompanied by an armed ethnic militia. Lissouba tried to arrest him and to disarm his militia before the election, setting off a six-month civil war. The government was overthrown, Sassou-Nguesso regained control, and Lissouba fled to neighboring Zaire. Kongo supporters of Lissouba continued in 1999–2000 to fight the government troops controlled by Sassou-Nguesso.

Laurent Kabila, from eastern Zaire, led a popular movement that overthrew the Mobutu government in 1997. Initially welcomed by the Kongos, his government soon proved as corrupt and divided as that of Mobutu. Kongo discontent, gradually recovering from the severe repression of the Mobutu era, came under renewed attack by the new Kabila government n 1997–98. Rebellions and continued fighting drew Angola and other African countries into what quickly became a widespread African war.

In July 1998, a self-proclaimed king, Bernard Mizele, who attempted the secession of the three provinces of the Democratic Republic of Congo dominated by the Kongos was arrested, tried for treason, and sentenced to 20 years in prison. Mizele and dozens of supporters were detained by soldiers in Bas-Congo province after eight soldiers were killed in clashes with the separatists. The separatists were well armed and organized. The three provinces, Bas-Congo, Bandundu, and Kinshasa, make up part of the ancient Kongo Kingdom. Mizele's secessionist sentiments led to his imprisonment, but he was released shortly after Kabila ousted Mobutu.

Rebels belonging to the UNITA group captured the Kongo city of Mbanza-Congo in northern Angola in January 1999, threatening the strategic oil corridor to the north. The rebels, often with the support of the local Kongo population, set up bases for operations against Angolan government troops. UNITA provided logistical support for a group of Kongo rebels fighting the Kabila regime in the Congo in 2000. The death of Kabila in January 2001 greatly increased the chaos and instability in the country.

Kabila's son, Joseph Kabila, became president of the Democratic Republic of Congo. Originally derided as too young and inexperienced, he soon proved more adept than his father. He made peace with the leaders of the Kongos in mid-2001 in an effort to diffuse growing Kongo nationalism.

SELECTED BIBLIOGRAPHY:

Friedman, Kajsa Ekholm. *Catastrophe and Creation: The Transformation of an African Culture*. 1992.

Jordan, Manuel. *The Kongo Kingdom*. 1999.

MacGaffey, Wyatt. *Kongo Political Culture: The Conceptual Challenge of the Particular*. 2000.

Okeke, Chika. *Kongo*. 1997.

Königsberg Slavs

Königsbergers; Kaliningraders; Prusans; Kaliningrad Slavs; Euro-Russians

POPULATION: Approximately (2002e) 865,000 Königsberg Slavs in northwestern Russia, concentrated in Kaliningrad Oblast, an enclave on the Baltic Sea separated from the rest of Russia by Polish and Lithuanian territory.

THE KÖNIGSBERG SLAV HOMELAND: The Königsberg Slav homeland lies in northeastern Europe, an enclave lying on the Baltic Sea between Poland and Lithuania nearly 500 miles west of the nearest Russian territory. Most of the region lies in the basin of the Pregolya River and its tributaries, including the two large freshwater lagoons just inland from the Baltic Sea. About half of the province's territory is under the direct control of the Russian military. The enclave forms a province, an *oblast*, of the Russian Federation. *Kaliningrad Oblast (Königsberg/Baltic Republic)*: 5,830 sq. mi.—15,103 sq. km, (2002e) 939,000—Russians (including Königsberg Slavs) 91%, Lithuanians 4%, Germans 1%, others 4%. The Königsberg Slav capital and major cultural center is Kaliningrad, often called Königsberg, (2002e) 424,000.

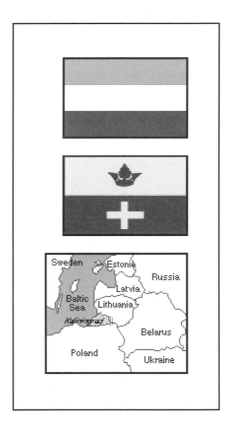

FLAG: The Königsberg Slav national flag, the flag of the national movement, is a horizontal tricolor of pale green, white, and blue. The flag of the Königsberg Movement is the traditional flag of the city of Königsberg, a horizontal bicolor of white over red bearing a centered red crown on the white and a white cross on the red.

PEOPLE AND CULTURE: The Königsberg Slavs are a subgroup of the Russian nation. The group, increasingly using the nationalist names Königsbergers or Euro-Russians, is Russia's newest group to claim separate national identity. Comprising the Russians, Ukrainians, and Belorussans settled in the region after 1945, the Slavs have begun to adopt the area's former German history and culture as their own. Separated from the Russian heartland for over five decades, they are culturally and linguistically

Russian but do not feel at home in Russia proper. They visit nearby Warsaw and Vilnius much more often than St. Petersburg, let alone distant Moscow. A unique German-Slav culture and identity is evolving from a fusion of the Russian present and the German past. The German minority, increased by the arrival of ethnic Germans from the Siberia and Central Asia since 1990, has become influential far beyond their small numbers.

LANGUAGE AND RELIGION: The Königsberg Slavs speak a western dialect of Russian, increasingly sprinkled with German words and expressions. The local regionalist and nationalist movements have promoted the use of the German language as a bridge between the region's pre–World War II identity and its present Russian-speaking population. German is now widely spoken as a second language, while English is becoming popular.

The majority of the Königsberg Slavs officially belong to the Russian Orthodox Church, but the population of Russia's smallest province is also among its least religious. Only about half the population claim religious beliefs, while atheism is widespread. Evangelical Protestant sects, mostly German, have gained support in the region since 1991.

NATIONAL HISTORY: The low, sandy area east of the Baltic Sea was the ancient home of the Borussi, a Baltic people related to the Lithuanians and Latvians to the north. Called Prussians by the Germanic peoples, the Baltic Borussi tribes fell to the Teutonic Knights in 1226. The crusading knights, theoretically on a mission to Christianize the pagan tribes, virtually exterminated or absorbed the Baltic Prussians.

The city of Königsberg, founded as a fortress by the Teutonic Knights in 1255, developed as a major trading center and a leading member of the Hanseatic League after 1340. The Order of the Teutonic Knights, expelled by the Poles to the south, made Königsberg the seat of their grand master in 1457. They retained control of the region called Prussia as vassals of the Polish kingdom. In 1525 Albert of Brandenburg secularized the Teutonic Order and took for himself the title duke of Prussia. The city of Königsberg was the residence of the dukes of Prussia from 1525 to 1618.

The German state of Brandenburg conquered Prussia from Poland in 1660. Frederick III, the elector of Brandenburg, in 1701 had himself crowned king of Prussia in Königsberg's famous gothic cathedral. Called East Prussia, the area formed a province of the kingdom of Prussia, a region of vast Junker estates and a stronghold of the Prussian landed and military aristocracy. Serfs in the region spoke Old Prussian until they died out in a plague in 1709. Following the plague, which killed about a third of the region's population, the Germanization of the region was promoted, and settlers from other areas were allowed to settle depopulated districts.

During the nineteenth century the opening of a railroad system in East Prussia and Russia gave new impetus to the region. Commerce made the city of Königsberg the principal outlet for much of the produce of the western Russian provinces. The city also became a major military port, with modern fortifications begun in 1843 and completed in 1905. The Russians unsuccessfully besieged Königsberg during World War I. It was a center of unrest following Germany's defeat in 1918.

The eastern outpost of German power and a major naval base during World War II, East Prussia fell to the advancing Red Army in autumn 1944. The East Prussian capital, Königsberg, was virtually destroyed before the Germans surrendered to the Soviets after months of siege. Its famous university and cathedral, the fourteenth-century castle, and most of the old city lay in ruins. The majority of the German population fled west. Forty thousand Germans who failed to escape were either executed or deported to make way for the settlement of displaced Slavs.

At the 1945 Potsdam Conference, East Prussia was divided into two parts. The Polish republic was given administrative control over the southern section, and the Soviet Union took control over the northern portion, which included the city of Königsberg. Although the division was meant to be a temporary administrative arrangement, it became permanent.

Königsberg and the surrounding territory, incorporated into the Soviet Union in 1945, received a new name to glorify the memory of Mikhail Kalinin, the Soviet Union's first president. The Sovietization of the region involved the renaming of the region's German monuments, cities, and place-names; all references to the German past were forbidden. Thousands of ethnic Slavs, displaced during the war, settled in the province. The Soviets laid out a new capital, Kaliningrad, in the former residential suburbs of Königsberg. The province, closed to foreigners, functioned as a virtual fief of the powerful Soviet military bureaucracy.

In the late 1980s, ethnic Germans from other parts of the USSR began to move to the region. Although Kaliningrad's German past had been mostly eradicated, it was still closer to Europe than the areas to which the Volga Germans* had been exiled during World War II. By 1989 an estimated 5,000 ethnic Germans lived in Kaliningrad.

The rapid changes overtaking the Soviet Union and its allies in the late 1980s began to filter into the closed province only following the overthrow of communist governments in neighboring Poland and Lithuania. Younger Slavs, disillusioned with decades of joyless socialism, began to question the belief that the province was merely a substitute for homes lost during the war and that the region had no past prior to 1945.

Influenced by resurgent Polish and Lithuanian nationalism, numerous organizations formed in the region, the largest being the Königsberg Memorial Association and the Russian-German Society. Determined to overcome official suppression, the nationalists began to rediscover and expose seven centuries of history, which they felt was by right of birth. Nationalists pressed for a reversion to the former names, heartened by the success of a similar movement to restore the old name of Leningrad, St. Petersburg. The effort to rehabilitate the region's past rapidly replaced the meager Soviet culture of sad war memorials with a fledgling European nation that combined the past with the present.

German interest in the region began with the opening of the formerly closed province in 1990. Over 50,000 Germans, most with historical roots in the area, visited Kaliningrad. Soon the region was speculating about "re-Germanization." The proposal to create a free economic zone brought offers of German investment, but interest in the dilapidated region quickly waned. A German-language newspaper was launched to encourage German investment. By 1995, only 5,000 German tourists a year visited the area, and plans for economic development were being hindered by the control of much of the territory by the Russian military forces and government.

The movement to reclaim the region's cultural heritage led to efforts to save the remains of the city's gothic cathedral, scheduled for demolition, and demands for the reopening of the university, originally founded in 1544. The university is famed for the tenure of Immanuel Kant, who has become a symbol of the new national movement. The Königsberg Movement, a coalition of several national and cultural groups, rapidly gained support following the declaration of a special economic zone in late 1990 and the opening of the *oblast* to foreign visitors in March 1991.

The abortive Soviet coup in August 1991 and the subsequent breakup of the Soviet Union accelerated demands for radical change. Pressured by an increasingly critical public, the provincial parliament voted to oust the local communist leadership, and it passed resolutions prohibiting the resettlement of Soviet troops returning from the former satellite countries.

The younger Slavs, increasingly calling themselves Königsbergers, pressed the local government to declare unilaterally the province a full republic within the Russian Federation. Republican status would give the region greater economic and cultural autonomy during the interim period of economic and political restructuring that the nationalists maintain must be completed before further political changes can be contemplated.

In 1994 the reconstruction of the medieval cathedral began, on the basis of prewar photographs and records. The city's ancient Germanic crest, a mermaid blowing a trumpet, was adopted as the region's official symbol in yet another step to recuperate Königberg's lost heritage. In spite of fear that Poland and Lithuania might resurrect old claims, the Königsberg Slav nationalists are pressing ahead with plans for the independence as a fourth Baltic state, the Free City of Königsberg. Legislation in 1996 declared the entire province a special economic zone, in the hope of offsetting the disadvantages of its location through favorable tax and tariff policies.

In October 1997, Russian and Lithuania signed a border agreement that allowed Russian transit rights across Lithuanian territory to Kaliningrad, but the region remains isolated. The military population, estimated at one in 10 of the total, grew rapidly during the pullback of troops from Eastern Europe, particularly Germany, and the number of troops in the enclave has remained very high in spite of a lessening of tension. Opponents of the border agreement in Lithuania, supported by groups in Poland and Kaliningrad, have demanded that the enclave be turned over to the United Nations, which would oversee its final disposition.

Efforts to win greater self-government were consistently blocked in the late 1990s by the Russian government. Kaliningrad is the only ice-free naval base that Russian still controls on the Baltic; plans to expand the North Atlantic Treaty Organization (NATO) to the east spurred a remilitarization and a crackdown on nationalist activities in the region in 1997–99. Russian hostility to NATO expansion was closely tied to the prospect of the enclave's being surrounded and cut off by states belonging to the Western alliance. A sign of progress was the agreement in 1999 to set up a European Union (EU) and Russian working group to study the options for the enclave.

The governor of Kaliningrad, Leonid Gorbenko, laid claim in 1998 to the adjacent city and district of Klaipeda in Lithuania. Using the city's original German name, Memel, he argued that the region historically belonged to East Prussia. The Memel district was seized from Germany by Lithuania in 1923, regained by Germany in April 1939, and came under Soviet rule with Lithuania at the end of World War II.

The economic potential of the region seems unlikely to be developed so long as the Russian hierarchy sees a need for a heavily armed presence on the Baltic Sea. To nationalists hoping for autonomy and economic ties to Western Europe, the Russian government seems to have settled on defying geography and history alike by pretending that the enclave remains as much a part of the Russian Federation as the regions and republics farther east. Politics in the region may prove that the future of the enclave is not quite as settled as the Russian government might wish.

Seen by the Russian military hierarchy as a precious trophy from the Second World War and a military bastion that must be protected, the region was held back to such an extent that a crisis developed: the inhabitants of the province asked for and received humanitarian aid from the Baltic States and Poland. Although much of the region is inhabited by Russian military personnel and their dependents, their supply situation in 1998 became critical. Moscow's inability to offer relief weakened the bonds between the central government and the Königsberg Slavs. In September 1998 the Kaliningrad government declared a "state of emergency" because of fear that food and fuel would run out and refused to send tax revenues to Moscow. In late 1998, local officials warned the Russian government that popular discontent could reach a level that would seriously undermine

Russia's sovereignty over the region. The provincial government, over protests from Moscow, allowed Germany to set up an economic mission in the region.

In 1999–2000 the reported deployment of nuclear weapons in the enclave spurred a renewal of the nationalist debate. The residents of the province, already among the poorest in the Baltic region, felt threatened by the presence of nuclear weapons. There were also many nuclear submarines in the port facilities, which posed a serious health risk should leaks of nuclear materials occur, as had happened in military ports in northern Russia.

Nationalist demands for elevating the province to the status of a full republic within the Russian Federation were again voiced in mid-2000. The creation of a Russian Baltic Republic, according to activists, would acknowledge the special situation of the region and the status of the Königsberg Slavs as Euro-Russians, the most European of the Russian peoples. One group advocates creating a federation with neighboring Lithuania, which would allow the states to enter the European Union (EU) together. Separatism is often fanned by a Russian government plan to revoke the region's special tax status.

Most Russian government officials oppose autonomy and republican status for the region, claiming that they could lead toward full sovereignty and final separation. The government has finally decided to allow Kaliningrad to retain its status as a special economic zone. From an economic standpoint, stronger ties to the West are a far greater necessity for Kaliningrad than for the rest of Russia. When neighboring Poland and Lithuania become full members of the EU and NATO, the Königsberg Slavs will be even poorer and more isolated. The current visa-free travel to neighboring countries will end, as will the import of duty-free goods for resale in Russia proper.

Elections for the governor of the province, held in November 2000, were won by opponents of the military hold on the region. A new government, even more determined to integrate the region into an economic and political Baltic region, will face opposition from the military, but economically the Königsberg Slavs must have the autonomy to make decisions and agreements that will allow them to survive as a Baltic nation.

The leaders of the territory in mid-2001 are far more relaxed about the territory's relations with the surrounding European states than their predecessors were in the years following the collapse of the Soviet Union. Königsbergers want to let workers and capital move relatively freely across the region's national borders. The Köngisbergers want closer ties to Europe, even at the expense of ties to the Russian motherland.

SELECTED BIBLIOGRAPHY:

Colton, Timothy, and Robert Levgold, eds. *After the Soviet Union.* 1992.
DuCastel, Viviane. *From Königsberg to Kaliningrad.* 1991.
Joenniemi, Pertti, and Jan Prawitz, eds. *Kaliningrad: The European Amber Region.* 1998.
Nordberg, Erkki. *The Baltic Republics: A Strategic Survey.* 1992.

Koryaks

Koriaks; Chavchu; Chavchuvens; Chawchvaj; Chav-chyvans; Nymylans

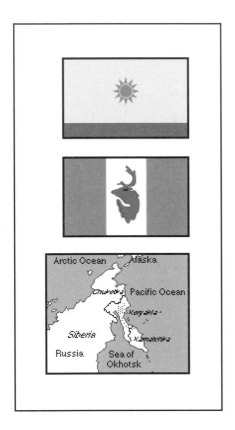

POPULATION: Approximately (2002e) 16,000 Koryaks, Itel'men, and Kamchadals in northeastern Russia concentrated in the Koryak Autonomous District and the Kovran district of Kamchatka Oblast of the Russian Far East. Other communities live in the Chukot Autonomous Okrug, Evenk Autonomous Okrug, and Magadan Oblast.

THE KORYAK HOMELAND: The Koryak homeland lies in the sub-Arctic region of northeastern Siberian Russia and the northern half of the Kamchatka Peninsula. Most of the region is a mountainous region around the Penzhina River basin, northeast of the Sea of Okhotsk. The Koryak heartland forms an autonomous district of the Russian Federation. *Koryak Autonomous Okrug (Chav' Chüv)*: 116,409 sq. mi.—301,499 sq. km, (2002e) 27,000—Koryaks 26% Russians 35%, Ukrainians 9%, Itel'men 5% Chukots* 2%, others 23%. The Koryak capital and major cultural center is Palana, (2002e) 4,000. The major cultural center of the Itel'men and Kamchadals is Kovran, (2002e) 2,000.

FLAG: The Koryak national flag, the flag of the national movement, is a white field with a horizontal green stripe at the bottom and a large gold sun and twelve rays representing the twelve clans centered. The flag of the Koryak Autonomous Okrug has three vertical stripes of pale blue, white, and pale blue with a centered brown reindeer on the white.

PEOPLE AND CULTURE: The Koryaks are a Paleoasiatic or Hyperborean people divided into twelve clans or tribes, Itel'men, Alutors, Nymylans, Chavchuvens, Kamen, Paren, Itkan Nymylans, Apuka, Kereks Palan, and Karaga. The Koryaks clans are ethnically related to the Native American peoples of the American continents. The majority of the Koryaks are reindeer herders, while the Itel'men are fishermen, harvesting salmon from the huge region's rivers and coasts. The Kamchadals developed from a mixture of Russians and Itel'men and Koryaks. The traditional occupations are used to classify the closely related peoples. Traditionally, marriage customs required a man to marry outside his clan. Dancing is an important part of Koryak social and religious life. Anthropologists have found striking parallels between the myths, rituals, and dwelling types of the Koryaks and the those of the northwestern indigenous groups of North America, particularly the Haidas* and Tlingits.* Atmospheric nuclear tests in the 1950s left a legacy of disease, particularly cancer, which exceeds the national average by three times. Infant mortality is also very high, and Koryak life expectancy is now less than 50 years.

LANGUAGE AND RELIGION: The Koryaks speak a Koryak-Alyutor dialect of the Chukotsko-Kamchatian languages of the Luorawetlan language group, which also includes the closely related Itel'men, Kamchadal, Kerek, and Alutor dialects. The language is spoken in nine dialects, two of which are regarded as possibly separate languages. The standard dialect, used in intergroup communications and in radio transmissions, is called Chavchuven, called Chawchvajejyl by the Koryak peoples. Some scholars believe that Itel'men, although heavily influenced by Koryak, is an unrelated isolated language, but studies are not conclusive. By 1989 only 52.4% considered Koryak their mother tongue, with 46.8% considering themselves Russian-speakers. Since the early 1990s, the cultural revival has reversed the trend, and the language is now more widely spoken. A Koryak written language, created in 1931 on the basis of the Latin alphabet, was forcibly switched to the Russian Cyrillic alphabet in 1936. Since the 1930s the language has been greatly influenced by Russian.

The majority of the Koryaks are Orthodox Christians; a minority has retained traditional beliefs. Their ancient shamanistic beliefs included the belief that wolves were their relatives, and accorded an important place to the raven. Spiritual forces in traditional religious beliefs are associated with a particular geography, like a district, a hill, or even a house. Each family has a person who is skilled in drumming and is thought to have influence with spirits.

NATIONAL HISTORY: Little is known about the prehistory of the Koryaks. People from the region of the Ural Mountains may have spread gradually eastward from 40,000 to 20,000 B.C. Also, populations from the Aral Sea area may have started moving north and east from about 20,000 B.C. There was also a movement of peoples from Lake Baikal. The Paleoasiatic Koryaks are probably a mixture of two or three of these population movements.

In prehistoric times small nomadic groups migrated across the vast stretches of wilderness in eastern Siberia. In pursuit of game, many of the bands crossed the land bridge that connected the continents of Asia and North America some 30,000 years ago. The small bands remaining on the

Asian side, gradually pushed north by strong peoples, spread out across the harsh landscape, some to take up herding in the interior grazing lands, others to settle on the coasts, where fishing became the tribal mainstay.

The ancestors of the Koryaks lived on the coast of the Sea of Okhotsk around 2,000 years ago, mostly as hunters of sea mammals. They gradually migrated to the Kamchatka Peninsula. Reindeer herding developed gradually among small inland groups between the eleventh and sixteenth centuries. Until they were called Koryaks by the Russians, the indigenous peoples lacked any term by which to designate their ethnic group as a whole.

Russian expansion, led by explorers and Cossack warriors, reached the Pacific coast in 1640. By 1649 the majority of the Koryak tribes, then numbering about 25,000, had come under Russian rule. They were subdued by Cossacks in the Morozko campaign in 1690 and the Atlasov campaign in 1697–98. There was no public authority among the groups, or any tribal or clan organization. Between 1697 and 1732 the Russians annexed the territories belonging to the southern tribes and the Itel'men of the Kamchatka Peninsula.

The Koryaks bravely defended themselves and refused to pay a required fur tribute. European diseases, particularly smallpox, decimated the tribal groups of the region. Armed clashes continued until the end of the eighteenth century, when the Russians decided to replace their inflexible and despotic policies with bribes. They offered the chieftains presents, alcohol, and a chance to retain local power in exchange for an alliance with the Russian authorities and assistance in tribute collection. The traders bartered items made of iron and cloth, as well as salt, tea, and tobacco for Koryak wares.

Resistance to the encroaching Russians weakened the Koryaks, and they became easy prey to the warlike Chukots to the north, whose raids, and a smallpox epidemic in the late eighteenth century, reduced the number of Koryaks by half. Exploited for its valuable furs, the region came under a Russian trade monopoly that forbade foreign trading in the coastal settlements. The Russians enforced their demands for furs by taking hostages and selling them as slaves or concubines when their demands were not met. Thousands perished in unprovoked massacres. Only a few thousand Koryaks and Itel'men survived the first half-century of Russian rule.

The tribes slowly recovered in the nineteenth century, and the long decline in population slowly began to reverse. Exiled Russian intellectuals deported to the region studied the Koryak and other indigenous peoples, and amateur linguists began to devise a written form of their languages. Orthodox missionaries introduced a system of education that produced the first educated Koryaks able to deal with the tsarist authorities.

The disturbances of the 1905 Russian Revolution, with its calls for equality and the redress of the empire's past mistakes, awakened a sense of grievance in the Koryak peoples. Led by their educated minority, the Koryaks began to demand land rights, particularly the right to fish in the streams and rivers of their ancestral lands.

In 1920 the Soviet authorities took control of Koryakia, as the region was called by the Russians. Until that time the Koryaks were virtually untouched by the world war and the revolution that had followed in Russia. The Soviets outlawed the nomadic lifestyle of the interior and collectivized the fishing communities along the Pacific coast and the Gulf of Shelekhov, east of Kamchatka. Collectivized by the late 1920s, the former nomads were forced to work for the state and to settle in permanent villages chosen for them.

The Soviet authorities suppressed their traditional religion and eliminated the shamans. Officials sent from European Russia banned their languages and traditions that conflicted with bureaucratic ideas of modern socialism. Alcohol abuse accompanied a sense of loss and the dreariness of Soviet life. By the 1930s alcohol had become a sort of money, used for barter. Official attempts to curtail the sale of alcohol to the native peoples met fierce resistance.

Soviet policy stressed production, not the well-being of indigenous populations. The communist ideology devastated the Koryak social structures, and communist development plans ruined the Koryak's fragile homeland. During the Stalinist terror, many shamans and reindeer herders were summarily executed. A campaign to collectivize the reindeer herds began in 1932. It met with bitter resistance; many Koryaks slaughtered their herds rather than surrender them to the government. The reindeer population fell by about 50% in less than four years. Many of the former nomads and fishermen, without experience or training, were assigned to the coal mines in the north of the peninsula.

Russian became the language of education and administration in the region. Koryak children were forcibly taken from their parents and sent to boarding schools, where they learned Russian, state socialism, antireligious propaganda, and scorn for shamanistic practices. Koryak customs and traditions were viewed with great suspicion. All religious services among the Koryaks were prohibited in the late 1930s.

During World War II, many ethnic Russians moved to the region from the war zones of western Russia. The Koryaks found their traditional lands rapidly decreasing, and more and more individuals were forced to give up reindeer herding to settle in the permanent villages and take up fishing or construction work. Many found work in the new oil and natural gas fields in the 1950s and 1960s.

The Soviet liberalization of the late 1980s, begun under the presidency of Mikhail Gorbachev, gradually seeped into the region from the west. The ideas of renewal and openness began a period of Koryak reawakening. In 1990 the Koryaks joined with other small northern nations to form the

Association of Northern Minorities, a coalition of nationalist and cultural groups dedicated to reclaiming the northern peoples' lands, cultures, and languages. Some Koryak nationalists declared the autonomy of the Koryak nation, a symbolic gesture designed to promote Koryak interests.

The region had been closed to foreign ships or journalists since just after World War II. In 1991, the official relaxation of the stringent Soviet authoritarianism allowed the Koryaks to renew their ties to the related peoples of northeastern Siberia and to integrate more closely into the Pacific Rim economic region. Since then, the new authorities in the Kremlin, whose aim is economic growth and development, have seen Siberia as offering a quick way to earn hard currency for the development of the rest of the country, a policy that has often gone against Koryak interests.

In February 1993 the Koryak leaders put forward a plan for an autonomous Koryak republic within the Russian Federation and unilaterally withdrew Koryakia from the authority of Kamchatka Oblast. The proposed republic would have extended to the Kovran region of Kamchatka, populated by the Itel'men people.

The breakdown of the Soviet command economy brought state-subsidized industry and mining to a halt. Thousands of the Russians settled in the region since the 1950s returned to European Russia. The end of the Soviet system forced the Koryaks to rediscover their past. In order to survive, they returned to the tundra and to their traditional way of life.

The small Koryak nationalist movement has gained support since the collapse of the Soviet Union in 1991, from the other small national groups and from many of the Slavic descendants of tsarist and Soviet exiles. The national movement has denounced corruption and abuses by officials, and it has given the Koryaks and the related peoples a voice to express their shared sense of outrage at the abuses they suffered under communist rule. The national claims put forward by the nationalist movement are based on the sovereignty of the ancient tribes, sovereignty that it claims was never surrendered to the Soviet Union or Russia.

In the late 1990s the revitalization of the fragile national identity led to a revival of the indigenous dialects, music, dance, and traditional occupations. Small groups long considered assimilated and not counted as indigenous ethnic groups increasingly returned to their roots, and national sentiment became popular, particularly among the young.

SELECTED BIBLIOGRAPHY:

Jochelson, Waldemar. *The Koryak*. 1994.

Krupnik, Igor. *Arctic Adaptations: Native Whalers and Reindeer Herders of Northern Eurasia*. 1993.

Mayer, Fred. *The Forgotten Peoples of Siberia*. 1994.

Slezkine, Yu. *Arctic Mirrors: Russia and the Small Peoples of the North*. 1994.

Kosovars

Kosovar Albanians; Kossovars; Shqip

POPULATION: Approximately (2002e) 2,400,000 Kosovars in southeastern Europe, concentrated in southern Yugoslavia, with smaller numbers in Albania, Macedonia, and Montenegro. There are Kosovar refugee populations in several European states, particularly in Italy, France, and Germany.

THE KOSOVAR HOMELAND: The Kosovar homeland occupies a mountainous upland in southwestern Serbia. The central part of the province is the valley of the Sitnica River, which forms a narrow plain ringed by mountains. Officially Kosovo forms a province of the Yugoslav Republic of Serbia, but since 1999 its status has been unsettled. *Province of Kosovo (Republic of Kosova):* 4,203 sq. mi.—10,888 sq. km, (2002e) 1,961,000—Kosovars 97%, Serbians 2%, Roms* 1%. The Kosovar capital and major cultural center is Pristina, called Prishtina or Prishtinë by the Kosovars, (2002e) 193,000. The major cultural center of the Metohija region in the west is Pec, called Pech by the Kosovars, (2002e) 78,000.

FLAG: The Kosovar national flag, the flag of the national movement, is a red field charged with the Albanian symbol, the Eagle of Scanderbeg, on the fly and bearing a large red five-pointed star, outlined in yellow, on the hoist, representing the Kosovar Albanians. The flag of the Kosovar Liberation Army is a red field bearing the Eagle of Scanderbeg within three concentric gold circles and the initials of the group above.

PEOPLE AND CULTURE: The Kosovars are ethnic Albanians whose culture and language have been influenced by centuries of contact with neighboring Slav peoples. The Kosovars are mostly peasant farmers, although a very high birthrate, possibly Europe's highest, has accelerated urbanization since World War II. Politically separated from the Albanians for most of the twentieth century, the Kosovars have developed a distinc culture that incorporates borrowings from neighboring peoples, although they retain strong historical and linguistic ties to Albania.

LANGUAGE AND RELIGION: The Kosovars speak a Gheg dialect o Albanian that has absorbed more Slavic and Turkic borrowing than hav the dialects spoken in Albania. The language is one of the major nationalis issues in the region, particularly following the suspension of education and publishing in Gheg in the early 1990s. Many Kosovars speak Serbian as second language.

The majority of the Kosovars are Sunni Muslim, with Orthodox and Roman Catholic minorities. The Muslim religion is an integral part o Kosovar culture, and repression under the former communists and the present Serbian government have only reaffirmed the Kosovar faith. Is lamic groups, unheard of until the 1990s, have gained popularity, partic ularly among young, unemployed men.

NATIONAL HISTORY: Ancient Illyrians, the ancestors of the Albanian peoples, populated the Balkan Peninsula as early as the second century B.C Latinized under Roman rule, the province of Illyricum became known for its wealth and culture. Destroyed by invasions of Germanic Visigoths in A.D. 376 and 395, Illyria, as it became known, later was ruled by the Byz antines of the Eastern Roman Empire. It had a mixed population of Illyr ians and Greeks when the first migrating Slav groups arrived in the sixth century. The Slav migration eventually pushed the Illyrian inhabitants into the mountainous southwest.

A Slavic state, the medieval Serbian empire, emerged in the twelfth cen tury and gradually extended its rule over much of the peninsula. In the fourteenth century the Serbs rallied the Christian peoples of the region to face the advancing Ottoman Turks. On 20 June 1389 a force of Christian Serbs, Albanians, and Bosnians met the Turkish army on an elevated plain called Kosovo. The Christian defeat began five centuries of Muslim Turk ish rule.

Conversion to Islam placed the Albanians in a favored position in the empire and sparked an enmity from the Orthodox Serbs that continues to the present. The Albanians, landlords and administrators, held large es tates, worked by mainly Christian serfs. The sporadic Serb uprisings gen erally focused on the Albanian landlords and merchant class rather than their Turkish overlords. Over several centuries many Serbs left the Kosovo region, while Muslim Albanians settled in the region.

The Turks granted Serbia considerable autonomy in 1829 but retained Kosovo under direct rule despite Serb claims. In 1867 the Serbs secured the withdrawal of all Turkish troops from Serbia proper, and in they 1878 won full independence from the weakened Ottomans. At the conclusion of the First Balkan War in 1913, Serbia annexed Kosovo and its large Albanian-speaking majority from defeated Turkey. The major European powers blocked Serbian efforts to annex Albania, which became an independent state, effectively partitioning the Albanian-speaking peoples of the Balkan Peninsula.

The Serbians' historical claim to Kosovo, vehemently rejected by the Kosovar majority is based on the Serbian assertion that Kosovo formed the heartland of medieval Serbia and that the Kosovars arrived only in the seventeenth and eighteenth centuries as lackeys of the Turks. The Kosovars claim descent from the ancient Illyrians and believe that their claim thus predates the Serbians'. The region, with its countless Serbian churches and monasteries, retains a powerful grip on Serbian emotions.

In the aftermath of World War I, a united South Slav state, later called Yugoslavia, became a kingdom under Serbian political domination. The government, in an attempt to dilute Kosovo's Albanian-speaking majority, settled thousands of ethnic Slavs, mostly Serbs, in the region between 1918 and 1940. The Serbs brutally crushed several Kosovar rebellions, further alienating the Albanian-speaking majority of the region.

During World War II, the Italians separated Kosovo from Serbia and added it to Italian-occupied Albania. Freed from Slav rule, many Kosovars joined attacks on the region's Serb settlers, setting off massacres that eventually claimed 50,000 lives, including those of Kosovars resisting Kosovo's reincorporation into Yugoslavia by the communists in 1945–46. Although the Kosovars had supported the communist insurgents in Albania, Serbia, and Montenegro, the returning Serbian forces brutally eradicated Kosovar military units and massacred alleged separatists.

Josip Broz Tito's postwar Yugoslav government added Kosovo to Serbia as an autonomous province, thus denying the Kosovars cultural and linguistic rights granted to Yugoslavia's other national groups. Neglected by the Serbian administration, the region stagnated. By 1960 the Kosovars had the highest birthrate but the lowest level of development in Yugoslavia. The Kosovars suffered from economic neglect, discrimination, forced assimilation, forced emigration, and political disenfranchisement. Kosovo was one of Europe's poorest, most illiterate, and least developed region in the 1960s and 1970s.

Kosovo's burgeoning population, high unemployment, and abject poverty fueled growing unrest and resistance to Serbian domination. In 1968 violent riots swept the province. The continuing disturbances provoked serious ethnic clashes. To defuse the rising tension, Tito granted the province autonomous status broadly comparable to that of the Yugoslav republics, as part of the new federal constitution of 1974.

The formation of an autonomous Kosovar government prompted many ethnic Serbs to abandon the province. Charging ethnic harassment, some 65,000 Serbs had left Kosovo by late 1975. Kosovar nationalists, demanding status as a full republic, sent petitions to the federal government and led mass demonstrations. Riots, especially severe in 1976 and 1981, ended only after the Yugoslav military intervened in April 1981.

Tito's death in 1980 began a process of disintegration in Yugoslavia. Student groups in Kosovar demanded full republican status equal to that of Serbia. The student demonstrations were put down, and many leaders were jailed. On their release, many left to join the growing Kosovar diaspora in Western Europe. There some joined nationalist organizations talking of uprisings and independence.

Renewed instability within the Yugoslav federation provoked a Serbian nationalist backlash in March 1989. The Serb government dissolved the Kosovar legislature and passed constitutional changes that effectively ended the autonomy granted the province in 1974. Many Kosovar leaders were arrested, and thousands of Kosovars lost their positions in local government, schools, and universities. A peaceful campaign for Kosovar rights began in late 1989, but Kosovar leaders were careful not to provoke an armed response against the unarmed civilian population. The Serbian government began offering financial incentives for Serbians to settle in the region.

On 28 June 1989, the 600th anniversary of the Battle of Kosovo was attended by over a million Serbs. The anniversary was seen by the Kosovars as a display of Serbian military and pan-Serbian nationalism. By January 1990, armed clashes had broken out in several regions in the province. In July the Serbian Assembly permanently dissolved the Kosovo Assembly and shut down Kosovar television, radio, and newspapers.

The disintegration of Yugoslavia in June 1991 spurred Kosovar nationalist efforts to break Serbia's military hold on the province. In September 1991 a clandestine referendum on independence organized by the major nationalist organization, the Democratic League of Kosovo, led by Ibrahim Rugova, resulted in a 90% vote in favor. On 11 October 1991 the Kosovar leaders symbolically declared Kosovo independent of Yugoslavia. Only neighboring Albania recognized the declaration. As far as they could, the Kosovars boycotted Serbian institutions. Kosovar students were denied admission to the region's schools and universities, which were mostly reserved for ethnic Serbians. Discrimination against Kosovars seeking employment or housing increased dramatically. The Kosovars set up their own schools and health care, and they refused to participate in Serbian elections.

Kosovo's national leaders, led by Rugova, who emphasized a non-violent resistance, fearing an extension of Serbian "ethnic cleansing" to Kosovo, frantically attempt to put the issue on the international agenda. In September 1994 the Yugoslav government refused to discuss a Kosovar demand that a neutral third party be brought in to mediate the growing conflict. With liberalization in Albania, many Kosovars began to contemplate ties between Kosovo and Albania, effectively splitting the Kosovar national movement between pro-Albanian and pro-independence factions.

The Kosovars were dismayed that the Dayton peace conference of 1995 that ended the war in Bosnia did not put Kosovo on the international agenda. They viewed the European Union (EU) recognition of the new Federal Republic of Yugoslavia, comprising Serbia and Montenegro, as a disaster. The EU had thus recognized continued Serbian domination of the province of Kosovo. Kosovar anger flared, and Kosovars increasingly rejected their earlier program of peaceful resistance.

In March 1996 the Serbian government offered to restore a degree of Kosovo's autonomy, but nationalists announced as their ultimate aim an independent Kosova republic, with close ties to, but not unity with, adjacent Albania. Rugova, the leader of the Kosovars' nonviolent campaign for independence, warned the West that the province was nearing a crisis, but he was largely ignored. Neighboring Albania virtually collapsed in 1997, and its armories were thrown open. Suddenly the Kosovars had access to modern weapons. Kosovars in western Germany raised money to buy more.

In 1999 the Kosovars, led by the Kosovar Liberation Army (UÇK), finally rebelled against oppressive Serbian rule. Disillusioned with the Democratic League's passive resistance, the Kosovars attacked army bases and police compounds. The Serbs retaliated by attacking Kosovar civilians, and eventually the Serbian government sent in the army. The Serbian counterattack sent hundreds of thousands of Kosovar civilians fleeing across international borders into Albania, Macedonia, and Montenegro. Negotiations failed, partly due to Serbian intransigence over autonomy for the Kosovars. The Serbian army began organized ethnic cleansing, driving the Kosovar population from cities, towns, and villages across the province. Entire towns were burned to prevent the Kosovar inhabitants from returning. Ultimately an estimated 1.5 million Kosovar refugees fled the region.

The United Nations and the North Atlantic Treaty Organization (NATO) demanded that Serbian forces withdraw from the province. When the Serbian government refused, NATO began a campaign of bombing military targets in Serbia, eventually forcing the Serbian military to abandon Kosovar, which allowed the Kosovar refugees to return to the devastated region. The Kosovar Liberation Army was officially disbanded, but Kosovar nationalist organizations continued to proliferate as independence became a real possibility. Suggestions by the EU and other international organizations that Kosovo should remain part of a democratic Balkan federation were rejected.

Increased violence between the Kosovars and the remaining Serb population in the province, particularly in the mixed city of Mitrovitsa, erupted in February 2000. The Kosovars' first democratic elections in July 2000 mostly excluded the remaining Serbian minority in the north of the province, due to the continuing ethnic violence. Kosovars in the region and abroad, however, were eligible to vote. Even though the United Nations continues to recognize Yugoslav sovereignty in Kosovo, the interim administration is building the trappings of an independent state in Kosovo, if only for want of any other means of administration.

In regional elections in October 2000, Ibrahim Rugova won the majority, displacing more radical groups allied with the Kosovo Liberation Army. The vote was seen as a vote against the guerrillas, who had taken control of several areas, often confiscating houses or businesses from local Kosovars. The decline in the popularity of the guerrilla groups marked a change in the political climate of the region. The Kosovars stated that they would settle for nothing less than full independence, even when Slobodan Milosevic was defeated in elections in Serbia and a new, more moderate government under Vojislav Kostunica promised to restore Kosovar autonomy in early 2000. At the turn of the twenty-first century, the Kosovar homeland remained in limbo, under UN military occupation, neither a functioning part of the Yugoslav Federation nor the independent state the Kosovars wanted to create.

The prospect of Kosovar independence sparked new problems in adjacent areas of Serbia, where the inhabitants of several Kosovar-populated districts sought to unite their areas with Kosovo, under UN/NATO administration. In November 2000, attacks by Kosovar militants into the region from Kosovar, forcing Serbian police to retreat, led to an influx of Albanian refugees into Kosovo. President Kostunica of Serbia demanded that NATO stop the violence that had spilled from Kosovo into southern Serbia.

The United Nations–sponsored elections for a Kosovar parliament passed peacefully in November 2001, including the participation of the small Serbian minority. The voters chose moderates for the 120-seat assembly, which later elected Ibrahim Rugova as the Kosovar president. Despite the success of the election, many Kosovars were disappointed that their new assembly will be prevented by the international community from proclaiming Kosovar independence.

SELECTED BIBLIOGRAPHY:

Judah, Tim. *Kosovo.* 2000.
Juka, S.S. *Kosova: The Albanians in Yugoslavia in Light of Historical Documents.* 1984.
Malcolm, Noel. *Kosovo: A Short History.* 1998.
Ramet, Sabrina P. *Balkan Babel: The Disintegration of Yugoslavia from the Death of Tito to the War for Kosovo.* 1999.

Kuban Cossacks

Kubanskie Kazaki; Kazaki Kuban; Kazaky Kuban; Kozaki Kuban; Chernomortsy

POPULATION: Approximately (2002e) 1,730,000 Kuban Cossacks in southern European Russia, concentrated in the Kuban, officially Krasnodar Kray, the Krasnodar Territory. There are large Kuban Cossack communities in other parts of southern Russia, and also in France, Germany, and Scandinavia. Outside Europe the largest Kuban Cossack communities are located in the United States, Canada, and Australia.

THE KUBAN COSSACK HOMELAND: The Kuban Cossack homeland occupies the Kuban Steppe and the valley of the Kuban River on the eastern shore of the Black Sea in southern European Russia. The northern districts of the Kuban are steppe lands, but in the south the Caucasus Mountains extend across one-third of the territory. The region, forming the Krasnodar Kray or Territory, is one of the so-called Cossack provinces, which also includes Rostov Oblast, the homeland of the Don Cossacks,* and Stavropol Kray, the homeland of the Terek Cossacks.* The historical Kuban Cossack homeland was organized as Krasnodar Territory 1937; in 1991 the Adyge Republic was separated as a member republic of the Russian Federation. *Krasnodar Territory (Kuban)*: 29,344 sq. mi.—76,001 sq. km, (2002e) 5,084,000—Russians 36%, Kuban Cossacks 32%, Ukrainians 21%, Adyge* 1%, Armenians 1%, Greeks 1%, others 8%. The Kuban Cossack capital and major cultural center is Krasnodar, called Ekaterinodar by the Cossacks, (2002e) 643,000, metropolitan area, 774,000.

FLAG: The Kuban Cossack national flag, the flag of the former Kuban Cossack republic, is a tricolor of pale blue, raspberry red, and pale green, the red twice the width of the other stripes. The same flag, with the addition of the territorial arms, is the official flag of Krasnodar Territory.

PEOPLE AND CULTURE: The Kuban Cossacks are a Slavic people of

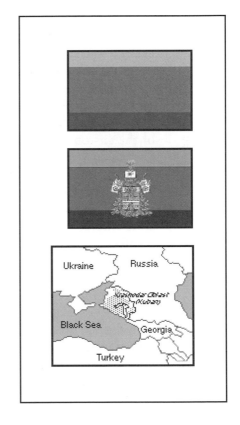

mixed Russian, Ukrainian, and Circassian background. They are traditionally divided into two groups—the Chernomortsy, descendants of Zaporozhye Cossacks and Ukrainian settlers concentrated in the lower reaches of the Kuban River; and Lineitsy (First Liners), descendants of Don Cossacks, Circassians, and Russian colonists in the middle and upper reaches of the Kuban Basin. A precise definition of the Cossack nations is still a matter of debate; the Russian parliament describes a Cossack "host" as "a community of people with their own traditions, areas of residence, culture, economic system, and a special attitude toward army service and their relationship with the state." The Kuban Cossacks claim they are a nation, while many scholars classify them as a historical phenomenon, a military caste, a social class, or a Russian cultural subgroup. The Kuban Cossack claim to separate national status is based on history, way of life, culture, and language. Nationalists claim that between a quarter and a half of the regional population has Cossack ancestry, although official figures put the Kuban Cossack regional population at about a seventh of the total. Many of the customs and traditions of the Kuban Cossacks have their origins in Circassian culture. Being a Cossack remains an essentially male pursuit, although military service has ceased to be an obligation.

LANGUAGE AND RELIGION: The Kuban Cossacks speak a Cossack language of mixed Russian and Ukrainian origin that developed as a separate language in the isolation of the Kuban Steppe in the seventeenth and eighteenth centuries. The Kuban Cossack language is spoken in three major dialects, Krasnodar, Upper Kuban, and Lower Kuban. The dialect spoken in the upper Kuban Basin has considerably less Ukrainian influence and has absorbed many Circassian words. The culture and dialects of the Kuban Cossacks have been strongly influenced by their long association with the neighboring Circassian peoples, particularly the Adyge. The language, outlawed from the Red victory in the Russian Civil War in 1920 until 1990, is rapidly being revived. Schools have been opened to teach young Cossacks in their own language.

The Kuban Cossacks are overwhelmingly Russian Orthodox, although there are small Muslim and Roman Catholic minorities, particularly outside Russia. The Orthodox religion is an integral part of the Cossack culture and history, and it remains an important ingredient in the modern Cossack revival.

NATIONAL HISTORY: The territory of the Kuban Cossacks was originally inhabited by fierce Circassian tribes that blocked further Slavic expansion to the south. Nominally a part of the first great Slav state, Kievan Rus,' the Kuban was overrun by the Golden Horde in 1241 and later formed part of the Golden Horde's successor state, the khanate of the Crimean Tatars.* The first Slavs fleeing south to escape serfdom appeared in the region, then under Turkish control, in the fifteenth century.

The Russians began to penetrate the area in 1774 and ultimately annexed the territory to the expanding Russian Empire in 1783. Many of the Zaporozhye Cossacks, defeated and officially dissolved following an uprising in the Ukraine in 1775, fled across the Danube River into Turkish-controlled territory. Those that stayed in Russian territory were allowed to settle along the Black Sea between the Dnieper and Bug Rivers and became the Black Sea Cossacks. At the end of the Russo-Turkish War of 1787–91, the tsarist authorities grew suspicious of the ties between the Black Sea and Zaporozhye Cossacks across the Danube. Forcibly relocated to the Kuban, newly annexed as part of the Crimean Tatar territory, the Black Sea Cossacks came to be called the Kuban Cossacks. In 1828, most of the remaining Zaporozhye Cossacks left Turkish territory to join the Kuban Cossacks in their new homeland on the steppes of the North Caucasus.

Called Chernomortsy, the Black Sea People, the Kuban Cossacks were allowed to govern themselves, in exchange for a vow of loyalty to the tsar and military service as the guardians of Russia's new southern frontier. Don Cossacks, from the Don River basin to the north, settled the interior of the territory in the 1830s and became known as Lineitsy, the First Liners.

Collectively rechristened the Kuban Cossacks in 1860, the Kuban horde, the civil and military organization, formed the largest Cossack community in southern Russia. The Muslim Circassian tribes farther to the south, finally defeated in 1864, mostly fled or were expelled to Turkish territory. Their confiscated lands became Kuban Cossack lands, held in common by the villages and clans; many Circassians were taken into the horde. Thousands of freed Russian and Ukrainian serfs migrated south to the fertile region following the abolition of serfdom in 1861. The Kuban Cossack communes absorbed many of the former serfs, while others settled on the Cossack's communal lands as tenant farmers.

The Russian and Ukrainian settlers greatly resented Cossack privileges, by which they traded military service for freedom from taxes and direct Russian control, and control of the Kuban territory. Under the tsars they formed elite military units with special statutes of self-government. Whenever their privileges were threatened, the Kuban Cossacks rebelled. In the latter part of the nineteenth and the early part of the twentieth centuries, the tsarist government used Cossack troops to perpetrate pogroms against the Jews.

Personally loyal to the tsar, not to the Russian state, the Kuban Cossacks formed frontline military units when war began in 1914. The Kuban Cossack units suffered heavy casualties, which fueled growing unrest among the military clans. Their oaths of loyalty were voided by the overthrow of the tsar in February 1917. Kuban Cossack units deserted the front in large numbers to return to their homeland to protect it from a threatened Turkish advance from the south. Kuban Cossack leaders convened a parliament, the Rada, in March 1917, creating a Kuban military government to replace the local tsarist administration. On 17 July 1917 the Rada declared the Kuban a sovereign state within the new democratic Russia.

The Kuban Cossacks joined the anti-Bolshevik White forces following the Bolshevik coup in October 1917. A minority, believing in Lenin's internationalist propaganda, fought with the newly formed Red Army. Confrontations between Kuban nationalists and the White leadership, who opposed the breakup of the Russian Empire, soon soured relations.

The Chernomortsy favored full independence for the Kuban but faced strong resistance from many of the Lineitsy, committed to Russian unity, and the Ingorodnie, Slavic tenant farmers won over by Bolshevik promises to redistribute the Cossack communal lands. The Kuban government insisted on forming a Kuban National Army, separate from the White military forces of Gen. Anton Deniken, which were based in the Kuban.

The Kuban separatists gained support as the Russian Empire collapsed and chaos spread across the region. On 16 February 1918, the Kuban Rada, dominated by the Chernomortsy, declared the independence of the Kuban as the Kuban People's Republic. The new state had a population of 3.5 million, 53% Russian, 47% Kuban Cossack, 10% Adyge. A delegation from the Kuban government traveled in 1919 to Paris to attend the Paris Peace Conference, in an effort to win allied recognition. In the fall of 1919 Deniken arrested the Kuban's leaders and executed 11 of them before moving his headquarters out of the breakaway state, which he claimed was dominated by nationalists.

The White defeat in 1920 was followed by the rapid occupation of the Kuban by the Red Army and the formation of a Kuban–Black Sea Soviet Republic. Widespread famine swept the Kuban in 1921–22, leaving many dead in its wake. Many of the Kuban Cossacks fled abroad or joined guerrilla bands that harassed the Soviet authorities until finally eradicated in 1924. The Soviet authorities revoked all traditional Cossack privileges, including military training. The authorities reclassified the Kuban Cossacks from Ukrainian speakers to Russian speakers, forcing them to use Russian in place of the Kuban's unique Ukrainian-Russian-Circassian dialect.

Collectivization in 1931–32 was followed by yet another famine in 1933, partly caused by the confiscation of all grains, including seeds and fodder, by the Soviet government. Thousands of Kuban Cossacks starved, their fate ignored by the Soviet authorities. The government of Joseph Stalin was accused of planning the famine in areas where Soviet rule was opposed, charges that were confirmed when the Soviet archives were opened in the 1990s.

In 1936, as Germany began to threaten from the west, certain privileges were returned, and the Cossacks were again allowed to serve in the military. The Krasnodar Territory was created in 1937, but the Cossack name of the region, Kuban, remained forbidden.

In 1941 Hitler turned on his Soviet ally and invaded the Soviet Union. The Germans, advancing on the Maikop oil fields in the southern Kuban in late 1942, decreed that the Kuban Cossacks were descendants of Germanic Ostrogoths, not "subhuman" Slavs, and therefore constituted acceptable allies. Thousands of Cossacks joined the Germans against the communists, and once again Kuban Cossacks faced each other in opposing armies. In October 1942, an autonomous Kuban government under Ataman Wasili Domanov was created, supported by a Kuban Cossack militia.

At the end of the war some 28,000 Cossacks with their families surrendered to the Allies in Austria. However, at Stalin's insistence, the British forcibly repatriated the Cossacks, including 4,000 women and 2,500 children. Thousands were sent to slave labor camps in the Arctic and Siberia. Many others were summarily executed or imprisoned for long periods.

A cultural revival in the 1960s began with the publication of the first Cossack dictionary and of works on Kuban Cossack history and culture that exile groups smuggled into the Soviet Union. The revival raised demands for recognition of the Kuban Cossacks as a separate ethnic and cultural group in the Soviet Union. The resurgence of their culture and traditions incited a parallel nationalist revival; Kuban Cossack nationalism emerged as a potent force following the liberalization of Soviet society in the late 1980s. Several powerful Kuban Cossack associations formed. At first the goals of the Cossack associations were cultural and historical in nature, to preserve Cossack traditions and improve the historical accuracy of Cossack lifestyles. Kuban Cossack leaders later began to demand local self-administration and the return of traditional lands.

Kuban Cossack nationalists, with the support of the Ukrainian minority, gained support for demands that the Kuban be granted republic status within the Russian Federation. More radical nationalists claimed that their separate history and culture were the basis of a viable national state, while even more nationalistic groups advocated the creation of a greater "Cossackia" of some 20 million inhabitants, to incorporate the traditionally Cossack lands between Kazakhstan, Ukraine, and the Caucasus Mountains. Several Kuban Cossack associations sought to form a semiautonomous republic within Russia, and demanded that Cossacks be considered a separate ethnic group. One group declared the sovereignty of an autonomous Kuban Cossack republic, called the Middle-Kuban Cossack Republic, on 14 December 1991. The republic, proposed as a member state of the Russian Federation, failed to receive official recognition or popular support.

In mid-1992, a decree signed by Russian president Boris Yeltsin partially rehabilitated the Cossacks. The decree granted them the status of an ethnic group and gave them land free of charge. The decree classified them as an oppressed people who qualified for "positive discrimination" and government subsidies as compensation for suffering in Soviet times. It also called for the use of Cossack forces to protect Russia's borders. In 1995, the administration of the Krasnodar Territory, again popularly called the Kuban, adopted the flag of the Kuban Cossacks, with the addition of the territorial coat of arms.

Some Russian officials opposed the Cossacks for reason of their inherent militarism, record of xenophobia, and historical anti-Semitism. They worried aloud about the dangers of encouraging the Kuban Cossacks to think and act as a national group, but the Cossacks' votes, important to the Russian government overrode all objections.

The Kuban Cossacks in August 1996 celebrated 300 years of the Kuban Cossack army, the Voisko, with a huge gathering in Krasnodar, with traditional music and a remembrance of their heritage. Many Cossacks attended in traditional uniforms, complete with swords. The crowd listened to speeches and waved the Kuban Cossack flag as speakers called for unity and the resurrection of self-government. Other Kuban Cossack groups, particularly a community in New Jersey in the United States, have claimed to represent pre–World War I Kuban Cossacks. (Many Kuban Cossacks settled in New Jersey after the Russian Civil War and more during and after World War II.)

At the beginning of 1996, the government of the region negotiated broad powers that included the right to regulate immigration, to pass legislation on land, and official rehabilitation of the Kuban Cossacks as a distinct Cossack group. In September 1997, the governor of Krasnodar Kray set up a regional Kuban Cossack militia. The provincial legislature is turning the region into an outpost governed by its own laws, many of which run counter to federal legislation.

The Kuban Cossacks continue to press for recognition as a special "cultural-ethnic" community. The movement is based in the strong nationalistic tendencies of the Kuban Cossack revival, with its cult of strength and nihilistic leadership. Kuban Cossack military formations strongly influence the regional government and authorities at lower levels, as the unofficial military wing of the territorial government.

The Kuban Cossacks preserve a strong sense of identity in their homeland. They were never uprooted wholesale from the Kuban under Stalin, as were many other peoples. They suffered terrible losses during the Soviet era, but enough remained in the Kuban to preserve their national sentiment. The Kuban Cossacks continue to insist on one of the pillars of Cossack nationhood, the independence of the Cossack community under its own elected *atamn*, the traditional leader of the Cossack horde.

The two basic principles of "Cossackhood," service and independence, have strong historical roots, and the contradiction between the two persist with the Kuban Cossack revival of the 1990s. As throughout the history of the Kuban Cossacks, their fiercest loyalty remains to be to themselves.

SELECTED BIBLIOGRAPHY:

Feodoroff, Nicholas V. *History of the Cossacks*. 1999.
Groushko, Mike. *Cossack: Warrior Riders of the Steppes*. 1993.
Sgorlon, Carlo. *Army of the Lost Rivers*. 1998.
Ure, John. *The Cossacks*. 1999.

Kumyks

Kumuks; Kumiks; Kumihs; Qumuqs; Kumuklars; Kumykis

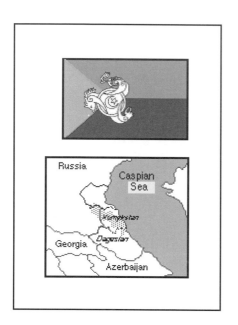

POPULATION: Approximately (2002e) 314,000 Kumyks in Russia, concentrated in the northern districts of the Dagestan Republic, a member state of the Russian Federation, in southern European Russia. There are smaller communities in neighboring regions of Chechnya, Ingushetia, North Ossetia, Stavropol Krai, and Kalmykia. Outside the Russian Federation there are Kumyk communities in Turkey, Kazakhstan, Syria, and Iran. Nationalists claim a regional population of over 500,000 in southern Russia and the Middle East.

THE KUMYK HOMELAND: The Kumyk homeland is primarily in the lowlands and foothills of the northeastern Caucasus region between the Terek and Samur Rivers and the Caspian Sea. Because there is no easily accessible pass over the Caucasus Mountains, the coastal plain bordering the Caspian Sea has historically been an important north-south passage. The region, called Kumykstan by the Kumyks, comprises seven districts of the Dagestan Republic—Khasavyurt, Babayurt, Kizilyurt, Buinaksk, Karabudakhkent, Kaiakent, and Kaitak. The region called Kumykstan has no official status, although the majority of the Kumyks have expressed a desire to separate their homeland from the multiethnic Dagestan Republic. *Region of Kumykstan*: 4,635 sq. mi.—12,004 sq. km, (2002e) 508,000—Kumyks 48%, Avars* 22%, other Dagestanis* (Laks 18%, Dargins 10%), Russians 2%. The capital and major cultural center of the Kumyks is Buinaksk, called Temir-Khan-Shura by the Kumyks, (2002e) 57,000. Makhachkala, the capital of Dagestan, (2002e) 336,000, is located in traditional Kumyk territory and is an important Kumyk cultural center.

FLAG: The Kumyk national flag, the proposed flag of the Kumyk Republic, is a horizontal bicolor of red over green with a pale blue trapezoid at the hoist. Over the joining of the three colors is a white circle, outlined in gold, bearing a gold crescent moon and five-pointed star. Around the edge of the circle are the symbols of the three Kumyk groups, in gold.

PEOPLE AND CULTURE: The Kumyks originated with Turkic nomads migrating to northern Dagestan from Central Asia. There they mixed extensively with the native Caucasian peoples, although traditionally they remained in the northern steppe lands as nomadic or seminomadic horse and livestock herders; some engaged in trading or farming. The Kumyks are divided into three traditional groups based on dialect and location. The northern Kumyks inhabit the Kumyk Steppe. The central Kumyks, the most influential of the three, inhabit the region around Buinaksk and Makhachkala. The southern Kumyks are highlanders, living in the Caucasian foothills. The situation of the pastoral peoples like the Kumyks deteriorated seriously during the twentieth century, with many settling in the cities as industrial workers. Although the Kumyks were somewhat dispersed during the Soviet era, 82% of the Kumyk population in Russia continued to live in their ancient homeland at the turn of the twenty-first century. The Sunni Muslim religion and their identity as a Turkic people in a region dominated by Caucasian nations has reinforced the Kumyks' culture and sense of identity. Although the rate of urbanization is high, they have maintained a strong ethnic identity and rarely marry outside their national group.

LANGUAGE AND RELIGION: The Kumyk language is a Turkic language, a Ponto-Caspian dialect, part of the Oghuz group of the Kipchak or West Turkic division of the Turkic language group. The Kumyk language, although basically a Turkic language, includes some elements of Bulgar, Khazar, and Oghuz Turkish. The language is spoken in three major dialects, Khasavyurt in the north, Buinaksk (Buynaksk) in the central districts, and Kaitak (Khaikent) in the south, as well as several subdialects. Because of centuries of ethnic mixing, the language has incorporated many Caucasian borrowings and is intelligible to the Azeris south of Kumykstan. The Kumyk language has become the lingua franca of much of central Dagestan. The language has a long literary tradition, but where the scale of population transfer was the greatest, there are neither newspapers nor radio programs in the Kumyk language. Many schools in these districts no longer teach in the Kumyk language. Most Kumyks use Russian as their second language.

The Kumyks are overwhelmingly Muslim, mainly Sunnis, with 70% adhering to the Shafiite branch and about 25% belonging to the Hanafite rite. There is a small Shi'a Muslim minority. The Kumyk culture emphasizes family ties and the Muslim religion, though their religious observance is less fervent than that of their Caucasian neighbors. Religious beliefs are, however, an integral part of the Kumyk culture and mark the yearly cycle. Traditional pagan beliefs continue to exist alongside the Muslim traditions, including ritual dances offered to the dead.

NATIONAL HISTORY: The origin of the Kumyks is not clear, although they are mentioned in chronicles of the second century A.D. Kumyk tradition sets the origins of their nation with the migrations of Turkic and Mongol peoples westward across the steppes of Central Asia to the region around the Caspian Sea in the fifth century A.D. The Turkic Khazars, by the year A.D. 650, had established a stable state in the region, with trading routes across the Caucasus. In spite of trading relations, the Caucasus Mountains, which separated the Khazar Empire from the Persian lands, became a scene of repeated and devastating wars in the eighth and ninth centuries. By the tenth century, some Turkic tribes had migrated to the area west of the Caspian Sea, where they mixed extensively with the indigenous Caucasian peoples.

The Kumyks consolidated their sense of nationhood and strengthened their hold on the lowland steppes between the eleventh and thirteenth centuries. During the fifteenth and sixteenth centuries, the Kumyks established an independent state, the Shamkhalat of Tarki, which controlled large areas inhabited by non-Kumyk Caucasians. From the fifteenth to sixteenth centuries, the state of the Kumyk prince, the Shamkhal, the leader of a rigid feudal heirarchy, was a dominating power in the eastern half of the North Caucasus. The Kumyks controlled the lowland winter pastures used by the Caucasian mountain herders, and their language was adopted as a second language by large numbers of the their Caucasian subjects.

The expansion of the Russians into the steppe lands weakened Kumyk power in the sixteenth century. To counter Christian Russian influence the Kumyks declared loyalty to the Safavid dynasty of Persia, which controlled the Caucasus highlands just south of Kumyk territory. The Kumyks were caught between the great powers during the wars for control of the Caucasus in the seventeenth and eighteenth centuries. When Peter the Great conquered Derbent in 1722 and defeated the Persians the Kumyks finally lost their independence. The Shamkhalat realm was dissolved, and the Kumyks were brought under direct Russian rule. The Kumyk homeland was divided into two Russian provinces.

The Kumyks managed to retain a degree of autonomy over the next century, but Russian influence divided the Kumyk clans. In the early 1830s Shamil, imam of Dagestan, called for strict observance of Shari'a, Islamic law, and for *gazawat*, holy war against the Christian invaders. The northern clans joined the anti-Russian Shamil movement, while the central clans sided with the Russians, and the southern clans maintained neutrality. When the Russians finally crushed the Shamil rebellion, the Kumyks, along with the other Caucasian nations, were brought under strict Russian control. During the period of Russian occupation in the late nineteenth century, the Kumyk national movement was centered mainly in Ottoman Turkish territory.

The nineteenth-century industrialization of the region, particularly the Caspian port cities, drew in large numbers of Kumyks, who formed an urban labor class. Many of the urbanized Kumyks were involved in the growing revolutionary movement. In the beginning of the twentieth century, the Kumyks started to develop a middle class of merchants and intellectuals. Both were destroyed after the Russian revolution.

The overthrow of the Russian tsar in 1917 was followed by the takeover of Russia by the Bolsheviks, who had considerable support among the urban Kumyks, although most Kumyks preferred pan-Turkic or Islamic nationalism. The Kumyk nationalists mostly joined forces with other North Caucasian nations in an effort to create an independent state in the North Caucasus region.

The civil war that followed the Russian Revolution devastated the Kumyk homeland. Villages and towns were destroyed and their populations dispersed. In 1920 the Red Army, victorious in the civil war, took control. The new Soviet authorities in 1921 created the Dagestan Autonomous Soviet Socialist Republic, formed from the tsarist region of Dagestan. Over the next year the borders of the republic were extended northward to include the lowland Kumyk region of Terskaia, which was later subdivided into three districts of the autonomous Dagestan Republic. The Kumyk national leaders were killed or repressed.

A policy of ethnocide, the oppression of ethnic identities, was implemented in order to create a new "Soviet people." The Soviet program of collectivization started in Kumykstan in 1928–29. Kumyk farming and pasture lands were confiscated, the clans were disarmed, and Muslim Shari'a law was abolished. The Kumyk leadership, accused of bourgeois nationalism and pan-Turkic policies, was annihilated or deported during the 1930s. Government functionaries sent from Moscow filled all posts in local government.

The situation in Kumykstan stabilized only in 1936, when the government formalized the structure of the Dagestan autonomous republic, but unregulated migration of mountain dwellers to the Kumyk Steppe threatened the Kumyk culture and traditional land use. Because the Caucasian immigrants received large portions of the Kumyk plains, land shortages among the Kumyks were chronic in the late 1930s and early 1940s. The introduction of monoculture cotton agriculture, overexploitation of the soil, and deforestation contributed to an economic and ecological crisis that continues to the present.

During World War II, the German army drove south toward the oil fields in the North Caucasus. The Kumyk homeland was occupied in 1942. *Kolkhozi*, collective farms, were closed, mosques were reopened in areas under German control, and promises of self-determination were given to Kumyks who were willing to listen. The majority, viewing the Germans as just another in a long line of invaders, refused to cooperate and thereby saved the Kumyk nation the brutal deportations suffered by other nations in the Caucasus region.

The postwar industrialization of the region again drew many Kumyks into the growing cities. Because of their concentration in Dagestan's central districts, the urban and rural Kumyks were able to stay in close communication, which reinforced their traditional culture and values.

Soviet policies forced many of the mountain peoples to move down to the lowlands, where they could be more easily controlled. By the 1970s, the Kumyks were sharing their traditional lands with Caucasian mountaineers. The agricultural practices and attitudes of the Caucasian peoples clashed with those of the rural Kumyks. Tension between the two groups accelerated during the reforms instituted in the Soviet Union in the late 1980s. The Kumyks resented the massive migration to their homeland. The forced resettlement of mountain peoples to Kumyk territory destroyed the traditional settlement patterns and deprived the Kumyks of half their arable land by the time the Soviet Union disintegrated in 1991.

The first Congress of Kumyk People, held in November 1989, formed a Kumyk National Council as the nation's representative body. The Kumyk People's Movement, called Tenglik (Equality), was created to oversee the development of the economy and cultural traditions, bring about the return of ancient Kumyk territory, and form administrative bodies for self-government. The delegates demanded the administrative reform of the Dagestan Republic as a federal state under which all its small nations could form self-governing republics.

In 1990, Tenglik, led by Salav Aliev, announced its intention to form a Kumyk national state out of seven districts of Dagestan. Originally, the national movement favored complete independence, but it later adopted a line favoring autonomy within the Russian Federation. According to Kumyk leaders, their nation was underrepresented in the republican structures and was economically deprived.

In November 1990, the Congress of People's Deputies of Dagestan voted to create a Kumyk republic within Dagestan, but the Kumyk representatives considered the level of autonomy on offer insufficient and negotiations between Kumyk leaders and Dagestani representatives of the congress broke down. In April 1991, the Kumyks voted against a resolution to create a sovereign republic of Dagestan, as there was no provision for a separate Kumyk homeland.

In October 1991, Tenglik mobilized virtually the whole of the Kumyk nation in protest against the dominant position of the Avars in regions with Kumyk majorities, as well as to express their dissatisfaction with the resettlement of mountain peoples in traditional Kumyk territories. In 1994, the Kumyk National Congress was formed. It was less radical than Tenglik and was believed to be an initiative of the Dagestani government to counterbalance the radical nationalists of Tenglik.

The Kumyks, who claim the Khazars as their ancestors, are increasingly unhappy in the multiethnic Dagestan Republic. A small but important group of militants works for complete independence for the Kumyk nation, arguing that only through full sovereignty can the Kumyk language and culture recover from decades of Russification and suppression.

The Kumyks are the only ethnic group to charge the Dagestani authorities with cultural repression. They claim their culture and language are threatened by the continuing program of settling excess populations from other areas, particularly Avars, Laks, and Dargins from the mountainous southern districts, to their traditional homeland in the northern steppe lands. The mountain peoples settled in the region dominate both urban society and much of the rural lowlands. Their cultivation techniques applied to areas traditionally used by the Kumyk pastoralists led to serious clashes after 1991.

In June 1996 Kumyk nationalist leaders demanded that the Dagestani authorities take tough measures to ensure order in the districts of the republic that border Chechnya. The Kumyks suffered kidnappings and violence as a result of the war in the neighboring republic. In October 1999, as the second Chechen war raged in Chechnya, the Dagestani authorities only allowed fleeing Kumyks registered in Dagestan to enter the republic, setting off protests by local Kumyks.

Their homeland is potentially rich, but the Kumyks remain among the poorest of the nations in the Russian Federation. In the late 1990s unemployment, particularly among urban Kumyks, added to growing unrest. The regional economy ran much as it had under the Soviet government, and most of the former communist officials continued to hold official positions in the Dagestan government. The precarious economic situation and the Kumyk's strong national identity continued to focus the growing separatist movement. The feeling that economic and political security could only be found within the national group and under an autonomous system dominated developments in the Kumyk homeland.

The Kumyks are the most active and contentious of the nations of Dagestan and the most frequently involved in intergroup disputes. The migration of Dagestani peoples into their traditional lands is seen an trespassing and as a threat to the survival of the Kumyks. The lands of historical Kumykstan are among the most valuable in Dagestan. Massive Dagestani immigration has reduced the Kumyks to a minority in their traditional homeland.

The overlapping cultural and religious identities among the Kumyks has allowed Islamic fundamentalism to become a powerful movement in the region. Although no Kumyks have been listed among the leadership of the radical Wahhabi movement in Dagestan, several Kumyk groups have adopted an Islamic ideology.

The terrorist attacks in the United States in September 2001, carried out by people closely associated with the Wahhabi movement led to a Russian crackdown on Islamic organizations in the North Caucasus. Although the Kumyk leadership condemned the attacks, some of the more radical organizations refused to do so. Islamic ideology, as in neighboring Chechnya, could become an integral part of Kumyk identity.

SELECTED BIBLIOGRAPHY:

Bremmer, Ian, and Ray Taras, eds. *Nations and Politics in the Soviet Successor States.* 1993.
Goldenberg, Suzanne. *Pride of Small Nations.* 1995.
Olson, James S. *An Ethnohistorical Dictionary of the Russian and Soviet Empires.* 1994.
Tutuncu, Mehmet, ed. *The Turkic Peoples of the Caucasus.* 2001.

Kunas

Cunas; Gunasdule; Thule; Dule; San Blasinos

POPULATION: Approximately (2002e) 64,000 Kunas in Central America, concentrated in the Kuna Yala autonomous region of central Caribbean Panama and the San Blas Islands. Outside Panama, there is a small Kuna community in Colombia. The number of Kunas in Panama and Colombia could be as high as 120,000, as census figures are based on stated mother language.

THE KUNA HOMELAND: The Kuna homeland lies on the Caribbean coast of eastern Panama, including the San Blas Islands. The San Blas Islands, home to about 40,000 Kunas, include 360 low coral islands that stretch from the border with Colombia to the Gulf of San Blas. Most of the Kuna population live on 38 islands in some 50 densely settled villages and 11 mainland coastal communities north of the San Blas Mountains. Inland there are Kuna villages along the Bayano and Chucuaque Rivers. Part of their traditional lands, both mainland and islands, now forms a reservation of three counties of the Republic of Panama, Emberá, Kuna de Madungandi, and Kuna Yala or the County of San Blas, collectively called Kuna Yala, or Dule Nega in the Kuna language. *Kuna Yala (Yala Kuna/Dule Nega)*: 3,517 sq. mi.—9,109 sq. km, (2002e) 45,000—Kunas 92%, Latinos 7%, other Panamanians 1%. The Kuna capital and major cultural center is Narganá, (2002e) 13,000.

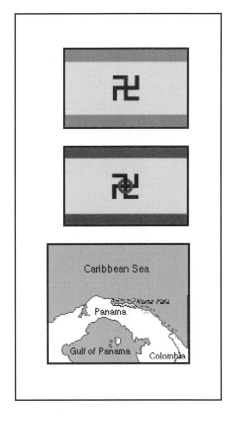

FLAG: The Kuna national flag, the flag of the national movement, has horizontal stripes of orange and yellow, the yellow four times the width of the orange stripes bearing a centered black swastika, an ancient Kuna symbol. The flag of the former republic, has horizontal stripes of red, yellow, and red, the yellow stripe four times the width of the red stripes and charged with a centered black swastika within a red ring.

PEOPLE AND CULTURE: The Kunas are an indigenous nation of Central America. Descent is reckoned bilaterally, with individuals tracing their ancestors through both the male and female lines. Marriage is matrilocal in extended families, of several generations, the son-in-law is under the authority of his wife's father. Kuna society includes two distinct groups the Mainland or Mountain Kuna and the San Blas Kuna. There was little contact between the two groups until the 1960s. Traditionally Kuna society is rigidly hierarchical and communal and focuses on the household and village. The major problems facing the Kunas are poor health (due to diet) and sanitation facilities. The so-called white natives of the San Blas Islands are actually albinos who make up about 0.07% of the Kuna population and are not permitted to intermarry. The Kunas are one of the most politically mobilized and active indigenous groups in Latin America They have doggedly held on to their culture and traditions, and they maintain a close connection with nature. The Kuna population is growing rapidly, making emigration to the mainland to search for work and land a necessity.

LANGUAGE AND RELIGION: The Kunas speak a Chibchan language called Dulegaya that belongs to the Eastern Chibchan group of the Macro-Chibchan languages. The majority of the Kunas speak Spanish as a second language. The Kuna language is not officially recognized, and education is in Spanish. Activists continue to demand schooling in their own language and official bilingualism in the Kuna reserve. The Kunas have long recognized the value of literacy; schools were first established in the region in the nineteenth century, though education was mostly in the Spanish language.

Traditional Kuna religion centers on shamans, who cure the sick and practice a form of witchcraft. The sun and moon were formerly the major deities, but Kuna mythology has been greatly affected by European beliefs. Officially many of the Kunas are Christians, both Roman Catholic and Protestant, although their beliefs are often mixed with pre-Christian traditions and customs.

NATIONAL HISTORY: The Kunas, prior to European colonization, occupied the central region of what is now Panama and the neighboring San Blas Islands. In the sixteenth century they were an important nation, living in federated clan villages under chiefs who had considerable power. The Kuna clans engaged in warfare with each other and with neighboring tribal peoples. Captives were generally enslaved. They were mostly farmers but also conducted an extensive trade, mainly by canoe, along the coast.

The Kunas had a well-developed class system. Important chiefs were carried in hammocks. After death the chiefs were preserved and buried in large graves with their wives and retainers, who are thought to have been killed to accompany the chiefs. Numerous gold ornaments have been found in the graves, along with fine ceramics and ornaments of shell and bone.

Europeans visited Kuna villages along the coast in the early sixteenth century. In 1510 the Spanish established a colony on Kuna lands at Darién. The colony became the center of Spanish exploration and colonization. The Kunas, at first welcoming, began to withdraw to less accessible areas following mistreatment and enslavement. The arrival of the Spanish began a period of deculturation and decimation. Many Kunas were killed in fighting the invaders or died of European diseases. European contact eventually destroyed the political structure of the Kunas and greatly modified their social and religious systems.

Before settling the San Blas Islands, the Kunas lived in inland settlements, concentrated on rivers and streams on a large territory in and around the San Blas Range. Their contacts were mostly confined to trade with pirates on the coast and with the European settlements around the Isthmus of Panama. In 1787 the Kunas signed with the Spanish authorities a treaty that began a century of profitable trade. The Kunas specialized in farming coconut, which continues to be their main cash crop.

Pressure from the growing Latino population gradually pushed the Kunas toward the coast. During the nineteenth century, the Colombian government sponsored immigration to the traditional Kuna lands as population pressure grew in the Colombian heartland. Conflicts between the Kunas and Colombian military forces increased as government policy hardened against the Kunas, who were seen as blocking progress.

At the end of the nineteenth century, the Kunas revolted against repressive local government rule. The revolt continued, mostly in the islands and in the rugged San Blas Range on the mainland, for several decades. In 1903, under U.S. pressure, the Colombian government recognized the secession and independence of Panama, but the new Panamanian government, like the Colombians, refused to recognize Kuna demands and land claims. Concessions by the new government in 1910–11 decreased the number of violent confrontations, but the low-level revolt continued.

Kuna contact with the outside world remained limited until around 1910. Panamanian settlement focused on the Isthmus of Panama region, mostly not on the traditional Kuna homeland. Missionary activity began with a Roman Catholic mission in 1907; several Protestant denominations were established in 1913. Mission-educated Kunas quickly took over leadership of a growing national movement. Non-Panamanian Protestants were banned following the revolt of 1925.

In early 1925 the Kunas again rebelled and drove out all Panamanian officials. On 8 February 1925 the Kuna leaders declared their homeland independent of Panama, as the Tule Republic (*tule* in the Kuna language means simply "men"). The flag adopted by the Kunas incorporated the Spanish flag, charged with a reversed swastika, an ancient Kuna symbol. (When the Nazis came to power in Europe, the Kunas wished to differentiate their flag; in 1942 they added a red circle, representing their traditional nose rings.)

The Kuna rebels were defeated in 1927–28. The Panamanian government established the San Blas Islands as a semi-autonomous zone in 1930. The autonomous *comarca*, county, of San Blas was created in 1938. A bill called the Carta Orgánica established the administrative structure of the reservation in 1953. Although officially the Kunas became self-governing, economic and political power remained with local administrators on the mainland.

Tension between the Kunas and the government increased in the 1960s, and the Kunas again rebelled in 1962. Relations worsened during the presidency of Omar Torrijos Herrera, who took power in 1968. His government attempted to alter Kuna political institutions, particularly by appointing Latinos rather than Kunas to sensitive posts in the reservation. A government plan to promote tourism in the reserve threatened its status. The Kuna region was the only part of Panama to vote "no" in the 1977 referendum on the Panama Canal treaties. Demands for reserved lands on the mainland became a nationalist issue in the 1960s, due to the rapid increase in population, particularly in the San Blas Islands. The Kuna population grew nearly 60% between 1950 and 1980.

In 1972 the government established the borders of a new reservation, including part of the traditional Kuna territories on the mainland. The Alto Bayano region, a national park of over 400,000 acres, was turned over to Kuna control in 1977. By the mid-1980s, the boundaries of the reserved lands, including the national park, had been established, and the Kunas had set up a functioning autonomous government. The Kuna reserve, called Yala Kuna, elects two representatives to the Panamanian legislative assembly. The Kunas are the most organized of Panama's indigenous nations; they have a strong sense of national identity that has allowed them to resist assimilation.

The reservation system allows the Kunas considerable autonomy, and they are free from taxation. Militants, however, object to the reservation on the grounds that it covers too little of their ancestral lands. They charge the Panamanian government is withholding most of their traditional lands because of mineral and other resources on the disputed lands.

In the 1990s one of the major concerns of the Kunas, particularly those living on the mainland, was the rapid increase of squatters on their reserve. In 1991, following a series of armed clashes between Kuna militants and illegal settlers, thousands of Kunas marched to protest government policies that failed to protect the boundaries of the Yala Kuna reservation. Some 5,000 Kunas, in early 1992, used force to remove some 200 squatter families who had settled in the Alto Bayano region since 1990. Government officials assured Kuna leaders that it will do all possible to keep squatters out of Alto Bayano National Park, but illegal settlements continued to appear. The Kunas petitioned for more reserved land to protect their homeland from squatters, but the requests were ignored.

A government project to build Bayano Dam to aid the development of Panama City and its rapidly growing urban area placed severe stress on the fragile environment and the Kuna population of the region. Roads built into the jungle allowed in even more squatters, increasing tension and causing clashes between the Kunas and the settlers. In April 1993 armed Kunas staged a rebellion near the park demanding the immediate passing of a bill guaranteeing the integrity of Kuna land reserves. They took two government officials hostage and set up roadblocks on the Pan-American Highway. The hostages were released unharmed after police were called in to restore order. In May, following serious disturbances and confrontations with police, the Panamanian congress voted on, but failed to pass, a bill establishing larger reserves for the mainland Kunas.

Government land concessions to mining companies increased dramatically after 1991. This effort to generate capital and employment is one of the major causes of the increasing tension between the Kunas and the Panamanian government. Many of the land claims are on traditional Kuna lands. Kuna nationalists have denounced the government practices and their treatment as a mere colony of the Panamanian state.

Migrant-wage labor is the most common form of nonfarm income. The Kunas have a long history of migrant labor, beginning with service on ships in the nineteenth century. In the late twentieth century, United Fruit Company banana plantations became a magnet for the Kunas, who were seen as exemplary employees; a few were promoted to managerial positions. Their experience in the outside world is mostly restricted to males; Kuna women rarely leave the homeland where they maintain the traditions, identity, and language.

In 1999, part of the territory turned over by the U.S. government to the Panamanian government at the eastern end of the Panama Canal was claimed as ancestral Kuna lands. The Kunas accumulated a large development fund from the salaries of Kunas employed in and around the U.S.-administered Panama Canal Zone after the 1970s. They plan to develop eco-tourism in the area once their claims are recognized by the government.

The prevailing culture of Panama is fundamentally Spanish, which disparages indigenous cultures. All aspects of Kuna culture are considered by the Latino majority as valueless, strange, and antique, although the exotic Kunas are seen as good for the tourist market.

SELECTED BIBLIOGRAPHY:

Calkins-Bascom, Willow. *Islands and Rainforests: Living in the Tropics with the Kuna People.* 1994.

Howe, James. *A People Who Would Not Kneel: Panama, the United States, and the San Blas Kuna*. 1998.

Salvador, Mari Lyn, ed. *The Art of Being Kuna: Layers of Meaning among the Kuna of Panama*. 1997.

Tangherlini, Arne E., and Andrew L. Young. *Kuna Yala: Unite and Change*. 1987.

Kurds

Kords; Kirdasis; Kurdi; Kurdistanis; Kordestanis

POPULATION: Approximately (2002e) 30,000,000 Kurds in the Middle East—4,600,000 in Iraq, 14,500,000 in Turkey, 7,400,000 in Iran, 1,400,000 in Syria—and smaller numbers in Lebanon (175,000), Armenia (90,000), Azerbaijan (70,000), Georgia (40,000), and Russia (50,000). Although there are no trustworthy figures, as Kurds are not usually counted separately in most countries, it is estimated that between 16 and 35 million Kurds inhabit large areas of Turkey, Iran, Iraq, Syria, and smaller territories in Lebanon, Armenia, Azerbaijan, and Georgia. Outside traditional Kurdish areas there are sizable communities in other parts of Turkey and Syria, and in Western Europe, particularly Germany.

THE KURDISH HOMELAND: The Kurdish homeland, Kurdistan, occupies a mountainous region of disputed extent in southeastern Turkey, northern Iraq, northwestern Iran, and northeastern Syria. The region straddles the major oil-producing areas of the northern Middle East and the major rivers, the Tigris and Euphrates, that supply water to much of the region. Kurdistan, with the exception of a small area in northern Iraq, has no official status; the region forms a number of administrative units of Turkey, Iran, Iraq, and Syria. *Region of Kurdistan (Kordestan)*: 224,540 sq. mi.—581,710 sq. km, (2002e) 42,000,000—Kurds 70%, Turks, Arabs, Iranians, Azeris, Assyrians,* Turkmens, Armenians 30%. The major cultural centers of the Turkish Kurds are Diyarbakir, called Amed by the Kurds, (2002e) 570,000, Gaziantep,

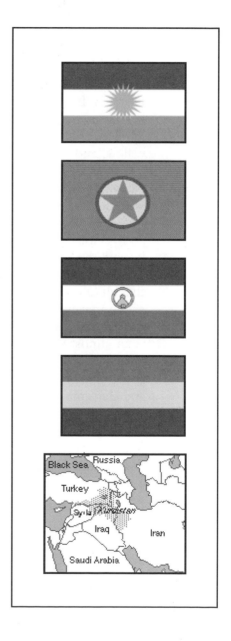

called Enteb, (2002e) 797,000; and Erzurum (Erzirom), (2002e) 333,000 The major cultural centers of the Iranian Kurds are Bakhtaran, called Kirmashan by the Kurds, (2002e) 769,000; Rezaiyeh (Wirmiye), (2002e) 481,000; and Sanandaj (Sina) 307,000. The centers of the Iraqi Kurds are Kirkuk, Karkuk in Kurdish, (2002e) 693,000; Irbil (Hawler), (2002e) 1,052,000; and al-Sulaimaniya (Silemani), (2002e) 721,000. The major centers of the Syrian Kurds is al-Qamishliye, called Qamishlo by the Kurds. (2002e) 176,000, and al-Hasakah, called Hassetche, (2002e) 190,000.

FLAG: The Kurdish national flag, recognized in all Kurdish areas, is a horizontal tricolor of green, white, and red bearing a centered, multi-rayed yellow sun. The flag of the Kurds in Turkey, the flag of the PKK, is a red field with a centered yellow disc, outlined in green, bearing a five-pointed red star. The flag of the Iranian Kurds, the flag of the Kurdish Democratic Party of Iran (KDPI), is a horizontal tricolor of red, white, and green bearing a gold mountain and sun within a gold circle. The flag approved by the Kurdish parliament-in-exile in 1995 is a horizontal tricolor of green, yellow, and red.

PEOPLE AND CULTURE: The Kurds are an Indo-European nation, a tribal, mountain people who trace their ancestry back to the Gutu of the ancient Assyrian Empire, the ancient Medes, and later admixtures of the region's many conquerors. The Kurds exhibit a variety of physical types and regional variations; many are fair and light-eyed. According to one legend, the Kurds are descended from 400 virgins who were raped by devils on the way to King Solomon's court. The fourth-largest ethnic group in the Middle East, the Kurds make up the world's most numerous ethnic group that has, with the exception of northern Iraq, no legal form of self-government. Race, culture, and language aside, what makes a Kurd a Kurd is an almost spiritual affinity with the highlands and snow-capped mountains of Kurdistan. Geography helps to define the Kurds, but it also divides them. The Kurds' geographic divisions into numerous tribes, subtribes, and clans makes Kurdish unity difficult to achieve. The major divisions are the Northern Kurds or Kermanjis of Turkey, Iraq, Armenia, Georgia, and Iran; the Southern Kurds or Soronis of Iran and Iraq; the Herki and Dimili Kurds of Turkey and Iraq; the Western Kurds of Syria and Turkey; the Shikaki Kurds of Iran, Iraq, and Turkey; the Surchi and Hawrami (Gurani) Kurds of Iraq. The Kurds are more an assemblage of clans than a united people, with great differences in religion, class, and regional cultures. This disunity is reflected in the myriad of Kurdish guerrilla armies fighting at cross-purposes, making statehood an almost impossible dream.

LANGUAGE AND RELIGION: The Kurdish language, a West Iranian dialect of the Indo-Iranian language group, is spoken in four major dialects that are not always mutually intelligible—Kermanji (Kurmanji) and Zaza in Turkey, Gorani in Iran, and Sorani in Iraq and Syria. The language is closely related to Farsi, the major language spoken in Iran. It remains a number of regionally defined dialects and subdialects, not all of which have evolved a written form; no unified literary language ever developed. In 1932 Kurds in exile developed a Latin script for Kermanji, the most widely spoken dialect, and this alphabet continues to be used by most Kurdish dialects. New technologies and a sharp increase in Kurdish immigration to the West have led to a new flowering of Kurdish publishing. The Hawar Latin script is becoming the accepted alphabet of the Kurdish literary language in Europe, while a Perso-Arabic script is used in most of Kurdistan. Illiteracy is a major problem amongst the Kurds due to chronic neglect by the central governments. Except for the minority in the countries of the former Soviet Union, illiteracy amongst Kurds stands at over 70%. There is a chronic lack of schools in all Kurdish districts and the many wars have negatively affected efforts at education.

The Kurdish majority is Sunni Muslim, with Christian and Shi'a Muslim minorities. Unlike the Turks, who follow the Hanafi school of Islamic law, the Sunni Kurds follow the Shafi'ite school. Adult male Kurds with religious inclinations tend to join Sufi brotherhoods, which have a powerful influence on Kurdish society. The Naksibendi and Kadiri orders have large followings among the Kurds in all areas, particularly Iran. The Faili Kurds of Iraq and Iran are mostly Shi'a Muslim. Some Kurds belong to Ghulat (extreme Shi'a sects) such as the Ahl-I-Haqq, Yezidis, and the Qizilbash. In Turkey all Shi'a groups, Kurdish and Turkish, are called Alevis and they were persecuted and in the past were massacred by the orthodox Sunni Ottomans. Many Kurds also belong to Sufi orders based on the veneration of saints. Belief in evil spirits who inhabit wells, caves, and mountains and must be appeased is still widespread. Protection from these spirits is sought by amulets and magic. There are many shrines of local saints who are regarded as healers or intercessors; pilgrimages to these shrines are very popular.

NATIONAL HISTORY: The Kurds trace their history back more than 4,000 years to a people called the Gutu, who predated the ancient Indo-Aryan Medes. The Kurds claim that they have been fighting for independence since their ancestors rebelled and captured ancient Nineveh in 612 B.C. The event is now celebrated as the Kurdish new year, Nev Roz or Nevruz, on 21 March; it is the most important holiday of the Kurdish year.

In the winter of 401 B.C. an army of Greek mercenaries making their way home from Mesopotamia after failing to overthrow the Persian king were attacked by bands of Carduchi, a fierce race of bowmen. They did more harm to the Greeks in seven days than had the Persians during the entire Mesopotamian campaign. The fierce Carduchi mountaineers are believed to be the ancestors of the modern Kurds.

In the second century B.C., tribal peoples occupied regions around the Zagros and Taurus mountains. Ancient Kurdistan, most often under Persian rule during its early history, fell to invading Muslim Arabs in the seventh century A.D. The Arab conquerors settled in the lowlands and pushed the native Kurds into the northern mountain regions. Converted to Islam, the Kurds formed an important part of the Muslim empire, the Caliphate. In the eleventh century Seljuk Turks overran most of Kurdistan, ending Arab domination. Briefly independent, Kurdistan produced one of Islam's greatest heroes, Saladin, called Salah ad-Din by the Arabs, who led the twelfth-century Muslim resistance to the Christian crusades and re-possessed Jerusalem and much of the Holy Land.

The rival empires of the Ottoman Turks and the Persians contended for power in Kurdistan, most of which came under Ottoman rule following a decisive Persian defeat in 1514. The Ottoman victory marked the first formal partition of the Kurdish lands between the Turks and Persians. The Kurds of the Turkish Ottoman Empire, ruled as a separate principality from the fifteenth to the eighteenth century, enjoyed considerable auton-omy as the guardians of the empire's eastern frontier.

The government of the decaying Ottoman empire centralized its ad-ministration in the nineteenth century and ended all minority self-rule. Resistance to direct Turkish rule sparked serious Kurdish revolts in 1826, 1834, 1853–55, and 1880. The sporadic revolts consolidated a national revival in the late nineteenth century, a period marked by widespread Kurdish participation in massacres of the empire's Christian minorities.

The beginning of World War I in 1914 finally brought allies for the Kurds' continuing fight against the Turks. Promised independence, most of the Kurdish tribes aided the allied war effort. which defeated the Ot-toman Empire in 1918. Encouraged by the Turkish defeat and U.S. pres-ident Woodrow Wilson's call for the independence of the non-Turkish peoples of the empire, the Kurds sent a delegation to the 1919 Paris Peace Conference. The allies incorporated a provision for an independent Kur-distan in the 1920 Treaty of Sèvres—a treaty that resurgent, nationalist Turkey led by Kamal Ataturk refused to sign. A second treaty, the Treaty of Lausanne, signed by Turkey and the allies in 1923, omitted the Kurds. Turkey, Iran, and the French and British administrations of Syria and Iraq partitioned Kurdistan over the opposition and pleas of the Kurdish inhab-itants. There also remained a number of Kurds in the Soviet Union and Lebanon.

Betrayed by the West, the Kurds began to mobilize. Rioting erupted across Kurdistan, followed by rebellion in northern Iraq in 1922. The rebellion spread across the new international borders, provoking harsh re-pression by the various regional governments and military incursions by the British military. Sporadic revolts continued in the 1920s and 1930s, but tribal divisions hampered unity and made it easier for the different governments to deal with uprisings.

In the period from 1923 to 1929, the Soviets created an autonomous egion called Kurdistana Sor—Red Kurdistan, in Azerbaijan. The region was created to export communism to the Middle East but was ultimately liquidated when Kurdish nationalism proved more persuasive than Soviet internationalism.

The resurgent Turkish republic created by Kamal Ataturk out of the ruins of the Ottoman Empire was to be a homogenous nation, with no room for ethnic or national minorities. On 3 March 1924 the use of the Kurdish language was prohibited. This was the beginning of the suppression of the Kurdish identity in Turkey. In February 1925 Sheik Said of Piran led a major uprising aimed at the creation of the independent Kurdish state promised in the Treaty of Sèvres. The rebellion was crushed, but it affected Turkish policy toward the Kurds.

The new Turkish state also came into conflict with the United Kingdom, which ruled Iraq under a mandate from the League of Nations. The Turks accused the British of inciting the Kurds to put pressure on the Turkish government to give up its claim to the Mosul region, now in northern Iraq. On 8 July 1937, Turkey, Iran, Iraq, and Afghanistan signed the Saadabad Peace; British saw the agreement as a vehicle to contain communism and its influence in the region, but the regional governments saw it more as a pact to contain Kurdish insurgencies.

Soviet troops, soon after World War II began, occupied the northern provinces of neutral Iran to ensure the southern supply route of the USSR. Encouraged by the Soviets, the Iranian Kurds declared independence at Mahabad on 22 January 1946. Granted generous oil concessions, the Soviets eventually withdrew, leaving their nationalist Kurd allies to face an Iranian invasion and years of brutal reprisals. The separatist leader, Ghazi Mohammed, was executed along with most other leaders of the breakaway republic. (To this day, photos of Ghazi Mohammed occupy a prominent place in Kurdish strongholds in Iran and Iraq.) Another influential figure in Mahabad, Mulla Mustafa Barzani, lived in exile in the Soviet Union for more than a decade. Barzani later returned to lead several rebellions in northern Iraq.

As a result of Turkish repression in the 1920s and 1930s, many Turkish Kurds migrated to Syria for safety. The Syrian government encouraged extremist Kurdish groups in their terrorist activities in neighboring Turkey. It has, however, firmly suppressed its own Kurdish population, especially in the 1960s and early 1970s. Arabization was enforced, and there was a large population transfer of Kurds from the border areas into the interior; their confiscated lands were given to Arab settlers. Kurdish books and music were forbidden and Syrian Kurds still suffer from constant surveillance by the security forces.

The Kurds of Iraq launched an armed rebellion against the government in 1961. In 1969 the Iraqi army attacked the Kurds in the northern provinces, leaving a reported 60,000 dead. Supported covertly by the United

States, Israel, and Iran, the Kurds again rebelled in March 1974. The Iraqi regime had to use tanks and planes to repel Barzani's forces. Thousands were killed, and 250,000 fled into Iranian territory. Following an agreement between Iraq and Iran in 1975, the shah of Iran withdrew his support of the Iraqi Kurds, and the revolt collapsed. The Kurdish rebels withdrew to their caves in the mountains, and Barzani went into exile in the United States, where he died in 1979.

Most Iranian Kurds initially supported the Iranian revolution, with the primary exception of the tribal chiefs who were benefiting from the shah's regime. When it became clear that the new Islamic regime had no intention of granting autonomy to non-Iranian national groups, the Kurds rebelled. The outbreak of the Iran-Iraq War in September 1980 provided the Kurds with another opportunity. Iraqi troops were preoccupied with the war front in the south, and fewer were available to confront the resurgent Kurds.

In 1984, the Kurdish Workers Party (PKK) began an armed rebellion against the Turkish government. Militants often targeted officials, Kurdish collaborators, and the Turkish military. Until 1991 the largest of the Kurdish populations, called Mountain Turks, were forbidden to use their language; their very existence was officially denied.

The Kurds of Iran rebelled in 1990 following the execution of 17 Kurdish activists. Between April and August 1990, Kurdish rebels mounted numerous attacks against government forces. Over 300 Iranian soldiers were killed, and another 150 were captured. In July, the Kurds released the prisoners as a humanitarian gesture. In early 1991, an estimated 1.3 million Iraqi Kurds, fleeing the Iraqi army's attacks in the wake of the Gulf War, crossed into Iranian Kurdistan. Fighting in Iran temporarily ceased until the majority of the refugees returned to Iraq under Western protection. The status of the Kurds in Iran remains basically unchanged since 1989. They are still engaged in a military campaign in an effort to gain regional autonomy, mostly from bases in northern Iraq.

After the Gulf War of 1991 the Kurds of northern Iraq created the first autonomous Kurdish state in modern history. Protected by foreign military units, the Kurds assembled a government and held free elections. In February 1993 representatives of Turkey, Iran, and Syria met to discuss the threat posed by the increasingly independent Kurdish entity in northern Iraq, and its powerful effect on their own Kurdish populations. The Kurdish region of northern Iraq is one of the major oil region, and the presence of an autonomous Kurdish state under Western air cover continues to threaten the viability of the Iraqi state. The northern mountains of Iraq are home to no fewer than five Kurdish guerrilla armies.

In 1998, the Turkish government moved troops to the border and threatened air strikes against Syria over the Syrian government's support or the PKK. The insurgency in southeastern Turkey had cost over 30,000 lives since the late 1980s. The Turkish government believed that the PKK rebels receive political indoctrination in Syria and training in Syrian-controlled Lebanon. PKK activists often targeted ethnic Kurds believed to be dealing with the Turkish government. Violence against civilian populations, both Kurds and Turks, caused the PKK to be branded as a terrorist organization.

Turkey began a vast 13-dam South-East Anatolia Project in the vicinity of the Kurdish city of Diyarbakir in the 1990s. The dam project will give the Turks control over how much water reaches Syria, which could become a powerful lever to end Syrian aid to the PKK rebels in southeastern Turkey.

In meetings in Washington in 1998, the two major Kurdish political organizations in northern Iraq, the PUK and KDP, held a series of meetings in an effort to unify the autonomous region, which has been the scene of severe inter-Kurdish conflicts. The meetings continued in 2000, but without agreement.

The capture of the PKK leader, Abdullah Ocalan, in February 1999 by Turkish authorities set off rioting in western Iran and throughout the Kurdish communities in Europe. Ocalan was later convicted of treason but was not executed. The PKK announced its willingness to negotiate an end to the conflict in Turkey. As Turkey's largest non-Turkish national group, the Kurds, concentrated in eleven southeastern provinces, are perceived as the only group that could pose a serious threat to Turkish national unity.

In northern Iraq, in the so-called safe haven established after the Gulf War, the Kurdish culture is flourishing. The Kurds read Kurdish books, watch Kurdish television, and sing a Kurdish national song every morning in school. With the help of the United Nations and protected by American and British air power, the three northern provinces, although officially part of Iraq, have become the de facto state of Kurdistan, with far more autonomy than the Kurds of Turkey, Iran, or Syria. The Iraqi Kurds use a different currency and patrol their own borders. They even set their clocks an hour ahead of Baghdad. They are also relatively prosperous, with an economy that functions while the rest of Iraq flounders.

The Kurds claim that they have survived where other nations have disappeared into history. The Kurdish leaders, in spite of differing ideologies, tribal divisions, and a lack of support or aid, all agree on one goal, the self-determination of the Kurdish nation. An old Kurdish proverb says, "The Kurds have no friends except the mountains." The pawn of regional politics, the Kurds desire for a united, sovereign Kurdistan has motivated generations of Kurds, but has brought them only horrible suffering, deportations, and massacres.

SELECTED BIBLIOGRAPHY:

Chaliand, Gerard. *The Kurdish Tragedy*. 1994.
Ciment, James. *The Kurds: State and Minority in Turkey, Iraq and Iran*. 1996.
Kreyenbroek, Philip, and Christine Allison. *Kurdish Culture and Identity*. 1996.
McDowall, David. *A Modern History of the Kurds*. 2000.